The Anglo-Saxons

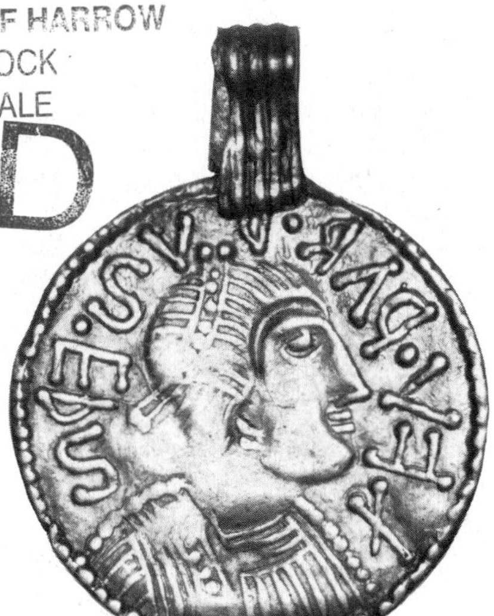

James Campbell, F.B.A., F.S.A., studied at Magdalen College, Oxford. He has been Fellow of Worcester College since 1957, a university lecturer in modern history at Oxford since 1958 and is now a Reader in Medieval History. He was also Visiting Professor at the University of South Carolina in 1969 and at the University of Rochester in 1986–7. His other publications include *Norwich* (1975) and *Essays in Anglo-Saxon History* (1986).

Eric John was born in Altrincham in 1922 and educated at Stand Grammar School, Whitefield, and Manchester University, where he read history. After a year as reader at the Institute of Historical Research of London University he returned to Manchester as a lecturer in history and retired in 1982 as Reader in History. He was Visiting Professor of History at the University of Massachusetts at Amherst in 1970–71. His publications include *Land Tenure in Early England: Orbis Britanniae*; and he has been editor and contributor to the *Book of Popes* and numerous articles in the *English Historical Review*, *Bulletin of John Rylands Library* and many others.

Patrick Wormald was born in 1947 and educated at Eton (King's scholar) and Balliol College, Oxford. He was a Prize Fellow of All Souls College, Oxford, from 1969 to 1973 and an external fellow from 1974 to 1984. He was Lecturer in Medieval History at the University of Glasgow from 1974 to 1989 and has been Tutor and Lecturer in History at Christ Church College, Oxford, since 1990. He was a British Academy Research Reader in the Humanities from 1987 to 1989. Much of his work has concerned Bede and the conversion of the Anglo-Saxons, seen in its European setting; he edited *Ideal and Reality in Frankish and Anglo-Saxon Society* (1983). He has since been working on Anglo-Saxon law and its place in English and European legal history and is author of *The Making of English Law*. His book *King Alfred to the Norman conquest* is forthcoming. He is married to the historian Jenny Wormald, and they have two sons.

The Anglo-Saxons

James Campbell
Eric John
Patrick Wormald

General Editor: James Campbell

With contributions from

P. V. Addyman, S. Chadwick Hawkes, D. A. Hinton, M. K. Lawson, D. M. Metcalf

PENGUIN BOOKS

Acknowledgements

PENGUIN BOOKS

Published by the Penguin Group
Penguin Books Ltd, 27 Wrights Lane, London W8 5TZ, England
Penguin Books USA Inc., 375 Hudson Street, New York, New York 10014, USA
Penguin Books Australia Ltd, Ringwood, Victoria, Australia
Penguin Books Canada Ltd, 10 Alcorn Avenue, Toronto, Ontario, Canada M4V 3B2
Penguin Books (NZ) Ltd, 182–190 Wairau Road, Auckland 10, New Zealand

Penguin Books Ltd, Registered Offices: Harmondsworth, Middlesex, England

First published by Phaidon 1982
Published in Penguin Books 1991
10 9 8 7 6 5

Printed and bound in Singapore by Kyodo Printing Co.

HALF-TITLE ILLUSTRATION
The Liudhard 'medalet' (cf. fig. 42). One of half-a-dozen varied coin-ornaments of the late 6th century said to be from the churchyard of St Martin's, Canterbury—presumably a necklace from a grave. The retrograde inscription, around an imperial portrait of Constantinian inspiration, has been read as LEU·DAR·DVS·EPS. The first two symbols are rune-like. Bishop Liudhard, who was Queen Bertha's episcopal chaplain, used St Martin's Church.

FRONTISPIECE
Relief sculpture, probably 8th century, in the church of St Kyneburgha, Castor, Cambs. It is possibly from a sarcophagus (cf. figs. 103, 107–9).

The publishers would like to thank the following for permission to reproduce photographs and works in their possession (numbers refer to figure numbers):
A. C. L. Brussels, 113; Society of Antiquaries, 177; Society of Antiquaries/K. Branigan, 13; P. A. Barker, University of Birmingham, 40; BBC Publications, 173; British Tourist Authority, 206; British Museum Publications Ltd, 137; Cambridge University Aerial Photograph Collection, 12, 58, 61, 100, p. 121 (2), p. 153 (3); Camelot Research Committee, 15; Canterbury Archaeological Trust, 99; Peter Clayton, 11; The Master and Fellows of Corpus Christi College, Cambridge, 45, p. 158 (3); Courtauld Institute of Art, Conway Library, 115, 172; R. J. Cramp, University of Durham (photos T. Middlemass), 66, p. 74 (2); University of Durham, Department of Archaeology, p. 75 (6) (photo T. Middlemass), p. 75 (7), 90; East Sussex County Council, Presentation Section, p. 235 (1); Department of the Environment (Crown Copyright), 3, 10; Peter Heppel, p. 171 (4); M. Holford, 60, & jacket photograph; W. A. How, 178; W. T. Jones (Mucking), 19, 59; Kremsmünster Cathedral Chapter (photo Elfriede Mejchar), 102; Lincoln Archaeological Trust, 55; Martion-Sabon/© Arch. Phot. Paris/S.P.A.D.E.M., 47; Studio Maurice Chemin, Mortain, 110; Dr Uwe Muuss, p. 121 (3) (FH 774–151); National Monuments Record, 4, 38, 49, 73, pp. 74–5 (1, 3, 4), 80, 83, 84, 86, 87, 94, 103, 108, 109, 116, 145, 150, 151, 152, p. 153 (5), p. 163 (3, 4), 195, 201, 207; National Monuments Record/W. A. Baker, 2; Norfolk Archaeological Unit of the Norfolk Museums Service (photo D. A. Edwards), p. 174 (1); Norfolk Museums Service, 20, 21, 28, 32, 68; Northampton Development Corporation, 104; Oslo, University Museum of National Antiquities, 140, 141, 174; Documentation photographique de la Réunion des Musées Nationaux, Paris, 181; Public Record Office (Crown Copyright reserved), p. 227 (3, 4); P. Rahtz, University of York, 162; Royal Commission on Ancient and Historical Monuments, Scotland, 89; Scottish Development Department, 17; P. Snelgrove, 67; G. Speake, p. 48 (3); The President and Fellows of St Johns College, Oxford, 198; The Master and Fellows of Trinity Hall, Cambridge, 209; Turners of Newcastle, 1; By courtesy of the Dean and Chapter of Westminster, p. 226 (1); R. L. Wilkins, Institute of Archaeology, Oxford, 23, p. 25 (2, 3, 4), pp. 48–9 (1, 4, 5, 6, 7); Winchester Research Unit, p. 175 (3); Reece Winstone, 136; Woodmansterne Ltd, 111; York Archaeological Trust, pp. 166–7 (1 (P. V. Addyman), 2–5 (M. S. Duffy)).

Contents

Preface

This book is meant to be a brief interpretative account of Anglo-Saxon history, of such a kind that illustration is relevant. To set its 250-odd pages beside the number of generations, men, and events in the six Anglo-Saxon centuries is to be tempted into quotation, not self-congratulatory, though blasphemous: 'A thousand ages in thy sight are like an evening gone.' It does not seek even summary comprehensiveness on all aspects of Anglo-Saxon history, though the Picture Essays make it more comprehensive than otherwise it would be. The authors of the main text are grateful to their colleagues who have contributed some of these. They have consulted together a great deal, but each takes individual responsibility for the chapters he has written. The book has been provided with a fairly substantial apparatus. It is intended to be enough to direct the reader to other relevant works and to provide references for statements which seem to need them.

The authors owe warm thanks to the following, who have helped one or more of them in important ways: Dr N. P. Brooks, Mr D. Kerfoot, Mrs S. Chadwick Hawkes, Professor P. H. Sawyer, Dr J. M. Wormald. The contribution of Dr M. K. Lawson to this book considerably exceeds the two essays he has signed. Mr P. Snelgrove discharged with efficiency the thankless task of finding the photographs. The editor responsible for the book at the Phaidon Press was Mr Bernard Dod: the authors wish to record that they have valued highly his help and care. Two of them, J. C. and P. W., take this opportunity to say something about the third, since he is about to retire. Their knowledge of and interest in their subject owe much to Eric John's very important contributions, published over many years, and they are grateful.

The Penguin edition of *The Anglo-Saxons* is an unaltered reprint of the original edition published in 1982. The best guides to the considerable literature published since then are the bibliographies published annually in *Anglo-Saxon England* and in *The Old English Newsletter*.

J. C.
August 1990

CHAPTER ONE

The End of Roman Britain

Roman rule in Britain began in AD 43 and ended in about 410. That is to say it endured for a span as long as from Shakespeare's time to ours. Its memorials in the landscape give a lasting and true impression of ordered power: the line of the great roads, the shadows of lost towns in the fields, the Wall running from sea to sea. Objects and the traces of buildings have survived in enough abundance from Roman Britain to permit a kind of familiarity with that lost world. There they are: the very dining rooms, dishes and tooth-picks of the rich; the huts and tools of the poor. But such familiarity is that of archaeology, not of history, deriving from things, not from words. The written record, after the first century, is one of episodic reports and scattered references. What we know of the course of events is a thin, interrupted tale; what we know of the organization of society is for the most part fragmentary and doubtful. If the right way to understand history is 'to go on reading till you can hear people talking', then the history of Roman Britain will never be understood. Its people have not left enough for us to read.

For the knowledge of any part of the civilized past to be lost is sad, but there is a more insular and a stronger reason for regret: our ignorance hinders our knowing whether or how far the roots of our own society lie in the Roman past. The ancient and deep interest in the fall of the Roman Empire is a social version of that personal instinct which makes a man concerned to know the origins of his own family.

1 The central section of Hadrian's Wall (see pp. 14, 18) looking east. It runs along the crags to the left. To the right is the *vallum*, an earthwork built to control access from the south, disused from the 3rd century.

2 A section of the Fosse Way, the Roman road running from Lincoln to Devonshire. It never deviates by more than 6 or 7 miles from a straight line linking its terminal points.

Britain in the Fourth Century

In the middle of the fourth century Britain was an integral part of the Roman Empire, much valued, badly threatened and strongly defended. A century later it had native rulers independent of outside authority; but many of them were about to lose their power to barbarians, and civilization was waning. It would not have been easy, in 350, to have foretold such a fate. Gibbon saw the second century as the apogee of the Empire; the succeeding period as one of decline, no less inevitable for lasting three centuries. He never appreciated the strengths and virtues of the later Empire. These are nowhere more apparent than in Roman Britain. Its best days were in the fourth century.

In important respects Britain in late Roman times was more like its medieval than its Anglo-Saxon self. For example, it now seems that it may have been nearly as populous in 300 as it was in 1500. A generation ago Roman Britain was supposed to have been thinly inhabited by a population of about 1,000,000 or 1,500,000; much of the country was thought of as hardly settled until later centuries. No one then and no one now has any means of making a reliable estimate of population. Crude guesses are built on such data as there are, the most important being those relating to density of settlement. It has become clear that this was more intense than had been thought. For example, in the Nene valley in the South Midlands 36 Romano-British settlements had been identified by 1930; by 1972, 434—though mostly small and by no means all there at the same time. More and more places are proving to have had a Romano-British past. Thus the deserted Yorkshire village of Wharram Percy, which has been carefully excavated over many years, at first seemed unlikely to have been much older than 1066, when it is first mentioned. It now proves to have had three Romano-British farms; and although we cannot be certain that they were inhabited in the later Roman period, the study of field boundaries suggests continuity of cultivation. Such discoveries, and they are numerous, have emboldened scholars to pitch their guesses for the population of Roman Britain higher than they once dared; up to 3 or 4 million.

Parts of the countryside were studded with the stone houses of landed proprietors or other prosperous men. About 600 such villas are known, and there must have been more. Their study provides strong evidence that men of the kind who owned them were doing well in the first half of the fourth century. Villas vary very much in size; most of the handful of very big ones, such as Woodchester—which was about as large as a medium-sized eighteenth-century country house, with 60 or more rooms—were built about the end of the third century. A high proportion of villas were enlarged or improved in the fourth century. It was then, for example, that nearly all the mosaic pavements characteristic of the luxury of many were laid. In short, there is no doubt that villa owners were doing well and living well during much of the fourth century.

Their prosperity must in large part have depended on the capacity to make money in a developed economy. Coin circulated widely in Britain. The abundance of the coins which are found would almost suffice to prove that this was a money economy. There is, however, better evidence of economic sophistication, for example the pottery industry. In the early part of the Roman period Britain had depended for pottery largely on imports 'on a truly colossal scale'. By the fourth century it had become in this, as in other ways, self-sufficient. Pottery for ordinary use was made on a large scale at about a dozen centres, and very widely used.

3 Plan of the villa at Chedworth, Gloucestershire. Perhaps originally three separate though related houses, it reached its maximum size in the fourth century (drawn by Roger Goodburn, scale 1:1182).

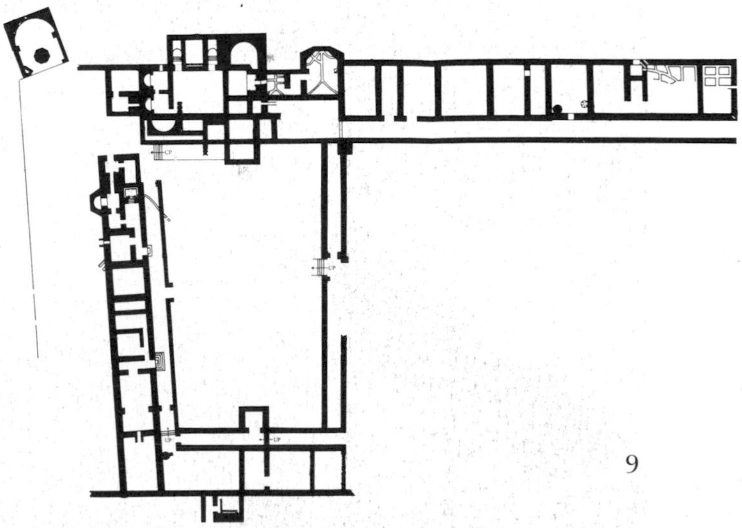

Towns provide further evidence of economic development. About 100 walled places have been identified; and, though the smallest of them, with only a few acres within the walls, can hardly be called towns, there were other unwalled settlements which were more than mere villages. The estimation of urban populations is desperately difficult. It depends largely on deductions from the extent of walled areas; but estimating the average density of population within such an area is guesswork, and the lines of fortification of most British towns were of second-century origin, thus no safe guide to the extent of areas inhabited later. The most extensive city was London. The 330 acres within its walls could have held 30,000 people. Cirencester had 240 acres, *Verulamium* (St Albans) and Wroxeter 200 each. So, they may have had populations of upwards of 15,000. On the same line of deduction there were some score of other places which could have had populations of between about 2,000 and about 10,000.

That is to say that the towns of Roman Britain may have been as important as those of late medieval England; indeed, perhaps rather more important, if there were three towns other than London with populations over 15,000, for no provincial town in medieval England is thought to have exceeded 14,000. Caution is needed in such comparisons. To the extent that historians of Roman Britain use medieval data as a guide in their speculations there is a risk of circularity in argument. Furthermore, the nature of towns can vary between one period and another. For example, no medieval town outside London had a governmental function as important as that of fourth-century Cirencester, which was (probably) the capital of the province of *Britannia Prima*. The provision of extensive public services may in itself have made towns larger than their later counterparts. Vast public baths and elaborate systems for the supply of water and the disposal of sewage all require considerable numbers of men to run them.

All the same, much of what went on in Roman towns was what went on in later towns: commerce and manufacture. Shopping centres and market halls were commonly provided, with other public buildings, in the first and second centuries. Many towns had numerous and varied shops and a wide range of crafts and manufactures. At least one town, *Durobrivae* (Water Newton), was primarily devoted to manufacture, that of pottery. The abundance of manufactured goods in much of Britain required a commercial and probably an essentially urban network for their distribution. The integration of such a network over a wide area required good communications: Roman Britain had better roads and better waterways than medieval England.

There are signs of many, though not all, towns flourishing in the fourth century. (The evasiveness of the formula warns of the patchiness of the evidence.) In some places public buildings were extensively rebuilt (such buildings nearly always dated from the first or the second century). In a number of towns both large and small the more imposing town houses dated from the fourth century. That so many towns were given improved for-

4 Stretch of Roman road near Blakeney, Glos.

tifications in the fourth century is a sign of their continued importance (see below, p. 14). The urban evidence fits with that for the villas and for the development of British manufactures. In the first and second centuries Britain had been provided with an admirable infrastructure of roads, canals and public buildings. It had escaped the worst of the crises of the third century; in particular the terrible invasions which devastated Gaul. In the late third and early fourth centuries it built on these advantages.

Economic development and civilized ways were not uniformly distributed. Although Roman rule had considerable effects in the highland areas of the north and west, not least an increase in the density of settlement, nevertheless such areas were in important ways less affected than others. Only one villa has been found in the whole of the modern counties of Devon and Cornwall. By contrast, there were at least 30 within ten miles of Ilchester, 20 within ten miles of Cirencester, and 25 within ten miles of Bath. In such areas one villa must always have been in sight of the smoke from the central heating plant of another. But even in the south-east there were wide tracts which were not at all like this. Thus there were no villas in the Fens, which the Romans drained.

Roman Britain was a very diverse country with a very diverse society, in some ways not unlike British India. The higher-ranking civil servants and soldiers (with many of the rank and file) came from elsewhere in the Empire (cf. p. 16 below). Trade created a cosmopolitan element in the towns. Thus the tombstone of the wife of a merchant from Palmyra has been found at South Shields (late second or third century); and in 237 a British merchant set up an inscription at Bordeaux showing that he was a member of the merchant guilds both at Lincoln and at York. Roman policy brought distinguished exiles and alien peoples. When Constantine was proclaimed emperor at York in 306 an Alemannic king called Crocus was prominent among his supporters.

However strong the cosmopolitan elements in the state structure and in the towns, there is no reason to doubt that a high proportion of the rich men of Britain, and very many of the villa owners, were British. We know too little about them. Some were doubtless the descendants of Britons of consequence who had come to terms with Rome. There are many villas which started as something like farmhouses in the first or second century and developed generation by generation to something rather grand by the fourth. The continuity of a house cannot prove the continuity of a family; but the continuity of many houses does suggest the continuity of a class. Men of the kind who owned the villas and the big town houses cannot by the fourth century have been as it were natives with a veneer of civilization. They were Roman citizens, bilingual in British and Latin, and living much as their counterparts lived in other parts of the Empire. By the fourth century many of the officers of the army in Britain are likely to have been British. At least in the towns knowledge of Latin extended further down society and was used for the ordinary purposes of everyday life, such as writing a curse on an enemy for deposit at a shrine.

5 One side of a lead sheet bearing a curse, 17.6 × 12.1 cm, from London (Museum of London). It reads: 'Titus Egnatius Tyrannus is cursed and Publius Cicereius Felix is cursed.'

There could hardly be a clearer indication of the way in which the island was open to distant influences than the establishment and development there of a religion whose origins lay in Palestine. There were some Christians in Britain by the second century. It was possibly in the third that Saint Alban was martyred near the place which has come to bear his name. By 314 there were bishops in Britain, for three of them attended a council at Arles in that year. It is clear that some of the owners of great fourth-century villas were Christian. This is most strikingly demonstrated by the mosaic with the head of Christ and the Chi-Rho monogram found in an impor-

6 Objects from the hoard of Christian silver found at Water Newton, Cambs. (*Durobrivae*), bowl diam. 17 cm, strainer 20.2 cm long (British Museum). Probably earlier 4th century, the earliest such collection known from anywhere in the Empire.

7 (*left*) A 4th-century mosaic from a villa at Hinton St Mary, Dorset (British Museum). The Christian Chi-Rho monogram behind the head in the centre of the lower panel probably indicates that it is of Jesus; if so it is the oldest such mosaic picture known. The whole mosaic measures 28 × 15 ft.

8(*above*) The prow of a ship, carbon-dated to *c.* 400, height 152 cm, presumably of the kind used by the Anglo-Saxons, found at Appels in Belgium (British Museum).

tant villa at Hinton St Mary in Dorset. Although paganism was not dead in late fourth-century Britain, there is reason to suppose that among the many great changes then taking place not the least was the widespread adoption of Christianity.

Of all the British inhabitants of Roman Britain only two have won lasting fame: Pelagius and Patrick. Both were Christians; both owe their fame to their role within the Church. Pelagius was a Christian teacher, whose heretical doctrines, emphasizing the extent to which salvation can be achieved by man's own efforts rather than by grace, were influential at the end of the fourth century and well into the fifth, not least in Britain. The little that is known of his origins, that he was British and went to Rome, probably to study law, in about 380, suffices to reveal something of the nature and aspirations of the British upper classes in the last generations of Roman rule. (It may also, indirectly, suggest the possibility of frustrations which could have had something to do with the end of Roman rule. If Britons had aspirations in an imperial context, they never reached the highest fulfilment. No Briton seems to have attained powerful office, except very unusually, *c.* 406 (see p. 16). Men from other provinces commanded and ruled in Britain: Britons did not command and rule in other provinces.)

Most of what is known of Patrick comes from his own writings. He was the son of a landowner, a decurion, that is to say a member of the council of prominent men who ran a *civitas* (see below, p. 16). At the age of about 16 he was captured by Irish raiders, ultimately escaped from Ireland, but later returned to be its bishop and evangelist. He gives no dates, and this is a major difficulty. It is usually supposed that he was born in about 390, kidnapped in about 405, returned to Ireland as a bishop in 432 and died in 461; but it is coming to seem increasingly likely that everything should be put about 30 years later. Nor for that matter can we be sure whence he came, though it could well have been from the neighbourhood of Carlisle.

Notwithstanding these difficulties, Patrick's autobiographical notes are important evidence about upper-class British society either just before or just after the end of Roman rule. Christianity was well established. Patrick's father was a deacon as well as a landowner; one of his grandfathers a priest. What Patrick says about his own education is striking. He regretted that he was not well educated, and his Latin is indeed of an unsophisticated kind. But he implies that he had or would have had the opportunity of a more elaborate education while young had he been less negligent (and, no doubt, had he not been kidnapped so young). Both the heresiarch's life and the saint's show that, whatever the stresses to which Britain was subject at the end of the fourth century, it was still a civilized country with an educated upper class.

The Enemies and Defence of Britain

Nevertheless, under stress Britain certainly was. The pressure came from foreign enemies: the Picts, the Scots and the Saxons. The Picts were the inhabitants of modern Scotland north of the Forth–Clyde line, and in particular of the valleys and coastal plain to the east. Picts first appear under that name in connection with an expedition against them in 297; but it is likely that they included the same people whom earlier Roman writers called *Caledonii*, and the name *Caledonii* may have been applied to one section of the Picts afterwards. The principal value of Hadrian's Wall (cf. p. 14 below) in the later years of Roman Britain must have been as a defence against these people, though it lay a long way south of their southern frontier, and in the wide intervening area dwelt Britons living under their own rulers subordinated to Roman authority. The Picts were also sea raiders, and raided the eastern coasts of Britain. Most of their history is desperately obscure. Sufficient of a threat to Roman Britain to bring the emperor Constantius there in 306, they were still fighting the kings of Northumbria 450 years later. No people had so long a history as a menace on the same frontier.

Second among the enemies of Roman Britain were the Scots, that is to say the inhabitants of Ireland. They had started to raid Britain before the end of the third century; and may have made settlements in parts of Wales before the end of Roman rule (see below, p. 20 and fig. 16). Last, but not by any means least, were the Saxons. Roman writers used this term to describe the inhabitants of the north German plain (approximately between the Elbe and the Weser) and of the southern part of the Danish peninsula (see below, pp. 30ff.). They had probably started to assault the coasts of the Empire early in the third century. By the later part of it they were a great danger, raiding all the way from the Rhine mouths to the Bay of Biscay. The most arresting account of their activities comes from the fifth-century landowner, poet and later bishop, Sidonius Apollinaris, describing their raids on the coast of Aquitaine. They outdo, he says, all others in brutality. Ungovernable, entirely at home at sea, they attack unexpectedly. When they are ready to sail home they drown or crucify one in ten of their victims as a sacrifice, 'distributing the iniquity of death by the equity of lot'. (Sidonius was writing in about 470; that is to say that the raiders he describes may have been Saxons based in Britain.)

Tacitus said of Britain, 'nowhere is the sea more widely master', and emphasized the extent to which the island was penetrated by estuaries and rivers. The problems which its defenders faced, then and later, were above all those of coastal defence and of holding the narrow seas. The dangers were like those created by the Vikings from the eighth century onwards. Sea raiders, operating from invulnerable bases, threatened almost the whole of a very long coastline in a country where much of what was most rich and vulnerable lay not too far from the sea.

The scale of the danger facing Britain in the fourth century is measured by the scale of the Roman response to it. Nothing is more astonishing, especially to the medieval historian, than the military effort of which Rome was capable. It has been calculated that at the end of the second century the Roman forces in Britain numbered over 50,000. This is a larger force than any medieval king of England ever managed to keep in the field, nor could any medieval king of England have maintained a standing force a tenth of that size. An impression, but no very certain estimate, of the strength of the Roman garrison in the fourth century can be obtained from the *Notitia Dignitatum.* This vital document lists and locates the units of the Roman army. As it has come to us, it was probably drawn up for the most part in about 395, with some later additions. While it is demonstrable that some of what it describes for Britain is a true indication of late fourth-century circumstances, it is also the case that some of its British sections were substantially out of date.

It is not easy to be sure of the strength, let alone the quality, of units of the late Roman army. Towards the end troops were withdrawn, in particular probably by Magnus Maximus in his bid for the Empire in 383, and never returned. All the same, the *Notitia* indicates that there was a powerful army in Britain at least until late in the fourth century and probably into the very early fifth. For example, it indicates, and here was certainly supplying up-to-date information, that apart from the two defensive commands under the *Dux Britanniarum* (Duke of the British provinces) and the *Comes Litoris Saxonici* (Count of the Saxon Shore) there was also a field army of 6,000 men under the *Comes Britanniarum* (Count of the British provinces). Such a force seems very small to historians of the ancient world, one of whom has described it as 'ludicrously inadequate' for the recovery of Britain. Still, it was probably three times larger than the force which Theodosius brought to restore order to Britain after a concerted attack by its barbarian enemies in 367 brought it near to collapse; and was probably about the same size as William the Conqueror's army at Hastings.

9 A page from the *Notitia Dignitatum* showing the forts of the Saxon Shore (see p. 18). A copy made in 1436 of a Carolingian copy of an original (Oxford, Bodelian Library, MS Canon. Misc. 378, fol. 153).

The fortifications of Britain were strong and repeatedly strengthened. The great northern wall which Hadrian built in the 120s was kept in repair and garrisoned at least till very late in the fourth century (see below, p. 18). Round the south and east coasts stood a series of powerful forts, those of 'Saxon Shore', from Brancaster in the north to Porchester in the west, mostly built between 270 and 285. In the fourth century new forts were built on the west coast against the Irish threat, for example Cardiff and Lancaster.

The internal fortifications of Britain were exceptionally strong. Not only were all the major towns protected by stone walls built in the third century, so too were a large number of minor places—far more than was the case in most other parts of the Empire. Many town walls were improved late in the fourth century, above all by the addition of towers; the river wall at London was strengthened not long before the end. There can be no clearer indication of the commitment of Rome to Britain than the great fortifications built to hold it. The magnificence of the legionary fortress at York, completed *c.* 300 or rather later, the most imposing of its kind anywhere in the Empire, is characteristic and symbolic of the imperial commitment to Britain.

It was at York that Constantine was proclaimed emperor in 306 on the death of his father Constantius, who had come on a campaign against the Picts. The extent to which Britain mattered to the Empire in the fourth century appears from the number of expeditions sent to secure it. Constantine himself may have returned there on one or more expeditions after 306. In 342–3 the emperor Constans came, hurrying from the Continent in winter, to deal with some crisis (whether a barbarian invasion or internal sedition we cannot tell). He was the last emperor to come to Britain while wearing the purple. But in 360 Julian sent a force to combat, yet again, the Picts and Scots. After a successful combined assault on Britain by the Picts, Scots and Saxons in 367, Valentinian sent Count Theodosius to restore the situation, which he did. Magnus Maximus, the commander in Britain who took away many of its troops in 383 to make a bid for the Empire, probably returned to reorganize its

10 (*above*) The Saxon Shore fort at Burgh Castle (see pp. 14, 18). The walls are 10 ft thick and still stand some 20 ft high.

11 (*below*) The Multangular Tower at York; one of 8 such added to the south-west wall of the legionary fortress, probably *c.* 300, and perhaps as much for show as for security. (Thc upper part is medieval.)

defences a year or so later. Very near the end of the century the great *Magister Militum* (commander-in-chief), Stilicho, led, or more probably sent, some kind of relieving expedition. While there was some effective central authority left in the western Empire Britain was not regarded as expendable.

The Collapse of Imperial Authority

But the central authority ceased to be effective and Britain was lost. Though little is known of the drama of the last years of Roman power in Britain, we do know something at least about the final scenes, thanks to a fairly detailed account provided by the early sixth-century Greek historian Zosimus, drawing on earlier authorities. According to him the dénouement came in 406–10. He indicates that some time in 406 the army in Britain set up (it was not for the first time) a usurping emperor. We are told nothing else of him, except his name, Marcus, and that he was killed by troops the next year. He was immediately replaced by another usurper, Gratian, a Briton. He too was killed within months and succeeded by a third usurper, a common soldier who called himself Constantine III. In 407 Constantine led most of the army out of Britain, to Gaul, to meet a crisis there: on the last day of 406 the Vandals, Alans and Sueves had crossed the frozen Rhine, and broken loose in Gaul.

This marked the true beginning of the end of the Roman Empire in the West. Constantine for a time checked the invaders and extended his authority into Spain; but was executed on the orders of the emperor Honorius in 411. In the meantime, according to Zosimus, Britain was heavily attacked by barbarians (we know from another source that there was a major Saxon incursion in about 408), and this 'brought the inhabitants of Britain and some of the nations of Gaul to the point of throwing off Roman rule and living independently as no longer obedient to Roman law. The Britons took up arms, and, braving danger for their own safety, freed their cities from the barbarians threatening them . . .' This probably took place in 409. Zosimus adds that in about 410 Honorius wrote to the cities of Britain telling them to take responsibility for their own defence. These events are generally taken as marking the end of Britain as part of the Empire.

It is probably right so to take them. That there was a transformation at about this time is plain from the history of the coinage. There had been no mint in Britain since 326. The large supplies of coin needed to pay the army and the bureaucracy had to be imported. The latest gold coins found more than occasionally in Britain are those of Honorius and of Constantine III. The latest silver found in any quantity is that struck at Milan in about 400; the latest bronze, issues of before 404. That the supply of new coin coming into Britain diminished in this way is a sure sign that Britain was no longer part of the imperial machine; though it has to be borne in mind that the cessation of the import of coin can be interpreted as a cause rather than as a consequence of the events of 406–7.

It is not easy to know what happened in Britain immediately after the crisis of 406–10. According to the story reported by Zosimus Britain was lost to the Empire not because it could not be defended but because its inhabitants defended it for themselves. One obvious question to ask is: who took power in about 410? The great officials and the more important army officers were probably all or nearly all from other parts of the Empire. We know a little about two of those who held the most important civil office of all, that of *Vicarius* (governor) of the diocese of Britain, in the last years of imperial authority. One was Chrysanthus, who ended his life as bishop to the Novationist heretics at Constantinople, an office his father had held before him. The other, Victorinus, was a friend of the Gallic poet Rutilius Namantianus, and after his service in Britain retired first to Toulouse, which seems to have been his home, and later to Italy. It is a reminder how cosmopolitan the Empire was to the end.

Perhaps all the non-Britons concerned with running Britain left at about the time of Constantine III; but some may have stayed. The British priest Gildas, writing shortly before the middle of the sixth century (see below, p. 20), mentions the deeds of Ambrosius Aurelianus, who defeated the Saxon invaders somewhere about the end of the fifth century. He writes of him as 'perhaps last of the Romans' among those who had survived the troubles caused by the first Saxon 'rebellion' (see below, p. 23). He may mean that Ambrosius was, as it were, the last Romanized, civilized British leader; but elsewhere he always distinguishes between 'Britons' and 'Romans' and so may have meant to convey that Ambrosius was not of British origin.

In any case some Britons had been in a position of power in the last years of imperial authority. The second of the usurpers of 406, Gratian, was a Briton, as was Gerontius, who commanded Constantine III's army in Spain and ultimately rebelled against him. Gratian was called by the contemporary historian Orosius *municeps*; exactly what he meant by *municeps* is not easy to say, but it probably had something to do with a town. The principal centres of British authority within Roman Britain were the *civitates*. These were approximately 30 in number and formed the main units of local government. They corresponded to a considerable extent to the tribal divisions of pre-Roman Britain, and the life of each centred on a capital which was a town of some significance. The responsibility for running the *civitas* lay with its *ordo*, a body of about 100 local men of consequence. It is a plausible guess that when imperial authority collapsed the *civitates* and the men who ran them became autonomous centres of power.

Another source of power in Britain may have been the rulers of peoples just beyond the frontiers and in the highlands generally. The British peoples who lived immediately beyond the Roman Wall had for a long time been apparently outside the area of direct Roman authority. Much of the interior of Wales seems to have been left without Roman garrisons through the later fourth century. Here, and in other relatively un-Romanized areas, there may have been local native structures of authority which could produce potentates capable of

12 Air photograph of *Calleva Atrebatum* (Silchester, Hants), the cantonal capital of the *Atrebates*. The line of the 3rd-century defences is easily visible; their extreme dimensions north–south and east–west are about 850 yards. Inconclusive evidence suggests it survived as a centre of British power till the 6th century. The date of its abandonment is not known.

taking advantage of the decline of central authority.

We do not know how far, and, if so, for how long, there was a central authority for independent Roman Britain after 410. In the early third century there had been a council, with largely ceremonial functions, for all the *civitates* of Britain. It could have been that this continued to meet, with greater powers, or that it was revived. It is not impossible that there was a series of British emperors, having authority over all or most of Britain. Gildas says that Ambrosius Aurelianus's parents (see above, p. 16) had 'worn the purple'. The natural meaning of this would be that they had been emperors of some kind; if so it could have been in Britain. The ninth-century 'Nennius' (see below, p. 26) refers to Ambrosius as 'king among all the kings of the British people', which would indicate some superior authority. These are the only shreds of evidence for some kind of united authority in independent Britain. It is almost absurd to trouble with evidence so slight and so inconclusive; but most of what we know of fifth-century Britain is little more than what can be extracted from such trifles.

If it is hard to tell who held authority in Britain immediately after 407, it is hardly easier to tell by what means it was defended. Nevertheless, defended it was. True, before long Saxons established themselves in force; but there was almost certainly a substantial interval between the evacuation, as it appears, of most of the army by Constantine III and the first major Anglo-Saxon conquests. The composition of the Roman army in Britain in the final decade or so of imperial power is very uncertain. The *Notitia Dignitatum* provides some answers but raises more questions. A crucial problem is to what extent the late Roman army in Britain was British. In the earlier years of the Empire, troops very seldom served in the province from which they were recruited. The names of the garrison units stationed in Britain show that they derived from all over the Empire; archers from Syria, cavalrymen from Illyria and so on. Many such units are listed in the British sections of the *Notitia*; but by the fourth century local recruitment had become normal for units of most kinds, and those (they were numerous) which had been based in Britain for several generations are likely to have been largely British, whatever their exotic names suggest. The mobile troops of the field army were probably of overseas origin.

A further crucial question is how far the regular, or irregular, troops were recruited from Germans. If there were such German forces in Britain it is of course a question whether they included Angles or Saxons. There is no evidence that they did; but the possibility is an interesting one. In any case Germans of one kind or another had long been active in Roman military service, both at low levels and at high. The *dux*, probably *Dux Britanniarum*, who was killed by the barbarians in the crisis of 367 had a German name, Fullofaudes.

The end of the Roman army in Britain is, up to a point, easy to trace. It is likely that permanent reductions were made in the garrison by Magnus Maximus in 383 and that most or a large part of the troops left in 407. We can be reasonably sure that after that date no troops in Britain were paid by authorities across the Channel. But this leaves much unanswered. For example, when was the Wall evacuated? The archaeological story used to be fairly clear: it appeared that after about 367 the military and civil settlements on the Wall became less distinct; the villagers moving into the forts, as if soldiers and settlers on the Wall were hardly to be distinguished. Then the forts seemed to be abandoned *c.* 383. But both these conclusions are now powerfully disputed. All that can be said is that some kind of military occupation of parts at least of the Wall continued till about 400 or even later. If, as is not unlikely, Saint Patrick's home was in the neighbourhood of Carlisle, then his autobiographical notes show that in an area immediately south of the Wall Romanized life was surviving, even if under threat, after the turn of the century (see above, p. 13). Whatever happened to the army must have made a vast difference to certain places and areas. Consider, for example, York. The Sixth Legion, *Victrix*, had been based there since 122, and was so much part of British geography that York could be called *Ad Legionem Sextam*. When it left we do not know. We cannot indeed be absolutely certain that it ever did leave; but probably it did, and its departure must have marked a sharp break in the life of York.

A major problem is that of the fleet. The fleet was undoubtedly very important in defending Britain against sea-borne enemies. The Saxon Shore forts must have been in large measure naval bases, and some can have been little but naval bases. For example, *Gariannonum* (Burgh Castle, Suffolk) was at the end of a peninsula. The cavalry who garrisoned it must have had a very limited radius of action; and the fort's siting makes no sense at all unless its primary function was to protect a harbour. We have a description of an element in the North Sea fleet from the Roman historian Vegetius, writing in the later fourth century. He describes light reconnaissance vessels which had their sails and ropes dyed blue, and whose sailors wore blue uniforms to camouflage them as they patrolled on the watch for invaders. It could be that some of the earliest settlements of Saxons, for example that at Mucking on the Thames estuary, were to provide naval assistance against their compatriots or other sea-borne invaders (see below, fig. 19). In any case we just do not know what happened to the arrangements for naval defence—and it is worth noticing that some of these, in particular the long chains of signal stations along the east coast, would have been very difficult to keep in operation without the control of a central authority.

The fate of the army is closely linked to that of the economy, and both to that of state power. The presence of big garrisons in Britain must have been a fact of major importance in its economic life, particularly as a source of career opportunities for Britons rich and poor. The departure of those garrisons or their transformation into entities of a different kind must have been correspond-

13 (*left*) The villa at Keynsham (Somerset) was destroyed at some time in the 4th century. This photograph shows evidence for a later reoccupation which, as often, has been impossible to date.

14 (*above*) Coin of Allectus who usurped authority in Britain 293–6, succeeding Carausius, himself a usurper (British Museum). The rise and fall of both depended much on naval power; it is appropriate that the reverse should show a light galley.

ingly significant. Important elements in the economy may have been declining and changing in the last generation of imperial authority. It looks as if a considerable number of villas may have been deserted or changed their use after the barbarian triumphs, devastating if transitory, of 367. Out of 135 villas where there are coin finds sufficient to enable some estimate to be made, 65 do not produce coins of after about 360. In some areas, such as Wiltshire, this is so of many villas. But in other areas, for example the Cotswolds, there is no indication of a break at this time. On the contrary, some villas were not only still inhabited, but were being improved very near to the date of the end of imperial authority. For example, that at Hucclecote in Gloucestershire has a mosaic laid in mortar which has a worn coin of 395 in it. In the towns the evidence is seldom, if ever, good enough to tell us whether a town was declining or not in the last imperial generation—though we do know that many had their fortifications improved in about the third quarter of the fourth century.

The economy of Roman Britain was one which depended in substantial measure on the circulation of coin in large quantities, and where mass-produced pottery circulated in abundance. Though we know when new issues ceased to be brought into Britain in any quantity, we do not know when the existing stock of coin ceased to circulate or became inadequate. One can see from the worn state of many of the Theodosian coins found, for example, at Silchester, that circulation could have gone on for a long time. It is generally thought that the production of mass-produced pottery ceased by about 425; but it is not easy to be certain of this. Here, and generally, the end of the importation of abundant new coin deprives us of much knowledge which archaeology could otherwise provide. The chief means of dating in the archaeology of Roman Britain is by coins, and because issue followed issue quite quickly, such dating can be fairly precise. After the early fifth century this crucial aid to knowledge disappears. All we can say, on many sites, is that the latest coins found are of the period *c.* 400, which does not always help in determining how much after 400 the site in question is; and may sometimes tempt archaeologists to date it nearer 400 than it really was.

The events of 406–7 marked an important break in the history of Britain. Quite how important we cannot be sure, not only because we know so little about what was happening after 410 but because we know so little of what was happening before. Thus we do not know whether any of the non-British upper echelons of the administration stayed on. We can see the army's withdrawal was important; but we cannot tell how many troops stayed behind, having become so territorialized as to be impossible to move; or how far barbarian settlers had already become established on an official or an unofficial basis (see below, pp. 31, 34).

The fall of Roman Britain poses sharply the problems of the fall of the western Empire as a whole. On the one hand, it can be seen as the inevitable culmination of processes which made its enemies stronger and its capacity to resist them less as the generations went by. On the other hand, one can regard it as the result of specially unhappy combinations of events. There was nothing demonstrably unprecedented about what was happening in Britain in the decade up to 410. The Picts, the Scots and the Saxons were far from being new enemies, and there is no reason to be sure that they were attacking in new strength. They had had successes often before, and often before they had been beaten back. There was nothing new about a usurper seizing power in Britain and establishing separate authority there; nothing new about such a usurper using the British garrison to establish himself over the Channel. It may be that the underlying circumstances in Britain changed greatly between Magnus Maximus's usurpation there in 383, and Constantine III's in 406. It is always too easy through the foreshortening which comes from distance in time and scanty information to forget that 30 years was as long a time then as now. But it may be that the collapse of imperial power was caused not so much by structural changes as by the misfortune of events, for example the bad luck of an unusually severe winter, which enabled too many barbarians to cross the Rhine frontier. The difficulty of coping with them was enhanced by the unfortunate fact that the Visigoths moved against Italy at just the same time. In the end it proved impossible for the central authority to restore order; there was just too much to deal with at one time. Crucial for the fate of Britain was the failure to restore authority not only in Britain but also beyond the Channel. After 406 the northern provinces of Gaul were never again secure in imperial hands. This had important and lasting effects for Britain.

Both in Britain and to a degree in Gaul, what we are seeing is not the overrunning of imperial provinces by invading barbarians. It is the secession of imperial provinces in circumstances created by barbarian invasions. Britain in the face of the crisis of the fifth century proved not the weakest, but the strongest, part of the Empire. In this sense; by 500 control of every part of the western Empire had passed to barbarian rulers, even if some of these sometimes left considerable power in the hands of the Roman ruling classes. There was one exception, Britain. There, although large areas of the island had passed under barbarian control, at least half was still under British rule. And although in the end none of Britain was left under British rule, the defeat of the Britons took a very long time. When Edward I defeated Llewellyn, Prince of Gwynedd, in 1282, and subjugated his principality, this marked the loss to a foreign ruler of the last piece of the Roman Empire in the West which was still in the hands of rulers of the race which had inhabited it before the Romans came.

The Lost Centuries: 400–600

The natural vice of historians is to claim to know about the past. Nowhere is this claim more dangerous than when it is staked in Britain between AD 400 and 600. We can identify some events and movements; make a fair guess at others; try to imagine the whole as a picture in the fire. That is all. Knowledge will creep forward by the accumulation of facts, especially archaeological facts, and by the dialectic of hypotheses. But what really happened will never be known.

The Transformation of Britain

The unknown men who took power in 410 (see above, p. 17) must have faced problems extending far beyond those of defence. Those of internal order, of the relations between the harder men of the hills and the more civilized of the plains, of the towns to the countryside may have been just as pressing. The life of Roman Britain had been in many ways determined by involvement in the structures and systems of imperial power. There can hardly be a stronger demonstration of this than the extensive use of coin in provinces which had no mint. The severance of the imperial link, and so of the flow of coin, must, sooner or later and probably sooner, have demanded new answers to such questions as how to pay an army, how to feed a city, how to curb a highland chief and, for many, simply how to make a living.

Some were answered, others proved unanswerable. By stages which can hardly be traced the ordered world of Roman Britain was destroyed, or transformed. The feelings of an educated Briton of the mid-sixth century could have been of despair had he looked to the east of the island, where destruction had come. Had he looked to the west he could have felt a degree of pride and confidence, for there there had been transformation. We know the views of only one such Briton, the priest Gildas, who produced a tract *On the Fall of Britain* in about 550. *His* view was never sanguine, no matter which point of the compass he faced. Everywhere he saw sin and anticipated Providential retribution. But what he says, and, still more, what he was, reveal much of the extent, as well as the limits, of British success.

By the time he wrote much of the island had passed under the control of Germanic invaders. But their advance had, he said, for some two generations been arrested. His work provides vague indications, and we have others somewhat more precise, of approximately which areas were still under British rule (they are indicated on fig. 50). These British lands were divided into kingdoms of varying size. Gildas names the kings of five of these. Their conduct was, he maintained, consistently damnable. He denounces it, and much besides, with an eloquence which would have jangled in the ears of a classical Latinist but which is, nevertheless, sophisticated and up to the best standards of his day. His work proves that he stood in a tradition of learning and came from an educated milieu. It reveals the most interesting contrast in the part of Britain which had remained British: that between the supersession of the Roman political order and the survival—or more than survival, the success—of the Church and its Latin learning.

We have few indications of the origins of the numerous dynasties which succeeded to power. Gildas hints that one or more were descended from Ambrosius Aurelianus; if so, they may have had aristocratic Roman origins (see above, p. 16). At least one dynasty, that of Dyfed in south-west Wales, had originated in Ireland. It is likely that the rulers of Rheged and Manau in the north were descended from those of the peoples who had lived north of the Wall in Roman days. It could have been that the kings of Dumnonia, the largest of the British kingdoms, were descended from native families there.

While the areas over which some of these rulers exercised authority are known approximately, the centres from which they exercised it are not. It is likely that some Roman towns survived as centres of power, if not of population (see below, pp. 39–40). There were also new centres. In many of the areas which remained British hill-forts were constructed or reconstructed. The most impressive of those which have been excavated was at South Cadbury (in modern Somerset). Here a major Iron Age fortified place, which had been stormed and destroyed during the Roman conquest of the south-west, was refortified, probably in the fifth century, and had its fortifications improved in the sixth. These consisted of a big bank of rubble, laced with beams and provided with two quite formidable gatehouses of stone and timber. The size of the fort, 18 acres, and the presence there of a hall-building more than 60 feet long, show its connection with some considerable authority, though whose is unknown. The re-use of this Iron Age centre four centuries after its abandonment is characteristic of a reversion to older patterns which made Gildas's Britain in important ways more like that which the Romans had found than that which they had ruled (see fig. 15).

15 (*above*) South Cadbury. In the left hand part of the excavation are the remains of the timber and stone bank of, arguably, *c.* 500; to the right, the wall of Aethelred II's *burh* (see pp. 152–3).

16 (*far left*) The Vortipor stone (see p. 22), height 211 cm (Carmarthen Museum). The inscription on the face is MEMORIA VOTEPORIGIS PROTICTORIS. The edge is inscribed in Ogam letters VOTECORIGAS ('of Votecorix').

17 (*left*) Stone from Whithorn (Dumfries and Galloway), height 87 cm, commemorating Latinus, a Christian (Whithorn Abbey Museum). Its date is disputed; the most recent opinion is 'not later than the first half of the 5th century'. It is probably the oldest such inscription from the North. Latinus's grandfather is mentioned, which suggests that Christianity extended at least two generations back.

18 (*left*) Tombstone of Hariulf from Trier, width 108 cm, late 4th century (Trier, Rheinisches Landesmuseum). It describes him as a member of the royal line of the Burgundians and as *protector domesitigus* (*sic*), which here indicates that he was in the imperial guard. It is a reminder of the long involvement of high-born Germans with Rome and suggests a possible origin for the title used of Vortipor (fig. 16).

In other ways, no less important, it was very different. The kings whom Gildas denounced were something more than late Iron Age potentates. They were Christians and lived in societies in which Latin was in fairly common use. Take for example Vortipor, whom Gildas mentions as 'tyrant of the Demetae'. Not only were his sins denounced in Latin ('the rape of a shameless daughter', etc.), but his tomb was marked by a Latin inscription. This memorial inscription is one of some 200, dating between the fifth century and the seventh, to survive in the Celtic west. Most are from Wales, some from the south-western peninsula, a few from the (modern) Scottish borders. In the areas in which they are principally found they are considerably more abundant than inscriptions of the late Roman period (see fig. 16).

Their evidence is reinforced by that of documents. Perhaps the most important recent discovery about Dark Age Britain is that we have records of a considerable number of documents from south-eastern Wales from the mid-sixth century onwards. They are in *The Book of Llandaff*, a twelfth-century compilation, long known and as long distrusted. Dr Wendy Davies has shown that it preserves the substance of genuine documents relating to gifts made to churches. They show us landowners, whose estates are measured in Roman units, making grants by means of written documents in Latin. At least 20 of these are of before 600. They, like the memorial stones and Gildas's Latinity, show that, at least in some areas, Latin-using culture survived into the sixth century and may sometimes have been stronger than it had been in the days of Roman power.

Its survival owed everything to the Church. Almost certainly by the time of Gildas all the Britons were Christian. Much about the British churches is obscure; for example we know very little about the way in which their episcopate was organized. But it is certain that they were very powerfully affected by monasticism during the sixth century. It is likely that numerous monastic settlements played a large part in ensuring that Christianity, and with it some elements of Roman culture, were taken to the countrysides of western Britain.

British Christianity had another achievement, and a major one: its important part in the conversion of Ireland. Thanks to the efforts of Saint Patrick (see above p. 13) and others Ireland had become a Christian island by the time Gildas wrote. Before the end of the sixth century Irish missionaries started to go to the Continent. During the seventh century they went to Gaul, Germany, Italy and, not least, to England, and Ireland had become one of the chief homes of Latin learning.

If Britons played a large part in the conquest of Ireland for the Church they had other conquests, less peaceful, further south. They secured control of Brittany. It is conceivable that the first stage in this was the settlement of Britons by the Roman authorities to defend the Armorican coastline; certain that Britons were established in strength in Brittany by the 460s; probable that they had come both as invaders and refugees; and in any case astonishing that they should have established a little Britain beyond the sea, with a Cornwall and a Dumnonia of its own (Cornouaille and Domnonée), and a distinct and still enduring identity and language. Some Britons went yet further. By the 570s there was a British settlement in north-west Spain, sufficiently numerous to have a bishop of its own.

There are other indications of how far the water routes could lead for the people who lived round the Irish Sea. From the late fifth century on, pottery (and probably wine and/or oil) was imported from the eastern Mediterranean and is found on sites associated with the rich and powerful in Ireland, Wales, and south-western Britain. Tableware imported from the Atlantic coast of Gaul is also found. Some of the memorial inscriptions (see above) tell a similar story of maritime connection; in particular some of those of the sixth century indicate links with the Mediterranean, even perhaps with North Africa. It could be that such distant connections had much to do with changes in the British Church from about 500, for example the development of monasticism and the cult of relics.

The transformation of western Britain, of Ireland and of Brittany in the generations following the Roman withdrawal from Britain is altogether remarkable. What had been the edge of the Roman world was becoming an increasingly civilized northern Mediterranean. Many Britons lost by the decline of Roman power; others gained: some gained Brittany. Important elements in Roman civilization seem not so much to have faded as the Empire collapsed, but rather, in some areas, to have flourished.

The Byzantine historian Procopius, writing at about the same time as Gildas, thought that Britain was not one island, but two: *Brettania*, lying opposite Spain, and *Brittia*, opposite the Rhine mouths. His confusion arose presumably because his knowledge of the British side of Britain came to him by one route, and that of the eastern, Anglo-Saxon,* side by another. The mistake is probably a fair reflection of the extent to which Britain had become divided into two worlds. By the late sixth century the eastern two-thirds of what later became England were in the hands of dynasties of German origin, and to a considerable extent settled by German peoples. Figure 50 gives indications of the situation there. It has to be vague. We know little about boundaries; there may have been kingdoms of which we know nothing; there may have been areas occupied by Anglo-Saxons but not ruled by kings.

Still, some generalizations are possible. First, it is at least plain, and important, that German Britain, like British Britain, contained many kings. It could well have been that the one set of these in many ways resembled and was much involved with the other (see below, pp. 41, 52). But, second, there was a crucial difference between them. All the British kings were Christian. All the Anglo-Saxon kings were pagan until Saint Augustine's mission of 597 (see below, p. 45). Their lands were the largest part of the Roman Empire as it had been in *c.* 400 to remain pagan so long. That this was so is an indication that what had happened in eastern Britain was in some sense catastrophic.

**The term* Anglo-Saxon *is used here and elsewhere to relate to all or any of the German peoples who settled in Britain, though they included others than Angles and Saxons. Later, all are called English.*

The Written Sources for the Coming of the Saxons

But what *had* happened to divide Britain into a British west, forming part of a Christian Celtic world, surviving, even prospering, round the Irish Sea, and an Anglo-Saxon east, forming part of a pagan North Sea world? Only one authority earlier than 600 attempts to tell us: Gildas. To illustrate the workings of Providence, and in particular to warn his countrymen of its markedly retributive nature, he sketched the history of Britain, as follows. Britain was an island conquered by the Romans. (He always distinguishes between Britons and Romans; the attitudes behind his work seem to be not those of a British ruling class which had come to regard itself as Roman, but rather of one which resented Roman rule.) By the 'fall of Britain' he means not the collapse of Roman power, but the subsequent collapse of British power. It began, he maintains, with the withdrawal of the garrison by Magnus Maximus in his bid for the Empire (383, as we know, though Gildas gives no dates). The Picts and Scots took advantage to harry Britain. The Romans sent a legion which restored the situation. On its withdrawal the Picts and Scots struck again. Once more a Roman army came to repel them; it fortified the island and left, this time insisting the Britons should defend themselves. They did not do so, but appealed for help to 'Aetius, thrice consul'. (Aetius was the Roman *Magister Militum*—commander-in-chief. The reference to his third consulship dates the appeal to between 446 and 454.)

No help came. Still, the Britons did have a respite of prosperity in which they devoted themselves to luxurious debauchery. (It is characteristically thus that Gildas reveals that for considerable periods the Britons did rather well.) During this period 'all the councillors together with the proud tyrant' imported Saxons to defend 'the east side of the country' against 'the peoples from the north'. Three shiploads came first; they were later reinforced. These forces were paid a regular allowance. They demanded more, mutinied, and caused fearful havoc. After a time the Saxons went home (*domum*), whatever he means by that. British power revived under Ambrosius Aurelianus (see above, p. 16), and a series of victories culminated in that of Mount Badon, which Gildas seems to date to about 500. The security thus gained had lasted till his own day.

Gildas's vehement narrative, without dates, without precise geographical locations, very sparing with names, is baffling. It is often impossible to know to what extent he is generalizing from what he knew about one area, rather than from a knowledge of Britain as a whole. *Sapiens* he came to be called, and indeed for our purposes he is too clever by half. His tale is not a record, but an attempt to work out what had happened from inadequate information (which included some written source from overseas). Nevertheless, he is very important. His account of how the beginnings of German power in Britain derived from the mutiny of mercenary forces is plausible, and uses a vocabulary suggesting that he may have been drawing on a fifth-century source.

19 Belt-furniture from a grave at Mucking, Essex, cast bronze 'chip-carved' with silver inlay, length of buckle 10.1 cm. Such fittings were Roman military issue in the later 4th century, and are found above all in German graves (including those of Saxons who had retired home to die). This early 5th-century set is probably of insular manufacture, perhaps issued by a British authority to an important German warrior.

Finglesham. A Cemetery in East Kent

Early Anglo-Saxon cemeteries have been explored since the eighteenth century, but until lately standards of excavation and publication were not good. Interest was concentrated on the grave-goods, especially the jewellery; skeletons were often disregarded and the historical value of the cemetery as a whole was largely ignored. Disenchantment with this state of affairs led a new generation to seek and excavate the sites of settlement, with excellent and varied results. But while they tell us much about such basics as house-types and the economics of daily existence, abandoned homes rarely yield more than building foundations and the kinds of objects people threw away. Their cemeteries, on the other hand, contain the things treasured by the Anglo-Saxons, their mortal remains and the precious possessions which they sought to take with them after death. The evidence recoverable from the two types of site is thus complementary, and in order fully to understand any given community, one should ideally have both. So far this has rarely been possible. However, cemeteries are in fashion again, the subject of enlightened new interest to exploit their full potential. Many have been dug properly and comprehensive publications are on the way, though their wealth of material evidence, and the various expertise required in post-excavation work on them, make them slow to appear in print.

Such a site is Finglesham. It was found by chalk quarrying: 31 graves were rescued in 1928/9 and another 215 were excavated more scientifically between 1959 and 1967. The plan (1) shows that, except for a few graves destroyed in its north-west corner and two inaccessible beneath the modern line of the ancient Whiteway, which formed its western boundary, we have an unusually intact cemetery. It tells an interesting story. Its very name, that of the nearest village, contributes: the 'Old English' form, contemporary with the cemetery, was *Pengels-hām*, the 'prince's manor'. Almost certainly it is no coincidence that the people who founded the site were among the wealthiest and most aristocratic yet to be found in the kingdom of Kent. Finglesham is close by the old royal vill at Eastry, and there is every likelihood that its leading family in the

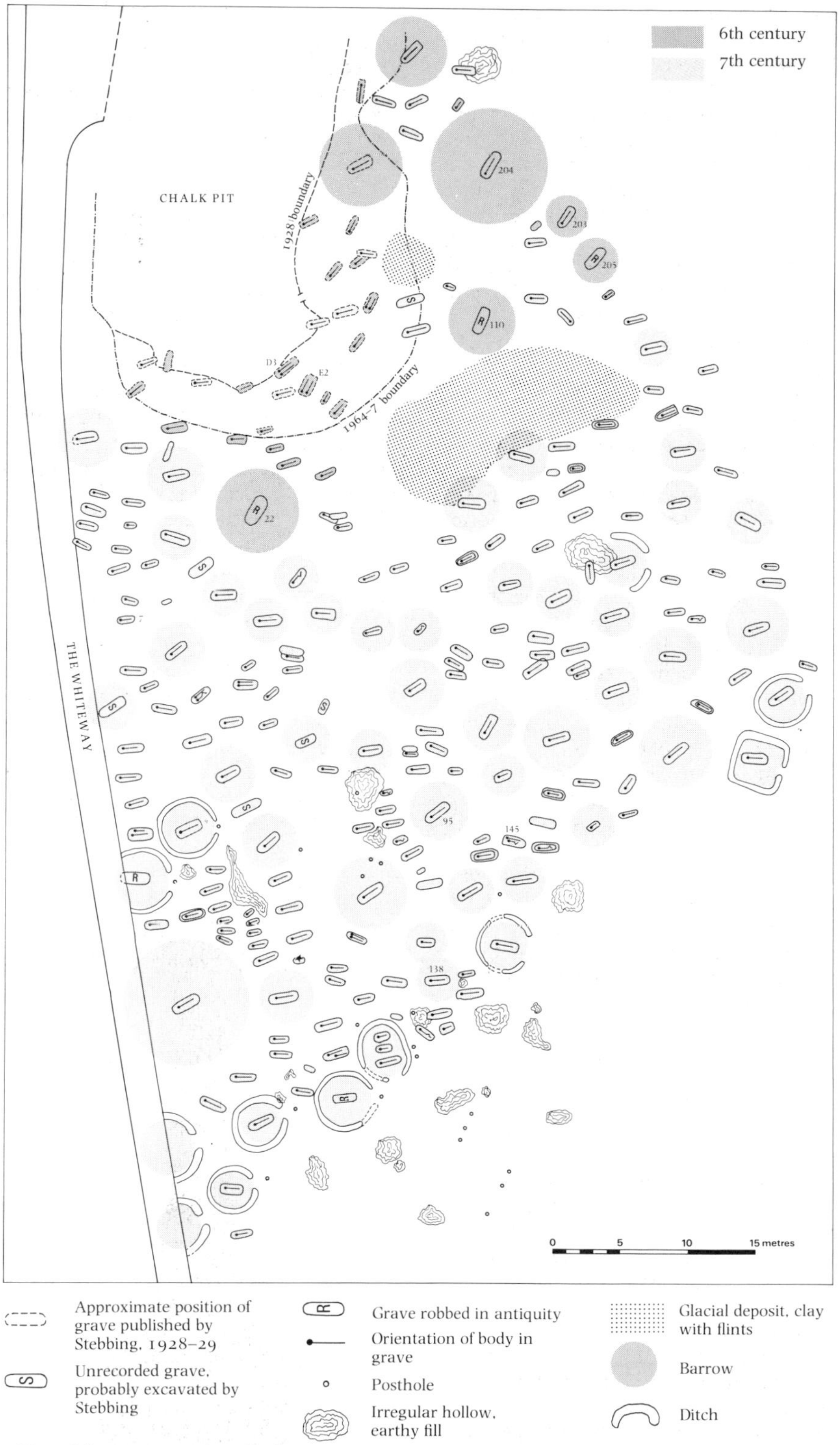

1 Plan of the cemetery showing barrows.

sixth century belonged to the royal kindred.

The burials of these aristocrats and their followers, not more than 30 in all, lie at the northern end of the cemetery, on high ground overlooking the presumed site of settlement. The founding male (buried in grave no. 204) died aged about 25 in about the year 525, and was buried in a large iron-bound coffin with his Kentish silver-gilt hilted ring-sword (3), silver-studded shield, spear and knife, Kentish glass claw-beaker (4), Frankish bronze bowl and well-datable but not new Frankish cloisonné belt-buckle (2), which might have belonged to his father. Of his kinsmen and successors, two robbed in antiquity (22, 110) had certainly been richly furnished, those in unmolested graves (G2 with sword, spear, shield, buckle, 211 with at least spear and shield) were less so. The rich womenfolk fared better: only one of their graves was robbed (205), leaving three intact. The earliest (D3), perhaps 204's consort, was buried with Jutlandic heirlooms, a very worn square-headed brooch and gold D-bracteates, newer Frankish radiate brooches and brand-new Kentish bird-brooches and claw-beaker. She also had an iron sword-shaped weaving-beater, apparently a status symbol; a similar beater was found in the later grave 203, of *c.* 550/60. Here there was another claw-beaker, a bowl like the man's and much jewellery: a double necklet with antique Jutish and Frankish gold elements; overlying it her cloak-fastener, a Frankish square-head brooch; at her waist an antique Frankish buckle-set; at her neck a Frankish garnet rosette-brooch; and on either breast new Kentish square-heads. It should be possible to reconstruct her entire dress. Finally, the third rich lady (E2) had a fine buckle-set, and four jewelled brooches, a disc and large and small square-heads, all made in Kent *c.* 540. Each woman's brooches were of gilded and nielloed silver, the luxury metal at a time when gold was in acutely short supply. These four intact graves reflect not just the family's wealth but also its history, and indeed that of the kingdom as a whole, from Jutish origins in the fifth century, Frankish connections in the early sixth, to Kentish cultural independence at least by the beginning of the reign of Aethelbert in *c.* 560.

This seems to have been the date at which our aristocratic family left Finglesham. Burial continued, perhaps after an interval, until the beginning of the eighth century, but the later people were less rich and their leading family socially

2 Silver gilt buckle with inset garnets and green and white glass from grave 204, width 6.3 cm (all the objects illustrated in this essay are from the Northbourne collection; Oxford, Ashmolean Museum).

less prestigious. The details of the changeover are less puzzling now that study of the spaces around graves has revealed that the sixth-century aristocrats were buried under barrows. Now quite ploughed away, in Anglo-Saxon times these must have been prominent, with the big mound over 204 a positive landmark. The seventh-century people therefore knew the whereabouts of the earlier burials and (unless they were the robbers) respected them, encroaching on them seldom. They emulated the custom of barrow-burial, and their mounds, with or without ditches, once clustered thickly on the site. In some cases one can see how barrows were built first and flat graves gathered round them, and obviously this will help determine the family groupings and chronological sequence in the seventh century, which remain a problem. Two graves (7,145) are coin-dated to *c.* 675 and 700 respectively, but though there are a few fine things, some glasses and the gilt buckle from grave 95 especially (p. 48, no. 1), most of the grave-goods, the pottery, the spears and buckles of the men, the simple necklaces and caskets of the women, are not closely datable. At present, in addition to more traditional methods of study, all available data are being processed by computer to wring the last drop of information from the site.

3 Sword from grave 204, length from tip of pommel to scabbard mouthpiece 14.7 cm.

4 Green glass claw-beaker from grave 204, height 19.9 cm.

Meanwhile, their bones tell us that, typically for pre-modern societies, these people could be short-lived. Though child mortality was not excessive, nearly half the population died by the age of 25. Of those who survived the hazards of youth, however, a good many lived to ripe middle age. Causes of death are rarely evident, but double burials suggest epidemic disease and childbirth casualties, and one man died of a sword-cut to the head. The absolute numbers alive at one time in the sixth century suggest a smallish household, while those in the seventh indicate perhaps the whole population of a substantial working farm. For a whole village community one must look elsewhere.

S. Chadwick Hawkes

The next effort to put together an account of the coming of the Saxons is that of Bede, *c.* 731. He used and filled out Gildas's account, adding the names of the 'proud tyrant' (Vortigern, which Gildas also may have supplied in one version) and of the leaders of the mercenaries (Hengest and Horsa); also a location for their settlement (Kent) and a date for their mutiny (between 449 and 456). Bede's account has dominated later historiography, but poses many problems (see below, p. 29). A fuller account appears in an early ninth-century collection made in Wales and associated with the name of Nennius. Like Bede's it supplies the names of Vortigern, Hengest and Horsa, and locates the settlement in Kent, but adds a variety of other information or, anyway, matter. Some of this is suggestive of the kind of thing which may actually have happened, for example that Hengest's son went to fight the Irish in the region of the Wall. Much of it, however, like the story of how Hengest acquired Kent by luring Vortigern into marriage with his daughter, reads as romance. Indeed 'Nennius's' account probably is largely romance; the relationship between history and fiction was often intimate in the Dark Ages. But, at the very least, the Nennian tales testify to vivid ninth-century interest in what had happened in the fifth.

The knowledge of that interest, and of the forms it could take, is salutary when one comes to consider the account of the beginnings of Anglo-Saxon power profered by the *Anglo-Saxon Chronicle*, a compilation of *c.* 892 drawing on earlier materials (see below, p. 253). What it has to say is perplexing. Its annals provide accounts of the origins of the three early kingdoms which were incorporated in Wessex by 892: Kent, Sussex, and Wessex. In each case a leader or leaders are described as landing in a small number of ships, and a brief annalistic account of their subsequent campaigns is supplied. The Kentish origin story is that of Hengest and Horsa, dated to 449–54, and draws heavily on Bede, though he says nothing about their campaigns against the Britons. That for Sussex starts with the landing of Aelle in 477 and has a little on his campaigns up to 491. For Wessex there are three origin stories: one beginning with the landing of Cerdic and Cynric in 495, the second with that of Port in 501, the third with that of the 'West Saxons' in 514.

20 The ankle-bone of a roe-deer, inscribed in runes, from a cremation urn at Caistor-by-Norwich, believed to be of the early 5th century, arguably earlier, length 2.8 cm (Norwich Castle Museum). Runes came into use among the Germans by the 3rd century, chiefly for magic. The meaning of this inscription is disputed: 'divine power', 'a marker' and 'roe-deer' have been suggested. The bone presumably relates to other ankle-bones and bone (? and shale) counters in the same urn. They may be the apparatus for a game, or, more weightily, for casting lots.

The fifth-century Anglo-Saxons were illiterate and cannot have kept annals. Wherever the material in the *Chronicle* came from the absolute dates required by an annalistic form were probably supplied by various processes of deduction and guesswork and are worth little. Some of what the *Chronicle* says looks as if it may have derived from materials reflecting fictionalizing historical interests which can be paralleled in the Celtic world. Thus on nine occasions the name of a place is associated with that of one of the *dramatis personae*; for example, '501 . . . Port and his two sons came to Wessex at the place which is called Portsmouth.' While it is true that the Anglo-Saxons sometimes did name places after great men, it is also true they they deduced the names of non-existent men from place-names. Thus of the Roman *Anderida* (Pevensey) they made 'the *ceaster* (their normal word derived from *castrum*, for a Roman fortified place) of Andred': *Andredesceaster*. So one may suspect that Port had more to do with the Latin *portus* than with a real man; and that Wightgar similarly never lived, but was conjured up from *Vectis*, the Roman name for the Isle of Wight. Such an interest in imaginatively relating place-names to events recalls the Irish *dindshencus*, 'traditions about places', and may have very little to do with what actually happened. Other statements made in these annals are more literary devices than facts. Thus they have three of the kingdom-founding expeditions sailing in three ships, and this may be merely a formula (one also used by the historian of the Goths, Jordanes, who has them migrate in three ships from Scandinavia).

But if substantial elements in the early annals had been transmitted through genres of writing or composing in which truth and fiction met, married and bred, still, some of them sound very plausible, for example: '456. In this year Hengest and his son Aesc fought against the Britons at a place called *Crecanford* and killed 4,000 men; and the Britons then deserted Kent and fled in great fear to London.' It is indeed likely that the Britons would have fled to London, and although the origins of such annals are deeply mysterious, and suspect, they cannot be simply discarded. (There is similar, and apparently related, material on the conquest of Kent in the Nennian collection.)

It is important to observe that the *Chronicle* has nothing at all to say about most of the English kingdoms. It supplies a date, 547, for the succession of Ida to Bernicia and another, 560, for that of Aelle to Deira; these may indicate the beginnings of the power in those kingdoms of the dynasties which were to rule them, and possibly of Anglian power there. For the other kingdoms there is nothing. Most strikingly, the *Chronicle* does not mention London, or the kingdom in which it lay, Essex, between 456 and 842, apart from two seventh-century references to Mellitus, bishop of London (see below, p. 51) derived from Bede. London had been the principal place of Roman Britain; its site is the most important in the south. The omission by itself suffices to damn any attempt to use the *Chronicle*, with no matter what reserves, to provide even an approximate outline of the main events of the fifth and sixth centuries.

To some slight extent its gaps can be filled from other, though doubtful, sources. A handful of annals preserved in chronicles of the twelfth and thirteenth centuries, but not impossibly derived from materials such as the compilers of the *Chronicle* used, may cast a little light on the origins of East Anglia, Mercia and Essex. These annals associate the origins of East Anglia and ultimately of Mercia with an invasion from Germany in 527, and begin the kingdoms (or dynasties) of Essex, East Anglia, and Mercia in 527, 571, and 585 respectively. No one would put much faith in such sources, least of all in the dates they give. Still, it is worth noticing that the origin of the rule in England of all the dynasties north of the Thames mentioned in these annals or in those of the *Chronicle* is put in the sixth century, not the fifth. In the case of East Anglia one can be reasonably sure that the annals are right, at least as to the century, for the evidence of Bede with that of Sutton Hoo (see below, pp. 32–3) strongly suggests that its dynasty came from Sweden in the sixth century.

21, 22 Saucer brooches are found chiefly in the Continental homeland of the Saxons and in England in areas identified by Bede (see p. 29) as Saxon, though not only in these. The upper brooch is bronze, from Caistor-by-Norwich, and of the later 5th century (Norwich Castle Museum). The lower pairs are gilded bronze, from Fairford, Glos., and of the 6th century (Oxford, Ashmolean Museum). All are about 4.5 cm in diameter.

In considering what we know, and how little we know, of the course of events in the dark centuries, it would be natural for a reader to ask: 'What about king Arthur?' No satisfactory answer is to be had. Arthur's late and continuing fame owes almost everything to a fictional history of the kings of Britain written by Geoffrey of Monmouth in the 1130s. The only early references to him are as follows. One, a statement in a Welsh poem, thought to be of about 600, that someone was *not* Arthur; it may be a late interpolation. Two, a list in the Nennian collection, of twelve battles fought by Arthur, there described not as a king but as *dux bellorum* (commander in wars). Three, two references in annals appended to the same collection: one, to his being at the battle of Mount Badon (here dated 516) and there 'carrying the cross of our Lord Jesus Christ for three days and nights on his shoulders'; the other, to his death at the battle of Camlann, 537. These annals do not indicate whether he was a king and in any case are unlikely to derive from contemporary materials. That is all. And on that little all the imagination of the learned and the unlearned has run riot. He has, for example, been seen as the last of the emperors of Roman Britain, or as the commander of a field army for such an emperor or for a federation of British rulers. Perhaps there were such emperors (see above p. 17; perhaps there was such an army. There is at least this to be said for the inexhaustible, if rather ridiculous, interest in trying to work out who the 'real' Arthur was. By provoking speculation it forces realization of how many great men and great events there must have been in the fifth and sixth centuries of which we know nothing at all.

The Archaeological Record

If in some ways we know very much less of the fifth and sixth centuries than we do of later periods, in others we know more. Thus far more objects survive from this period than do from, say, the late Middle Ages. This is because the Germanic invaders and settlers were accustomed to bury grave goods with their dead or else to cremate them and to bury the ashes in decorated pots. At least 1,500 cemeteries have been dug up, in whole or in part, containing probably not fewer than 30,000 burials from the early fifth century to the early eighth. A handful of settlement sites have been explored; but the bulk of the evidence is funerary. The early Anglo-Saxon archaeologist must be a Resurrection Man; the grave his haunt.

Nothing could be more exacting than the effort to decode so many thousands of *things* to try to make them tell a historical tale. Dating them is often terribly hard. Because coins were not in use nearly everything depends on the correlation of typological series; that is to say on elaborate chains of argument which can grow progressively weaker as they are extended. There are dire basic problems in the interpretation of the archaeological evidence which must be faced but cannot be solved. Two are particularly vexing: that of the reliability of what has been found and studied as an index to what once was there; and that of the almost total absence of archaeological traces of the Britons.

No one knows how many people lived in the lands under Anglo-Saxon control in the centuries concerned. But it would be surprising if we have the graves of 1 per cent of them, and possible that we have those of not more than, say, 0.2 per cent. How far is such a proportion representative, for example in its geographical distribution? In some very general ways it must be; the absence of pagan cemeteries in, say, Lancashire certainly tells one something. But to consider the ease with which ploughing could destroy a large cremation cemetery if the urns were fairly near the surface is to realize how far our distribution maps must represent, not what once was there, but a complicated and unknowable relationship between the Anglo-Saxons' choice of cemetery sites and agricultural practices over many later centuries. Worse still is the problem of the Britons. During much of the fifth and sixth centuries wide areas of what became England were in British hands. Where is the British archaeology of, say, fifth-century East Anglia? A few odds and ends, a few speculations apart, there is none. Yet the history of East Anglia in the fifth century must have been in large measure a British history. However low one puts the survival rate of Anglo-Saxon graves, it is inconceivable that the few score pre-450 burials from East Anglia can indicate that all the British inhabitants had been driven out. Indeed, for all we know, all or part of the area may have been ruled by Britons till the sixth century.

Those who wish for certainty in history and who like to feel the ground firmly under their feet are best advised to study some other period. For those who care to venture into a quagmire, the archaeological evidence, and the truly remarkable intellectual effort of archaeologists to make sense of it, are of basic importance. The starting point, in many ways for good, though in some for ill, in the use of archaeology to illustrate the meagre written record and to fill its gaps is the fifteenth chapter of the first book of Bede's *Ecclesiastical History*. His account there of the origins of Anglo-Saxon power in Britain was based on Gildas's narrative, with additions. One of these looks as if it came to him late, probably in a letter, and as if he inserted it, not quite with his usual deftness, into a narrative which he had already written. It comes after he has repeated Gildas's narrative of the employment of Germans to defend Britain (see above, p. 23):

'Those who came over were of three of the more powerful peoples of Germany; the Saxons, the Angles and the Jutes. From the Jutes are descended the men of Kent, the *Victuarii* (that is to say the people who inhabit the Isle of Wight) and that people who are today called the Jutes and are located in the kingdom of the West Saxons, opposite the Isle of Wight. From the Saxons (that is to say from that area which is now called Old Saxony) came the East Saxons, the South Saxons and the West Saxons. Next, from the Angles (that is to say from the country which is called *Angulus* and which is said to have re-

23 (*left*) Jewellery and glass objects from Sarre, Kent, grave 4, width of larger square-headed brooch 4.1 cm, probably before the middle of the 6th century (Maidstone Museum). The glass beaker is Frankish, the six gold bracteates Scandinavian, and all the jewellery Kentish.

24 Gilded bronze 'equal-armed' brooch from Haslingfield, Cambs., length 9.3 cm, mid-5th-century or somewhat later (Cambridge University, Museum of Archaeology and Anthropology).

25 From an early or mid-6th-century grave at Little Wilbraham, Cambs., came this square-headed brooch, 14.3 cm long, and two cruciform brooches, which had secured a woman's cloak at the neck and her tunic at the shoulders; also a pair of sleeve-clasps (Cambridge University, Museum of Archaeology and Anthropology).

26 Brooch in the 'quoit' style from Sarre, Kent, mid-5th-century, diameter 8.5 cm (British Museum). The significance of such brooches is debated. Though the form and style are probably of Scandinavian origin, the craftsmanship has a Roman pedigree.

27, 28 Urn from a cremation cemetery at Wehden, Lower Saxony (above), and fragments from another from a similar cemetery at Markshall, Norfolk (below) (Hannover, Niedersächsisches Landesmuseum, and Norwich Castle Museum). Each is very unusual in its own country in showing human faces. It is likely that they were made by the same probably mid-5th-century potter. Height of urn 21.5 cm, width of larger fragment *c.* 11.5 cm.

mained deserted from that time to the present, between the lands of the Jutes and those of the Saxons) are descended the East Angles, the Middle Angles, the Mercians, all the race of the Northumbrians (that is to say of those peoples who live to the north of the river Humber), and the other Anglian peoples.'

This paragraph, put by Bede with Gildas's highly plausible account of the mutiny of Germans who had been hired to defend part of Britain, and supplied with an indication of date, ensured that for many centuries readers of Bede had plain answers to the main questions about the arrival of the Anglo-Saxons in Britain: Who? How? When? Bede knew less than many of those many generations of readers thought; but to the first question the answer he gave is demonstrably in large measure right. The archaeological evidence is plain that a high proportion of the invaders and settlers were indeed Angles, Saxons, and Jutes. The Angles were a people who lived in the southern part of the Danish peninsula and on some of the Danish islands. The Saxons were to the west of them, occupying the North Sea coastal plain up to approximately the mouth of the Weser (and, in the fifth century, increasingly further west). These are the peoples most prominent in the English archaeological record. For example, cremation cemeteries full of urns, just such as they used, appear in England as they do in south Denmark and north Germany, most strikingly in a series of big cemeteries found in eastern England from Norfolk to Yorkshire, for example at Caistor-by-Norwich, Markshall and Spong Hill in Norfolk, Loveden Hill in Lincolnshire, and Sancton in East Yorkshire. The objects found in the inhumation cemeteries of southern and Midland England tell the same story; their connections are generally Angle or Saxon (Angles and Saxons were more involved together both on the Continent and in England than Bede implies).

For many years Bede's account of the role of the Jutes caused trouble as that of the Angles and Saxons did not. He seems to indicate that the *Iutae* came from Jutland, and philologists claimed, in bold defiance of apparent common-sense, that this was philologically impossible. However, it has become plain that there were indeed strong connections between Kent and Jutland. They appear in much that is found in Kentish graves: in pottery, in jewellery, and most strikingly in bracteates, decorated discs of gold. Here too Bede was right; archaeology also shows a special connection between Kent and the Isle of Wight. Even Bede's suggestion about the desertion of some of the areas from which the immigrants came is confirmed. During the fifth century large parts of the North Sea littoral were affected by rising sea-levels. Villages which had for long been inhabited were deserted, and it is a fair guess that the inhabitants of some of them came to England (see fig. 29). It is remarkable how much Bede's informant knew; and the more remarkable in that, except in the passage in question, Bede seems to regard Angles and Saxons as hardly distinguishable, and to know nothing of Jutes.

Angles and Saxons (with Jutes in Kent) did indeed then compose the bulk of the fifth-century invaders and

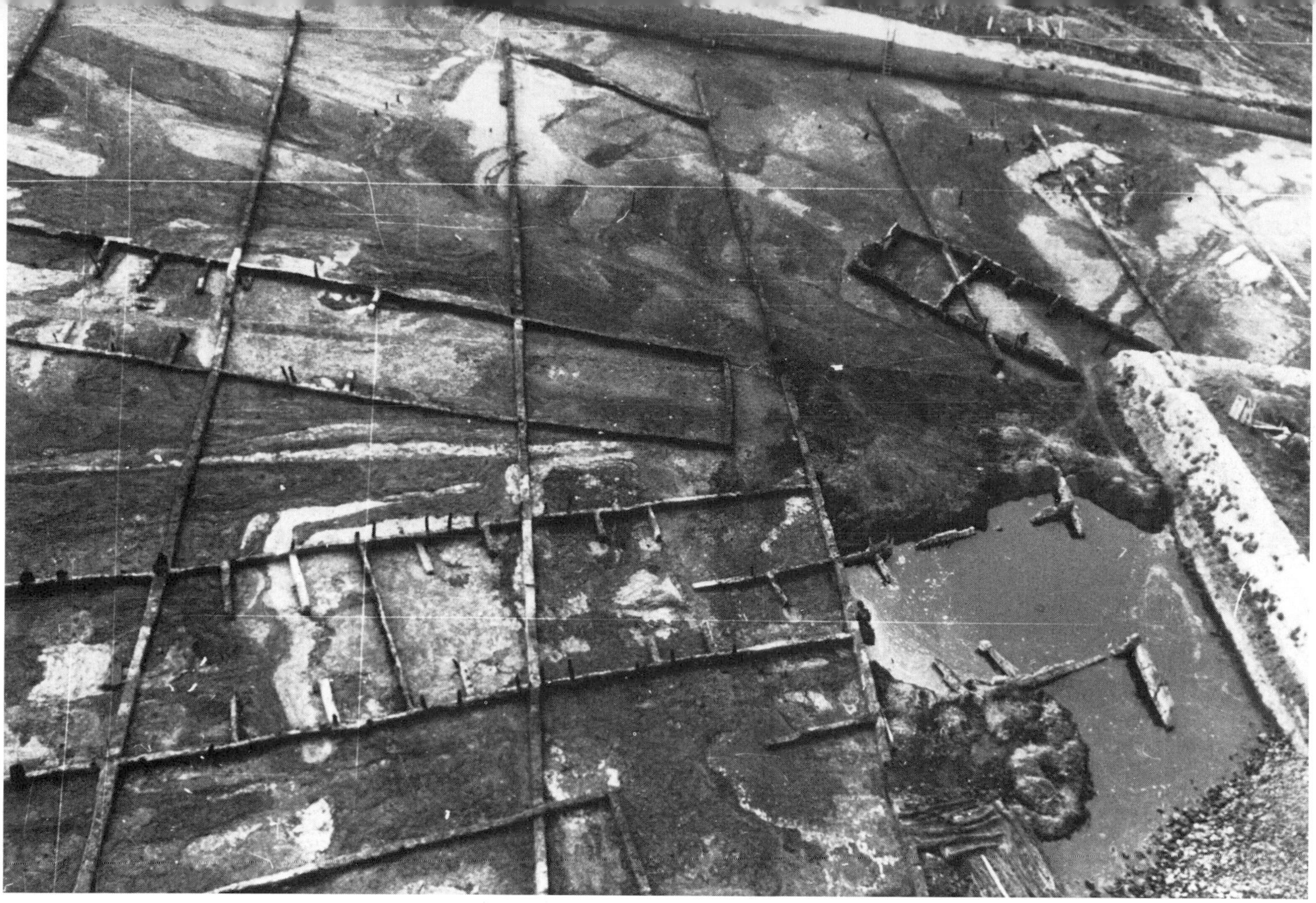

29 Early levels at Feddersen Wierde, near Bremerhaven. This settlement developed from a farmhouse of the first century BC to a radially planned village of about 30 houses, standing on a mound for security from sea-flood. It was abandoned in about 450; its inhabitants may well have come to England (see above, p. 30).

settlers in Britain. Other peoples and other areas of the German world were also represented. Procopius (see above, p. 22) regarded Britain as inhabited by Britons, Angles, and Frisians. There is no doubt that many of the settlers did come from Frisia. Both Angles and Saxons were settling in Frisia in the fifth century, and for some it was a staging post on the way to England. In later centuries Frisian resembled English more closely than did any other Germanic language. The most important non-Anglo-Saxon element was probably Frankish. The Franks and Saxons, pressing on Gaul from the east, had long been associated together in attacks on the Empire. Franks had participated in the great barbarian assault on Britain of 367 (see above, p. 14). The archaeological evidence suggests they played a considerable part in southern England in the fifth century. In another passage Bede says that there were many peoples in Germany from whom the 'Angles and Saxons who now live in Britain' derive their origin. 'They are', he says, 'the Frisians, the *Rugini*, the Danes, the Huns, the Old Saxons and the *Boructari* (*HE*, V.9). He may have been writing loosely and not really meaning to imply that all these peoples were actually represented in the settlement of Britain. But it is what he says; and he does not generally write carelessly. The mention of Danes could fit with the archaeological evidence for extensive settlement in eastern England, from the late fifth century, by people whose Continental homes lay considerably to the north of the Angles and Saxons, from modern north Denmark and south Norway. The *Boructari* were a people who lived in the general area of the Ruhr and are usually counted as Franks. The *Rugini* were a people who had moved in the fourth century from the Baltic to Moravia. This would not seem likely to have brought them near Britain, but their participation in Attila's invasion of Gaul in 451 might have done so. Whether or not it is right to take Bede as meaning just what he says, it is certain that men came to Britain from many parts of the German world, from Norway to south Germany.

If Bede was well-informed on the 'Who?' of the coming of Germans to Britain, he was very ill-informed on the 'When?' He made various guesses at the date of the coming of the Saxons, putting it at various points between 445 and 455. He was doing no more than making what deductions he could from the meagre chronological data provided by Gildas. An earlier date, 428, is provided in the Nennian collection. It is probably no better-based than Bede's, but the archaeological evidence suggests that it is, nevertheless, rather nearer the truth. In considerable areas the earliest Germanic objects found seem to belong to somewhere near the beginning of the fifth century. Some of the earliest German pottery in England is sometimes judged to be even earlier.

Sutton Hoo

1 The ship under excavation. The timbers had disappeared but the rivets, and stains in the sand, permitted their reconstruction, except for the high tips of bow and stern. Nearly 90 feet long and, at its widest, 14 feet wide, the ship is larger than any other from the early Dark Ages so far found.

In 1939 the tomb of a seventh-century king was found at Sutton Hoo, near Woodbridge in Suffolk. He had been buried like this. A ship had been dragged from the river Deben up to the top of a 100-foot-high bluff, and laid in a trench (1). A gabled hut had been built amidships to accommodate a very big coffin and an astonishing collection of treasures and gear. The trench had then been filled in and a mound raised over it to stand boldly on the skyline. The burial was found untouched. Simply to list what was there would exhaust this small space. The weapons included a helmet (fig. 70), a sword and a shield, all magnificent. There were numerous personal ornaments, most of gold inlaid with garnets (e.g. fig. 77), silverware, kitchen equipment (3) and much else. Most enigmatic was the 'ceremonial whetstone' (fig. 69).

Whose was the grave? With the body was a purse containing 37 Merovingian gold coins. The latest of these date from the 620s. So the tomb could be that of Redwald; its wealth would match his great power (see p. 56), and the presence of Christian objects in an apparently pagan context would accord with Bede's account of him as having syncretized pagan and Christian practices (*HE*, II.15, p. 116). These arguments are inconclusive. It could just as well be one of his successors (see p. 56) who lay here.

Other treasures have survived from seventh-century England; but those from Sutton Hoo are outstanding not only in number, but in quality. In that they are unsurpassed, indeed unsurpassable. Consider, for example, the shoulder-clasps (fig. 77). They are cloisonné: that is to say they consist of plates of gold on to which were brazed gold strips, set on edge in such a way as to create a pattern of cells into which were fitted thin slices of garnet or millefiori glass. The skill displayed is at it height round the edges of the clasps. The garnet interlace there seems set into solid gold. In reality 'the plain fields between and around these garnet elements . . . are . . . cells, just like those which carry the garnets, often of the most irregular shapes, with thick gold lids brazed over their tops' (Bruce-Mitford). They were wealthy kings indeed who could afford such jewels and such craftsmen.

The finds reveal distant influences and wide connections. Most emphasized have been those with Sweden. Ship burials have been found in only two parts of the Germanic world, east Suffolk and east Sweden. The impression of a Swedish connection is reinforced by the nature of the helmet and shield, such that Mr Bruce-Mitford can say that they were probably 'made in Sweden or by armourers from Sweden working in Suffolk exclusively in their traditional Swedish manner and with Swedish dies, moulds and other equipment'. Perhaps the East Anglian royal house and kingdom had been established by Swedes in the sixth century. There are other indications there of migration from Scandinavia, though they suggest in the main connection with areas west and/or south of those indicated at Sutton Hoo (see p. 34).

Other elements in the treasure point to Gaul. The coins are Merovingian. No two are from the same mint, which suggests their selection from a large hoard. Such a hoard need not, but could, have been

2 The great gold buckle, length 13.2 cm, weight 414.6 gm. The design is a complex of animals, snakes and bird heads, picked out in niello (all the objects from Sutton Hoo are now in the British Museum).

that of the East Anglian kings; if it was, it need not, but could, have been the fruit of trade with Gaul, for example the export of slaves. Equally suggestive, and yet more enigmatic, is the great gold buckle (2). Mr Bruce-Mitford regards it as locally made but 'unmistakably Swedish' in style. It leads his mind to the pagan shores of the Gulf of Bothnia. Dr Werner, however, emphasizes a singular thing about it, that it is hollow, with a hinged back which opens like that of a watch. He believes it to be a reliquary. *His* mind is led to parallels in the Christian world of Gaul and Burgundy.

Some of the finds undoubtedly came from the far south. The great silver dish (3) was made in Byzantium in about 500. A set of 10 silver bowls had a more recent Mediterranean origin. A bronze bowl had come from Alexandria fairly recently; among the animals incised on it is a camel. The three 'hanging bowls' had a very different and probably Celtic origin (see fig. 64). Links of a different kind are suggested by close resemblances between the pattern of the shoulder-clasps and that of a carpet-page in the Lindisfarne Gospels (see figs 76, 77).

The interpretation of many of the objects found at Sutton Hoo is a matter for speculation, whose pleasures, however exquisite, do not satisfy. Perhaps the spoons (4) were a christening present to Redwald: perhaps they were not. Dr Werner's view of the great buckle makes one reflect that Sigbert (see p. 45) was converted in Gaul and that his bishop was a Burgundian; who can say how much the reflection is worth? Mr Bruce-Mitford suggests that the whetstone may have been a symbol of bretwaldic power (cf. p. 53). Fascinating: but there is a risk of circularity here, for if he is right, it is by far the best evidence for bretwaldaship as an institution. More secure is what the treasure taken as a whole tells us. For example, it emphasizes how much of the Germanic world England had links with, directly or indirectly. The animal ornament of some of the jewellery was of a kind which became fashionable over nearly all that world. So minor a decorative device as the use of mushroom-shaped cloisons is paralleled *c.* 600 in objects found from Sweden to Lombardy. Or again, in more ways than one the treasure shows the pervasive influence of Rome (see p. 66). But the most important function of archaeology is its simplest: to recover the physical reality of the past. If anyone wishes to know the true importance of Sutton Hoo, the answer is: read Bede's *Ecclesiastical History* II.12, II.15 and III.18 without having considered that treasure; then read those chapters again, having done so.

J. Campbell

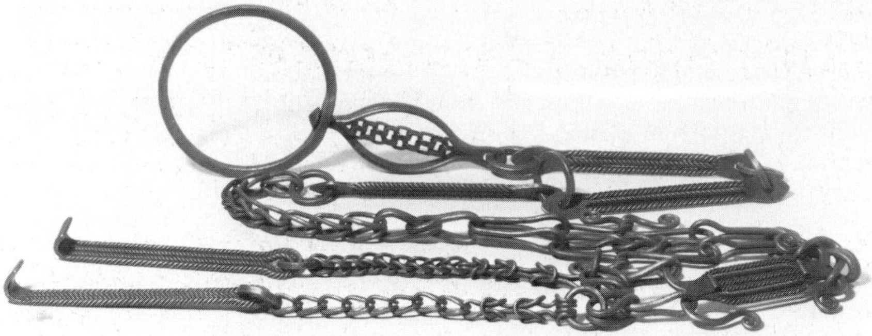

3 A modern reproduction of a chain-work complex for the suspension of a bronze bucket. It is 12 ft 6 in (3.75 m) long and its elaboration suggests that it was not just kitchen equipment, but rather that it hung for some purpose in the king's hall.

4 A pair of silver spoons of late classical type, length 25.4 cm. One is inscribed, in Greek letters, PAULOS, and the other SAULOS, which suggests the possibility of their having been a christening gift to Redwald.

5 The Anastasius silver dish, diameter 72.4 cm. It is of Byzantine origin and bears control stamps dating its manufacture to between 491 and 518.

In the south and centre of England some of the grave-goods tell a story of a similarly early date. Certain objects, in particular belt-buckles found in cemeteries south and just north of the Thames, are of the kinds associated with German, probably for the most part Saxon and Frankish, settlers, who appear in Gaul during the later fourth century, having been established there by the imperial authorities for military purposes. Among the earliest such settlers were men wearing belt-furniture of the kind worn by Germans in Roman military service, and of types which can be dated with some confidence to a decade or so on either side of 420. Their graves (always in small numbers) have been found at, for example, Croydon, Dorchester-on-Thames, Milton (in Kent), and Mucking on the Essex side of the Thames estuary. In Midland England, in particular along the Icknield Way (see fig. 30), rather differently furnished graves of the early fifth century are found, containing brooches which are unambiguously Saxon and suggesting fairly direct contact with the Saxon homeland on the North Sea. There are many doubts and difficulties; dating objects of the kinds concerned is a very approximate business. Still, it does seem reasonably certain that there were Germanic settlers in various part of England from the Channel coast to north of the Humber in the earliest decades of the fifth century (see figs. 19, 21, 22, 24).

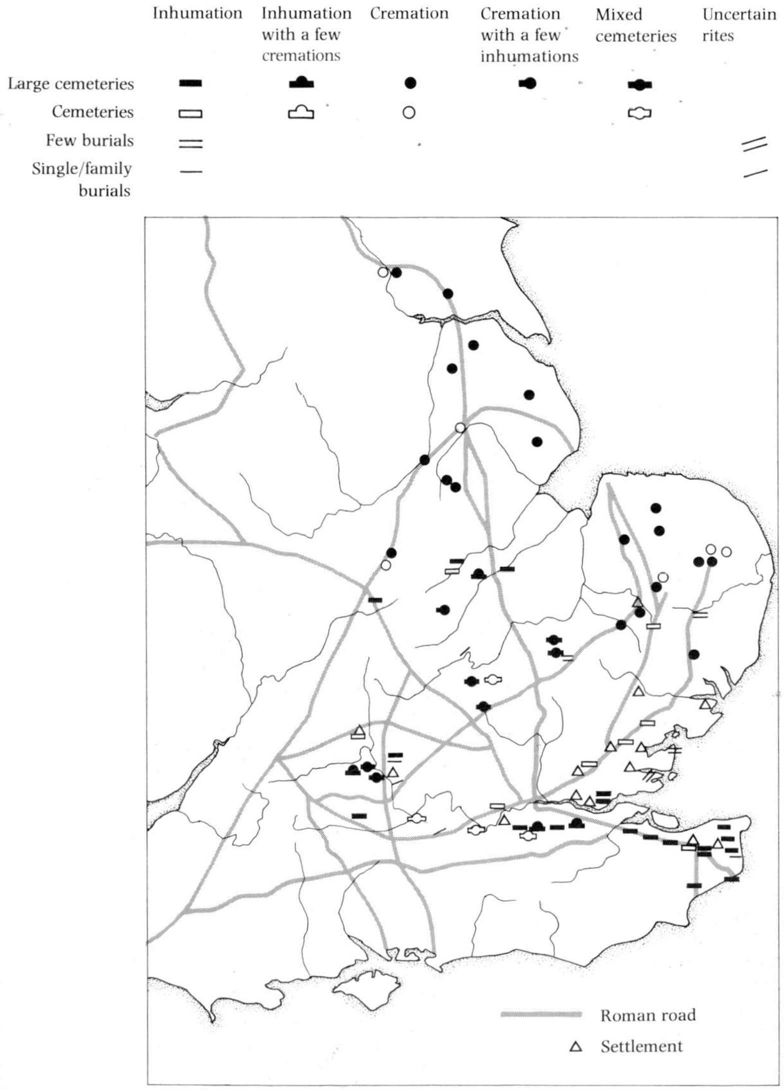

How had they come there? There is no doubt that Gilda's account, which Bede follows, is very credible. The use of Germans for defence against Picts, other Germans, or indeed other Britons is something which could easily have occurred to British authorities. But something much more complex than what Gildas describes must have happened. He indicates that there was one settlement of Germans; but while it could well be that there was some particularly important arrangement made by some major British authority, which first brought Angles and Saxons in, the very diversity of the archaeological evidence suggests that the settlement of Germans for defence must have been by a variety of arrangements made by various authorities.

Archaeology can reveal a great deal. It cannot, however, provide unambiguous evidence as to the nature of the authority under which men were living. Any of the early fifth-century German settlements, of whatever kind, could have been made under the control of British authorities for a defensive purpose. Perhaps all were. On the other hand many may have been the result not so much of controlled settlement, as of intrusion by force. The distinction between settlers and invaders may often have been unclear, and, as Gildas indicates, one could prepare the way for the other. The kind of thing he describes probably happened in many areas apart from Kent (and it should be emphasized that he does not indicate Kent as the place; that the settlement and mutiny he describes took place there may be just a guess by his successors). Nothing is more difficult than to imagine the circumstances which led from the appearance of the first German settlers in the early fifth century to the establishment of German dynasties, many of which need not have come to power before the sixth century. Often there may have been no close connection between the first German settlers and the later German kings; an extreme case is East Anglia, where the fifth-century settlers were Angles and Saxons, but the sixth-century kings seem to have come from Sweden (see above, pp. 32–3). Here, and elsewhere, it is improbable that there was a simple development from fifth-century settlements to sixth-century kingdoms. There may well have been ebbs and flows of power between Anglo-Saxons and Britons, and between various German peoples and rulers.

In the consideration of what may have happened in the fifth and sixth centuries two issues are of special importance. One is that of the number of the Germanic incomers, the other is that of the nature of power in the world from which they came. Although there are burials certainly or probably from the early decades of the fifth century in many parts of southern and eastern England they are not numerous; probably a few hundred at most. The problem at once arises of what relation the number of modern finds bears to the demographic realities of the past (see above, p. 29). No one knows. But it does seem to be the case that there are in most of the areas concerned many more graves dating from later in the century; that sixth-century graves are more numerous than fifth-; and that sixth-century graves are found in some areas where

31 (*above*) Gold jewellery of the late 7th century from Roundway Downs, Wilts., height of triangular pendant 2.8 cm (Devizes Museum). The linked pins with garnets in their heads, animal heads at the ends of the chain and a moulded blue glass stud of Irish type in the centre setting probably fastened the head veil. The pendants are set with cabochon garnets and lignite; alternating with the biconical gold beads, they would have formed a choker necklet (cf. fig. 41, 46).

32 (*left*) This lid, presumably from a cremation urn of the pagan period, was found in the cemetery at Spong Hill, Norfolk (Norwich Castle Museum). The seated figure, 14.5 cm high, is unparalleled, and of uncertain significance.

33 (*right*) 'Claw-beaker', imported from the Rhineland in the 5th century, found at Castle Eden, Co. Durham, height 19 cm (British Museum).

30 (*opposite page*) The Anglo-Saxon settlements by the middle of the 5th century (after J. Morris, *The Age of Arthur*, Weidenfeld & Nicolson, 1973, with additions by S. C. Hawkes). Unpublished research shows that the density of settlement in East Anglia is in fact considerably greater than indicated here.

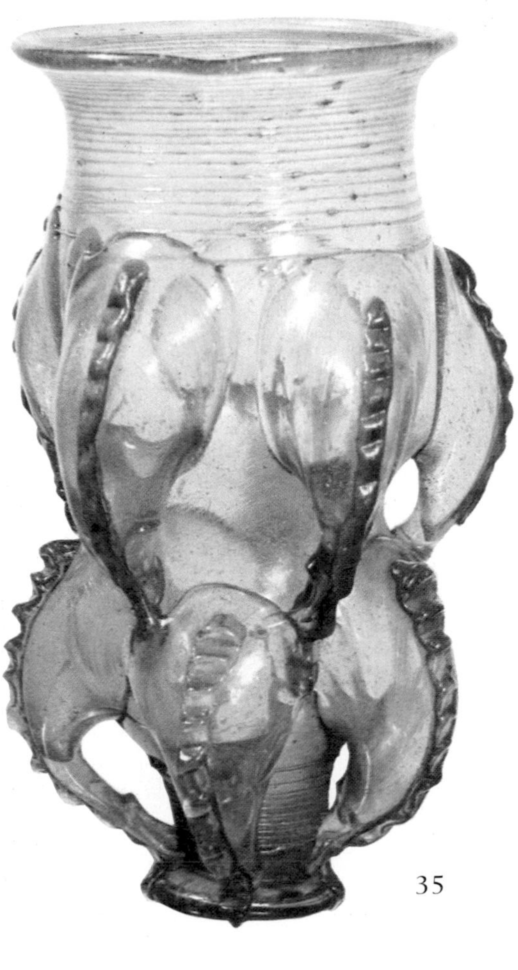

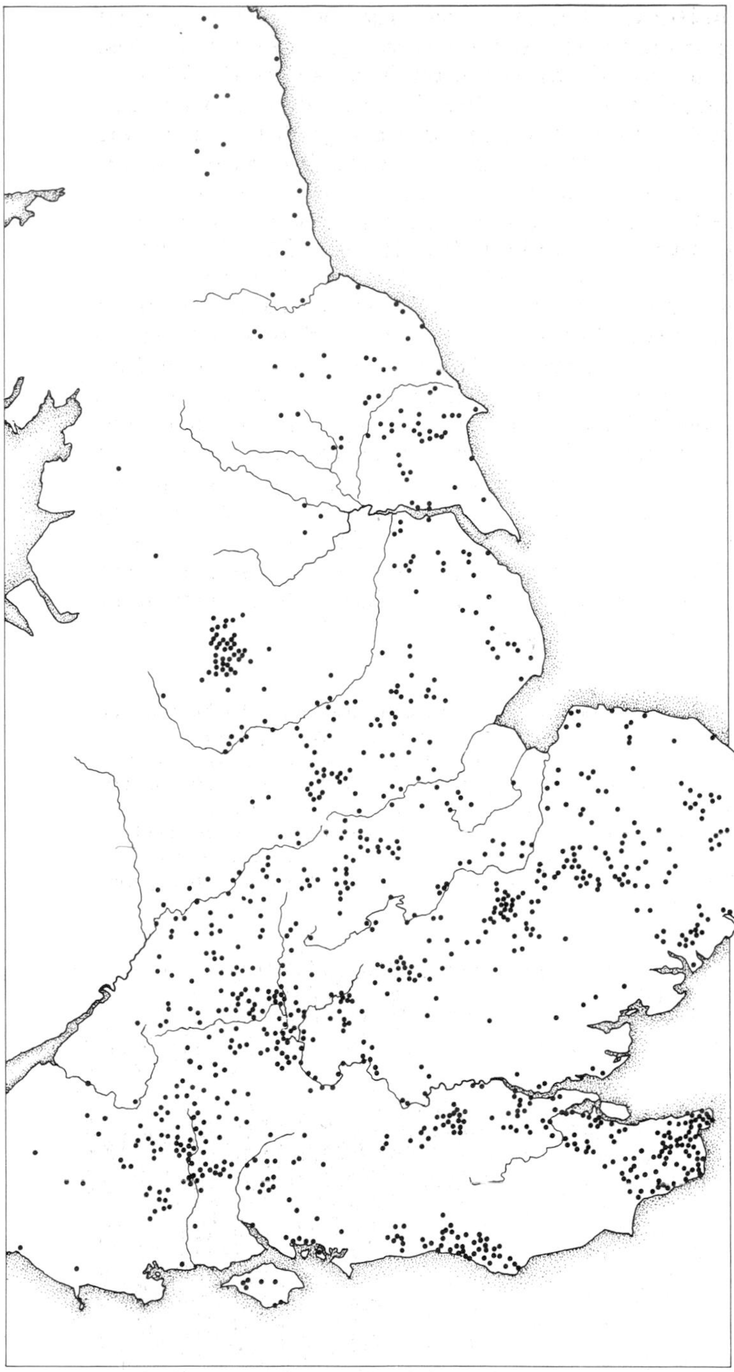

34 Anglo-Saxon cemeteries and single burials in England, showing the extent of Anglo-Saxon colonization by the end of the 7th century (after S. Chadwick Hawkes).

fifth-century graves do not occur. What lies behind these changes must be, to an important extent, continued immigration from overseas, in the fifth century, from the Anglo-Saxon homelands, and later also from Scandinavia (see above, p. 30). The increase in the number of discovered graves may also relate to natural increase of the Anglo-Saxon population; possibly, but if so very importantly, it may relate to the use of Germanic objects and the adoption of Germanic customs by Britons. The

35 Cremation urn from the 'Illington/Lackford workshop' height *c.* 19 cm (Bury St Edmunds, Moyses Hall Museum). 222 vessels and shards from 10 sites in East Anglia and Cambridgeshire have been identified, by the impressed stamps used for decoration, as the product of one late-6th-century potter or group of potters. This is suggestive, though not conclusive, for distribution by some commercial means.

contents of sixth-century graves may tell one more about customs, tastes, and the sources of supply of metal goods than they do about the ethnic origins of the corpses. The appearance of Anglo-Saxon cemeteries in the later pagan centuries in areas where they do not appear in the earlier is, of course, often simply an indication of such areas having passed under Anglo-Saxon control. Thus the absence of pagan cemeteries round about St Albans until the seventh century probably reflects St Albans having remained in British hands till the late sixth century (see below, p. 51). Though conversely it has to be remembered that Anglo-Saxon graves do not prove Anglo-Saxon rule. For example, there is no necessary incompatibility between the discovery of early sixth-century graves very near Cirencester (fig. 34) and the *Chronicle*'s date of 577 for its conquest by the West Saxons.

36 A stamp of deer-antler, used for the decoration of potter (cf. fig. 35); found at West Stow, Suffolk (Bury St Edmunds, Moyses Hall Museum).

The sheer bulk of the archaeological evidence, the extent to which it can by intelligence and labour be made sense of, the fact that some archaeologists do deploy mind and work on these complicated matters with a resourcefulness which puts historians of other kinds to shame, all these things can create an illusion: that archaeology can tell you what happened. It cannot; by its nature it cannot do more than provide an imperfect echo of what happened.

The Politics behind the Archaeology

Perhaps the best way of glimpsing the complications of the politics behind the archaeology is to consider the relations of Britons and Saxons with Gaul, where the sources, if poor, are better than they are for this island. Late Roman Britain was closely linked to Gaul. For most of the fourth century the imperial capital to which it looked was not Rome, but Trier. The soldiers and administrators who ran Britain and those who ran Gaul were men of the same kind, and they may have had a common loyalty, not to Britain, or to Gaul, or to the Empire, but rather to that part of the Empire which included both Britain and Gaul. It is striking that when Constantine III led the last Roman army from Britain it was not so much, so far as we can tell, to seize power, as to save Gaul. The close connection across the Channel continued in the fifth century. Saint Germanus, bishop of Auxerre, came to Britain in 429 and again in the 440s to repress Pelagian heresy (see above, p. 13). His *Life*, by Constantius, is the only near-contemporary source to reveal a little about the British ruling class at the time. (It appears civilized, prosperous and factious.)

In the mid-fifth century the authority of failing emperors was maintained, insecurely, in northern Gaul by Aetius, *Magister Militum* (see above, p. 23). After his death in 454 Roman noblemen, first Aegidius, then his son Syagrius, maintained a kind of independent power. Both Britons and Saxons were important among the many forces with which the last Roman rulers had to cope. In the late 460s a British king, Riothamus, appears as a man to be reckoned with in Gaul, engaged in an unsuccessful campaign against the Visigoths. He raises problems. Professor Fleuriot has suggested that he was none other than Ambrosius Aurelianus (see above, p. 16). He points out that 'Riothamus' may be a title, in British 'supreme ruler', rather than a name; and that the Irish version of Nennius says that Ambrosius ruled over the Franks and the Britons of Brittany. There are severe difficulties about this identification. Still, there would be nothing implausible about a British ruler having authority on both sides of the Channel. In any case it is important that Britons were a force, not only in Brittany, but elsewhere in Gaul. Saxons were also active there at just the same time. Some served in Aetius's army against the Huns in 451. A Saxon king, Adovacrius, was active in the Loire valley from about 464. Saxons settled around Boulogne, in Normandy, and near the mouth of the Loire.

Gildas's account of the appeal to Aetius is a clear indication of links between the men in power in Britain and those in Gaul. We have no details of such links, apart from the archaeological evidence (see above, p. 31), just semi-possibilities. For example, when the *Chronicle* relates that Wessex was founded by two Saxons, who came by sea, one of them, Cerdic, bearing a British name, one can guess that some involvement of Britons and Saxons in Gaul lies behind. Or again, Gregory of Tours, the historian of the Franks, has an account of a dialogue between the Frankish king Childeric (died 482) and his future wife Basina. He asked why she had deserted her husband to come to him. She replied: 'I know you to be capable and strenuous in action . . . be sure that if in the parts beyond the sea I knew someone more capable than you, I should have sought him for my husband.' The 'parts beyond the sea' sound like Britain, and the implication could be that this was where Frankish and other German adventurers were doing well in the third generation of the fifth century, providing in principle the most promising hunting-ground for this demanding lady. The archaeology does indeed suggest that there were such men there at that time, and as far afield as the upper Thames Valley.

37 A wooden stoup covered with bronze stamped with biblical scenes (Baptism of Jesus shown), from a boy's grave at Long Wittenham, Berks., height 15.2 cm (British Museum). Such stoups were made in northern Gaul in the later 5th century; this one corresponds closely to one found in a grave of *c.* 500 at Lavoye (Meuse). The Long Wittenham grave was orientated and also contained a cauldron of Frankish origin. Its evidence is among that which proves contact between the Upper Thames and Gaul in the 5th century and suggests the presence of Franks.

Procopius, our only major sixth-century source besides Gildas for the history of Britain, retails an odd story about it. He says (writing *c.* 560) that 'not long ago' a people called the *Varni* were ruled by a king called Hermegliscus. He was married to a sister of Theudebert, king of the Franks (534–48) and had a son, Radigis, by an earlier wife. He intended Radigis to succeed him and had engaged him to the sister of an Angle king in *Brittia* (see p. 22). One day, as he was out riding, a bird, perched in a tree, croaked to him a disconcerting prophecy: that he would die within 40 days. He reflected that Radigis would do better to marry his step-mother, rather than the 'island princess', for the Franks were nearer, just the other side of the Rhine, and so more dangerous. Hermegliscus did die; Radigis did marry his step-mother. The island princess was understandably put out. She sailed to the Continent with her brother and a vast army, captured Radigis, and made him marry her.

It is an odd tale, a far cry from the subtle speculations of modern historians. But the prophetic bird and the marriage to the step-mother prove it to be a German tale, and, notwithstanding fabulous elements, it probably has a real basis. It warns us of the likely importance of relations between rulers in Britain and others in Germany beyond the former imperial frontier. (The *Varni*, alias *Werini*, were a people, associated with the Angles, who in the late fourth and fifth centuries had moved from the Baltic coast and, perhaps, Jutland, into Thuringia.)

Procopius has other things to say about Britain. Its population is, he says, so great that every year people migrate from the island, and are allowed to settle in Gaul by the Franks, who thus intend to win authority over Britain. Not long ago, he says, the king of the Franks had sent an embassy to Justinian (527–65), in which Angles were included to support a claim to overlordship in the island. Elsewhere he says that Justinian was so extravagant in giving subsidies to barbarians that he gave them as far away as Britain. A late life of a Breton saint says that Childebert I, who ruled in Paris from 511 to 558, also had power in *Brittania transmarina*.

Such tales have weight. They may be garbled or exaggerated; but still, they take us into a world of rulers and of power, whereas archaeology usually can tell us only of peoples and settlements. They are a reminder that although cemeteries reveal much they cannot reveal who led, sent, paid or lured Germans to come to this island to be buried. Very likely some just came, driven by economic necessity. But many must have had rulers, the confused connections of whose struggles for power linked Britain to Gaul, to Germany, to Scandinavia, and even perhaps ultimately to Byzantium.

Aethelbert's England and the Problems of Continuity

The first English king who can be a little more to us than a name and a handful of dates is Aethelbert (*c.* 560–616), King of Kent, the first English ruler to become Christian (see below, p. 45). Bede tells us that he was the third king who had authority over all the others south of the Humber; the first having been Aelle of Sussex, who had reigned a century or so before, the second Ceawlin of Wessex, who died in 592. We cannot tell what this authority amounted to, except that it enabled Aethelbert to send missionaries under safe-conduct to the upper Thames (see below, pp. 45, 53).

The most obvious question to ask about Aethelbert's England, and the hardest to answer, is the nature of its links to the Roman, or Romano-British past. These must have differed considerably from one area or kingdom to another. 'Continuity' would have meant something very different in Bernicia, north of Hadrian's Wall, and in the once civilized Cotswolds (see above, p. 11). Furthermore, its nature would have differed with the date of the Anglo-Saxon conquests. The kingdom of Kent had probably been founded about the middle of the fifth century, when a great deal which was truly Roman must have survived. Much of the territory in English hands by 600 had been conquered much more recently. If the *Chronicle* is to be believed (and its late sixth-century dates have more claim to indicate at least approximate truth than its earlier ones), considerable areas in what later became Oxfordshire and Buckinghamshire were not conquered from the Britons by the West Saxons till 571; and they did not gain Gloucester, Cirencester and Bath until 577. It is perfectly possible that considerable elements of civilization did survive in such areas (see below, p. 40) but what survived to influence the Saxons would have been very different from what had been there a century before.

There have been scholars who would have regarded it as largely beside the point to consider variations in Romano-British influence from one part of England to another, believing that the invaders destroyed and exterminated on such a scale that they were able to create a new and purely Teutonic world. One can understand the temptation to take such a view, granted that there are almost no British words in the English language and that the overwhelming majority of place-names in all parts of England except Cornwall appear to be of Germanic rather than British origin. Striking though these phenomena are, they prove little about what happened in the Dark Ages. Peoples often adopt the languages of those who dominate them. That is how the Irish come to speak English, or for that matter how the French and Spaniards come to speak languages largely derived from Latin. Most place-names were given, or passed into the forms in which they are first recorded, centuries after this period. So their predominantly Germanic character need tell one little more than that the English in later centuries spoke English, and most of those who have studied them have in any case been more sensitive to Germanic than to Celtic derivations.

It is certain that something more survived into Anglo-Saxon England from Roman Britain than residual groups of enslaved Britons. The difficult thing is to know how much more. Consider Aethelbert's Kent. Kent had kept its Roman name: the men of Kent called themselves *Cantware*, which is simply *Cantiaci*, Germanized. It had kept its Roman capital. Bede implies that Aethelbert had a palace there and states that it was the *metropolis* of his dominions. Traces of what were probably Jutes living in huts in one part of Roman Canterbury in the fifth century have been found, but nothing from the sixth. One could be tempted to think of Canterbury, which like other ruined Roman towns must have been a dangerous place, as simply having been abandoned, were it not for Bede's reference to it as the king's *metropolis*. Here the evidence from another town, York, is most apposite. At York there is even less evidence for early Dark Age occupation than there is at Canterbury, with one crucial exception. It has been shown that the great headquarters building of the legionary fortress was, at least in part, used and kept in repair. (See above, p. 14). This discovery puts fifth- and sixth-century York in a new light. It did not survive as a centre of population; but it probably did survive as a centre of authority. So much could be found out only because it was possible to excavate part of the one crucial site. The corresponding site in Canterbury would be that of Aethelbert's palace, could it be found. There may be, there probably are, similar sites to be found in other once-Roman towns.

The fate of the towns of Roman Britain is everywhere mysterious. The economic changes which came with the collapse of imperial authority must have ensured that towns lost most of the functions which would have required, and provided for the sustenance of, large populations. In many towns there is evidence for some kind

38 The excavations under York Minster. The column is one of those of the basilica of the headquarters building of the legionary fortress (see p. 14). Mr Phillips has found evidence that this and adjacent buildings remained 'standing and in good repair' at least until the 9th century. Edwin's first church at York (see p. 45) may have stood in one of the courtyards here. Ultimately, the Roman buildings did not fall, but were demolished.

39 The belt-buckle from a princely grave at Taplow, Berks., of about 600, length 10 cm (British Museum). It is of gold inlaid with garnets, may well have come from Kent, and is one of the few contemporary objects which can be set beside the jewellery from Sutton Hoo.

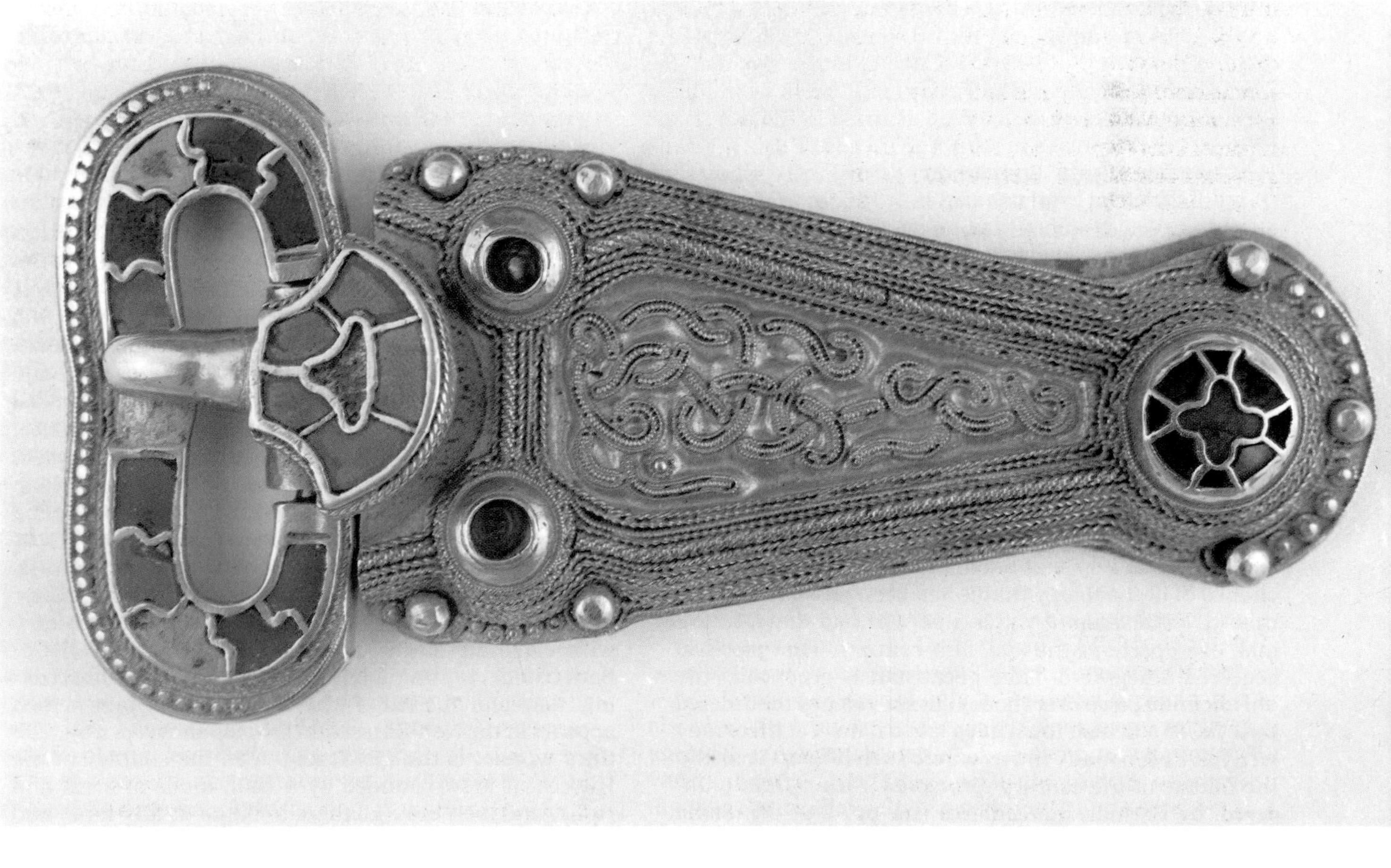

in connection with extractive industries. In the Nennian list of Wonders of Britain (see above, p. 40) are salt springs. 'Salt springs are found there, from which salt is boiled, with which various foods can be salted.' This probably refers to the salt springs at Droitwich. These had been exploited by the Romans. As soon as we have any records which can tell us what was happening there under the Anglo-Saxons—charters and notices of charters from the late seventh century—we find that the salt springs were exploited and valued. Certainly by the eleventh century Droitwich was a major source of salt and of revenue for the Crown. The name Droitwich may mean something likely 'princely trading place'. Continuity here could have meant continuity in control of a valuable source of revenue.

Similarly with lead mines. Britain had been a major source of lead for the Romans. Considerable quantities of lead seem to have been available in England by about 700. For example, Bede describes a bishop's covering a church with plates of lead. There is no doubt that by the ninth century at least, the Derbyshire mines were in production again (see below, p. 143). Either lead-mining

41 Gold and garnet jewellery of the mid 7th-century or somewhat later. The pins are from Cowlow, Derbys., the cross from Winster Moor, Derbys., the pendant (diameter 3 cm and inset with a stylized boar's head) from Womerseley, Yorks., and the necklace from Brassington, Derbys. (see also pp. 48–9, figs. 31, 46) (Sheffield City Museum).

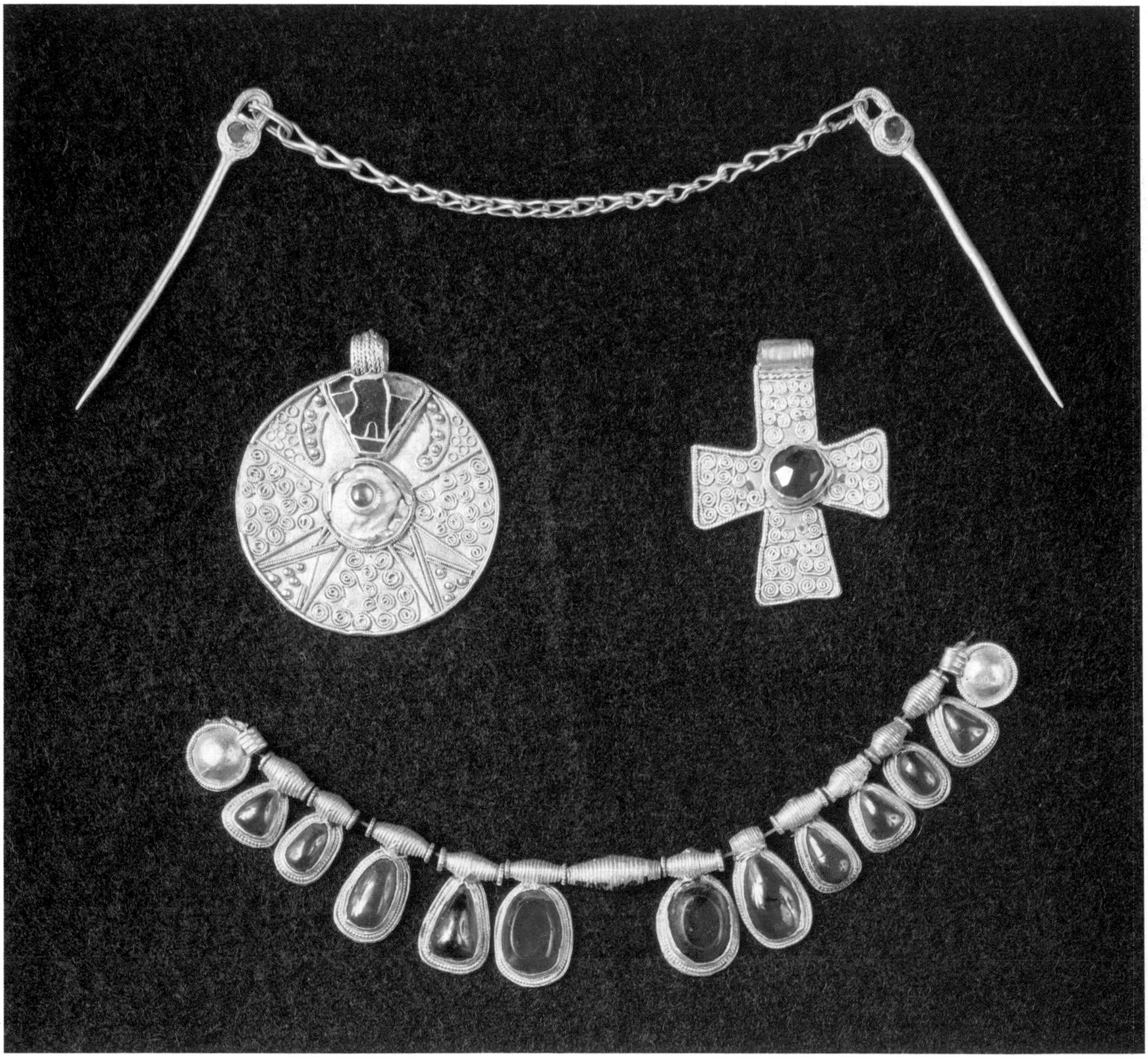

42 A brooch, a Roman intaglio, five imperial (or pseudo-imperial) and Merovingian gold coins and a 'medalet' mounted as pendant, found near St Martin's church, Canterbury, and presumably from a grave or graves, late 6th-century (Liverpool, Merseyside County Museum). The 'medalet' (second in the top row, diameter 1.2 cm) is inscribed LEUDARDUS EP(ISCOPU)S. Bede says (*HE*, I.25, p. 45) that a bishop Liudhard came with Bertha when she married Aethelbert (see p. 44 and half-title page).

43 The crest of Benty Grange helmet (see also fig. 57) of hollow bronze and most elaborately made, length *c.* 9 cm (Sheffield City Museum). Boar-crested helmets are mentioned in *Beowulf*.

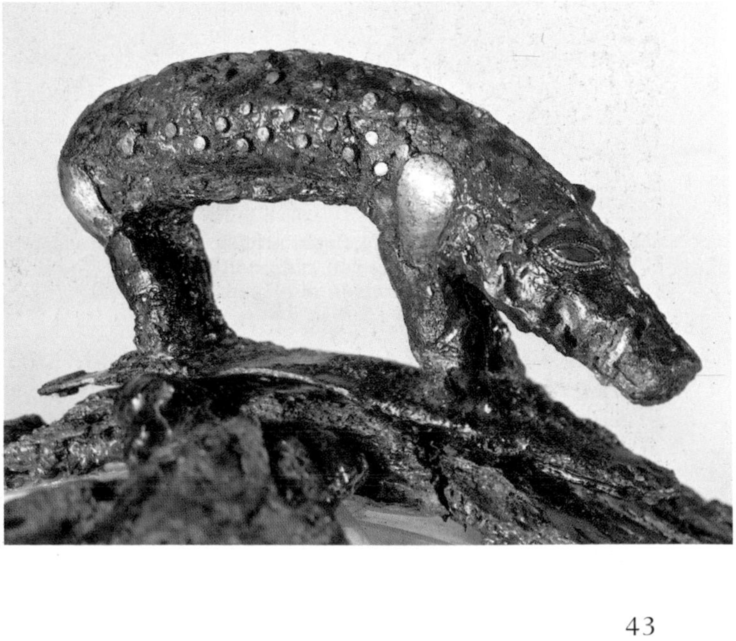

was continuous from the Roman period or else its techniques were reintroduced some time before the late seventh century. If the former was the case, then here too mines may have meant revenues and power for princes.

Although the sixth-century economy was obviously and fundamentally less sophisticated than that of Roman Britain, it had much about it that was far from primitive. Perhaps the most striking thing about it was the number of techniques which were available: in metal-working as we know, in carpentry as we may reasonably feel sure. To see the most elaborate Anglo-Saxon jewellery, such as some of that made in Kent in the early seventh century, is to have no doubt of the range of techniques which were available to their craftsmen and the skill with which they used them. In a sense even more impressive is the variety, number, and skilful (if often ugly) manufacture of the brooches and other ornaments worn by men and women more ordinary than such as could wear a great treasure like the Kingston Brooch (fig. 48). The Anglo-Saxons were people whose style of dress depended on an abundant supply of small metal goods. Knives and spears were common among them, though swords were not. There was probably little that a Roman smith or carpenter could have made that his Anglo-Saxon equivalents could not have made equally well. The pagan Anglo-Saxons did not build in stone and until the seventh century did not use the potter's wheel except in Kent, but the sharp break which this creates between their archaeology and that of the Romans can deceive. They were in important ways very advanced.

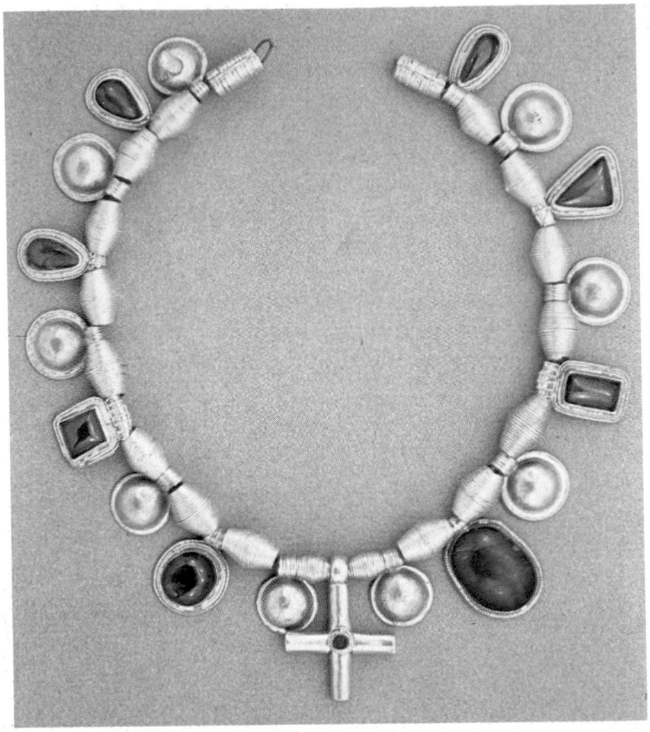

46 A necklet from a late 7th-century cemetery at Desborough, Northants., comprising cabochon garnets, gold bullae, biconical gold beads, and a central cross (height 2.5 cm) which indicates that the lady who wore it was a convert (British Museum).

The next generation saw the conversion of most of the kings of England. The power which accomplished this was in origin Irish. While Edwin ruled, the sons of his predecessor and enemy Aethelfrith were in exile in the Irish kingdom of Dalriada, in western Scotland (see below, fig. 50), and were converted there. When one of them, Oswald, succeeded to Northumbria in 634 he sent to an Irish monastery for a missionary. The monastery was Iona, founded by Columba in the 560s, the capital of the Church in Dalriada and much of northern Ireland, and situated on an island between the two. The missionary was Aidan; he and his followers, based on Lindisfarne, had great success in Northumbria. Oswald and his brother and successor Oswy (642–71) were for periods dominant in Britain. Their power influenced other kings, and so kingdoms, to conversion: *c.* 635 Wessex, *c.* 653 Essex, a little later Middle Anglia. Most important, in 655 Penda of Mercia, the last great pagan king, died in battle, defeated by Oswy. His successors were Christian. The last dynasty known to have stayed by the old gods was that of the Isle of Wight. Caedwalla established his power there, and Christianity with it, *c.* 686.

The Church in the Third Generation of the Seventh Century

By 660 there was tension between the triumphing missionaries from Lindisfarne and others. At issue was the method of calculating the date of Easter. It was determined for most by Oswy's deciding for the Roman

47 Tomb of bishop Agilbert (see p. 47) in the crypt of the monastery church at Jouarre, near Paris (Seine-et-Marne). The side shown has Jesus enthroned in the centre with (probably) the Apostles in attitude of prayer. This tomb is the most important figure sculpture from 7th-century Gaul. Much more may have been lost, and with it the possibility of full understanding of the origins of such sculpture in England.

48 'Composite' early 7th-century brooch from Kingston Down, Kent, diameter 8 cm (Liverpool, Merseyside Country Museum). Cloisonné, inlaid with garnet, glass, white shell and gold filigree panels, it is the finest of its kind and demonstrates the ostentatious wealth of the great in Kent.

method at a meeting held at Whitby in 664. The matter was passionate, for contemporary theology was such as to invest it with deep religious significance. Among the last words of Saint Cuthbert, greatest of Northumbrian saints, as he lay dying in 687 were: 'Have no communion with those who depart from the unity of the Catholic peace, either in not celebrating Easter at the proper time, or in evil living.' Some have been inclined to see Easter as a mere *casus belli*, in a conflict between Churches with opposed principles and systems; the Celtic, holy, humble but ill-organized, and the Roman, conventional, proud but efficient. Reality was simpler. They did care about Easter.

Reality was also more complicated. Something of this may be seen in the careers of the main Roman protagonists at Whitby: Agilbert and Wilfrid. Agilbert was a Frank. He had been educated in Ireland, an indication of the influence which Irish missionaries had gained in Gaul from the 590s. This was presumably in southern Ireland, whose churches had accepted the Roman Easter in the 630s. (There was no 'Celtic Church', but rather Celtic churches.) In about 650 he became a bishop in Wessex, one of several churchmen who came to England in the period, having no known connection with either Lindisfarne or Canterbury. Expelled from Wessex, he afterwards (666 or later) became bishop of Paris. His friend Wilfrid was by origin a Northumbrian nobleman. His adolescence had been spent at Lindisfarne, while Aidan was still alive. But in about 652 he went on a six-year journey to Rome and to Lyons. He was not the only young noble in Aidan's Northumbria to be drawn to Rome. Benedict Biscop, later founder of Bede's monastery of Monkwearmouth/Jarrow (see below, pp. 74–5,

The Archaeology of Conversion: Cemeteries

1 Gilt buckle from grave 95 at Finglesham, Kent, length 7.8 cm (Northbourne collection). The figure of the naked man wearing a headdress terminating in eagle heads and holding two spears indicates the cult of Woden.

2 Gold pectoral cross set with garnets, from Ixworth, Suffolk, height 4.5 cm (Oxford, Ashmolean Museum).

3 Silver gilt 'fish' buckle from Crundale, Kent, length 15 cm (British Museum).

Anglo-Saxon cemeteries are rich in information, supplementing that from history, about the effects of Christianity during the early years after the conversion. They show that pagan-style burial, clothed and with grave-goods, on sites outside the settlements, ceased in England during the early eighth century. At Finglesham (see pp. 24–5), as elsewhere, the latest datable objects from graves are small purse-hoards of silver coins, notably the *sceattas* of Kent's king Wihtred (*c.* 691–725), which have been interpreted as perhaps the purchase-price of goods which had been alienated, possibly by gift to the Church. By the middle of the century Christianity seems to have been well enough organized to provide new graveyards, associated with high crosses, minsters and newly founded local churches. Excavated cemeteries of the middle and late Saxon periods (Elstow, North Elmham and Raunds, for example) show serried ranks of west–east oriented burials, without dress-items or grave-goods, which appear thoroughly Christian.

During the seventh century, however, there was an interesting phase of transition before Christian ideas were fully assimilated. At Finglesham, for example, though they continued to use the heathen burial place, the seventh-century people changed to west–east orientation, using sunrise bearings, and were probably at least nominally Christian. Elsewhere, in places where the conversion came later (Leighton Buzzard and Winnall, for example), we find new cemeteries with west–east burials slightly distanced from an older burying place. We thus have a series of early or proto-Christian cemeteries, often quite short-lived, in which deposition of grave-goods was not yet abandoned and pagan practices still lingered. Indeed, it has been suggested that there is increased evidence of superstitious behaviour in the seventh century, from decapitation or stoning of corpses to simple provision of more pagan amulets, as if people doubted the power of the new religion over potentially unquiet dead who had been denied accustomed pagan rituals. That old ideas died hard and slowly we know from historical sources, and objects overtly symbolic of the cult of the god Woden in two graves at Finglesham (1, 7) probably date from the period of pagan reaction in Kent during the reign of Aethelbert's son Eadbald. Redwald of East Anglia's known ambivalence after conversion early in the seventh century is well represented by the Christian baptismal spoons and bowls in his otherwise heathen ship burial at Sutton Hoo (see pp. 32–3). Later instances of symbolic dualism are the boar figure and crosses in the helmet-grave at Benty Grange, Derbyshire (fig. 43), and the Christian and pagan pendants in grave 56 at Riseley, Horton Kirby, in west Kent (**5**). Obviously Redward was not the only convert to need the double insurance of protection from the old gods alongside the new (see p. 32).

However, Christian amulets are relatively frequent in the richer graves of seventh-century England, and presumably these indicate the progress of conversion amongst the various kingdoms' upper-class families. Pectoral crosses were worn not just by clerics like Saint Cuthbert (see pp. 80–1) but by wealthy women too, and fine jewelled gold examples survive from early in the seventh century at Ixworth, Suffolk (2) and Wilton, Norfolk, from slightly later at Milton Regis and Thurnham, Kent, White Low, Derbyshire, and, as the centrepiece of an elaborate necklet, at Desborough in Northants (fig. 46). Circular gold and silver pendants with the cross motif in filigree or repoussé were a cheaper alternative. More rare is the cross-decorated blue glass stud, probably a gift from the Irish community at Malmesbury to a prestigious lady convert, which forms the centrepiece of the jewelled gold pin-suite in the barrow-grave at Roundway Down, north Wiltshire (fig. 31). The cross motif also occurs on a relatively frequent ingredient of seventh-century female assemblages, the so-called thread-boxes, cylindrical bronze capsules which may in fact have been Christian reliquaries. One from Updown, Kent (4), contained the only fragment of silk so far recorded from early Anglo-Saxon England, and since the site seems to have been the early Christian cemetery of the royal vill at Eastry, it may not be too fanciful to imagine it a clipping from a sacred textile—a vestment of Saint Augustine? Probably Christian, too, though more cryptic, is the symbol of the fish which appears quite often on seventh-century jewellery, most notably on a fine silver-gilt buckle from Crundale Down, Kent (3). Both this and the famous sword found with it bear versions of animal ornament and zoomorphic interlace not long antecedent to those used in the first insular Gospel books.

Finally, the coming of Christianity with the mission from Rome and the trafficking between kingdoms which ensued seem to have led to a total change in women's dress during the seventh century. Gone are the old fashions, with their plethora of brooches and great festoons of beads; gone too are the regional differences. The last clear view we have, before grave-finds fail us, is of a uniform culture, with the great ladies of Kent, Wessex, East Anglia and Mercia all dressed alike in a sewn costume, requiring no metal fasteners, with gold and silver jewellery consisting only of delicate chain-linked headdress-pins and elegant necklets of beads and jewelled pendants (5); and figs. 31, 41, 46. This is a uniquely English adaptation of the classic style of Byzantium.

S. Chadwick Hawkes

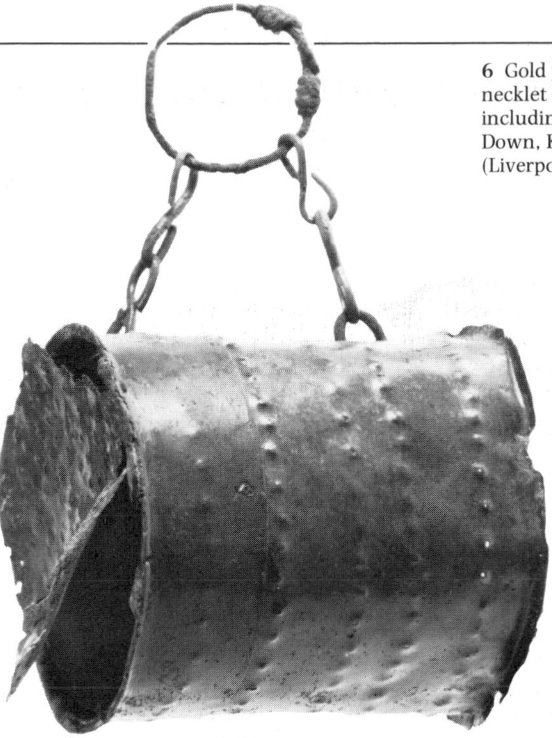

4 Bronze 'thread-box' from Updown, Kent, found in the grave of a small baby, height *c.* 8.7 cm.

6 Gold pendants and silver gilt crosses from a necklet consisting otherwise of beads including 12 amethysts, found at Kingston Down, Kent, height of upper cross 2 cm (Liverpool Museum).

7 Bronze pendant from grave 138 at Finglesham, in the form of a head with a horned headdress with bird heads, length 2.5 cm (Oxford, Ashmolean Museum, Northbourne collection). This piece is clearly related to the buckle from grave 95 (no. 1).

5 Necklet from Risely, Kent, with amethyst beads and pendants including two with crosses and one with a pagan motif of a man wrestling with two snakes (top right), diameter of centre pendant 3.6 cm (Dartford Museum).

78–83), set off with Wilfrid and arrived before him; it was the first of five such journeys. This was not a world divided between 'Celtic' and 'Roman'. The Irish were active in Gaul as well as England and the triangular relationship between the three lands was weighty. Perhaps most important, it was a world in which the magnetism of Saint Peter's see might be felt anywhere, in Ireland or in Lindisfarne as well as in Kent (cf. pp. 82–3).

If Englishmen were attracted to Rome, Romans were not attracted to England. The problem was a sharp one for Pope Vitalian in about 667. He had been asked by Oswy to provide a new archbishop of Canterbury in succession to Deusdedit, who had died in 664. No one would go. All said it was too far. In the end a candidate was sent, though not, one would have thought, *prima facie* a very suitable one. Theodore was a refugee from the Arab invaders of his home in Asia Minor and was 66 years old. In May 669 he arrived in Canterbury and began to transform the English Church.

49 The remains of an early church at Bradwell-on-Sea, Essex, standing partly in the Saxon Shore fort of *Othona* (*Ythancaestir*), where according to Bede (*HE*, III. 22, p. 173) the Northumbrian missionary Cedd built a church in *c*. 653. The surviving building is generally taken to be the nave of that church. It may have been. If so, the odd and interesting thing is that when complete with its curved apse and side-chapels this church bore detailed resemblance to early churches in Kent.

What did he find when he arrived in the strange world of Britain? For us, to seek to guess is like looking from a mountain into a misty valley. There something stands out quite clearly; somewhere else is an indistinct outline; every so often a shaft of light shows how one feature joins another; for the most, one can only peer and guess. In the rich maritime kingdom of Kent he probably found secure Christianity. If any of the Gregorian missionaries still lived they were old indeed. But, at least in Kent, they had trained up a native clergy. The first English bishop, Ithamar of Rochester, had been consecrated 25 years before. Pagan worship had been forbidden in Kent for some years.

Canterbury was recognizably a Christian capital. A short distance from its cathedral church of Christ stood the monastery of St Peter and St Paul, the burial place of the archbishops and the Christian kings of Kent. It cherished relics of Saint Augustine, one of which, his Gospel book, still survives. (It may not have been so diligent in keeping records of his mission: it is odd that Bede does not seem to have learned its true date, probably from Rome, until after 703, and that he was unable to record the year of Augustine's death.) Just beyond St Peter and St Paul stood St Pancras' church; just beyond St Pancras', St Martin's. There were other churches within the city walls. Canterbury was probably not unlike some of the Gaulish cities through which Theodore had passed on his way to England. Kent had as much, or more, to do with Gaul than it did with Mercia or Northumbria; its Church may have been strengthened by the growing strength (which had much to do with Irish missionaries) of the Church in northern Gaul at this time.

Outside Kent there was diversity amounting to chaos. Though all the major dynasties had been converted, there were only three or four bishops between them. Of these one, Wilfrid, had been made bishop of Northumbria in 664, but had soon after been displaced by Chad, the validity of whose consecration was doubtful. Wini was bishop of London; he had bought his see, an indication that ecclesiastical office could already be a source of profit. Boniface was bishop of East Anglia; that this was so is nearly all that is known of the contemporary history of the Church there. The Christianity of some kings was weathercock. One king of Essex had temporarily reneged a few years before, frightened by the plague of 664. (Well might he fear; if, as is likely, it was bubonic plague, it was probably the most terrible event in seventh-century history.)

All was not black. Wilfrid and Benedict showed that already there were zealously devout noblemen with, certainly in Benedict's case, the means to endow their faith. The great age of monastic foundation (see below, p. 72) was beginning. In a previous generation devout English princesses had gone to Gaulish nunneries. Now their families were founding similar institutions for them at home. Whitby (founded 657), where the council was held, was one of the first. In the north, far to the north of the Wall, Lindisfarne survived as a powerful force, though its bishop and some of his followers had fled to Ireland rather than accept the Roman Easter. There were other, more obscure monasteries. For example, there was an Irish foundation, unconnected with Lindisfarne, at Malmesbury in Wessex, and perhaps already another at Bosham in Sussex; there had been another, Cnobheresburg, in East Anglia, but Penda had destroyed it. How many more there were we cannot tell, any more than we can tell how many Franks, less successful than Agilbert, had come to England to save souls or make a career.

How many souls had already been saved? The extent and nature of the conversion of the population as a whole by 669 is dark. In Kent and elsewhere where the power of kings was put behind that of the Church it may well have sufficed to ensure conformity — not necessarily conviction. Priests were not numerous (though they may have been more numerous than we know, and monks undertook pastoral work, as in later centuries they did not). Much depended on bishops and others touring the countryside. We are told that when Cuthbert went on such tours in remote and mountainous areas the people would come to him at appointed places to receive his ministrations, making little huts of branches for shelter. For many the new faith may have been largely a matter of seasonal festivals. So too, probably had the old been. It is highly suggestive that for the greatest of festivals, in spring, though the rites changed, the names did not. 'Easter' is *Eostre*, according to Bede the name of a pagan goddess whose feast was celebrated at the same time of year. But burial rites also mattered, and here the evidence of archaeology is decisive that great changes, which must have been due to Christianity, came about in the seventh and early eighth centuries (see the Picture Essay, pp. 48–9). That really does mean something. Bede implies, though only by silence, that paganism was extinct by his day. The *Penitential* of Theodore, though its legislates against pagan practices, suggests that organized pagan cults did not survive, for it does not mention pagan priests. Perhaps some had changed sides.

Many of the subjects of the kings with whom Theodore had to deal may have already been Christian, or not entirely pagan. The problem is in part that of British survival and of how Germanized surviving Britons became. It is far from certain that Christianity survived in areas of early conquest and fairly dense settlement; but it is certain that the wide conquests of seventh-century kings in the north and west gained them Christian subjects.

The plainest case is that of Wessex. There is no doubt that the West Saxon conquest of most of the south-western peninsula, in full swing when Theodore arrived, brought many Christian Britons under Saxon rule. Such an abbey as Glastonbury may well have had a history which began under the kings of Dumnonia, to end under that of Henry VIII. Its earliest abbots (as they appear in a late list) have apparently British names. Mercian and Northumbrian conquests must also have involved the subjugation of British Christians. Whether those who were conquered by pagan kings could have kept their faith as more than a memory for a generation or so is questionable. Conquest by Christian Kings would have been another matter. When one learns of Wilfrid's being given the endowments of British churches whose priests had fled (*EHD*, I, p. 69) one may doubt that their flocks had all fled with them; indeed it is certain that he had Britons living on his estates.

The most singular case of possible Christian continuity in the part of Britain which became England is that of St Alban's. Bede says that from the time of the martyrdom (see above, p. 11) until his own day, miracles had not ceased at Alban's tomb. The case for continuity is strengthened by the situation of the later abbey of St Alban's: outside Roman *Verulamium*, where an extra-mural cemetery, and so Alban's tomb, could well have been; there are many Continental parallels for such a site. St Alban's could have been within an area not conquered from the Britons till the 570s. That the later abbey, astonishingly, never claimed such continuity gives pause. Still, it is a fair case; and to reflect that when Mellitus went to be bishop of Essex in 604 there may already have been a centuries-old Christian shrine in his diocese, is to learn how little we know.

Similar problems and possibilities can be found all round the Gallic and German fringes of the once-Roman world. It is not easy for us to gauge the possibilities of survival; the nature of half survival; the limits of pagan tolerance; or the extent to which organized Christianity could survive, leaving no record. Distant parallels suggest that Christian communities could continue for many generations, isolated in an alien world. Archaeology almost proves that in the sub-Roman Rhineland this happened. If such communities kept records they could easily be lost. There must have been a Christian Church in the little British kingdom of Elmet, conquered by Northumbria in the early seventh century. Of its Latin learning just one faint possible trace remains: Bede was able to give the right Roman names for two minor places in Yorkshire.

In any case, and for many reasons, Christians and Christianity must have been familiar to many Anglo-Saxons. It is unlikely that Aethelbert was the first pagan king to have a Christian wife; he is after all the first English king of whose wife we know anything. The recurrence of British names among the kings of Wessex suggests the recurrence of British queens. As soon as we have a little information we find pagan Saxons going into exile in Christian Celtic courts and forming alliances with Christian British kings. Contacts with Gaul must similarly have brought acquaintance with Christianity. When Augustine came to Aethelbert's court what he brought with him which was new was probably not so much Christianity as the idea that Saxons should become Christians. In sixth-century Britain religion must generally have been determined by race.

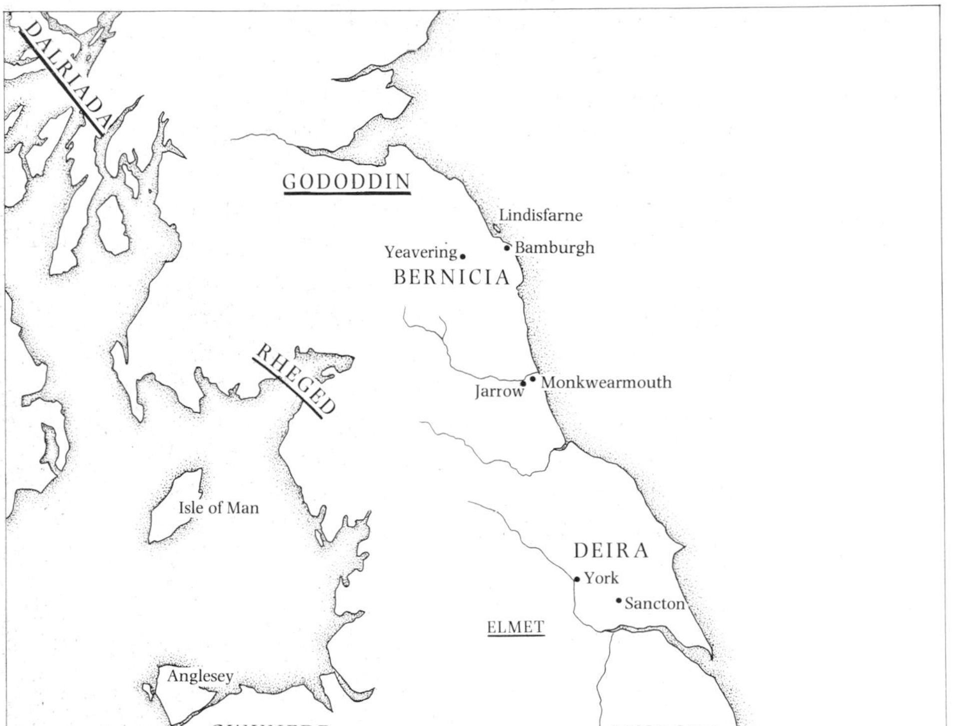

50 The kingdoms and the principal sites and towns of southern Britain, *c.* 600, including places mentioned in Chapter 4. Note that it is uncertain whether Middle Anglia ever existed as more than a description of an area; and it is possible that in the early period there were kingdoms and sub-kingdoms of which we know nothing. The so-called heptarchy comprised East Anglia, Essex, Kent, Mercia, Northumbria (combining Bernicia and Deira), Sussex, and Wessex.

51, 52, 53 Cross from Wilton, Norfolk, height 5.6 cm, and pendants from Bacton, Norfolk (centre), and Forsbrook, Staffs. (below), early 7th-century (British Museum). Imperial gold coins (of 615–32, 585–602 and 375–9) in cloisonné garnet settings: that of the Wilton Cross closely resembles the garnet-work at Sutton Hoo (see fig. 77).

Theodore was to be archbishop for 21 years, and brought authority and order. He soon started to fill vacant sees and was concerned to create new ones by the division of old. Within months of his arrival he went to Northumbria, something no archbishop had done before, and made his power felt there. Within three years he called the first known council of the English bishops. A particularly remarkable thing about it is that its proceedings were efficiently recorded in an act drawn up by a notary. This is a sign of his bringing legal order to the English Church. Theodore was a learned man; his learning included canon law, and he taught it, with much else, at Canterbury. Its implementation in regular synods was essential for order and continuity in the Church. The spirit is very apt to die, the letter preserves life. Even more important was Theodore's holding synods of the English Church at which no king was present, and which acted on the assumption that the appointment and dismissal of bishops should be in ecclesiastical hands. That Theodore and his immediate successors were able to act to a degree independently of kings was a passing phenomenon, but a significant one.

Seventh-Century Kings and the Nature of their Power

It is to kings that we must now turn. The written records produced by the Church make seventh-century rulers intelligible as those of the sixth are not. Fundamentally important is the *Ecclesiastical History* of Bede, completed *c.* 731. Copious, intelligent, drawing on documents where possible, the fruit of wide inquiries, it tells most of what will ever be known of the events of the age. It is supplemented by saints' lives, above all those of Wilfrid and Cuthbert, and by laws, charters and annals. The first written laws are those of Aethelbert of Kent. Two other Kentish codes and one West Saxon survive from the last generation of the century. The earliest surviving charters (i.e. formal documents recording the transfer of land) are from the 670s. The annals of the *Chronicle* from this period onwards must often derive from contemporary records.

These sources show England full of kings (in this respect resembling Ireland and Scandinavia). Although it has long been convenient to think of a heptarchy of seven kingdoms (see above, fig. 50), reality was richer. For example, we hear of kings of Wight, of the West Midland kingdoms of the *Hwicce* and the *Magonsaete*, and of Lindsey. There were probably others of whom we know nothing. Although Deira had been united with Bernicia into Northumbria, it retained an identity, and sometimes a king, of its own. Some kingdoms could be divided among co-heirs (as Essex occasionally was), or more widely among several members of the royal clan (as not improbably in Wessex). At the bottom of the pyramid of power were petty kings, some the subordinated heirs of once-independent dynasties, some members of conquering dynasties, others the beneficiaries of divided inheritance. Above them were greater kings; and sometimes above these greater kings yet. Kingliness was relative.

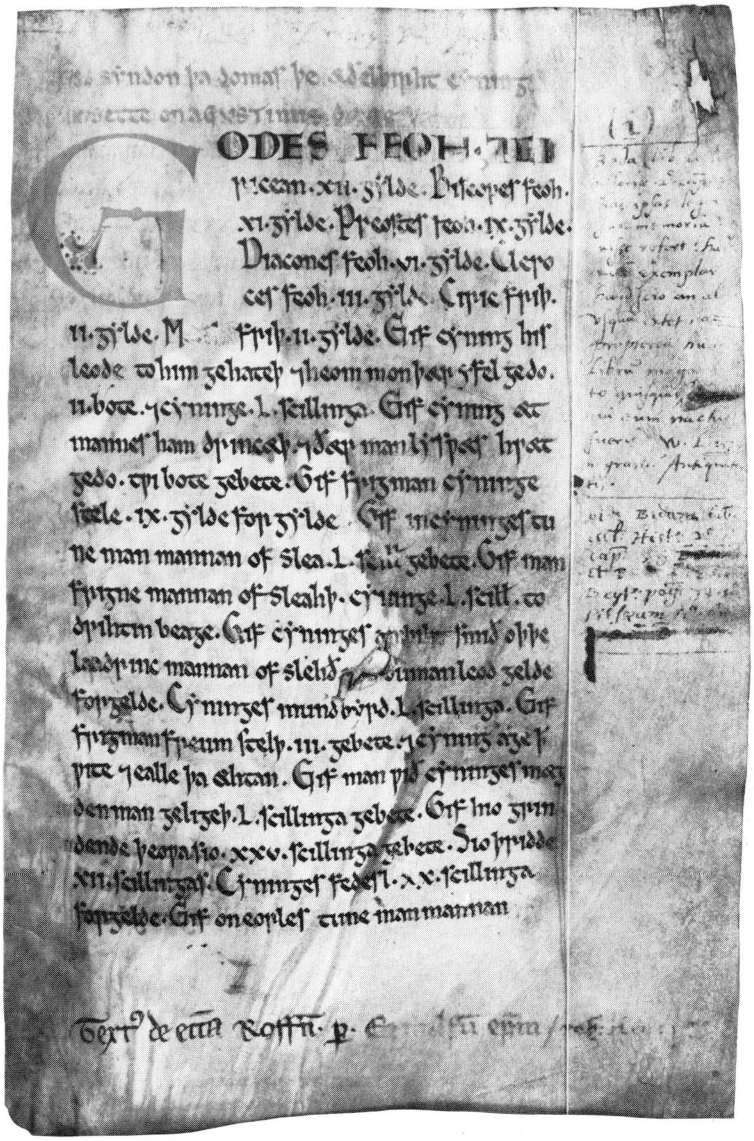

54 Opening page of the Textus Roffensis, showing the beginning of King Aethelbert's law code (Rochester Cathedral Library, MS A.3.5, now in Kent County Record Office, Maidstone). This 12th-century manuscript is the only surviving copy of early Kentish legislation.

The power of the greatest kings extended over most of the Anglo-Saxon lands and sometimes beyond. Bede provides a list:

Aelle of Sussex (? late 5th century)
Ceawlin of Wessex (560–91 or 2)
Aethelbert of Kent (560–616)
Redwald of East Anglia (?–616/27)
Edwin of Northumbria (616–33)
Oswald of Northumbria (634–42)
Oswy of Northumbria (642–70)

The *Chronicle* (written *c.* 892) calls these kings *bretwaldas* (or perhaps *brytenwaldas*) ('ruler of Britain', or 'wide ruler'). There is a substantial gap between Aelle and Ceawlin. The reigns of Ceawlin, Aethelbert and Redwald overlap, but that is not to say that each succeeded the other in a defined office. It is more likely that the word was used, and Bede's intention was, to indicate rulers

55 A bronze-hanging bowl, diameter 24 cm (cf. fig. 64) lies in a cist grave in the earliest (7th-century) phase of the church of St Paul in the Bail, Lincoln. Erected in the courtyard of the Roman forum (compare p. 40) this church may be that which Bede says Paulinus (see p. 45) built at Lincoln, then under Edwin's control. No body was detected in the grave.

whose authority, at least for part of their reigns, extended over other kingdoms. Others may for periods have been as powerful, or nearly so, for example Penda of Mercia (?632–55) (and see below, pp. 67, 70, 73, 99).

The list indicates the instability of hegemony. First one kingdom has it, then another. Although Northumbria has a long run at the end, all three of its *bretwaldas* faced the rising power of Mercia; the first two died facing it in battle. If their power was wide it was never safe for long. But it *was* wide. Bede says that the first four of these rulers had authority over all the kingdoms (he may mean just the Anglo-Saxon kingdoms) south of the Humber. He goes on to say that Edwin had wider authority extending over all the peoples of Britain, British and English, except Kent; and including Anglesey and Man, which he subjected to English rule. Oswald ruled within the same bounds. Oswy had authority over much the same lands for some years, and also subjugated most of the Picts and the Scots and made them tributary. Historians, quiet men always liable to confuse the less interesting with the more plausible, are apt to leave what Bede says here with some such phrase as 'vague overlordship'; but we do not know how vague or otherwise it was. If Bede is right, then Oswy had wider power in this island than any ruler till James I and VI. That of the Mercian overlords of the eighth century was much less extensive; it stopped at Wat's or Offa's dyke (see below, pp. 120–1) and the Humber, whilst that of their predecessors had run from sea to sea.

It is significant that after the death of Redwald no southern or eastern kingdom was supreme. Dominance went to the frontier states of Northumbria, Mercia and Wessex. It probably had much to do with the conquests they made at British expense. Between the late sixth and the late seventh century Northumbrian kings subjugated vast areas west of the Pennines and north of the Tweed. In the early seventh century the western boundary of Wessex was about that of modern Wiltshire; by *c.* 700 it was the Tamar. Much of the West Midlands passed from British to Mercian hands in the seventh century. Rulers making such conquests had lands to give, slaves to sell, and (possibly) minerals to exploit. The dynamics of power in early England are likely to have been such as to ensure that these advantages enabled them to gather armed power sufficient to dominate their neighbours to the south and east.

In understanding those dynamics the poem *Beowulf*, the only secular epic in Old English to survive, is useful. Its story is of how Beowulf, a prince of the Geats, a Swedish people, ridded Hrothgar, king of the Danes, of two monsters, returned home, and ultimately himself was killed by another monster, the guardian of a treasure hoard. It is the poem's assumptions about power, rather than the nature of its plot, which concern us. (It has to be borne in mind that the date of the poem is uncertain; it may be considerably later than its often suggested date of the eighth century; it cannot provide answers, but it can provide clues to answers about the nature of the world of power.)

In the political world of the poem four things stand out: the importance of the king's noble retinue, some of whose members may derive from kingdoms other than his own; an indissoluble connection between success and gifts of gold; the store set by good weapons, which are regarded as treasure; and the endless insecurity associated with feud. A king lives surrounded by noble warriors who feast with him, sleep in his hall by night, fight for him and are ready, or anyway sincerely hoped to be ready, to die for him. Their number and loyalty are crucial to royal power. As king Hrothgar prospered, so did the number of his young retainers increase. A king's followers can come from abroad, as Beowulf comes from Geatland to Denmark. Adventure or the hope of profit brings some; the harsher compulsion of exile others.

To secure followers and power treasure is essential. Kingship and treasure-giving go hand in hand. Kings are 'treasure-guardians', 'gold-friends', 'ring-givers'. A good king gives. Hrothgar was 'the best of earthly kings . . . the best of those who bestowed gold'. A bad king 'begins to hoard his treasures, never parts with gold rings'. Treasure rewards service, creates the expectation of loyalty, and is the outward sign of honour. The gift of a splendid sword ensured that the recipient was 'more honoured on the mead-bench thereafter'. The social and emotional significance of gold-giving and gold-wearing was complex and deep; and it was not for nothing that Beowulf died to win a treasure hoard. With the poet's interest in treasure goes a similar interest in weapons. Gifts of armour and of pattern-welded swords are treated as treasures.

All the kings and kingdoms mentioned in the poem ultimately come to grief, and the poet is at pains to remind his audience of this. The world he describes is an unstable one in which it is all-important for a king to give

57 (*right*) This later 7th-century helmet from Benty Grange, Derbys. (Sheffield City Museum), is the only one to survive from early England other than that from Sutton Hoo (fig. 70). They differ greatly. This was composed of an iron framework covered with horn plates. It has a splendid boar crest (see fig. 43). Such crests were probably thought (as Tacitus indicates much earlier) to give protection in battle. If so, the warrior who wore this helmet was doubly protected; for its nose-piece has a silver cross set in it.

treasure, which includes arms. If he has gold to give, and is successful in war (these things feed one another), he can attract followers from other kingdoms, because noblemen are often on the move through hunger for reward or the necessities of exile. To keep giving he has to keep taking, and so adds feud to feud. No kingdom or king can hope for long success. When a great king grows ill or old or mean there are always enemies waiting at home or abroad. They seize their advantage and other kings rise, taking the treasure, the men, and the glory.

The great treasure found at Sutton Hoo (Picture Essay, pp. 32–3) shows how strongly, at least in some respects, seventh-century reality resembled what the poet described. To see the splendid jewellery is to apprehend how men might live and die for such treasures. There is no problem in understanding how arms like those found here might be regarded as treasures, and some of them correspond very closely to descriptions in the poem. This is particularly true of the helmet. Indeed one particularly difficult passage describing a helmet would be securely translated only by considering the real helmet from Sutton Hoo; it refers to 'a comb passing over the roof of the helmet wound round with wire inlay'. The poem fairly frequently mentions mail shirts, as if they were normal gear for the great. The only certain find of such armour from early England is that from Sutton Hoo. (There may perhaps have been some in association with the only other known helmet, that from Benty Grange.) Although spears and knives are common in Anglo-Saxon graves, swords are not common, and the really good, pattern-welded swords, such as could shear armour, are rarer. That is to say that, however many men may have been liable to serve in war, the best equipment was confined to those who were royal or noble. If so, the movement of such men from one kingdom to another to seek shelter or service could have had a military significance far outweighing their small number.

56 (*left*) The blade of a 'pattern-welded' sword (Cambridge University, Museum of Archaeology and Anthropology). Such swords were very elaborately made. The centre of the blade is an iron strip. To it were welded two steel edges. The channels left on either face were filled with strips made from layers of iron and steel twisted together, then beaten to shape.

The history of the dynasty part (perhaps only a small part) of whose treasure was buried at Sutton Hoo also has echoes of the *Beowulf* world. Redwald, who is probably buried at Sutton Hoo, is the first East Anglian king of whom we know more than his name. He was the fourth *Bretwalda* (see above, p. 53), and Bede's account shows that on occasion his power stretched even north of the Humber. When Aethelfrith, king of Northumbria, drove Edwin, prince of a rival house, into exile, Edwin wandered through many kingdoms, and ended at Redwald's court. Aethelfrith offered gold and silver and uttered threats of war to have Edwin handed over. Doubtless he wished to kill him. Though tempted, Redwald declined to sell. Instead he fought, defeated and killed Aethelfrith, taking him unawares before he could gather his army. Redwald's son was killed in this fight, which made Edwin king of Northumbria.

On his death (sometime between 616 and 627) Redwald was succeeded by another son, who was, however, soon murdered. After an interval Sigbert (another son or step-son) came to power, after having been in exile in Gaul. He later abdicated, to be followed by a king whose relationship to him is unknown. Both were killed by Penda. Next came Redwald's nephew Anna; he too was killed by Penda. Anna's brother and successor met the same fate at a different hand: he was killed by the Northumbrians, while fighting *for* Penda at the battle on the Winwaed in 655.

Much in this sparse and bloody tale is characteristic of seventh-century kingship. Of six East Anglian kings in less than 40 years five died violently; the manner of the sixth's, Redwald's, death is unknown. One of the great differences between medieval and Dark Age kings is that while the former were rarely killed in battle (a king's ransom was worth too much for that), the latter often were, for it seems to have been normal to kill kings and nobles if they were captured, the milder fate of enslavement being reserved for lesser men. A king, no matter how great, was quite likely to end, as Oswald of Northumbria did in 642, slain in battle, with his head and hands stuck up on stakes on the battlefield.

There were threats within as well as without. Neither in East Anglia, nor in any other kingdom was there a settled system of succession. It seems that any male member of the royal family, widely defined, could succeed if he could get the required support and acceptance. This meant that a king's most dangerous enemies could be his own relations, especially if he sought to determine his own successor (see pp. 114 ff.).

Such circumstances were among those which generated feud; and feud made exile common. Sigbert was in exile before he became king; so was Edwin. This is characteristic of many seventh-century royal careers; for example, Oswald, Oswy and Aldfrith of Northumbria, and Cenwalh and Caedwalla of Wessex were also at some time exiles. We hear of kings as exiles, because we hear most of kings. Feud must often have driven lesser men into exile also. Thus early in the eighth century some noble exiles with an armed force, 'ravaging because of some injustice done to them', burned Oundle monastery.

Exile must have ensured that all kings recruited to their service nobles from kingdoms other than their own. This is found both in early England and also in *Beowulf*. But when Beowulf arrived in Denmark, his bearing suggested not that he was an exile but that he had come in search of adventure. It was common, probably normal, for an Anglo-Saxon nobleman to go to fight for a king or for his own hand when he reached adolescence. The clearest instance is that of Guthlac (see below, p. 82). When he was about fifteen (*c.* 690), 'a noble love of command began to glow . . . he gave himself up to arms . . . laid waste the towns and dwellings, the villages and fortresses of his enemies . . . brought together comrades of diverse peoples and gathered vast booty.' It is important that his retinue, like a king's, was from various peoples. The mobility, free or forced, of great men, with their retinues, must have been one of the determinants of power, just as it appears in *Beowulf*.

The game kings played in endlessly repeated wars was a harsh one. If the prize was authority over many other kings, great wealth, many followers and a blazing name, the likely end of it all was violent and often early death. Redwald had flirted with Christianity. His successors were the first Christian kings of the East Angles. How did their new faith relate to the violent and threatened lives of them and their like? The circumstances of their conversion often derived from the nature of such lives. Redwald became a kind of Christian presumably because that was the wish of his overlord Aethelbert. Other kings were converted in similar circumstances (see above, p. 46). Sigbert was converted while an exile; so too were Oswald and Oswy of Northumbria; so too was Cenwalh of Wessex reconverted, while in exile at the court of Anna of the East Angles.

What did Christianity offer such kings? Among other things, the assistance of divine power. One missionary message was that God could give victory. Oswald erected a cross before he fought the battle which made him king. In that sign he conquered. They called the site of the battle and of the cross Heavenfield. When Bede says that Edwin not only learned to hope for heavenly kingdoms unknown to any of his ancestors, but also won earthly kingdoms far larger than any of theirs, he is implying a lesson. It is a good Old Testament lesson; there was a good deal more to match Anglo-Saxon experience in the early history of the Jews than there was in Roman Palestine. Christianity could, however, and did, affect some kings otherwise. Sigbert of East Anglia abandoned the world for a monastery. Others later were to do likewise. Bede says that Sigbert of Essex was murdered (between 650 and 664) because he would forgive his enemies. Such a predilection could indeed have been shocking in a society to whose passions, and also to whose regulation, feud was intrinsic.

This story is a reminder that there could be more to kingship than an endless struggle to shed blood and gain gold. Something of other sides to the lives of kings may be found in the discoveries made at Yeavering. Yeavering lies in what was the kingdom of Bernicia, about 40 miles north of the Wall, some 20 miles inland from the great

; This air-photograph of Yeavering shows above and to the left the
.rving line of what was probably a corral for cattle. Below and to the
;ht are the outlines of successive royal halls. Below these and
ghtly to the right is the 'grandstand'.

) The excavated post-holes of an early Saxon timber 'hall' from the
rly settlement site at Mucking, Essex (see also p. 18 and fig. 19).
ie ground plan measures about 22 feet wide by about 44 feet long.
ie photograph shows the east end; the rest of the plan is obscured by
:onveyor.

Bernician fortress of Bamburgh, quite high up in the Cheviots. It is a desolate and often a very cold place. Bede mentions it as a royal vill, saying that Paulinus spent 36 days there with Edwin, teaching and baptizing continuously, and that at some later time it was abandoned. In 1949 an air photograph showed the marks of extensive buildings there. Over many years the site was excavated by Dr Hope Taylor. His was the infinitely difficult and subtle task of discovering the nature of numerous timber buildings from the faint traces they had left in the ground. His success was brilliant.

What he found was this. As a place of burial, and so presumably as a centre of cult, Yeavering had a very long prehistoric past indeed. It had been a focus of some kind for the British regime which preceded that of the Bernician kings; what is almost certainly a big and elaborately defended cattle corral is likely to have gone back to so early a date. A series of buildings dated from the end of the sixth century to somewhat later than the middle of the seventh. Among the most important were a succession of halls. The finest of these, which was probably Edwin's, was as grand a piece of carpentry as can be imagined. It was over 80 feet long and nearly 40 feet wide. Its walls consisted of planks, $5\frac{1}{2}$ inches thick. Their height can only be guessed, but it must have been great, for their timbers would not otherwise have been set up to eight feet into the ground. It may have had a clerestory. Its successor, probably Oswald's hall, was hardly less fine. More remarkable still was a kind of grandstand, rather like a segment of a Roman amphitheatre, which stood facing a platform. When first built, possibly under Aethelfrith, it had accommodated about 150 people; later, perhaps under Edwin, it was enlarged to hold about 320. Much else was found, for example what may have been a pagan temple later converted to Christian use, and what may have been a small Christian church.

The halls take us straight to the world of *Beowulf*. The magnificence of Hrothgar's great hall is dwelt upon there. Its roof was gilded and it had a name, like a ship, 'Heorot'. Whether the halls at Yeavering were gilded we cannot tell. That they were very grand we can. The setting of the dinings and drinkings of the Northumbrian kings was as fine as most great Roman buildings. (The halls were plastered, perhaps to make them look more Roman.) And Yeavering, though a major centre for Bernicia, was by no means the only such centre these kings possessed. There was another, much more important, at Bamburgh, 20 miles away, and other royal vills scattered through their kingdom, many of which may have had halls as grand. Even more remarkable is the 'grandstand'. Its only purpose can have been for meetings; and of a kind where one man on the platform, presumably the king, faced many. It gives a kind of reality to Bede's description of Edwin consulting his *amici, principes*, and *consiliarii* (friends or relations, great men and counsellors) on the adoption of Christianity (though this debate more probably took place in the headquarters of the legionary fortress of York). That 'grandstand' is the oldest item in the constitutional archaeology of England. The royal buildings at Yeaver-

ficially appear 'tribal' could be used to indicate what were really administrative areas. This raises very hard questions about the nature of government. For example, does 'East Wixna 300' indicate a 'tribe' with a past extending back to the invasion period, perhaps with a *princeps* who paid tribute to a Mercian king at the round sum indicated, which is simply an indication of what the king reckoned to get out of that 'tribe', or does 'East Wixna' denote a unit in an elaborately organized system in which the 300 hides were apportioned through the area village by village, not a tribe, rather a governmental area?

It is not easy to do more than play jesting Pilate on the Tribal Hidage, not least because the truth could have lain somewhere between the two poles stated. But at least this can be said. The Hidage looks rather like a kind of administrative document. It need not be so early as the seventh or even the eighth century; but Bede mentions in passing hidages for certain kingdoms, which suggests that he may have had access to a similar list by *c.* 730. Quite likely it *is* early, or is derived from early lists. If so, whatever it is, and whatever it means, it indicates a degree of orderliness, or coherence in the exercise of power, which, if it can be glimpsed in the early laws and charters, is less easy to detect in the narrative sources. Orderliness in governmental arrangements is something which has a long history, probably extending far into the prehistoric past. The nature of political development would have been much affected if, as is likely, most of the lands of the English (and indeed those of their British neighbours) were organized with some regularity and on similar systems. The collection of tribute, the absorption of one kingdom by another, the regulation of subordinated powers would all have been simplified.

The power of kings and the relative orderliness of their systems of government had its effect on the Church. Some of the laws indicate at least aspirations towards close royal control of the whole population. Thus those of Ine prescribe heavy penalties for failing to have a child baptized within 30 days or for breaking the Sabbath. The impression of peoples much under the control of their kings is reinforced by such an account as Bede's of what Paulinus did at Yeavering. Paulinus's teaching and baptizing for 36 days continuously suggests that Edwin brought conversion about by royal edict, just as, a little later, Earconberht of Kent forbade pagan worship. Such things chime with other indications of extensive royal power given by the early laws; in which we see, for example, Kentish kings entitled to a fine for the slaying of any freeman. It may be that one reason for the relative speed and effectiveness with which the population as a whole became formally Christian is that kings, acting through their agents in fairly close networks of royal vills, really could determine what their subjects did.

61 (*left*) The East Wansdyke runs for over 10 miles over the downs, eastwards from somewhat east of Bath. It is probably post-Roman and 5th- or 6th-century. Another earthwork to the west, also called Wansdyke, may be related. Though not on the scale of Offa's Dyke, such works indicate the extensive power of some rulers (cf. fig. 67).

Governmental systems affected the development of the Church in other ways; it looks for example as if, particularly in Kent, but also elsewhere, it was usual to have a church for each royal vill, or the area dependent on it. A striking feature of the early English Church is the speed with which it established the power to tax. It is likely that it was able to do so by grafting its exactions on to existing royal systems. When Bede complained that there were villages so remote that they had never seen a bishop, but not one of which was exempt from paying *tributum* to the bishops, it is a fair guess that those hill villages had long been accustomed to paying *tributum*, via a royal vill, to a king.

England and Europe

The English were a maritime people. Each of the three seas which surrounded them led into a different world. They themselves were North Sea people; and they did not lose contact with its southern and eastern shores after they came to Britain. It is a question when they ceased to come. The royal house of East Anglia was probably of Swedish origin and had arrived in the sixth century, perhaps not much before 550. More than a century afterwards Saint Guthlac was succeeded at Crowland (in 714) by Cissa who, some years before, had been still a pagan and not yet come to this island. Presumably he came from Germany or Scandinavia. The way in which new styles of ornament became rapidly diffused all round the North Sea, the fact that *Beowulf* is a Scandinavian story, the zeal which the Anglo-Saxons showed for the conversion of their Saxon homeland: all these things show to what an extent the North Sea united as well as divided.

The Irish Sea, the Celtic Mediterranean, had a still stronger unifying force. How maritime the Celtic world

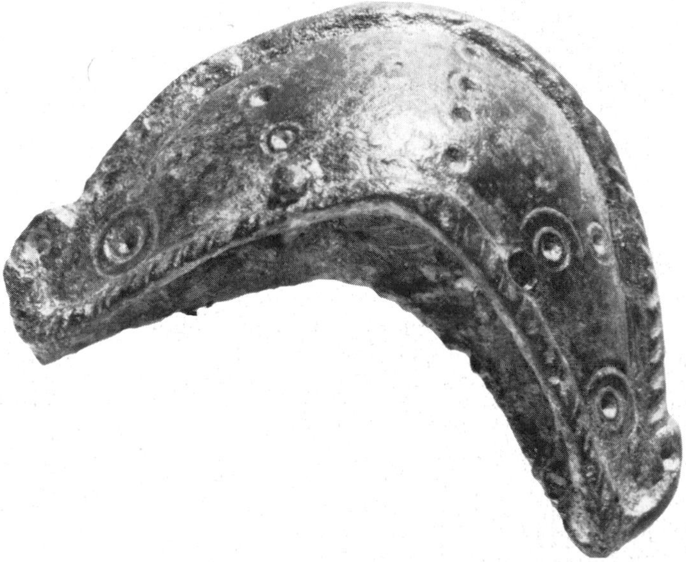

62 The pommel of a seax (single-edged long dagger) of the 7th century from Sibertswold, Kent, length 3.9 cm (Liverpool, Merseyside County Museum). It is most unusual in representing a ship (upside down).

Anglo-Saxon Coins 1: Seventh to Ninth Centuries

(All the coins illustrated in this Essay, except nos. 4 and 10, are in the Ashmolean Museum, Oxford, size × 2.)

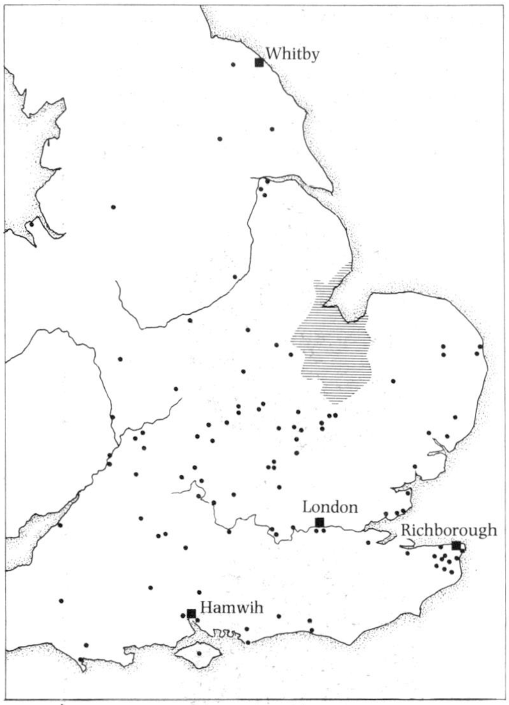

Map showing all the find-spots of *sceattas* in England.

It is doubtful whether there was ever a period when coinage was completely unknown to the Anglo-Saxons; but for the first 200 years or so, only foreign gold coins were in use. Because of their high unit value, the monetary functions they could perform were restricted, and they were in any case prized for use as jewellery, which took some of them out of the monetary sector. Byzantine, Provençal, Italian, Burgundian, and—increasingly—Merovingian coins accumulated in England in quantity. At first there were two denominations, namely the *solidus*, weighing something over 4 g, and its third, the *tremissis* (see p. 118). After the early seventh century the *solidus* was rarely seen, and nearly all the coins were little gold pieces of the smaller kind, about the size of a modern halfpenny. In the second quarter of the seventh century the Anglo-Saxon kings found it expedient to take matters more firmly into their own hands, by striking these *tremisses*—or, in English, *thrymsas*—themselves. There are none in the Sutton Hoo treasure, concealed *c.* 625 and including only Continental coins, but many, of several different varieties, in the Crondall hoard, concealed *c.* 640. Some are likely to be Kentish, some were minted in London (1), and there were probably other mints as well.

1 Gold *thrymsa*, London mint.

The two great treasures of Sutton Hoo and Crondall dominate our knowledge of the Anglo-Saxon gold currency, which is otherwise thin and patchy in the extreme. The information on which we have to rely is purely archaeological in character, and it is important to distinguish between the evidence of grave-finds and of stray losses. Their geographical distribution is different, both in detail and in its broader regional pattern. The grave-finds, which are in effect jewellery, are concentrated more heavily in east Kent. The stray finds which make up nearly all the remaining discoveries tend to be of later date, and are found almost as widely throughout England as are eighth- or ninth-century coins, with the exception that there are extremely few from Mercia. One must assume that they make up only a minute fraction of the coins that were once available, for gold was so valuable that people took very good care not to lose it. There is one instance where we can put some rough figures against this argument. Statistical analysis of the dies of the 'Two Emperors' coinage (2) has prompted the suggestion that between 1 and 2 million pieces were struck. Yet they have left us with only three provenanced finds. As there are scores of finds of other types, what are we to conclude about the stock of gold coinage in England?

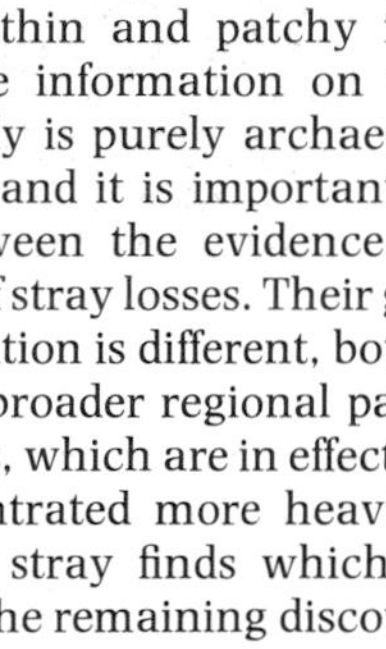

2 Debased gold *thrymsa*, 'Two Emperors' type.

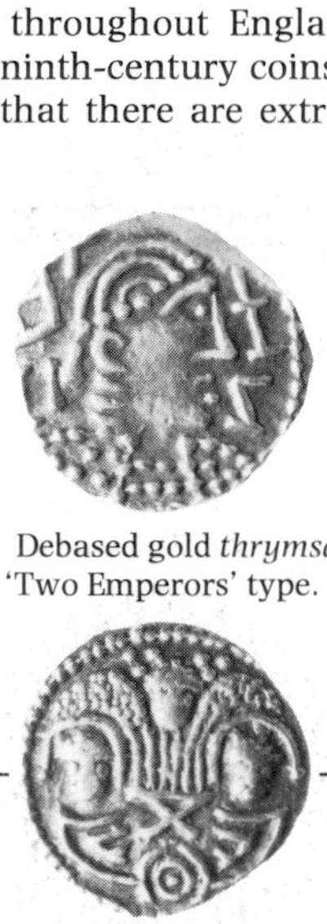

Late in the seventh century the gold currency, which had become more and more debased, was swept away and replaced by a coinage of pure silver. The new pieces, which were of the same size, weight, and general appearance as the *thrymsas*, had only a fraction of their value, and this is reflected in their much higher loss-rate. Because there are many more stray finds, we are better informed about their regional circulation. Again, one must distinguish the evidence of the grave-finds, which are concentrated in east Kent. Numismatists call the silver coins *sceattas* (see p. 59), but what their original users called them is quite uncertain. In effect they were pennies. Although, unlike Offa's more famous pennies, they were rarely inscribed with a king's name (indeed, they usually have no inscription at all, or else a meaningless jumble of letters), it should not be doubted that they were royal coinages, in which the various heptarchic rulers took a close interest. Their correct attribution has to be deduced through a combined study of their find-spots and the interrelationships of their designs. No. 3 is an early *sceat* from the kingdom of the East Angles. It imitates a Roman coin on which the emperor is shown wearing a radiate crown, and the reverse is an illiterate copy of a Roman *Vota* type. In front of the bust, runic letters have been added. Runes are a particular feature of East Anglian coinage until *c.* 800.

Before many decades had elapsed the silver coinage, like the gold, was progressively debased. At the same time it flowered into a profusion of different pictorial designs, often of great charm. The East Saxon kings, for example, chose as a symbol for their issues a standing figure

3 Silver *sceat*, primary series, runic legend, from East Anglia.

of a sphinx (**4**), which they copied from a coin of Cunobelin—found by chance, no doubt, in the soil of Essex. Looking back to Cunobelin and the first century was perhaps a way of asserting their independence from the growing power of Mercia.

4 Silver *sceat*, secondary series, Sphinx, from Essex.

Archaeological excavations of the trading emporium of *Hamwih*, the modern Southampton (see pp. 102–103), have yielded numerous *sceattas* (**5**) of types which were evidently minted locally, for they are not found in other parts of England. The Northumbrian kings, too, issued their own coins at York, sometimes jointly with the arch-

5 Silver *sceat*, secondary series, Southampton type.

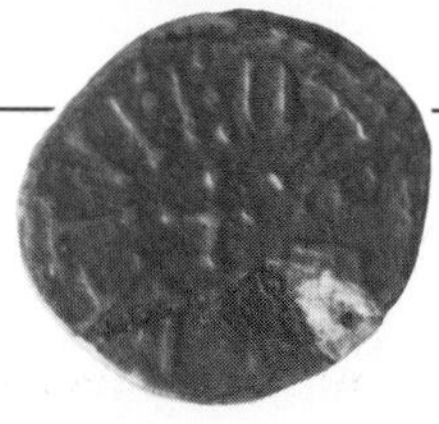

6 Silver *sceat*, Northumbria, Archbishop Egbert.

bishop (**6**). These provided the local currency, and are hardly ever found south of the Humber. Right up until the fall of York in 867 (see p.135) the Northumbrian rulers continued to mint coins of the same general style and weight as *sceattas*, but containing even-

7 Brass *styca*, Northumbria, Archbishop Wigmund.

tually no silver at all (**7**). Numismatists call them *stycas* (see p. 135). They are of considerable interest, both as a source of information about the personal names of the moneyers, and because they offer the earliest secure evidence for the manufacture of brass in medieval England.

8 Early silver penny, Beonna, East Anglia.

Meanwhile, in the south another reform restored the purity of the silver coinage, and changed its fabric to match more closely the *denarii* of the Frankish King Pippin. A King Beonna of East Anglia, about whom little is known, was among the first to make the changeover (**8**), but the new style of coinage is associated most closely with the name of King Offa (see p. 118). The weight of the pennies remained about the same, but the flans are broader and consequently thinner. A few of the Mercian coins are in the name of Offa's queen, Cynethryth (**9**).

9 Early silver penny, Offa, for Queen Cynethryth.

Offa made a variety of other monetary changes and experiments, of which one of the most surprising was the production of a gold coin closely imitating an islamic gold dinar. The royal name, OFFA REX, has been inserted among the lines of Kufic script—upside down! (**10**).

D. M. Metcalf

10 Offa's gold dinar (plaster cast from a coin in the British Museum).

was can be seen, for example, by considering Iona. How could a monastery on an island off the coast of Mull have been the head of a major family of monasteries had not sea travel been frequent and easy? The sea linked even northern Ireland to Gaul. Frankish pottery is found all round the northern end of the Irish Sea (see above, p. 22). It is interesting that the first Anglo-Saxons we know to have been Christians (*c.* 560) were living in the diocese of Nantes, at the southern end of the western sea routes; the first two insular Anglo-Saxons known to have become Christians were monks in the Irish monastery of Iona, at the northern end of those routes (before 597). It was of major importance that from the late sixth century Northumbria extended to the Irish Sea.

The third of the British seas is the Channel, and the third of the culture provinces whose circles intersected in Britain was northern Gaul. Anglo-Saxons had settled to the south of the Channel. Kent was nearly as Continental as it was Insular. It is unlikely that Aethelbert was the first Kentish king to marry a Frankish princess; or that Edwin's family were the first English royal exiles in Gaul. The Frankish gold coins at Sutton Hoo may well speak for many relationships.

Much that happened in the English Church in the seventh century is to be explained in terms of associations which had to do with the sea. It is not uncommon for surprise to be expressed at the development of Northumbrian religion and culture in the age of Bede; Northumbria seems so remotely northern. This was so in Roman, but not in British terms. Northumbria was the central state of the island; its northern border was about as far from the Pentland Firth as its southern was from the Channel. If the island has a natural capital it is York. Northumbria occupied the neck of Britain, where the Irish and the North Seas come closest together. Its seamen were active on both seas. Without maritime power its kings could not have held the key islands of Anglesey and Man. Its great monasteries of Lindisfarne, Monkwearmouth/Jarrow and Whitby all lay beside harbours. The contacts of the last three with Gaul speak for the importance of the seaways. When Abbot Ceolfrith left Jarrow for Rome, he sailed from Jarrow to Gaul. When a princess came to Northumbria from Kent she came by sea. From York to London by road would have taken far longer than by sea. The sea route to Frisia was hardly longer than that to London. When the first great Northumbrian missionary to the Continent, Willibrord, went to Utrecht it would not have been a very long journey nor may it have been at all an uncommon one. That Northumbrian religious culture embraced elements from Ireland and from Gaul and extended its influence from the monastic sea-base of Iona to the Rhine mouths reflects some of the same geographical circumstances which were to make the Viking rulers of York formidable on two seas (see below, pp. 145, 154–5).

To consider foreign contacts is to think of trade. How extensive was foreign trade in England? Rich objects certainly came from abroad; for example, it is curious to think that at the very time when Gregory was writing to the patriarch of Alexandria to tell him of the success of his mission, bronze vessels from Alexandria were being imported into Kent. Objects of elephant ivory are not very rare in early England—for example, Saint Cuthbert's comb. That English missionaries going abroad sometimes simply paid their fares and got on a ship; that English *sceattas* were soon imitated in Frisia; above all, the existence of great trading places at Hamwih, London and Ipswich; all these things suggest quite extensive trade (see the Picture Essay, pp. 102–3). But nearly all the evidence other than the import of luxuries—which need not necessarily have come by commercial means—relates to the late seventh century (see figs. 44, 63).

But there is important evidence for one important trade much earlier: that in slaves. The earliest reference to the export of slaves from England is a letter from Gregory I seeking to have English slaves bought in Gaul. The next is the famous story, already current in early eighth-century Northumbria, of Gregory's being moved to attempt the conversion of England by seeing English slaves exposed for sale in the market-place at Rome. The story may be false; the circumstances in which it is set can hardly be. Bede provides evidence that the humbler captives of war were exported; and he tells of a captive (not humble, but there were special circumstances) being captured in a battle on the Trent (679) and sold to a Frisian slave merchant, who took him to London for export. There is quite extensive evidence for English slaves in Gaul. One of them, Balthildis, ultimately became queen and regent of Neustria.

Conversion to Christianity was part of a wider process of change. For example, it was accompanied by, and

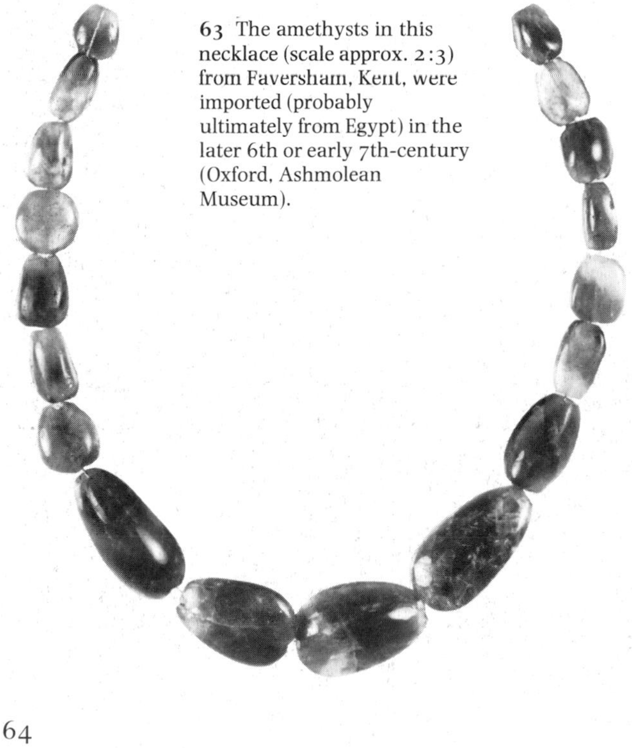

63 The amethysts in this necklace (scale approx. 2:3) from Faversham, Kent, were imported (probably ultimately from Egypt) in the later 6th or early 7th-century (Oxford, Ashmolean Museum).

64 (*right*) The enamel and millefiori glass escutcheons of the largest of the hanging bowls from Sutton Hoo (that illustrated is 5.7 cm in diameter) link East Anglia to Celtic lands or craftsmen (British Museum).

connected with, the writing down of laws and the striking of coin. Christianity, coins, and written laws all made England more like Gaul. There are indications of change in dress at the same time, again to styles prevalent in Gaul. Some of the things which Gregory of Tours says about Merovingian kings acquire a somewhat different ring when one thinks of them in relation to England. For example, he says of Chilperic that he ordained that new letters be added to the alphabet. He makes this sound like a despot's whim. But to know that such matters were considered in Gaul is to understand more easily how Aethelbert's laws came to be written in Old English, when a major problem must have been to find the letters to fit the sounds. When Bede refers to Aethelbert's making written laws he says they were *more Romanorum* ('in the Roman style'). And indeed, if the immediate influences were often from Gaul, what was unfolding was part of a much longer story, that of the effects on Germanic rulers and peoples of influences ultimately derived from Rome.

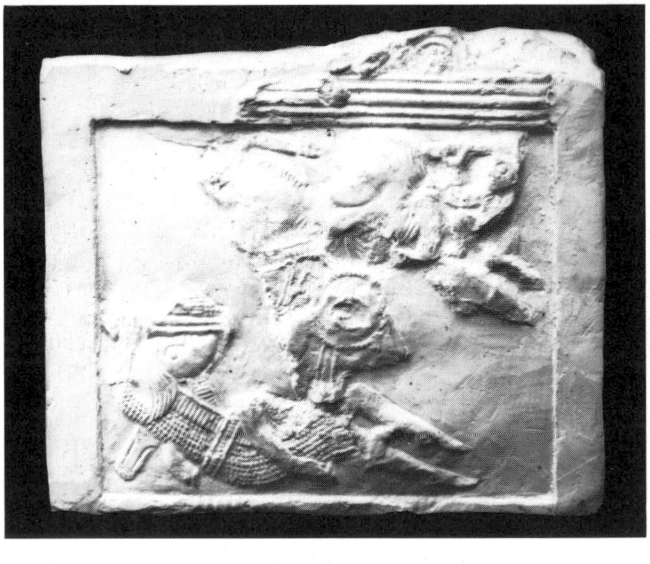

66 Tomb of Flavinus, a Roman cavalryman of the late 1st century, height 264 cm (Hexham Abbey), and one of the cast plates of the Sutton Hoo helmet, width 5.7 cm (British Museum).

65 This silver gilt cover was part of the helmet of a Roman officer (probably, since it is stamped STABLESIANA VI, of the *Equites Stablesiani*) who was drowned in a bog at Deurne (Holland) *c.* 320 (Leiden, Rijksmuseum van Oudheden). Remains of a similar helmet have been found at Burgh Castle (fig. 10).

Consider the glimpses we get of this in East Anglia. The Sutton Hoo treasure gives a mighty impression of barbarian magnificence. Yet in various ways it is Roman. The silver plate is plainly Roman. The helmet is a German version of a late Roman parade helmet. Its decorations, for example the six plates showing a cavalryman riding down a foot-soldier, have a barbaric air; but to look at a Roman depiction of the same scene is to think again about that. The helmet's nearest ancestors come from Sweden, but they are a reminder that even so far north a barbarian potentate could wish to look like a

67 The Devil's Dyke is one of several dykes in Cambridgeshire which were apparently intended to control the main route into East Anglia from the south-west. It may well be Dark Age, and is about 5 miles long, 40 yards across and 30 feet from ditch bottom to bank top (cf. fig. 61).

Roman general. It is essentially the same kind of helmet that an officer of a Roman regiment based in Suffolk, say the *Equites Stablesiani* at Burgh Castle, would have worn three centuries before. Even the ceremonial whetstone, which has struck some as very barbaric indeed, is capped by a naturalistic statuette of a deer which could almost pass for Roman. The garnet-inlaid jewels are not Roman. But they take one south rather than north; they are similar to, if finer than, those buried in the tomb of Childeric, six generations before. The potentate buried at Sutton Hoo belonged to a German world which had for centuries been influenced by Rome. Not only Roman goods and Roman techniques, but plundering the Empire and serving the Empire had had deep effects.

A Roman influence appears in a quite different way in the later history of the East Anglian kings. Bede says a little of their genealogy, taking it back to Wuffa, perhaps the Swedish founder of the line. By the late eighth century they claimed a grander descent, with a unique feature, the inclusion of Caesar among the royal ancestors. They seem to have taken this claim seriously; for Romulus and Remus appear on East Anglian coins, and on them alone; and one of the only two other early Anglo-Saxon depictions of Romulus and Remus comes from East Anglia (fig. 68).

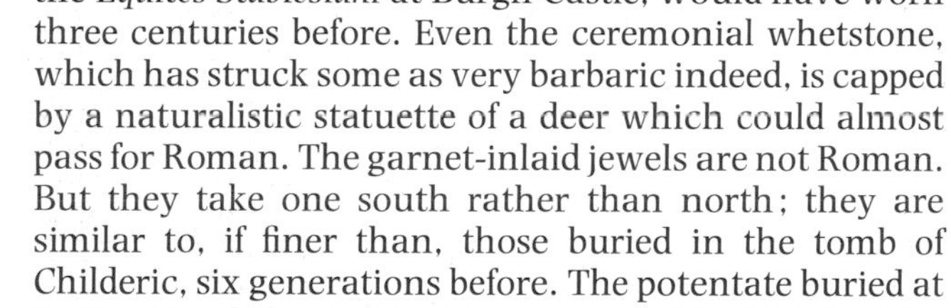

68 Part of a bone casket (or book-cover) from Larling, Norfolk, width 7.1 cm (Norwich Castle Museum). The wolf and twins also appear on a coin of Aethelbert, king of East Anglia (d. 794), to whom Larling church is dedicated.

Roman or Roman-style plate and gear (such as barbarians had been using for centuries) and a claim to descent from Caesar are not the same; but they may be part of the same story. The treasures indicate at least that when Sigbert went into exile in Gaul (see above, p. 56), the East Anglia he left was in some ways part of that penumbra of the Roman world in which his Merovingian hosts flourished. By that time the Merovingians had been equipped with pseudo-Roman claims to descent from a Trojan exile. In becoming a Christian a barbarian moved from a world in which he could eat his dinner from a Roman dish to one in which he could enjoy the idea that he actually was in some sense a Roman.

Conclusion

The England to which Theodore came differed very much from that to which Augustine had come. The balance of power among the kingdoms had shifted drastically. There was no question of Kentish supremacy. Kent had been exempt from the authority of the Northumbrian overlords, but within seven years of Theodore's arrival it was to be ravaged by Aethelred of Mercia (later to die a monk). This foreshadowed its loss of independence in the next century. Oswy was the last king to enjoy authority over nearly the whole island. But by the late 660s, though he still had a great empire in the north, and Northumbria was never to fall under the lordship of another Anglo-Saxon dynasty, his power in the south must have been diminished by that of Mercia. Wulfhere, building on the gains of his father Penda, who had extended Mercian power from a relatively small area on the Trent to include the whole of the Midlands, had

69 The 'ceremonial whetstone' or 'sceptre' from Sutton Hoo (British Museum) is nearly 84 cm long (diameter of the ring at the top 10.2 cm) and had never been used as a whetstone. Its significance is for speculation; it has been plausibly suggested that whetstones were associated with the thunderbolts of a sky god.

gained authority over Essex during the 660s, and so access to the sea at London, which must have been crucial. The dominions of the kings of Wessex were being expanded fast in the west; and Ine was one of the greatest kings of his day. It is unlikely that any king had overlordship over the whole of southern England. This may be a reason why Theodore and his successors were able to establish a degree of independence; the authority of the archbishops of Canterbury stretched over a wider area than that of any king.

In the building up of the greater kingdoms many small dynasties, perhaps even great ones, had been subordinated or, we may fairly assume, wiped out and their memory lost. Anglo-Saxon kings sought to extirpate enemy lines; that is why, for example, the wife, children and household of Edwin had to flee as far as Gaul from the conquering Oswald; somehow they seem to have felt that his Christian faith did not guarantee their safety, as no doubt it did not. With failure went oblivion. The history we have is of, or written largely from the point of view of, the dynasties which survived and flourished.

Theodore found all the successful dynasties Christian. In considering those kings and the nature of their faith two things have always to be borne in mind: our ignorance and their diversity. There are so many things that we only just know—for example, it is only the immense good fortune of having found Sutton Hoo and Yeavering that gives us any idea of the magnificence of these rulers. There must be many things we do not know at all. We can only guess at what their culture was like. Almost certainly there was a great deal of verse; their minds would have been well-stocked with quasi-knowledge of the past derived from poems perhaps resembling *Beowulf*. But it would be rash to assume that the later poetry produced after the coming of Christianity gives an adequate idea of what earlier verse was like. Or again, it could be that wood carving was a major art form in the pagan period; if so, it is bad luck, for none survives.

In some ways what had happened to kings, as to their subjects, was a development, almost a natural development, a matter of assimilation of their ways and beliefs to those of the lands to the south and of new beliefs to old. Christian kings still fought and slew, killed members of rival families and killed rivals within their own. The Church in many ways fitted itself remuneratively enough into their world, taking tribute and claiming its share of booty. Saints of a new kind appeared very well suited to dynastic needs and heroic values. In the later years of the century cults developed both of Oswald and of Edwin, warrior kings who had died in battle; their principal claim to sanctity being that among their enemies were pagans. They were in a sense among the first crusaders. But the contrast, seen earlier at its extreme between Redwald and Sigbert, between those who conformed and those who were transformed, continued. If some kings sat very easily to their faith, others were led by it to enter a monastery or to go to Rome to die. The England of Bede and Aethelbald, if in some ways an old world with new things in it, was in others a very new world.

70 (*right*) The Sutton Hoo helmet (British Museum). Although this type is of late Roman (and ultimately Sassanid) origin, the nearest immediate connections are with eastern Sweden. For example, the decorative bronze panelling closely resembles similar work on a helmet from Old Uppsala (see fig. 65 and pp. 66–7).

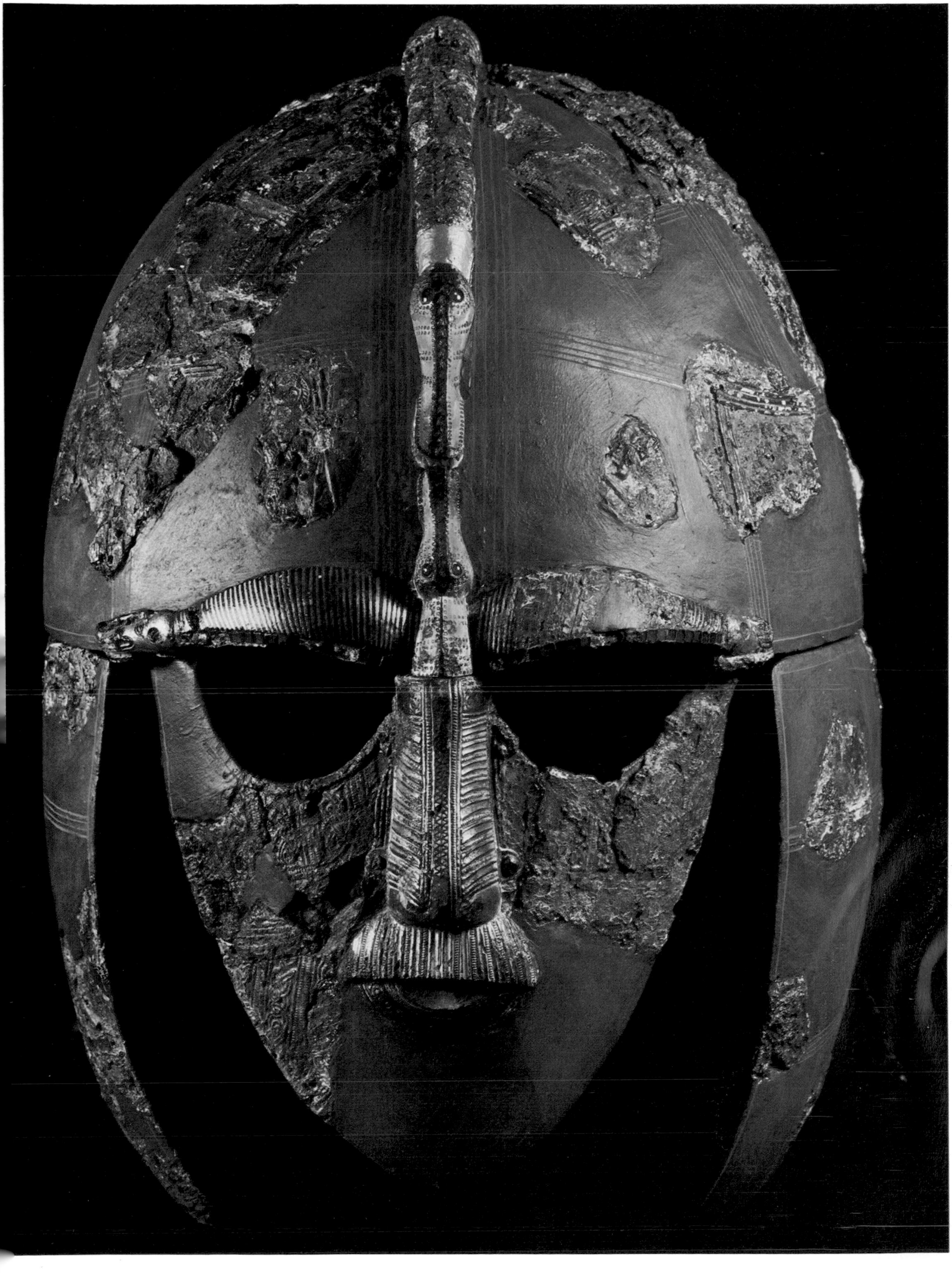

73 The Anglo–Saxon church at Bradford-on-Avon, Wilts. This exquisite little church (its nave measures 25 × 13 ft and is 25 ft high) was identified by William of Malmesbury in the early 12th century as built by Aldhelm. Opinions vary (as often with Anglo–Saxon churches) as to whether it was built then, or *c.* 1000, but an early date is certainly possible.

rightly) to Archbishop Theodore (669–90). Finally, from *c.* 670, we have charters, the most valuable records of the effect of Christianity on Anglo-Saxon society and politics. In the process of converting themselves from 'northern' to 'Mediterranean' standards of civilization, the Anglo-Saxons in fact left the most richly varied set of sources for any period of their history.

Second, Bede's passage reflects both of the most important conditions of the flowering of Christian culture: the organization of dioceses, and the proliferation of monasteries. When Theodore arrived in 669, Christianity was established in all but one of the English kingdoms, but its organization was still precarious: there were only seven dioceses, of which only four were occupied, and only two of these by canonically unobjectionable bishops. Christian history offers few parallels to the achievement of this Greek-speaking refugee from an utterly different environment, 67 when he arrived and 88 when he died, in creating a stable diocesan structure under the close supervision of Canterbury. By 690, there were 13 or 14 bishoprics, and Theodore's immediate successors added three or four more. This diocesan pattern was to be disrupted in the north and east by the Vikings, and modified by reformers from the tenth to the twelfth centuries, but otherwise it survived until the Reformation.

Similarly, it is unlikely that there were many more than a dozen English monasteries in the mid-seventh century, and Bede himself commented on their scarcity. A century later, as he implies in his conclusion, monasteries had become very numerous. By the end of the pre-

74 Symbol of St Matthew with interlace border from the Book of Durrow (Dublin, Trinity College, MS A.4.5, fol. 21b). Quite apart from its Irish provenance (Durrow was a dependency of Iona), the manuscript has several Irish features, including the possibility that this figure is wearing the 'Celtic' tonsure which was rejected at the Synod of Whitby. But the script and some 'Germanic' decoration, suggest that it may have been produced in Northumbria under Irish influence, and later went to Iona. If so, this is not only the first of the great insular *codices de luxe* (p. 93), but also one of the very first surviving English books.

75 Conjectural reconstruction of glass fragments from Building D—perhaps the guest house—at Jarrow (see pp. 74–5) (Jarrow, Bede Memorial Museum). The reconstruction is based on the distribution of excavated fragments. Window-glass was unknown to the pagan Anglo–Saxons, and glaziers had to be imported from Gaul by Benedict Biscop. 900 glass fragments were recovered from this building alone, and Monkwearmouth and Jarrow have produced more early medieval glass than anywhere else in the West.

Viking period, it is possible to count over 200 monastic communities in England as a whole; given the patchy nature of the evidence, this is probably an underestimate. Some of these communities were very small, but others, like Bede's own, were apparently enormous. Though the number, wealth and organization of monasteries were also to be affected by the Vikings and reform, it seems likely that the age of Bede was decisive in the formation of the landed wealth of the medieval English Church; and certainly the history of many of the greatest monasteries began then, if not earlier: Glastonbury, Canterbury (Christ Church), Abingdon, Peterborough, Winchester (St Swithun's), Canterbury (St Augustine's), Worcester, Evesham, Ely and Crowland. All in all, the religious changes of the century after 650, and their social and cultural ramifications, were probably as significant as those of the Reformation itself.

The third point to emerge from what Bede says is Aethelbald of Mercia's dominance over the southern English kingdoms. Bede describes this power in terms almost identical with those he earlier used of the seven holders of the *imperium* (see above, pp. 53–4). But unlike theirs, Aethelbald's supremacy is documented elsewhere. In an important charter of 736, the 'Ismere Diploma', Aethelbald is entitled (in the grant proper), 'king not only of the Mercians but of all provinces called by the general name "South English"'; and (in the witness-list), 'king of Britain' (Birch, *Cart.*, no. 154; *EHD*, no. 67). The first title certainly reflects what Bede had said about the *imperium*; the second is a Latinization of the vernacular *bretwalda*, which was otherwise first used by the *Anglo-Saxon Chronicle* for the year 829, when adding Egbert of Wessex (802–39) to Bede's list. The charter thus proves that some such resounding title as *bretwalda* was indeed given to overlords of southern England, and that Aethelbald did indeed belong to the series.

Whether, and to what extent, such power was held by other kings between the death of Oswy and Aethelbald's accession is a more difficult question, better deferred (see below, pp. 99–100). However, it does seem that Wulfhere of Mercia (658–74) was dominant in southern England, since he led a powerful southern coalition to defeat by Egfrith of Northumbria, *c.* 674. Any prospect, arising from this battle, of a revival of Northumbrian supremacy was checked by Egfrith's own defeat at the Battle of the Trent (679), and then by the annihilation of himself and his army at Pictish hands (685). The victor of the Battle of the Trent, Aethelred of Mercia (674–704), and his successors, Cenred (704–9) and Ceolred (709–16), were effective overlords between the Humber and the Thames, but were challenged and even rivalled in the south by Wihtred of Kent (692–725), Caedwalla of Wessex (685–8) and Ine. Aethelbald's power thus seems to represent a return to the clearer political pattern of the seventh century, after a period of some confusion. More important, there is now more material with which to assess it.

The last point to make about Bede's summary is that its euphoric tone is probably misleading. Only three years later, he wrote an important letter to his pupil, bishop Egbert of York, in which he expressed his real

Monkwearmouth and Jarrow

Monkwearmouth and Jarrow, the twin monasteries where Bede spent his life, are the best-known of all early Christian foundations in England. We have two detailed histories by inmates: Bede's *History of the Abbots*, and an anonymous *Life of Ceolfrith*. Bede's many writings enable one to compile a catalogue of the community's impressive library, and the fact that the great Bible, the Codex Amiatinus, is now known to have been written there (**5**) means that other manuscripts can be ascribed to its *scriptorium* by palaeographical comparison (e.g. fig. 71). Significant parts of the fabric of the original churches survive (**1**, **6**), and Professor Cramp's excavations, among the most exciting in the history of Anglo-Saxon archaeology, have revealed many, if not all, of the other monastic buildings (**2**).

Benedict Biscop founded Monkwearmouth in 674, and Jarrow followed in 681 or 682; Ceolfrith was first abbot of Jarrow, and then abbot of the double community from just before Biscop's death in 690 until his own resignation and death on the way to Rome in 716. Two things about the early history of these foundations need particular emphasis. First, the community was very large and very rich. We are told of endowments from King Egfrith (**3**), his successors, and the local nobility, totalling *c.* 150 hides (p. 93), among the largest endowments of an early Christian foundation in England. We also read that, when Ceolfrith set off for Rome, he left almost 600 brethren behind, and took another 80 with him; no later medieval English monastery had anything like this complement, though many were probably what would later be called lay brothers. Jarrow was probably the smaller of the two abbeys: its site is relatively constricted, and it is unlikely that many significant buildings have yet to be discovered, yet those which are now known could scarcely accommodate one-fifth of the total recorded. At Monkwearmouth, on the other hand, local conditions have made excavation much more difficult, relatively few buildings have yet been unearthed, and it seems that the area involved was much bigger than that so far investigated.

Second, the cultural atmosphere of the community in its early years at least

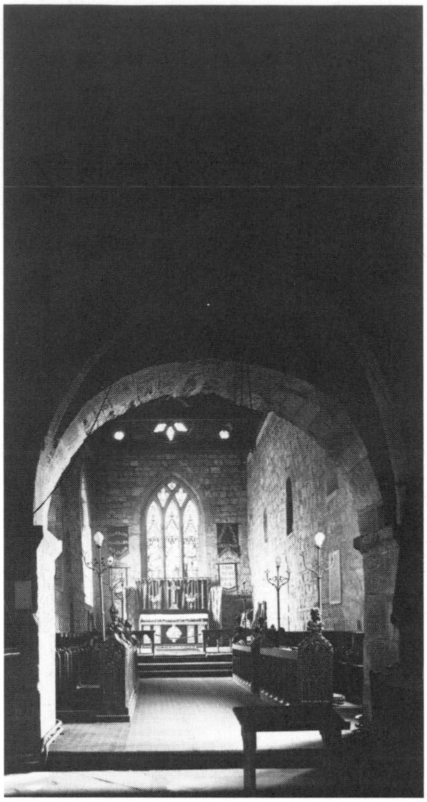

1

1 Chancel of St Paul's, Jarrow. The original internal dimensions were $39\frac{3}{4} \times 15\frac{3}{4}$ feet, and it had a gallery at the west end. The squared stonework may have come from a Roman building on the site; the three little windows in the south wall are original.

2 Model of the excavated section of the monastic buildings at Jarrow in the late 8th century, looking north, reconstruction by Rosemary Cramp (Jarrow, Bede Monastery Museum). The chancel of the modern church (**1**) was originally a separate chapel to the east of the main basilica. The basilica itself stood on the site of present nave until the eighteenth century; it measured 90×19 feet, and apparently had a west porch of two stories and *porticus* to the side, like Brixworth (see fig. 84). To the south of the church lay the main monastic buildings. That to the west was probably a refectory, measuring $91\frac{1}{2} \times 26$ feet. That to the east, measuring 60×26 feet, contained what was possibly a chapter-house, a cell and an oratory; the latter may well have been the place of Bede's famous and beautiful death scene. Both buildings had floors of Roman *opus signinum* (pounded tile), painted plaster walls, and coloured glass windows. The building on the river at the south-east corner was possibly a guest house for lay dignitaries, and may later have been a workshop; it also had coloured glass windows (fig. 75).

2

3

must have been markedly 'Mediterranean'. Biscop sent to Gaul for masons to build a stone church, 'in the Roman manner which he always loved' (*HA*, c. 5, p. 368); later he sent to Gaul again for glaziers (see fig. 75). He had already acquired books on foreign travels; from two further visits to Rome, in 678–9 and 684–7, he brought back more books, relics, vestments, a teacher of Roman chant, and pictures of saints and scenes from the Bible with which to adorn his churches. Archaeology amply confirms the sophistication of his buildings, and significantly it was to Abbot Ceolfrith that the King of the Picts wrote in the early eighth century, not only to be put right on Easter, but also for architects to build *him* a church 'in the Roman manner' (*HE*, V.21, p. 333). Similarly, the Codex Amiatinus is very Italian in style—indeed, had the *Life of Ceolfrith* not quoted the verses on its dedication page in their original form, it might never have been identified as English. Insular art styles left some mark on the community, but one has the impression, at least in Bede's lifetime, of an island of Mediterranean culture in a barbarian sea.

4

3(*left*) Dedication stone of St Paul's, Jarrow, now in the wall above the chancel arch. It dates the dedication of the basilica on 23rd April, in the 15th year of King Egfrith, and the 4th of Ceolfrith's abbacy (i.e. 685).

6 (*right*) West front of St Peter's, Monkwearmouth. This is all that survives of the original fabric, and it shows that Biscop's church was 18½ feet wide × 50 feet high; if, as is probable, the modern nave is on the old foundations, it was 64 feet long (thus significantly smaller than the Jarrow basilica, despite what is said above about the size of the two communities). The porch was originally two-storied and *c.* 33 feet high, with lateral *porticus*; the upper reaches of the tower are late Saxon. This sort of west structure is paralleled in what is known of the early church of St Martin, Tours, which is what the sources' mention of Gallic masons would lead one to expect.

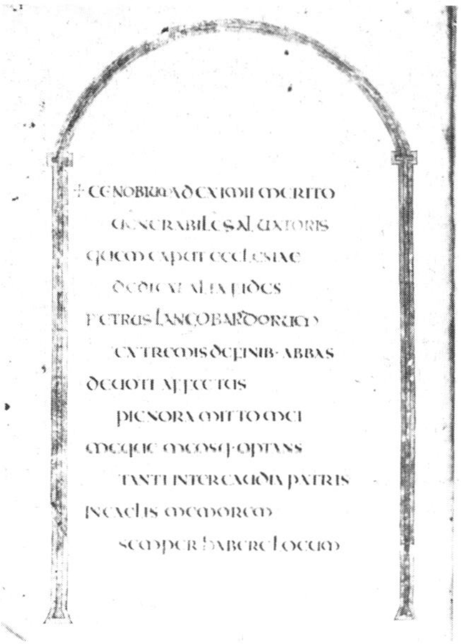

5

5(*above*) Dedication page of the Codex Amiatinus (cf. fig. 91). As can be seen, the verses have been tampered with. The otherwise almost identical verses quoted in the *Life of Ceolfrith* show that the first two lines should read: 'Corpus ad eximii merito/ venerabile Petri', and the fifth: 'Ceolfridus Anglorum'. The manuscript, one of the earliest and best of Saint Jerome's Vulgate translation of the Bible, is thus identified as one of the three Bibles which Ceolfrith commissioned, the one he took with him as a present for the Pope in 716. Rightly described as 'one of the great books of the world', it further underlines the community's wealth: it has been calculated that to prepare the vellum for the three Bibles it would have been necessary to slaughter 1,550 calves.

4(*left*) Sculptured stone panel from Jarrow, now in the church porch. The 'inhabited vine-scroll' has close affinities with that of the Ruthwell Cross (fig. 89), which has led to the suggestion that the Ruthwell sculptor was linked with the Jarrow community.

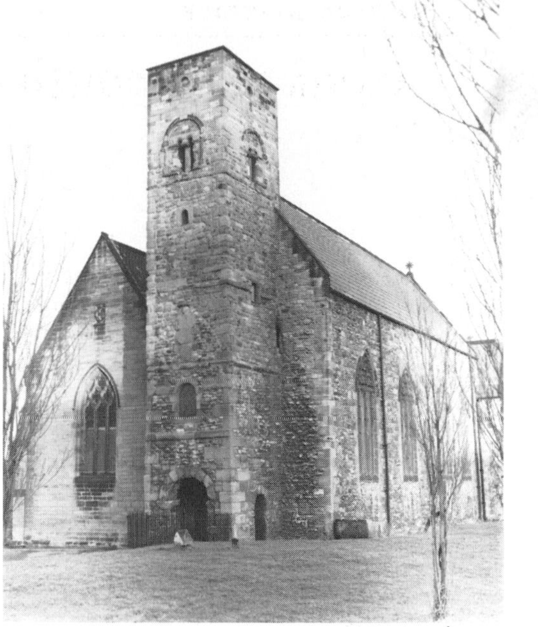

6

7(*below*) The Herebericht stone from the west porch of Monkwearmouth, now in the church itself. One of the most beautiful tombstones of the whole Anglo-Saxon period, it commemorates the rest 'in the body' of the otherwise unknown priest Herebert.

7

P. Wormald

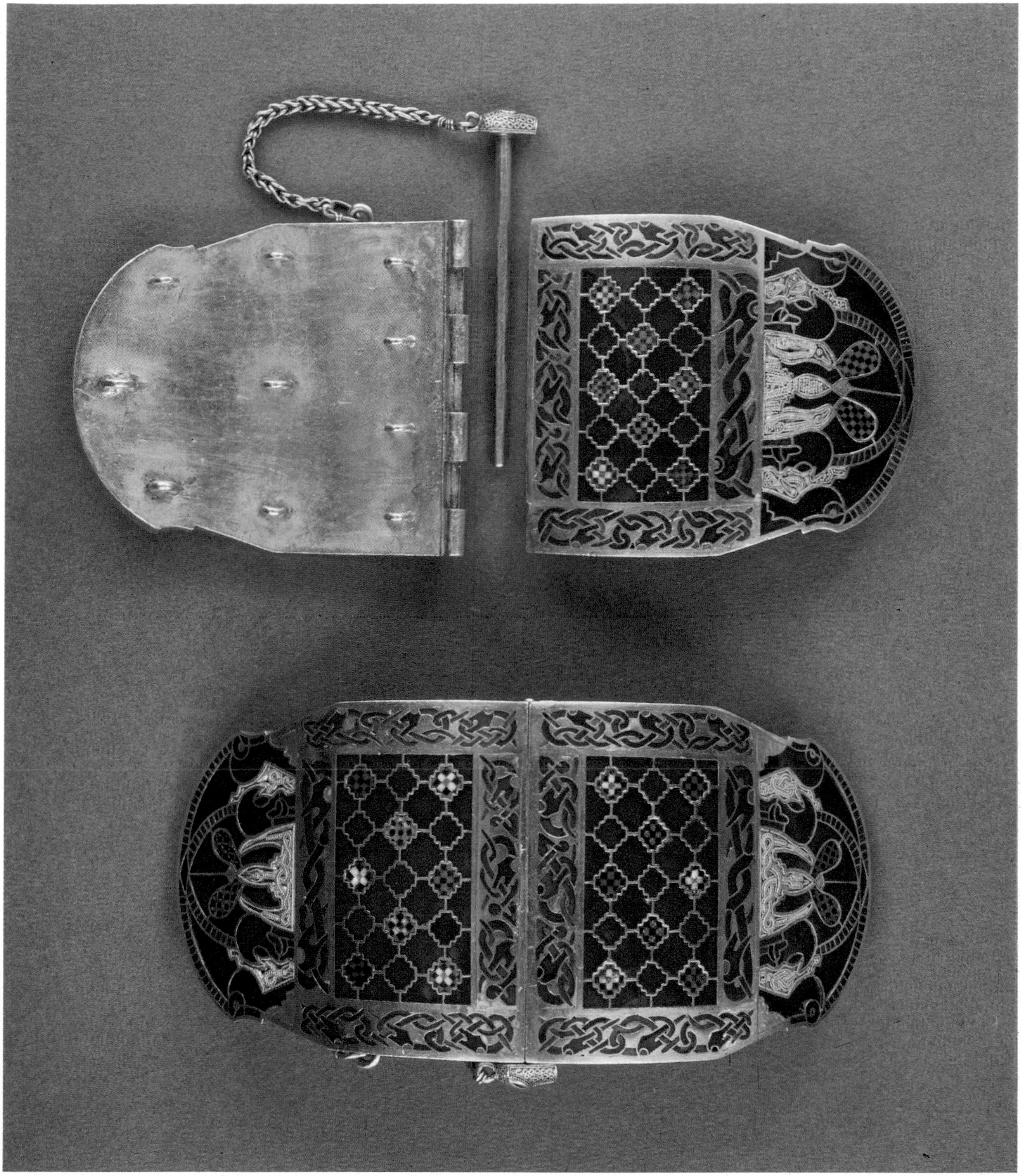

76, 77 A carpet-page from the Lindisfarne Gospels (British Library, MS Cotton Nero D.iv, fol. 94b), juxtaposed with two enamel and gold shoulder-clasps from the Sutton Hoo treasure, width *c.* 10.5 cm (British Museum). The inspiration of secular metalwork in the design of the holy book is clearly apparent (cf. p. 93).

feelings about the state of the Northumbrian Church. There were still not enough bishoprics, because of episcopal greed for the revenues of large dioceses. Most of the new monasteries were monasteries only in name: noblemen were receiving chartered endowments on the pretext of founding monasteries, but living there like secular lords, with their families and retainers. In consequence, there was now a shortage of land with which to endow not only more bishoprics but also youthful warriors, who might defend the country from 'barbarians'—a hint that Bede was perhaps less complacent about Celtic revenge for the Anglo-Saxon conquests than he seemed in his *History* (*Ep. ad Egb.*, pp. 414–17). If we put this letter alongside the *History*, which begins with Gildas's denunciation of the sins of the Britons, and the terrible punishment of the Anglo-Saxon invasions which God visited upon them, it emerges that one reason why Bede may have written the *History* was out of anxiety that the failings of the English Church would lead to similar disasters.

Bede's letter is the most important, but not the only, evidence for the 'secularization' of ecclesiastical life in early Christian England, and for the growing tension between the needs and aspirations of 'Church and State'. In 745/6, the great Anglo-Saxon missionary, Boniface, wrote to Aethelbald (described as 'wielding the glorious sceptre of the empire of the English'), and complained vigorously of the king's interference with nuns and impositions on other holy institutions (Tangl, no. 73, pp. 146–55). This letter, and another of the same time addressed to Archbishop Cuthbert of Canterbury (740–60), prompted an important council of the southern English bishops, where Aethelbald presided, and which was dominated by the issue of secular influence on the Church. Two years later, Aethelbald was obliged to define the services to which the king was entitled from churchmen and their estates. The age of Bede and Aethelbald ended with conflict between its two most obvious beneficiaries, the Church and the Mercian monarchy. It was perhaps inevitable that such prodigious ecclesiastical development should prove hard to reconcile with the scarcely less evident increase in the stature of the Mercian kings.

Six Early English Saints

Just as Bede pinpointed the major themes of the period, so he remains the most important source in tracing them throughout the rest of this chapter, and it is right that the age should bear his name. Nevertheless, the most remarkable product of an age is not necessarily the most typical, and Bede may have been exceptional, not only in his learning, but also in his background and outlook. Moreover, his *History*, unlike that of Gildas, is remarkably discreet about the sins and controversies of which he disapproved. It is, above all, 'a gallery of good examples', designed to teach the kings and churchmen of his own day their duties, by focusing their attention on the edifying achievements of their predecessors. One paradoxical result is that it is much less informative about the period of his maturity, after 687, than it is about the age of conversion. The story of the growth of the English Church and Christian culture is thus, in some ways, better told in the lives of six other saints of the period: Benedict Biscop, Hilda, Cuthbert, Guthlac, Boniface and Wilfrid. Their careers are better recorded (and more eventful) than Bede's own; for only two of them is Bede the main source; and each brings out different aspects of the development of Anglo-Saxon Christianity, aspects that can then be isolated and discussed in their turn.

It is right to begin with Bede's own founder-abbot, Benedict Biscop (628–90), whose story Bede told himself in the *History of the Abbots* of his community. Biscop was a Northumbrian nobleman, a young retainer at Oswy's court, who presumably grew up under the influence of the Irish mission. When, at 25, he became eligible for a land-grant from the king, he renounced the world and began 20 years of almost continuous pilgrimage. He visited Rome six times, began a book collection, and sampled the customs of 17 different European monasteries, including the famous Lérins off the south coast of Gaul, Saint Augustine's house at Canterbury, where he was briefly abbot, and (probably) Jouarre, near Paris, spiritual home of Agilbert, who had led the *Romani* at Whitby (see above, p. 47). Returning finally to Northumbria, he founded the monasteries of Monkwearmouth (674) and Jarrow (682), importing masons and glaziers from Gaul, and books and pictures from two further Roman visits. The buildings and manuscripts of Biscop's community are discussed in a Picture Essay (pp. 74–5).

The spiritual atmosphere Biscop created is best conveyed by his last words to his monks. He reminded them of his Rule, which he had based on his wide experience of European spiritual life, but he made special mention of the *Rule* of the sixth-century Italian abbot, Saint Benedict, whose *Life* Pope Gregory had written, and whose name Biscop took. Bede's familiarity with the *Rule of Saint Benedict* (which was to become the blueprint for all western European monasteries) is one of several indications of its importance at Monkwearmouth–Jarrow. Biscop dwelt on his library, stressing its Roman origin; Bede's vast learning is the best witness to its range. Above all, he insisted that he was not to be succeeded by his brother, or anyone else on account of birth, but by an abbot chosen for spiritual qualities from the community. Bede saw Biscop as a rich young man who *had* observed the Gospel precept to leave home and kindred for Christ, and Biscop's denial of family claims to his monasteries is of a piece with his determination to renounce the values of his class.

It is itself an interesting point that the second (and chronologically the first) of the saints considered here was a woman. Hilda (614–80) is known largely from a long chapter in Bede's *History*. She was a princess of the Deiran dynasty, and was baptized by Paulinus. Her sister became queen of the East Angles, where the influence of the Gallic Church was strong, and she originally planned to take vows at Chelles. But she was recalled by Aidan, and eventually made abbess of Whitby, which Oswy

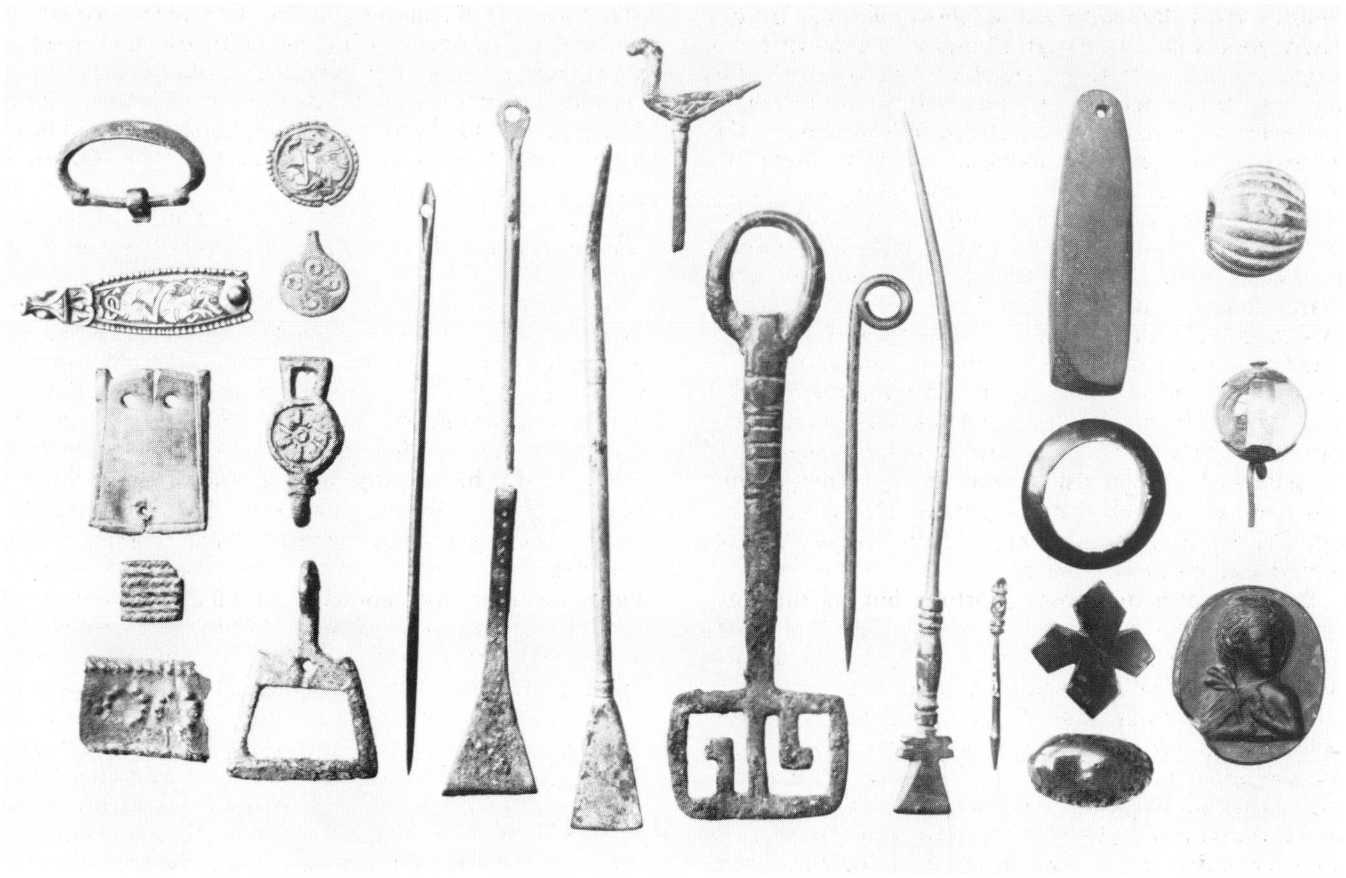

78 A few of the finds from the pre-Viking abbey of Whitby (British Museum). They include a key, styluses, needles, pins and tweezers, and precious, or semi-precious, items of personal adornment, suggesting, that the abbey's inmates were living in some style.

founded in gratitude for his victory over Penda. Hilda and Whitby are significant in several ways. Whitby was of course a nunnery, but it also contained a community of men; it was one of many such double monasteries in early Christian England and Gaul. It was very much a royal establishment: Oswy and eventually Edwin were buried there, and Hilda, herself Edwin's cousin, was succeeded by Aelfflaed, Oswy's daughter: claims of kindred did matter at Whitby. Inadequate excavations make it difficult to be certain of the monastic layout, but it may have been cellular, not communal and regular like Biscop's houses; perhaps more significant, the number and variety of 'small finds' made suggest that its residents were living in some style. Whitby was the source of one of the earliest saint's lives written in England, a *Life of Gregory*, the English apostle; its Latin is unimpressive, and it contains some bizarre stories, but it does at least show good knowledge of Gregory's own works. Finally, one of Bede's best stories tells how Caedmon, a cowherd attached to the monastery, was inspired by a dream to compose the first vernacular religious poetry; the poem survives, and is essentially an adaptation of the techniques and idioms of secular verse to the theme of God's glory. Hilda's life and community show not only the importance of women at this stage of English Christian history, but also that not all houses were as concerned as Biscop's to shut out the values of the world outside.

Cuthbert (?630–87), the most famous saint of the series, is best known from a *Life* by Bede. But this is really an attempt to add elegance, edification and some more miracles to an earlier anonymous *Life* written at Lindisfarne, where Cuthbert was buried, and Bede allowed the Lindisfarne monks to vet what he had written; it is thus Cuthbert's own community that gives us our knowledge of him. Cuthbert, perhaps of humbler origin than Biscop, was, from the outset, a disciple of the Irish mission; he followed Aidan's pupil, Eata, from Melrose to Lindisfarne itself, where Theodore made him bishop in 685. Much in his life is reminiscent of the Irish tradition, and of Columba especially: his miracles, involving not only cures but also prophecies and angelic visitations; his close relations with birds and animals; his missionary journeys, as far afield as the Picts of Fife; his hermitage on Farne, whither he retired to die, though still a bishop; and finally the anxiety which, like Columba, he felt about his funeral. But there is more to Cuthbert than this. His monastic regime, as described by Bede, was like Benedict's rather than the Irish, and his episcopal values, as reflected in the anonymous *Life*, were in line with the prescriptions of Gregory the Great (Bede, *Life*, c. 16, pp. 206–13; Anon., *Life*, IV.1, pp. 110–13). Moreover, the splendid relics with which he was buried, especially his

The Tomb of Saint Cuthbert

Saint Cuthbert (for whose life see pp. 79–82) died on 20 March 687, on Farne Island. The same day his brethren from Lindisfarne rowed his body to the mainland and buried it in their church. Eleven years later they determined to treat it as that of a saint, that is to say, to move it to a shrine raised above the ground. They were confirmed in their decision, and deeply touched, to find it uncorrupted. So began one of the greatest of medieval cults.

The history of Cuthbert's body is very remarkable. In 875 the Viking assault drove the community to leave Lindisfarne, taking their saint with them. For seven years they wandered, but in 883 settled at Chester-le-Street, coming to terms with the invaders (see p. 154). In Ethelred II's reign the renewal of Viking attacks led to a further move, to Durham in 995. Throughout the Middle Ages Cuthbert's shrine there attracted pilgrims and wealth; Durham's greatness derived from the power of his cult. In late 1539 or early 1540 the commissioners of Henry VIII destroyed and despoiled it. In 1827 the grave in which Cuthbert's body was believed to have been reburied was reopened.

There he was. There were three coffins. The innermost had figures incised in its wood: on the lid Jesus surrounded by the symbols of the four Evangelists (1); on one side the 12 apostles, on the other five archangels; at the head two more archangels; at the foot the Virgin and Child. Within, enclosed in many wrappings, was the skeleton of a man. On his breast was a pectoral cross of gold set with garnets (2). Also in the coffin were an ivory comb (3), a wooden travelling altar enclosed in plates of silver (4), and numerous fragments of rich textiles. The coffin and its contents were such as to make it certain that it was Cuthbert's. While any of the objects could conceivably have been added to the tomb on one of the occasions of its opening in later centuries it is likely that all were there in 698, except for the rich fabrics, most of

1 The lid of Saint Cuthbert's coffin, 167.6 cm long, up to 40.6 cm wide. All the objects illustrated here (except the Gospel book) are in Durham Cathedral and reproduced by permission of the Dean and Chapter.

2 The pectoral cross, 6.4 cm across.

which must have been put in later. To what was found in 1827 must be added a little manuscript of the Gospel of Saint John, removed in 1104, and now on loan to the British Library (**5**). Other things were found in 1104 which have disappeared since: a paten, scissors, and, most remarkable, 'a chalice . . . its lower part representing a lion of purest gold, which bore on its back an onyx stone, made hollow by the most beautiful craftsmanship' (anonymous account of the opening of the tomb in 1104, Battiscombe (ed.) 1956, p. 103).

All the surviving objects are in some sense unique in England. The coffin is the only decorated wood to survive from the period; the Gospel book is the only seventh-century English manuscript whose binding is certainly early and probably original; the cross is the only such treasure from the north; the comb and altar are unparalleled in England. They reveal much. First, an extremely high level of craftsmanship. The cross is a phenomenally intricate piece of work. Up to a point this is no surprise; the Sutton Hoo treasure is by itself enough to show what seventh-century jewellers could do, though the Cuthbert cross differs in important ways from the gold-and-garnet work of the south. The binding of the Gospel book is very accomplished, especially in the use of moulded leather, and is anything but the work of a man who had never bound a book before. Similarly with the embossed silver-work on the altar. Its skill is such as to suggest very strongly that there must have been quite a lot of such work, just as the binding suggests that such bindings were fairly numerous.

3 The ivory comb, 12 × 16.2 cm.

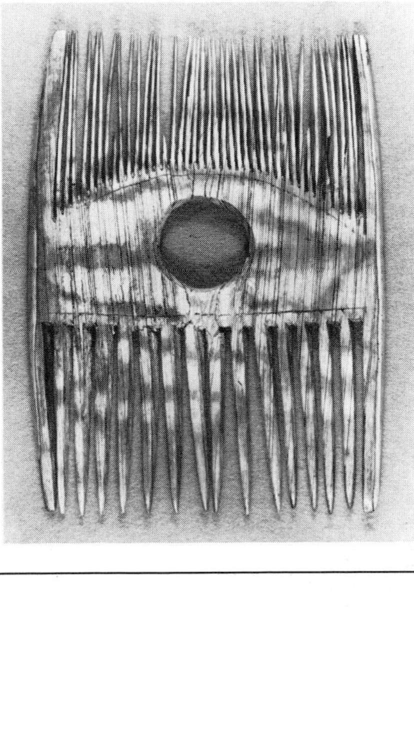

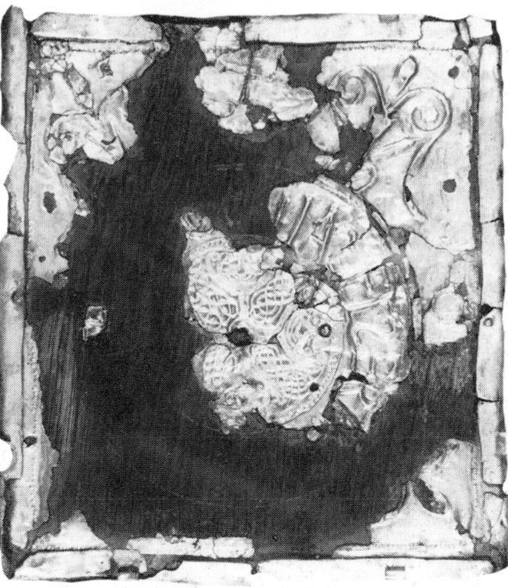

4 The travelling altar, 13.3 × 12.1 cm. The central roundel with interlace is part of a repair, perhaps of *c*. 900. The letters just outside are original and read . . . NIA EC ERA . . .

Another tale these objects tell is of contacts with distant lands. The comb is of elephant ivory. The shell backing to the central garnet in the cross probably came from further afield than the Mediterranean. Though the coffin's decoration has a superficially barbaric air all its figures are in fact derived from Mediterranean models: for example the figure of Christ on the lid comes, ultimately, from a probable Hellenistic source of the fifth or the sixth century, the Evangelist-symbols from a western Mediterranean source of the sixth century or later. The complete absence of abstract ornament from the coffin is striking. These are Lindisfarne treasures, yet the influence on them of Ireland is faint; it is possibly to be seen in the form of lettering incised into the wooden altar, more certainly in the selection of seven archangels for the coffin. What is most powerfully demonstrated here, as in the Codex Amiatinus, the figure illuminations in the Lindisfarne Gospels, and the Ruthwell Cross (figs 89, 91, 92), is the force in the far north of Mediterranean examples, and the capacity of northerners to copy and adopt them.

Perhaps the strongest impression the relics give is one of magnificence. When Bede emphasizes Cuthbert's simplicity, one does not think of the saint's wearing, as he almost certainly did, that fine pectoral cross; when he describes the body being wrapped in 698 in a 'new garment' one does not imagine it as being made, as quite likely it was, from figured Byzantine silk with a repetitive pattern of a 'nature goddess'. Bede did not seek to deceive, but to teach. In teaching he to an extent transmuted reality, a reality in which treasures could matter as much to

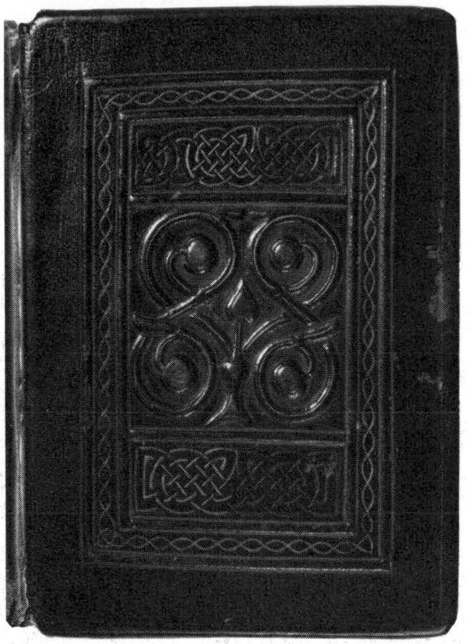

5 Front cover of the Gospel book originally in Saint Cuthbert's tomb, known as the Stonyhurst Gospel from its long association with Stonyhurst College. Page size 13.3 × 16.5 cm. Now on loan to the British Library (reproduced by permission of the English province of the Society of Jesus).

churchmen as they did to their lay relations (see p. 82 top).

There is something about the shrine of Saint Cuthbert even more remarkable than its contents: its power. The community which treasured and served it became the dominant authority in the far north, with wider estates and wider franchises than any other church in medieval England. They played an important part in the establishment of Danish power in Northumbria (see p. 154), and Danish kings may have played a similar part in establishing theirs. The splendid vestments and the book which Aethelstan gave (see below, fig. 153) are mere fragments from the many gifts which showed how later kings sought to please Cuthbert and his men. The extent to which Cuthbert's body and goods were undisturbed when they were found in 1827 suggests that even Henry VIII's agents did not find it prudent to meddle too far with a saint who, for a period as long as that from King Stephen's time to ours, had been the great focus of loyalty in the far north.

J. Campbell

gold-and-garnet pectoral cross, show that he could cut a magnificent figure (see pp. 80–1). Cuthbert had been exposed to other influences than the Irish, not least his native society's love of display.

Guthlac (675–714) belongs to a new generation, to Mercia rather than Northumbria, and to an apparently East Anglian biographer, Felix, of whom Bede knew nothing. Like Hilda, he was of royal blood, a descendant of the putative founder of the Mercian dynasty. Like Biscop, his early life was that of a nobleman, except that, instead of serving at court, he led his own war band on a career of pillage and rapine. Reminded suddenly of, 'the shameful ends that the ancient kings of his family had met' (*Life of Guthlac*, c. 18, pp. 80–3), he joined the double monastery of Repton (where Aethelbald was to be buried), and then, two years later, became a hermit at Crowland in the Fens. Guthlac's life as a hermit recalls Cuthbert's, in his miracles of healing and foresight, his relationship with the local fauna, and his role as spiritual guide to the many who consulted him, including kings. Felix had read Bede's *Life of Cuthbert*, as well as the *Life of Anthony* (of Egypt), the original inspiration of all hermits. But what is interesting about Guthlac is the way his biographer sees his spiritual war with devils in heroic terms. Guthlac made his home in a barrow, like Beowulf's dragon, and lived, like Grendel, in a loathsome fen. Unlike the demons who haunted Anthony, in the form of 'normal' animals, Guthlac's foes were authentic monsters, deformed in every limb, and this one-time raider of the Britons was visited by armed British demons! For Felix, Guthlac had exchanged one form of the hero's life for another, not dissimilar; he thereby gave an aristocratic Anglo-Saxon audience the sort of saint they could understand and admire.

Boniface of Wessex (?675–754) was in marked contrast to his contemporary, Guthlac, except that he too was unknown to Bede. This time, there is not only a *Life*, by Willibald, but also a magnificent collection of letters by Boniface himself, many to his English friends. Neither of these sources says much of the first, English, half of his life, but three things seem clear. First, he was of at least moderately wealthy background, and his father was ambitious for his worldly career. Second, either in his first monastery at Exeter, or later at Nursling, he was deeply soaked in the *Rule of Saint Benedict*, which he did much to popularize on the Continent. Third, he was learned: he wrote books on grammar and metrics, like Bede, and his style owed a lot to his older fellow countryman, Aldhelm.

The turning-point of Boniface's life was his decision to take the faith to the Continental homelands of his people. In 719, he secured a papal mandate to preach to the gentiles, and joined the Northumbrian, Willibrord, who had been Archbishop of the Frisians since 695. From this point until his martyrdom by pagans when nearly 80, he threw himself into his Pauline mission in Germany and Frisia, and the reform and reorganization of the Frankish Church. Both exercises were conducted in close collaboration with the Pope, who made him an archbishop in 732, and with at least some assistance from the Frankish authorities. Though he remained a monk, and

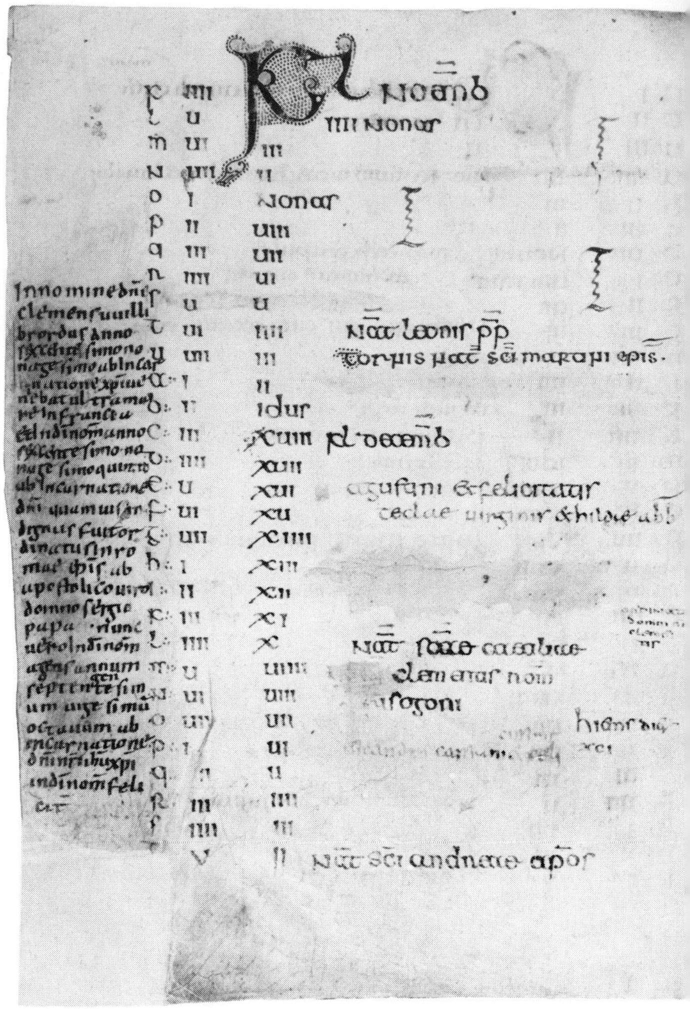

79 A page from the calendar that belonged to St Willibrord (Paris, Bibliothèque Nationale, Lat. 10857, fol. 39b). The feast of Abbess Hilda is marked on 17 November, and in the left margin is a note in Willibrord's own hand, recording the dates of his arrival in Francia (690), his consecration by the Pope (695), and the year of writing (728).

founded the great German monastery of Fulda, he was a man of action and Church government, like none of the others considered so far. But he may have had one thing in common with all save Biscop. It has been pointed out that his death-scene, with pagans closing in on a small band of individually identified men, owes much to the world of saga, and Fulda was to become a centre of vernacular religious literature, as well as preserving the only known Continental fragment of vernacular heroic verse. Perhaps aristocratic values left some mark on Boniface too.

Wilfrid (634–709) comes last, out of chronological order in the series, because, though by no means the most revered (then or since), he combines many of the features of the others. Though Bede has much to say of him, the major source is a *Life*, probably by his choirmaster, Eddius Stephanus, which ranks second only to Bede's *History* as a document of early English Christianity. Like Biscop, Wilfrid was a Northumbrian nobleman, and, like Cuthbert, he was an early disciple of the Irish mission, spending a happy spiritual adolescence at Lindisfarne. With Biscop, he travelled to Rome in 653, and, like him, he then spent some years in the ambience of southern Gallic Christianity, in his case at Lyons. On his return, he became the protegé of Alchfrith, sub-king of Deira, and was ordained by Agilbert, the Frankish ex-bishop of the West Saxons; he was thus the natural choice as spokesman for the *Romani* at Whitby, and for the Northumbrian bishopric that fell vacant on Colman's defeat and withdrawal. But thereafter his career was extraordinarily turbulent. Three times (664–9, 678–86, 691–706), he was deprived of his see. Twice, he appealed to Rome successfully, only for the Northumbrian king to ignore the verdict. Even when he died at peace, his diocese had been reduced to the area dependent on his own monastery at Hexham. Eddius significantly describes his *Life* as an *excusatio*, and it is indeed markedly apologetic, even by hagiographic standards: Wilfrid's miracles tend to be wrought in defence of himself and his community.

Whatever the explanation for this embattled career, its interest lies in the variety of Wilfrid's spiritual interests, and of the influences upon him that they reflect. He was a bishop, like Boniface, who sought papal support; like Cuthbert, he cultivated a splendid episcopal image, and this he may have owed to his Frankish masters, like Agilbert. As a monk, he claimed, perhaps rightly, to have introduced the *Rule of Saint Benedict* to Northumbria, and, like Biscop, had a papal charter protecting his monasteries at Ripon, Hexham and elsewhere from outside interference. But he was also a patron of hermits and an enthusiastic advocate of the religious life for women: he encouraged the Northumbrian queen in her virginity through twelve years and two husbands. Like Cuthbert and Boniface, he was a missionary: he was the first Englishman to preach overseas when in Frisia on his way to Rome in 679; he converted Sussex, nearly the last pagan English kingdom, and Archbishop Willibrord was his pupil. He was an ambitious builder, and his crypts at Ripon and Hexham can still be seen. Eddius says less of his interest in learning, but his disciple and successor at Hexham, Acca, had a notable book collection, and Eddius himself, as will be seen (p. 90), had a remarkable knowledge of the Bible.

Above all, the values of the Northumbrian nobility shine through in many episodes of his life. When attacked on a Sussex beach, he and his (notable) following of 120 men resolved, 'that they would either find death with honour or life with victory' (*Life of Wilfrid*, c. 13, pp. 28–9). His dedication of Ripon was followed by three days and nights of typically heroic feasting. His relations with his enemies in the Northumbrian Church have something of the quality of a feud, and, like secular feuds, they led to exile; indeed, Aldhelm, in a letter, compared the obligation of Wilfrid's followers to share his exile, with those of laymen to their lord. On his death-bed, he arranged, unlike Biscop, that he *would* be succeeded at Ripon by a kinsman, and divided out his extensive treasure: after providing for the poor and the churches of Rome, he gave one share to the abbots of Ripon and Hexham, 'that they might . . . purchase the friendship of kings and bishops', and the other to 'those who have laboured and suffered long exile with me, and to whom I have given no lands' (*Life of Wilfrid*, c. 63, pp. 36–7). Not only was Wilfrid very rich, he also, in his last hours, remembered what a nobleman, as well as a Christian, should do with wealth. Wilfrid was a great saint, of colossal spiritual energy and commitment, but his life retains much of the flavour of the Germanic warlord.

This roll-call of early English saints shows the intense response of the Anglo-Saxons to their new faith. They were exceptional, as saints by definition are, but we know about them because they were admired, because they were genuinely heroes, albeit of a new type, to Anglo-Saxon society. The variety of influences so apparent in Wilfrid was characteristic of the others too. Even Biscop, whose Roman orientation seems so clear, took his builders from Gaul, resembled the saints of Lérins in that no miracles were attributed to him, and is more like the Irish than anyone else, in the concept of abandonment of his kindred for the sake of Christ, and in his surprising failure to become a bishop. In almost all aspects of the Anglo-Saxon Church, once the missions were completed, Roman, Gallic and Irish features in-

80 St Wilfrid's crypt at Hexham Abbey, Northumberland. Wilfrid used dressed stone from nearby Roman buildings.

tertwined with each other and with other influences from further afield, like Spain and the eastern Mediterranean.

Nearly all these saints show the marks of their secular background in one way or another. The conversion of the Anglo-Saxons to Christianity was being followed, as it often has been, by the conversion of Christianity itself. The exception is Biscop, and this in itself may explain Bede's contempt for the secularized monasteries of his own time, and the focus of his *History* on an idealized past, rather than a devalued present.

The Making of the Early English Church

The story of the earliest English saints thus seems to have two contrasting themes. One is the vigour of the Anglo-Saxon response to the ecclesiastical and cultural inspiration flooding in from several quarters. The other is the survival and re-expression of traditional values in the new context. Both themes are crucial to all aspects of the making of the early English Church: the organization of bishoprics, the growth of monasticism, the further spread of the Faith by internal and external missions, and the development of Christian learning and art.

Gregory the Great had envisaged two English ecclesiastical provinces, each of twelve dioceses, and each ruled by metropolitan bishops (or archbishops, as they would later be called), based at London and York. This scheme probably reflected the administrative, and perhaps too the ecclesiastical, structure of Roman Britain. But it also reflected Gregory's own experience of episcopal organization in central and southern Italy, and the principles of episcopal life he had set out in his *Book of the Pastoral Rule*. The bishopric was originally based on the Roman city, and, because cities were densely packed around the Mediterranean littoral, bishoprics were too. Moreover, the bishops of central and southern Italy were under much more effective metropolitan authority from Rome itself than was normal elsewhere. In his book, Gregory made two main demands of a bishop: first, that he closely supervise the spiritual health of his flock; and second, that he retain his humility amidst the pomp of episcopal office. Both purposes were best served by small dioceses, since, as Bede later wrote to Egbert, these meant easier visitation and a lower revenue. Theodore himself came from Asia Minor, where cities and bishoprics were likewise thick on the ground; he had spent much of his adult life in or around Rome; and he was undoubtedly soaked in Gregory's writings. It is thus no surprise that the ninth canon of his Council of Hertford (672) was: 'That more bishops be created as the number of faithful increases' (*HE*, IV.5, p. 216).

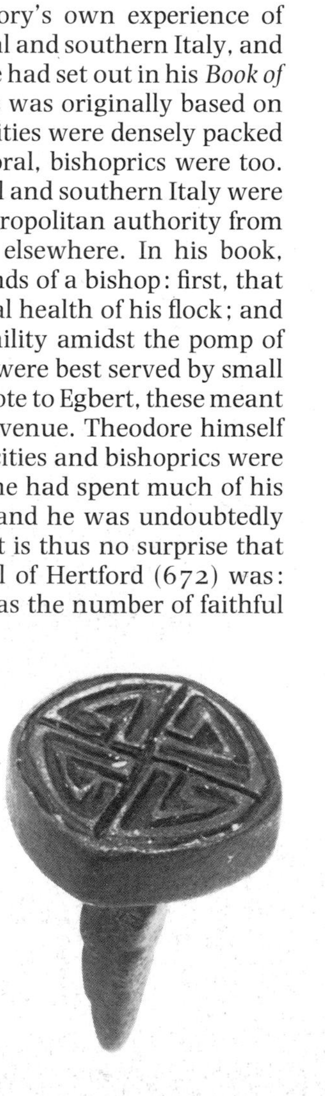

81 Stamp for the decoration of book-bindings height 2.2cm, found at Swanley, Kent (British Museum). Similar tools, with similar designs, had long been used for the decoration of Anglo-Saxon pottery – another example of the re-expression of old values in a new context.

82 Silver plaque from Hexham, 10 × 7.5 cm (British Museum). This crude but appealing object may depict a saint holding a book, and wearing the *pallium*. Its closest affinities are with Merovingian work, and it could reflect the Frankish inspiration behind Wilfred's episcopal style.

However, the canon goes on to say: 'At the time we came to no decision on the matter.' Theodore had encountered opposition. Not long afterwards, Bishop Wynfrith of the Mercians was deposed for 'disobedience', probably because he resisted the subdivision of his see, which soon followed (*HE*, IV.6, p. 218). In 705, the division of the West Saxon bishopric was accomplished only after some controversy. Above all, Wilfrid's expulsion from Northumbria in 678 was at least parly prompted by his opposition to the breaking up of his enormous diocese, and the accusations against him in his last exile included 'contumacious' rejection of the decisions of Theodore's successor, Berhtwald (*Life of Wilfred*, c. 53, pp. 110–11). It is likely that the opposition to the archbishops was inspired by the very different episcopal ideals of Frankish Gaul, whose influence was strong on Wilfrid and many other early English churchmen. Cities in Gaul were relatively few, and dioceses correspondingly big. Bishops were normally members of the Roman or Germanic aristocracy. Hence, for all their private austerity (which Wilfrid shared), Gallic bishops' public *persona* was one of wealth and splendour; Gregory objected to their habit of wearing the *pallium*, the vestment indicating metropolitan status, in the streets.

Moreover, neither in Gaul nor elsewhere did a metropolitan have the sort of authority over suffragan bishops that Gregory had at Rome, and gave the leaders of the English provinces. The resistance of Wilfrid and the others may thus have been based on a sincere sense that large dioceses were appropriate to episcopal dignity, and that metropolitans had no right to carve up dioceses and depose bishops by their own *fiat*.

However, part of the appeal of the Gallic model in England may have been simply that England was much more like Gaul than Italy; its vestigial Roman cities were thinly distributed, and its society was dominated by a warrior aristocracy. For all Theodore's energy and success (and by 737 Gregory's scheme for twelve southern dioceses under a metropolitan had been realized), it seems clear that the structure and style of episcopal government in England were deeply affected by social and political realities. There is other evidence than Eddius that early English bishops increasingly resembled secular lords. Theodore's *Penitential* stipulates that tribute to the Church is not to burden the poor, and that,

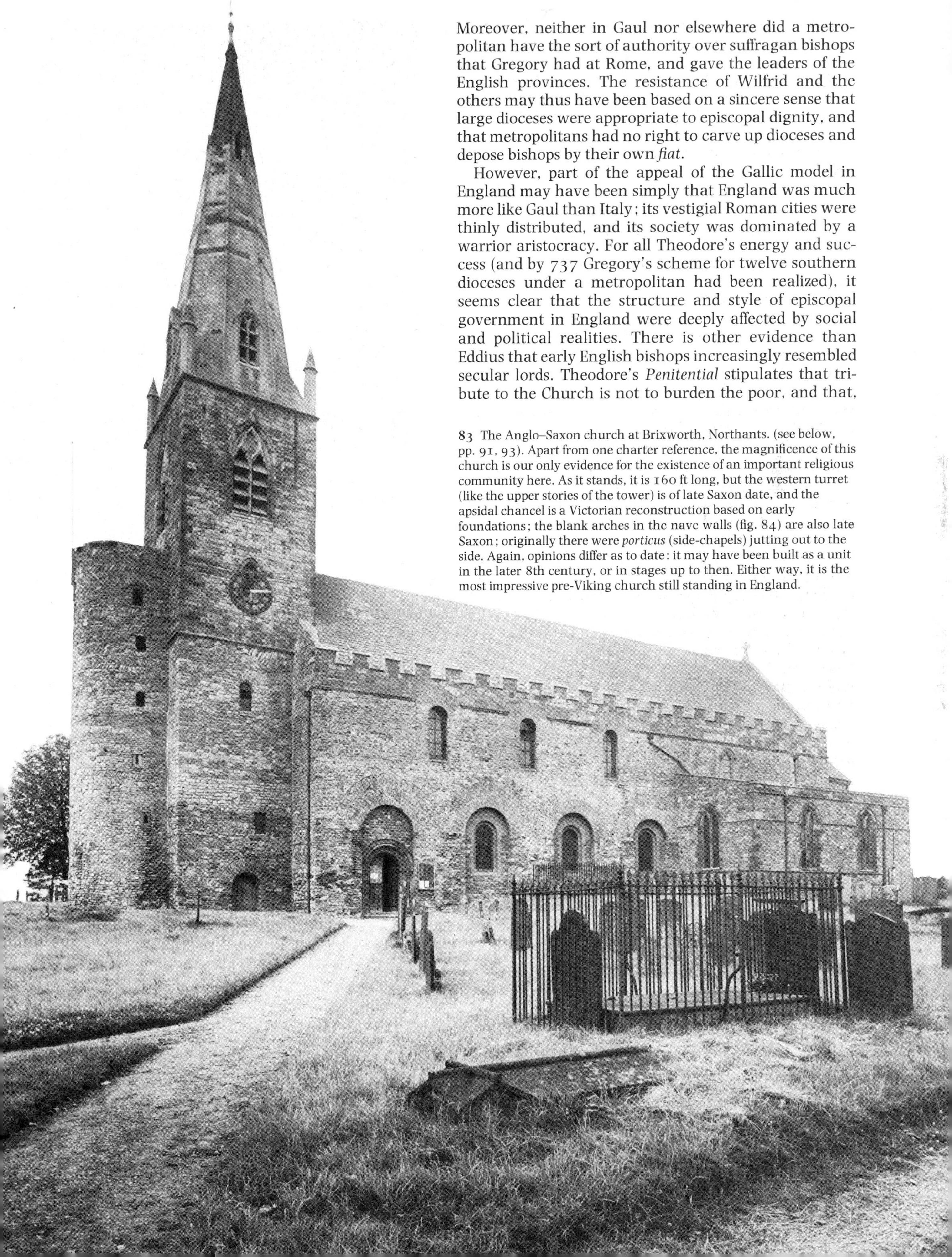

83 The Anglo–Saxon church at Brixworth, Northants. (see below, pp. 91, 93). Apart from one charter reference, the magnificence of this church is our only evidence for the existence of an important religious community here. As it stands, it is 160 ft long, but the western turret (like the upper stories of the tower) is of late Saxon date, and the apsidal chancel is a Victorian reconstruction based on early foundations; the blank arches in the nave walls (fig. 84) are also late Saxon; originally there were *porticus* (side-chapels) jutting out to the side. Again, opinions differ as to date: it may have been built as a unit in the later 8th century, or in stages up to then. Either way, it is the most impressive pre-Viking church still standing in England.

84 The interior of Brixworth church (see fig. 83).

though servants of God should not fight, the Church was to receive one-third of the booty taken in war, and could accept conquered lands from kings. The Roman council which heard Wilfrid's appeal in 679 also decreed against clerics bearing arms and having 'harpists'. A society which, as will be seen, gave churchmen status equal to, or greater than, that of the lay nobility, would expect bishops to have the wealth and tastes of noblemen; and, as has been seen, even Cuthbert responded to the expectation.

Episcopal wealth demanded a fairly substantial diocese; and bishoprics tended to be based, if not on whole kingdoms, as in 669, or on Roman *civitates*, as in Gaul, then at least on recognized sub-kingdoms, and on Roman cities that may have retained some administrative role. A good, because unusually well documented, example is Worcester, centred on a Roman *ceaster*, and probably corresponding to the province of the *Hwicce*. The resulting size of diocese was such as to enable most medieval English bishops to be powerful and wealthy men. Likewise, Canterbury rather than London became the primatial see, because Kent dominated Essex when Augustine arrived; and when York regained its planned metropolitan status in 735, the division of the English Church into northern and southern archbishoprics reflected a basic fact of Anglo-Saxon politics. The structure of the Anglo-Saxon Church was a triumph for Gregory's and Theodore's 'Roman' model, and Boniface re-exported it to Francia. But the very permanence of the arrangements indicates that they suited the English scene, partly because most English dioceses were larger than would have seemed normal to Gregory.

Presumably because he disapproved of the form many monasteries took, Bede says much less about monastic growth than episcopal organization. But there is other evidence that monasteries became very numerous indeed. By 850, there were at least 30 in the diocese of Worcester alone. We know about them only because so many reliable early Worcester charters survive, and this inspires more confidence than one might otherwise feel in late and legendary traditions of early houses in areas where there are few or no charters, like East Anglia and the Midlands. *The Resting-places of the English Saints*, a tract originally compiled in the ninth century, lists, among more familiar names and places, various otherwise obscure saints and communities: Rumwold at Buckingham, Aethelbert at Bedford, Frideswide at Oxford, and so on. Not all these need belong to this period, but some do; and since the likely point of the list was the encouragement of pilgrimage, it is a fair guess that some were important.

Traditional accounts of early English monasticism see it as a blend of the Benedictine model of the Roman missionaries with that of their Irish rivals. It now seems unlikely that Augustine sought to spread the *Rule of Saint Benedict* in the exclusive way that tenth-century churchmen did. At this stage, each founding abbot was responsible for drawing up his own Rule, as Saint Benedict himself had done, though, since Gregory knew and admired Saint Benedict's *Rule*, it is not unlikely that Augustine, like Biscop, used it as an ingredient in his own. The most important specifically Roman contribution to English monastic life was the episcopal monastery. Monasticism had originally flowered as a layman's quest for spiritual purity when the Christian Church became 'established' after Constantine's conversion; its principles of prayer and contemplation were theoretically incompatible with a bishop's active duties. But Gregory had insisted on living with his monks, even as Pope, and strongly encouraged Augustine to do so. This was the model followed not only by Wilfrid and Boniface, but also, if Bede is right, at Lindisfarne.

Irish influence was certainly important on early English monks. Saint Anthony of Egypt inspired imitation all over the West, but the hermit's life was especially popular in Ireland, and Irish inspiration seems obvious in Cuthbert. Wilfrid himself may have been influenced by Irish monastic organization, in that he regarded his many monasteries, scattered throughout England, as a single family under his authority, and his third exile was probably connected with his defence of this system against the jurisdiction of local bishops. But, in this instance Irish influence was possibly indirect, through the families of Continental monasteries founded by Columbanus; Wilfrid vested his rights in a papal charter of exemption, and the earliest known such charter was granted to Columbanus's Bobbio in 629.

This point introduces a third source of influence on early English monasticism that was neither Roman nor Irish. Hilda had planned to go to Chelles, one of the great Gallic double monasteries, and it is likely that this anomalous form of the religious life for women was inspired by Gallic example; the cellular structure recorded of other English double monasteries, if not Whitby, is also attested in their Gallic counterparts. Perhaps more important, it was probably in Gaul that Wilfrid, Biscop and Boniface's West Saxon masters found the *Rule of Saint Benedict*. The first to make extensive use of it in the monastic Rules they drew up themselves were the Frankish disciples of Columbanus, and their foundations included Jouarre, burial-place of Agilbert, the ex-bishop of the West Saxons and friend to Wilfrid and Biscop. However this may be, the early English, out of respect for Gregory, their apostle and Benedict's biographer, probably had a more intense admiration for this *Rule* than anyone before; its earliest manuscript is English.

As with bishoprics, however, it is wrong to see the monasteries of the period simply in terms of ecclesiastical ideals. Bede thought that the monasteries of his day were almost indistinguishable from secular establishments, and there is good evidence that many were 'private churches' or *Eigenkirchen*, in the parlance of the German scholar who first recognized the institution. Unlike Biscop, most noblemen and kings who endowed monasteries were unable to forget their family's interest in its

85 Anglo-Saxon manuscript of the *Rule of St Benedict* (Oxford, Bodleian Library, MS Hatton 48, fol. 29a). This sumptuous uncial MS, datable 700–50, is the earliest of the *Rule* known anywhere. Its handwriting has some connection with manuscripts from the Worcester area (see fig. 95), and its medieval provenance was Worcester.

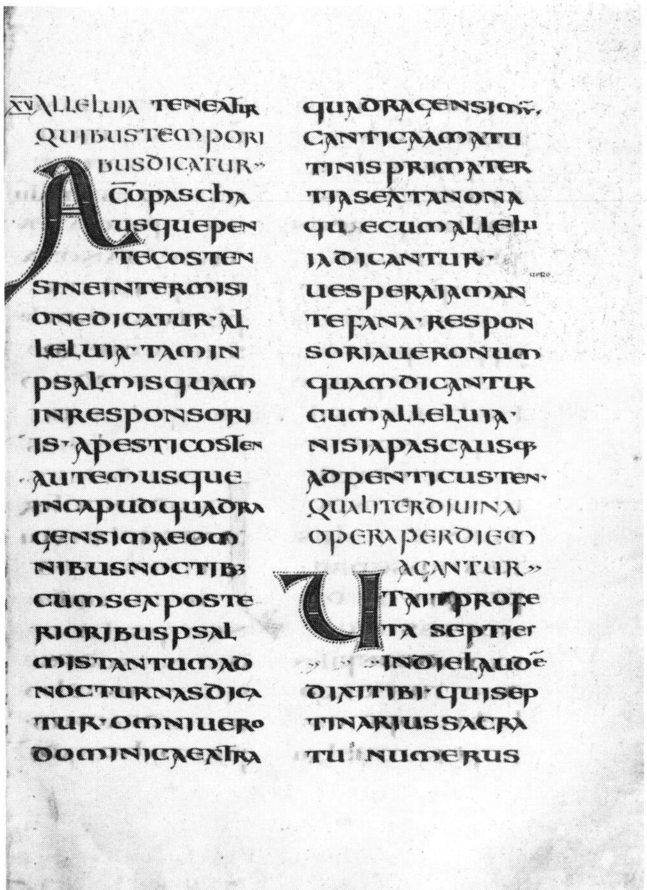
XV ALLELUIA TENEATUR
QUIBUS TEMPORI
BUS DICATUR
A CO PASCHA
USQUE PEN
TECOSTEN
SINE INTERMISSI
ONE DICATUR AL
LELUIA TAM IN
PSALMIS QUAM
IN RESPONSORI
IS A PESTICOSTEN
AUTEM USQUE
IN CAPUD QUADRA
GENSIMAE OM
NIBUS NOCTIB;
CUM SEX POSTE
RIORIBUS PSAL
MIS TANTUM AD
NOCTURNAS DICA
TUR OMNI UERO
DOMINICA EXTRA
QUADRAGENSIMA
CANTICA MATU
TINIS PRIMA TER
TIA SEXTA NONA
QU ECUM ALLELU
IA DICANTUR
UESPERA IAM AN
TEFANA RESPON
SORIA UERO NUM
QUAM DICANTUR
CUM ALLELUIA
NISI A PASCA USQ;
AD PENTICUSTEN
QUALITER DIUINA
OPERA PER DIEM
AGANTUR
UT AIT PROPE
TA SEPTIES
IN DIE LAUDE
DIXI TIBI QUI SEP
TINARIUS SACRA
TU NUMERUS

subsequent history. The head of the community would be founder's kin, and its revenues might be diverted to the kindred's secular uses. Whitby is a good example of family succession, and, among the Worcester charters, there is an unedifying record of a dispute over Withington between the daughter and the granddaughter of the foundress. The *Dialogue* of Bede's correspondent, Archbishop Egbert, even poses the question, whether a monastery can be partitioned between heirs. Occasionally, such houses might become wholly secularized, their abbots laymen who were succeeded by sons, and their property sucked back into the family inheritance. More often, it was simply a matter of recognizing the right of a founder's distant kinsman to be head or member of the community, and standards might not suffer; ten out of twelve abbots of Iona itself were related to Columba. These arrangements look like a shocking breach of monastic principles, and so Bede saw them. But, in practice, noblemen could no more be expected to ignore their kindred when founding monasteries than to lose their aristocratic style when becoming bishops. On any other terms, it is unlikely that so many monasteries would have been founded at all.

The missionary zeal of the early English Church is important not only for what it achieved on the Continent (Boniface has been called, with pardonable exaggeration, the founder of Germany), but also for what it shows about the way the faith was spread in the English countryside itself. It has often been attributed to further Irish inspiration. It is nowadays stressed that the primary purpose of the famous pilgrimages of the early Christian Irish was not evangelization, but martyrdom, in the form of exile from the kindred and the legal protection they offered. But for those who were converted as a result of such pilgrimages, like the English, it may well have seemed that conversion was the object of the exercise.

86 The tiny Anglo-Saxon church at Escomb, Co. Durham (nave 24 ft 6 in × 14 ft 6 in), almost certainly of 7th/8th-century date. It could well have been the sort of 'private' church that Bede records two Northumbrian noblemen as putting up on their estates (*HE*, V. 4–5).

Wilfrid, Willibrord and the other Northumbrians, who were the first to preach on the Continent, were all in some sense the pupils of the Irish. But, according to Eddius, Wilfrid first conceived this ambition when praying to Saint Andrew in Rome—probably in Gregory's own foundation on the Coelian hill, itself dedicated to Saint Andrew, whence he had sent his missionaries to England. Wilfrid was in many ways at his most 'Roman' in his approach to missionary activity. Where the Irish, and to some extent Boniface, went about like Old Testament prophets, striking awe in their audience, whether kings or peasants, by their defiance of pagan gods and social conventions alike, Wilfrid preached 'gently', and 'with sweet and marvellous eloquence'. He also used more concrete inducements: we are told that, while some South Saxons were converted willingly, others, 'were compelled by the king's command' (*Life of Wilfred*, c. 41, pp. 82–3); and both in Frisia and in Sussex, one result of his arrival was a marked improvement in local fishing technique. Such a blend of reasoned argument, political force and material incentive had been characteristic of Gregory himself, who, on the one hand, advised Augustine that pagan temples be converted into Christian churches, and, on the other, told King Aethelbert that he was to suppress the worship of idols and destroy their shrines. The two approaches were complementary rather than contradictory, and both were important in the spread of Anglo-Saxon Christianity. Thus Theodore's *Penitential* is flexible on illicit marriages, but the contemporary laws of King Wihtred are not, as will be seen. The second approach is a warning against the facile interpretation of the first as meaning that paganism was allowed to live on, 'in disguise'.

Wilfrid's dedication of himself (and many of his churches) to Saint Andrew is important in another way. In the Apocryphal Gospels, Saint Andrew was the missionary *par excellence*, with many brave feats against cruel barbarians. This literature was certainly known in early England, and there is a long Anglo-Saxon poem on Saint Andrew, which very probably shows some knowledge of *Beowulf*, and which sees the Saint's confrontations with pagan cannibals in very much the heroic idiom. It is neither possible nor sensible to ascribe the *Andreas* to Wilfrid's circle, but it may give some idea of how Wilfrid, and perhaps other Anglo-Saxon missionaries, saw their enterprises. One could almost say that, whereas the Irish saw exile as a penitential severance of the ties of kin, their Anglo-Saxon converts saw it as a new kind of warrior adventure, in the service of their Heavenly Lord.

With the final aspect of the making of the Anglo-Saxon Church, its explosive literary and artistic achievement, Bede inevitably resumes the spotlight. From references in Bede's own works, one can build up an extraordinarily impressive catalogue of the library Biscop had collected. Although the number of classical authors listed may be exaggerated, since Bede could have quoted them from grammarians, the list of Christian authors, on the other hand, may not be complete, and it certainly featured most of the major writings of the important western Fathers. For Bede, the purposes of scholarship all centred around the understanding of God and his ways with the world. Grammar was important, because, without a knowledge of Latin, the Bible could not be understood; chronological science because it enabled one to chart the time-scale of the Divine Dispensation; Biblical exegesis of the Old Testament because it gave an allegorical under-

87 The Bewcastle Cross, Cumbria. This imposing, if mutilated, monument stands 14 ft 6 in high even without its head. The west face shows (in descending order) John the Baptist, Christ in Majesty, and John the Evangelist; the south face, like the north, has panels of scroll and interlace, and the east face a continuous vine-scroll. The inscription beneath Christ in Majesty is no longer legible. It was once, but very disputably, said to be a memorial for Alchfrith, son of Oswy, and his wife. The cross is now dated to the first half of the 8th century, perhaps later than the Ruthwell and Acca crosses (figs. 89, 90). The church is modern, but its dedication to St Cuthbert and location in a ruined Roman fort may indicate a connection with Cuthbert's missionary journeys to remote areas, where a cross offered a liturgical focus, in the absence of a church (cf. p. 51); the lowest panel on the south face is certainly very like the interlace of the Lindisfarne Gospels (fig. 76).

88 Two scenes from a manuscript of Sedulius's *Carmen Paschale* (Antwerp, Plantin-Moretus Museum, MS M.17.4, fol. 33b, 31b), showing St Peter's betrayal and remorse and Christ entering Jerusalem. The manuscript was produced at Liège after 814, but on fol. 65b is the name 'Cuduuini', and he is probably to be identified with the East Anglian Bishop Cuthwine, whom Bede records as having brought an illustrated copy of the 'Passions' of St Paul from Rome. The style of the illustrations in this manuscript is 5th-century Italian: the manuscript thus probably represents a Carolingian copy of an insular copy of an Italian manuscript.

standing of Christian Truths. In all these respects, Bede was in the orthodox tradition of the western Church Fathers, and helped to pass their legacy on to the Carolingian Renaissance.

Yet Bede should not be allowed to dwarf the learning of his contemporaries. Very few manuscripts actually survive from early Christian England, and we would have little idea of the scale and range of Biscop's collection, did we not have Bede's writings; for this reason, we may underestimate what was available elsewhere. The otherwise obscure Worcester double monastery of Inkberrow possessed a fine manuscript of Saint Jerome on Ecclesiastes, for example, but this is known only because it was taken to the Continent, with its one-time owner's *ex libris* still on it. The most important of Bede's fellow scholars, the only one whose works survive to any great extent, was Aldhelm, whom most historians have hurried past with derogatory mutterings about his Latin style. But it is now clear that his classical and patristic learning was comparable to Bede's, and that he owed less of it than was once thought to the Irish, more to the Canterbury school of Theodore and his North African assistant, Hadrian. Though little is known of Canterbury teaching, Aldhelm's respect for it is borne out by the fact that Hadrian was in correspondence with Julian of Toledo, probably the most distinguished European grammarian of the age.

Again, not all scholars shared Bede's view of the purposes of learning. Aldhelm's style is obscure mainly because of his sheer joy in the riches of Latin vocabulary, and Guthlac's biographer evidently felt the same. Most of Bede's Biblical commentaries were sent to Bishop Acca of Hexham, who commissioned Eddius's *Life of Wilfrid*, but Eddius made a very different use of the Old Testament. To Bede, it was mainly important as an allegorical foretaste of the life of Christ and the Church; to Eddius, it supplied a way of understanding his hero. For almost every episode in Wilfrid's life, he has an Old Testament parallel, most of them with the Judges, Kings and Prophets of ancient Israel. The Israelites, with their warrior kings and tribal law, must have looked very like themselves to the Anglo-Saxons, and the 'Germanic' aspects of Wilfrid's career might be legitimized (if necessary) by comparing him to an Old Testament prophet. Bede stands for the earnest commitment of the Anglo-Saxons to the new scholarship, Eddius for their ability to see it in their own terms.

Both views are relevant to an understanding of the remarkable corpus of vernacular Christian poetry, some 30,000 lines of which survive, in the form of stories from the Bible, Saints' lives, and what might be classified as homiletic meditations. It is nearly always anonymous and undatable, but is at least unlikely to be earlier than this period. There have been two main approaches to this literature. One, generally the older, dwelt on the heroic imagery which made Moses and Christ into warrior kings, and saw the Apostles as 'twelve glorious thegns'. The other, more recent, stresses the Christian learning underlying many poems, seeing *Exodus*, for example, as an allegory of the Redemption. Both approaches have been overdone, but both are justifiable.

The milieu of early Anglo-Saxon Christianity was aristocratic, and poets drew naturally on the idioms of aristocratic poetry; but they also expressed their perception of Christian mysteries, as expounded by the Fathers. In the *Dream of the Rood*, one of the greatest English poems, and dated to this period by its appearance, in part, on the Ruthwell Cross, all Creation, including the tree from which the Cross was fashioned, is seen as Christ's war band; thus the tree participates in its

Lord's death, at His command: 'I was raised up, a rood. I raised the great King, liege lord of the heavens, dared not lean from the true' (lines 44–5). It is an extraordinarily poignant heroic image of the Redemption. Yet the poem also bears the impress of seventh-century theological controversy about the nature of Christ, and of the introduction by Pope Sergius (687–701) of the feasts of the Annunciation and the Exaltation of the Holy Cross. Traditional poetic imagery enhanced rather than compromised the subtleties of Christian Revelation.

For the visual arts of the early English Church, Biscop and Wilfrid are again the central figures, because Bede and Eddius say so much about their activities, and because so much that is associated with them survives, or has been excavated. The story here is largely one of identification with the new Christian civilization. Wilfrid's churches seem to have been modelled on the Roman basilicas, and the sculptural fragments at Hexham, including what is perhaps the first high cross erected in the British Isles, are wholly Mediterranean in artistic repertoire. Bede says that Biscop also built 'in the Roman manner', and the pictures in his churches came from Rome, even if his Gallic masons had some influence on the decoration, and perhaps the design, of his buildings. The carving on the Ruthwell Cross, which is linked with sculpture found at Jarrow, is the supreme Anglo-Saxon example of realistic figure-work in the classical tradition. The Codex Amiatinus, designed by Biscop's successor, Ceolfrith, as a present for the Pope, is so like an Italian book in its dignified uncial script, and late Antique style of decoration, that it was long thought to be Italian (see figs. 89, 91 and pp. 74–5).

With the visual arts as with learning, however, it is important to remember achievements and traditions other than those most closely associated with Bede. There are a substantial number of seventh- or eighth-century churches and sculptures throughout England, most of them at places of which we know little or nothing from documentary sources. The church at Brixworth, perhaps the finest substantially intact structure of the period, is a counterpart to the Inkberrow Jerome, in that the existence of a monastery there is known only from fragmentary Peterborough records, and we should never guess at the wealth and style of the church in the East Midlands, had it not survived (see figs. 83, 84).

Brixworth shows the same architectural ambitions as

89 *(far left)* The Ruthwell Cross, Dumfriesshire. This most famous of Anglo-Saxon crosses has been reconstructed to a 17 ft height, after being broken up at the Reformation; the cross-piece is modern. The runic version of the *Dream of the Rood* can be seen on either side of the 'inhabited vine-scroll' on the west face.

90 *(left)* Part of the 'Acca Cross' in Hexham Abbey, Northumberland. Like that of the Bewcastle Cross (fig. 87), the inscription here is illegible, and it is not certain that it is to be identified with one of the two splendid crosses recorded in a 12th-century source as standing at the head and foot of Bishop Acca's grave. Art-historical opinion indicates a date early in the history of Northumbrian sculpture for the magnificent and wholly abstract scroll decoration, whose nearest affinities lie as far away as the Dome of the Rock, Jerusalem.

CODICIBUS SACRIS HOSTILI CLADE PERUSTIS
ESDRA DO FERVENS HOC REPARAVIT OPUS

Wilfrid's and Biscop's churches, but the Lindisfarne Gospels, probably made for the translation of Cuthbert's relics in 698, belongs to a quite different artistic tradition from that which they espoused. This manuscript is among the greatest surviving examples of 'Insular' art, in a tradition that has usually been fathered on Lindisfarne's Irish founders. For some of the elements in script and decoration, this is probably right, but there is another way of seeing this manuscript. Unlike earlier Insular *codices de luxe*, such as the Book of Durrow (fig. 74), it does contain serious attempts at realistic figure-work in its Evangelist portraits, and one of these, Saint Matthew, is clearly modelled on the source of the Ezra portrait in the Codex Amiatinus. On the other hand, the panelled or interlaced 'carpet' and initial pages resemble nothing so much as the treasures of Sutton Hoo (see figs. 76, 77), and it has been shown that they were designed in the same way. The Insular style represents the transfer to the page of the motifs and techniques of secular treasure; what had once glorified a proud and warlike aristocracy was now to glorify God. The Lindisfarne Gospels thus makes the same two fundamental points about the growth of the Anglo-Saxon Church as so much of the rest of the evidence. The Anglo-Saxons showed remarkable determination to transform their civilization in the light of the multifarious influences to which they were exposed. But what gave vigour and originality, as well as some less desirable features, to their achievement, was the ability to articulate their commitment in traditional terms.

Three Contemporary Kings

For most of this chapter, the emphasis has been on what the Anglo-Saxons, individually and collectively, did with their Christian heritage; and it is right that by far the most vibrant and creative phase in the history of the Anglo-Saxon Church should have a more than equal share of the attention given to the period. But it is still necessary to tackle the more difficult, because less accessible, question of what Christianity did to Anglo-Saxon kings and society. As with the Church, so with the laity, one way of doing this is to consider the careers of three particular kings: Egfrith of Northumbria (670–85), Caedwalla of Wessex (685–8), and finally Aethelbald of Mercia himself. All three were closely associated with saints, the first two with Wilfrid and the third with Guthlac.

Egfrith succeeded his father, Oswy, in circumstances that may not have been entirely smooth. He had an elder half-brother, Alchfrith, who had rebelled in 664/6, probably because of the threat to his own succession that Egfrith posed as son of the reigning queen, and another half-brother, Aldfrith, who suggestively spent his reign in exile. Rivalry between the sons of different mothers but the same king was to pose several problems in the tenth and eleventh centuries. At all events, Egfrith did establish his authority, and, for Eddius, his career divided symmetrically into two halves. In the first, he was on excellent terms with Wilfrid, and lavishly endowed his churches; significantly, the endowments included lands west of the Pennines taken from fleeing British clergy. In this phase, he defeated the Picts, and crushed Wulfhere of Mercia's large southern confederacy (674). However, Egfrith was turned against Wilfrid by his 'Jezebel' of a queen, and his fortunes turned too. The Mercians were revenged for their early debacle at the Battle of the Trent

92 St Matthew portrait from the Lindisfarne Gospels (British Library, MS Cotton Nero D.iv, fol. 25b). The inspiration of the Ezra portrait (fig. 91) behind the figure is quite clear, and the manuscript from which the Codex Amiatinus picture was copied was presumably lent to Lindisfarne. Other features, such as the figure (probably Christ) behind the curtain, indicate that at least one other 6th-century manuscript was also used as a model.

91 (*left*) Frontispiece of the Codex Amiatinus (Florence, Biblioteca Medicea-Laurenziana, MS Amiatinus 1, fol. 4). As the inscription indicates, the picture shows Ezra working at the sacred texts in the garb of an Old Testament prophet. However, the nine volumes in the cupboard suggest that this is also a 'portrait' of the 6th-century Italian scholar Cassiodorus, who edited the Bible in nine books, and whose great single-volume Bible, the Codex Grandior, was taken to Monkwearmouth and Jarrow, and provided the immedate inspiration both of this picture, and of the Codex Amiatinus itself. The picture is probably the work of an Anglo-Saxon artist striving to recapture the technique of a 'Mediterranean' original (see also pp. 74–5).

(679), and, after attacking Ireland in 684 against Saint Cuthbert's advice, Egfrith was defeated and killed at Nechtansmere in Pictland (685). Egfrith's career has several useful lessons. First, he had not in fact 'gone bad'. Cuthbert was grieved at his death, and he was the principal patron of Monkwearmouth/Jarrow. But he had fallen foul of one saint (or more), and there were contemporaries willing to ascribe his fate to the equivalent of a witch-doctor's curse. Second, more prosaically, his power, like any early Anglo-Saxon king's, depended on his ability to increase his holdings, and so keep rewarding his followers. But Wilfrid and the Church now claimed a share of his largesse; the queen referred pointedly to 'all the temporal glories of Wilfrid, his riches, . . . his countless army of followers' (*Life of Wilfrid*, c. 24, pp. 48–9). In such circumstances, a king could either attack the Church, or push ever further outwards. Egfrith did both, and the result was disaster.

Caedwalla was the son of an otherwise obscure West Saxon king, Cenbert, who may or may not have been, as was claimed for him, a descendant of Cerdic and Ceawlin; at best, his family were sub-kings, of a cadet branch of the royal house. He is first encountered in Eddius as, 'a certain exile of noble birth', roaming the wastes of the Chilterns and the Weald, presumably in refuge from the current king of Wessex (*Life of Wilfred*, c. 42, pp. 84–5). He was apparently not yet baptized, and killed King Aethelwealh of Sussex, patron of Wilfrid's mission there, but Wilfrid threw in his lot with his fellow exile; he thereby secured not only confirmation of his substantial Sussex lands, but also a quarter of the Isle of Wight, when Caedwalla, now King of Wessex, disposed ruthlessly of its ruling family (686). There is evidence that Caedwalla went on to conquer Surrey, London and even Kent; but, within two years of his accession, he created a sensation by retiring to be baptized and die at Rome.

Caedwalla's career also has two lessons. On the one hand, the presence on the scene of a Holy Man made no difference to the conduct of Anglo-Saxon secular politics. As an exile, who made good at the expense of his kindred and neighbouring kingdoms, Caedwalla is straight out of the heroic world, and Wilfrid had no objection so long as the Church got its cut. On the other hand, Caedwalla himself was apparently aware of the tension between God and Mammon, because he retired at the height of his power. His successor, Ine, was a comparable case. Also the son of an obscure king, distantly related, if at all, to the main dynastic line, he ruled for 38 years, keeping up the pressure on Sussex and Kent, expanding south-west at British expense, and issuing an important law code; but he too retired to Rome in the end, leaving the kingdom to a distant kinsman. There were several other such cases in the period, and Bede regarded them with nothing but enthusiasm, but it is difficult to resist the conclusion that they were a force for instability in English politics.

Aethelbald of Mercia, the greatest king of the period, has some of the features of both the other two. Like Caedwalla, he began as a royal exile with genealogically somewhat tenuous claims to the throne. He sought consolation from Guthlac, who prophesied his future greatness, and he rewarded the saint with an elaborate shrine when the prophecy came true. Here, however, one can leave the shadowy world of curses and prophecies for that of sheer ecclesiastical politics. Among Guthlac's other visitors was Bishop Haedde of Lichfield, perhaps one-time abbot of Breedon, and an important member of the Mercian establishment; Guthlac's support for Aethelbald may thus have had political value. Conversely, it is tempting to identify two other figures in the *Life of Guthlac*, Tatwine and Wilfrid, with Tatwine of Breedon, who became archbishop of Canterbury in 731,

93 The lid panel (now in Museo Bargello, Florence) from the Franks Casket, the rest of which is in the British Museum. These famous whalebone panels are assigned to early 8th-century Northumbria by the language of their runic inscriptions, and depict a series of scenes from pagan and Romano-Christian cosmogony, the best-known of which is the juxtaposition of the Adoration of the Magi with a scene from the grisly adventures of Wayland the Smith. The scene shown here probably represents Wayland's brother, Egil, defending his house (the name Aegili appears in runes immediately above the archer); it is noteworthy for the impression it gives of contemporary warfare, featuring helmets, breastplates and swords, as well as arrows, shields and spears. (Length of panel 22.4 cm.)

and with the Wilfrid who was bishop of Worcester from *c.* 718. The identifications would suggest that kings could give office as well as land to the circle of their patron saint.

Aethelbald's career is oddly obscure once his greatness was assured, since Bede gives no details of his power. Annalistic references suggest that he attacked the Welsh, the Northumbrians and the West Saxons (several times), and that he may have been allied with King Angus of the Picts. More important, Kentish charters show that he was in control of London, and a patron of the Kentish churches; the next two archbishops after Tatwine were also Mercians. Above all, there are the spectacular claims of some of his charters, including the Ismere Diploma of 736, which almost explicitly rank him with Bede's seven overlords, and the documents associated with the Council of Clovesho (746/7), which make him partly responsible for the reform of the English Church. There is thus evidence to suggest a king of formidable power. Yet, as has been seen, Boniface saw him as responsible for many of the Church's troubles, and threatened him with divine vengeance for his violation of ecclesiastical personnel and privileges. He may have seen the error of his ways, but his 41-year reign (the longest reliably recorded in Anglo-Saxon history) ended in anti-climax. He was murdered by his bodyguard, and, though perhaps buried in a splendid Roman-style mausoleum at Repton, was seen by an anonymous visionary in Hell.

Church and King

The overall impression made by these royal careers is one of some tension between traditional political and social patterns and the demands of the new dispensation. To an extent, the problems are inherent in the nature of Christianity itself, which has never been exclusively contemplative, like Buddhism, but which has never admitted specific objectives in this world, like Islam. The difficulties experienced by the first generations of Anglo-Saxon Christian kings were not dissimilar from those of later Roman emperors, or the Protestant monarchs of sixteenth-century Europe. Nevertheless, there were particular, and not always adverse, ways in which the Church affected Anglo-Saxon kings, and their relations with their subjects, and three will be considered here: the problem of property and of the charter; the problem of security, and of the law code; and the problem of peace, and the high-kingship.

Charters are grants of land and/or privilege. Later in the Anglo-Saxon period, they include dispute-settlements and wills, are sometimes in the vernacular, and are granted by and to laymen; but at this stage nearly all are Latin grants by the king to the Church. They are among the Anglo-Saxon historian's essential tools, but nearly everything about them is controversial. Different answers have been given to such questions as: who introduced the charter to England, and from where? Who actually wrote them, the king's own clerks (what would later be called a chancery), or the grant's recipient? What legal rights did a charter convey, an immunity from specific obligations to the king, the entitlement to break the entail on a hereditary estate and alienate it to the Church, or simply permanent and heritable tenure of a grant that would have been revocable if not chartered? The difficulty of answering these questions is enhanced by the fact that many texts are forgeries, doctored or simply invented in later centuries by churches claiming particular properties and rights. But one way of getting round this problem is to find charters which survive in the original version, instead of later copies. Aethelbald's Ismere Diploma of 736 is one of these (Birch, *Cart.*, no. 154; *EHD*, no. 67).

94 The crypt from the double monastery of Repton, Derbys., where Guthlac began his spiritual life, and where Aethelbald, and later Wiglaf and Wystan (see p. 138) were buried. The remarkable 'barley-sugar' columns, and the vault, are secondary features; it is not certain whether they date to Aethelbald's time, or to Wiglaf's.

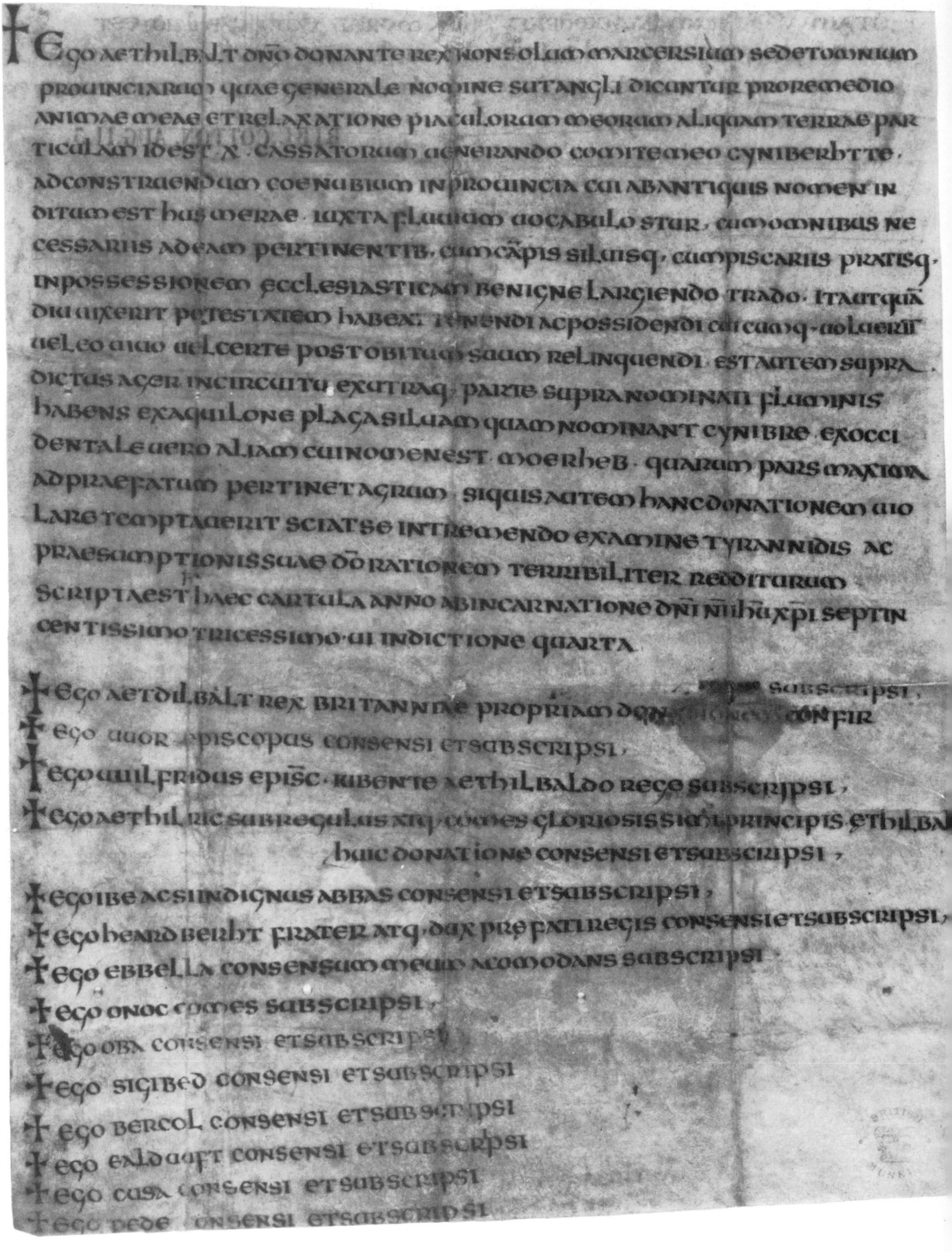

Ego Aethilbalt dno donante rex non solum marcersium sed et omnium
prouinciarum quae generale nomine sutangli dicantur pro remedio
animae meae et relaxatione piaculorum meorum aliquam terrae par
ticulam id est X cassatorum ueneranda comite meo Cyniberhtte
ad construendum coenubium in prouincia cui ab antiquis nomen in
ditum est husmerae iuxta fluuium uocabulo stur, cum omnibus ne
cessariis ad eam pertinentib, cum campis siluisq, cum piscariis pratisq,
in possessionem ecclesiasticam benigne largiendo trado, ita ut quam
diu uixerit potestatem habeat tenendi ac possidendi cui cumq uoluerit
uel eo uiuo uel certe post obitum suum relinquendi. est autem supra
dictus ager in circuitu ex utraq parte supranominati fluminis
habens ex aquilone plaga siluam quam nominant Cynibre ex occi
dentale uero aliam cui nomen est Moerheb. quarum pars maxima
ad praefatum pertinet agrum. siquis autem hanc donationem uio
lare temptauerit sciat se in tremendo examine tyrannidis ac
praesumptionis suae do rationem terribiliter redditurum.
Scripta est haec cartula anno ab incarnatione dni nri ihu xpi septin
centissimo tricessimo ui indictione quarta.

Ego Aethilbalt rex Britanniae propriam do… confir … subscripsi
Ego Uuor episcopus consensi et subscripsi
Ego Uuilfridus episc iubente Aethilbaldo rege subscripsi
Ego Aethilric subregulus atq comes gloriosissimi principis Ethilbal
huic donatione consensi et subscripsi
Ego Ibe acsi indignus abbas consensi et subscripsi
Ego Heardberht frater atq dux pre fati regis consensi et subscripsi
Ego Ebbella consensum meum acomodans subscripsi
Ego Onoc comes subscripsi
Ego Oba consensi et subscripsi
Ego Sigibed consensi et subscripsi
Ego Bercol consensi et subscripsi
Ego Ealdauft consensi et subscripsi
Ego Cusa consensi et subscripsi
Ego Pede consensi et subscripsi

It is a grant by Aethelbald, 'to my venerable companion Cyneberht, for the construction of a monastery', of ten hides, with the appurtenant fields, woods, fisheries and meadows, 'in the province to which was applied by the men of old the name Ismere'. Cyneberht was entitled to possess it, and, whether in life or death, to leave it 'to whom he shall wish'. The charter gives the estate boundaries, and threatens anyone who violates it with fearful reckoning, 'at the terrible Judgement'. It is then dated by the Incarnation, and attested by the king, by the bishops of Lichfield and Worcester, by the sub-king of the Hwicce, by the king's brother, by an abbot, and by eight others, presumably lay noblemen; each name is preceded by a cross, and neither the names nor the crosses are autograph: they are in the main hand of the text. On the back, in a different hand, is another grant by Aethelbald to Cyneberht. An indication that the document is an 'original' is that the names of some witnesses were added later with a new pen.

This document, and the others of the early English series, are like neither the charters of south Wales, which probably went back to Romano-British practice, nor those of Frankish Gaul, which were probably descended from the official documents of the later Empire (though some early Wessex charters have Merovingian features). Generally, their affinities are with Italian private charters of the sixth century, and the formulas of some (though not this one) are strikingly like those of grants by Gregory himself. It is therefore clear that the Anglo-Saxon charter was not a hangover from Roman Britain or Roman government but a re-introduction by the missionaries, most of whom were Italians, but some of whom, including two early bishops of the West Saxons, were Franks. It is also possible that, though the earliest extant charters date from Theodore's time, the idea was Augustine's.

The formulas of the Ismere Diploma are much more like those of other royal grants to Worcester itself and to laymen of the diocese in this period than they are those of Aethelbald's charters elsewhere. Only two years before, he gave the church at Rochester remission of toll at London for one ship; the formulas differ in almost every way, including the royal title and the dating-clause, which need not have been affected by the different subject-matter (Birch, *Cart.*, no. 152; *EHD*, no. 66). Given the fondness of bureaucrats in all ages for fixed forms of words, the contrast would hardly exist if Aethelbald had been using his own clerks. Until the tenth century at least, it seems in fact that the writing of charters was the responsibility of the local bishop, the local abbot or their scribes (the important proviso being that such men were often in attendance on the king). The script of the Ismere Diploma is very like that of other books produced in the Worcester area, including the Inkberrow Jerome. Like other early 'originals', the whole document *smells* ecclesiastical. It is written in uncials on vellum, like the most solemn liturgical books, and it threatens violators with Hell, rather than secular punishment as one might expect (and as one finds in Frankish charters). One concludes that, having been introduced by the missionaries, charters remained essentially ecclesiastical instruments, designed to protect the beneficiary from theft rather than a chancery from fraud. The king's part in the proceedings was an oral grant and/or symbolic gesture, such as putting a sod of the granted land on an altar, and the transaction, with the names of its witnesses, was then written up.

95 (*left*) The Ismere Diploma (British Library, MS Cotton Augustus ii.3). Note the uncial script (cf. fig. 96), and the fact that the 2nd and 9th–14th subscriptions were added with a different pen.

The question of the legal rights conveyed by charter is the most controversial of all, and the ambiguous and inconsistent terminology of the documents does not help. But it does perhaps rule out the theory that charters gave immunity from forms of royal service, because formulas of immunity do not appear in early charters, and the distinction between immunity and mere possession was well known on the Continent; if immunity was what charters gave, why do they not say so until later? The language of the Ismere Diploma and others implies that what was conveyed was simply land; more precisely, the food-rent, or *feorm*, of an estate, assessed in hides (see above,pp. 58–9), was transferred to a new lord. The terms of tenure of chartered land (*bookland*, as it came to be called) are more difficult to assess. A possible solution may be found in the distinction, widespread in Germanic and other societies, between inherited property, inalienable from a kin, and property otherwise acquired, which could be disposed of as the owner wished. It is unlikely that the Anglo-Saxons had no concept of heritable land; if it rarely features in the sources, this may be because it was taken for granted. But inalienable land could not be used to endow the Church. Acquired property could be so used, but there is evidence (for example in heroic poetry) that property acquired from the king could be revoked by him. A charter helped to solve the problem by making an acquisition from the king permanent, and giving the Church the perpetual right it needed. Hence, most early charters are royal grants, either to the Church directly, or to a layman for pious purposes. Unfortunately, a kin was apt to overlook the distinction between heritable and permanently acquired property. Cyneberht was given Ismere to build a monastery which he could dispose of as he wished. A later charter (Birch, *Cart.*, no. 220) shows that he passed it to his son, who succeeded him as abbot, but that when this son wished to give it to Worcester, he had to beware the claims of his kindred.

This analysis of the rights conveyed by charter may explain two problems that loomed large in the ecclesiastical history of the period. In the first place, kings were now permanently losing lands which they might earlier have withdrawn from one warrior and given to another. Wilfrid faced Egfrith with the same difficulty as that complained of by a sixth-century Frankish king: 'All our wealth is in the hands of bishops; our honour perishes.' Secondly, charters offered anyone a permanent form of royal donation, to be added to his kindred's stock of heritable land, provided he founded a monastery, and kept its government in his family's hands. Bede's letter to

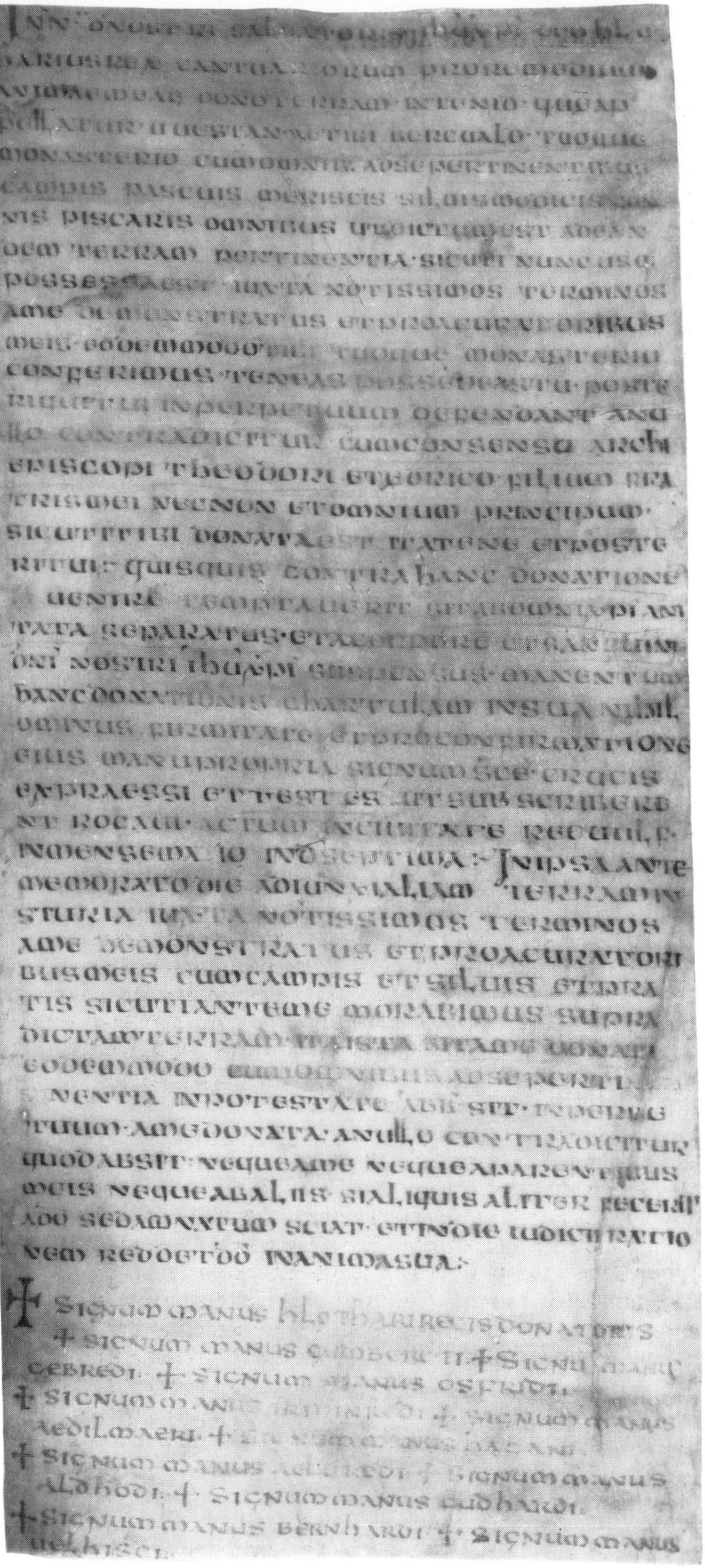

96 Charter of King Hlothere of Kent, 679 (Birch, *Cart.*, no. 45, British Library, MS Cotton Augustus ii.2). This grant to Abbot Berhtwald of Reculver (later archbishop of Canterbury) is the earliest extant 'original' Anglo-Saxon charter. Like the Ismere Diploma (fig. 95), it is in uncials, and there is once again a difference of script in the attestations.

Egbert, and the history of the Ismere estate, show that this is what happened. Paradoxically, what the charters had originally called 'perpetual' or 'ecclesiastical' right came to be known as 'hereditary right'. One reason why so many monasteries were founded in this period may have been that they actually enriched the founding family.

If the Church needed wealth from a king, a more basic and obvious need still was security, and, by the seventh century, it was the Church's well-established principle to seek security in secular legislation as well as divine vengeance. This brings us to the early Anglo-Saxon law codes, whose evidence has already been considered in part (above, pp. 57, 59, 70). The problems to be considered are the purposes of this legislation, and the difference that it made to the king's role. There are many paradoxes about the earliest English laws. Bede says that Aethelbert legislated, 'according to the example of the Romans' (*HE*, II. 5, p. 90), and it is possible to detect parallels, between his code and seventh-century Continental laws; yet it and the others are in the vernacular. They give the impression of a sophisticated and wide-ranging approach to the establishment of custom and royal right; Aethelbert's code is well organized, and some of its gaps are filled by his successors in Kent, Hlothere (?685) and Wihtred (695). But gaps remain (for example on land tenure), and the series ceases. Ine's West Saxon code (688/94) begins in an ordered way, but becomes very jumbled and repetitive. The value of such texts to judges who presumably knew their customary elements already, and who were probably illiterate, may be doubted. In the end these codes, like their Continental counterparts, seem to be attempts to civilize the image of Germanic kings by giving them a role for which Roman emperors were famous; it was thus more important to write *something* of a people's custom or a king's judgements down, than to organize the material in a comprehensive way. Churchmen, and kings too, aspired to live by written law, and the ambition went a surprisingly long way in early Kent; but the mood passed, and legislation of this type stopped until the time of Alfred.

The greatest difficulty posed by early codes (and one on which the texts themselves lend no assistance) is to decide whether what they describe is traditional custom or governmental innovation. Historians have therefore seen them either as evidence of the persistence of the society described by Tacitus, or as evidence of increasing royal power; and we cannot know whether the king was significantly more powerful as a result of issuing them, or whether his power was already well established. But two things may be said. First, early English justice was essentially that of the blood-feud. Anthropologists working on 'primitive' societies of the modern world have shown that blood-feud can paradoxically bring social peace, provided that a man's kindred is liable to vengeance for whatever he does, and provided that handsome compensation is acceptable to the injured party or his kindred instead of vengeance. The threat of revenge remains, as a disincentive to crime, and as an incentive to pay compensation for it, but the vested interest in peace of both kindreds involved should ensure settlement. Thus, Aethelbert, Hlothere and Ine give the wergelds, or blood-prices, of various social classes, and Aethelbert and later Alfred list the appropriate compensation for a long list of injuries, from the 'generative organ' to the lesser toenails, but kings expect crime to be amended between parties rather than punished by their officers. Their role is to cover marginal cases, like the kinless man, or the man killed in the act of theft who could not be avenged. Yet within this context, kings already have formidable power. They take fines for many offences, on top of the compensation payable to the injured party. Those in their service have special status. Trade and traders are carefully monitored, perhaps because the merchant was the kinless man *par excellence*. A seventh-century English king was more closely involved in justice than his Scandinavian, Scottish or Irish counterpart for many centuries.

Secondly, one undoubtedly new royal responsibility was the Church, and kings took it very seriously. Aethelbert gave churches a heavier compensation for theft than himself. Wihtred exempted the Church from taxation in return for its prayers, and heavily fined illicit sexual unions. Ine enforced infant baptism and Sunday observance with severe penalties, and put the highest fine at his command behind the payment of taxation to the Church. This is the sort of legislation for which Boniface hoped from Aethelbald. It presupposes a frightening degree of royal power, but frightening is perhaps the operative word: as Boniface was complaining, such power could be used against the Church as well as in its favour. Ultimately, it does seem probable that being made solemnly and permanently responsible for the statement of law enhanced a king's power. Law was issued in the king's name, and became the king's, in a way it may not have been before, and was never to be in Scandinavia. If the early laws are most important as evidence for a stage in the history of English society, they are also a powerful symbol of the post-conversion transformation of English kingship.

The last to be considered here, but not the least, of the Church's needs from kings was peace. A Church given responsibility by Gregory for the faith throughout English Britain and beyond could hardly welcome the incessant warring of the English kingdoms. Bede says that after Egfrith's brother was killed at the Battle of the Trent, there would have been a prolonged feud, had Archbishop Theodore not intervened, and ensured that compensation for the prince was paid instead. A very interesting letter of 704/5 from Bishop Wealdhere of London to Archbishop Berhtwald, which survives in its original text, shows the former desperately trying to make peace between Ine and Wihtred. With this objective, it might be thought that the Church had much to gain from the existence of a *bretwalda*. Some of the problems of this exalted, if shadowy, status have been discussed above (pp. 53–4, 74). That the title mattered is clear; that Germanic kings could erect vast hegemonies in remarkably little time is also clear, from Continental analogy; that the status conferred specific institutional rights is only possible. When Wulfhere of Mercia confirmed a grant by the sub-king of Surrey (Birch, *Cart.*, no. 34; *EHD*, no. 54), this may be because he was entitled to, or it may just be that he was powerful enough to put his own nominee into the government of Surrey, and insist on being consulted about his grants. References to one king paying tribute to another (and there are not many) might merely be a mark of the latter's strength and ruthlessness; the Tribal Hidage (p. 59), which never, unlike the Burghal Hidage (see pp. 152–3), gives a rate of assessment on the hide, only *may* be a tribute-list.

A further difficulty is the issue of who was *bretwalda* and who was not. Redwald led a southern army into Northumbria (617) and is on the list; Penda (655) and Wulfhere (674) also did, but are not. In the 40 years between Wulfhere's death and Aethelbald's rise to power, there is evidence that Caedwalla and Ine of Wessex, and Aethelred of Mercia, were considered *bretwaldas* by some, but clearly not by all. Despite what Bede says about Aethelbald's power at the end of his book, neither he nor his even mightier successors, Offa and Cenwulf, are listed by the *Anglo-Saxon Chronicle*. Indeed, all the charters that indicate Aethelbald's title were probably written at Worcester, whose bishop, Wilfrid, may have been the king's close friend.

The likelihood is that the status of *bretwalda* was always to some extent subjective. Some kings were very powerful indeed, and could impose their will beyond their own borders. But their power was resisted and resented, so their claims to the title were not acknowledged in retrospect; Bede tells how the monks of Bardney in Lindsey knew Oswald was a saint, but refused to accept his bones, 'because he belonged to another kingdom and had once conquered them' (*HE* III. 11, p. 148). On the other hand, kings of one's own people, or kings whose success had not been gained at its expense, might be given the title enthusiastically: hence the anomalies in Bede's and the *Chronicle*'s lists, and the confinement of Aethelbald's titles to Worcester charters. High-kingship in England was perhaps like the Irish kingship of Tara from the tenth to the twelfth centuries: a political myth for which rival kingdoms competed vigorously. It was not, in most respects, like Frankish or Lombard kingship of Roman provinces which still retained a sense of their basic unity, because they still retained an articulate Roman population.

But if this is so, the church at Canterbury nevertheless had a special interest in making the title stick, because it offered a prospect of unitary control and peace throughout its province. It is perhaps suggestive that both Bede's list of *bretwaldas*, and his account of Aethelbald's power, come in a context of material probably derived from Canterbury. It is very suggestive that Alcuin described Kent as the '*origo imperii Anglorum*', and that the appearance of Aethelbald's titles in the 730s coincides with Mercian takeover of the archbishopric. Canterbury had been entrusted by Gregory with the southern province of Britain, which squares with the emphasis of all early sources that the overlordship was of the southern English; yet until 735, and to some extent thereafter, it claimed responsibility for all Britain, and *bretwalda* means 'Britain-ruler' (but cf. p. 53): Wihtred's code described Archbishop Berhtwald as a 'high-bishop of Britain'. The concrete realization of high-kingship made sense for Canterbury whoever held it, whereas it made most sense for other Englishmen when held by their own patron. But there was a catch. An overlord was all very well, so long as he respected the susceptibilties of Kent in general and the church of Canterbury in particular. It is striking that Edwin and perhaps the other Northumbrian *bretwaldas* are said *not* to have held sway in Kent. Aethelbald had much to recommend him too; apart from the fact that Mercians held the see, there is no evidence in charters of his active power, as opposed to patronage, in Kent. But with Offa, Cenwulf and the West Saxon kings of the ninth century, it would be a different story.

If it is right that Canterbury was particularly interested in the overlordship of southern England, the policy bore fruit. Theodore held his synod himself, with no kings present, but in 746/7 the Council of Clovesho met under the presidency of Aethelbald, much as Frankish and Visigothic kings were presidents of their Church's councils. The documents associated with this council encapsulate many of the themes of this chapter, and help to draw them together. By the middle of the eighth century, the anxieties expressed in Bede's letter to Egbert were shared by other churchmen, and extended to the behaviour of kings themselves. Between 745 and 747, Boniface sent a whole series of letters to England, of which the most important were to Archbishop Cuthbert and Aethelbald himself. Aethelbald was greeted with enthusiasm, and praised for his charity and good order. But Boniface went on to denounce him for his unchaste life with nuns, and to accuse him of depriving churches of privileges and property, and allowing monks to be treated with unprecedented violence and extortion. What he meant by these last remarks is revealed in his letter to Cuthbert, which refers to 'forced labour of monks upon royal buildings and other works' (Tangl, no. 78, p. 171). Otherwise, this letter urges the archbishop to condemn the take-over of monasteries by powerful laymen, the drunkenness of the clergy, and their extravagant clothes (apparently modelled on those of old Roman senators).

Boniface's words were heeded. The Council of Clovesho, under Aethelbald and Cuthbert, sought to reform monasteries where 'tyrannical greed' corrupted the Christian life. It also forbade monks to mix with laymen, or conduct secular business, condemned 'ludicrous arts' and drunkenness in monasteries, and prohibited priests from singing 'in the manner of secular poets' (Clovesho, 5, 11, 16, pp. 364, 366, 369). In a final canon, it protested at secular suspicion and envy of the clergy, and ordered prayers for king and laity. Then, at Gumley in 749, Aethelbald issued an important privilege, freeing the Church from 'all works and burdens', and from 'feeding of kings and princes', insisting only on its contribution to the building of bridges and forts, which had been enjoined on the whole people 'by royal edict' (Birch, *Cart.*, no. 178). It was witnessed only by Mercian bishops, and may have been confined to Mercia. But its presence in the same manuscript as the Clovesho *Acta* and Boniface's letter to Cuthbert suggests that it was seen as part of the reform programme.

The impression one gets is of a Church in decline and oppressed by kings. But the matter may be seen otherwise. Christianity has always had its reforming idealists, like Bede and Boniface, but most Christians seek to reconcile the faith with the norms of life in this world, and the Church always tends to become part of the 'Establishment'. No doubt there were abuses, but what the reform programme of the 740s amounted to was that the Church was too identified with secular values; and, as has been seen, these values also inspired some of the most vibrant aspects of the early English Church. It is no more justifiable to deny Wilfrid's sincerity because of his resemblance to a secular nobleman than it is to suppose that the Lindisfarne Gospels was made without reference to its contents because it looked like a secular treasure. On the other hand, the Church's success in establishing itself did pose problems for kings. Some of Aethelbald's nuns may not have been easily distinguished from noble ladies. Aethelbald himself may have realized that many of the monasteries that drained his landed and manpower resources were not too different from secular halls, and have felt entitled to treat them as if that is what they were. His Gumley privilege was perhaps a sensible compromise, and its implications must be considered in the next chapter, but it did not save his reputation, and the fundamental dilemmas of Christian government, dramatized by Egfrith's fate and Caedwalla's retirement, remained. For all the achievements of the early English Church and the Mercian monarchy, it is some comment on the realities of eighth-century England that both Bede and Aethelbald, when they died, had reason to feel disillusioned about their age.

The Age of Offa and Alcuin

Offa, Alcuin and Charlemagne

'Charles, by the grace of God king of the Franks and Lombards, to his dearest brother, Offa, king of the Mercians. Having perused your brotherly letters, we first give thanks to Almighty God for the sincerity of the Catholic faith set down in your pages; recognizing you to be not only a most strong protector of your earthly country, but also a most devout defender of the holy faith . . . Concerning pilgrims who desire to reach the thresholds of the blessed Apostles, they may go in peace. But we have discovered that certain persons fraudulently mingle with them for the sake of commerce: they are to pay the established toll at the proper places . . . You have also written about merchants, and we allow that they shall have protection in our kingdom. And if they are afflicted with wrongful oppression, they may appeal to us. Similarly, our men are to appeal to the judgement of your equity . . . . Regarding the priest Odberht, who desires to live abroad, we have sent him to Rome with the other exiles who in fear of death have taken refuge under our protection . . . As for the black stones which your reverence begged to be sent we will willingly order them to be given. But as you intimated your wishes concerning the length of the stones, so our people make a demand about the size of the cloaks, that you may order them to be such as used to come to us . . . We have sent a gift to the various episcopal sees of your kingdom and of Aethelred's, in alms for the apostolic lord, Hadrian, our father and your friend. Also to your love we have sent a belt and a Hunnish sword . . . May Almighty God preserve the excellence of your dignity for the protection of his Holy Church' (Dümmler, no. 100; *EHD*, no. 197).

These are extracts from a letter of 796 from the Frankish king Charlemagne (768–814) to King Offa of Mercia (757–96). It is the only one extant from a European king to any Anglo-Saxon ruler; it is the only one to survive in which Charlemagne calls another western king his 'brother'; and it is also the first known letter between European kings about trade. By any standards, it is among the most remarkable documents of Anglo-Saxon history, and it also epitomizes many of the main themes of the age.

In the first place, it underlines the mighty power of Aethelbald's successors as kings of Mercia. Charlemagne's conquests in Germany, Italy and northern Spain made him the most powerful ruler that western Europe had seen for four centuries; and his achievement was acknowledged when, on Christmas Day 800, the Pope crowned him Roman Emperor. In the very year of his letter to Offa, his armies obliterated the Avar (Hunnish) empire in central Europe, and rifled its great treasure hoard. That Charlemagne could give Offa a cut of the proceeds, and address him as an equal, conveys some idea of the status to which Mercian kings could now aspire, as does an earlier (though abortive) proposal for a marriage alliance between Offa and Charlemagne.

Charlemagne, moreover, saw England as if it were ruled by two kings only: Aethelred ruling Northumbria, and Offa everything to the south. Early in his reign, Offa was indeed a more effective overlord of Kent and Sussex than Aethelbald seems to have been; and, after an apparent setback in the 770s, he re-emerged as the unrivalled king of much of England. The local dynasties of Kent, Sussex, the Hwicce and (temporarily) East Anglia disappeared; Offa's daughters married Kings Beorhtric of Wessex (786–802), and Aethelred of Northumbria (774–9, 790–6), which may denote his superiority in some form even over these kingdoms. He raided deep into Wales in 778, 784 and perhaps 795/6, and built a dyke up to 25 feet high the entire length of the Welsh border—the most impressive monument of this type ever constructed by a known European king (see below, pp. 120–1). He was the first Anglo-Saxon king to be called 'king of the English' in reputable charters.

The achievement of Offa's almost immediate successor, Cenwulf (796–821), was scarcely less impressive. From 798, his control of the south-east was as real as Offa's. There is less evidence of his influence in Wessex or Northumbria, but he increased Mercian pressure on the Welsh; and, after his death at Basingwerk, at the northern end of the dyke, his brother and successor, Ceolwulf I (821–3), virtually overran the principality of Powys. Cenwulf was the only English king before the tenth century to be styled 'emperor' in one of his charters (Birch, *Cart.*, no. 289). In England as in Francia, royal power seems to move onto a new plane in the second half of the eighth century.

Second, the commercial concerns of Charlemagne's letter hint at the sources of this new level of power. It was in the second half of the eighth century, on both sides of the Channel, that a new silver coinage appeared. It was bigger and thinner than the old, its weight and silver

Hamwih

The objects illustrated are in Southampton City Museum.

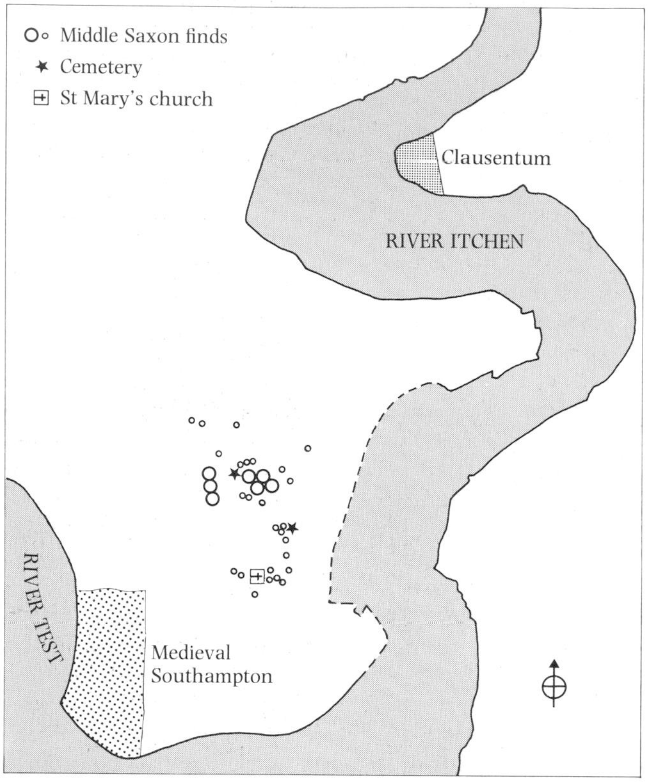

1 Map showing Hamwih, *Clausentum* (?), and medieval Southampton.

2 Excavations in progress on a site in *Hamwih*. Preliminary cleaning is taking place; the gravelled area in the foreground is probably a street surface, and the darker marks in the ground behind the diggers are pits and wells.

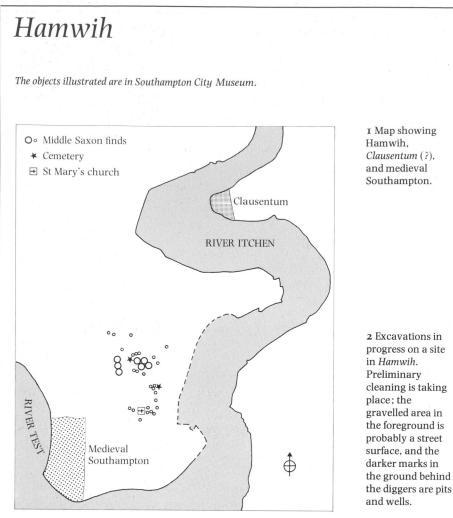

The development of a trading network in the post-Roman era in north-western Europe led to the establishment of a number of mercantile centres. Favoured sites for these were river estuaries which offered shelter, a sloping beach onto which boats could be hauled, and good communications inland. The Solent estuary is well placed for trade between the south of England and northern France, and the Southampton peninsula in the eighth and ninth centuries was the site of one of the largest of the north European ports.

The former existence of a major Saxon settlement at Southampton (for the problem of names see below) was recognized in the nineteenth century, when the development of land which had previously been open fields revealed deep pits filled with bones and various other refuse but including occasional coins. Not until the 1940s were serious efforts made to investigate the size and nature of the settlement. Intermittent excavations began then and large-scale campaigns were undertaken in the 1960s. Every site revealed more of the deep pits which had led to the first identification of the site, but it was also possible to locate traces of timber buildings, gravelled roads and cemeteries. No trace of a boundary ditch or palisade was identified, so the precise extent of the occupied area is unknown. It extended, however, over at least 30 hectares. This indicates how large an eighth-century English trading centre could be. Southampton could well have been the most populous place in England at that time.

The mid-Saxon port was on the west bank of the river Itchen, downstream of a Roman fort and harbour (*Clausentum*) which may have remained in some sort of use. A late fifth-century brooch has been found there. As 'Stanham' it may have given its name to the whole Southampton area. The Roman fort may have been re-used in the late ninth century since its wall-length fits that which the Burghal Hidage (see pp. 152–3) implies for *Hamtun*. The west bank of the river provided a more attractive site for merchants in the Saxon period: it had mudflats for beaching boats and space for houses and other buildings. It is no longer thought, as once it was, that there was a lagoon there providing a sheltered harbour. No jetties, wharves or purpose-built warehouses have been found, so that little is known about the physical operation of the port.

The coin finds show that the port was established by the end of the first decade of the eighth century. Its rise may be connected with that of the power of the West Saxon kings Caedwalla (685–8) and Ine (688–726). The extent to which such rulers interested themselves in trade is uncertain. It could be significant that they did not put their names on the coins which were struck locally (see pp. 62–3). But traders brought goods of the kind which kings needed to maintain their status, and merchants needed royal protection. They may also have been attracted by the commodities and livestock which kings probably collected from their subjects and from their defeated enemies. Enormous quantities of animal-bones have been found in the port. They demonstrate the large-scale slaughter of stock, suggesting perhaps the collection of hides for export. The gathering of such herds was more likely to have been achieved by the exercise of royal power and the collection of royal dues than via the mechanisms of a formal market network which probably did not exist.

The goods exchanged for this agricultural surplus certainly included glass vessels, since many broken fragments are found, and probably quantities of wine, gold and silver. No precious objects, except coins, have been found at Southampton, but there were many gold or silver sword-hilts, finger-rings and other precious objects in southern England, and the metal for them may have come from overseas.

Occasional royal presence at Southampton is attested by the issue of a charter there. The place's administrative importance is shown by its having given its name to the surrounding shire, *Hamtunscire*, which first occurs in the *Chronicle* under 755. The port was called *Hamtun* when contemporaries were referring to its administrative role, *Hamwic* when referring to its mercantile role. The two names do not necessarily apply to two separate places. But, as these names were also used in the tenth and eleventh centuries for the port which developed on the east bank of the Test it has become conventional and convenient to call the mid-Saxon site *Hamwih* (a variant of *Hamwic* coined on the Continent), while the later site to the west is called Southampton.

The active life of *Hamwih* seems to have been quite short. The trade on which it depended was disrupted by the Vikings. Its low-lying position was not easily defensible and it was raided in 842 (see fig. 142). A few late ninth-century coins have been found, but they suggest activity on a much reduced scale. A ditched enclosure on the higher ground by the Test came into use, and became the nucleus of medieval Southampton, which flourished after the Norman Conquest. The mid-Saxon site was almost totally abandoned, though its church, St Mary's, remained and was the 'mother church' of the medieval port. Until the thirteenth century all the citizens had to be buried there. The rest of the site of *Hamwih* returned to agricultural use until the nineteenth century.

D. A. Hinton

3 A bone plaque, perhaps from a casket, late 7th century, 3.5 × 4.7 cm. The decoration of a pair of interlaced snake-like creatures is paralleled in such 7th-century works of art as the Sutton Hoo shoulder clasps and the Book of Durrow (figs. 74, 77).

4 A sherd from a jug of Tating ware, 8th–9th century, 5.8 × 6.5 cm. This high-quality pottery is thought to have been made in the region of the Eifel mountains. The decoration is applied tin foil.

5 Pieces of combs, made from antler and bone, 8th–9th century, length of top left comb 10 cm. Manufacture of small bone objects leaves much debris of this sort, although it is unlikely that bone-working was more than a relatively minor craft.

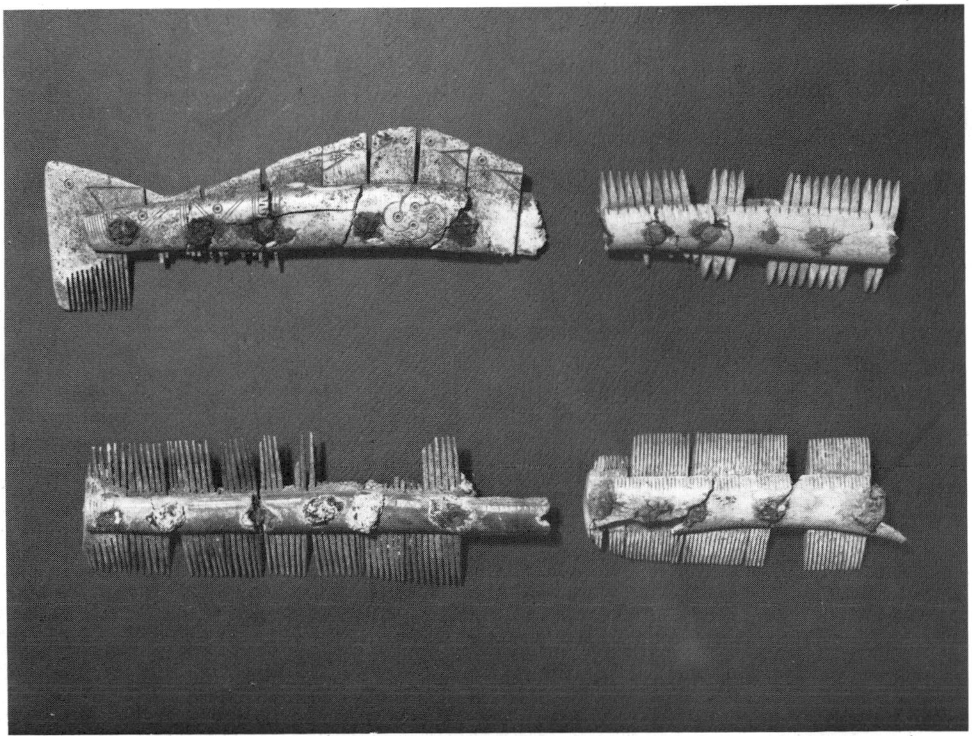

97 (*above*) David and court musicians, now fol. 30b but probably once the frontispiece of the Vespasian Psalter (British Library, MS Cotton Vespasian A.i). The manuscript is almost certainly from Canterbury, and datable in the first or second quarter of the 8th century. Its exemplar may have been a 6th-century Italian Psalter under Byzantine influence (note David's purple robe), but the harp is very like the reconstructed instrument from Sutton Hoo, and strongly 'Celtic' motifs may be seen in the arch.

98 (*right*) Initial from the Book of Kells (Dublin, Trinity College, MS A.I.6, fol. 34a). This famous Gospel book is variously dated between the mid-8th and early 9th-century, and is understandably considered the climax of the insular tradition of *de luxe* manuscripts. As with the Book of Durrow (fig. 74), its origin is disputed; an Irish provenance (Iona moved to Kells in the early 9th century) and 'Celtic' decorative elements are again matched by 'Germanic' decoration and characteristically Northumbrian script. One solution is to ascribe the manuscript to Iona, whilst noting how strong Northumbrian influence had become there; Alcuin had Irish pupils and friends.

h generatio
34

content were improved, and it bore the name of a king. Offa was probably not the first English king to produce it, but he was among the first, and his coins are much the finest and most numerous of the period. Cenwulf emulated him in quantity of coinage, if not quality. Now Charlemagne refers to 'black stones' being imported, and 'cloaks' being exported by the English; Rhineland lava-stones, which were used for the making of querns, are indeed found fairly widely in England, and excavations at Hamwih (see the Picture Essay, pp. 102–3) have revealed quantities of spindle-whorls and loom-weights which suggest intensive and concentrated cloth manufacture. Moreover, the letter shows clearly what early laws only hinted at: that merchants were the king's responsibility and under his protection; and its reference to customs evasion implies that merchants were having to pay heavily for the privilege. It is thus more than likely that the appearance of a royal coinage marked a new determination by kings to harness their subjects' wealth; and it is also likely that this was because their subjects were getting wealthier.

Third, Charlemagne sees more in kingship than the mere exercise of power. Offa was 'a most devout defender of the holy faith', was a friend of the Pope, and was expected to protect the Church. Charlemagne, who wept when Pope Hadrian died (795), had an intense awareness of his responsibility to God for his kingdom's spiritual health. His reign saw repeated royal and conciliar legislation aimed at Church reform, and a major effort to raise the level, and widen the distribution, of learning—hence the term Carolingian Renaissance. Offa seems to have had the same priorities. In 786, he became the first English king (and the last before 1070) to hold an ecclesiastical council under the auspices of papal legates. It probably led to the anointing of his son, Egfrith, as king, apparently the first instance of royal unction in Anglo-Saxon history, and perhaps modelled on that of Charlemagne's sons by the Pope in 781. Offa also used his contacts with Pope Hadrian to set up a new archbishopric at Lichfield for the Mercian part of Canterbury's province. His motives may have been political (see below p. 126), and the scheme certainly outraged Canterbury; but it may be significant that the conversion of bishoprics into archbishoprics, in order to create more manageably sized metropolitan provinces, was an aspect of Carolingian reform. Cenwulf also presided over an important reforming council, at Clovesho in 803. Unfortunately, he too fell foul of Canterbury, when one of the greatest Anglo-Saxon archbishops, Wulfred (805–32), launched a strong attack on secularized monasteries (see above, pp. 87–8), with a special eye on the Kentish houses of Reculver and Minster-in-Thanet where Cenwulf's daughter was abbess. Church reform, as Aethelbald and the Carolingians also found, was not always convenient for kings.

Fourth, Charlemagne's letter foreshadows the frailty of even such power as Offa's and Cenwulf's. Aethelred of Northumbria, Offa's son-in-law, to whom Charlemagne also sent gifts, had had a troubled reign, divided into two halves by 11 years of exile. Before he could receive his gifts, he was murdered. He was one of a long series of Northumbrian kings to meet an untimely fate in this period. Royal succession was open to vigorous competition, leading to murder and feud. The way in which Offa and later Cenwulf came to power shows the potential for equal instability in Mercia, notwithstanding the long reigns of some of its kings. Neither was at all closely related to his predecessor. Offa succeeded the murdered Aethelbald only after fighting a civil war with one Beornred. When he died in 796, shortly after receiving Charlemagne's letter, his son and successor, Egfrith, survived him for only five months. Cenwulf's brother, Ceolwulf, was deposed in a palace *coup*, in favour of Beornwulf (823–6); and so it went on (see below, pp. 115, 116, 138).

In such violent and unstable politics, exile and exiles played a major part (see above, pp. 56, 94). When Charlemagne refers to 'the priest Odberht and other exiles', he is evidently seeking to assuage Offa's anxiety about the exiles he was harbouring; and well might Offa be anxious. The fugitive priest, Odberht, was probably Eadbert, a claimant to the throne of Kent, who led a major Kentish rebellion at Offa's death, and was not deposed (and mutilated) by Cenwulf till two years later. Probably the most important of the exiles of royal blood sheltered by Charlemagne was Egbert, a distant relative of Offa's son-in-law and possible protegé, King Beorhtric of Wessex. As often, distance of relationship proved no bar to succession. When Beorhtric died in 802, Egbert returned from Francia and made himself king of Wessex, in full independence of Cenwulf. In 825, he defeated Beornwulf of Mercia at Wroughton in Wiltshire; and when Beornwulf was killed while trying to suppress an East Anglian rebellion, Egbert seized his chance to conquer the south-east, and even temporarily occupied London (829–30). He was the founder of West Saxon greatness. In the end it was Wessex and Egbert's grandson, Alfred, who inherited what Offa had built.

Finally, there is the way in which this letter survives. It was preserved in one manuscript of the letters of Alcuin of York (*c.* 735–804), the dominant intellectual of the age of Charlemagne and Offa. That Alcuin was English is one of the most important facts in the history of relations between Britain and the Continent in the early Middle Ages. He was educated in the cathedral church of York, whose history he wrote in a poem which has been called 'the first historical epic in the extant Latin literature of the medieval West'. In 782, he became the master of Charlemagne's court school, and a central figure in the Carolingian Renaissance. He returned to England for the legatine council of 786, and was again in Northumbria from 790 to 793; but most of his last years were spent on the Continent, where he died as abbot of St Martin's, Tours. He was one of the foremost grammarians, liturgists and theologians of Charlemagne's Europe. About 300 of his letters, many to English kings, prelates and noblemen, and a major source for the English history of the period in their own right, have been preserved: more than we have from any other Englishman in the entire Middle Ages.

99, 100 Ruined church and sculpture fragment from Reculver, Kent, the minster which received the earliest extant 'original' Anglo-Saxon charter (see fig. 96), and was one of the subjects of Archbishop Wulfred's great dispute with King Cenwulf. The aerial photograph shows the outline of the 7th-century church, enlarged in the 8th century, which was located in a Roman Saxon Shore fort now destroyed by erosion; the foundations of the pillars of the arcade separating nave and apse (now removed to Canterbury Cathedral) can clearly be seen. Also at Canterbury are fragments, including that shown, of the remarkable cross which apparently stood in front of the arcade. The cross was probably destroyed at the Reformation; the church was pulled down in 1809 at the instance of the vicar's mother, in what H. M. and J. Taylor have called, 'an act of vandalism for which there can be few parallels even in the blackest records of the nineteenth century'.

Alcuin is very interesting and important in himself, but he also symbolizes the continuing English commitment to the Continental Church, which had begun with Willibrord (see pp. 82, 88 and fig. 89) and still flourished in the age of Charlemagne. Alcuin's Northumbrian contemporary, Willehad, was the first bishop of Bremen, one of several Englishmen to hold episcopal office in the new German Church. An otherwise wholly unknown Anglo-Saxon, Cathwulf, wrote a learned and important letter to Charlemagne about kingship, probably before Alcuin reached his court. Objects as striking as the Gandersheim Casket, the Tassilo Chalice and the Rupert Cross, which are strongly under English influence, if not of English manufacture, demonstrate the Anglo-Saxon impact on Continental culture, though they cannot be associated with any known personality (figs. 101, 102, 121).

Yet it will be observed that almost all the evidence for the richness and vigour of Anglo-Saxon culture in the age of Offa comes from the Continent, not, as in the age of Bede, from England *and* the Continent. Very few of Alcuin's voluminous extant works were written in England, and most belong to the last phase of his life. No one after 750 is known to have written the life of an English saint who stayed in England, as opposed to an English missionary abroad. There is little surviving in an English context which can confidently be placed alongside a

101 (*left*) The 'Rupert Cross' from Bischofshofen, Austria (158 cm high) (Salzburg, Dommuseum). The decoration has affinities with Northumbrian sculpture of the later 8th century, and is probably the work of an English artist on the Continent.

102 (*above*) The 'Tassilo Chalice' from Kremsmünster, Austria (silver gilt, 27 cm high). It was presented to the new foundation of Kremsmünster by Tassilo, Duke of Bavaria, between 777 and 788. Its sumptuous decoration is again under strongly English influence, and may represent the work of a Continental artist trained by an Anglo-Saxon master.

masterpiece like the Tassilo Chalice. It is impossible to say whether such works once existed and have been lost. While it is clear that Alcuin's stature was comparable to Bede's, and the age of Offa may well be inscribed with his name also, as that of Aethelbald was with Bede's, most of his known and knowable history belongs to Continental rather than to English history. Though a vitally important witness to the England of Offa and Cenwulf, he is, unlike Bede, a witness from without.

Our knowledge of the age depends entirely on such witnesses. We have less direct information about the period of Mercian greatness than about any comparably significant part of Anglo-Saxon history after 597. There is a shocking contrast here with the profusion of annals, laws and learned works which illuminate the achievement of Charlemagne. There is no Mercian counterpart to the Northumbrian annals of the period, in many ways the fullest of the whole Anglo-Saxon series, which graphically illustrate the chaos of Northumbrian politics. There may never have been such a source, but it is virtually certain that royal charters were once preserved in the great churches of the Mercian heartland: Lichfield, Repton, Crowland, St Albans and Peterborough; yet all that survive are a few Peterborough fragments. In the early Middle Ages, the reputation of kings depended heavily on the churches which had benefited most from their patronage, and in which they were buried. One of the most significant things about Offa is that no one even claimed to know where he was buried until the St Albans chroniclers of the thirteenth century. They said that it was at Bedford, a church of which we know almost nothing; yet their report is all the more plausible for the fact that they regarded Offa as their second founder and would certainly have claimed him for themselves if they could have done. It would seem that the historical traditions of the churches who might have told us most about Offa were at some subsequent stage drastically interrupted (see below, pp. 145, 149).

We are thus forced back on the evidence of the neighbours of the Mercians, who were not infrequently their enemies. For example, it is Welsh annals, not English sources, that tell us all we know about the western campaigns of the Mercians. The *Anglo-Saxon Chronicle*, compiled in King Alfred's Wessex almost a century after Offa's death, has no more than seven entries on his reign, and four on Cenwulf's, including those recording the dates of their accessions and deaths. What it does say is not overtly hostile, but tends to concentrate on the bare facts of violence, like Offa's execution of an East Anglian king in 794, or Cenwulf's suppression of the Kentish rebellion in 798; its account of Egbert's conquests after

103 The so-called 'Hedda stone' from Peterborough cathedral (107 × 76 cm). The artistic affinities of this sarcophagus/shrine are with the 'Breedon school' (figs. 108, 109); it is thus too late to be genuinely connected with Hedda, abbot of Breedon and bishop of Lichfield (p. 94). It does, however, underline the importance of Peterborough in Offa's period: Offa confirmed a charter there, and its abbot was often at his court.

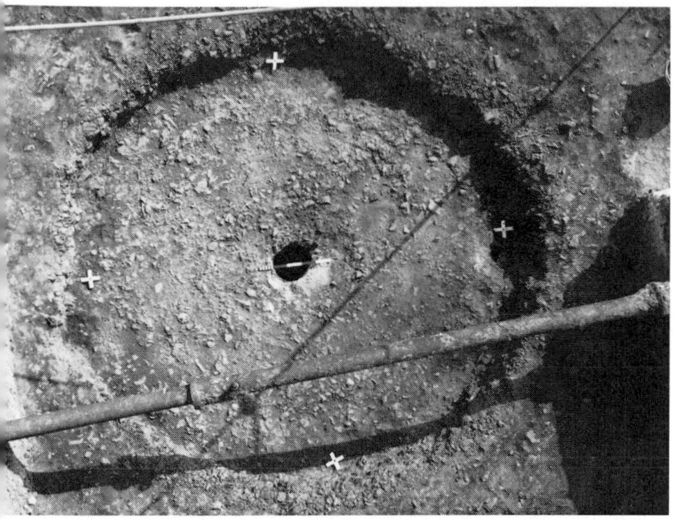

104 Mortar-mixer discovered in recent excavations at Northampton; it consists of a bowl scooped out of the ground, with a central post-hole for a 'paddle' with which to mix the mortar. Apart from its considerable technological interest, its presence (with two others) suggests the nearby construction of another important church, of which nothing is otherwise known; perhaps it was an 8th-century predecessor of St Peter's, Northampton, only about 50 yards away. (Diameter of bowl approx. 3 m.)

825 is much more sympathetic. An extraordinary story in Asser's *Life of Alfred*, describing how Offa's daughter lived tyrannically 'in her father's manner', and poisoned her husband, King Beorhtric (Asser, *c.* 14, p. 12), gives some idea of the feelings of Egbert's dynasty about Offa, and of what may lie behind the *Chronicle*'s reticence.

Charters can do something to fill the gaps in narrative sources on Mercian supremacy. But most of those that survive were preserved (and probably written; see above, pp. 95, 97) by the churches of the Mercians' neighbours, and so victims. The important group of Worcester charters are admittedly a special case; for though they tell us almost all we know of the subjugation of the kings of the Hwicce by those of Mercia, this was a long and old story, going back to the seventh century. Charters from Kent and Sussex, on the other hand, provide clues to the new growth of Mercian power under Offa, and of how it was received. All that the *Anglo-Saxon Chronicle* says of Offa's campaigns in the south-east is that a battle was fought between Mercians and Kentishmen at Otford in 776; though it vouchsafes the additional information that 'marvellous adders were seen in Sussex', it does not give the battle's result (*EHD*, p. 178). Stenton, however, showed from charters that Offa was dominant in Kent as early as 764, and that 10 years later he was being styled '*rex Anglorum*' (king of the English), and '*rex totius Anglorum patriae*' (king of the whole fatherland of the English) (Birch, *Cart.*, nos. 213, 214). Both these charters are suspect; but a Sussex grant of 772 not only calls Offa '*rex Anglorum*', but also shows that Osmund, previously king of Sussex, was now a mere *dux* (Birch, *Cart.*, no. 208). On the other hand, charters of 778 and 779 are grants by Egbert II of Kent, without any reference to Offa, and a South Saxon ruler also granted land without consent in 780. It thus emerges that Otford was a Mercian defeat, leading to the recovery of independence by Kent and Sussex.

But its effects were only temporary, as appears from the most remarkable charter of the whole series (Birch, *Cart.*, no. 293; *EHD*, no. 80). It seems that a Kentish gentleman had received lands from King Egbert II of Kent, and transferred them to Christ Church Canterbury. Offa seized them on his return to power in Kent, and gave them to his own followers, 'saying that it was wrong that his *minister* should have presumed to give land allotted to him by his lord into the power of another without his witness'. So Offa apparently regarded the Kentish king as his *minister* and felt entitled to annul the grants Egbert had made without his consent. The meaning of the charter can be disputed (see below, p. 126), but it is undeniably impressive evidence of Offa's power. It may be just as significant, however, that Christ Church ultimately got the land back, and were far from endorsing the transaction's legitimacy. A memorandum by Archbishop Aethelheard (792–805) refers pointedly to 'the rapacity of a certain king' (Birch, *Cart.*, no. 319), and a charter of Archbishop Wulfred says that Offa acted, 'as if Egbert had no right to bestow lands in hereditary right' (Birch, *Cart.*, no. 332)—the implication being that Egbert did have such a right. We do not really have Offa's side of the story. Thus, the Mercian hegemony can look more violent than that of the West Saxons later, not because it necessarily *was*, but because it lacks contemporary endorsement, because its violent elements were highlighted by its victims, and not least because it did not last.

105 Silver-gilt sword-pommel, inlaid with niello, from Fetter Lane, London (British Museum). 'One of the best surviving late Saxon pieces', its artistic affinities are with manuscripts of the late 8th and early 9th centuries. An early 11th-century prince's will bequeathed a 'sword that had belonged to King Offa'; it could well have been such a splendid weapon as this.

106 David in a decorated border from the Durham manuscript of Cassiodorus's Commentary on the Psalms (Durham, Dean and Chapter Library, MS B.II.30, fol. 172b). This is sometimes ascribed to Monkwearmouth/Jarrow in the second half of the 8th century, but the most recent research suggests that it could be an almost unique survival from the library which Alcuin used at York.

Similar considerations apply to the more peaceful activities of Offa and Cenwulf. Alfred refers to a law code of Offa in the preface to his own, and it is usually thought to have been lost. If, as will be suggested (p. 125), Alfred was actually referring to the decrees of the 786 council, the reason this has not been realized is that these decrees are extant only in the report of the papal legates, where Offa's presidential role is much less prominent than it might have been in a native record. Offa's Lichfield project is known only from the correspondence with the Pope who suppressed it, at the instance of hostile Canterbury. The long and bitter dispute over the Kentish ministers between Cenwulf and Archbiship Wulfred is recorded only in a Canterbury document. In both cases, the king's case goes by default, and looks more cynical than it may really have been. Again, Alcuin's letters to Offa and his entourage hint that Offa was interested in learning, and may even have had his own copy of Bede, like Charlemagne. But these hints are virtually all there is to show for Mercian culture in this period. Almost no manuscripts can be safely assigned to Mercian *scriptoria*; and, though eighth-century Mercian sculpture exists, it is so lacking in cultural context as to have received comparatively little notice.

What gives one pause about this situation is how little one might think of Northumbrian culture after Bede's death, if all one had was the bloody record of the annals. Alcuin wrote almost nothing before he left England, but most scholars form their intellect long before they are 50, and Charlemagne would hardly have taken Alcuin into his service and rewarded him well, unless Alcuin had much to offer. It therefore seems reasonable to attach weight to the remarkable list of books in the York library, which Alcuin included in his epic poem. It has a full complement of Church Fathers, all the major grammarians, a wide selection of Christian and classical poets, and some classical prose. Several of the writers listed, including Vergil and Cicero, were used by Alcuin in other writings, but may not have been known to Bede. It seems clear that behind Alcuin lie very high cultural standards indeed, and his masters, Archbishops Egbert (732–66) and Aelbert (766–80) can be called the founders of the first cathedral school of the Middle Ages.

York and Alcuin might of course have been exceptions. But there is also a poem by one Aethelwulf, datable 803/21, about the abbots of his monastery. He describes a spiritually and culturally respectable community, with a fine church and ecclesiastical ornaments; and his poem shows knowledge of Vergil, Ovid and the Christian poets, including Alcuin, whose work on York was his model. Yet the community cannot be identified, and might be any known or unknown Northumbrian monastery. These poems are almost all the evidence we have for Northumbrian civilization in the age of Offa; few, if any, manuscripts survive from the York library, and, apart from some churches, there are few clear examples of artistic attainment. What, then, are we to make of Breedon in Mercian Leicestershire, which preserves some very fine eighth-century sculpture indeed, and which had already produced one learned archbishop of Canterbury (see above, p. 94)?

Thus, while it is possible to see that Offa and Cenwulf were extremely powerful, they emerge, in the nature of the sources, as starker, more violent, more resented rulers than the Northumbrian *bretwaldas* before, or the West Saxon kings afterwards. It is important to appreciate that they may have been neither less cultured nor more aggressive. Moreover, if much of their history can only be informed guesswork, the corollary is that we do know something of the neighbours of the Mercians, each of whom illustrates at least one major theme of the period. The Northumbrian annals illuminate the turbulence of dynastic politics, which was certainly a feature of Offa's Mercia too. The Worcester and Kentish charters not only demonstrate the reality of Mercian power, but

107 (*below*) Fragments of a cross from St Andrew's church, Bishop Auckland, Co. Durham. This cross of *c.* 800 or rather earlier has 'inhabited vine-scroll' on its lateral face, with an archer shooting at a bird just visible on the photo. The central panel to the front shows Christ bound rather than nailed to the cross, a motif of Syrian origin. The unknown monastery described by Aethelwulf (p. 112) was presumably a community with the same sort of artistic standards as this wholly undocumented church.

108, 109 Sculpture from Breedon church, Leics., datable perhaps to the late 8th century. These striking fragments were only identified as Saxon in 1927, and reflect the very sophisticated culture of the little-known abbeys of Offa's Mercia. The cocks and hens (above) are among a large number of architectural friezes, with human, animal, plant or wholly abstract ornament. The panel (below) probably represents the Virgin, whose cult was developing in 8th-century England, though she is rarely shown holding a book.

110 The Mortain Casket, late 8th-century. This house-shaped reliquary (13 × 5 × 12 cm) from the treasury of Notre Dame de Mortain, France, is made of beech, with copper plates. On the side, Christ is flanked by two figures, identified (in Latin Script) as the archangels Michael and Gabriel; the inscription shown is in early Anglo-Saxon runes, and reads: 'May God help Aeadan who made this casket.' The name is Irish, and though it is not known when this casket reached Mortain, it might be a further indication of the cultural links between Ireland, England and France in the 8th century.

also show bishops organizing their cathedral chapters, and continuing the campaign against secularized minsters (both significant aspects of Carolingian reform). Across the channel, it can be seen that the Carolingians were seeking, and to an extent getting, control of their own landed resources, that tolls on trade were as carefully monitored as revenue from land, and that changes in Frankish coinage, which closely mirror those in England, were directed by the government. An Anglo-Saxon king did not necessarily resemble his Frankish neighbour (least of all when that neighbour was Charlemagne), but to consider Charlemagne's empire is at least to enlarge one's sense of eighth-century possibilities. By casting a spotlight on the peripheries of the Mercian kingdom, each of which has its own interest, it may also be possible to illuminate the darkened central stage.

Northumbria and Dynastic Politics

The history of King Aethelred of Northumbria, the other recipient of Charlemagne's gifts, gives a good idea of eighth-century dynastic politics, and, with the help of the splendid set of northern annals, may be recorded annalistically:

759: Seizure of the throne by Aethelwold Moll (Aethelred's father); Oswulf, son and successor of the relatively successful King Eadbert (737–58) had been killed by his 'household' (*EHD*, p. 266).

765: Aethelwold loses his throne; succession of Alchred, 'sprung, as some say, from the stock of King Ida' (founder of the Bernician dynasty) (p. 267).

774: Alchred 'deprived of the society of the royal household and nobles by the counsel of all his people'; succession of Aethelred (p. 269).

779: Aethelred driven into exile; succession of Aelfwold, son of Oswulf (above, year 759) (p. 270).

788: Aelfwold killed by a conspiracy of one of his 'patricians'; succession of Osred, son of Alchred (above, year 765) (p. 271).

790: Osred 'deceived by the guile of his nobles, taken prisoner, tonsured and forced into exile'; return of Aethelred (above, year 774) (p. 271).

791: Aelfwold's sons, Oelf and Oelfwine (above, year 779) enticed from York cathedral by Aethelred and killed (p. 272).

792: Osred (above, year 788), invited back from exile by 'certain nobles', but betrayed, and killed by Aethelred; Ealdorman Eardwulf captured and ordered to be killed by Aethelred, but (? miraculously) revived (pp. 271–2).

796: Assassination of Aethelred; 27-day reign of the 'patrician' Osbald, followed by succession of Eardwulf (above, year 792) (p. 274).

In line with their belief in the continuity of Anglo-Saxon 'democracy' from Tacitus to 1066, nineteenth-century historians saw the fall of Alchred at least (774) as an example of a king's 'constitutional' deposition. But it is possible to see a different pattern behind the apparent chaos of the story as a whole. What we have is usurpation of the throne by noblemen of marginal, if any, claims in 759 and 765, followed by dynastic feud between their families and that of the original royal line. Each family held and lost the throne at least twice in 38 years, and all then made way for a fourth:

1 Eadbert (737–58)			
2 Oswulf (758–9)	3 Aethelwold (759–65)	4 Alchred (765–74)	
	5 Aethelred (774–9)		
6 Aelfwold (779–88)		7 Osred (788–9)	
	8 Aethelred (790–6)		9 Eardwulf (796–)

The feud between these families caught up in itself the resentments of their followers, so that kings were murdered by members of their bodyguard whose secret

111 The Ormside Bowl (diam. 14 cm). Probably found in a Viking's grave at Ormside, Cumbria, and now in the Yorkshire Museum, this sumptuous little silver bowl with gilt copper lining may be an indication of secular taste in late 8th-century Northumbria. Its plant ornament is in Northumbrian style, but its 'menagerie' has Carolingian affinities.

sympathies lay elsewhere, or deposed by members of a court party who hoped for better things from an available rival. Fear of usurpation turned a king not only against his rivals' heirs, as in the case of Aethelred with the sons of Aelfwold, but also against members of the nobility who might be suspected of supporting someone else, or of harbouring ambitions for themselves (as presumably in the case of Aethelred and Eardwulf). The more a king like Aethelred acted on his apprehensions, doubtless often justified, the more likely he was to foster corresponding apprehensions in his nobility, which could bring him down.

There is reason to believe that the less well-documented politics of other eighth-century English kingdoms were similar. The *Anglo-Saxon Chronicle* shows that no West Saxon king from 685 to 802 was more than distantly related to his predecessor, and raises the question whether the politics of open succession did not create as much turbulence there as in Northumbria. In particular, it tells a remarkable story for the year 757. Cynewulf and the West Saxon 'councillors' deposed Sigebert 'because of his unjust acts', and Cynewulf became king. Sigebert soon shed light on the meaning of 'unjust acts' by killing the ealdorman 'who stood by him longest', and was then murdered in revenge by the ealdorman's swineherd; but that was not the end of the story. Twenty-nine years later, Sigebert's brother, Cyneheard, attacked Cynewulf, who was visiting his mistress. The king's escort defended him bravely, but he and they were all killed, bar one British hostage. The main body of Cynewulf's army then arrived. Cyneheard offered them money and land if they would allow him the kingdom, and pointed out that their kinsmen were among his following. 'They replied that no kinsman was dearer to them than their lord, and they would never serve his slayer'; and they cut Cyneheard and his war-band down, kinsmen and all. (*EHD*, pp. 175–6). This story too has a hint of 'constitutional' procedures at the outset, and it is famous for its flavour of heroic saga. But what lies behind it is another dynastic feud.

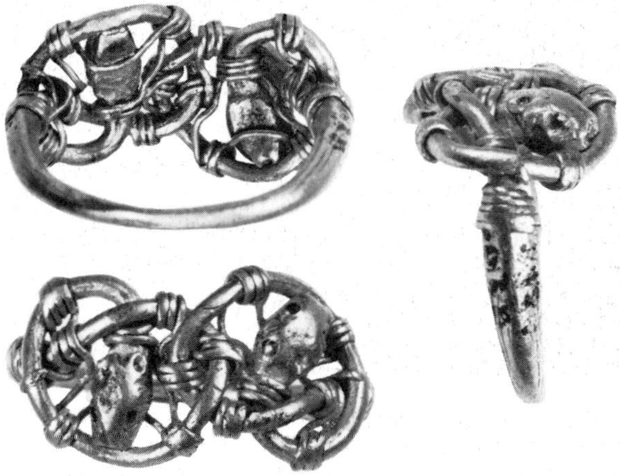

112 Gold ring (diam. 2.5 cm), from Dorchester, Dorset (Oxford, Ashmolean Museum). The design is of interlaced snakes, with wire decoration, and the ring is datable *c.* 800.

The Mercian evidence has already been considered briefly (p. 106). Aethelbald was the second cousin of Ceolred, his predecessor, if the royal genealogies are to be believed. Offa was the first cousin twice removed of Aethelbald. Cenwulf was *fourth* cousin twice removed of Offa. Aethelbald had started as an exile, and Cenwulf may have done so too (there is no trace of him in Offa's charters). Offa's ruthless efforts to protect his son against such dangers are well reflected by Alcuin's comment on Egfrith's death, in a letter to the Mercian ealdorman, Osbert: 'Truly, he has not died for his own sins; but the vengeance for the blood shed by the father has now reached the son. For you know very well how much blood his father shed to secure the kingdom on his son' (Dümmler, p. 179; *EHD*, p. 855). As compared with the seventh century, when the descendants of Aethelfrith of Bernicia and Penda of Mercia had established their grip for 90 years and three generations respectively, there seems to be an almost complete breakdown in the eighth century of the principles of regnal succession. Kingship was now up for grabs by the most distant claimants, and the kings who were the most secure were those, like Offa, who were most ruthless.

But the apparent contrast between the two centuries may only be a function of the greater discretion of seventh-century sources. Violence and chicanery were always inherent in early English regnal succession, and were to remain so long after the Norman Conquest, perhaps as long as the office of sovereign was still worth fighting for. The principles that were supposed to operate can be summarized in the formula: election from the blood royal of a candidate of suitable maturity. Unfortunately, each of the three elements in this formula is ambiguous. It is obvious that electing a king might mean little more than a prudent pledge of loyalty to a candidate who was already in a commanding position; and that deposing a king could involve no more than a *coup d'état* which owed as much to constitutional procedures as Latin American changes of government. Again, the candidate mature enough to defend his kingdom is also likely to be the candidate in the best position to press his claims, inasmuch as his power would enable him to dispose of his rivals as well as his people's enemies. In practice, a successful candidate was most likely to be the designated choice of his predecessor, because he would be best-placed for a smooth take-over; but there was still scope for a *coup* by a disappointed relative, close or distant.

The most interestingly ambiguous principle is that of royal blood. The Anglo-Saxons were undoubtedly among those peoples for whom in theory royal blood was a vital qualification for kingship. The royal genealogies of the later eighth century trace the ancestry of most contemporary kings back to at least one royal predecessor, and beyond him to a pagan god (Woden or, in one case, Saxnot), suggesting that the blood of kings was even semi-divine. However, it is clear that the upper reaches of these genealogies are fiction, including as they do not only gods, but also Germanic heroes who are most unlikely to have had anything to do with sireing the Anglo-Saxon race. If they were fictional for the distant past, they may also have been fictional in parts of their more recent sections. A successful usurper might graft his line onto the royal genealogy at a point so remote that no one could dispute the claim; or he might come to be believed to have divine descent because he was successful. The work of anthropologists has shown that, in preliterate societies, genealogies exist as much to legitimize claims as to record facts. In a case like that of Cenwulf of Mercia, the suspicion can hardly fail to arise that he had no real connection with the Mercian royal house, and in Alchred's case (see above, p. 114) such a suspicion was actually voiced by the Northern Annalist. The evidence does not therefore prove that all Anglo-Saxon kings were of royal blood. It merely proves that royal blood was in principle important: so important that, if it did not exist, it had to be invented.

'The eventual arbiter in matters of succession was the sword', concludes the most recent discussion of these matters (Dumville 1979, p. 33). Strong candidates with dubious claims could promote themselves by force, with election merely the acknowledgement of a *fait accompli*; the required ancestry could be supplied later. This is why Anglo-Saxon royal heads lay so uneasy. Yet one is struck by the fact that two different eighth-century sources go out of their way to use 'constitutional' language for what may have been fairly sordid affairs. Principles did exist, even if they were distorted in practice. A quest for stability is second-nature to nearly all societies, because, as in blood-feud, the alternative is ultimately appalling. Among the Anglo-Saxons, society's need for a focus of common loyalty encouraged belief in the special quality of royal blood, and election was the cosmetic process whereby it reconciled itself to political realities. Peaceful and regular succession was the preferred norm, and blatant infringement of basic principles put the usurper himself at risk. Successful kings could, if they were lucky in their children (as Aethelbald, Offa and Cenwulf were not), found dynasties which might long outlive their effectiveness, as the Merovingians did in Francia. An important feature of eighth-century politics was that efforts were made to fortify the principles of royal succession, perhaps because they were now so often violated.

One of these efforts was the compilation of a corpus of royal genealogies, tracing the real or alleged ancestry of most contemporary Anglo-Saxon kings, except those of Sussex and Essex. The earliest manuscript, one of the very few extant from pre-Viking Mercia, was written about 810. The most recent research suggests that the collection originated in Northumbria during the reign of Alchred, was characteristically adapted by Offa to include his son Egfrith at the end of the Mercian line, and reached its earliest extant form with the inclusion of Cenwulf's ancestry, immediately after his accession. It therefore now seems unlikely that it was inspired by the dynastic and imperial pride of Offa himself, as used to be assumed. Offa had reason to be proud of his ancestry, if the collection was right to trace it back to an earlier Offa, hero of the Anglian homeland; and one of Offa's charters calls him 'King of the Mercians, sprung from the royal stock of the Mercians' (Birch, *Cart.*, no. 195)—perhaps a pointed comparison with the parvenu Carolingians across the channel. But Offa was not the only one to stress the importance of royal descent. One other at least was Alcuin.

In a letter to the men of Kent of 797, to which reference has already been made (p. 99), Alcuin wrote: 'The very peoples of the English, their kingdoms and their kings, fight among themselves. Scarcely anyone can now be found from the ancient stock of kings, and the more uncertain their origin, the more they lack valour' (Dümmler, p. 192). For Alcuin, as for Bede, it was no embarrassment to have kings descended from pagan gods (who could anyway be written off as deified heroes), so long as this descent was illustrious. Even sophisticated churchmen sought political stability in the ancient, originally pagan, concept of hereditary royal charisma, and lamented its disappearance from England. This is a useful clue to the sort of milieu in which the genealogical collection may have arisen, and the sort of reasons why.

But Alcuin's concern went further than this. He was present at the 786 legatine council, and very probably drafted some of its decrees. One canon reads: 'Kings are to be lawfully chosen by the priests and elders of the people, and are not to be those begotten in adultery or incest' (Dümmler, pp. 23–4; *EHD*, p. 837); this is in fact the first western European statement of the principle that only the children of legitimate marriages, as opposed to anyone of royal descent, could hold or pass on claims to the throne. Now it is also an interesting feature of the genealogical corpus that it omits not only apparent usurpers, like Aethelwold Moll in Northumbria or Beornred in Mercia, but also apparent bastards, like Oswy's son, Aldfrith, and his descendants. When it is remembered that the collection originated in Northumbria, when Alcuin was still there, and when it is further noted that it was transmitted to Wales, which was also visited by one of the 786 legates, it becomes tempting to see a close connection between it and Alcuin. At any rate, the genealogical collection, the 786 council, and Alcuin's views may all be seen as different aspects of the same movement to reinforce belief in the special quality of genuine royal blood, for an age which may well have needed reminding of the point.

The 786 council's canon goes on: 'Let no one conspire to kill a king, for he is the Lord's Anointed' (Dümmler, p. 24; *EHD*, p. 838). This reference to the 'Lord's Anointed' may well be connected with the fact that, then or in the following year, Offa had his son 'consecrated king' (*EHD*, p. 180). Ten years later, Eardwulf of Northumbria was 'consecrated' at York (*EHD*, p. 274). These are the first such references in Anglo-Saxon sources, and what

113 (*right*) Ivory panel (30 × 18 cm) from the Genoels–Eldoren diptych (Brussels, Musées Royaux d'Art et d'Histoire). The inscription is in 8th-century Northumbrian script, and the subject-matter (Christ in Majesty trampling the lion and the dragon of Psalm 90 on this panel, the Annunciation and the Visitation on the other) recalls the iconography of the Ruthwell Cross (fig. 89), while its style resembles that of the St Andrew's, Bishop Auckland, Cross (fig. 107). For English ivories in general, see pp. 196–7. Splendid ivories were a significant feature of Carolingian art; and whether or not early English ivories reflect Carolingian influence, the availability of elephant ivory in 8th-century England indicates its far-flung contacts.

114 (*below*) Ivory panel (10.8 × 30.7 cm) from an 8th-century Anglo-Saxon casket (Munich, Bayerisches Nationalmuseum). The scene is apparently an Ascension, with the Virgin between candlesticks, Evangelist symbols and Apostles gazing upwards; style and subject-matter recall figs. 107–9.

they probably amount to is that kings or kings-designate were now being anointed by churchmen with holy oil. It is a question whether this ritual was introduced by the Franks in 751, as a way of legitimizing the *coup* by Charlemagne's father, Pippin, against the old Merovingian dynasty, and copied from them by the English; or whether it originated among Celtic Christians, and was borrowed by the Anglo-Saxons and then the Franks. It is, however, undeniable that the ceremony was noticed by later eighth-century sources, Irish and English, as it had not been before; and this raises the perhaps more important question of why unction came to matter so much at this stage in English history.

The idea of royal unction came from the Old Testament, and the anointing by Samuel of Saul and David, as slightly later liturgies show. It is yet another of the ways in which 'barbarian' peoples in north-western Europe found a model they could understand and imitate in ancient Israel. But why did this particular form of imitation become so prominent in the later eighth century? The ritual has been interpreted as a substitution of divine authority, mediated by the Church, for the ancient charisma of royal blood; as an ecclesiastical take-over of the sanctions supporting kingship. The English evidence suggests rather that unction was intended to reinforce royal charisma; the Church gave its blessing to the election of suitably qualified candidates. Unction then emerges as a further symptom of society's quest for stability in an age when, on both sides of the channel, traditional systems of king-making had been abused or challenged. But it did not, of course, protect kings in fact, any more than had traditional systems. Though eighth-century kings refined the ideology of kingship, and though, as will shortly be seen, they had great administrative power, the moral of the period's political history is that kings were not secure. The paradox of sophisticated ideology and institutions as against political instability will be met again, not least in 1066.

The Carolingians, the Coins and the Dyke

It seems no more credible that eighth-century kings were capable of sophisticated administration than it does for their seventh-century predecessors, and it is no more demonstrable from 'bureaucratic' documents. Yet now we have the facts of Offa's coinage, Offa's dyke, and the brutal control revealed by Offa's charters, to face. Moreover, the administration of Offa's Carolingian contemporaries *is* documented. It has been argued that few of Charlemagne's administrative methods were in fact new; what was new was that so much was now written down. If this is right, Carolingian evidence does more than simply show what was possible for eighth-century kings. It also suggests that even kings like Offa who apparently made little use of writing in government might nevertheless have been capable of effective administration. Carolingian analogies illuminate much in Mercian government. But their most important function is to warn us not to expect too little of Offa and Cenwulf.

The relationship between English and Frankish history in this period is particularly important in coinage. In England, unlike Francia, we have only the coins to help interpret the major changes, and much in eighth-century English numismatic history is still unclear and/or controversial. But the outline history at least is now established, and is set out in the Picture Essay (pp. 62–3). The English development closely mirrors that of Francia. The gold *scillings* reflect the influence of the coins the Anglo-Saxons knew best, the *tremisses* of Merovingian Gaul. The gradual adulteration, and eventual replacement, of the gold content in these coins by silver happened at much the same time in both countries. The early penny, or *sceat*, had its counterparts in the late Merovingian *denarius*, and coins of the same style and fabric were also made in Frisia. Similarly the appearance of the 'new' penny in England (see pp. 59 and 62–3) coincides closely with the introduction of a royal coinage by Charlemagne's father, Pippin, in 755.

The earliest 'signed' English coinage was almost certainly not that in Offa's name, but that in the name of Northumbrian, East Anglian and Kentish kings, which is datable *c.* 758–82. But when Offa's magnificent coinage did appear, it was once again linked with Continental developments. Both Charlemagne's early and his late coinages were influenced by Offa's designs; on the other hand, the still heavier pennies of Offa's last years were probably an attempt to bring the English weight up to the new standard set in the early 790s by Charlemagne. Such a close relationship between the monetary histories of England and Francia is probably an important clue to the economic context of the reform, because it suggests that coins were passing between the two countries as a result of trade.

The place of money in early English economic life, and the extent of trade in north-western Europe as a whole, have been very controversial issues. The evidence is partly numismatic and partly literary and archaeological. With early medieval coinages, it is possible to distinguish between the different 'dies' used for making the same series of coins. It has been shown that an Anglo-Saxon moneyer could probably make up to 10,000 pennies from one die before replacing it with a new one of the same design because the first had worn out. A single coin hoard of, say, 50 coins might contain the products of between about five and about 45 different dies. If a large number of dies is represented in a hoard, and one reckons that each die had at some point produced nearly 10,000 different coins, then it becomes clear that a very large number of coins indeed was in circulation. Calculations of this sort have produced staggering figures for Offa's coinage, from a conservative 2 million up to 10 million; and the implication is that coined money was extremely significant in Anglo-Saxon economic life.

The distribution of coin-finds, and perhaps of mints, is also suggestive. Canterbury remained the major English mint until the Viking Age, and coin-finds are generally most intensive in Kent. But more often than not there was a separate East Anglian mint, producing coins for Offa and Cenwulf as well as local rulers; there was almost certainly a mint at Hamwih, and at times at London; York minted for the Northumbrian kings; and there may also have been mints in the Upper Thames area, and in West Sussex. The distribution of coin-finds extends from Kent along the south and east coasts, up the Thames, and well into the Home Counties. Find-spots include ecclesiastical sites, like Reculver and Whitby, known *emporia* like London and Hamwih, and Roman, or more ancient, roads and cross-roads, as well as, more mysteriously, ex-Roman villas and Iron Age hill-forts. Taken as a whole, this evidence suggests a fairly wide circulation of money, and a connection between it and trade, both external and internal.

Some non-numismatic evidence which points in the same direction has already been cited (p. 101). The implication of Charlemagne's letter to Offa is that trade between England and Francia was significant and extended beyond luxury goods. Both Alcuin and a Frankish source suggest that Charlemagne imposed a trade embargo on English merchants when his marriage negotiations with Offa collapsed, which was presumably a weapon that was calculated to hurt. London had already been described by Bede as an '*emporium* of many peoples coming by land and sea' (*HE*, II. 3, p. 85), and its commercial status under Aethelbald and Offa is implied by an important series of charters granting remission from its tolls to ecclesiastical communities in Kent, in Worcester, and in London itself. Toll was also remitted at Fordwich in Kent and perhaps at the salt-wells of Droitwich in Worcestershire; while Hamwih was described as a *mercimonium* (trading place) in an eighth-century saint's life, and we know from another life that there was a colony of Frisian merchants at York. Place-names and archaeology offer further useful evidence. London was called *Lunden-wic* in Hlothere's laws (pp. 22–3), and York's name was original *Eofor-wic*. The same *-wic* suffix occurs in Hamwih, Fordwich, Droitwich, and across the channel at Quentovic. It also occurs in Ipswich, for which there is no early literary reference to trading, but which, like Hamwih (pp. 102–3), has supplied copious archaeological evidence of industry and commerce. The suffix derives from Latin *vicus*, which may already have acquired the sense of 'market centre' in late antique times, and certainly seems to have done so by the eighth century. All the evidence combines to suggest that money and trade were widespread and went together.

What, then, is the significance of the coinage reform that occurred in Offa's age, and is usually associated with him? It has been suggested that some anonymous *sceattas* of the late seventh, and early eighth centuries were already the responsibility of kings, chiefly on the grounds that the series are so homogeneous as to suggest official backing, and that some of their designs look like royal portraits. But it is a little hard to understand in that case why the king's name does not appear (as non-royal names occasionally did). Late Merovingian coinage, probably the inspiration of the English series, was the responsibility not of kings but of civic authorities and their moneyers. The odds are, therefore, that early English coinage was produced by the merchants who used it, as a convenient unit of mercantile exchange, a known weight of precious metal whose value was guaranteed by its 'trade-mark' design; the more homogeneous series are those of the most prosperous traders (but cf. pp. 62–3).

But we know from the toll-charters of Kentish and Mercian kings that trade was already being exploited in the royal interest. It is therefore possible that a royal currency was introduced as a further way of exploiting the profits of trade at a time when they were growing faster than ever. Both the Carolingians and post-Conquest kings of England took a cut from the conversion of bullion into coin in their name; Anglo-Saxon kings probably did so too. This seems the more likely because, in the later eighth century, Frankish coin-finds become rare in England and *vice versa*. The systematic exclusion of foreign coin in the interests of the royal monopoly was certainly royal policy in the tenth century; the policy perhaps began at the same time as a royal currency appeared. If this policy was not Offa's invention, even in England, all the evidence suggests that he applied it on a new scale. Two conclusions follow. First, the government of Offa and Cenwulf was in this respect no less sophisticated than Charlemagne's; and second, one reason why those Mercian kings were so powerful was that they were tapping the wealth of an increasingly rich society.

Offa's dyke is described elsewhere (pp. 120–1); but something must be said here of why and how the longest and, from the engineering point of view, the most demanding earthwork known to European history was made. Once again, there is no written evidence to help us, other than Asser's statement, 100 years later, that Offa built a '*vallum magnum*' (a great dyke) from sea to sea between 'Britain' and Mercia (*Life* of Alfred, c. 14, p. 12), a point which no archaeological investigation of the structure has either proved or gainsaid. Excavation has, however, begun to yield clues to its purpose. It used to be argued that the dyke was an 'agreed frontier', because it has many gaps, or 'gates', and because it seems to represent a withdrawal from already established English settlements. However, it turns out that most of these gaps were not originally gaps at all, and there were too many Welsh kings at this stage for such an agreement to be plausible. The evidence of the Welsh annals suggests that relations with the English were largely hostile, and it is possible that the English retreat from earlier settlements was the result of Welsh pressure. The dyke may then have been conceived as a barrier against further Welsh penetration, and as a base for the sort of attacks that Offa and Cenwulf are known to have launched in force. It is not probable that it was garrisoned, like Hadrian's Wall. A determined Welsh force could cross it; but their horses would have found it hard to scramble up its 25-foot bank, and any cattle they carried off would have found it even harder to scramble down.

Archaeology cannot say so much about how the dyke was built, but Continental analogies and earlier English parallels may put the achievement in better perspective. The *Danevirke*, across the southern end of the Jutland peninsula, was probably built a generation earlier than Offa's dyke, and shows that another eighth-century ruler could put up a great earthwork without written docu-

Offa's Dyke

Offa's Dyke is the largest archaeological monument in Britain, and the most impressive structure of its kind in Europe. For all that, it has been the subject of only one major survey, and until recently it was largely neglected. Sir Cyril Fox, one of the greatest British archaeologists, published his detailed survey in 1955, though the work on which it was based was completed over 20 years before. His conclusions were generally accepted, and the problems of the dyke considered to have been solved, until David Hill and the Extra-mural Department of the University of Manchester began a long series of piecemeal excavations in 1972. The results have been such as to cast serious doubts both on Fox's methods and on his conclusions; so far from being solved, the problems of the dyke now seem more mysterious than ever.

It is perhaps best to begin with what *is* agreed. The frontier covered by the dyke is nearly 150 miles long (longer than the two Roman walls in northern Britain put together). About 80 miles of earthwork are extant, consisting of a ditch to the west about 6 feet deep and a rampart rising up to 25 feet above it to the east, the whole structure being about 60 feet across. Where the earthwork survives, it generally commands an impressive view to the west. It may be seen at the very south end, from just east of the mouth of the Wye on the Severn estuary along the Wye to a point about four miles south of Monmouth. There is no visible sign of it for the next 37 miles up the Wye to Bridge Sollers, where it strikes out across country, though with many gaps, until it reaches hilly country at the headwaters of the River Arrow. From here to Buttington on the Severn, it is almost continuous and extremely impressive, often rising to points as high as 1,400 feet above sea-level. There is another gap along the Severn from Buttington to Welshpool; thereafter, the dyke again crosses generally hilly country until it peters out as a visible structure near Treuddyn in south Flintshire. Associated with Offa's Dyke are a series of short dykes to the west of the central section, and the very similar, and therefore presumably roughly contemporary, structure known as Wat's Dyke, which runs east of Offa's, from Basingwerk-on-Dee to Morda Brook in Shropshire (about 38 miles). We have the word of Asser (see p. 119) that Offa built a dyke from sea to sea along the Welsh frontier, and a variety of place-names and later traditions establish what is now known as Offa's Dyke as that structure. A very suggestive passage in the early poem *Widsith* (see p. 122) attributes a dyke along the Eider to Offa's Continental ancestor and namesake; the same poem celebrates a certain *Wade*, and a more or less unreliable twelfth-century source associates this *Wade* with Offa in a fight against the Romans. Although such sources prove nothing, nevertheless they show that Offa's connection with such a dyke is an old-established tradition; and there is no archaeological evidence that disproves this tradition.

If this much is clear, most of the rest is not. Fox was quite happy to accept that many of the large and small gaps that are now apparent in the dyke were original. He thought they reflected unfinished work, areas of 'forest so dense' that no delineation was possible, or lines where rivers and ravines rendered fortification unnecessary. Underlying these conclusions, and much of the rest of his work on the dykes, was his view that they constituted an 'agreed frontier'; in support of this view, he pointed to places where the dyke apparently left Welsh fortresses or settlements intact to the west. He believed that the short dykes to the west were early attempts by Anglo-Saxon colonists to block possible lines of Welsh advance, that Wat's Dyke was a first general attempt to protect the rich Cheshire plain, and that Offa's own dyke was the culmination of this to-ing and fro-ing, whereby the English and Welsh settled down to a frontier that they could both live with. In short, Offa's Dyke was an act of peace.

This view does not square with the evidence of Welsh sources for more or less continuous war between Welsh and English in the eighth and early ninth centuries (see p. 119). But, in addition,

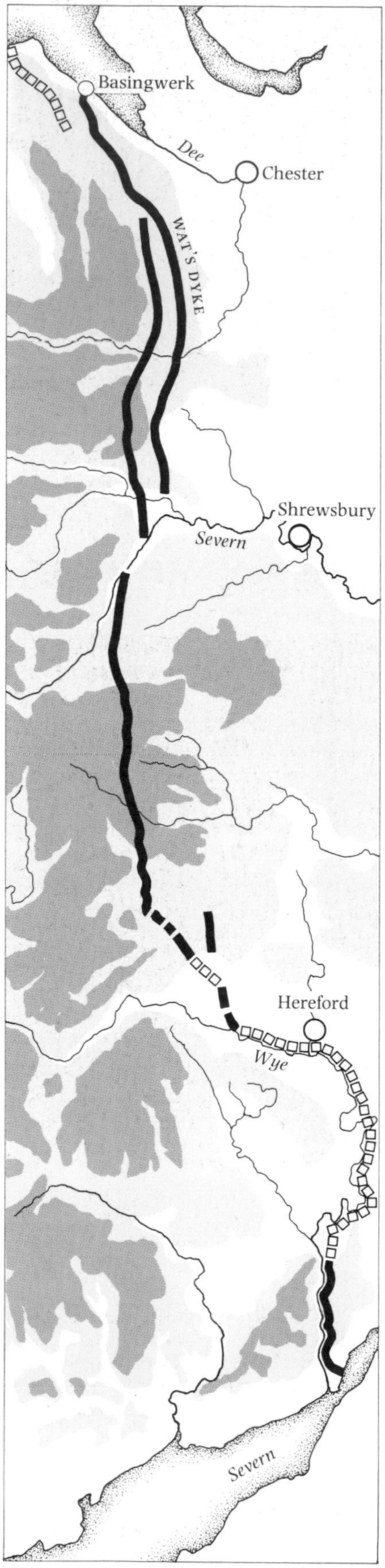

1

Postulated frontier *(after Fox)*   Known earthwork

1 Map of Offa's and Wat's Dykes (from D. Hill, *An Atlas of Anglo-Saxon England* (Blackwell, 1981)). It now seems clear that the postulated N. end of Offa's Dyke, through Flintshire to Prestatyn, never existed; the frontier was completed by the north end of Wat's Dyke, terminating at Basingwerk-on-Dee, where King Cenwulf died in 821. On the other hand, it now seems possible that many of the gaps that exist today were not originally gaps at all; exceptions are the line of the River Severn from Buttington to Welshpool, and perhaps the line of the Wye in the south.

2

3

4

2 Aerial photograph of Offa's Dyke 3¼ miles west of Mainstone, Shropshire (Cambridge University collection).

3 Aerial photograph of the Danevirke, across the base of the Jutland peninsula, and sufficiently formidable to serve as a major military feature in the nineteenth century. It is now known that the main structure dates *c.* 737; that is, it is even earlier than its main English counterpart.

4 Offa's Dyke at Baker's Hill, Gloucs. (photo: C. J. Wright). The ditch was originally 6 feet deep, and the rampart measured from the bottom of the ditch 24 feet high.

the excavations of David Hill and his colleagues have now seriously modified Fox's conclusions. For example, there is no archaeological evidence for the dyke along the most northerly section of Fox's line; it seems that Wat's Dyke served as the northern end of the frontier. There is now some evidence that Offa's Dyke was surmounted by a stone wall, at least in places. So far from areas of dense forest being left ungarded, the analysis of excavated pollen samples has suggested that waste ground was burnt off in order to build the dyke. Above all, almost all the gaps which Fox thought to have been original have now been shown not to be original at all; the ditch can still be detected beneath the latter-day efforts of farmers. Even where no trace of the dyke can be discovered, there is no indication that the gap was deliberate. On the evidence now available, Offa's Dyke was indeed continuous, from sea to sea, the only gaps being rivers that themselves constituted adequate obstacles. It must be emphasized that the Manchester excavations are not complete, and that they have had to concentrate on selected sites where little or no visible evidence survives; to 'dig' the whole dyke would be the largest and most expensive project in British archaeological history. Nevertheless, what we now know suggests that Offa's Dyke was an act not of peace but of war. It was intended to put a stop to the apparently successful Welsh counterattack, which had swallowed up early English settlements to the west; and for at least two centuries it seems to have succeeded in doing so.

Archaeology can say a little about how the dykes were built. There is evidence of a marker-ditch for the work-gangs to follow, and indications of where one gang's stretch ceased and another's began. More important, archaeology can supply a perspective which makes the achievement of Offa's Dyke at least less incredible. Quite apart from contemporary earthworks, like the Danevirke (3), major public works of this order were being erected in Britain as far back as the early Bronze Age. The historian's imagination is defeated by the capacity of an apparently illiterate government to organize this sort of enterprise, but the prehistorian is quite used to such things. The proper conceptual counterpart of Offa's Dyke is not Hadrian's Wall but Stonehenge. To a real extent, it marks not the first great public work of English government, but the last great prehistoric achievement of the inhabitants of Britain, in a tradition stretching back thousands of years.

P. Wormald

115 St Luke from the Lichfield Gospels, probably 8th-century (Lichfield Cathedral Library, p. 218). This sadly mutilated manuscript was evidently once a Gospel book to compare with Lindisfarne or Kells (figs. 76, 98). It appears to have been in wales in the late 8th century to judge from the South Welsh style 'charter' (cf. p. 22) shown on this page, which relates to Llandeilo Fawr; by the 11th century it was at Lichfield. It is impossible to say whether the manuscript was made in Wales; it is in any case a striking testimony to cultural standards among Offa's Welsh neighbours that a church should acquire such a fine manuscript.

ments, since the Danes, as pagans, were still effectively illiterate. More instructive still, becaust it *is* documented, is Charlemagne's abortive project of 793 for a canal between the Rhine and the Danube. Part of what was reportedly achieved in two months is still there, and it suggests that the annals were not exaggerating in their estimates of up to 8,000 labourers involved. Offa's dyke would have posed different, if equally difficult, logistic problems; its construction would certainly have taken more than two months, for it is at least 50 times as long as the *Karlsgrab*. Even supposing that it took the whole reign to build, the calculations for Charlemagne's enterprise suggest that it can hardly have used fewer than 5,000 workmen, and if it was a defensive barrier rather than an agreed frontier, it is likely to have been built much more rapidly. Just as we must reckon with a coinage for Offa running into millions, so we may have to assume his ability to conscript labourers in tens of thousands.

Evidence has already been adduced to suggest that dykes were something of an Anglo-Saxon speciality, as their low-lying homeland would lead one to expect. The enigmatic Anglo-Saxon poem, *Widsith*, ascribes a dyke on the River Eider to Offa's eponymous ancestor in Angeln, though this may be a flattering echo of Offa's own achievement. More significantly, it was in fact from the mid-eighth century, as has been seen (p. 100), that Mercian royal charters begin to stipulate the duty of bridge and fortress work on estates otherwise immune from public services; the terms of Aethelbald's Gumley privilege suggest that, even if the obligation was ancient, it was now being emphasized to a new extent, and reference is made to a 'royal edict'. Offa's charters seem to be concerned not so much with dykes as with fortified places: perhaps such as Hereford and his 'capital' at Tamworth in Staffordshire, where evidence for fortification of about his period has been excavated. But the same system could have been applied to dykes, and a Worcester charter of 836 refers to 'ramparts', rather than fortresses (Birch, *Cart.*, no. 416; *EHD*, p. 518). So it seems that Anglo-Saxon kings may have had an ancient right to the labour of their subjects for common defence, just as they may have had traditional responsibility for the kinless merchant. But just as patronage of merchants now extended to royal control of the coinage, so conscripted labour was now applied to a new scale of fortification, culminating in Offa's stupendous dyke.

Worcester and Canterbury: Bishops, Nobles and Kings

It has been seen that much of what we know of the policies of the Mercian Kings is derived from charters, but that these charters were probably written by scribes of the local cathedral rather than royal clerks. Good examples are the records of King Beornwulf's very important council of Clovesho in 825, whose judgements in favour of Canterbury, Selsey and Worcester were not preserved in official minutes, but in separate charters, each differently formulated and significantly biased in favour of the beneficiary, in the archives of the churches concerned. This means that charters are, in the first instance, evidence of the way kings were seen by bishops and their entourage, but this does not make them any less revealing about the churches that produced them. In the age of Offa and Cenwulf, there are especially good collections for Worcester and, from 798, for Christ Church, Canterbury.

One of the most revealing series of Worcester charters concerns the estate at Ismere, which was the subject of Aethelbald's famous grant in 736 (see above, pp. 95, 97). Some time in the first half of Offa's reign, the grantee's son, Ceolfrith, 'abbot by gift of God and the right of paternal inheritance', gave Ismere to Worcester, 'with the permission of Offa, king of the Mercians' (Birch, *Cart.*, no. 220). But in 781 it was one of a series of estates which Offa complained that Worcester was 'wrongly holding in its power', inasmuch as it was 'the inheritance of his kinsman, King Aethelbald' (Birch, *Cart.*, no. 241; *EHD*, p. 506). Worcester was allowed to keep Ismere and the other estates in dispute, provided it handed over Bath Abbey, and a strategic slice of territory south of the Bristol Avon. But in 816, Ismere was transferred to Cenwulf in return for the 'liberty' of various other Worcester estates 'from all secular services, and from the feeding of the king, princes and their subjects, except only the three cases, fortress and bridge building and army service . . . And if a wicked man be caught three times in flagrant crime, he is to be handed over to the royal vill' (Birch, *Cart.*, no. 357).

Three points can be made about these charters. First, Ismere had evidently become the sort of *Eigenkirche* or family monastery discussed above (pp. 87, 88). Ceolfrith succeeded his father as abbot, and when he decided to transfer it to Worcester, he thought it necessary to anathematize 'anyone of my kindred' who might interfere. Ismere is one of a number of such private minsters that Worcester made a sustained attempt to take over in this period; others were Inkberrow, and Offa's own family monastery at Breedon, Worcestershire. Among the bishops' motives was doubtless the concern to maintain spiritual standards in such communities, but the families involved could be excused for resenting a campaign that cut across their property rights. Second, there is Offa's remarkable behaviour in 781. He had no obvious case for claiming that Worcester was wrongly holding property of his kinsman Aethelbald in Ismere's case, because Aethelbald had formally granted it away, and Ceolfrith had Offa's own permission to pass it to Worcester. The episode can be set beside others in Kent (below, pp. 125–7) indicating that Offa was less concerned with legal niceties than with securing land on any pretext.

Finally, there are the terms on which Ismere was given to Cenwulf in 816: an immunity for other Worcester estates from some, but not all, forms of public service. Immunities, which were important in Carolingian government, first appear in English royal charters at the very end of the seventh century, and become regular in the second half of the eighth. As here, they usually involve the freeing of an estate from the duty of feeding the king, his officers, and even his horses, hounds and hawks. They might also give a landholder the right to keep the fines levied for offences committed on the estates concerned; this is implied by the specification in many charters that the necessary compensation is still to be paid to the victim, even if he lives outside the area covered by the immunity. In the case of this particular charter, the provision that only if a man has been caught three times is he to be transferred to royal authority shows that the immunity did include judicial rights. But nearly all grants of immunity also specify that the lands still owed bridge and fortress service, and were also to supply troops to the army, as this one does. Certain basic royal rights were reserved. Such, it would seem, was the compromise Aethelbald offered the Church at Gumley in 749 (see above, p. 100): they could have so much freedom from royal dues, but no more. To a modern eye, the surrender of rights and responsibilities over an area scarcely seems evidence of strong government; yet this only proves how unfamiliar early medieval methods have become. The exercise of royal rights anyway demanded the co-operation of local officials. By giving a bishop, or even a layman, a vested interest in the proceeds, their loyalty was rewarded at little effective cost to the crown; and in any case, not all royal rights were alienated. Immunities are better evidence for governmental realism than weakness.

A second interesting case in the Worcester archives is that of the ealdorman Aethelmund and his family: it gives us a very unusual glimpse of the sort of powerful men who thronged Offa's court and conducted his business. Aethelmund first appears receiving a grant which Uhtred, 'ruler of the Hwicce', made with Offa's permission; it has an immunity clause, couched in the same terms as the Gumley privilege, which shows that such rights were now given to laymen (Birch, *Cart.*, nos. 202–3; *EHD*, no. 74). In the last years of his reign, Offa himself gave Aethelmund a large estate at Westbury on similar terms. There is now no reference to a ruler (*regulus* or *subregulus*) of the Hwicce; the dynasty had apparently been suppressed, and probably Aethelmund was now himself ealdorman of the province, since he was killed leading a Hwiccian attack on Wessex in 802. His son, Aethelric, took the trouble to prove his right to Westbury, where there was now a monastery, before a royal council in 804; he then promised it by will to his mother, Ceolburh, to protect her from 'the Berkeley people', but he insisted that it was to revert to Worcester after her death (Birch, *Cart.*, nos. 313–14; *EHD*, no. 81). Ceolburh had probably become abbess of her own family monastery at Berkeley after her husband's death; and Aethelric was presumably trying to protect *his* family monastery from the claims of his mother's kindred by promising it eventually to Worcester. At any rate, Berkeley certainly disputed Worcester's claim in 824, and the bishop had to swear to his rights, together with a large number of priests; a long list of oath-takers is recorded on the charter, and some can be identified as members of the Worcester community (Birch, *Cart.*, no. 379; *EHD*, no.84).

This complex and often obscure story also has useful lessons. It shows the local dynasty of Hwiccian *subreguli* being replaced by an ealdorman in Offa's service, as the Kentish and South Saxon dynasties also were. It is another example of the conflicting claims of kindred to a family monastery, and of the way that the bishops of Worcester were taking over such places with the connivance of some members of the kin, if not all. It brings forward the names of the cathedral community at Worcester, and shows that they were called priests, not monks (cf. below, pp. 124–5). Finally, there is an unexpected twist to an apparently rather sordid story. Aethelric's will made bequests to Deerhurst in Gloucestershire, where he expected to be buried, as his father had been. Deerhurst still stands as one of the finest Anglo-Saxon churches, and, significantly, it was enlarged in the

116 The Anglo-Saxon church at Deerhurst, Gloucs. The complex architectural history of this church appears to have included a significant enlargement in the pre-Viking period, which might have involved the addition of either the second or the third storey of the tower shown in this picture of the west wall, as well as the building of *porticus* to the side; it is tempting to associate these developments with the patronage of Aethelmund and Aethelric.

ninth century. Offa's ealdormen could patronize the arts as well as fight his enemies and quarrel over property.

Canterbury cathedral was apparently sacked in Eadbert's rebellion of 796–8 (see above, p. 106), since few of its documents survive from before that date. But for most of the century that followed, a superb series of charters, frequently extant in their original form, ensures that we know more about Kent and its primatial see than about any other aspect of Anglo-Saxon history in that period; and from Offa's time the archbishops also issued their own coinage. It emerges that Archbishop Wulfred (805–32) in particular, a man of whom we should know almost nothing otherwise, was one of the greatest Anglo-Saxon churchmen. Canterbury evidence is interesting in itself (for its magnificent set of illuminated manuscripts, see below, p. 143, and figs. 122, 124), and it also pulls many of the separate threads in this chapter together.

Archbishop Aethelheard (792–805) was from the Mercian monastery of Louth in Lincolnshire (of which, like Tatwine's Breedon—above, pp. 94, 112—little is known). He was probably Offa's appointee, and was driven from his see in 796–8. Then, and also earlier, he was reminded of his duties by Alcuin. These were two in particular. First, he must 'boldly raise the standard of the Holy Cross', and 'counsel your bishops carefully to work with all urgency for the word of life' (Dümmler, p. 46). Second, he must 'bring into the house of God the zeal for reading, that there may be young men there reading . . . and the study of holy books, that they may have among their number him whom they can elect as their pontiff' (Dümmler, p. 190; *EHD*, p. 857). In other words, an archbishop should assert his authority over his subordinate bishops, which included summoning them to regular councils, and he should regulate his cathedral community. Archbishops Aethelheard and Wulfred showed both concerns. Among the earliest surviving Christ Church records are professions of faith and obedience to the archbishop from newly appointed bishops in the Canterbury province, and nearly 30 survive from the ninth century. They are the earliest known professions in Europe, which raises the possibility that they were inspired by the trauma of Offa's attempt to create an archiepiscopal see at Lichfield, at Canterbury's expense. They are certainly evidence of efforts to assert Canterbury's authority, sustained over three generations. The records of archiepiscopal councils are more uneven; but the regularity with which a full complement of southern bishops turns up to witness charters issued in connection with royal councils under Offa and Cenwulf suggests that they were more frequent than extant texts show.

The fact that in 805 Wulfred was indeed appointed from the Canterbury community suggests that Aethelheard had also done something to raise its standards, as Alcuin insisted. But the major achievement in this sphere was apparently Wulfred's own. In a charter of 813, Wulfred said that he had rebuilt the 'holy monastery' at Canterbury. He went on to say that the individual members of the community could dispose of their own 'houses' however they liked, provided that they did not grant them away out of the community, and provided that they regularly frequented the church, the refectory and the dormitory 'according to the rule of monastic discipline' (Birch, *Cart.*, no. 342). The monastic bias of most medieval ecclesiastical history, and of Anglo-Saxon history in particular, has obscured the interest of these arrangements. The communities of priests surrounding a bishop (his *familia*) had an ambiguous status in the pre-Carolingian Church. On the one hand, monastic contemplation was theoretically incompatible with episcopal activity; on the other, the *Rule* of Saint Augustine, which was the normal model for a bishop's *familia*, was almost indistinguishable from any other monastic rule; and, as has been seen, Gregory strongly encouraged bishops and their communities to live as monks (see above, p. 87).

It is a significant illustration of the difficulties of telling

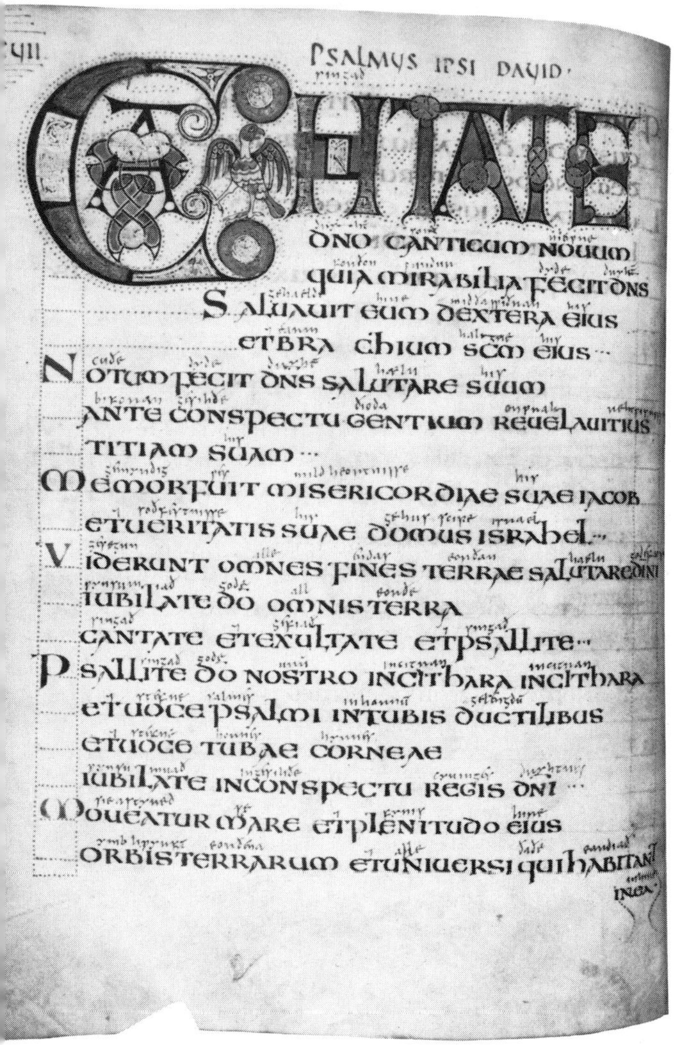

117 The Vespasian Psalter (British Library, MS Cotton Vespasian A.i, fol. 93v; cf. fig. 97). This page, from the opening of Psalm 97, shows the elaborate decoration of initials in the manuscript (which has Frankish as well as insular elements), and also the vernacular gloss to the text. This gloss is usually considered Mercian; if, as seems almost certain, this is a Canterbury manuscript, it is interesting evidence of the Mercian dominance of Canterbury in the 8th century.

monks and ordinary cathedral priests apart that there was much discussion until recently whether Alcuin was a monk or not (It now seems clear that he was not.) But the eighth century, which saw a developing Benedictine monopoly of the monastic profession, also produced a revised rule of Augustine for the bishop's *familia*. Monks and canons (as they came to be called) were now carefully distinguished; the 786 legatine council has a decree to this effect (Dümmler, p. 22). Wulfred's reform was essentially a reflection of this new position. His community, like that of Worcester, was to consist of priests not monks; and since its members were not monks, they were entitled to some private property.

Wulfred also carried through interesting property transactions on behalf of himself and his community. He was apparently from a very rich Mercian family, with extensive property in Middlesex. In a long series of charters, he exchanged lands with Cenwulf or his successors, and bought land outright. The object was evidently to build up consolidated blocks of territory in east Kent, where it could more easily be defended and administered. The sums he disbursed, apparently from his personal fortune, have been added up to 18,000 pence—itself a significant reflection of an individual's monetary resources in the age of Offa, even if not all his payments were in monetary form. Most of these lands were either themselves passed by Wulfred to his community, or left to his kinsman, Werhard, who became its priest-abbot by 833, and left them in his turn to Christ Church. By 833, Wulfred had greatly enriched the church at Canterbury; perhaps equally important, he had given it room to breathe by acquiring a high proportion of the surviving royal land in Kent.

Archbishops of Canterbury were inevitably closely involved with royal power, and the history of their relations with Offa and Cenwulf is clearly the most important thing about them. As has been suggested (p. 100), there was a fundamental ambiguity in Canterbury's attitude to powerful kings. On the one hand, they provided a political context in which the archbishops could hold their province together; on the other, they might threaten the rights of the see. The policies of Offa and Cenwulf illustrate the problem well. A striking feature of the period of Mercian supremacy was the regularity with which all the bishops of Canterbury's province and a number of powerful layman assembled under the presidency of the archbishop and the Mercian king to resolve the grievances of particular churches, and occasionally to issue ecclesiastical decrees. These meetings resemble the *placita* of the Carolingian empire, which often issued secular as well as ecclesiastical legislation, and they show what both king and archbishop had to gain from good relations.

The most significant of Offa's assemblies was that which met the papal legates in 786, though it is only known from the report which the legates sent back. Its decrees are mostly ecclesiastical, like that distinguishing a monk from a canon, but there is also what amounts to secular legislation (or at least exhortation); on qualification for royal office and its sacrosanctity; on the need for powerful men to give just judgements; on the disinheriting of the illegitimate child, and so on. These decrees were expounded both in Latin and the vernacular, and it is a reasonable guess that the text issued in southern England (the same decrees were approved by a comparable Northumbrian assembly) was in Offa's name. This raises the possibility that it was the 786 decrees that Alfred was thinking of when he referred to Offa's laws. There are traces of their influence in Alfred's own code; while a letter of Alcuin, referring to the 'good, moderate and chaste customs which Offa established', which is usually taken as a reference to Offa's lost code, is pretty clearly thinking of the 786 decrees (Dümmler, p. 180; *EHD*, p. 855). At least the latter probably give an idea of what laws Offa did issue.

But if Offa's councils had much to give Canterbury, he could also be a danger. The most serious affront to its dignity was the Lichfield scheme (see above,

p. 106), and the Pope was persuaded to abandon it after Offa's death, on the grounds that it had been promoted by 'enmity against the venerable [Archbishop] Jaenbert and the people of Kent' (*EHD*, p. 860). But it has been seen that Offa also seized Canterbury land, apparently insisting that no Kentish king had a right to grant it (p. 111). Whether Offa was here exercising the 'rights' of the *bretwalda*, or was simply taking opportunities for rapacity as they arose, is not clear on this evidence. But there is another Canterbury charter restoring lost property, and it describes how Offa had clung on to the minster at Cookham, which had originally been granted to Christ Church by Aethelbald (Birch, *Cart*., no. 291; *EHD*, no. 79). As in the case of Ismere (see above, pp. 97, 123) there is no question here of an underking having overstepped the mark, because the original grantor was Offa's Mercian predecessor, A notorious feature of early Carolingian government was their seizure of church lands, on what amounted to extended forced loan, in order to reward their followers. It is possible that Offa's treatment of Worcester and Canterbury property (and of Selsey's too) should be seen in the same light. Lands were of the essence of barbarian kingship, and some kings at least did not much care how they got it.

118 Map showing places mentioned in the text of chapters 5 and 6, down to 865 (other than bishoprics and minsters, for which see fig. 72). Also marked are the locatable meeting places of the Mercian 'grand councils', wics and places where tolls are known to have been levied by Mercian kings, the battles which determined or challenged Mercian supremacy, and places where early Viking attacks are recorded.

From Offa's point of view, Archbishop Jaenbert was too closely linked with Kentish resentment of his overlordship. His lands were fair game.

Cenwulf had the advantage of working with Mercian archbishops, and he began his reign in Kent with some regard to the resentments which had presumably inspired Eadbert's rebellion (see above, p. 106). The Canterbury lands seized by Offa were restored. Kent had its own sub-king in Cenwulf's brother, Cuthred. Lichfield was scrapped and its incumbent deprived of episcopal office by a great council at Clovesho (803). The council was a good example of the sort of assembly that Mercian kings held with their bishops and leading laymen, and it also issued a decree against secularized monasteries, and resolved disputes between three pairs of bishops. The coinage of the archbishops, which, under Offa, had borne the king's name on the reverse, now dispensed with Cenwulf's name, and featured on the obverse a tonsured prelate wearing the *pallium*; the style was probably borrowed from the papacy, and it is striking testimony to the self-confidence of the archbishopric under Wulfred.

But in the 803 decree on secularized monasteries lay the seeds of another great crisis between king and archbishop; and, like the age of Aethelbald, that of Offa and Cenwulf can be seen as ending with tension between 'Church and State'. Wulfred's Council of Chelsea (816) was characteristically Carolingian in its emphasis on the rights and duties of bishop and archbishop, extending even, like early ninth-century Frankish councils, to the condemnation of Irish churchmen, because they lacked an orthodox structure of episcopal government. But the English council was ahead even of the Franks in its sustained attack on lay lordship of monasteries, and in the drastic remedies it sought. In virtual defiance of canonical norms, it gave a bishop the right to appoint a community's abbot or abbess, in order to protect it from the vices of seculars. This is the sort of control that the bishops of Worcester were looking for in their diocese. It deserves some attention as an approach to a problem for which tenth-century reformers were to find a better-known, and more permanent, solution. But it went far beyond what Cenwulf was prepared to accept.

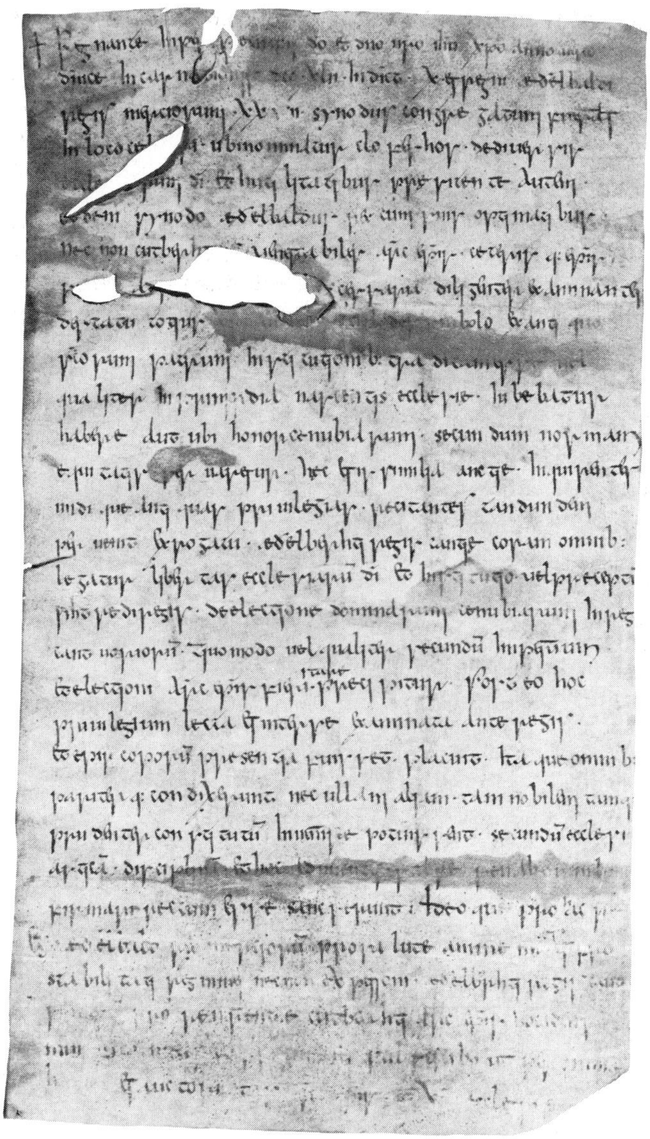

119 Alleged privilege of King Aethelbald of Mercia to the Kentish churches, 742 (Birch, *Cart.*, no. 162, Canterbury Cathedral Library, Chart. Ant. M.363). This charter is in a fine insular minuscule of the early 9th century, which may well be in the hand of Archbishop Wulfred himself. From this, and the document's anachronistic formulae, Brooks 1983 argues that it is a forgery, concocted by Wulfred to reinforce his case against Cenwulf.

What happened next is known only from a long and often almost unintelligible Canterbury record of the Council of Clovesho in 825, which sought to end the dispute (Birch, *Cart.*, no. 384). It seems that Wulfred followed up his council by claiming 'lordship' of the rich minsters at Reculver and Minster-in-Thanet. But Cenwulf's daughter, Cwenthryth, was abbess of these places; they had in effect become royal family monasteries. Cenwulf reacted with fury and almost frightening power to this attack on royal rights. We are told that Wulfred was suspended from active duties for almost six years; and the assertion is to some extent confirmed by the Kentish coinage, which, for a significant time, omits the names of either king or archbishop. We are also told that Cenwulf was able to threaten Wulfred with permanent exile, and it is implied that he enlisted the support of the Pope himself in his struggle with the archbishop (a further hint of the often close relations between the Mercian kings and the papacy). In the end, Wulfred was forced into a very unfavourable settlement, whereby he recovered his rights over the Kentish abbeys, but in exchange for surrendering a huge estate at Eynsham in Oxfordshire, and for a payment of no less than 120 pounds (or 30,000 pennies). Even then, the abbeys withheld 'obedience', and Wulfred had to be satisfied with estates in Middlesex as compensation. Wulfred obviously had a point in his stand over the religious status of the abbeys, but it has now been shown that he had recourse to forgery in order to buttress his claims; and even the Pope seems to have seen the force of Cenwulf's objections, when family monasteries were a fact of life.

Mercian power south of the Thames collapsed suddenly under the assault of Egbert of Wessex within years of Cenwulf's death. It is tempting to seek an explanation in Kentish resentment of Cenwulf's vigorous behaviour, and the *Anglo-Saxon Chronicle* certainly implies that Egbert was welcomed in the south-east. But this impression may be false. Wulfred apparently remained loyal to the Mercian monarchy, and his coinage ceases abruptly at the time Egbert's Kentish series begins. We know that, like Offa, Egbert seized Canterbury property, because in 838 he agreed to restore it (see below, p. 140). The West Saxon kings were either unwilling or unable to summon the sort of council of all the southern bishops that the Mercian kings held. If the Kentishmen did welcome Egbert's conquest, Canterbury may have remembered the point that, as well as threatening its rights, Mercian hegemony had much to offer its campaign to assert its authority throughout the southern province of the English Church. In the end, the real reason for the Mercian collapse may have been the sort of dynastic instability that was studied earlier in this chapter. Mercian kings commanded great resources of money and manpower, but the deployment of their power, and the control of government machinery, depended on a stable relationship with their officers in the localities. In the 820s, Mercian dynastic feud became chronic. We do not know whether Ceolwulf I (821–3), Beornwulf (823–6), Ludeca (826–7) or Wiglaf (827–40) were related to one another, and Wiglaf was to have his own troubles (see below, pp. 138–9). Uncertainty at the top bred tension in the locality; in the circumstances, local society might be glad enough of a new master altogether. The Carolingian empire took longer to die than the Mercian, but was ultimately broken by the same malady.

A final comment on the Age of Offa and Alcuin is provided by yet another possible parallel between the Mercian and Carolingian kings. Charlemagne had ordered the ancient songs of the deeds and wars of kings to be collected, and Fulda's *Hildebrandslied* (see above, p. 82) may be one of the results. Now *Beowulf* is undatable, and modern fashion favours a much later date than used to be accepted. But there remains a temptation to fit it into Offa's period, or that of his immediate successors. The poet seems to go out of his way to discuss Offa's illustrious namesake and claimed ancestor, Offa of Angeln (though he is not polite about his wife). The name Beornwulf is close to Beowulf, and Beowulf's last loyal supporter was called Wiglaf. We know that Offa's age cultivated the ancient heroes, because their names were used to add lustre to royal genealogies. The royal and aristocratic minsters of the period give the right social and cultural context for a literate work that glories in aristocratic and kingly values. But if *Beowulf* was indeed written in the early ninth century, it is significant that the poem is also strongly marked by nostalgia for the heroic days. After about 800, the Anglo-Saxons stopped naming their sons after saga heroes. As well as dispensing land and treasure to his followers, a king like Offa also sold land and privileges for money; and instead of exercising a traditional form of gracious, if sometimes brutal, overlordship over subordinate kings, he did away with them altogether. In his most famous letter, Alcuin asked the monks of Lindisfarne: 'What has Ingeld to do with Christ?' referring to a hero who appears briefly in *Beowulf* itself (Dümmler, p. 183). The assimilation of the new Christian dispensation with the old aristocratic values was not after all acceptable, as Wulfred's campaign against secularized monasteries also showed; Charlemagne's son and successor, Louis the Pious (814–40), would have nothing to do with 'pagan songs'. The Age of Offa was perhaps the end of England's heroic age. And if a poem which begins by singing 'the bygone glory of Danish kings' was indeed composed then, it is a striking irony that the Anglo-Saxons already had reason to think very differently about Danes.

120 (*opposite above*) The Witham Pins: silver gilt, central pin 12.1 cm long, discovered in the River Witham, Lincs. (British Museum). The spectacular ornament has parallels with the Gandersheim Casket, and with other known products of late 8th-century Mercia and southern England.

121 (*opposite below*) Walrus ivory casket, 12.6 × 6.8 × 12.6 cm, from Gandersheim (Brunswick, Herzog Anton-Ulrich Museum). Its runic inscription suggests that it contained a relic of the Virgin and came from Ely, and its ornament may be compared with that of the Witham Pins (fig. 120). It was presumably taken to the Continent by an Anglo-Saxon pilgrim or missionary before the Viking sack of Ely.

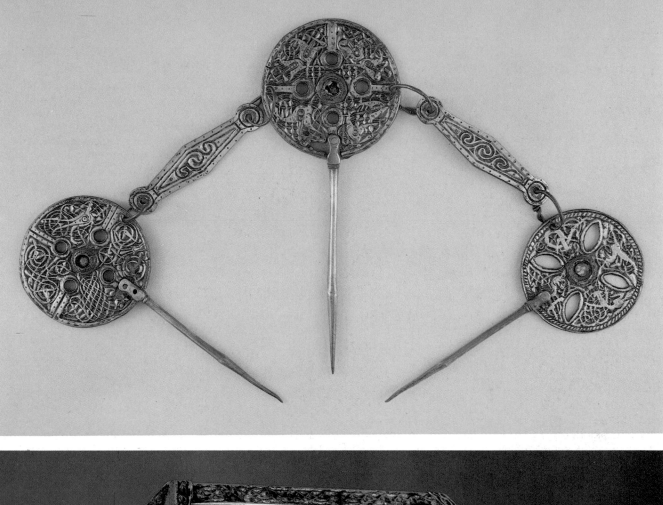

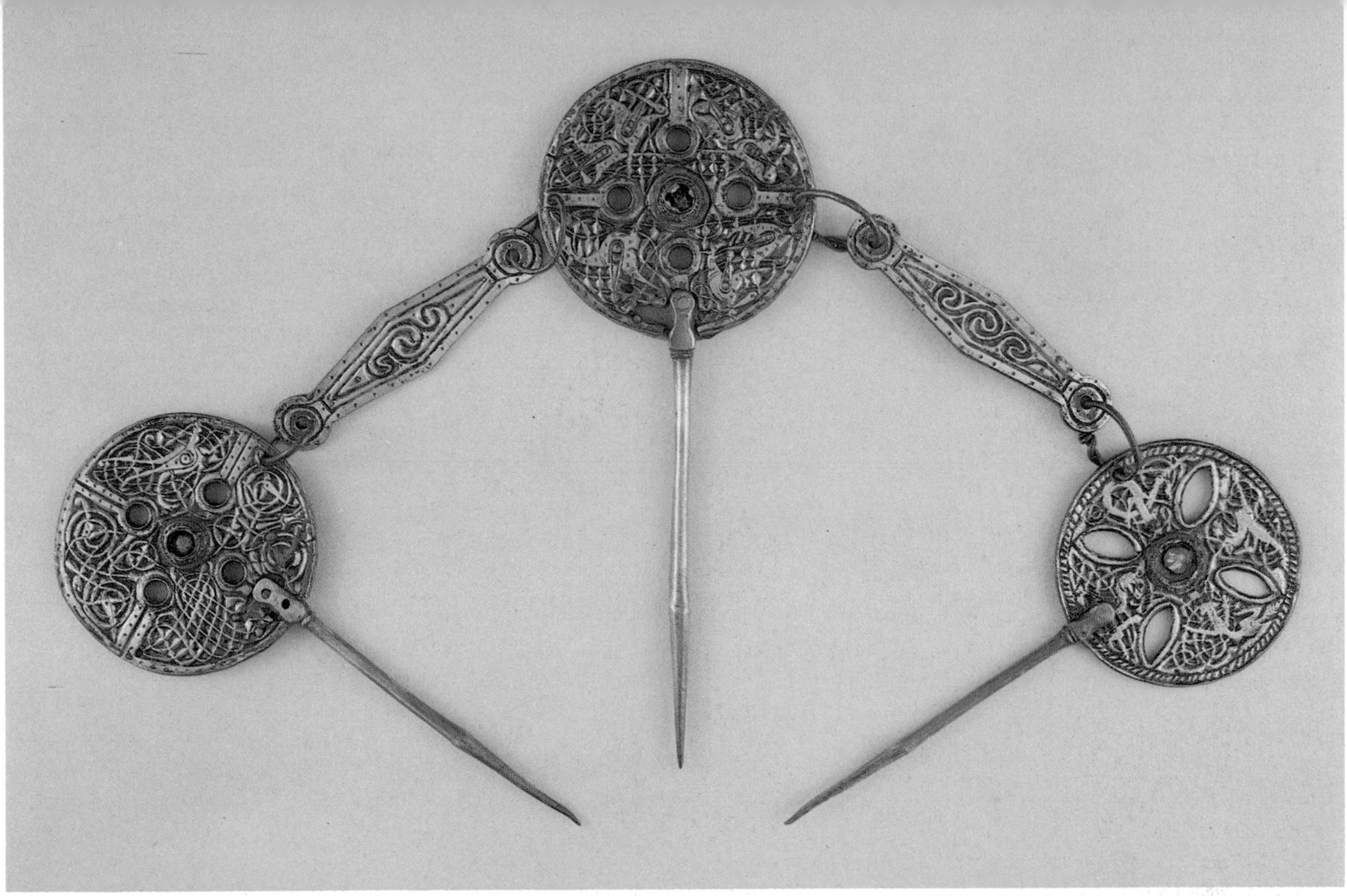

Anglo-Saxon Coins 2: Alfred to Edgar

(All the coins illustrated in this Essay are in the Ashmolean Museum, Oxford, size × 2.)

Before England was partitioned in the 880s, a unified national currency had evolved. Coins of a single design were issued by agreement between the kings of Wessex, the kings of Mercia, and the archbishops of Canterbury, and the issues of each mingled freely together throughout most of England. Periodically the design was changed by all three issuing authorities, and the currency was renewed. The coins were minted chiefly at Canterbury and at a second mint in the south-east, probably Rochester or London—not because the use of coinage was greatest there, but because of the need to convert foreign coin, flowing in as a result of cross-Channel trade, into English money at the ports of entry.

1 Silver penny,
Alfred, early type.

No. 1 is a silver penny of Alfred, struck before 874 by the moneyer Heremod. The same design was produced for Burgred (King of Mercia 852–74) and for Archbishop Ceolnoth (833–70). No. 2, also of Alfred, is a special issue of fine quality minted at London, and with a monogram of the city's name, Londinium, as its type. It is thought to have been struck following Alfred's occupation in 886 (see p. 132).

The creation of the Danelaw destroyed the political framework within which a national currency had functioned, but it could not as easily destroy the monetary and economic realities of inter-regional trade. Because shipping followed coastal routes, contacts with the Continent and between the Danelaw and the Continent, and even with Scandinavia, were normally by way of the Thames estuary or Kent. In the south-east, after the destruction of the Mercian kingdom, a shared issue of coinage was limited to Alfred and Archbishop Plegmund (3, struck for Plegmund by the moneyer Sigehelm), but the same design was copied in the eastern Danelaw. The imitations, which still bore Alfred's name, were clumsy, and, more important, they were on a lower weight-standard than their prototype (4).

2 Silver penny,
Alfred, London monogram.

3 Silver penny,
Archbishop Plegmund.

4 Silver penny, Danelaw,
imitation of Oxford penny of Alfred.

5 Silver penny,
Edward the Elder, Tower type.

6 Silver penny, Vikings of York, *Mirabilia fecit* type.

7 Silver penny, Vikings of York, *Mirabilia fecit* type.

8 Silver penny, Vikings of York, Saint Peter, Sword type, with Thor's hammer.

A special issue by Edward the Elder (**5**, with an imposing architectural reverse design) shows the elegance of which die-engravers were still capable in the south.

No clearer sign of political independence could be given within England than by the issue of a separate coinage. Thus, the Danes of East Anglia struck an extensive series of pennies in the late ninth and early tenth centuries. Yet they too copied an existing design, which had been used by the murdered king Edmund (pp. 135, 148). The coins are anonymous in the sense that they name only him, and they are of interest in showing how swiftly and firmly his cult became established (**6**, slightly blundered, but other specimens suggest that the legend is in the vocative case, *Sce*[=*Sancte*] *Eadmunde Rex*; the large A stands for *Anglorum*).

The coins of the Vikings of York are more original in their designs: there were no earlier silver pennies for them to copy, as the Northumbrian kings had minted *stycas*. It is again noticeable how quickly they saw fit to use Christian symbolism and inscriptions. On no. 7, EBRAICE refers to York, but no ruler is named. The obverse legend, exhibiting political self-justification, is MIRABILIA FECIT, 'He hath done marvellous things.' Another York coin (**8**) combines a reference to Saint Peter with Thor's hammer.

The unification of England by the tenth-century kings was followed by a long struggle to re-establish a unified national currency, successful only from *c*. 973. The creation of *burhs* throughout southern England prompted legal arrangements for the minting of coins in each *burh*. In the form in which they have survived, the laws are part of the decrees issued at Grateley by Aethelstan (924–39), but they would seem to be somewhat earlier in origin. As well as insisting that there is to be only 'one coinage over all the king's dominion', they specify how many moneyers there are to be in each of the principal towns of southern England, listing the places in the order of their seniority and importance as mint-towns: 'In Canterbury seven moneyers; four of the king, two of the bishop, one of the abbot; in Rochester three, two of the king, one of the bishop; in London eight; in Winchester six; in Lewes two; . . .' and so on. The names of the *burhs* as well as those of the moneyers are now often included in the reverse inscription. In all, 35 mints scattered throughout England are known from Aethelstan's coins. No. **9** is a handsome portrait coin from Norwich. But most of his coins, and those of his successors until *c*. 973, bear no mint-name, and can at best be attributed to a region (such as 'the midlands' or 'the north-east') on grounds of style.

In spite of its advantages, the provision of facilities for local minting was ill-matched to the realities of bullion movements, and many of the moneyers at inland places found that there was hardly any work for them to do. Canterbury, Rochester, and London enjoyed much of their traditional importance, and Winchester's role as a fiscal centre is marked out even at this early date.

What distinguishes the tenth century from the ninth is a dramatic shift northwards in the balance of minting. Great quantities of coins were struck, for example, at York, Lincoln, Derby, Leicester, Nottingham, Tamworth, Stafford, Shrewsbury, and Chester. It would seem that there was a general increase in the wealth of the northern regions, and in particular an expansion of the overseas trade that flowed through York, Lincoln, and Chester. Chester seems often to have had more moneyers at work than London. The same geographical pattern persists from Aethelstan's reign through to that of Edgar. No. **10** is a typical coin of the period, attributed to Chester on grounds of style and of its occurence in hoards.

D. M. Metcalf

9 Silber penny, Aethelstan, Norwich mint.

10 Silver penny, Edgar, Chester mint.

CHAPTER SIX

The Ninth Century

The Vikings and King Alfred

'In this year, dire portents appeared over Northumbria. They consisted of immense whirlwinds and flashes of lightning, and fiery dragons were seen flying in the air. A great famine followed, and a little after that, on 8 June, the ravages of heathen men miserably destroyed God's church on Lindisfarne.' Thus the 'northern' recension of the *Anglo-Saxon Chronicle* for the year 793 (*EHD*, p. 181). Seldom in English history has so dramatic an event been so dramatically announced as the coming of the Vikings—a word meaning 'sea-borne adventurer' or 'pirate', which historians apply to the Norwegian and Danish invaders of much of north-western Europe in the ninth century.

There were other Viking raids in other parts of England at about the same time. The *Chronicle*'s main text says that, at some point between 786 and 802, 'the first ships of Danish men which came to the land of the English' landed at Portland, and their crews, commanded by the local reeve to report to the royal vill at Dorchester, promptly killed him (*EHD*, p. 180). Already by 792, a possibly genuine charter of Offa provides for Kentish defence against 'pagan sailors' (Birch, *Cart.*, no. 848). But it is the sack of Lindisfarne above all which seems to set the tone for a century in which the conquests and settlements of the Vikings profoundly altered the history of Church, state and society in England.

Despite the traumas of the 790s, the England of Offa and Cenwulf was not much disturbed by the Vikings. Little more is heard of them in narrative sources until 835. But from then on raids in the south and west of England are regularly recorded, and at some point between 830 and 845 the Lindisfarne monks (happily recovered from the experience of 793) thought it prudent to move Saint Cuthbert's relics inland to Norham-on-Tweed. In 865, a 'great army' invaded England, and it was reinforced in 871 by 'a great summer army' (*EHD*, pp. 191, 193). These forces proceeded to conquer Northumbria (867), East Anglia (869) and most of Mercia (874–7). Wessex itself barely escaped after a number of bloody battles in 871. Its new king, Alfred (871–99), was under heavy presure until, in midwinter 878, the Danish king Guthrum surprised him at Chippenham, and, as the *Chronicle* says, 'occupied the land of the West Saxons and settled there, and drove a great part of the people across the sea, and conquered most of the others' (*EHD*, p. 195).

It was with Alfred's subsequent flight into hiding in the Somerset marshes that later legend associated consolatory visions of Saint Cuthbert, or Saint Neot (or both), as well as his less happy culinary experiences. But he rallied his forces. The *Chronicle*'s words are all the more moving for their restraint: 'In the seventh week after Easter, he rode to "Egbert's stone", and there came to meet him all the people of Somerset and Wiltshire and of part of Hampshire, and they rejoiced to see him. And then after one night he went from that encampment to Iley, and after another night to Edington, and there fought against the whole army and put it to flight . . .' (*EHD*, p. 196). It was apparently a decisive victory. Guthrum agreed to be baptized, and withdrew to become king of East Anglia in 880. In 886, Alfred captured London, and gave it to his son-in-law, Aethelred, who was now ruling the rump of Mercia as ealdorman. In a subsequent treaty between Alfred and Guthrum, the terms of which survive, the boundary between English and Danish spheres of influence was fixed on the line of Watling Street, running from north of London up to Chester. Between 893 and 896, a third 'great army' attacked southern England, but Alfred had used his 15-year breathing space well; with Aethelred's help, he beat it off. In the last decade of his reign, he was able largely to devote himself to the revival of learning, which he undertook with a court of imported scholars. But though Alfred had saved Wessex and part of Mercia from Danish domination, the Northumbrian, Mercian and East Anglian kingdoms had disappeared for ever; the history of every bishopric and monastery north-east of Watling Street was drastically disturbed (with the partial exception of York); and wherever they settled, the Vikings left an enduring legal and linguistic impact.

This stirring tale is usually seen in terms of that familiar English experience, glorious national victory snatched from the jaws of shattering national defeat. The Vikings are a national enemy, like the French, the Spaniards and the Germans later. Alfred is the greatest hero among English rulers, because he led the nation's successful resistance to them. This impression is not just a matter of patriotic hindsight. It also reflects the influence

122 (*opposite*) A page from the Royal Bible (British Library, MS Royal 1.E.vi, fol. 43a). This manuscript was almost certainly produced at Canterbury, and has strong artistic links with the Codex Aureus (see fig. 124 and caption for further discussion).

of the main contemporary source for the period, the *Anglo-Saxon Chronicle*, compiled in Wessex *c.* 892. The *Chronicle* was understandably obsessed with the Danish armies, who dominated the last third of the century, and must, in retrospect, have seemed to dominate the earlier decades also; equally understandable, it has little good to say of them. Its point of view is naturally that of the ascendant West Saxon kingdom, under Egbert (802–39), his son Aethelwulf (839–55), and his grandsons Aethelbald (855–60), Aethelbert (860–6), Aethelred (866–71) and Alfred. Moreover, because the Vikings destroyed the other English kingdoms, the *Chronicle*'s information on events and attitudes beyond Wessex is even sparser than hitherto. But while one can understand the *Chronicle*'s slant, it can also be argued that it seriously distorts one's picture of the period up to Alfred's triumphant defence of Wessex, and thereby distorts one's impression of Alfred's quite remarkable achievement.

In the first place, intensive study of the Vikings over the last 20 years now permits them to be seen in their own terms, and not just as The Enemy. The major difficulty for students of the Vikings is that, as pagans, they wrote little or nothing about themselves, and, as pagans, they had no hesitation in attacking the holiest shrines of the churchmen who did write about them. And whereas most Germanic peoples produced later historians who at least give the impression of reconstructing their pre-Christian past, the Scandinavians produced only the colourful and fictionalized tales known as sagas, or, at best, saga-like histories. We therefore depend, even more than with the Mercian kings, on information supplied by their victims. Whether, as has been suggested, clerical scribes exaggerated the scale of Viking destruction, is another question (see below, p. 147); but, in emphasizing only destruction, and only by Vikings, they undoubtedly present a wholly negative image of their enemies.

Fortunately, being pagans, the Scandinavians still buried their dead with grave-goods, so that we know more about how Scandinavians lived in the Viking age than how their victims did. Archaeology has helped to balance the traditional view of Vikings by highlighting the role of trade as well as plunder in their culture; it shows, for example, that Birka, Hedeby and Kaupang in Scandinavia, and York and Dublin among overseas settlements, were focuses of major commercial enterprise. Similarly, the study of place-names in north-eastern England shows that, whatever damage they did to start with, the Vikings ended by beating their swords into ploughshares, and settling the land (see pp. 162–3).

Second, the concentration of the sources on Alfred's struggle with the Vikings has tended, like a telescope, to foreshorten the history of ninth-century England, and to blur the historian's vision of Anglo-Saxon kingdoms other than Wessex. Probably, the Vikings did not seriously disrupt the rhythm of English life and culture until the arrival of the great army in 865. Kentish charters continue to reflect precautions against Viking incursions, but they also reveal the establishment of West Saxon control in Kent, the increased urbanization of Canterbury, the relations of a prosperous local aristocracy with the Kentish churches, and, for a time, the maintenance of calligraphic standards at Christ Church. The Worcester charters of the same period show some of the same things in the surviving Mercian sphere of influence. Fragmentary annals show something of a temporary revival of political stability in Northumbria. Numerous coins of both Mercian and Northumbrian kings survive, and there are enough from East Anglia to document its recovery of independence. An obsession with the Vikings can lead us to forget that there are positive things to be said about English politics, society and culture in the first half of the century.

Nor should the *Chronicle*'s West Saxon bias deceive one into thinking that all Englishmen saw Alfred as their natural leader against a foreign foe. The very much more abundant literature of the Carolingian empire proves that kings and noblemen sought Viking support in pursuit of private ends, and the Irish annals show the same thing. England had never been politically united to the same extent as Frankish Gaul, and it is unlikely that the English sense of being one people was stronger than the Irish. In the ninth century, a man's first loyalty was not to his country (which was not in any case England, but Northumbria, Mercia, East Anglia or Wessex), but to his family's rights and traditions, and beyond that, to his lord. Inherent in the ethic of lordship was the principle that bad lords—those who did not offer protection and reward, or who cut across family rights—could be disowned. Grievances about power and property could simply override all other loyalties. Moreover, the early medieval aristocracy was to some extent cosmopolitan; they respected their enemies, and may have felt more in common with them than with their own peasants. *Beowulf* shows that Danish kings and warriors of the past could be heroes to the Anglo-Saxon nobility. Alfred, therefore, could not take English national solidarity for granted. He had to create it, and it will be seen that even Alfred did not always succeed.

The fact that, by and large, we have only the West Saxon view of the Viking wars is part of a third and wider problem about the sources for Alfred's achievement in general. Whether or not the *Anglo-Saxon Chronicle* was actually written under Alfred's auspices (see below, p. 156, 253), it certainly gives a more detailed and sympathetic account of him than of any previous king, West Saxon or otherwise. Alfred is also the first English king whose will is extant, which more than compensates for there being relatively few charters from his reign. His law code is the first to survive (at least in its original form) since Ine's, and reflects not only his administrative methods but also his legislative ideals. There are also the books written at Alfred's court. Asser, from St Davids, wrote an intimate biography of the king. Bishop Waerferth of Worcester translated the *Dialogues* of Gregory the Great into Anglo-Saxon. Bede's *History* was translated by an anonymous Mercian, and Orosius's *History Against the Pagans* by a West Saxon. Above all, Alfred wrote translations himself: of Gregory's *Pastoral Rule*, of Boethius's *Consolation of Philosophy*, and of Augustine's

Soliloquies. He was the only European king of the early Middle Ages, or long before and afterwards, known to have written books, and it will be seen how these give a unique opportunity to explore a royal mind (pp. 156–7). Where, then, the problem with Offa is that we don't know enough, and what we do know comes largely from unsympathetic circles, the problem with Alfred is almost that we know too much, and too much from the king's own circle. It is typical that the beautiful Alfred Jewel is the first and only elaborate treasure that can be connected with near certainty to a particular Anglo-Saxon king (fig. 125). Alfred is three-dimensional, as no other early English ruler is. The danger is therefore that one will either take his achievement for granted, or else make him too good to be true.

England before the Great Army (865)

A survey of the English kingdoms before the main Viking assault can begin in East Anglia, where there is a particular temptation to forget that the Vikings did not occupy a vacuum. In the seventh century, we can see that East Anglia was a rich and powerful kingdom, and there are hints of its distinctive ecclesiastical culture. In the eleventh century, Domesday Book shows a wealthy and densely populated area, supporting powerful nobles and churches. But in between our ignorance of East Anglia is almost total. Its kings, from Aethelbert, beheaded by Offa in 794, to Edmund, slaughtered by the Vikings in 869, are literally no more than names. It is only coins that show that a certain Eadwald led an East Anglian rebellion like Eadbert's in Kent after Offa's death; and that after the Mercian kings, Beornwulf and Ludeca, had been killed fighting the East Angles, the latter recovered full independence under kings Aethelstan, Aethelweard and Edmund. But we do at least know that East Anglia *was* powerful enough to remain independent, and it is probably significant that the evidence which shows this comes from coins. From the origins of the English coinage, there was usually an active East Anglian mint, operating even under Mercian kings. The implication is that, as earlier and later, East Anglia was rich, and we know that it remained an important source of wheel-turned pottery. Such evidence is just sufficient to show what we miss in our ignorance of East Anglia.

123 The bronze seal-die of Bishop Aethelwald together with its impression (6.9 × 3.2 cm), from Eye, Suffolk (British Museum). If, as is very probable, this is the seal of Bishop Aethelwald of Dunwich in the mid-9th century, it is of great interest as an almost unique testimony to East Anglian ecclesiastical culture in the 9th century.

Northumbria is rather better known, because, though the splendid series of northern annals stops in 801, the community of Saint Cuthbert preserved isolated details about Northumbrian kings, and later medieval sources contain fragments of a lost northern chronicle. It seems that the early ninth century saw a temporary restoration of political stability. Eardwulf (see above, p. 114) lost his throne in 806, but recovered it two years later, and was the first Northumbrian king to pass the kingship peacefully to his son for over 100 years. The son, Eanred, reigned for over 30 years, the longest recorded Northumbrian reign, and was in turn succeeded by his son, Aethelred II. Only in 844 does the chaotic pattern of the later eighth century recur. Aethelred was expelled after four years' reign, then restored after a brief exile, then killed in 848. His successor, Osbert, reigned for well over 10 years, but was overthrown by Aelle. Osbert and Aelle were still disputing the throne when the great army arrived at York, and killed them both. It is possible that the shadowy kings, Egbert (867–73) and Ricsige (873–6), who ruled Northumbria under Danish domination before the Danes set up their own kingdom, were also descendants of the feuding Northumbrian dynasties.

Northumbria, like East Anglia, produced a coinage in the ninth century, which survives in greater quantities than any other type of Anglo-Saxon coin. These '*stycas*' have been much criticized by numismatists. They were certainly small, and progressively debased until they were almost wholly copper on the eve of the Viking attack. But the coinage was under royal or archiepiscopal control for most of the period, and the lower the value of a currency the more use it is in everyday transactions. It is possible, then, to suggest that the Northumbrian economy was quite heavily monetarized and exploited by the Northumbrian authorities. Yet there is evidence of declining control at the end of the series, as blundered and/or anonymous coins appear. There might be a temptation to ascribe this to the Viking attack, were it not that coins from Osbert's relatively long reign are few, while there are none for Aelle. Monetary collapse apparently preceded the Vikings. Moreover, the mid-tenth century *History of Saint Cuthbert* alleges that these last two kings were robbing Lindisfarne of land. Such scrappy evidence admits more than one interpretation, but it may be argued that civil war had undermined the wealth of Northumbrian kings, who sought to make good their losses at the Church's expense.

AUTEM
GENERATI

124 (*left*) A page from the Codex Aureus (Stockholm, Royal Library, MS A.135, fol. 11a). This manuscript was quite possibly produced at Canterbury; it has strong artistic links with the Royal Bible (fig. 122) and with other probable Canterbury manuscripts (figs. 130, 135; cf. p. 143). The badly mutilated Royal Bible is datable 800–50, and might well have been comparable in size and magnificence to the Codex Amiatinus itself (fig. 91, and pp. 74–5); the Evangelist symbol of Saint Luke in its arch recalls the iconography of the Gospels of Saint Augustine (fig. 45), and the illustrations it is known to have once had of scenes in the life of Christ have parallels in early 9th-century Carolingian manuscripts. The perhaps rather earlier Codex Aureus has Evangelists even more reminiscent of the Gospels of Saint Augustine, and has panelled lettering similar to the Vespasian Psalter (fig. 97) and the Royal Bible (with which it also shares purple-stained pages). The page shown has an inscription recording its purchase from the Vikings and presentation to Christ Church, Canterbury, by Ealdorman Aelfred and his wife (see p. 148).

125 (*above right*) The Alfred Jewel (6.2 × 3.1 × 1.3 cm), found 4 miles from Alfred's one-time refuge and later abbey at Athelney, Somerset, and the Minster Lovell Jewel (diam. 2.3 cm), found at Minster Lovell, near Oxford (Oxford, Ashmolean Museum). The Alfred Jewel has an openwork gold frame, with the inscription AELFRED MEC HEHT GEWYRCAN ('Alfred had me made'), and a decorated gold back-plate enclosing a rock crystal over a figure in cloisonné enamel; the gold animal head at the base has an aperture for a small rod. In spite of the absence of a royal title, there is little reason to doubt that King Alfred commissioned this remarkable piece. The iconography has presented more problems; there is some resemblance to the Sight figure on the Fuller Brooch (fig. 126), which has led to the suggestion that Sight is depicted here also; more plausible, perhaps, is the suggestion that Christ as Wisdom is represented, since he is shown holding two similar objects on Irish crosses and in the Book of Kells. The aperture at the base has led to the suggestion that this is one of the *aestel*, or book-markers, which the king circulated with his translation of the *Pastoral Rule* (see p. 157 below). The Minster Lovell Jewel was apparently made in the same workshop, and perhaps for the same purpose.

126 (*below right*) The Fuller Brooch (diam. 11.4 cm), silver and niello, provenance unknown (British Museum). The style indicates a date in the second or third quarter of the 9th century; the iconography represents a striking and unique depiction of the five Senses: Sight in the centre, Taste upper-left, and then clockwise, Smell, Touch and Hearing. As a homiletic theme, the five Senses was used by Gregory the Great, and later by Abbot Aelfric (below, pp. 201ff.).

127 Bronze bucket (26.3 × 25.6–17.5 cm) from Hexham (British Museum). This unlovely, if unusual, object is of interest because, when unearthed near the abbey wall, it contained up to 8,000 Northumbrian *stycas* of the 9th century. There were more Anglo-Saxon coins in the bucket than have survived from the whole of southern England before 900.

Narrative evidence for the last decades of the Mercian kingdom is even sparser than for Offa and Cenwulf. The *Chronicle* for 853 records how King Burgred (852–74) mounted a major attack on the Welsh which may have administered the *coup de grace* to Mercia's old enemy, Powys. It could be indicative of declining Mercian power, however, that he sought the help of Aethelwulf of Wessex to do so, and the alliance led to his marriage to Aethelwulf's daughter, Aethelswith (a lady whose ring survives). There are also hints of dynastic trouble in Mercia. Anglo-Saxon royal families sometimes had alliterative names, most obviously in early Wessex and Essex, where names beginning in 'C' and 'S' respectively are almost universal. On this far from conclusive basis, it can be suggested that three different families were competing for the throne from 823 onwards. Cenwulf's brother, Ceolwulf, was deposed in favour of Beornwulf, whose name suggests the possibility of a link with Beornred, Offa's rival in 757. To judge from their names, neither Ludeca, who replaced Beornwulf in 826, nor Wiglaf (827–40) were related to their predecessors. In 840, the 'B' dynasty returned in Berhtwulf (840–52) and Burgred. But when Burgred retired to Rome, in apparent despair at the Viking onslaught, his successor was Ceolwulf II (874–?81). The *Chronicle* scornfully dismisses him as a Danish nominee, and only a 'foolish king's thegn' (*EHD*, p. 194); but, on charter evidence, he was acceptable to the Mercian bishops and nobility, and his name suggests that he came from the house of Cenwulf.

These impressions are given some extra force by the cults of two ninth-century Mercian royal saints. Kenelm, alleged son of Cenwulf, was supposed to have been murdered by the lover of his sister, Abbess Cwenthryth (see above pp. 106, 127), and was commemorated at Cenwulf's family monastery of Winchcombe. Wigstan, son of Wiglaf, was killed, more suggestively, by Berhtferth, son of King Berhtwulf, and was buried and revered at Repton. Whatever the truth of the stories, the cults are fact; and in some other cases in Anglo-Saxon history (most obviously, Edward the Martyr, killed in his half-brother's favour in 978), dynastic trouble seems to underlie cults of this type. It may be that the cult of murdered kings and princes focused or released the social and political tension of a dynastic feud. If these conclusions about Mercian dynastic instability are right, the case of Ceolwulf II shows how useful to the Danes such disputes could be.

Such shadowy evidence apart, Mercian history in this period is illuminated, like Northumbria's, by coins, and, unlike Northumbria's, by large numbers of charters. Mercian coinage was prolific, especially under Burgred, whose coins are commoner today than those of any one Anglo-Saxon king before him. But if coinage evidence suggests, as in Northumbria, a more effective kingship than one might otherwise expect, an ominous feature, as in Northumbria, is that from 871, Burgred's pennies were debased, and their diameter reduced. It is possible that Mercian royal wealth was by this time in decline. The charters of the Mercian kings, after their loss of Kent, are preserved largely in the Worcester archives, but are still sufficiently numerous to show something of the power of Wiglaf, Berhtwulf and Burgred. Two examples are perhaps particularly instructive.

In 836, Wiglaf gave the minster at Hanbury immunity from feeding the king, his officers and his messengers, 'and from all building of the royal residence', reserving only 'the construction of ramparts and bridges' (Birch, *Cart.*, no. 416; *EHD*, no. 85). The charter is extant in its original form, and has several significant features. In the first place, it is witnessed by the archbishop of Canterbury, and by an almost complete list of southern bishops; in other words, it suggests that Wiglaf was still able to hold the sort of great council that earlier Mercian kings held, despite Egbert's victories in the 820s. West Saxon supremacy may not yet have been secure.

Secondly, like many late Mercian royal charters, it is a grant not of land but of immunity; and its endorsements reveal that, whatever the pious sentiments of the main text, such privileges were not had for nothing. Wiglaf was given a life interest in one estate, and his earldorman, Mucel, received another on the same terms, while Ealdorman Sigered received 600 shillings in gold. Late Mercian kings were not simply alienating their rights and those of their officials; they were selling them for land and treasure. It is a more constructive policy than it looks at first sight, but it could imply that the Mercian kings were running short of land.

These implications are perhaps further brought out in a second Worcester charter, dated 840. We are here told that King Berhtwulf had robbed Worcester of lands, and granted them to his own men. The bishop achieved restitution under the terms of the charter, but he had to pay even for this; it cost him 'four very choice horses, and a ring of 30 mancuses' (a sum in gold worth 30 silver pennies), 'and a skilfully wrought dish of three pounds, and two silver horns of four pounds' (Birch, *Cart.*, no. 430; *EHD*, no. 86). This is one of a number of charters of this period in which Mercian kings are accused, like their Northumbrian contemporaries, of robbing the Church. In another document of 849, Berhtwulf received a long lease on various estates from the bishop of Worcester, the condition being that 'the king be more firmly the friend of the bishop and his community', and would not rob them in future (Birch, *Cart.*, no. 445)!

It is not possible to be certain what these transactions mean. Just as Wiglaf seems to retain some of his predecessors' role with Canterbury and the southern English Church, so Berhtwulf can be seen as exercising the same ruthless power over Church rights and property as Offa and Cenwulf. Neither Wiglaf nor Berhtwulf gives the impression of an effete kingship. Yet it is tempting to remember in this connection what Bede had written to Archbishop Egbert over a century before about the long-term consequences of excessive generosity to bogus monasteries: 'a complete lack of places where the sons of nobles and of veteran thegns can receive an estate' (*Ep. ad Egb.*, p. 415). It may be that the reason why Mercian and Northumbrian kings were robbing the Church in the mid-ninth century, and the reason why so many Mercian royal charters are grants of privilege rather than land, is that their landed resources were drying up, and there was little left with which to endow either the Church or their secular followers. At any rate it is fairly clear their policies caused resentment in churchmen. The history of Northumbria after the Viking attack would reveal the possible results (see below, pp. 154–5).

The West Saxon kingdom was obviously the success story of the first half of the ninth century, even if, by and large, we have only its own word for it. In 829, Egbert followed up his conquest of the south-east by an outright conquest of Mercia and Essex, and by marching on up to Northumbria, where, in the *Chronicle*'s words, the Northumbrians 'offered him submission and peace' (*EHD*, p. 186). It is at this point that the chronicler proudly adds Egbert to Bede's list of *bretwaldas*. Egbert does indeed appear in one list of Mercian kings, and he issued coins from the London mint as king of Mercia. But his triumph did not last. The Northumbrian chronicle incorporated in Roger of Wendover's thirteenth-century history shows that the Northumbrian campaign was a bloodier affair than the West Saxon annalist implies. 'When Egbert had obtained all the southern kingdoms, he led a large army into Northumbria, and laid waste that province with severe pillaging, and made King Eanred pay tribute' (*EHD*, p. 281). This is a good illustration of how a king claimed as *bretwalda* by sources from his own kingdom can look much less acceptable when we have sources from elsewhere; it also shows the sort of resentments that still divided England on the eve of the main Viking attack.

It is thus no surprise that Wiglaf recovered his throne and the London mint within a year. In 831, he made a grant to Archbishop Wulfred, who may not have been enthusiastic about West Saxon overlordship, as has been seen (p. 128). In 836, he presided over a council of the whole southern Church (see above, p. 138). Even the shadowy East Saxon kingship, last survivor of the 'minor' kingdoms, lived on under Mercian dominance, to disappear at an unknown point in the ninth century. The West Saxon kings were called 'King of the Southern English', and so on, in their charters, like Mercian overlords earlier; but unlike them they never held great

128, 129 Gold rings, decoratd with niello, of Aethelwulf (above), king of Wessex, and his daughter, Aethelswith (below), queen of Mercia (see pp. 138, 140); the former (diam. *c.* 3 cm) found at Lavenstock, Wilts, the latter (diam. 2.6 cm) at Sherburn, Yorks, both now in the British Museum. Aethelwulf's name and title can be read around the base of his ring, and are an integral part of the design; Aethelswith's are merely scratched on the inside of hers. The designs (?peacocks in confrontation, and an Agnus Dei) perhaps reflect the pronounced piety of Alfred's family.

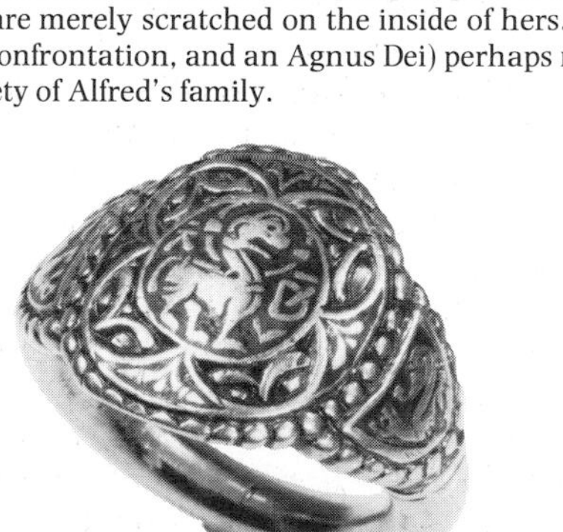

councils of all southern bishops. Though certainly the most powerful kings of the day, they were perhaps further from uniting England than Offa.

But one thing Egbert did achieve was to solve the West Saxon dynastic problem. Aethelwulf was the first West Saxon king to succeed his father since 641. Two important charters show how it was done. The record of the Council of Kingston (838), which survives both in Canterbury and West Saxon 'originals', shows that Egbert restored property he had seized from Canterbury (p. 128), on condition that 'we ourselves and our heirs shall always hereafter have firm and unshakable friendships from Archbishop Ceolnoth and his congregation at Christ Church' (Birch, *Cart.*, no. 421). A grant of the same year to Winchester has the same condition in the same words (Birch, *Cart.*, no. 423). Egbert had only a year to live; he was buying support for his son. Moreover, Kingston was, by the early tenth century, the place where West Saxon kings were crowned; it is not impossible that, on this occasion, the bargain was sealed by the unction of Aethelwulf, just as Offa sought to secure Egfrith's succession before his own death by having him anointed.

Aethelwulf himself, however, had to face the problem that he had four sons when his turn came. Even if there was no question of dividing the kingship between them (and there may have been, as in Frankish Gaul), each brother was entitled to a share of the royal land, as also were each brother's heirs; this could only deplete royal landed resources. Exactly what Aethelwulf did about this is not entirely clear. But, to judge from the extant will of his youngest son, Alfred, he insisted that each brother was to succeed to the throne in turn, and that the younger brothers were to allow the oldest survivor a life interest, as king, in their share of the royal lands. Alfred's will shows that this arrangement caused some controversy, and it will be seen that Alfred's own nephew was very far from satisfied. We know that Aethelbald, the eldest son, launched a serious rebellion when his father was away in Rome (855–6). But the four sons did succeed their father in turn, and apparently did so peacefully. Whether by good judgement or good luck, the West Saxon kingdom was spared the sort of dynastic trouble that beset Northumbria and perhaps Mercia as they faced the Viking threat.

For the West Saxon kings of the ninth century, as for the Mercians earlier, the most important charters survive from the archives of Christ Church, Canterbury, and the other Kentish churches. They show West Saxon rule in Kent as differing significantly from that of Offa and Cenwulf. There are few grants by the kings to Archbishops Ceolnoth (833–70) and Aethelred (870–89) or to other churches, though there are no apparent cases of their seizing Church lands either. Instead, there are a number of royal grants to Kentish laymen, and of grants by these laymen to the Church. Excellent examples are two texts associated with Badanoth Beotting. The first is a grant of 845 by Aethelwulf to his official, Badanoth, at the instance of Ealdorman Alchere, and in exchange for fifteen mancuses of gold (cf. p. 139), of lands in and around Canterbury, free of all obligations (Birch, *Cart.*, no. 449). The second is Badanoth's will, written in the same Christ Church hand as the royal charter, and dating between 845 and 853. Badanoth declares that he is giving himself to Christ Church, and entrusting his wife and children to the patronage of the community. His family is to enjoy the land he obtained from Aethelwulf, and entertain the community 'at my anniversary'. After their death, the land is to go to the community in perpetuity, and whoever receives it from them is to 'observe the same custom of providing a feast at my anniversary as my heirs may previously establish, and therewith attain to the divine reward of my soul'. We are told that two copies are to be made, one to be kept by the community with its deeds (which is presumably the text that survives), and the other by Badanoth's heirs (Birch, *Cart.*, no. 417).

Badanoth's will is one of a series of such documents from ninth-century Kent. The family of the Ealdorman Alchere, who appears to have been important in Kentish government before being killed by the Vikings in 853, made several bequests of food-rents to various churches; in one case, with the significant proviso that, 'if . . . any panic should arise through a heathen invasion, so that this cannot be provided that year, then twice the amount must be given in the following year' (Birch, *Cart.*, no. 501). Among the interesting features of Badanoth's case are the evidence it supplies of royal grants of urban property; of the fact that laymen kept their own copies of transactions that involved them, even if their grants, like those of kings, were actually written in the local church; and of a sincere lay piety, however much inspired by fear of the future life, in an age more notorious for secular 'oppression' of the Church. Thanks to the survival of so many ninth-century Canterbury charters, we not only learn about kings' relations with their greatest officers and followers, but can also, for the first time, see something of a whole local society going about its business.

The charter collections of the main churches in Wessex proper, Winchester, Abingdon, Malmesbury, Sherborne and Glastonbury, have aroused much scholarly suspicion, and only one text of the period survives in its original form. But the Abingdon cartulary, in particular, contains a number of interesting documents. One is a text of the general privilege of 854 in which Aethelwulf granted a tenth part of all his lands to the churches of his kingdom (Birch, *Cart.*, no. 471). This transaction has been regarded with positively aggressive suspicion, and neither the Abingdon text nor those in other Wessex cartularies can be genuine as it stands. But we know from Asser that the grant took place, and while all extant texts have probably been tampered with, it is inconceivable that a number of different churches could all have forged the same sort of text in the same sort of words. What Aethelwulf gained from it is still unclear. What does seem clear is, first, that Aethelwulf was a king of perhaps more than conventional piety, as his pilgrimage to Rome with the young Alfred in 855 also suggests; and, second, that Aethelwulf was anyway both rich and generous.

130 Evangelist portrait and symbol (St Mark) from the Book of Cerne (Cambridge University Library, MS Ll.1.10, fol. 12 b). This collection of devotional texts, datable to the first or second quarter of the 9th century, has often been ascribed to Bishop Aethelwald of Lichfield (818–30), but it now seems likely to be a 9th-century copy of a collection put together for an earlier Aethelwald, Bishop of Lindisfarne (721–40); the strong iconographical resemblance between this manuscript and the Royal Bible (fig. 122) would imply that this was another Canterbury manuscript.

This last point, and its possible implications, are further suggested by other Abingdon documents. In 844, Berkshire must still have been in Mercian hands, as it probably had been since Offa's day, if not before. We know this because, in a charter of that year, Berhtwulf of Mercia persuaded the bishop of Leicester to give him an estate at Pangbourne in perpetuity, in exchange for an immunity for certain unnamed monasteries; and he then transferred it, with a wholly unqualified immunity, to an ealdorman, Aethelwulf (Birch, *Cart.*, no. 443). The transaction is typical of the Mercian kings of the period, and one wonders how the bishop of Leicester felt about royal 'persuasion'. About 20 years later, however, the same Aethelwulf received ten hides at Wittenham from King Aethelred of Wessex (Birch, *Cart.*, no. 534). Here, there is no suggestion that the land came originally from the Church, and the immunity is qualified by the three customary services of bridge, fortress and army. Were the West Saxon kings then richer in land than their Mercian counterparts? Could they afford not to pressurize the Church in the same way, and to be less generous in the immunities they gave laymen? If so, it may not be coincidence that Berkshire passed from Mercian to West Saxon control in this period, presumably in time for Alfred to be born at Wantage in 848; and that Ealdorman Aethelwulf, a Mercian who was buried at Derby, was killed fighting the Danes for King Aethelred in 871.

The wealth of the West Saxon kings is brought out by other evidence. In his will, King Alfred disposed not only of numerous estates, but of movable wealth running into thousands of pounds; and Asser spends some time on his munificence, whether in the decoration of buildings, or

131, 132 Silver-gilt chalice (12.6 cm high), and silver horn-mounts engraved with niello decoration (21.4 cm, 18.2 cm), from the Anglo-Saxon silver hoard found at Trewhiddle, Cornwall (British Museum). The hoard contained several other items, including a striking silver scourge, and coins (one from Northumbria) which dated its deposit 872–5. It is impossible to say how this impressive collection came to be left down a Cornish tin-mine at this date; Viking loot is perhaps a possibility. The hoard is at least evidence of the silver wealth of late 9th-century England.

the reward of his secular followers and craftsmen, or charitable causes. The West Saxon kings inherited the main English mint at Canterbury, and established others at Rochester (which they may have shared with Mercian kings) and Southampton. There is little evidence of debasement. On the contrary, in the 880s, Alfred raised the weight of the West Saxon penny to that of Charlemagne's heaviest currency. What his motives were is not clear; it is not impossible that he was consciously imitating Charlemagne's imperial image, and it will be seen that he had reason to do so. Alfred's heavy penny does at least show that he had access to ample reserves of silver.

Several conclusions may be drawn about pre-Viking England. Perhaps the clearest, and most significant, is the strong position of the house of Wessex even before Alfred. If they did not actually dominate the other kingdoms, they were nearer to doing so than their rivals. They had established their prestige in a series of spectacular victories, not only against the Mercians, but also, as late sources make even clearer than the *Chronicle* itself, at the expense of the Cornish and Welsh. Their dynasty was by Northumbrian, and perhaps by Mercian, standards stable. There is some, if not conclusive, evidence that they had more landed and movable wealth than Northumbrian and Mercian kings. The Pope wrote to Archbishop Aethelred of Canterbury in 878 implying that even Alfred had his eye on Church lands and privileges, but there is little charter evidence that West Saxon kings had outraged the saints of their kingdom by rifling their property. In any assessment of Alfred's achievement, due credit must go to his predecessors as kings of Wessex.

133 Cast bronze brooch (diam. 3.5 cm), found at Boxmoor, Herts (Oxford, Ashmolean Museum); it is apparently modelled on a gold *solidus* of the Frankish Emperor, Louis the Pious (814–40), and is itself a Frankish piece. As such, it is a further small hint of abiding Frankish contact with England.

Perhaps the most striking illustration of the West Saxon dynasty's confidence and prestige is Aethelwulf's second marriage. On his way home from Rome in 856, he married Judith, daughter of the Frankish King Charles the Bald (840–77), the only known case, apart from Aethelbert's (see above, p. 38) of an Anglo-Saxon king marrying into a Continental royal family. The marriage is generally notorious for Judith's scandalous subsequent behaviour: on Aethelwulf's death, she married Aethelbald, his eldest son, in express defiance of the ecclesiastical prohibition which had also been breached by Aethelbert's son; and, not content with that, she eloped with Baldwin of Flanders when Aethelbald was dead. But Judith, like most ninth-century Frankish princesses, was a cultivated lady; and it is a reasonable guess that she brought with her to the court where the young Alfred was growing up some of the culture as well as the aura of the Carolingian monarchy.

In general, the glimpses that we get of English society before the main Viking onslaught show a powerful and wealthy aristocracy, profiting from government service (or from the sale of their privileges to churches), and from the labour of a well-subordinated peasantry. Worcester charters of the 880s show men and their families being transferred with estates, like serfs (Birch, *Cart.*, nos. 547, 559). The Alfredian translation of Orosius used *ceorl* as if it meant a *freed* man, rather than a *free* man, implying that *ceorls* were at least to some extent at a lord's disposal. Alfred's laws insist that all 'free men' are entitled to public holidays, as if they might otherwise have been forced to work (*Laws of Alfred*, c. 43, pp. 84–5). In general, Alfred's laws make more of class distinctions, and the rights of lords, than Ine's. Charters as well as coins suggest the further growth and monetarization of the English economy. Prices are normally paid for lands or privileges. Payment was not always in coin, as opposed to precious objects of a given weight. But the will of a Kentish royal reeve, perhaps the brother of Ealdorman Alchere, says, among other things, that a silver penny is to go to every 'servant of God' in Kent (Birch, *Cart.*, no. 412), as if minted bullion was widely available. One Canterbury charter refers to a by-law that two feet of 'eave's drip' be left between two houses in the town, showing that its population was becoming densely concentrated (Birch, *Cart.*, no. 519). King Burgred granted the bishop of Worcester 'a profitable little estate in the town of London', with the right to free use of 'the scale and weights and measures as is customary in the port' (Birch, *Cart.*, no. 439; *EHD*, no. 92); London property was worth having, as was dispensation from payment (presumably to the king) for the use of authorized weights and measures. One reason why the Vikings attacked England was its movable wealth in coin. But the towns where trade was increasingly concentrated would, under Alfred, play a critical part in their repulse (see below, p. 152–4).

In a famous letter, with which he prefaced his translation of Gregory's *Pastoral Rule*, King Alfred bemoaned the decay of learning in England, even before 'everything was ravaged and burnt' (*EHD*, p. 889). His strictures are

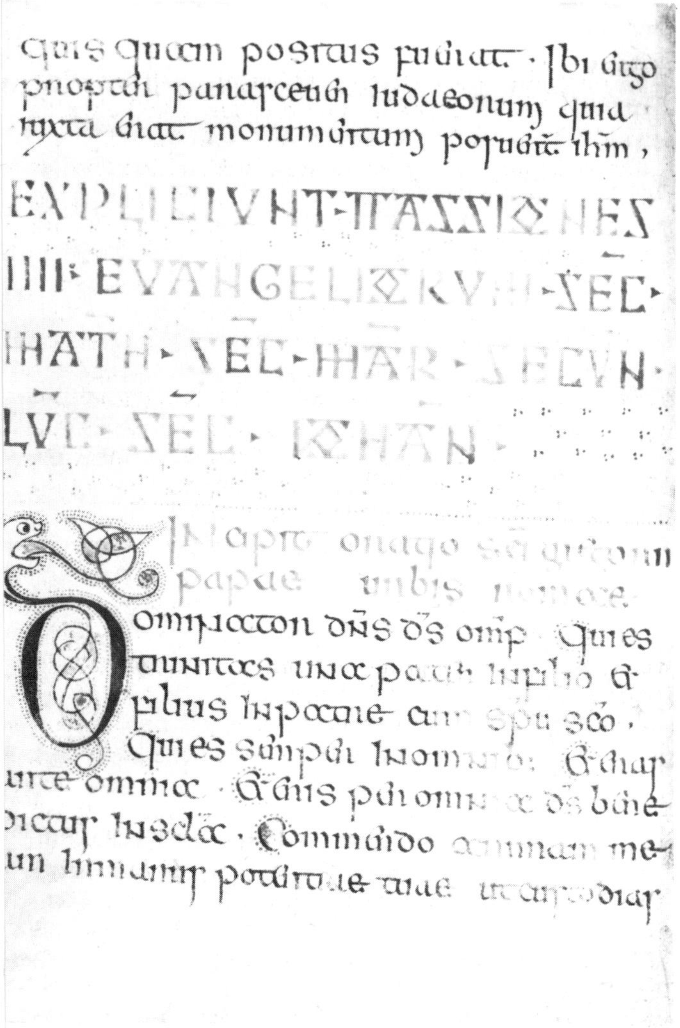

134 Page from the 'Book of Nunnaminster' (British Library, MS Harley 2965, 16b). A devotional collection, like the Book of Cerne (fig. 130), focusing especially on the sufferings of Christ, its script and decoration are of 8th/9th-century date, but later inscriptions show that it belonged to Alfred's queen, Ealhswith, who perhaps gave it to the convent of Nunnaminster which she founded at Winchester. As such, it is a rare illustration of a manuscript that was available in Wessex throughout the period of disruption by Viking attack.

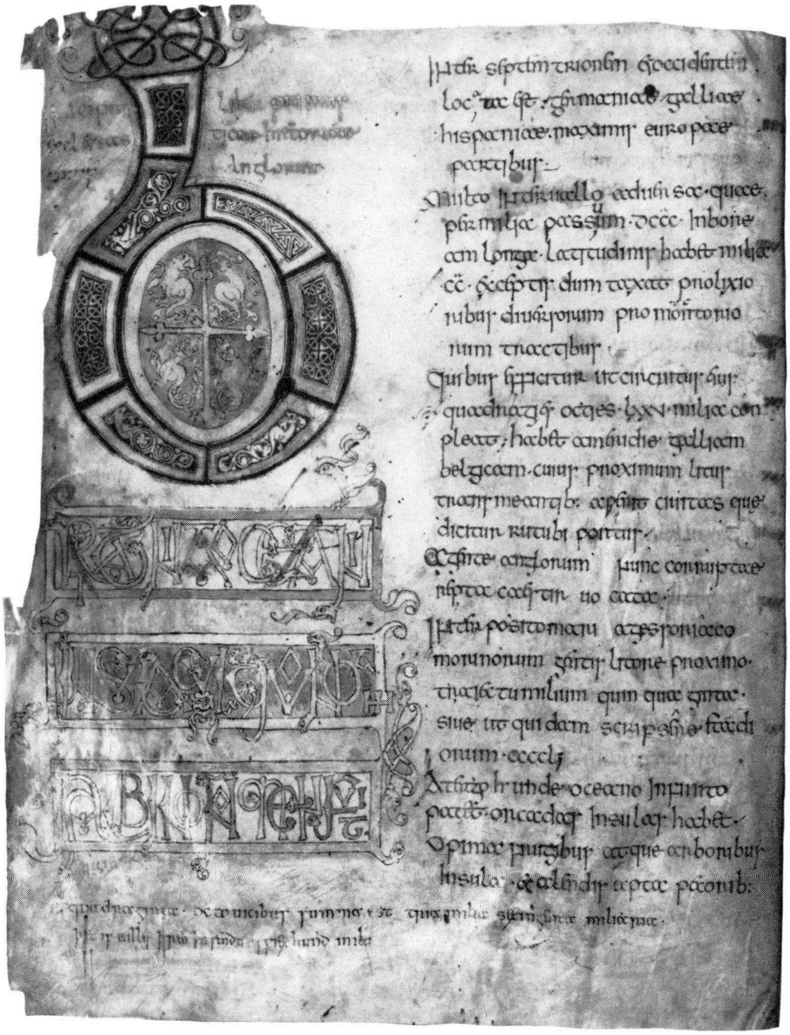

135 Page from the 'Tiberius Bede' (British Library, MS Cotton Tiberius C.ii, fol. 5v), showing the beginning of Book I, chapter 1. Although a contemporary gloss describes Saint Cuthbert as 'ours', suggesting a link with Lindisfarne, the decorative style of this manuscript links it with others of the 'Canterbury' school (figs. 122, 124, 130).

borne out by the Latin of ninth-century charters, especially from Canterbury, which becomes increasingly ungrammatical, if not incomprehensible. Yet Canterbury presents another side to the picture. One reason for the decline of Latin was that the vernacular was increasingly used for documents, like Badanoth's will. The handwriting of Canterbury documents in the first half of the century represents the climax of early Anglo-Saxon calligraphy. The Kentish churches, perhaps especially St Augustine's at Canterbury, maintained a splendid tradition of manuscript illumination, a tradition going back to the books Saint Augustine brought from Italy, but also perhaps influenced by Carolingian taste. The Royal Bible, a Canterbury manuscript of the early or mid-ninth century, would rank high among Anglo-Saxon works of art were it not so sadly mutilated (see fig. 122).

There are other hints of better things than Alfred implies, though, as always since the death of Bede, they remain hints. Two are especially suggestive, since we would not even have them, but for the importance of the mineral resources that helped to make England rich. First, the distinguished Carolingian scholar, Lupus of Ferrières, wrote to King Aethelwulf and his secretary for lead to roof his church; in the process, he revealed the interesting detail that the secretary was a Frank (*EHD*, nos. 217–18). Quite apart from Aethelwulf's second marriage, cultural contacts between England and the Carolingian empire had not died with Alcuin (and Lupus also sent to York for works which even he did not possess).

Second, in about 835, the abbess of Repton gave the Mercian ealdorman, Hunberht, land at Wirksworth in Derbyshire, provided that he supplied Canterbury with 300 shillings of lead annually (Birch, *Cart.*, no. 414). The church at Wirksworth has fine sculpture of this period or slightly earlier, and its iconography has been linked with a poem on the Ascension by Cynewulf, the only Anglo-Saxon poet who 'signed' his work. Is it

138 (*opposite*) Silver hoard from Cuerdale, Lancs, (now in British Museum and Ashmolean Museum, Oxford). This hoard, weighing 88 lb. in all, and surviving, unlike the Croydon hoard (p. 145), substantially intact, was found in the bank of the River Ribble in 1840. Besides numerous items of 'hack-silver', and brooches and arm-rings of Hiberno-Viking style, the hoard contained over 7,000 coins, of which over 1,000 were English (mostly of Alfred), over 1,000 were Frankish, nearly 5,000 were from Viking-controlled England, and 27 were oriental. These coins date the hoard to the very early 10th century, and suggest that it may have been deposited when the descendants of Ivarr, expelled from Dublin, made for north-west England and south-west Scotland. Although this hoard is the largest ever found in western Europe from this period, it is tiny compared to the treasure disposed of by King Alfred in his will, to say nothing of the much larger sums which some of his successors had at their command.

Modern views of the Vikings tend, nevertheless, to play down the size and ferocity of Viking attacks even in this later stage. It is argued that medieval chroniclers were always prone to exaggerate numbers and the extent of any disaster. Ocean-going Viking ships could not carry much more than 30 men, and fewer if horses, camp followers and prisoners were also on board (as we know they were in the 890s). The numerous Scandinavian place-names of the Danelaw (see below, pp. 162–3), and the considerable impact of Scandinavian languages on English, give an impression of dense settlement, but such effects could be achieved by a relatively small number of Danish landlords and governors. The consequences of the Viking invasions for the English Church, and English culture, look serious, but the Vikings were not fanatical pagans, out to kill priests and destroy churches for the sake of it, but raiders looking for loot where it was conveniently available, and Church and learning were already in decline. In other words, Vikings remained raiding bands of aristocratic warriors, rather than hordes of heathen savages. Their adverse effects were largely incidental, or else further contributions to pre-existent political and cultural crises. What is more, Vikings had beneficial effects too, notably on commercial and urban growth.

Yet each of these arguments can be challenged. Medieval chroniclers did exaggerate; but what is impressive about the sources for the Viking attacks is that the same sort of figures are given by wholly independent sources in different parts of Europe. In particular, both the Frankish annals and the *Anglo-Saxon Chronicle* number the great army of the 890s at 200 ships, and that of Haesten, which reinforced it after 20 years of raiding on the Loire, at between 50 and 100. This ability to agree in apparent exaggeration suggests in itself that no exaggeration was involved. If the 893 army was really transported in a total of up to 300 ships (including Haesten's fleet), then we must reckon with thousands of men, even if most ships carried no more than 10 men. Scandinavian settlement in the Danelaw is considered in a Picture Essay (pp. (162–3), and it is argued there that a mere change of landlords will not account for all the evidence. If, as has been suggested, the armies of the 860s and 870s were concentrations of war-bands from all over Europe under ambitious royal leadership, they could very well have numbered thousands.

Again, some of the evidence for Viking destruction is difficult to attribute to any other cause. In the Danelaw, the episcopal lists of every diocese except York and Lindisfarne are interrupted for decades; and the Lindisfarne community preserved a moving story of its wanderings with Saint Cuthbert's relics for several years after Healfdene's settlement in the old Northumbrian kingdom. Three bishoprics disappeared altogether: Hexham, Leicester and that of southern East Anglia. Although sees were re-established for Lindsey and for East Anglia in the tenth century, we do not know whether they were on the same sites as their ninth-century predecessors. Medieval bishoprics were durable institutions, which seldom, if ever, disappeared because of mere 'decay'. Such disruption in the history of the Danelaw bishoprics argues that the effects of Viking invasion were very serious indeed; as serious, locally, as the Anglo-Saxon invasions themselves. And once again the impression one derives from the English evidence is confirmed by comparison with Viking exploits elsewhere: the history of the dioceses in what was to become Normandy, as a result of Viking settlement there in the early tenth century, was also interrupted.

Moreover, how else can one explain the almost complete disappearance of books and charters from Northumbria, Mercia and East Anglia, which makes the reconstruction of the age of Offa so difficult? King Alfred's

139 Gilt bronze Northumbrian book-mount of 8th-century date (9.7 cm × 9.7 cm), converted into a pendant, and found in a woman's grave at Björke, Norway (now in Historisk Museum, Bergen, Norway). It must presumably represent the loss of at least one Northumbrian book to Viking raiders.

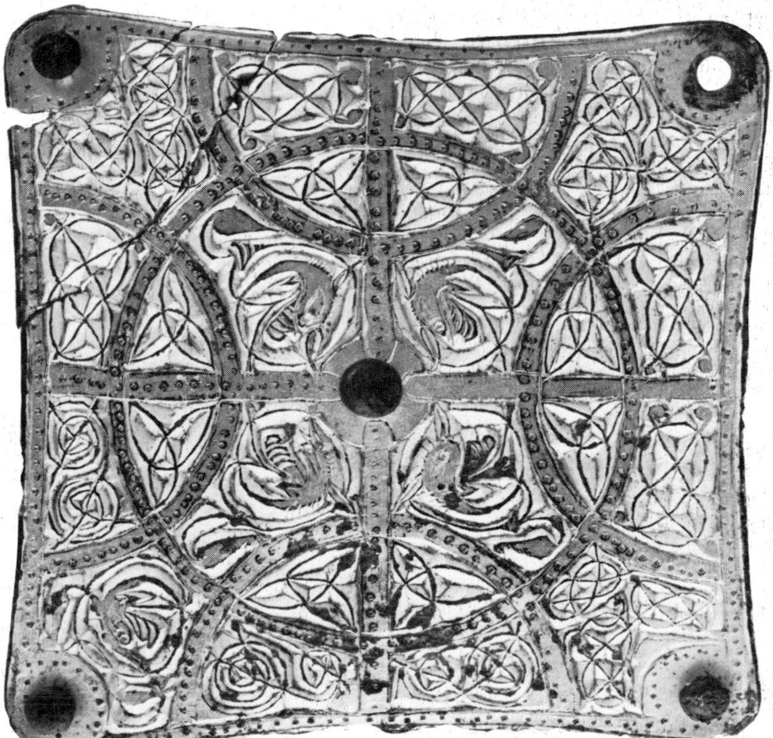

preface to his *Pastoral Rule* does assert that learning was being neglected before everything was burnt, but he can hardly have thought that the burning itself was the work of idle monks rather than Vikings. The evidence of the Canterbury and Rochester charters in the ninth century is clear on this point. Calligraphic, if not grammatical, standards were maintained until the recorded attacks on Kent in the early 850s. Thereafter, script deteriorates as rapidly as language and sense, and charters become scarce. One Kentish Gospel book, the beautiful Codex Aureus (fig, 124), has an inscription recording that Ealdorman Aelfred and his wife obtained it 'from the heathen army with pure gold' (*EHD*, no. 98). If this suggests that not every book was at once consigned to the furnace, it also shows that libraries could not expect to survive Viking attacks intact.

Some of this evidence gives one pause about the modern confidence that Vikings were not fanatically pagan. Some, clearly, were not, since we know of cases of a ready, if somewhat cynical, acceptance of baptism; and Scandinavian settlers seem to have been converted fairly soon after their arrival in England. Yet it may not be coincidence that Scandinavian sagas preserve most of what we know of ancient Germanic religion, whereas *Beowulf* is uncompromisingly monotheist; and that the Christian sculpture of northern England after the Viking settlement draws on pagan myths unlike the Ruthwell Cross (cf. pp. 162–3). If the memory of paganism survived better among Scandinavians than other Germanic peoples, it may have been more strongly rooted to start with. It has, moreover, been suggested that Kings Aelle of the Northumbrians and Edmund of the East Anglians were sacrificed by Ivarr to Othinn (the Scandinavian Woden) in a particularly gruesome way; the 'blood-eagle' involved ripping a victim's lungs out of his rib-cage, and draping them across his shoulders like an eagle's folded wings. Writing a century after Edmund's death, Abbo of Fleury gives an account of his sufferings that is without real parallel in early medieval hagiography. If there is anything in these stories (and Scandi-

140 The Gokstad ship, excavated in 1880 with a rich, albeit robbed, burial, and now in the Viking Ship Museum at Bygdøy, near Oslo (Oslo, University Museum of National Antiquities). This most famous of all Viking ships is largely of oak, and 76 ft 5 in long, with a keel of 60 ft. Its remarkable seaworthiness was demonstrated in 1893, when a replica crossed the Atlantic in 28 days, and won high praise from its experienced captain.

navian tradition was rather proud of them), it would explain why Vikings struck such terror into Christians, and also why their effects were so very disruptive.

It is true that there were positive aspects to Viking expansion. Trade was stimulated in some parts of northwestern Europe. New towns were founded, like Dublin and perhaps Norwich, and old ones received a new lease of life, like York and perhaps London. A fine silver coinage replaced the old Northumbrian *stycas*, and coinage was introduced to Ireland. Trade and piracy are often closely related, and Viking commerce, like that of the Anglo-Saxons in the seventh century (see above, p. 64), was probably heavily dependent on the inherently predatory slave-trade, but this does not affect the point that in the long run the prosperity of some of the areas they settled was much increased.

Again, Scandinavian settlers in Iceland founded the first European republican constitution since classical times, and Scandinavian administrative systems left several traces in the Danelaw (see below, pp. 161–4); like the Anglo-Saxons, Vikings could organize government as well as war-bands. And, like the Anglo-Saxons, they commissioned and produced works of great technical skill and artistic beauty; their ships were perhaps the most effective ocean-going vessels hitherto designed by man; their swords and tools represent, in quantity if not quality, a significant advance on those of earlier 'barbarian' invaders; their metalwork and later their sculpture compare well with those of seventh- and eighth-century England. But to say that, like other Germanic peoples including the Anglo-Saxons, the Vikings had their constructive side is not to deny that, like the others, they could be extremely destructive when confronted with a culture they did not understand. And if it is true that Anglo-Saxon and Viking society in the ninth century were much more similar than Anglo-Saxon and Romano-British society in the fifth, it may also be true that Viking paganism was more strongly rooted than that of earlier Germanic invaders, and it is very probable that Christianity was more closely woven into the social fabric of England in 800 than of Britain in 400.

Whatever the long-term beneficial effects of the Viking invasions, there can be little doubt that they caused a massive crisis in Anglo-Saxon society. There are reasons to believe that England after 865 was confronted by something like conquering armies under royal leadership, as the Roman Empire had been. We can see in Roman accounts of earlier Germanic peoples how the growth of predatory war-bands disrupted traditional tribal society, and led ultimately to the creation of whole new peoples, numbering tens of thousands and led by kings of substantial power. There is thus no reason why early raids by seaborne Viking war-bands under chieftains should not have developed into relatively massive invasions under kings. And the effects of the Viking invasions in England really speak for themselves. Three kings were killed (two, perhaps, in a ghastly way), and a fourth pushed into premature retirement. Three out of four remaining kingdoms lost independence for ever, and the Vikings established their own kingdoms in Northumbria and East Anglia (albeit not for long). Five dioceses lost bishops for a long period, and three were never reconstituted. Almost all churches north and east of Watling Street lost their libraries and charters, and laymen also suffered in the latter respect: several charters of the period were commissioned to replace documents which had been lost. Peasants in much of northern and eastern England received new lords, and probably new neighbours, speaking a different language. Whatever the explanation for the Vikings (and no one has yet 'explained' the Anglo-Saxon invasions), the central point for the Anglo-Saxon historian is that they inflicted on England much more than mere plunder-raids which were insufficiently sensitive to local religious susceptibilities. This in itself removes the temptation to write off all aspects of ninth-century English society save the House of Wessex as foredoomed to collapse like a house of cards at one Viking sneeze. It also enhances Alfred's own achievement.

The Achievement of Alfred

If we ask why Alfred survived Guthrum's surprise attack in 878, when all his fellow kings had gone under, the short answer is that we don't know. The first decade of his reign is obscure, except for the evidence of almost constant Danish pressure. But the significant point, perhaps, is that within months of humiliating defeat Alfred was able to rally sufficient forces to crush what was presumably a substantial and self-confident Danish army. Apart from the role of his own courage and determination, some of what was said earlier about the relatively strong position of his dynasty may also be relevant here. In Northumbria, the Vikings found two kings at feud, and killed both. In Northumbria and Mercia, it is possible that they were able to back disaffected royal dynasties against their hitherto more successful rivals. But Alfred's grandfather, father and brothers had apparently smoothed away any similar tensions in Wessex, and in 878 there was none of the dynastic splintering that the analogy of other kingdoms might lead one to expect. Again, Alfred's dynasty may well have been richer in land and treasure than the others, and had not felt the same temptation to rob the Church. As a result of its victories, its prestige was probably greater among its own people than that of Mercian or Northumbrian kings. Alfred's family, in short, were good lords, and, in Germanic societies, good lords were not so readily deserted. But if Alfred may have owed his initial survival to his family's efforts as much as his own, there is no doubt that what happened after 878 was all his own work; and it amounted to the most sustained programme of military, administrative, diplomatic and cultural change in the West since Charlemagne.

Alfred's problems with the Danes were threefold: military, political and religious. The military problem is of course the most obvious. Viking armies were very mobile; they used ships to descend at any point on the coast and to penetrate high up rivers, and they used horses to move fast overland. The *Chronicle*'s long and confusingly detailed account of the 893 campaign again-

141 Reconstruction (by Mary Storm) of tapestry fragments found in another ship burial at Oseberg (Oslo, University Museum of National Antiquities). The tapestry was 23 cm wide, and was perhaps designed for hanging around a hall. The scene underlines the importance of horses as well as ships to Viking mobility.

st the third great army shows how the Danes could turn up wherever the West Saxon army was not: 'When the king had turned west with the army towards Exeter, and the Danish army had laid siege to the borough, they went to their ships when he arrived there. When he was occupied against the army there in the west, and the other two Danish armies were in Essex, they went both together up along the Thames, and a great reinforcement came to them both from the East Angles and the Northumbrians' (*EHD*, p. 203). And yet, when the wars of 893–6 are compared with the desperate struggles of the 870s, a striking difference emerges. Whereas the Danes had earlier penetrated deep and repeatedly into Wessex, their successors of the 890s hardly got into Wessex at all (see maps, fig. 142). There is little doubt that the reason for this decisive contrast was the military reforms introduced by Alfred in the meanwhile: the navy, the army, and above all the *burh*.

The *Chronicle* for 896 tells how Alfred had 'long ships' of 60 oars, 'built neither on the Frisian nor the Danish pattern, but as it seemed to him they could be most useful' (*EHD*, p. 206). His ships were not an unqualified success (they ran aground on their first outing), and it is unlikely that Alfred was, as the Victorians had it, 'the founder of the English navy', if only because Edwin's exploits in the seventh century (see above, pp. 53, 64) could hardly have been managed without a royal fleet. The building of ships was a fairly obvious way to cope with Vikings, and Charlemagne had done it, as Alfred may have known. But the *Chronicle*'s reference to a new 60-oared design may well be significant, because the naval organization of later Anglo-Saxon England was based on 60-oared ships. Alfred was quite possibly the founder of a system whose importance to tenth- and eleventh-century kings was considerable (see below, p. 173).

Again, the *Chronicle* for 893 says that Alfred divided the army, or *fyrd*, into two, 'so that always half its men were at home, half on service' (*EHD*, p. 202). The point of this, as normally understood, was to let peasants alternate their military and agricultural duties. The value of an army of peasants with half a mind on their return to the harvest is doubtful, and the *Chronicle* does indeed record that in 893 the English besieging the Danes on Thorney Island abandoned their posts when their term of service expired. But we may be seeing here a trace of the sort of army reforms the Carolingians had introduced. The Frankish army was no longer a mass levy of all freemen; instead, peasant resources were pooled, so that for each one on service, there were one, or more, at home supplying him with provisions and equipment. This was also the principle of the 'select *fyrd*' of Domesday Book,

- □ Danish base
- △ Danish victory
- ▽ Danish defeat
- ⊙ Danish hoard
- (solid line) *1st phase:* Arrival of 'Great Army' and conquest of Northumbria and E. Anglia, 865–9
- (dot-dash line) *2nd phase:* First attack on Wessex and arrival of 'Great Summer Army', 870–1
- (dotted line) *3rd phase:* Settlement of Northumbrian revolt, conquest of Mercia and division of the army into N and E forces, 872–5
- (dashed line) *4th phase:* Second attack on Wessex 876–8

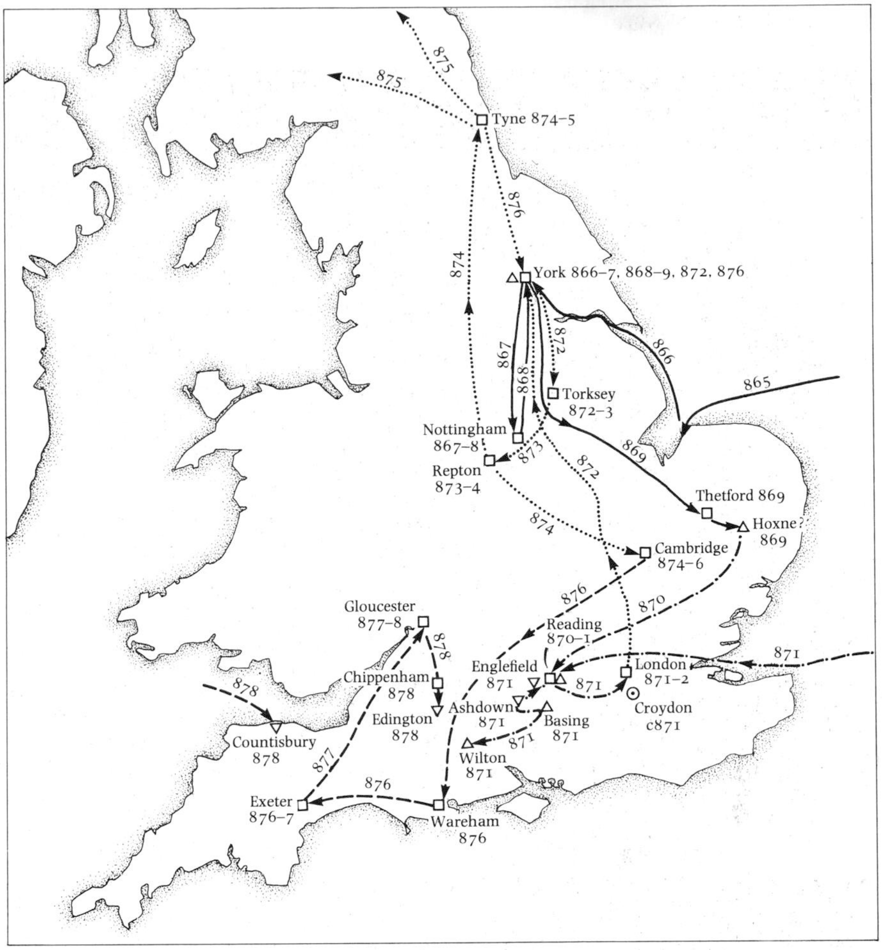

- □ Danish base
- ▽ Danish defeat
- ⊙ Danish hoard
- (dashed line) Invasion of the 'Great Army' and Haesten, 892
- (dot-dash line) Campaign of 893
- (solid line) Campaign of 894
- (dotted line) Campaigns of 895–6, down to dispersal of army from Bridgnorth

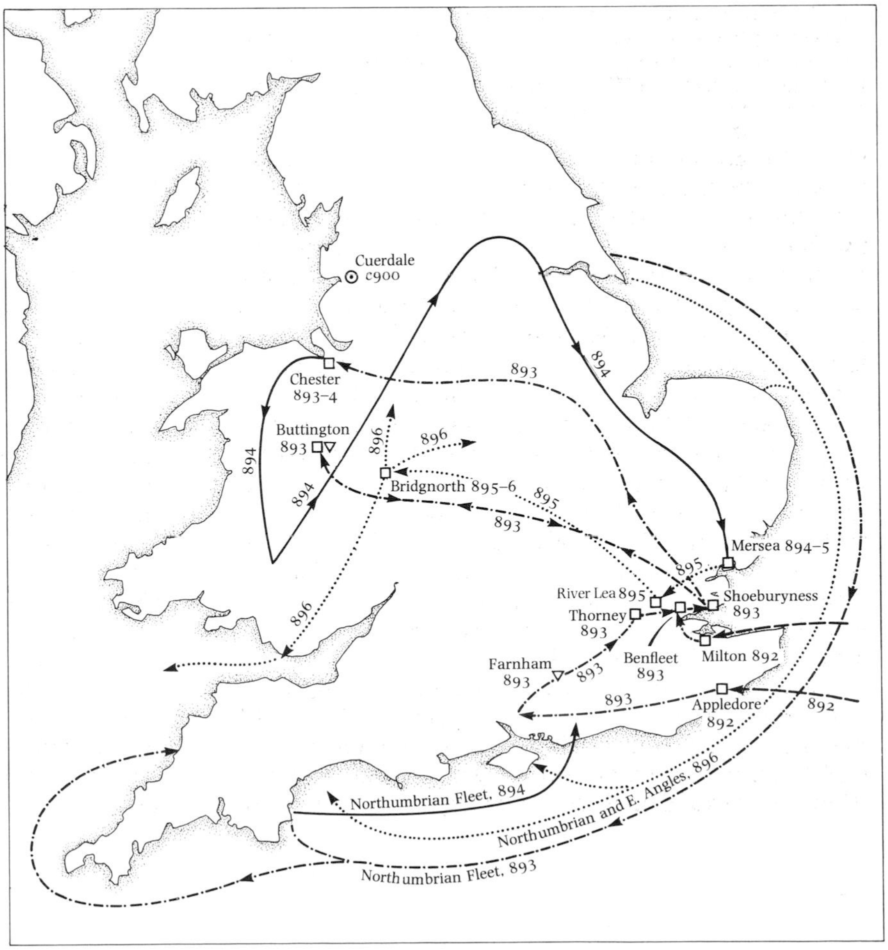

142 Maps showing the campaigns of and against the Vikings (after D. Hill, *An Atlas of Anglo-Saxon England*, Blackwell, 1981). These maps point the contrast between the operations of the 'Great Army' of 865 and the 'Great Summer Army' of 871, on the one hand, and those of the third 'Great Army' of 892–6, on the other. In the 860s and 870s the Danes moved freely not only up and down eastern England, but on three occasions well into Wessex. In the 890s an army based mainly in the Thames estuary crossed England to the north-west on three occasions, but, after the initial raid of Spring 893, did not penetrate Wessex. The main danger to Wessex came from coastal raids by Danes settled in Northumbria and East Anglia.

The Burhs

The *burhs* of Wessex are among the most impressive administrative achievements of Anglo-Saxon government, and the first of which there is direct documentary record. This record is known as the Burghal Hidage. It survives in a sixteenth-century transcript of an eleventh-century Winchester manuscript, and in several post-Conquest texts; none of these agree precisely with the others. 33 places are listed, together with the number of hides said to belong to them; thus, 'to Winchester belong 2,400 hides . . ., and to Wareham belong 1,600 hides . . ., and 1,500 hides belong to Cricklade . . ., and to Wallingford belong 2,400 hides. . .' etc. Worcester and Warwick do not appear in the transcript, and are clearly later additions; the others are listed in an approximately clockwise order around the borders of Wessex, from *Eorpeburnan* (unidentified, but probably in the Romney Marsh area) to Southwark. Cornwall is omitted, presumably because still independent; London is also missing, perhaps because it was a Mercian responsibility; and Kent too was apparently left to make its own arrangements.

The transcript, but not the post-Conquest manuscripts, has an important appendix, stating: 'If every hide is represented by 1 man, then every pole of wall can be manned by 4 men. Then for the maintenance of 20 poles of wall 80 hides are required, and for a furlong 160 hides are required by the same reckoning', and so on. The post-Conquest manuscripts have a different appendix; in its original form, this probably read: 'That is all 27,000 hides (and 70 which belong to it); and 30 burhs belong to the West Saxons'. This total of hides and *burhs* can be achieved if Buckingham, as well as Worcester and Warwick, is omitted. We thus arrive at a list of *burhs* confined to Wessex proper, together with an arrangement whereby no fewer than 27,000 men were assigned to their defence and maintenance.

The document is normally dated on the following basis: Oxford, together with London, only came into the hands of Edward the Elder (pp. 160–1) in 911, when Ealdorman Aethelred of Mercia died. The *burh* at Buckingham is said by the *Anglo-Saxon Chronicle* to have been built in 914, and the whole of Mercia, which by then had its own *burhs*, was seized by Edward on his sister's death in 919. Thus, the document's inclusion of Oxford, but exclusion of other Mercian *burhs*, should indicate a date between 911 and 919; and if Buckingham is really an interpolation, we can narrow this down to 911–14. However, the fact that London is omitted, though it also came to Edward in 911, may mean that the original form of the document is considerably older: it is possible that Oxford was originally in Alfred's hands, and only given to Ealdorman Aethelred when London was captured and transferred to him in 886 (see p. 132); this would explain why both London and Oxford were given back to Wessex when Aethelred died, though the rest of Mercia retained its autonomy. On this basis, the Burghal Hidage might be dated before 886.

However this may be, there is little doubt that the burghal system was Alfred's creation. Asser writes of 'the cities and towns he restored, and the others he constructed where there had been none before' (Asser, c. 91, p. 77). The *Chronicle* tells how the Danes overwhelmed a few peasants in a half-completed fortress on the River Lympne (perhaps *Eorpeburnan*) in 892. And finally, William of Malmesbury in the early twelfth century claims to have seen an inscription in the chapter-house at Shaftesbury recording that Alfred 'made this town' in 880; a fragment of the inscription was actually excavated early this century, and though it is now lost, a rubbing of it was preserved.

The *burhs* of Wessex were so distributed that nowhere was more than about 20 miles (or a day's march) away from one. They were of various types. Some were old Roman towns, whose surviving walls provided fortification, like Winchester. Others were re-used Iron Age or Roman forts, like Chisbury and Portchester, or new forts, like Eashing, the site of a royal manor mentioned in Alfred's will. Others again were fortified promontories, like Lydford or Malmesbury. Finally, some were new towns

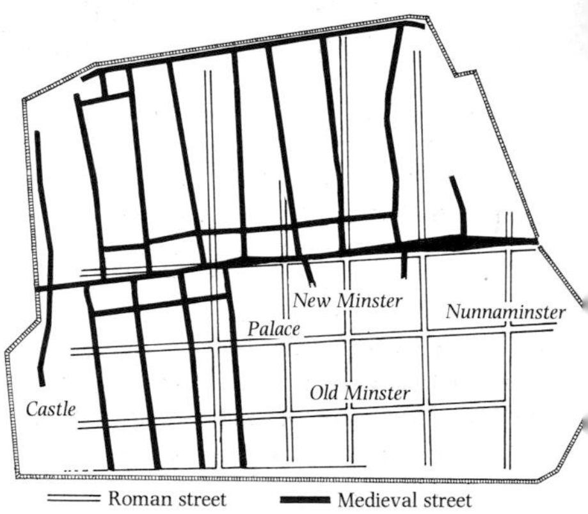

2 Town-plan of medieval Winchester from M. Biddle and D. Hill, 'Late Saxon Planned Towns', *Antiquaries Journal*. 51, 1971, p. 72). The rigidly rectangular Roman street-plan does not correspond to that of the medieval town (scale approx. 1:7,000).

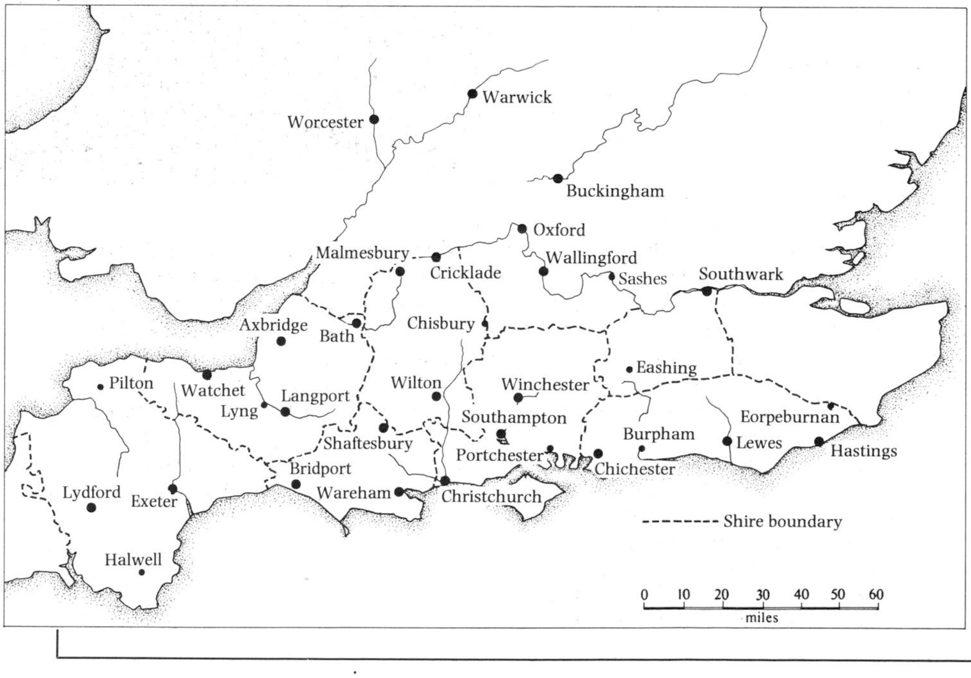

1 Map of the *burhs* listed in the 'Burghal Hidage' (from D. Hill, *An Atlas of Anglo-Saxon England* (Blackwell, 1981)). Worcester, Warwick and perhaps Buckingham are later additions to the list.

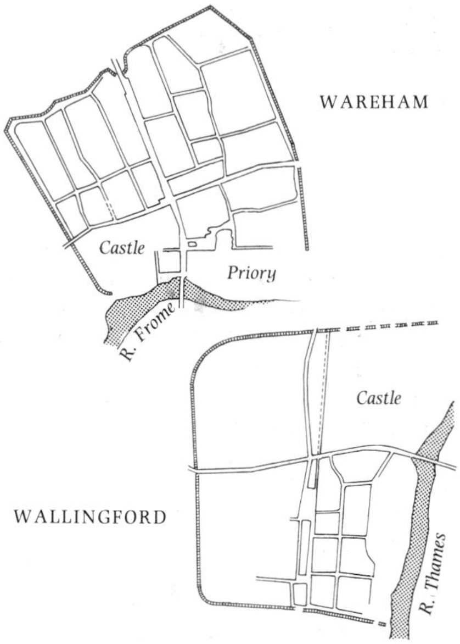

4 Town-plans of Wareham and Wallingford (from Biddle and Hill, op. cit., p. 80). The similarity between these *burhs* and that of Winchester is evidence that they were laid out as part of the same scheme (scale approx. 1:5,280).

on open sites with a rectangular perimeter, like Wareham, Cricklade and Wallingford. Excavation of the ramparts of the new *burhs* is inconclusive as to date and structure; any timber revetment for the earthworks was cut away in a subsequent phase of reinforcement; and an Alfredian date is not proven though not excluded. But what is clear is that in nearly all cases the length of the fortifications corresponds to what the formula in the Burghal Hidage would lead one to expect; thus Winchester's 2,400 hides would provide, on the basis of the formula, for the defence of 9,900 feet of walls, and the Roman walls of the town are in fact 9,954 feet long—a discrepancy of less than 1%. In short, the logic of the Burghal Hidage worked.

But it now seems clear that the *burhs* represented more than places of temporary refuge for the entire population of Wessex. Excavations at Winchester and elsewhere have shown that they share a common town-plan, with back streets running parallel to the main street, other streets at right angles to them, and a street around the inside of the wall. At Winchester, this plan is demonstrably post-Roman, yet it is known to have been in existence by the late tenth century, and there is both documentary and archaeological evidence that it was already there *c.* 900. The similarity of plan between other *burhs* and that of Winchester, which can be dated to Alfred's time, seems to indicate that many *burhs* were

3 Aerial view of Wallingford (from the Cambridge University Collection). The line of the ramparts can be made out, together with the High Street, and one of the back streets running parallel to it.

also planned as places of permanent habitation and trade. Laws of tenth-century kings demand that trade should take place in towns, and there is an interesting parallel in arrangements made by the German king, Henry the Fowler, in the 920s: every ninth 'agrarian soldier' was to live in a town, and build dwellings for his eight colleagues, who were to keep him supplied, and to hold councils, meetings and parties in the town, 'that they might learn in peace what they would have to do in emergency against enemies'. We might well imagine that similar arrangements were made in Alfred's England, and it is not improbable that Henry's policy was copied from them. In late Saxon England, many such *burhs* became mints, and their inhabitants paid a profitable rent for their burgages to the king; the *burhs* were in fact a key factor in the wealth and power of English kings, and it is not impossible that they were designed as such from the outset.

To sum up: the Burghal Hidage may well date to Alfred's reign, and almost certainly reflects Alfredian policy. It involves the conscription of up to 27,000 men in a scheme of defence that worked out in practice. Refuge was thereby provided for the persons and movable property of all West Saxons, together with a serious disincentive to Danish settlement in the area. And many *burhs* were planned not merely for defence, but also for settlement and commerce. There is no more impressive testimony to the power and efficiency of Anglo-Saxon government in general, and of the greatest of Anglo-Saxon kings in particular.

5 The ramparts at Wareham. These were reinforced in the Second World War, but were originally almost equally high and steep: perhaps 9 feet from the bottom of the ditch to the top of the rampart.

P. Wormald

whereby a well-equipped warrior was levied on each unit of five hides, and supported by the resources of the other men in the unit. The purpose was not so much to let peasants get on with the harvest, as to bridge the ever-widening gulf between the resources of the peasant and the expense of specialized warfare. Alfred's grandson, Aethelstan (924–39), ordered 'that every man shall provide two well-mounted men for every plough' (*Laws of Aethelstan*, II. c. 16, pp. 136–7). The meaning of plough in this context is obscure, but the law's tone is reminiscent of the principle of selective conscription found in contemporary Continental, and later Anglo-Saxon, practice. Just possibly, this is what Alfred's army reforms were also about, and it may be significant that, by 895, the *Chronicle* has the English army *riding* after the Danes.

Whatever the significance of Alfred's navy and divided army, there is little doubt that the crucial element in the exclusion of the 893–6 army from Wessex was the *burh*. Alfred's burghal system is discussed in a Picture Essay (pp. 152–3), but three points about it may be made here. First, unlike Offa's dyke, Alfred's *burhs* were 'bureaucratically' documented; the Burghal Hidage is the earliest unquestionably administrative document in English history. In its present form, it dates to the reign of Alfred's son, Edward the Elder (899–924), but it may well have Alfredian origins. It ends with a calculation of the number of hides, at one man per hide, needed to garrison a given length of wall. Where the known or ascertainable length of any *burh* wall, like Winchester itself, is compared with the length that may be deduced from the hidage formula, the correspondence is usually almost exact; and the formula envisages a total garrison force of 27,000 men. In other words, the burghal system involved the deployment of colossal manpower resources, and yet it worked. There is no more impressive evidence before Domesday Book of the capacities of Anglo-Saxon government.

Second, as their common lay-out shows, *burhs* were planned as more than defences; they were also to become markets, and eventually mints. A Worcester charter of the 890s shows Ealdorman Aethelred, with Alfred as witness, organizing borough defences at Worcester and also a market-place, some of whose tolls were remitted for the bishop, with the rest going to the king (Birch, *Cart.*, no. 579; *EHD*, no. 99). Royal *burhs* were not only to supply the scaffolding of the later Anglo-Saxon military and administrative structure (see below, p. 176), but were also to become extremely lucrative as trading centres both for their inhabitants and for the king. The rapid success of the burghal system (after its own initial hiccups) should perhaps be put down not only to Alfred's energy, but also to the incipient urbanization and commercialization of southern England which has been seen in this and the previous chapter.

Finally, *burh*-service was a traditional, and perhaps very ancient, right of Anglo-Saxon kings (see above, p. 122). Charles the Bald in Francia actually seems to have acknowledged English inspiration when arranging for fortification against the Vikings in his Edict of Pitres (864). But it is possible that some influence also flowed the other way. The bridge with which the *Chronicle* records Alfred as trapping a Viking fleet up the River Lea in 895 looks very like an expedient that Charles the Bald had used on the Seine. If one lesson, then, of this and other military reforms by Alfred is the remarkable administrative capacity of Anglo-Saxon government, another is that, whether or not they were influenced by Carolingian techniques, they belong to the same European trends in defence against the Vikings. It is worth adding that, for all the special lustre of Alfred's achievement, these trends also in the end enabled Frankish kings to contain the Viking threat.

143 Silver sword-pommel inlaid with gold (6.9 cm across), found in the River Seine at Paris. It seems to be English work of *c.* 900; it may have been looted by Vikings in progress from England to France, but in any case, it is an indication of the important connections between England and the Frankish empire (cf. fig. 133, and p. 150).

The political problem posed by the Danes is less obvious, but was real enough. It arose from what was said earlier about the absence of any 'patriotic' response to attack in ninth-century Europe. A Frankish case like that of Pippin II of Acquitaine, who secured Viking support, and even adopted Viking religion, in pursuit of his feud with his cousin, or the Irish example of the northern Ui Neill dynasty, who enlisted Viking aid in their long struggle with the southern branch of their family for the kingship of Tara, suggest that Alfred could not necessarily expect support from within his own dynasty, let alone from the populations of hitherto independent Northumbria, Mercia and East Anglia. Our West Saxon sources are in general characteristically discreet about comparable English cases to those in Francia and Ireland, but it is possible to cite two.

As has been seen, the *History of Saint Cuthbert* shows that the last Northumbrian kings were robbing the Church. This may explain the strange story it goes on to tell. After its several years' wandering, Saint Cuthbert's community was instructed by a vision of the saint to go to the Danish army and select a certain slave-boy as their king; the condition was that the new king was to give Saint Cuthbert a very substantial endowment between the Rivers Tyne and Wear. The monks did as they were told, and when the boy had been made king, 'Bishop

Eardwulf brought to the army the body of Saint Cuthbert, and over it the king himself and the whole army swore peace and fidelity' (*EHD*, p. 287). There are circumstantial as well as legendary elements in this story, and there is no reason to doubt its basic truth. It shows that, for a religious community, loyalty to the patron saint mattered more than loyalty to a native king. Osbert and Aelle had robbed the saint; a new Danish king might enrich him, and, if so, there was no objection to sanctioning a Danish regime with his own relics. This in turn suggests why it may have been important that West Saxon kings were less ruthless with Church property than others. It also suggests that Alfred and his successors would have to earn Saint Cuthbert's favour if they were to rule the north; they could not take it for granted that they would be preferred even to the Danes.

The other interesting case shows how dangerous dynastic tension might have been to Alfred. Aethelwold was the son of Alfred's elder brother, King Aethelred I. In accordance with Aethelwulf's will, he was passed over for the succession in 871, but Alfred's account of this in his own will suggests that Aethelwold had his backers even then. When Alfred died in 899, he was succeeded not by Aethelwold but by his own son, Edward, and Aethelwold burst into furious revolt. He fled to the Danes of Northumbria, who made him their king, and then led the East Anglian Danes against his cousin, as Pippin II had done in Francia. Fortunately for Edward, Aethelwold was killed at the Battle of the Holme in 903. But the sort of danger he represented is further suggested by another of the battle's casualties on the Danish side: Brihtsige, described as son of the *Aetheling* Beornoth by the *Chronicle*. *Aetheling*, by this stage of Anglo-Saxon history, almost certainly meant a prince of royal blood; and both Brihtsige's name, and that of his father, make it look very much as if a scion of the old Mercian 'B' dynasty also preferred the Danes to the new masters of southern England. If this could happen after Alfred's victories, it is all the more likely that it might have happened earlier. However destructive the Vikings were, princes and noblemen might take their side if it suited their interests.

Alfred, then, had to secure the loyalty of his own kingdom, and he had to woo the support of others. The first purpose was probably served by the opening chapters of his law code: that 'each man keep his oath and pledge', and that plotting against the king's life or harbouring his enemies was punishable by death and forfeiture (*Laws of Alfred*, cc. 1, 4, pp. 62–5). Apart from the exhortation of the 786 legatine council (see above, p. 117), this is the first Anglo-Saxon treason legislation, and the first reference to the oath of fidelity which all subjects had to take to later Anglo-Saxon kings. Such oaths were a favourite expedient of Charlemagne, and Alfred's law is quite likely to have been modelled on his example. Moreover, we know that the oath was enforced. A charter of 901 describes how a Wiltshire estate was forfeited by Ealdorman Wulfhere, 'when he deserted both his lord King Alfred and his country, in spite of the oath which he had sworn to the king' (Birch, *Cart.*, no. 595; *EHD*, p. 542). Wulfhere can be identified as a West Saxon nobleman who was especially associated with King Aethelred. If his treason was connected with the revolt of Aethelred's son in 899, we have further evidence of the sort of threat from within West Saxon society itself which Alfred's treason law was designed to combat.

In spite of these dangers in his own kingdom, it seems clear that, by the end of his reign, Alfred was laying claim to the old status of *bretwalda*. In the later 880s, charters from six different archives all give him the title 'King of the English', or something like it, and the coincidence rules out the possibility of retrospective forgery. One, if only one, of his new heavy pennies has the legend '*REX ANGLO* . . .,' the first such title on an English coin. Asser addressed Alfred as 'Ruler of all Christians in the island of Britain, king of the Angles and Saxons' (Asser, Prol., p. 1). Such claims were not of course new, even if Alfred, unlike his predecessors, had no rivals left. But what is impressive is the diplomatic offensive with which he sought to make his title acceptable to others than his own subjects. He married his daughter, Aethelfleda to the Mercian ealdorman, Aethelred; Alfred was in the last resort Aethelred's overlord, but Worcester charters, like that recording the town's fortification (see above, p. 154), show the Mercian council retaining effective autonomy. Offa had pursued this sort of policy in Wessex, without happy results (see above, p. 111); but Offa is not known to have made any such striking gesture as Alfred's return of London to Mercian lordship when he captured it in 886. Even more significant, perhaps, is the treaty Alfred made with Guthrum in about 886. Here Alfred is the leader and spokesman of 'all councillors of the English race'; and the terms of the treaty seem to have involved Danish recognition that Englishmen under their rule would have the same wergeld as Danes of their own class, and as Englishmen in Wessex (*EHD*, no. 34). This was a major concession by any standards, for which the East Anglians had cause to thank Alfred. Such policies probably paid off. Aethelred lent Alfred decisive support from 893/6, and the *History of Saint Cuthbert* in Northumbria rightly or wrongly began the history of the community's increasingly close and profitable relations with West Saxon kings from Alfred's time. The spectacular success of Edward the Elder within 20 years of Alfred's death may have had much to do with his father's diplomatic groundwork.

The religious problem posed by the Danes is in many ways the least expected to modern eyes, but was central for Alfred himself. In his preface to the *Pastoral Rule*, he wrote: 'Remember what temporal punishments came upon us when we neither loved wisdom ourselves nor allowed it to others' (*EHD*, p. 889). If the relevance of a revival of learning to the defeat of the Danes is scarcely obvious to us, except in so far as literacy might contribute to administrative efficiency, its relevance for Alfred was that, without God's help, no amount of fleets, divided armies or *burhs* would do any good at all; and God's help could only be won by learning to read and understand his word. Moreover, Alfred's biographer, Asser, knew, and in places copied from, Einhard's great *Life of Charle-*

Alfredian Manuscripts

King Alfred's translations are important for the history of vernacular English prose, and fascinating for what they convey of the King's own ideas. But, in addition, one survives in a contemporary manuscript; a second is extant in a manuscript of about a generation later, which may be ascribed to Winchester; while the *Anglo-Saxon Chronicle*, whether or not it was directly inspired by Alfred, exists in a near-contemporary text, which may itself have been written at Winchester, and which was almost certainly continued there. Therefore, as with Bede's *Ecclesiastical History* (cf. fig. 71), we have manuscripts which bring us very close to the context in which the works of Alfred and his circle were apparently actually composed.

The Oxford manuscript of the translation of the *Pastoral Rule* (1) was sent to Worcester, and is of late ninth-century date; the photograph shows the first page of the Preface. Its Worcester destination can be read in the first line, and in the second King Alfred greets Bishop Waerferth warmly. (The page also has some glosses in the hand of Archbishop Wulfstan, himself bishop of Worcester for a time, which confirms that the manuscript reached its target.) The handwriting of the Preface in this manuscript is in fact different from that of the main text, but it is apparently by the same scribe as that shown in no. 2. This is the sole surviving leaf of another contemporary manuscript of the *Pastoral Rule*, otherwise now totally destroyed, which was copied out in the seventeenth century. Very significantly, the transcript shows that there was a blank in its first line where the name of Waerferth stands in the Oxford manuscript. Moreover, another 'ancient hand' had apparently written on its first page: 'Archbishop Plegmund has been given his book, and Bishop Swithulf (of Rochester) and Bishop Waerferth'; we do in fact have later copies of the texts sent to the bishops of London and Sherborne, as well as the actual text sent to Waerferth. We can thus see some of the mechanics of the distribution of Alfred's *Pastoral Rule*, and presumably of his other translations too. More than that, the hand of the preface in the Oxford manuscript and of the lost manuscript—apparently a 'master-copy'—seems to be that of someone very important indeed.

The 'Parker manuscript' of the *Anglo-Saxon Chronicle* (so-called because it is in Archbishop Matthew Parker's collection, which he left to Corpus Christi College, Cambridge) is now, and probably always was, a very complex manuscript. No. 3 shows a page from the first section, which takes the *Chronicle* down to 891. The late ninth or early tenth-century hand is not unlike, though not the same as, that of the two *Pastoral Rule* manuscripts. Its closest affinities are with manuscripts likely or known to have been written in Winchester, where Alfred himself planned the 'New Minster', and where his queen founded Nunnaminster (see p. 143). Moreover, the *Chronicle* was later continued in the Parker manuscript by a scribe who was identical with, or at least trained in the same *scriptorium* as, the scribe of no. 4, the 'Helmingham' manuscript of the translation of Orosius, which was not Alfred's own work, but was probably written in his circle (see p. 134). And it has been shown that the beautiful and distinctive initials of the Helmingham Orosius were the work of an artist who also decorated a third manuscript, the 'Junius Psalter', which was probably a Winchester product. The evidence thus indicates that the Parker manuscript of the *Chronicle* was written and kept at Winchester, which was already important to Alfred, and very important indeed for his descendants. (An important proviso is that the Parker manuscript text is at least two removes from the original of the *Chronicle*, so that there is no proof that the *Chronicle* was compiled at Winchester.)

The manuscripts show us something of what the Alfredian revival of learning

1

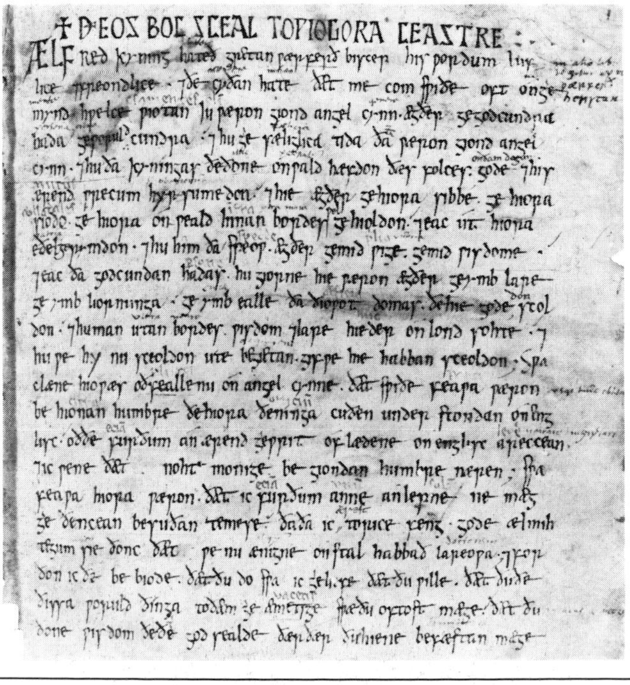

1 Opening page of the Oxford MS of Alfred's *Pastoral Rule* (Bodleian Library, Hatton MS 20, fol. 1a). The top line reads '*Ðeos boc sceal to Wiogora Ceastre*' ('this book shall [go] to Worcester'); the first line is: '*Aelfred kyning hateð gretan Waerferð biscep his wordum luflice . . .* ('King Alfred sends greeting to Bishop Waerferth in loving words . . .').

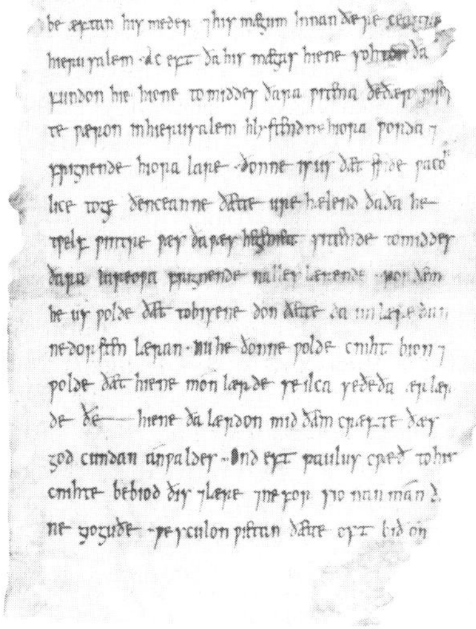

2

2 Leaf (now Kassel, Landesbibliothek, 4°MS Theol. 13) from the destroyed British Library MS Cotton Tiberius B.xi—perhaps a 'master-copy' of the *Pastoral Rule*.

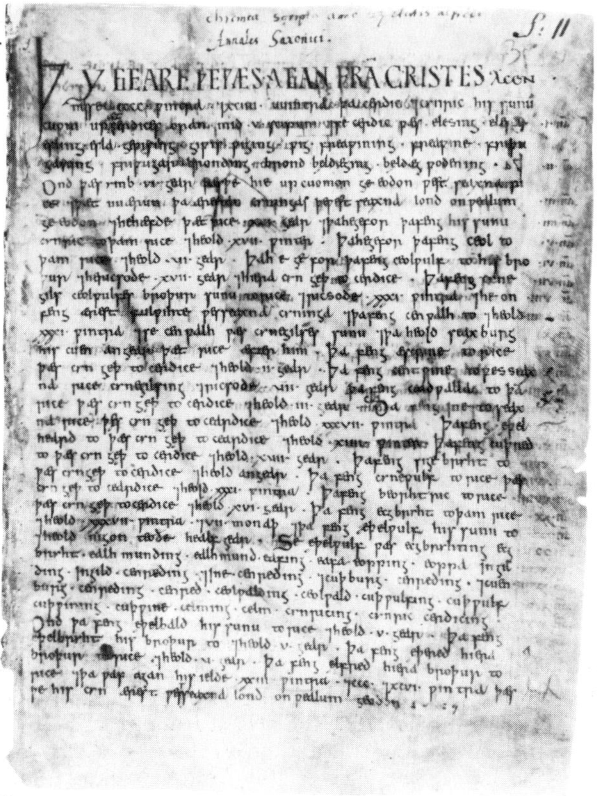

3

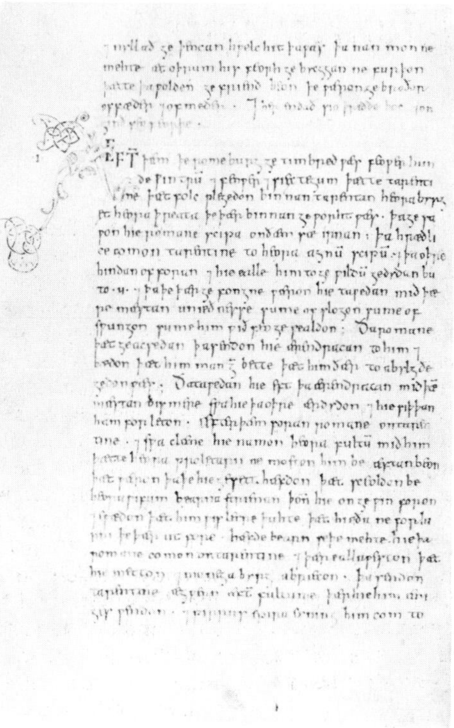

4

meant for handwriting. At least in Kent, where we have many original charters, the standard of handwriting deteriorated fast in the second half of the ninth century. Christ Church, Canterbury, itself was apparently obliged to employ a scribe who could not see what he was writing by the time he finished his stint; while three Rochester charters were the work of a scribe who produced what have been described as 'among the worst examples of medieval writing' (no. 5). The scribes of the Oxford *Pastoral Rule* and the Parker *Chronicle*, however, write a clear if not beautiful hand, which looks back to the 'insular minuscule' of the eighth and ninth centuries (cf. figs. 71, 119) but which also marks the beginning of a new style. By the time of the Helmingham Orosius, this has developed into the stately 'square minuscule' of the first half of the tenth century, which remained the basic script for writing the vernacular until after the Conquest (cf. figs 174, 187–9, 200). It has features in common with the 'Caroline minuscule' of the Carolingian Renaissance, including the use of square capitals as a display script, as at the top of the Oxford *Pastoral Rule*; and at the same time, English scribes began to use Continental methods of preparing parchment. In handwriting, as elsewhere, the age of Alfred seems to mark a new beginning, in which Continental exemplars played a part; and even here, the king's own energetic initiative may perhaps be detected. P. Wormald

3 Page from the first section of the 'Parker Manuscript' of the *Anglo-Saxon Chronicle* (Corpus Christi College, Cambridge, MS 173, fol. 1r), showing the genealogical preface.

4 Page from the 'Helmingham Orosius' (British Library, Additional MS 47967, fol. 94b); the initial is the work of an apparently Winchester artist of *c.* 925 or slightly later.

5 Rochester charter of 860 (later altered to 790), recording a grant of King Aethelbert of Wessex to Bishop Waermund II (British Library, Cotton Charters *viii.29; Birch, Cart.*, no. 502). The hand is so execrable as to have led to a suggestion of late copying and forgery; but it is apparently identical with that of two other charters (Birch, *Cart.*, nos. 506, 562), recording a grant to a layman in 862, and a grant *by* the Bishop of Rochester in 889; there was no motive for forging these at a later date. Apart from its altered date, this charter is discredited only by its incompetence.

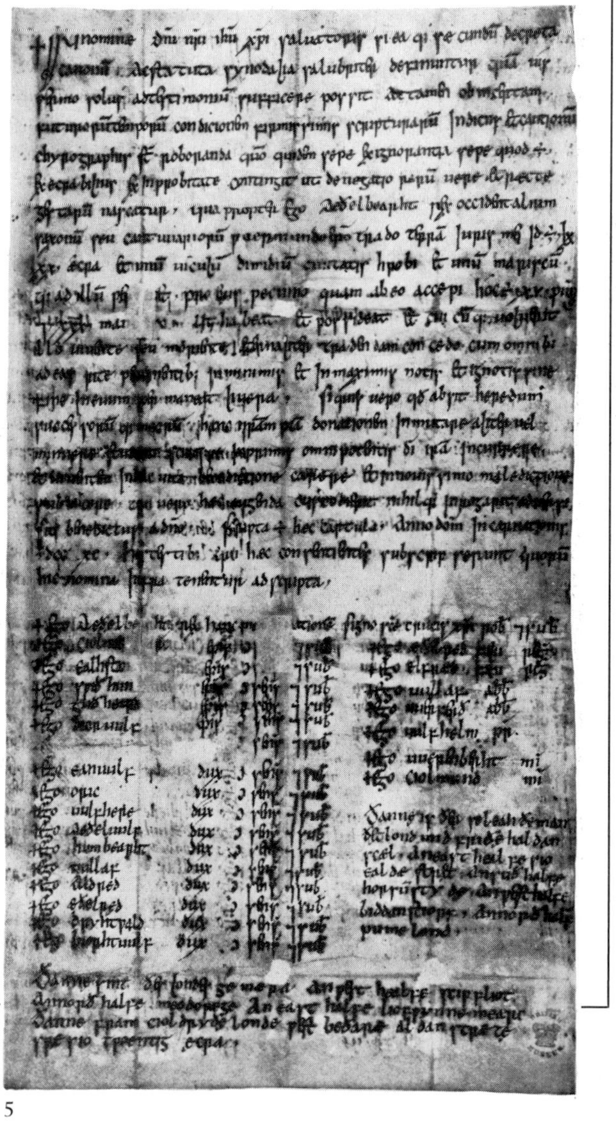

5

The Age of Edgar

'975. In this year died Edgar, ruler of the Angles, friend of the West Saxons, and protector of the Mercians. It was widely known throughout many nations across the gannet's bath [the sea], that kings honoured Edmund's son far and wide, and paid homage to this king as was his due by birth. Nor was there fleet so proud nor host so strong that it got itself prey in England so long as the noble king held the throne.' Thus one version of the *Chronicle* records the death of Edgar. He died young, at about 32, having been king of all England since 959, and of Mercia for two years longer. His reign marks the high point in the history of the Anglo-Saxon state.

One sign of this is, paradoxically, that we know little of secular events in Edgar's time. Violent incident was staple fare for annalists. Edgar, as the obituarist emphasizes, kept England free from invasion; so, there was less to record. The emphasis on the king's overseas reputation is also significant. He was the head of the oldest royal house in Europe, with a pedigree stretching back to Cerdic and the fifth century (see above, p. 26); and he was connected by marriage to the greatest families on the Continent. Such connections were not so common in this period as they were later to become. Tenth-century royal families normally married into the high nobility of their own kingdoms. But for a brief period the West Saxon royal family had done otherwise. Between *c.* 916 and *c.* 930 five of Edgar's father's sisters had been married to foreign potentates: the Carolingian Charles the Simple, Hugh the Great, duke of the Franks, Otto, later to be king of Germany, Sihtric, the Viking king of York, and, perhaps, Conrad, king of Burgundy (see below, pp. 164–5).

The European dimension is very important. To see Edgar and his England as insular and isolated is to misunderstand them. This is most plainly so in relation to his transformation of the Church (see below, pp. 181–9). It is the English part of a European movement. The framework of secular institutions which was by this time making England a powerfully organized state also owed much to the Carolingian as well as to the English past (see below, pp. 170, 241). The ways and links of English society make best sense if they are compared, and not always contrasted, with their Continental counterparts (see below, pp. 170–1). The creation of the English state was perhaps the most remarkable, and certainly the most lasting, feat of statecraft in tenth-century Europe. After Edgar's death, and until the Norman Conquest, England was to be wracked by succession disputes with deep effects on the nature of politics and of power. Nevertheless, very much of what had been accomplished by 975 endured.

The Making of England

The foundations of Edgar's power were not of his own laying and must be sought in the generally successful holding, and then conquest, of the Vikings, first by Alfred, then by his eldest son Edward the Elder and his three grandsons, who succeeded in turn, Aethelstan, Edmund and Eadred: five reigns that between them covered the years 871–955. If the Vikings were ever simply raiders or would-be traders with a penchant for cutting up their potential customers, they had become much more by Alfred's day (see above, pp. 147–9). It is clear Alfred was faced with an enemy bent on taking over most, or all, of England permanently. After 878 Wessex was no longer in serious danger of conquest: about the same time what was left of the kingdom of Mercia, in effect the old kingdom of the Hwicce or the medieval diocese of Worcester, is seen to be ruled by an ealdorman who regarded himself as Alfred's subordinate and soon became his son-in-law. In 886 Alfred seized London and this marks the turning of the tide. The *Chronicle* notes that 'King Alfred occupied London, and all the English people submitted to him, except those who were in captivity to the Danes.' If one needs a date for the beginning of an English kingdom this is as good as any (see above, p. 155). By the end of the next century the homilist, Abbot Aelfric (see below, pp. 202–4), could write of England, and use the word to mean substantially what it has meant ever since.

Alfred saw only the beginning of the West Saxon conquest of midland and eastern England. His son Edward made everyone who lived south of the Humber and east of the Welsh recognize him as king. At first he was preoccupied with a dangerous coalition between resident Vikings and one of his cousins who had been passed over for the succession to the kingdom (see above, p. 155). Not until 909 was Edward ready to take the offensive. In 910 he gained a decisive victory over an army of Northumbrian Vikings, probably alongside representatives of the old 'English' Northumbrian aristocracy, at Tettenhall in Staffordshire. This deprived the Vikings settled in eastern England of allies, even though in 919 an army of Norse Vikings from Dublin reconquered York and

145 Tower, St Peter's, Barton-on-Humber, Humberside (once Lincolnshire). The top storey is from about the time of the Conquest. Thomas Rickman (1776–1841) used the sequence of styles in this tower in his pioneering identification of Saxon architecture.

again established a northern kingdom there. In 915 Edward built a new *burh* at Buckingham, and this led within months to the submission of the Vikings of Bedfordshire and Northamptonshire. In 916 he entered Essex and established a permanent garrison at Maldon. Edward's sister, Aethelflaed, widow of the Alfredian ealdorman of the Mercians (see above, p. 155), began a programme of building *burhs* all over Mercia. Garrisons had been set in Hereford and Gloucester before 914; Chester had been restored as an English military centre in 907. In 913 the ancient Mercian royal centre of Tamworth was made into a *burh* and within two years Chester had been joined by another Cheshire *burh* at Eddisbury; and a very important strategic *burh* had been created at Warwick. By January 918 there remained south of the Humber only four Danish armies based on Leicester, Stamford, Nottingham and Lincoln. The Anglo-Danes of Northumbria, under threat from Norse invaders from their Irish base (it was by no means the case that all Scandinavians loved one another), offered to make common cause with Aethelflaed of the Mercians, whose death in June ruined the project. By this time the English Vikings retained only two important bases, Nottingham and Lincoln, and they had both submitted before Edward's death in 924.

The death of Aethelflaed gave Edward the chance of imposing direct West Saxon rule over the Mercians. He seized Tamworth and took Athelflaed's daughter prisoner by late 919. It tends to be assumed that it was 'natural' that Mercia should submit to Edward and thus begin its 'English' destiny: this is a false assumption. Until the establishment of the Vikings in Northumbria on a permanent basis in the middle of the ninth century, which to a degree united southern England in the front line, Mercia and Wessex had been bitter enemies. It was common necessity that thrust the land-holding classes together in the two kingdoms. The uniting of Wessex and Mercia still awaits its historian, but what studies have been made suggest that, Vikings or no Vikings, there remained an important and intransigent Mercian faction opposed to the West Saxon connection. In 918 Edward was in a very strong, although threatened, position. He was plainly poised to eliminate Viking power south of the Humber. Yet by 919 the Dublin–York axis was again in being; the Vikings held Northumbria, and Mercians must have feared that they would again be reduced to misery. No wonder Edward felt he could risk what amounted to a *coup d'état* to secure Mercia.

The Welsh, too, were impressed by Edward. Their main enemy was Mercia, and the man who had subjugated Mercia was a man they could deal with. After Mercia submitted to Edward, so did the most important Welsh princes, and he became overlord of West Wales; if the *Chronicle* can be believed, smaller princes followed suit and his power extended over all Wales.

The extent of Edward's success is sometimes summed up in the phrase 'conquest of the Danelaw', but it is in fact hard to be sure exactly what the Danelaw was. Legal compilations of *c.*1100 or later assume that England falls, as far as the law is concerned, into three divisions, of which the Danelaw is one. It used to be assumed that the maximum area of Danish dominance, that is England east of Watling Street, was meant. The earliest reference to the Danelaw is found in the laws of King Aethelred II, where it seems to mean only the more northerly areas of Danish influence, i.e. Lincolnshire and Yorkshire. Post-Conquest sources, sources from an age that cared greatly for official inquiries into the state of things as they were 'on the day King Edward [the Confessor] was living and dead' and incorporated them into legal records of various kinds, of which Domesday Book (see below, pp. 226–7) is the most famous, are adamant that all eastern England from Middlesex to Yorkshire lay in the Danelaw. There is no question that a very substantial part of the aristocracy of this area was of Viking origin or that they had dominated the whole of it for 38 years without intermission before Edward the Elder's conquest. Since both Edward and his successor tended to pay attention to local sensibilities even when promoting West Saxon penetration in the conquered areas, there is nothing improbable in supposing that Danish-derived customs were imposed on eastern England in the last quarter of the ninth century

Scandinavian Settlement

The problem of Scandinavian Settlement in ninth-century England is in some ways similar to those posed by that of their Anglo-Saxon predecessors (see pp. 23–37). The evidence is of five main types. First, there are the blunt statements of the *Anglo-Saxon Chronicle*, echoed by other narrative sources, that land in Northumbria, Mercia and East Anglia was 'shared out', 'ploughed', or 'settled' (cf. p. 147). Second, much, though not all, of the area north and east of the frontier agreed by Alfred and Guthrum, which came to be known as the 'Danelaw' (pp. 132, 161, 164), was marked by distinctive forms of social and administrative organization which seem to be Scandinavian in origin; for example, King Aethelred II's Wantage Code was apparently addressed to the territory of the Five Boroughs (Lincoln, Nottingham, Derby, Leicester and Stamford), and the code is strongly Scandinavian, both in language and in institutions. Third, there are numerous place-names of Scandinavian origin in the same general area, which are themselves of two main types: names with a Scandinavian suffix, like *-by*, usually compounded with a Scandinavian personal name or place-name element, and 'hybrid' names with an English suffix but a Scandinavian name element, like Grimston (1). This place-name evidence may be placed alongside the very strong Scandinavian influence on the English language generally, which extends to many items in everyday vocabulary and even to personal pronouns ('they', 'them', 'their'). Fourth, there is archaeological evidence from Viking burials, but, unlike those of the pagan Anglo-Saxons, these are extremely rare (2), and their distribution has been described by a noted expert as 'to all intents meaningless'; it is perhaps characteristic of the problems of Scandinavian archaeology in England that the only substantial Viking cemetery ever found was at Ingleby, Derbyshire—a Scandinavian place-name denoting an English settlement! Finally, however, there is evidence of the impact of Viking art and legend in the very considerable amount of Viking Age sculpture that survives in the north of England (3–4).

To decide the density and disruptiveness of Scandinavian settlement on this evidence is very far from easy. The narrative sources are straightforward, but they say nothing direct about numbers, nor do they enable one to distinguish between settlements of peasant soldiers in large numbers and the takeover of existing settlements and their workforce by a smaller number of warrior nobles. The institutional evidence is discussed in the text (p. 164); it is now doubted whether much that was once thought Scandinavian, like the substitution of 'ploughgang' or '*carucate*' for hide, is Scandinavian at all; and institutional evidence, in any case, could merely reflect the influence of a landlord class.

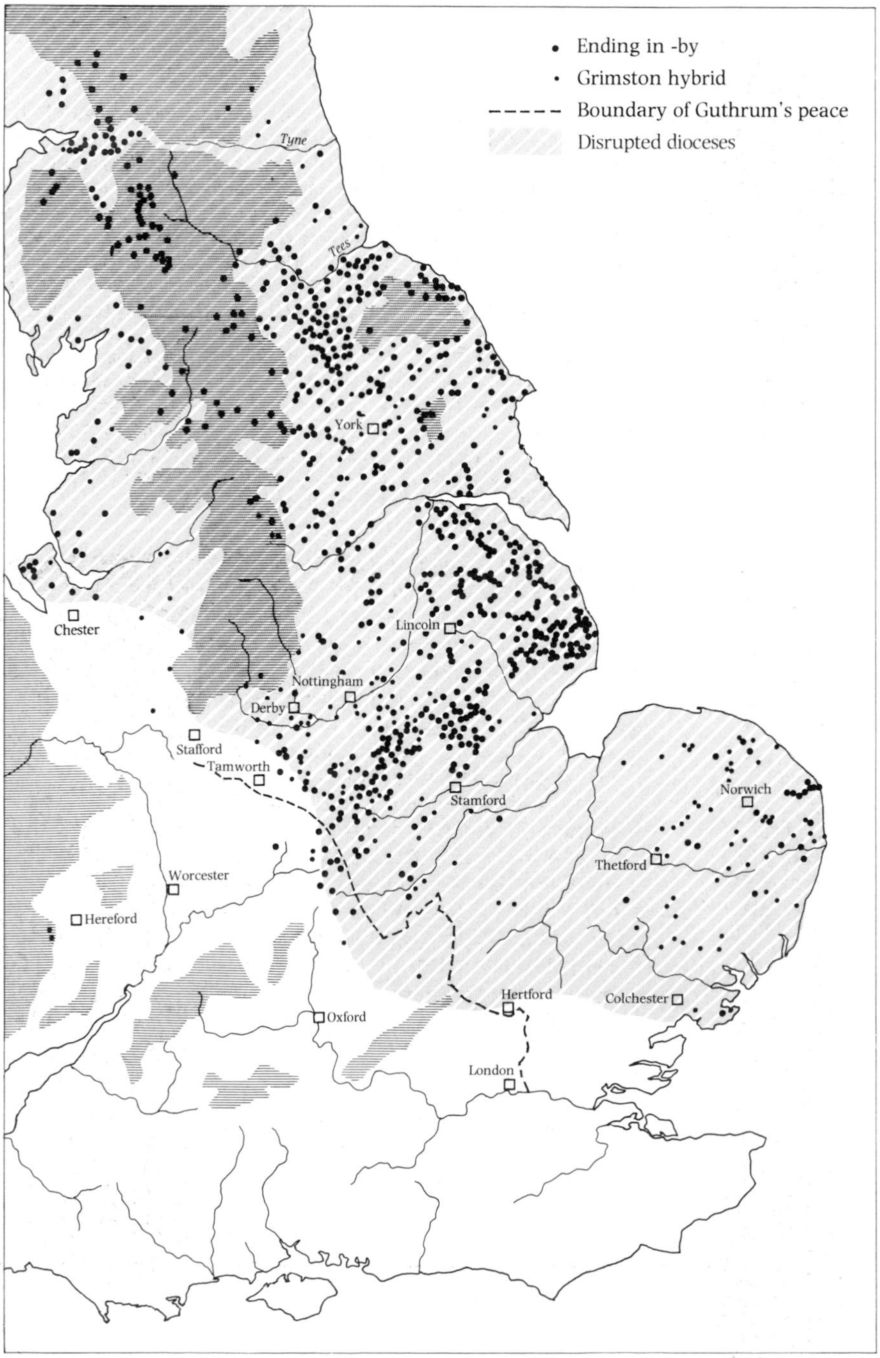

1

1 Map of Scandinavian place-names in eastern England (from D. Hill, *An Atlas of Anglo-Saxon England* (Blackwell, 1981)). Note the heavy concentration of *-by* names in Lincs, Leics. and the North and West Ridings, by contrast with the preponderance of 'hybrid' names in the East Riding, around most of the Five Boroughs, and in East Anglia. The large number of 'Hiberno-Norse' names in Cumbria indicate settlement by Norsemen from Ireland and western Scotland *c.* 900 or later, and raise rather different problems.

Place-names and general linguistic evidence seem more promising, but have been no less controversial. No one really knows what makes a language change (cf. p. 38), and it is extremely important to remember that one determinant of nomenclature is the *proportion*, not the absolute number, of different linguistic groups in a district. A virgin settlement by a single Danish family would provide a wholly Scandinavian place-name, while settlement by hundreds in an already populated area might nevertheless be linguistically swamped; this might explain why purely Scandinavian names are common in the North and West Ridings, but Scandinavian names are much rarer, and usually of the hybrid type, in East Anglia, the most heavily populated part of England in 1086. Two things about this evidence do, however, seem to be agreed. First, even in areas with large numbers of Scandinavian names, English survived, and a majority of field-names remained English. Second, settlements on relatively good land, where there was already an English population and where Scandinavian names are therefore few and often hybrid, constituted the earliest settlement phase. To this one can add that purely Scandinavian names, which are often found on relatively bad, and arguably previously unoccupied, land, are nevertheless also early, because they show no sign at all of the sort of assimilation with English which we know to have occurred later. That early settlers were occupying not only good settled land but also less good and perhaps unoccupied territory at the same time, suggests that pressure on landed resources was heavy, and settlement relatively dense. Linguistic evidence does therefore lend qualified support to a theory of considerable, if not overwhelming, settlement.

Such a theory is apparently contradicted by the scarce archaeological evidence, but here too there are complications. Quite a high proportion of what pagan burials there are seem to have been in pre-existent, or at least subsequent, churchyards (one was even in an old Roman cemetery which continued in Saxon use at Saffron Walden—**2**). Churchyards were of course constantly disturbed down the ages, and a great deal of archaeological evidence could thus have been lost. It is also argued from churchyard burials that the Scandinavians were not militantly pagan, and simply added the Christian God to their pantheon. With the proviso that pagan rites are pagan rites, whether or not they take place in churchyards, this may well be right. In the mid-tenth century, a poem in the *Anglo-Saxon Chronicle* distinguishes between the Norse army of the redoubtedly pagan descendants of Ivarr in Dublin and the Christian Danes of the Five Boroughs, suggesting that the latter had been rapidly converted. All the same, this evidence needs to be qualified by the fact of episcopal disruption in the Danelaw (**1**, and p. 147), and by the evidence of sculpture like that at Gosforth (**3**) that memories of pagan traditions, died hard in Scandinavian England, as they also did in Iceland; there is no counterpart to this in early English sculpture. Viking Age sculpture in northern England is sometimes found on earlier Christian sites, it shows points of continuity with Anglian traditions, and it duly, as at Gosforth, assimilated the Christian message; but it did not ignore the pagan Scandinavian past. The stress of the sources on the paganism of their Viking enemies may not have been misplaced.

P. Wormald

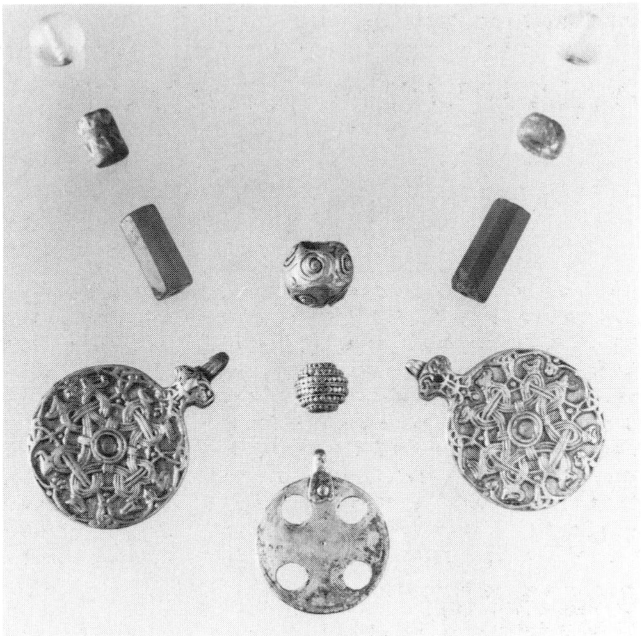

2

2 Necklace, with ornamented silver-gilt pendants, a plain silver pendant, and beads of silver, cornelian, crystal and glass (diam. of ornamented pendants 3.8 cm) from a woman's grave in the once-Roman cemetery at Saffron Walden, now in the Saffron Walden museum. The pendants are decorated in a Scandinavian style, and have been variously dated to the late ninth or late tenth century, but a pagan burial of a Scandinavian lady in Essex would suit the earlier historical context better.

3

3 The east face of the high cross in the churchyard at Gosforth, Cumbria. A crucifixion, attended by Longinus and a lady with a distinctively Scandinavian hair style can be seen at the base; above is a scene reflecting the vengeance of Viðarr, son of Oðinn, on the Great Wolf, an episode in *Ragnarök*, the Norse Doomsday. Other episodes appear on other faces.

4

4 Sculpture from the church at Middleton, North Riding, Yorkshire. In the foreground is one of several Middleton crosses of the period; it has a badly debased vine-scroll, showing continuity with the Anglian tradition (cf. figs 89, 90). In the background is a panel, presumably from another cross, showing a helmeted warrior with sword. It was made from the same template (or stencil), and perhaps by the same artist, as the more famous warrior on another Middleton cross (cf. Sawyer, 1971, pl. xiv). The latter was once considered of late ninth-century date, and to show a pagan warrior stretched out with his weapons in a grave, but it is now thought to show an enthroned warrior, and to be of rather later date.

146 One of eleven 'hogback' stones from Brompton, North Yorkshire (Dean and Chapter, Durham). Most such stones, probably grave-covers, occur in northern England; they are 10th/11th century. The bears which sometimes hug the roof-ridge of the formalized house possibly had Scandinavian cultic significance.

and that, in some shape or other, they survived even the Norman Conquest.

It used to be taken without question that the Viking invasions involved mass migration from Denmark to eastern England and that the many instances of apparently distinct peasant custom and status in this part of the world were of Danish origin. In particular, the strikingly large number of sokemen, or peasants with a high degree of freedom from the more onerous incidents of servitude, can be explained by supposing the sokemen to be the descendants of the rank and file of the Danish armies. The numbers involved in the Viking invasion are now much disputed, though they were certainly considerable. In any case, irrespective of the question of the size of the Viking armies, it is increasingly clear that sokemen represent an ancient, pre-Danish, form of tenure. What requires explanation is not the sokemen of eastern England but the absence of sokemen in many midland and southern counties, and the abundance of slaves there. The more servile areas seem to coincide with the sphere of influence of the more enduring and the more onerous of the early English hegemonies, the Mercian and the West Saxon, and perhaps this is where an explanation should be sought (see pp. 162–3).

If it was Edward the Elder who converted the kingdom of Wessex into a kingdom of England it was his eldest son, Aethelstan, who consolidated it. He was crowned at Kingston in 925. He had been brought up in Mercia, was clearly familiar with the Mercian aristocracy and so far as we know was accepted by the Mercians without question. Aethelstan was thus enabled to have a genuine and persistent policy for the north. He married his sister to the Norse king of York, Sihtric, in 926. Apart from anything else this was a useful counter to Mercian disaffection. But Sihtric died the next year, leaving a young son by an earlier marriage, Olaf, as his heir. Guthfrith, Olaf's uncle and king of Norse Dublin, came over to support him. Aethelstan decided the time had come to add Northumbria to his kingdom; he utterly defeated the two Vikings in a short but effective campaign. He seized York and razed its fortifications, an indication that he still regarded it as a possible centre of trouble. The kings of Scotland and Strathclyde, and the English lord of the great fortress of Bamburgh, all became his men. He then went south and west and extended his domination over the Welsh princes, gaining a substantial yearly tribute.

In 934 war broke out between what we must now call the English and the Scots. There was no pitched battle but Aethelstan humiliated the Scottish king by harrying his kingdom both by land and sea. In 937, realizing that Aethelstan was too powerful for any other single island ruler to tackle, the Dublin Norse allied with Strathclyde and Scotland and invaded England. The campaign reached its climax in the great battle of Brunanburh which the English won. There were heavy casualties on both sides, but the invaders were crushed. Although much about Brunanburh is obscure, including its location, its importance is not in doubt. Mercians fought for the first time as an integral part of an English army. The threat to the new kingdom had been great; it is probable that the northern enemies penetrated far into England before Aethelstan repelled them. Half a century later, the homilist Abbot Aelfric (see below, pp. 201 ff.) had no doubt that Brunanburh was a great and decisive victory. At any rate, Aethelstan had no more trouble with the north.

It must not be thought Aethelstan, or any of his pre-Conquest successors, incorporated Northumbria into England as successfully as they did Mercia. It was always necessary for the late Anglo-Saxon kings to go carefully with the north, and shortly before the Conquest the Godwine family's fall began with the failure of an attempt to increase the weight of southern control over Northumbria (see below, p. 232). The main lever these kings had in the north was the power to appoint the senior churchman of the region, the archbishop of York,

147 Silver brooch, diameter 3.5 cm, found with a large hoard of English silver coins in Rome, and likely evidence of an English visitor there early in the 10th century (British Museum). The central roundel imitates a coin of Edward the Elder.

148 Viking weapons, plus tongs and anchor, from a hoard found at London Bridge (Museum of London). They probably date from about the time of Aethelred II.

who was in some sense their representative there. From the time of Edgar, York was sometimes held in plurality with Worcester; this gave the archbishop a larger income and a tie to the south. The king of the day also appointed the earl of Northumria (or sometimes earls, since the area was not always treated as a whole but at times was split into its northern and southern components). It is significant for the extent of persistent Viking influence that by Edgar's reign these officials were given the Anglo-Danish title of earl in Northumbria and other areas of Danish influence. Their equivalents elsewhere were given the old English title of ealdorman until the reign of Cnut, during which earl became the universal term.

Aethelstan had important connections with the Continent, which had lasting consequences. The common problems of the Franks and West Saxons had already by Alfred's time led to mutual interest and sympathetic understanding between the East Frankish and West Saxon courts. A sign of English interest in Continental affairs is that when Charles the Fat was deposed by Arnulf of Carinthia in 887, much the best and most judicious account of what happened is to be found, not in the Frankish annals, but in the *Anglo-Saxon Chronicle*. It is significant that behind the *coup* was Charles's refusal to take the Viking threat seriously (he was a Swabian and his interests lay in the southern part of his empire), and Arnulf's willingness to face it. Arnulf was in many ways the German Alfred, and he inflicted on the Vikings a decisive defeat. It is not surprising that he found an interested audience in Alfred's England. After 919 the Saxon ducal dynasty established themselves as the rulers of Eastern Francia. Their first king was Henry I, 'the Fowler'. He married his son, the future Otto the Great, to Aethelstan's half-sister Edith; many German kings descended from this union. Henry I had to deal not so much with Vikings as with the Hungarians, who were worse. It is interesting to see him borrowing West Saxon techniques a generation or so later. In 929 he imitated King Aethelwulf (see above, p. 140), and made his kingdom impartible, ending the division of the crown's resources at every succession where the last king had left more than one son. About the same time he built a series of *Burgen*, sharing many features with the Anglo-Saxon *burh* and defending Saxony as Alfred's *burhs* had defended Wessex.

It is not surprising, then, to see Aethelstan involved in Continental affairs. Edward the Elder had married another of his daughters to the last surviving Carolin-

gian of the direct line, Charles the Simple, who by Aethelstan's accession had fallen on evil times. Charles spent the last years of his life as a captive and Aethelstan provided a refuge for his son, incidentally earning him the title of Louis d'Outremer. As the Carolingians declined, the rising family in western Francia was that later known as the Capetians, headed by Hugh the Great under the title of duke of the Franks. He married another of Aethelstan's half-sisters. Thus both old and new power in the old Carolingian Empire sought alliance and favours from the house of Wessex, and in 936 Aethelstan must have played a large part in the restoration of his protégé and nephew Louis as king of the West Franks.

The political relationships Aethelstan promoted proved ephemeral, but there were important cultural consequences, notably the first contacts between English churchmen and the Continental reforming monks (see below, p. 181). The cult of Saint Ursula and her 11,000 virgin companions probably reached Cologne via the English court at this time. In turn the English got a number of important manuscripts; important both for their contents and the quality of their illuminations. The debt of tenth-century English manuscript illumination to the Continent has been fairly well charted; the debt of tenth-century law codes to Continental and Carolingian example has not (see below, pp. 170–1).

For all Aethelstan's greatness he had not dealt with the Viking threat for good. It came again when he died in 939, to be succeeded by his 18-year-old brother, Edmund. The Norse Vikings from Dublin had what was al most their final fling in England, and Olaf Guthfrithson, king of Dublin, reconstituted the united kingdom of Dublin and York without difficulty in 939. In 940 Olaf invaded Mercia and East Anglia, the archbishops of York and Canterbury mediated, and Edmund surrendered much of the south-east Midlands and Lincolnshire. Olaf died soon after in 942, and Edmund recovered the territories south of the Humber and eventually drove the Norsemen out of the city of York itself. In 946 Edmund was murdered, leaving two sons, Eadwig and Edgar. They were, however, only small boys, and so he was succeeded by the last of the sons of Edward the Elder, Eadred, who had to deal with a new crisis in the north. Eric Bloodaxe, a former king in Norway noted for his bloodthirsty ways, descended on Northumbria and maintained himself in power there intermittently until 954, when he was expelled and then fell in battle. Eadred was able to extort recognition as king of all England from the Northumbrians. This victory left its mark on Eadred's charters, which give him such grand titles as 'Eadred, king, emperor of the Anglo-Saxons and Northumbrians, governor of the pagans, defender of the Britons' (Birch, *Cart.*, no. 911).

The Vikings were still a danger even though one of their greatest leaders, Eric Bloodaxe, had failed utterly in drawing a force of Vikings around him and seeking to restore Viking fortunes in the north. Prudent men did not write them off altogether. Eadred himself provided in his will for a contingency fund should it be necessary to buy the Vikings off. Nevertheless, it is obvious that the new Englishmen were gaining confidence. King Alfred had kept his *fyrd* in the field for three months, and those not on *fyrd* duty had still, presumably, to provide the garrison for the *burhs*. Aethelstan probably required two warrior to serve for one plough (p. 154). By the end of the century, and probably by Edgar's reign at the latest, one warrior served for each five hides of land. One senses that the pressure was off, although these changes could also mean that weaponry was becoming more expensive.

The Governance and Institutions of the English Kingdom

It will be apparent that the English kingdom put together out of the traditions of Mercia and Wessex under the pressure of the Vikings was a real entity. A study of its governance in general and the growth of its institutions in particular will confirm this.

The Anglo-Saxon kingdoms had some common institutions from early in their history. It has earlier been pointed out that in all of them the chief sources of the protection of the individual were his kindred and his wergeld, or man price, which was, of course, his obvious badge of status and which the kindred would exact for him should he be killed. Throughout the Anglo-Saxon period, a man's position in life depended largely on the nature of his kin and of his relations with them. Kinship relations were the chief source of protection, but also the chief source of obligation; if one's kin should happen to be involved in a feud this obligation might be very onerous indeed. Some of this survived the Conquest, and it is important to emphasize that the family as a source of social power or powerlessness was to have a long history that has not yet reached its end. A society composed of kindred groups is usually called a tribal society, but from its inception Anglo-Saxon England was more than tribal.

The kinship network was reinforced by the institutions of lordship and vassalage. Assumptions about Anglo-Saxon society have often been coloured by nineteenth-century beliefs that early England was so primitively, so Romantically, Teutonic as to be a kind of peasant commonwealth. This myth can feed another: that a strongly stratified society and the social institutions which expressed aristocratic authority came with the Conquest. These myths should be dead. No historian would accept them. But they won't quite lie down. It is therefore necessary to emphasize that the society of late Anglo-Saxon England, like that of early Anglo-Saxon England, had great inequalities of wealth and position, and a very powerful aristocracy. This society was held together by the bonds of lordship, or perhaps better by the bonds and privileges of lordship. The great magnates were the vassals of their lord the king; they would, in turn, have a number of ordinary warriors subordinate to them. It is probable that the bonds were symbolized by the ceremonies of homage and fealty. Homage was the bowing of the vassal before his lord, placing his hands within the hands of the lord. Since the sources treat bowing down to a lord and subjecting oneself to a lord as synonymous, it seems that they are taking the ceremony of homage for

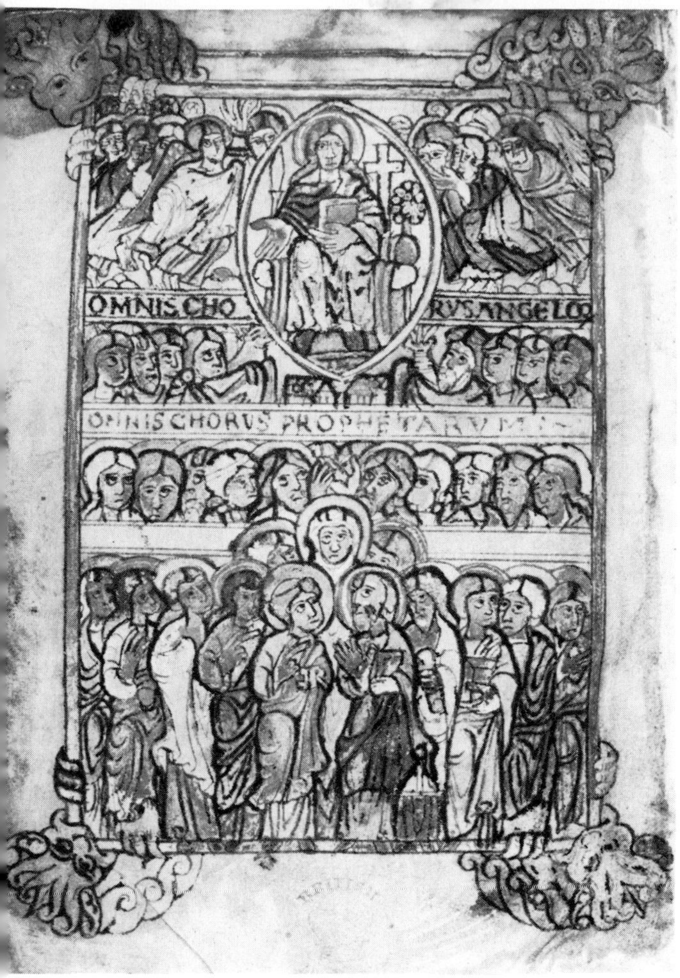

149 Christ in Majesty surrounded by the implements of his Passion, from the Aethelstan Psalter (British Library, MS Cotton Galba A. xviii, fol. 2v (see also fig. 154). Note the biting beasts in the corners.

granted. Fealty was a verbal oath, that might be varied for special occasions, taken with the hand on relics. Since one of the earliest texts of the fealty oath in its commonest form comes from a tenth-century English source, it is obvious that the English were familiar with the ceremony.

This kind of society is usually called feudal, except in the special case of English history. This exception has been made because scholars have traditionally agreed that 'feudalism' was introduced by William the Conqueror in 1066, although they have totally failed to agree about what this entailed. The Conquest did introduce important differences in English society, as well as preserve important continuities (see below, pp. 233 ff.). There is, however, no need to refuse ourselves the use of the term feudal for Anglo-Saxon society. It is, in a sense, important to use it in so far as it points to certain fundamental family resemblances between early insular and Continental societies, and even non-European societies. Nevertheless, we must never forget that feudal societies differ amongst themselves as much as capitalist societies do, and when looking at a particular society must describe it in its own terms before making comparisons.

Feudal institutions have been traditionally studied in terms posited by legal historians, who have sought a quite improbable precision and uniformity. The greatest legal historian of all, Maitland, pointed out that particularity and local variation are of the essence of a feudal society. It is what has been called sociological feudalism that matters. In the light of this one can see that a feudal society is as much a society made up of families as any tribal society. The king and his magnates will normally be related, by marriage if not by close ties of blood. The warrior, or the peasant, will acquire his bonds of lordship and his privileges as a vassal, normally by inheritance. What you were in this society depended basically on what family you were born into. The introduction of lordship brought different layers of kinship groups into association and mutual dependance, and thus made it possible for a society to cover a much greater territorial extent than a tribal society could. For a large part of its history Anglo-Saxon England managed with only the most primitive bureaucratic institutions. It was a face to face society. The feudal element allowed this essential personal element to be reconciled with the need to enforce obedience 'at a distance' by the reigning king. By the end of the period Anglo-Saxon kings met their magnates at least three times a year, usually at great feasts of the Church. During such sessions of the royal court a magnate was at the mercy of the king. Everything suggests that absence without a suitable excuse was conspicuous and dangerous. The magnates themselves must have often met their warriors in their neighbourhoods.

There is a very strong element of mutual dependence in all this. Great as the difference between the social position and wealth of an ordinary warrior and a king obviously was, the class of warriors was not large. It is generally reckoned that there were about 5,000 knights in England after 1066 and it is not likely that the Anglo-Saxons military aristocracy was much larger. We know from a contemporary source that the presence or absence of as few as 50 warriors at a battle could turn the fortunes of the armies. The warriors, as individuals never mattered, as a group they provided all the coercive power there was in that society and a comparatively small group of defectors could destroy a very great man. Could and did: it happened to King Sigeberht of Wessex in the eighth century, and to Earl Godwine in 1051; and the refusal of the West Saxon warriors to fight the Mercians and Northumbrians in 1065 marked the beginning of the end for the whole Godwine family (see above, p. 115, and below, p. 232).

The point of discussing what were largely perennial features of Anglo-Saxon society in the tenth-century context is that these institutions were under pressure to change and develop, pressure that came from the top, from the king. Aethelstan held numerous councils of his magnates. His predecessors had done so too, but what is new is the scatter of venues. We know of the location of these councils mainly from charters authorized by them for some great religious house or preserved in the archives of such a house. As great religious houses were mainly found in southern England at this time, the

Late Anglo-Saxon England and the Continent

Little evidence survives on Anglo-Saxon foreign relations, but there is enough to suggest that they were very important. The royal marriages alone—of Aethelstan's half-sisters (see p. 160), of Aethelred and Cnut with Emma of Normandy, of Cnut's daughter with the future Emperor Henry III—imply that England was far from isolated from its neighbours. In fact, nearly all Anglo-Saxons—kings, churchmen, nobles and peasants—were touched by foreign influence in some way, and not a few in many ways.

Kings could be great imitators, and some English rulers behaved like their foreign counterparts. If Edgar's coronation at Bath in 973 was an imperial ceremony to celebrate his dominion over the rest of Britain (but see p. 189), it hints at awareness of Otto of Germany's coronation as Holy Roman Emperor at Rome in 962. Moreover, it has been suggested that some of the most impressive features of late Anglo-Saxon government—including national taxation, general oaths and perhaps even the remarkable coinage system—were based on Carolingian precedent. Some legislative measures, too, may have been of foreign inspiration. In 1006, Henry II of Germany prohibited the sale of Christians to the heathen, a measure which appeared in one of Aethelred II's law codes shortly afterwards.

The tenth-century monastic reform movement was also indebted to Continental influence (see p. 181). Foreign ecclesiastics visited England, English churchmen went abroad. The synod which drew up the *Regularis Concordia*, an important manual of monastic usage, during Edgar's reign, was attended and advised by monks from Fleury and St Peter's, Ghent. English travellers were not simply major figures like Dunstan and Oswald. In the late tenth century Anglo-Saxon artists were illustrating manuscripts in Fleury (2, 3). Such visitors could carry important objects and see important things. The Carolingian Utrecht Psalter was in Canterbury by about the year 1000, whence, perhaps together with other Carolingian manuscripts, it had a major influence on English figure drawing (1). Similarly, the westworks of some late tenth-century English churches, including Winchester, had Carolingian and Ottonian models. If the tide of reform was slackening under Cnut and Edward the Confessor, by their day foreigners were joining the English episcopate.

Kings and laymen could also be connected with foreign churches. Cnut's gifts to them seem to have been considerable, and included a sacramentary and a Psalter sent to Cologne. Aelfgar of Mercia sent a Gospel book to Rheims in memory of his son Burchard, who was buried there after he died on pilgrimage to Rome (5). The noble pilgrim was probably a common sight in these years. In 1061, Tostig Godwineson visited Rome with his wife, his brother Gyrth and a sizeable party.

English magnates may also have had other important continental links for which evidence is largely lacking. It is suggestive, however, that late in the tenth century, Ealdorman Aethelweard sent a Latin translation of the *Anglo-Saxon Chronicle* to Matilda, abbess of Essen (4), a grand-daughter of Otto I by his English wife. As Aethelweard and Matilda were only distantly related, one would gladly know how they came to be in touch in the first place. Possibly her English blood was less important from this point of view than might be thought, and English and German aristocratic contact far more extensive than can be proved.

Of extensive trade there is sufficient indication. Links with Scandinavia were especially important. York is said to have been much visited by Danish merchants (see pp. 166–7), and among their wares

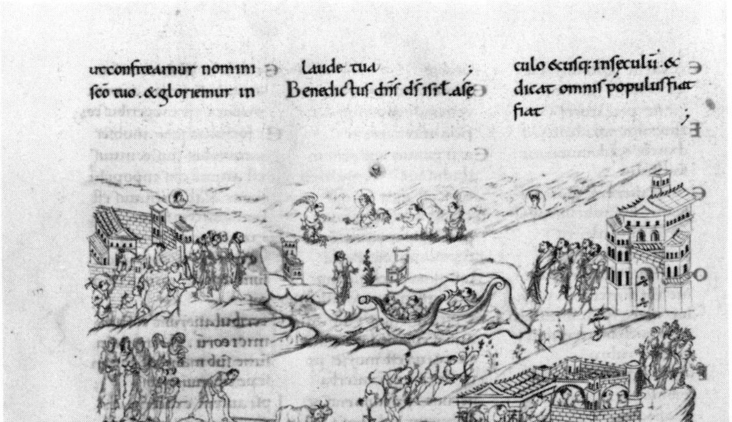

2

1 Page from the earliest of three surviving English copies of an early ninth-century Psalter from Rheims (now in Utrecht), Christ Church, Canterbury, early 11th century (British Library, MS Harley 603, fol. 54v, 380 × 309 mm).

2 Historiated initial I by an English artist working at Fleury, late tenth century (Paris, Bibliothèque Nationale, MS Lat. 6401, fol. 159r, 275 × 195 mm).

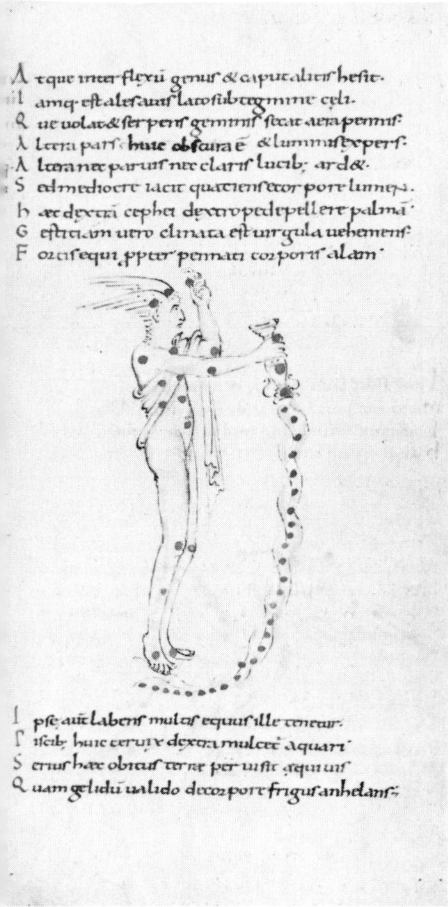

3 Drawing of the constellation Aquarius by an Anglo-Saxon artist in Fleury, late tenth century (British Library, MS Harley 2506, fol. 38v, 293 × 212 mm).

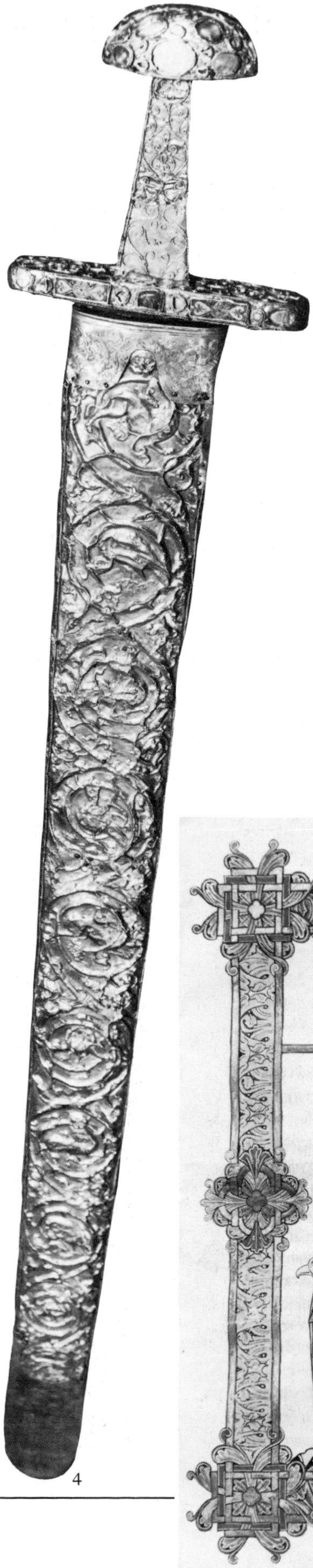

4

4 Sword and sheath covered with stamped gold, probably given to Essen by the Abbess Matilda (Essen Minster, length 95.5 cm). They are not English but have been included to indicate the richness of the very great in this age.

were probably hone stones, essential to many of the country's agricultural workers (for one in use, see fig. 193), and sometimes imported from Continental sources which included southern Norway. Bristol may have owed its early development to commerce between the west country and Norse trading centres in southern Ireland. Indeed, merchants from Ireland were in Cambridge on at least one occasion during the tenth century, when some of their merchandise was stolen by a priest. However, to be convinced of the sheer range of foreign merchants operating in England one must turn to the text known as IV Aethelred. This identifies some of those who passed through London: men from Flanders, Ponthieu, Normandy and the Île de France; and men of the emperor—Germans. The renders which these latter were required to make at Christmas and Easter are presumably an indication of the commodities they were dealing in—lengths of cloth, gloves, pepper and vinegar. That trade was evidently expected to carry on in mid-winter, when even raiders (though not those of 1015–1016) tended to settle down into winter quarters, is suggestive of its importance.

England's lack of isolation from her neighbours was from one point of view unfortunate. The Danes who came to York, the merchants of Rouen whom IV Aethelred reveals bringing wine and blubber-fish into London, such men were the news-bearers of their day, and one of the means by which foreign kings learnt of English wealth and perhaps of political divisions which invited conquest. There were at least five attempts to conquer England in the eleventh century, three of them—two Danish and one Norman—successful. It is ironic that they are much better documented than most of the other matters discussed here. Nor can it have been much to English comfort that their enemies, if unwelcome, were far from unknown.

M. K. Lawson

5 Saint Luke from the Gospels sent to Rheims by Aelfgar (Rheims, Bibliothèque Municipale, MS 9, fol. 88r, 320 × 238 mm).

evidence must exaggerate the number of West Saxon and south Mercian venues. Even so Aethelstan is found at Nottingham, Tamworth, Whittlebury (near Northampton), and Colchester, as well as London and Exeter. The peripatetic monarchy taking government all round England, which was so marked a feature of English medieval rule, begins with Aethelstan.

Aethelstan seems also to have made an important change in provincial organization and so in the status of the most senior magnates, the ealdormen. In ninth-century Wessex each shire (see above, p. 58), had an ealdorman. Mercian arrangements are less well-known, but seem to have been similar. A law of Aethelstan's nephew, king Edgar (959–75), strongly suggests that by that time there were ealdormen with much wider authority, and that those of Mercia, East Anglia and Northumbria were, in effect, viceregents for their respective regions. Because the ealdorman of East Anglia, Aethelwine, came from a family with close ties to the great Fenland abbey of Ramsey, a community more than usually literate, we know something about his family. Its founder, a contemporary of king Aethelstan's, was himself called Aethelstan; he first appears as an ealdorman in his namesake's reign, and was nicknamed 'half-king'.

It looks, therefore, as if ealdormen with very wide authority were the creation not of Edgar, but of Aethelstan. Aethelstan 'half-king's' sphere of authority is called not an ealdordom but a kingdom by the Ramsey monk Byrhtferth. (It is convenient to use the Old English term 'ealdordom' to denote the area over which an ealdorman had authority, since 'earldom' can have anachronistic implications if applied to the tenth century (the word 'earl' is worse).) This quasi-regal authority was inherited by the half-king's son Aethelwold, and after his death passed to his younger brother Aethelwine, who is indicated as having extensive authority in Edgar's fourth code. Two other brothers are named at Ramsey as having the position of ealdorman, but clearly were in some sense subordinate to the man bearing the title of ealdorman of East Anglia. It is only the accident of the Ramsey connection that reveals a continuity of semi-regal status in East Anglia and in the family of Aethelstan 'half-king'.

Much remains to be done before history of ealdormen and their spheres of office in tenth-century England is fully understood. It is clear that in tenth-century Wessex there was no longer a single ealdorman for each shire; the whole of the former kingdom was divided between two, and sometimes three, ealdormen. There are indications that the creation of exalted ealdormen elsewhere was Aethelstan's solution to the problem of how to govern his so recently extended kingdom. Mercia, as Offa knew it, was basically England between the Humber and the Thames. Aethelstan may have divided this area into two main provinces. The western province, comprising the medieval dioceses of Lichfield, Worcester and Hereford, is what was thereafter meant by Mercia. The eastern province cannot be so neatly defined in ecclesiastical terms, but geographically it stretched from Lincoln to the Thames and included Cambridge and Northampton. This area was usually called 'East Anglia' but occasionally and significantly 'East Mercia'.

The family of Aethelstan 'half-king', after dominating East Anglia for close on a century, lost its consequence on the death of King Aethelred II. In 1017, according to the *Chronicle*, Cnut divided England into four parts: Mercia, East Anglia, Northumbria and Wessex, having an earl over each of the first three but having Wessex 'for himself'. By the 1020s there was an earl for the whole of Wessex (see below, p. 209). It seems that the existence of superior earls (earlier ealdormen) with extensive authority in East Anglia, Mercia and Northumbria may go back to the tenth century and that the major innovation of Cnut's reign was the addition of an earl of Wessex to the original triumvirate. Certainly until 1066 some earls were very much more important than others. It looks as if the office of ealdorman developed along lines laid down in Aethelstan's reign, until William the Conqueror felt himself strong enough to begin to reduce the title of earl to a mere badge of status.

Well before the Norman Conquest England was divided up into shires; nearly all the historic shires of England, as they were to remain until 1974, were there. Each ealdordom consisted of a group of them. Some were very old; those of the old kingdom of Wessex—Hampshire, Wiltshire, Dorset, Devon, Somerset—were in existence by the late eighth or the ninth century and probably long before. Some, Essex, Kent and Sussex, were former kingdoms. The shires of the Midlands were laid out at some time after 900 and before 1016. There is dispute about the precise date, and the issue is complicated by the problem of the relationship of the shires to the burghal districts which appear in the tenth-century laws (see below, p. 176). It is certain, however, that the introduction of the regular system of shires, which was to be the basis of English government for a millennium, was the work of the late Saxon kings.

The shires had sub-divisions called hundreds (in parts of the Danelaw, alternatively, 'wapentakes'). They certainly often have ancient connections. Some of them, which are called after their meeting-places, have names with clear pagan elements. The hundred court, which in the tenth century met monthly and was supposed to be attended by all free tenants, must have had much local business of which we know nothing. But increasingly in the tenth century it was used as a means of extending the weight of royal government to the countryside. The hundred probably always had military functions. The Latin chronicle of Ealdorman Aethelweard, a contemporary of King Edgar, uses 'hundreds' as a synonym of *fyrd*. In the tenth century the military obligations owed by the tenants of the hundred were being reshaped to provide a new royal weapon, a fleet that was led by the king. Florence of Worcester (see below, p. 222) says that Edgar circumnavigated Britain annually. This was presumably to overawe the princelings of Viking descent or inclination who clustered round the Irish Sea. (For Alfred's fleet see above, p. 150).

The early twelfth-century compilation known as the 'Laws of Henry I' tells us that English shires were divided into hundreds and shipsokes; the latter seem to have been groups of three hundreds, each group being required to produce a ship and a crew of 60. What looks like the first mention of this arrangement and the levying of a fleet (*shipfyrd*) based on it is the *Chronicle* entry for 1008. It is, however, likely that the institution had already been established because the bishop of Sherborne alludes to the shipsoke in a letter and makes clear that his predecessors were concerned in the matter too. It is most likely that Edgar invented the system, and if the at least partially corrupt Oswaldslow Charter (Birch, *Cart.*, no. 1135), which claims that he subdued much of Ireland, including Dublin, can be believed, he may have taken his *shipfyrd* there on an expedition before 964. (What we now know about the links between the Vikings of Dublin and those of York would explain the likely reason for such an expedition.) Naval power would do much to explain the unwonted peace of Edgar's reign, culminating at Chester in 973, when a number of princelings from the Irish Sea area did him homage, probably by rowing him on the Dee. The shipsoke system also continued the process of royal intervention in social arrangements.

The bishop of Sherborne tells us that other bishops got a shipsoke, and it is probable some abbots did. Edgar seems to be borrowing a policy of Otto the Great, best exemplified in the creation of the great liberty of Cologne for Otto's brother Bruno, archbishop of Cologne. (Indeed a Worcester author, describing the position of the bishop of Worcester as head of his shipsoke, uses a title, *archiductor*, similar to the one invented by Bruno's biographer, *archidux*.) With the creation of the shipsoke the bishop or abbot who held the soke replaced the ealdorman as head of the contingent to the *fyrd*. The local warriors 'followed his banner' to war and probably became his men. Our one description of the *fyrd* in action, the poem *The Battle of Maldon*, reveals that the *fyrd* consisted of men who regarded themselves as the men of their lord, the commander, in this case Ealdorman Byrhtnoth.

The creation of shipsokes must have had important effects on the distribution of power in the provinces. This can be seen most clearly in the case of Worcester. The church of Worcester was reformed in Edgar's reign (see below, p. 185). It was given a liberty (that is to say an area in which exemptions and responsibilities in regard to the exercise of justice were enjoyed) of three hundreds. This liberty came to be called Oswaldslow, after Edgar's bishop of Worcester (see below, pp. 181–5), and it constituted a shipsoke. Its establishment was associated with major changes in the organization of landed society. We have a remarkable and unique series of some 60 local charters from late tenth-century Worcester. These stress that their recipients had submitted to the bishop as their lord and counted as tenants of the church. It is likely that some at least of these men had once held their lands by royal charter, with hereditary tenure, and had not been tenants of the church of Worcester. That is to say the new arrangements of Edgar's reign had curtailed their rights of inheritance and reduced their status.

These changes would have had serious effects on the power of the ealdorman of Mercia. The *burh* of Worcester was his responsibility and also one of the sources of his power. Oswaldslow lay all round the *burh*. So the ealdorman had to cope with new circumstances in which his strong-point was surrounded by warriors subject to another lord, one whose loyalty to him could not be taken for granted. No wonder Aelfhere, ealdorman of Mercia, reacted sharply against the new policy once Edgar's death made it safe to do so (see below, p. 192).

Because the holders of the liberties were reformed and reforming churchmen, the monastic sources call Aelfhere the enemy of the monks, and he may well have been. But the reaction was really against the shipsokes and the liberties they conferred on the holders, as well as the military power the holders had filched from the ealdormen. We have details of what this new policy meant in the countryside only in a very few cases, but we do know that the reaction was very widespread and not confined to Worcester, so we may well think that Edgar enforced a policy that bit. Once again we see a West Saxon king who meant to be obeyed.

The tenth-century kings legislated on a substantial scale, like the Carolingians, on whose laws theirs were in part modelled. Early medieval kings regarded written law as a status symbol: 'real law' was customary and verbal. King Alfred's law code reeks of status with its recitation of the Ten Commandments, patristic titbits, quotation *in extenso* of the largely obsolete code of the seventh-century West Saxon king, Ine, and its clever emphasizing of the fact that Alfred was the heir to a Christian and West Saxon heritage and had by this time become the representative of even wider traditions (see above, p. 157). Something of this kind of law-making clings to tenth-century legislation, and this is especially marked in the numerous codes of King Aethelred II (979–1016), who sometimes seemed to think that pious moans in legislative form might scare off the Danes when all else failed, as all else usually did. But there is more to tenth-century legislation than propaganda and piety. For example, King Edmund tried to outlaw the feud; Aethelred II offered the status of a thegn and a wergeld of 1,200 shillings to priests of ceorlish origin, that is to say those whose birth entitled them to a wergeld of only 200 shillings, if they would remain celibate. It is not likely that either of these laws had much effect, although by the last years of the century it was held that a ceorl who had gained as much as five hides of land and answered for its military service counted as a thegn, with the higher wergeld, whatever his birth. Service was replacing birthright as a mark of distinction. What is interesting here is the habit of mind these laws display. Edmund and his grandson were legislating for major changes in regard to two major areas of socially determinative custom, feud and wergeld. It seemed to them perfectly within their power and competence to do so. What is more, it is possible to prove that, even if in these two cases their legislation was not much regarded, in other and important cases it was obeyed to the letter.

The plainest evidence is that of coinage (see the Picture Essays, pp. 130–1, 204–5). The coins themselves demonstrate that such legislation as Aethelstan's on the cur-

Norwich and Winchester

By 1066 Norwich and Winchester were among the greatest towns in England. Domesday Book suggests that in that year Norwich had between 1,437 and 1,518 burgesses. If so, the population cannot have been less than 5,000 and may have been as high as 10,000. Winchester, like London, is unrecorded in Domesday; but a survey of 1148 suggests a population of the order of 5,500, and archaeological evidence indicates that the city had not grown very much since the Conquest. Such figures may not sound high, but they are; if one reflects that no English provincial city is thought to have exceeded 14,000 until the sixteenth century.

The plans of the two towns contrast strongly. The core of Winchester's is a neat grid laid out almost certainly by Alfred (see p. 152) within the Roman walls; though by 1066 there had been extensive suburban growth. The sprawling tangle of Norwich says more about evolution than about planning. There is a second contrast. Over a third of Edward the Confessor's Winchester was occupied by monasteries and palaces. Beside the cathedral church and monastery, the Old Minster, stood another monastery, the New Minster. They were about 13 feet apart. Both were impressively built; the west tower of the New Minster stood six storeys high, each storey richly adorned with carving. Over the way was a royal nunnery, the Nunnaminster. To the west of the Old Minster stood the king's palace, to the east, the bishop's. Norwich had many churches and chapels; by 1086 there were at least 49, their wide distribution being the best evidence for the spread, and scatter, of the town. But there was no monastery at Norwich and no royal palace, though the earls of East Anglia may have had an establishment there.

At root of these differences lay a contrast in royal involvement. Winchester lay in the heartland of the power and affection of the kings of the house of Wessex. It was almost a capital, and they were often there and kept their treasure there. Norwich was in East Anglia, liberated, or conquered, by Edward the Elder (see pp. 160–1). Norfolk, Lincolnshire and Suffolk were the three most populous shires in England (see fig. 204). No late Anglo-Saxon king is known to have visited them in time of peace; no council was held in them; no charter dated from any place in them.

That Winchester was more closely linked to kings and their monks than was Norwich ensures that we know more about it. There is written record to supplement the major discoveries of archaeology. Together they make it possible to outline its development: a major ecclesiastical centre (probably a royal one also)

1 Thetford ware cooking-pot, height 12.5 cm (Norfolk Archaeological Unit).

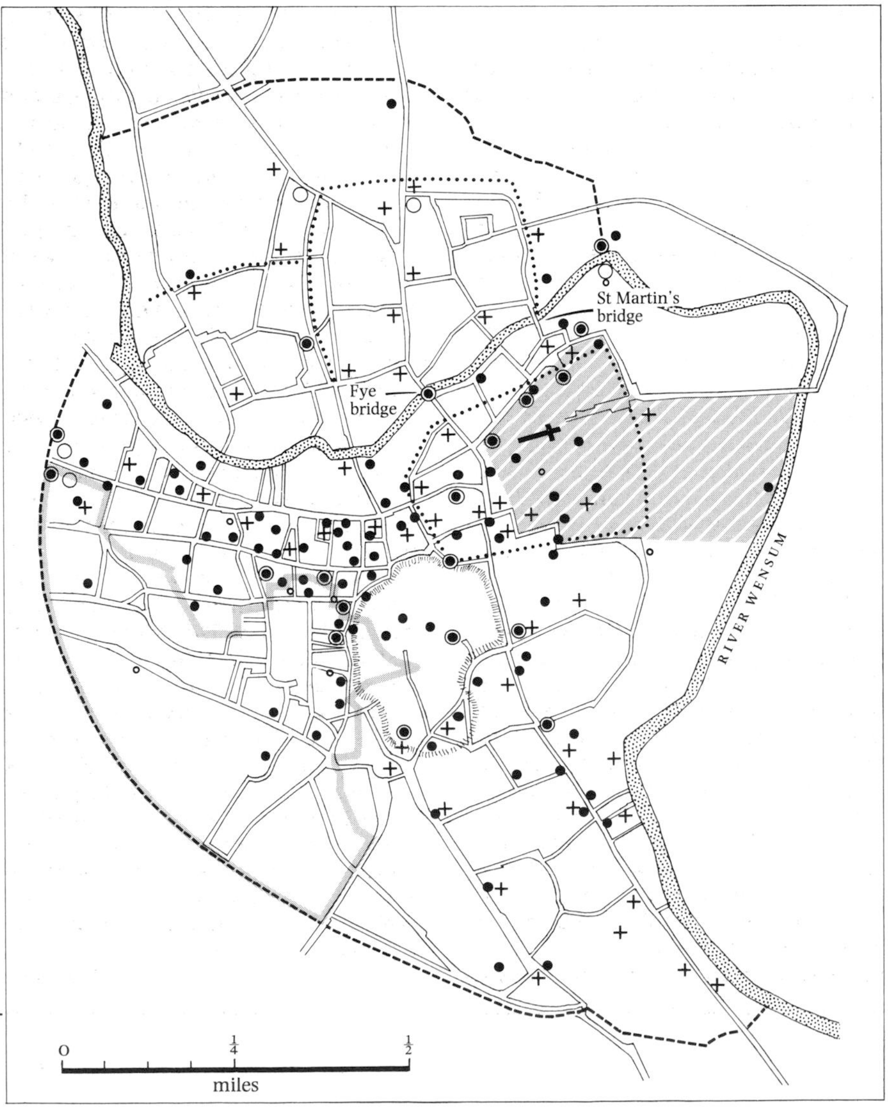

2 Norwich in the late Anglo-Saxon period (after Carter).

- ° Roman coin
- • Late Saxon pottery
- ○ Middle Saxon pottery
- ◉ Late and middle Saxon pottery
- + Churches
- ········· Saxon ditch lines
- - - - - - Medieval city wall
- Castle earthworks, post-conquest
- Approximate boundary of new Norman borough
- Medieval cathedral precinct

from the seventh century; probably acquiring its urban character through the successful implementation of Alfred's policy; developing and prospering in the following century and a half. There are saints' lives and charters to provide illuminating details. Above all there is a survey of the royal property in Winchester, made *c.* 1110 but based on one of the Confessor's reign.

The corresponding written record for Norwich is a famished little thing. The earliest document to mention the city derives from the last generation of the tenth century and shows it was one of four places in East Anglia enjoying burghal privileges. It is mentioned in writing earlier, but as a mint-signature, on coins, the earliest being of *c.* 900. The *Chronicle* records that Sweyn came with his fleet and burned it in 1004. An Old Norse poem mentions Cnut's fighting there (probably late in Ethelred's reign). There are no other written references to the town except in two wills, which permit the not very helpful deduction that there were at least two churches and one urban tenement there.

Yet Domesday proves that Norwich was one of the four or five most important towns in England. Even without Domesday we could guess as much from the output of its mint. In trying to guess how it rose to such greatness we depend on archaeology. Its evidence, while indicating settlement on parts of the site from Roman times onwards (the major Roman town of the area was three miles south, *Venta Icenorum*), provides nothing to suggest urban development until the ninth century at the earliest. The most important evidence is pottery, Thetford ware (1). It is important, not only because its distribution (2) helps to indicate the spread of the late Saxon town, but particularly because there is clear evidence that it was manufactured in Norwich on a substantial scale, in an industrial area in the west centre of the city.

Thetford, and similar late Saxon wares, were the first to have been made in really large quantities in Britain since the Romans left. Their manufacture seems to have been largely concentrated in towns. There is evidence for extensive manufacture in other towns: Stamford was another major pottery producer; bone and leather were worked on a large scale in York; a street in Thetford was four feet deep in iron-working residues. It may be that the production of consumer goods for a countryside in which coin circulated freely was a major reason for the extent to which late Anglo-Saxon England was urbanized. Such developments may have done more to transform the economy in the last Anglo-Saxon generations than any which took place for some centuries afterwards.

It is hard to know when pottery manufacture begins in Norwich. The wares concerned begin to be made in England in the ninth century and continue into the twelfth. It is likely that the Norwich industry goes back at least to the ninth century, and its start, and that of Norwich as a town, could have come during, and have been connected with, Danish rule in East Anglia, *c.* 870–*c.*917.

Late Anglo-Saxon Norwich was also a major port. Its site was characteristic of many such at this time: some way inland at a low crossing point on a major waterway; compare Lincoln, Cambridge and York. Ports actually on the coast, such as Orwell, Dunwich, Great Yarmouth, Lynn, Boston and Hull, often begin their development at around the time of the Conquest or later. Finds of imported pottery, mainly from the Rhineland, suggest the possible importance of overseas trade at Norwich, as does the Domesday render of a bear. Its importance as a fishing centre and as the key point in a network of river and coastal routes may have mattered more. Winchester too had river-traffic; but Southampton was its port, as *Hamwih* had been earlier.

The contrast between Winchester and Norwich cannot be pressed too far. Norwich was a major centre of government. Winchester had important concentrations of craftsmen and, probably, a pottery industry. The Normans made Norwich more like Winchester by moving the *seat* of the East Anglian see there (knocking down a good deal of the Anglo-Saxon town to build their cathedral and castle). Still, basic differences remained, and they are part of a pattern of distinction between East and West, which owes much to the policies and attitudes of the kings of the house of Wessex, and which has become an ingrained element in the personality of England.

J. Campbell

4 A fragment of wall-painting found on a stone re-used in the foundations of the New Minster, Winchester, and so earlier than *c.* 903, length 58.6 cm (Winchester City Museum). Its style resembles that of 10th-century manuscripts of the Winchester school and the probably Winchester-made vestments in Saint Cuthbert's tomb (see fig. 153).

3 Bronze strap-end from Winchester, length 7 cm (Winchester City Museum). Resemblances between its foliage and that of, for example, the New Minster Charter (fig. 164) have suggested a late 10th-century date. It is one of a number of rather luxurious small objects found at Winchester which intimate the importance of the city (cf. pp. 196–7).

rency was effective. The well-organized and elaborate system on which an abundant currency was managed from the last years of Edgar proves the power of royal government. Royal power to command depended in part on a crude but powerful bureaucracy. A crucial question here is whether there was a royal writing-office or 'chancery'. Students of the charters, the largest surviving source of evidence for the activities of the royal government, have long been and still are divided as to whether they were centrally produced from such an office or whether they were drawn up by the beneficiaries or their agents. The party in favour of a royal chancery, at any rate in the tenth century, seems in the ascendant at the moment. There is no doubt that many charters of about the same date addressed to many different beneficiaries and kept throughout the Middle Ages in many different archives exhibit features common to each other. One of the reasons why kings could have wanted to control the writing of charters is that they were one of the nearest things to a medium for propaganda purposes. Such things as royal titles and the political generalities usually found at the beginning of a charter exhibit regularities of theme and formula, in matters of vital concern to the kings concerned, that speak for central direction and control. But it must be observed that as well as such undoubted uniformities, there are also some charters, often very important ones, that deviate from norms and show singularity rather than uniformity. One is driven to a complicated and in a sense unsatisfactory conclusion: that there was something like a chancery; but some charters were drawn up by their beneficiaries.

In any case, there was more to the administrative machine than a chancery. In the provinces the burghal system was crucial. *Burhs*, essentially an Alfredian development, had probably done more than anything to hold the Viking invasions (see above, pp. 152–3). They were, of course, primarily garrisoned fortresses. The actual forts had dependent tracts of territory on which lay the obligations to build, maintain and garrison them. The area of land so burdened varied but was often large. For instance, that Worcestershire consisted of 12 hundreds in Domesday Book (see below, pp. 226–7) probably indicates that the whole shire (see above, p. 172) had been attached to the *burh* of Worcester, with an assessment of 1,200 hides. (One of the many complications of the history of the hundred is that, with its other functions, it could also be a fiscal unit; in Domesday Book many hundreds, especially in the Midlands, were assessed at 100 hides.) From their almost entirely military beginnings the *burhs* implied some permanent administrative apparatus. They seem to have early been centres of judicial authority; we know that in the second half of the tenth century the *burh* court met three times a year, and the little evidence we have of such courts suggests that very important people might sometimes be present. By the time of the Conquest, the *burh* court had merged with the shire court (see above, p. 172) The *burh* court must have been responsible for the enforcement of the burghal obligations, but soon after Alfred's day the *burh* and its administration take on far more than military tasks. From the laws of King Aethelstan it is evident that the *burh* was synonymous with the *port*. In the tenth century *port* meant any trading centre, not just a maritime one. The change in nomenclature is significant because it shows the importance of the non-military functions of the *burh*. The legislation about coins (see the Picture Essay, pp. 130–1) required that they be minted only in *ports*, and not in all of those. It was through the *burh*, in other words, that the regulation of the coins was achieved. The degree of success and the extent of that regulation are a measure of the power and efficiency of this arm of local government under the West Saxon kings.

Another theme running through tenth-century laws is that of royal concern for law and order, and again the measures that translated this concern into action operated through the *burh* or *port*. Edward the Elder tried to ensure that all buying and selling should be done in a *port* with the witness of a reeve, that is to say a royal official, so that the sale of stolen property could be hindered. Cattle was almost certainly what Edward had chiefly in mind; and a struggle against cattle-rustling is one of the predominant themes found in these law-codes.

150 Fragment of a 10th- or 11th-century cross shaft from East Stour, Dorset, height about 71 cm (British Museum). It is not known why such crosses are more common in the north than in the south.

151 (*above*) St Mary's, Breamore, Hampshire, from the south-east. Most that is shown here is late Saxon, although the chancel has been rebuilt on its Saxon foundations. A church on a royal manor; there may have been many such on a similar scale.

152 (*right*) The opening from the nave to the south chapel, Breamore. The inscription (perhaps early 11th century) may have been continued elsewhere in the church, and can be translated either as 'Here is manifested the Covenant unto thee', or as 'Here is manifested the Covenant which . . .'

Aethelstan (II Aethelstan 12) relaxed Edward's law so that it applied only to goods worth more than 20 pence. Clearly Edward's original ordinance had overloaded the system, and so Aethelstan modified it. There were limits to what royal government could do; but equally this is government trying out how far it could go and prepared to make adjustments in the light of experience.

Particularly important for the development of machinery for the maintenance of law and order are the codes known as II and VI Aethelstan. II Aethelstan was promulgated at Grately and contains the essentials of his law and order campaign. It was reiterated on a number of occasions, and VI Aethelstan is not so much a 'code' as an account of what was done in one important locality to meet Aethelstan's requirements. The early, perhaps contemporary, title of this 'code' was *Judicia civitatis Lun-*

153 (*left*) John the Evangelist, from a maniple, width 6 cm, found with a stole in the tomb of St Cuthbert (Dean and Chapter, Durham); see pp. 80–1. Both maniple and stole were originally made for Frithestan, Bishop of Winchester 909–31, on the orders of Queen Aelfflaed (died 916), and were later given to St Cuthbert's shrine by King Aethelstan.

154 (*right*) Christ enthroned with choirs of martyrs, confessors and virgins, from the Aethelstan Psalter (British Library, MS Cotton Galba A.xviii, fol. 21r, 128 × 88 mm). This 9th-century Psalter, probably from the Liège area, was given by King Aethelstan to the Old Minster in Winchester, where it almost certainly received the various English additions which include this illustration and fig. 149.

21
OMNIS CHORVS
MARTYRVM
VIRGINVM

doniae, the judgements of the 'city' of London. There is nothing urban about the contents. The area covered is obviously vast and rural. Several bishops and other great men are involved; that is, they were envisaged as normally resident and therefore landholders in the *civitas*. The code provides for those involved to form posses and ride after cattle rustlers and to combine against family groups who harboured thieving kinsmen or subordinates. The *civitas* of London must be the district attached to the *burh* of London, which we suspect from a remark in the *Chronicle* to have covered several shires even as late as the time of Rufus.

In addition to the arrangements for harrying cattle-rustlers and their powerful protectors, more general provision for the maintenance of law and order was prescribed. All local males, of free status, were divided into groups of nine with a senior over them to see they fulfilled their duties. These groups were called tithings and were in their turn combined into groups of 100 men. They provided the posses and undertook the policing duties. There was a frankly business side to this: a primitive insurance policy by which all combined to recover the rustled livestock of any member. There was also a social side: at least the officials ate a common dinner once a month and there is mention of butt-filling, with beer of course, which implies a common drinking session. The sources relating to the *Burgen* of Henry the Fowler, which are relevant parallels here (see above, p. 153), indicate that such banquets could also be occasions when important business was transacted. There is nothing unusual in this. Anglo-Saxons at the highest level were accustomed to take decisions of the most serious import at drinking sessions, the frequency of which helps explain why this was such a violent society.

VI Aethelstan reveals the kind of local institution which Aethelstan sought to develop. There is no reason to suppose that only the *burh* of London responded in this way; it is likely that its response was the one preserved because it was the greatest *burh*. The Ordinance of the Hundred, which is probably to be dated from Edgar's reign but could be earlier, takes the system further. The groups of a hundred were now endowed with jurisdiction. The fulfilment of their duties and the punishment of the delinquents they rooted out seem to have been put under the hundred court. Thus that ancient and customary institution was brought into the new scheme of things and linked with the burghal organization—unless it had been a component of that system from the beginning, as the frequency with which the Burghal Hidage (see above, pp. 152–3) attributes a round number of 100 hides, or multiples thereof, to *burhs*, suggests may have been the case. (It has to be admitted that the complications of the history of the hundred as a judicial, fiscal and military unit are easier to observe than to solve

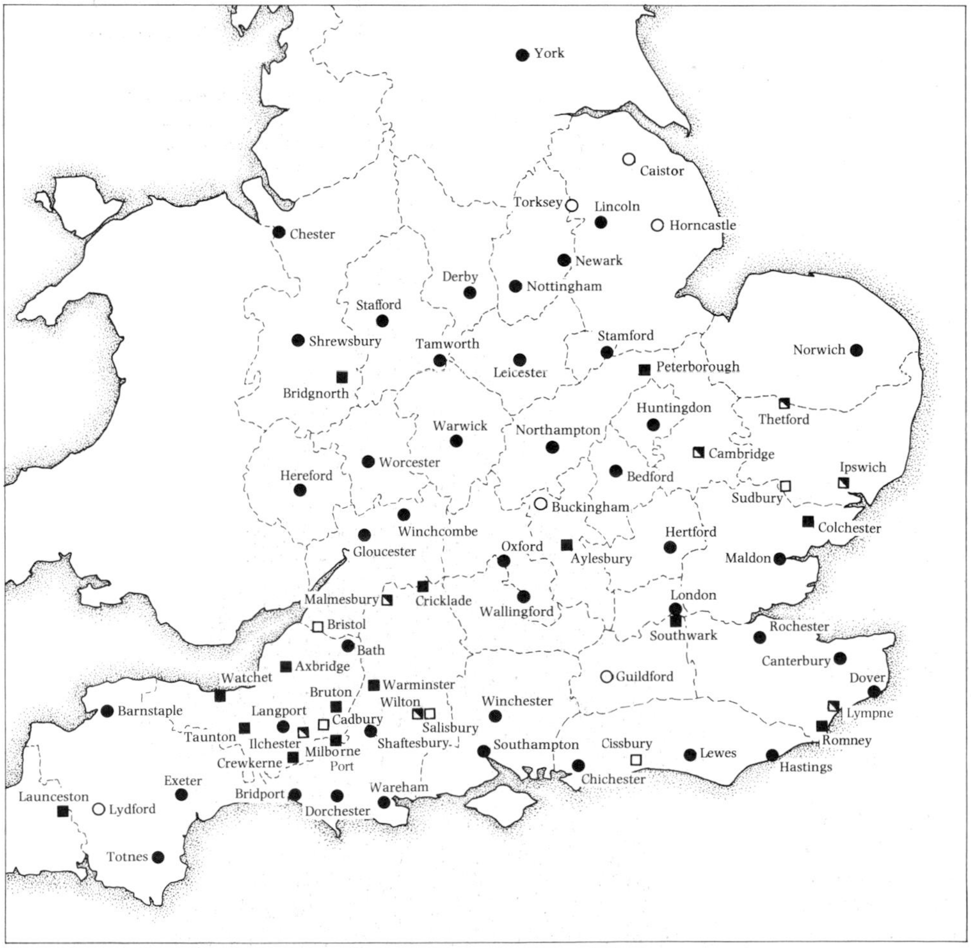

155 Mints in late Anglo-Saxon England (from D. Hill, *An Atlas of Anglo-Saxon England* (Blackwell, 1981). Bridgnorth should perhaps be regarded as doubtful, and Louth perhaps added.

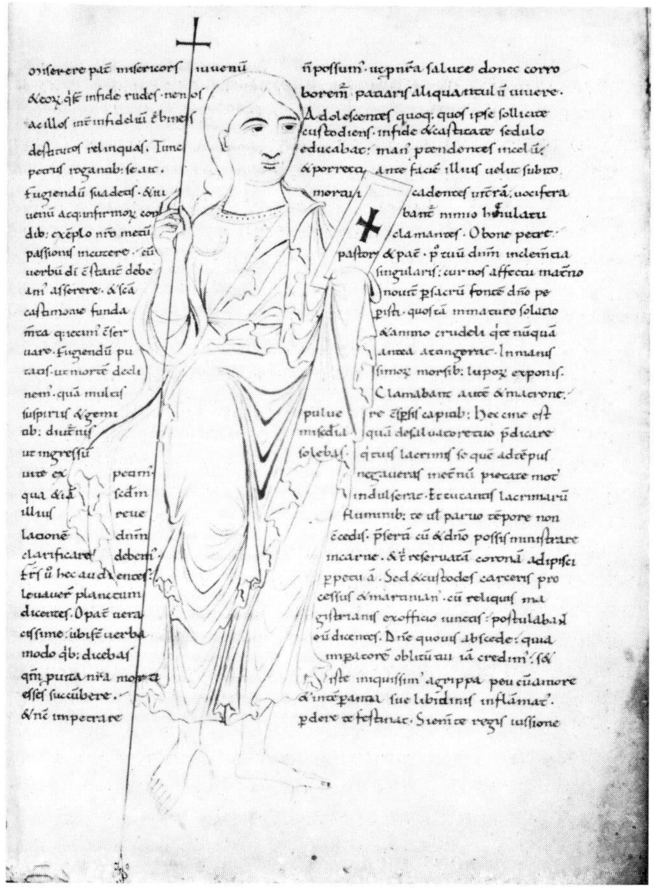

156 Christ, in a mid-10th-century drawing (Oxford, St John's College, MS 28, fol. 2r, 328 × 237 mm). Most of the manuscript which contains this outstanding example of the earliest phase of English outline drawing is from St Augustine's, Canterbury, but the drawing itself may be from Glastonbury.

(see above, pp. 172, 176).) Perhaps one of the more revealing things brought out by the legislation comes from a code of Aethelstan's younger brother, King Edmund. The local posses must round up thralls (that is slaves) who have abandoned their masters and taken to banditry. It is likely that such banditry was endemic in tenth-century England. Certainly in Aethelred II's reign thralls ran off and joined the Vikings, and it is possible to think they did much the same in Alfred's day. By the middle of the century they could no longer do this, but they could and evidently did go into banditry on their own account. Edmund instructed the local posses to hunt them down, hang the leaders out of hand and punish the rest, but not so as to destroy their economic usefulness. They were to be flogged three times, scalped and have their little fingers cut off. (Scalping, according to the laws of Cnut, was sometimes used as a punishment for men of much higher social class than Edmund's thralls.)

To sum up: success against the Vikings had been achieved by a remarkable feat of military organization, the burghal system. In later times of relative peace that organization was turned into an instrument of royal government at a distance and applied to a variety of practical needs. Clearly royal government was prepared to experiment and adapt, and the adaptation was usually, if not invariably, by increasingly tight regulation from the top. By the reign of Edgar, such regulation was affecting every social group from the magnate down to the thrall. The most ancient and traditional institutions, such as the feud, the wergeld, the fyrd, the hundred and the shire, were altered, experimented with and left rather different from what they had been. The change was always in the direction of greater power for the crown.

The Reform of the Church

While all this was going on a group of well-born and influential churchmen were getting ideas about the reform of the English Church. The influences on them were plainly Continental. By the middle of the tenth century there were reformed communities in Lower Lotharingia (what is now the Benelux countries), in the lower Rhineland, and most important of all, the great abbey of Cluny, in south-eastern France, founded in or about 910. Odo, second abbot of Cluny and the founder of its true greatness, had, through his family connections, got the major abbey of Fleury, on the Loire, to reform. Fleury and St. Peter's, Ghent, another great reformed house, at various times housed important English churchmen. Dunstan, a future archbishop of Canterbury and at the time abbot of Glastonbury and leader of the reform party, went into exile at Ghent during the brief reign of Eadwig, the elder son of King Edmund, who succeeded his uncle Eadred in 955. In Aethelstan's reign Bishop Oda of Ramsbury was ordered

157 Tenth-century bronze censer cover with the inscription 'Godric made me' found at Pershore, Worcestershire, height 9.7 cm (British Museum). Like the 'hogbacks' (fig. 146), it and other censer covers take the form of a building with animal ornament.

to escort Aethelstan's nephew, Louis d'Outremer, back to France (see above, p. 165). He took the opportunity to visit Fleury and publicly declare for the monastic party by having himself tonsured there. He later became archbishop of Canterbury and sent his nephew Oswald to be a monk at Fleury for some years. Oswald returned to become bishop of Worcester and later archbishop of York as well. He, like the other great reformer of the day, Aethelwold, bishop of Winchester, sent a number of his disciples to Fleury for training, some of whom became abbots and bishops in their turn. What principles did a reformed community stand for?

The difficulty has been that the tenth and early eleventh centuries are the least studied and most taken for granted periods of both English and Continental history. Historians have tended to see the problem of early tenth-century monasticism in twelfth-century terms. Almost all monasteries, by then, were communities of bachelor clergymen sharing a common way of life laid down in certain documents, i.e. *Rules*. The Rules of the different orders (associations of monasteries observing a common rule) differed in detail; some were much more austere in their attitude to the necessities, as well as the luxuries, of life than others. Monks of one order engaged in polemics to extol their own way of life and denigrate their rivals. For example, Saint Bernard and the Cistercians savaged their rivals of Cluny. Such disputes can lead one to exaggerate the differences between one twelfth-century monk and another, and lead one to forget that nearly all had more in common with one another than they did with those who lived in religious communities before the reforms of the tenth century.

In the tenth century the reformers had to cope with an over-successful integration of the religious life into that of the secular world of kindred groups. The family of the founder of the community expected to nominate its abbot. Even Iona was ruled in the time by Bede by kinsmen of Saint Columba, its founder (see above, p. 88). The great Alcuin, in Charlemagne's day, thought it no shame that he inherited a community as a member of Saint Willibrord's connection. If a family which owned an abbey had no eligible candidate to be abbot, the right of promotion could be and was sold. In the middle of the tenth century Saint Oswald began his monastic career, not as a novice monk in a settled community, but as abbot of a community in Winchester, the office being

158 (*above left*) Christ in Majesty, from the Benedictional of Saint Aethelwold (British Library, MS Add. 49598, fol. 70r, 293 × 225 mm). The lavish nature of the illustration indicates the magnificence which could go with reformed monasticism. (See also fig. 166.)

159 (*left*) The King's School, Canterbury, disc brooch, maximum diameter 14.2 cm (British Museum). Made in gold and silver perhaps in the early 10th century, its ornament has parallels in objects from France and Germany, but is thought generally to represent an English attempt to imitate the Scandinavian Jellinge style.

160 (*opposite*) late 10th-century crucifix reliquary of walrus ivory mounted on gold with a cedar wood core, height 18.5 cm (London, Victoria and Albert Museum). The figure, which is very similar to that in fig. 180, covers a cavity for relics.

bought for him by his uncle, Archbishop Oda. To his credit, when he found he could in no way influence his monks, he resigned and went to Fleury to be a real monk.

In an unreformed community the monks were not subject to any real authority, though the abbot was clearly intended by the *Rule* of Saint Benedict to wield an absolute, paternal and authoritarian power. But the *Rule*, of course, was still only one of many. In 817, at the synod of Aachen, the emperor, Louis the Pious, for the first time gave the *Rule* of Saint Benedict legal force as the rule for the monks. He did not succeed. Although the Benedictine *Rule* had been known, and importantly influential, in England from the late seventh century (see above, p. 87), it had later lost its power to determine the life of religious communities. At the beginning of the tenth century members of such communities did not have to live in poverty, holding their property in common and obeying their abbot. They enjoyed their own *mensa*, literally 'table', but what was meant was a block of estates, belonging by title to the patron saint of their community, that had probably been given by some ancestor and of which they were the holders by family descent.

In the days of the Mercian hegemony a reform of the cathedral community at Canterbury had been proposed (see above, p. 124). The archbishop envisaged that his community should live under a rule which was not so much for monks as for canons (see above, p. 125). Its members were allowed to have their own houses, though they were supposed to sleep in a common dormitory and eat in a common refectory. (Alcuin seems to have supposed the members of a similar community at Lindisfarne used their houses for gambling and giving parties.) They could still leave their property by will, though they were supposed to leave it within the community. How far this regime was observed by the early tenth century is merely for speculation. What is certain is that in England and everywhere in Europe, monastic communities lived lives in which family connection, the individual or quasi-individual ownership of property, and often enough marriage, played parts which were far from what Saint Benedict and other founding fathers of monasticism had intended.

Saint Odo of Cluny's biographer says his aims were to make the monks under his rule live chastely, abstain from meat and hold their property in common. He was not concerned, any more the English reformers were, with quarrels of the twelfth-century type about the niceties of ascesis, the quantity of psalms to be sung on any one day or the appropriate style of decoration for churches, but rather with the creation of the basic essentials of the monastic life. But this creation struck at the interests of those families important enough to own monasteries. Before the tenth century many of the lands of the Church were in fact family properties; their ecclesiastical nature merely meant that the secular head of the family had

161 Sites connected with the monastic revival of Anglo-Saxon England (from D. Hill, *An Atlas of Anglo-Saxon England* (Blackwell, 1981)).

somewhat limited control over them. The monks of the unreformed communities were not as a rule celibate. The reformers' polemics go on *ad nauseam* about the unchaste and lascivious clerks (*clerici*, to distinguish them from right-living *monachi*) whom they sought to displace. Reformed monks held the near-monopoly of writing and could say what they liked without much fear of contradiction; most of them had been brought up from childhood in all-male institutions and so there could well be a neurotic element in what they say. Some authors from the mid-tenth century to the mid-eleventh make detailed accusations of a degree of debauchery remarkable even by present-day standards, and these cannot be altogether dismissed. At the very least the unreformed clerks were often married with children.

The reformers proposed to counter this by creating a clerical status group with its own ecclesiastical loyalties which took precedence over loyalty to the kindred group. They hoped that they could then supply trained and educated clergy for the highest places of the Church, and in a comparatively short time succeeded. Nowhere was this policy more successful than in England.

Reform came to partial power when King Edmund (939–46), was led by an escape from a nearly fatal accident in the hunting field to make a pious gesture by appointing Dunstan, the leader of the reforming party by this time and a member of the royal family, as abbot of Glastonbury. Edmund himself had no sympathy with the reform movement and gave the abbey of Bath to unreformed clerks, refugees from the reform of St. Peter's, Ghent. His brother and successor, Eadred, was much more sympathetic. When Dunstan was unable to impose the new style of monasticism completely at Glastonbury, the leader of the reformers, Aethelwold (another high-born young man moved by a new monastic piety), wished to withdraw to the Continent. He was persuaded to stay when the king gave him the estates of a deserted monastery at Abingdon that had passed into royal possession, on which to build a monastery after his own heart. Eadred was prepared to make personal financial sacrifice, but not to incur the opposition which an attempt to write off traditional family loyalties in an established community would arouse. Eadred was soon succeeded by his two nephews. The elder, Eadwig, reigned for fewer than two years as ruler of England. In 957 England north of the Thames rejected him and recognized his younger brother Edgar as king of Mercia. Eadwig died in 959 and Edgar became king of all England.

Eadwig's attitudes are hard to understand. He sent Dunstan into exile. But it is unlikely that this was a basic cause of the king's unpopularity, which is still not understood. Aethelwold remained faithful to Eadwig until his death, and Aethelwold seems to have been Edgar's tutor and was certainly one of his principal advisers after his accession. Dunstan adhered to Edgar as did the lay magnates, both those who can later be identified as for the new monasticism and those who were against it. As soon as Edgar became king of England things began to move. Beohrthelm, recently appointed archbishop of

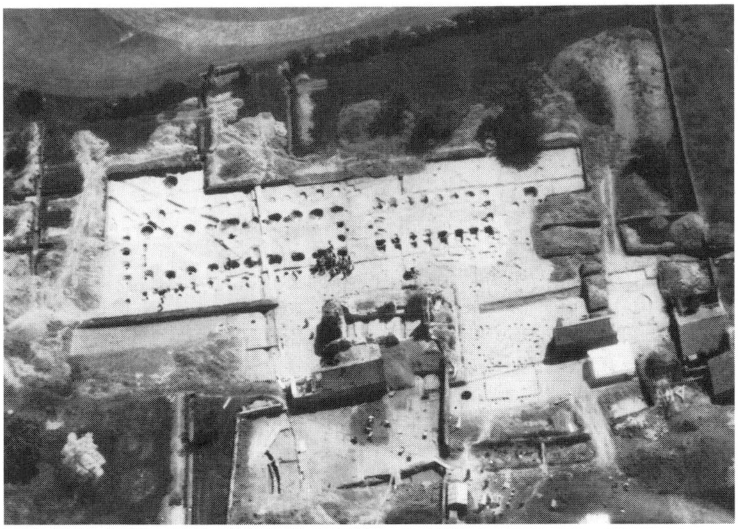

162 Excavations of the royal palace complex at Cheddar, from the north. The site on the right (eight post-holes long) was occupied by two late Anglo-Saxon halls in succession. That on the left is from the twelfth century. The structures included a stone chapel, and may have been intended to accommodate meetings of the national council, the *witan*.

Canterbury, was sent packing back to the diocese of Wells whence he had been promoted, and Dunstan, who had briefly held Worcester and London, was appointed in his stead. This was, of course, in total defiance of canon law. Kings could *de facto* promote bishops; this was taken for granted. It was not taken for granted that they could demote them. Had the papacy been in better condition Dunstan might have had the same troubles that befell the reforming scholar Gerbert a generation later. Gerbert had been appointed to Rheims in much the same situation that attended Dunstan's appointment to Canterbury. The pope intervened, probably from motives of personal spite, but the law was clear and Gerbert had to go (to Ravenna first and then, as it happened, to the papacy itself). Dunstan was more fortunate. Within five years Aethelwold had got the second see of Southern England, Winchester; and Oswald, Worcester. From Worcester and Winchester (Canterbury was not reformed until the next reign), an attempt was made to monasticize the English Church. Aethelwold's abbey at Abingdon was the source from which new reforming abbots and, later, monastic bishops were recruited. At Winchester and Worcester the abbot-bishops forced the communities to accept the full Benedictine discipline or abandon their property. Those who would not conform were expelled and their property expropriated; they and their (probably often grand) families had grounds for resentment. Royal provisions for reformed monasteries involved loss of status for the Church's tenants, as has been explained in the discussion of military service and the creation of the great ecclesiastical liberties (see above, p. 173). This at once joins what was being done in the English churches with the wider extension of royal power over the neighbourhoods and the kindred groups. No doubt something like what was done at, for example,

Worcester (see above, p. 173) would have been attempted even without the occasion offered by monk-bishops whose religious attitudes broke established social moulds, who needed royal support, and who might be used to break such moulds further, to the royal advantage. But if the king was to reduce the power of local establishments he needed alternative holders of the powers he had taken away, and they too had to be locally based. In other words he needed bishops and abbots he could trust and bishops, and abbots of the new dispensation were just what he needed. Celibate and self-conscious members of a clerical caste, they could be relied on to pursue the interests of their churches as they saw them, but Edgar and other reforming kings who were patrons of the monks of the day saw this as a small price to pay. The monks could also be relied on to act as a counterbalance to deeply entrenched local families, and as they were dependent on the king in a way the ealdormen were not, their loyalty could be taken for granted. Ealdormen were members of great families (see above, p. 172); so too were the greatest reformers. But in order to innovate on the scale their principles required, they needed the support of the only other force in society with innovatory power, the king. By the year 1000 pretty well the whole English episcopate had been recruited from the new monasteries.

166 The Nativity in the Benedictional of Saint Aethelwold (British Library MS Add. 49598 fol. 15v, 293 × 225 mm). This collection of episcopal blessings was written for Bishop Aethelwold of Winchester (963–984) probably at the Old Minster. It is an outstanding example of the 'Winchester School'. (See also fig. 158.)

165 King Edgar, palm in hand, with thc saints Dunstan and Aethelwold (London, British Library, MS Cotton Tiberius A.iii, fol. 2v, 240 × 177 mm). From a mid- 11th-century Christ Church, Canterbury, copy of the *Regularis Concordia*, the monastic manual drawn up in Edgar's reign.

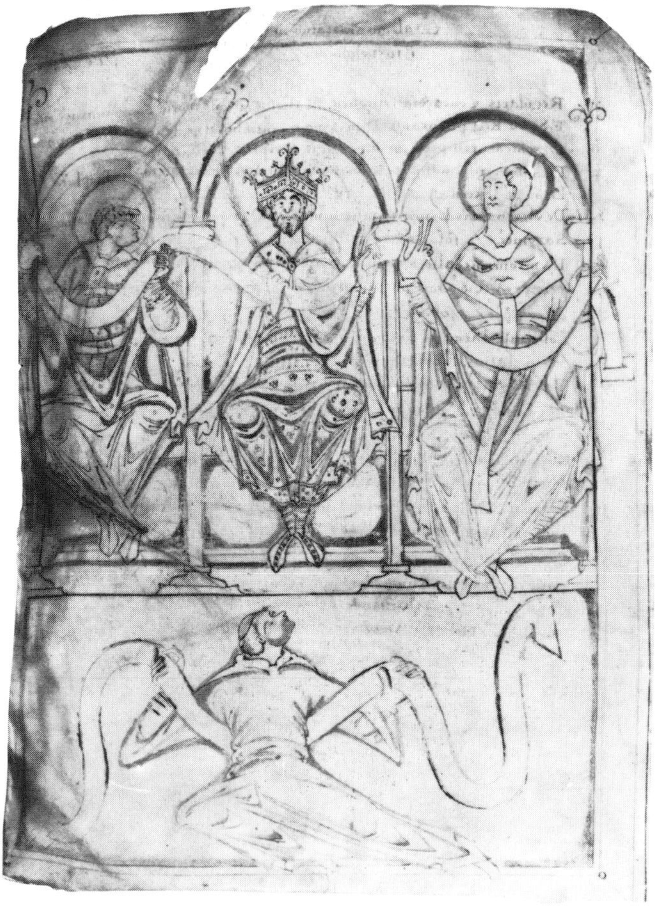

Something of the reasons for Edgar's predilection for the new churchmen can be got from a glance at the most spectacular public event of the reign, his coronation at Bath in 973. It seems clear that Edgar had not been crowned on his accession, as was customary. The sources emphasize that he was in his 29th year when he was crowned; since the same sources get the year of grace wrong, they clearly knew Edgar's age as an ideological not a chronological fact. The reference is to Saint Luke, who says that Jesus began his public ministry in his 29th year. The reformers, probably Dunstan himself, devised a grand new coronation ritual for the occasion, based on West Frankish models. It has been argued that Edgar had already been crowned on his accession, which would have been usual, and that what he underwent at Bath in 973 was an 'imperial' coronation. It is difficult to accept this. The parallel between Edgar's coronation and Christ's entry into his public ministry implies that something was beginning, and that something can only have been Edgar's career as *Christus Domini*, the Lord's Anointed. In any case the same ritual, which in a modified form is still in use, has ever since been understood as inaugurating a royal king or queen.

It could be held that the Bath ceremony was an

'imperial' coronation in the sense that it related not so much to the solemnization of Edgar's power in England as to that of his power in a more extensive sphere. If so, it could only refer to Edgar's authority (probably none the less real for our difficulty in defining it) over various kinglets and princelings of the west and north of Britain. But this authority was publicly celebrated shortly after the Bath ceremony, separately, in an 'imperial' ceremony held at Chester (see above, p. 173). This matter has a certain importance. There is no doubt that the Anglo-Saxons always had a conception of kingdoms with hegemony over other kingdoms, and that their literary men sometimes expressed this hegemony in Latin formulas redolent of ancient Rome and her empire. But an 'Imperial' idea or ideal probably weighed relatively little with Anglo-Saxon kings (less than it did with Carolingians or the Ottonians). Their power was real, and though it probably mattered to them how it was presented (see above, p. 176) ceremony was not of its essence for them.

The identification of a Christian king's functions with those of Christ himself was not specially new in 973. An older view had favoured comparisons between a king and some Old Testament exemplar, usually David. The replacement of David by Christ seems to have originated in circles close to the ninth-century archbishop of Rheims, Hincmar. It had certainly reached Fleury by Edgar's time, and there had been many contacts between the English reformers and Fleury (see above, pp. 169, 181). The idea of comparing a Christian king with Christ was not merely a matter of spiritual flattery but had a double edge. Bad Old Testament kings had to be put up with, but a bad Christ was unthinkable, and the way was open, if reforming churchmen were able and minded to take it, to hurl accusations of tyranny with some effect. Some of them were to do just this, though English churchmen never took this route. It is clear that, alongside such fulsome compliments as the comparison between Edgar as king and the Good Shepherd found in the *Regularis Concordia*, a supplement to the *Rule* of Saint Benedict which Saint Aethelwold drew up for English use, these churchmen had other thoughts. It is clear from the anathemas of charters and from the voluminous sermons of the monk of the next generation, Abbot Aelfric of Eynsham, that the reformers knew bad laymen to be common and that bad kings were commoner than good ones.

The best king they had, Edgar, died young in 975. He had never brooked opposition in his lifetime, nor apparently met it. But his policies towards both the magnates and the thegns and their kindreds, who bore the real cost of the monastic reform policy, had created hostility, disappointment and faction in most of England south of the Trent. (Monastic reform was not to come to most of the north until after 1066.) The reformers had seen a golden opportunity to accept the alliance the king offered them for a short cut to power. It is clear that they were not doing this out of ambition. Dunstan, Aethelwold and Oswald had very powerful connections that must have assured them a distinguished ecclesiastical career in any case. Because they adhered to reforming principles for decades before these were fashionable they were subject to some persecution. Dunstan was beaten up at the court of Aethelstan for his religious views. He and Oswald both experienced exile, and Aethelwold must have expected it from time to time. It was for the cause they believed in that they worked. In the short run they were more successful than their counterparts anywhere. In 959 there was hardly a reformed monastery anywhere to be found in England. By the end of Oswald's life in 992 (he lived the longest of the saintly trio, Dunstan, Aethelwold and Oswald), some of the greatest of the monasteries that were to become powers in the land until they were dissolved by Henry VIII had been founded. The English episcopate was in the hands of the new monks, and a very good job most of them did. But this had been done at the price of a legacy of dissent and bitterness never entirely overcome before 1066. Disunion and dissent always acted like a magnet to Vikings and back they came in the reign of Edgar's younger son, Aethelred II: the effect of their return was to produce dynastic instability in a political community that only worked with an undisputed king. There was a crisis when Edgar died in 975 and there were to be crises at every accession until 1066, with by this time no fewer than four great families disputing the succession. Subsequent kings, notably Cnut and Edward the Confessor, gave their subjects long period of peace and prosperity, but the days of the thrusting, reforming, constantly active kings of the tenth century were gone for good.

167 Christ in Majesty on a bronze (originally gilt) reliquary cover, length 7.3 cm (Oxford, Ashmolean Museum). Round the edge is a Latin inscription which can be translated: 'What is hidden within, may it release us from all sin.' Perhaps English work of the 11th century.

168 A page from the Grimbald Gospels, produced in Canterbury or Winchester early in the 11th century (British Library, MS Add. 34890, fol. 10v, 320 × 245 mm). Saint Matthew is shown seated at a lectern, gazing at an angel holding a scroll.

169 David and Goliath open Psalm 101 in a Psalter produced in Christ Church, Canterbury, between 1012 and 1023 (British Library, MS Arundel 155, fol. 93r, 292 × 170 mm). Even here, interlace ornament and biting animal heads make their appearance. Monastic artists capable of producing such beautiful miniatures probably had years of training behind them.

D
N̄E EXAUDI
ORATIONEM MEAM·
ET CLAMOR MEUS
AD TE UENIAT

CHAPTER EIGHT

The Return of the Vikings

Edward the Martyr and the Crisis of 975–979

The death of King Edgar in 975 was immediately followed by a serious crisis over the succession, a crisis exacerbated by the inevitable reaction to the monastic reform movement (see above, p. 173). The result was summed up by the first biographer of Saint Oswald, Byhrtferth, in these words: 'Strife threw the kingdom into turmoil, moved shire against shire, family against family, prince against prince, ealdormen against ealdormen, drove bishop against the people and folk against the pastors set over them.' By princes he probably meant Edgar's two surviving sons, the half-brothers Edward (later known as the Martyr) and Aethelred, the famous Unready.

Edward, a teenager, was old enough to take some political part and was certainly the candidate of the monastic party. Aethelred was not old enough to play any personal part, but was used as a figurehead by the anti-monastic party. The lay leader of the monastic and Edwardian party was Aethelwine, ealdorman of East Anglia, supported by his two brothers and his henchman, Ealdorman Byrhtnoth. The leader of those who wanted an end to, or drastic curtailment of, the monastic liberties was Ealdorman Aelfhere of Mercia, the chief victim of the aggrandisement of the bishop of Worcester. He was for Aethelred and the probable murderer of Edward the Martyr in 978. He may have had an ally in the other superior earl, Oslac of Northumbria, who disappears from history about this time and was perhaps replaced by Byrhtnoth, Aethelwine's right-hand man. The bishops who were opposed by their flock would be Oswald of Worcester and Aethelwold of Winchester. We have some idea of what form this opposition took.

Ealdorman Aelfhere seems to have personally sacked the Worcestershire abbey of Evesham and to have dispersed its monks. Abbot Germanus of Winchcombe, one of the men closest to Oswald, fled overseas to Fleury. Pershore, also in Worcestershire, was temporarily destroyed and never recovered its former glory. (A substantial part of its endowment was taken into the possession of the crown and never returned, later being used to endow the royal abbey of Westminster instead.) Deerhurst in Gloucestershire—and therefore also in the diocese of Worcester—was another of Aelfhere's victims. The West Saxon and East Anglian abbeys were safe enough, though not even Aethelwine could prevent smaller landholders bringing suits against some of them, claiming the monks had cheated or coerced them. Most of the evidence for this comes from the *Liber Eliensis*, a history of the estates of the abbey of Ely (twelfth-century, but deriving in large part from tenth-century sources). It shows that the way in which Bishop Aethelwold had built up the Ely estates had indeed been such as to create understandable grievances. The Ely monks seem to have come to some kind of settlement with their opponents.

The crisis was not entirely over the new monasticism, however. At this time monastic reformers had much wider aims than enforcing the *Rule* of Saint Benedict strictly, and one of their policies was the strict enforcement of the canonical rules about matrimony. According to canon law a man could not marry a woman with whom he shared a common great-grandparent. As with incest taboos in other parts of the world, it was not always observed. In the tenth century it is clear that among aristocrats at any rate there was no great guilt attached to unions that were canonically incestuous. But, it must be remembered, the canon law had a powerful weapon with which to enforce its discipline. Churchmen were by general consent the sole arbiters of the law of marriage. They could not do much directly about magnates who married their kinswomen, but they could declare the unions incestuous and any children produced by them illegitimate. A magnate who wished his son to succeed him could not afford altogether to disregard the canons; if he did, that son might find himself, at the dangerous moment of succession, when he would be faced by uncles, half-brothers, cousins anxious to grab all or part of his inheritance, confounded by a canonical declaration of illegitimacy, which would at the very least be an embarrassment. The laws and customs of tenth-century matrimony were in rather a fluid state, and not surprisingly the reformers sometimes got themselves into serious political difficulties. The senior and reforming prelates of the late Carolingian empire inadvertently cast doubts on the legitimacy of every surviving Carolingian after the death of Louis the Child in 911. Something similar seems to have happened in England in 975.

Edward the Martyr was certainly Edgar's eldest surviving son, but his mother was perhaps related too closely to the king and was put on one side. In the important and magnificent codex made to mark the monachizing of the royal abbey of New Minster, Winchester (Birch, *Cart.*, no. 1190; see fig. 164), the witness list makes it clear that Edward was only the King's 'procreated' son while his younger brother was his 'legitimate' son. Stress is also laid on the legitimacy of Edgar's second marriage. When Edgar died, his 'legitimate' son Aethelred was not yet 10 years old, so that Dunstan and Aethelwold and their supporters had to do a *volte-face* and recognize Edward as legitimate enough to succeed after all. It is also clear that some contemporaries judged Edward to have serious faults of temper and character as well.

There is also a curious regional factor in the crisis. The Edwardian monkish party is also an East Anglian (or East Mercian) party. The opposition was mainly West Mercian, though it had its supporters in Kent and perhaps Northumbria. The main target of Aelfhere of Mercia was Oswald's connection. Oswald himself, who by now was also archbishop of York as well as bishop of Worcester, was an East Anglian of Danish descent. It is not known if he were related to Ealdorman Aethelwine, but he was certainly a kinsman of one of Aethelwine's main supporters, Aethelstan Mannessune. When Oswald was given his liberty of Oswaldslow it was made as unpalatable as possible to Aelfhere, being such as to surround *burh* of Worcester, which was important to him, with landholders who owed their primary allegiance and their military service to another man, the bishop of Worcester (see above, p. 173). In the east the church of Ely got a great liberty called Wicklow in south-east Suffolk (it contained the site of Sutton Hoo). But Ely simply handed Wicklow to Aethelwine to run, the monks getting only a modest pension from him. When Oswald became bishop of Worcester and a power in the land in West Mercia, he seems to have brought a surprising number of kinsmen with him, to judge by the number of leases surviving in the Worcester archives which describe the lessee as connected in some way with Oswald. Oswald had no connection with Worcester before he became bishop, so he must have imported these relatives. It seems clear then that from the beginning of his reign Edgar had pursued a policy of alliance with eastern against western Mercia, and that this too played its part in the events of 975. It may also hclp cxplain why the Mercians played so equivocal a role in the reign of Aethelred II, when their ealdorman, Eadric Streona, twice turned his coat in the struggles of Aethelred, and then his son, Edmund Ironside, against the Danes (see p. 199).

170 Eleventh-century bronze-gilt disc brooch found at Pitney, Somerset, diameter 14.2 cm (British Museum). The body of the interlaced animal is represented by a band of plain and beaded lines. The neck is being bitten by a snake. Both Continental and Scandinavian influences on its styles have been suggested.

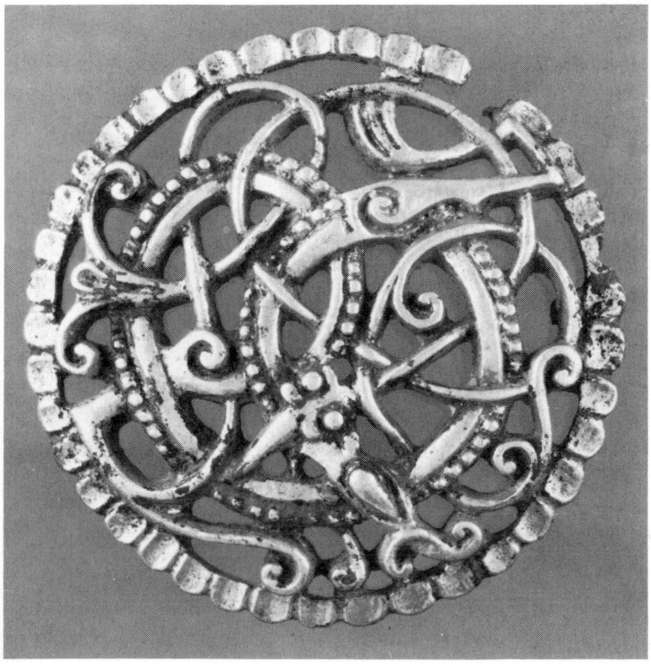

There is much we do not yet know about the whys and wherefores of English politics in the tenth century. But we do know that the monks and the Edwardians gained a partial victory in 975. Of Edward's brief reign we know only that it ended with his murder at Corfe in 978. No one was punished for the murder and perhaps no one was accused of it, but Ealdorman Aelfhere of Mercia did penance for it. Edward was succeeded by his younger half-brother Aethelred II.

Aethelred II and the Return of the Vikings

Aethelred had one of the longest reigns in English history, 37 years (979–1016), a reign of almost unremitting disaster that has impressed itself on the folk-memory of the English. Everyone has heard of Aethelred the Unready, and his name, joined to that of King John, is even now sometimes invoked by politicians as a jibe to throw at their opponents. There is more than incapacity to Aethelred, however, as there is more to King John. Firstly, Aethelred was never called the Unready. His nickname is a pun on his given name, Aethelred, *Aethelred Unraed*, literally 'good advice the ill-advised'. Pre-Conquest aristocratic names were commonly meaningful, and their meanings were still in Aethelred's day thought about and commented on. So, although we have no record of the nickname until after the Conquest, it could be contemporary. In Aethelred's favour it must be said the source of his difficulties lay partly in his father's policies and partly in events in Denmark that would have provoked trouble whoever had been king. His government, even perhaps he himself, proved remarkably fertile in new policies and sensible courses of action. In the end they provided the means by which some of the problems were solved, but not in Aethelred's day.

One of the difficulties in understanding the reign is that the fullest narrative of it which we have is such that we see the course of events through the eyes of a clever, misleading, and very defeatist contemporary, the author of the account of the reign in the *Chronicle*. Our earliest manuscript of this was probably written at the abbey of Abingdon, and so this narrative is sometimes called the *Abingdon Chronicle*; for the reign of the Confessor it probably was actually composed at Abingdon, but this is unlikely to be the case for the annals dealing with Aethelred's reign. The annalistic form gives an impression of objectivity and suggests that what we have is a sort of diary kept annually. This is almost certainly false. Its most recent commentator has argued very strongly that the bulk of the text was written by one man on a single occasion, and that occasion was after Aethelred's death and probably after Cnut's accession (1016). In other words it was written in the depths of national defeat and humiliation, and this colours its whole account of the reign. It is likely that its author was an East Anglian, and had a special interest or connection with the abbey of Ramsey; he also seems to have had first-hand knowledge of London. In the light of what has been said above (p. 193), it is interesting to note the hostility of this anonymous author to the ealdorman of Mercia, Eadric Streona. Although it shows little animus against the king personally, this chronicle is the source of Aethelred's later reputation. It is possible to argue that the defeatism of the author was more a feature of the end of the reign than of its beginning. But before moving on to the course of events it is necessary to say something about the enemies of the English, the Danes.

The new Viking invaders were rather different from their predecessors. This time they were closely associated with the Danish royal government and were usually led by the Danish king. By the middle of the century the Vikings had been contained everywhere in Europe. The defeat and failure of even so characteristic and charismatic a leader as Eric Bloodaxe (see above, p. 168) was a warning to the Vikings that the methods which had for generations brought success could no longer be relied on. Further, the strength of the Ottonian dynasty in Germany effectively sealed off Germany from the Danes. Their best hope of conquest and plunder was the British Isles. They seem to have deliberately prepared for conquest with a remarkable talent for organization of men and material. Four fortifications which have been found in Denmark (at Trelleborg, Fyrkat, Aggersborg and Nonnebakken) indicate the organized power of the Danish monarchy by *c.* 980. Their ordered plan and their similarity to one another (though Aggersborg is larger than the others) suggest a state with the capacity to plan and control on a large scale. That capacity was reflected in the fleets and armies which its rulers sent against England.

It was not only Danish kings who had ordered military power. The career of Thorkell the Tall (see below pp. 199, 208) suggest that the raiding armies were partly made up of the followings of independent warlords, who obeyed kings only so far as it suited them. Their forces may have been as well-disciplined as those of kings. The thirteenth-century *Jomsviking Saga* describes the career of Palnatoki, an exiled Danish nobleman. He made himself a power base in the Baltic by constructing a great fortress. It says that within this a remarkable discipline was enforced. The Jomsviking had to be a proven warrior. He could not take part in the feuds of his kindred and had to swear to avenge his fellow warriors should they fall. No women were allowed in the fortress. The saga is late and it is doubtful how much historical reality it contains. But at the very least its emphasis on discipline serves to remind us that it need not have been only kings who had tightly organized forces at their command. The power of kings and warlords was such as to ensure that the new Viking invasions confronted the English under Aethelred with the most formidable enemy they had yet encountered.

The raids began soon after Aethelred's accession. In the early years of the reign they were not particularly successful. Aethelred seems to have shown both energy and ability. Particularly important was the conclusion (with the mediation of papal legates) of a treaty with Richard, duke of Normandy, in March 991. A significant factor in Viking success was their ability to obtain rest, shelter and supplies in the ports of Normandy, the French Danelaw. The treaty of 991 sought to deny them these advantages. It marks the beginning of a policy which was to have lasting consequences. Although Aethelred was not on consistently good terms with Normandy—indeed at some stage in his reign he seems to have invaded it—he was, in 1002, to marry Duke Richard's daughter, Emma, and the Norman dukes were to prove the last and most steadfast allies of the house of Cerdic.

However well-judged the agreement of 991 was, it did not protect England from a severe reverse later in the year. The Vikings had last mounted a campaign in 988. If later Ely traditions are to be believed (see p. 195), this had ended with their defeat by the aged but active Ealdorman Byrhtnoth, at Maldon, on the Blackwater, in

171 Stirrup irons with brass inlay (not a pair), heights 23.7 cm, 19.2 cm (Oxford, Ashmolean Museum). Probably early 11th century. Found on the banks of the River Cherwell.

Essex. In 991 they returned, and fought again at Maldon, defeating and killing Byrhtnoth.

Our sources for the battle are curious. The earliest is the nearly contemporary *Life* of Oswald written by Byrhtferth of Ramsey and known only in a rather inaccurately copied Worcester manuscript dated some 50 years later. There is an important Ely account not known to have been recorded until the twelth century but which, since quite a lot of it can be checked, must have been based on earlier written, nor oral, traditions. There is also an unparalleled vernacular poem, *Thc Battlc of Maldon* (scc above, p. 173). This used to be thought of as an Ely source too, but this is unlikely. The one manuscript that has come down to us is no longer legible (it was badly damaged by fire), but it seems to have been written in an eleventh-century hand and to have belonged to Worcester. Its best editor remarked of its version of Old English, 'the *Maldon* text has linguistically the appearance of being a western copy of an eastern original'. An eastern manuscript copied at Worcester and used, as *Maldon* probably was, by the Worcester chronicler, 'Florence' (see below, p. 222), could easily be explained as part of the copious borrowings by the Worcester scriptorium from Ramsey. The founder of Ramsey, Oswald, was of course the bishop who introduced monks into Worcester.

From all this we can learn quite a lot about the battle. The poem has been taken by almost all commentators as

172 Eleventh-century carving on Caen stone from St Nicholas's Church, Ipswich (about 53 × 86 × 15 cm). Possibly part of a more extensive frieze, and inscribed 'Here Saint Michael fights (or fought) against the dragon.' Literacy was evidently expected of some of the faithful.

virtually contemporary with the battle. It uses traditional poetic techniques in a rather prosaic way. It is unwise to stress its literary conventions too much. (The late Dr Harmer, probably the greatest Anglo-Saxon scholar of her generation, once remarked too me apropos of the lack of real poetic ability in *Maldon*, 'You could write a poem as good as that if you only knew enough Anglo-Saxon). The point of the poem is to name those who behaved like heroes and died for their country and those who fled. It is a kind of literary cenotaph, and it is

173 The causeway between Northey Island and the Essex mainland near Maldon, at high tide. In 991 the Vikings left their ships on the island and crossed the causeway to defeat Byrhtnoth (see p. 194). The flooded area was narrower then than now.

Anglo-Saxon Ivories

1 Detail from a walrus ivory cross made for Gunhild (died 1076), daughter of Swegn Esthrithson, king of Denmark (Copenhagen, National Museum). If it is not English, then it is strongly influenced by English work. The whole cross is 28.5 × 22 cm; the roundel from the end of one of the arms illustrated here shows the personified Synagogue and is 3.8 cm in diameter.

'He bestowed upon it two episcopal crosses and two large ornamented crosses, besides other little neck crosses, and two large ornamented Gospel books and three ornamented reliquaries and one ornamented altar and five silver chalices and four corporals and one silver tube and five complete mass vestments . . . and two ornamented bowls and four horns and two large ornamented candlesticks and six smaller ornamented candlesticks and one silver censer with a silver incense spoon and eight basins. . .' (From the list of the gifts of Bishop Leofric (1046–72) to Exeter.)

Englishmen were pious; England was rich; its churches were full of treasures. Few of them survive, apart from manuscripts, and of those which do most are ivories. Some 50 carved objects of ivory or some other bone remain from Anglo-Saxon England. They have been beautifully published by Mr Beckwith (Beckwith 1972) from whose work nearly all this essay is derived. Simply to consider them as a body is instructive. Of those thought to be of before *c.* 800 not one is known to have been continuously in England; the Franks casket turned up in central France in the nineteenth century, the Genoels-Eldoren diptych was preserved in a Belgian church, the Gandersheim Casket in a German (figs 113, 121), and so on. Of the later, more numerous group, some have been continuously in England, but generally for much of the time buried in the ground, never in the continuous possession of a church. Henry VIII made a very clean sweep. That is a principal reason why such a high proportion of treasures of Anglo-Saxon origin (or possible Anglo-Saxon origin) are abroad (e.g. figs 102, 181).

Mr Beckwith dates nine of the ivories to before 800 and the remainder to after 900, none to the ninth century. The gap is significant, though it must be remembered that the dating of ivories usually depends on the analysis of style and so is sometimes inconclusive. The panels among the early group reveal how well English craftsmen had mastered the Mediterranean technique of ivory carving. The two caskets (figs 93, 121) are altogether different; in particular the Franks casket seems to belong to an entirely northern tradition of narrative depiction. Resemblances between ivories and stone carving are important. Compare, for example, the frieze round the Munich ivory (fig. 114) with that at Breedon (fig. 108). One answer to the question, 'How was it that (presumed) Anglo-Saxon craftsmen could carve figures in so classicizing style as that of Reculver or Ruthwell?' (figs 89, 99) could be that they had ivories as models. The most important ivories in England may have been not those which were carved there, but those which were not.

The later ivories present contrasts to the earlier in subject-matter and in material. From about 1000 the most popular subject is the Crucifixion; no earlier ivory represents it (cf. fig. 160; p. 206). Nearly all the ivories of the early period are elephant ivory; some of those of the tenth century are, but most are of walrus ivory; all the eleventh-century examples are of walrus. Both kinds of ivory came from a distance, both were available from an early period. But the shift from elephant suggests the greater importance of northern luxuries (perhaps furs also; among Leofric's gifts to Exeter were three bear skins) in the later period.

2 Part of a late Anglo-Saxon bone spoon found at Winchester, 4.9 × 2.2 cm (Winchester City Museum). It shows a bird and an acanthus leaf.

3 Two angels, probably part of a casket or portable altar, late 10th-century, 7.5 × 5 cm (Winchester City Museum).

4 The Nativity in walrus ivory, late 10th- or early 11th-century, 8 × 6.5 cm (Liverpool Museum).

Alfred's Norse informant on the far north said that he had gone to the Arctic chiefly in search of walruses, 'because they have very noble bones in their teeth'.

In the later period as in the earlier the ivories show close connections with other forms of art. This can be seen most strikingly in a comparison of the Nativity as shown on an ivory now at Liverpool and in the Benedictional of Saint Aethelwold (fig. 166 and 4). In their original condition ivories may have resembled manuscript illuminations even more closely that some now do; for there is evidence that some at least were painted. Many of those that survive are fragments, or removed from their settings. The special importance of the reliquary crucifix now in the Victoria and Albert Museum (fig. 160) is that it is complete, and shows the significance of colour and of the combination of materials. The metalwork may be German, but still may have been made in England. We are told that when archbishop Ealdred of York built a pulpit 'of incomparable workmanship', all of bronze and gold and silver, at the entrance to the choir at Beverley, flanked by two arches, and spanned by another with a cross on top, all of the same materials, it was *opere Theutonico*. All that is left of the magnificence of the Anglo-Saxon Church is words, manuscripts and fragments. Among those fragments which give a glimpse of lost splendours the ivories are not the least important.

J. Campbell

5 Seal matrix of walrus ivory, 8.5 × 4.4 cm, with impressions (British Museum). The handle shows God the Father and God the Son with their feet on a prostrate man. The inscription on one side is SIGILLUM B GODWINI MINISTRI ('the seal of thegn Godwine' – the significance of the B is unknown), on the other SIGILLUM GODGYÐE MONACHE D(E)O DATE ('the seal of the nun Godgytha, dedicated to God'). Godwine may be the *minister* of that name who attests a number of Aethelred II's charters between 980 and 987. Two other seal matrices of *ministri* of approximately the same period are known. It is a question for what purposes they were used. This matrix is unique in being two-sided. Perhaps the Godgytha side represents a re-use.

unlikely that the names of most of those whom it commemorates meant anything more than a few years after the battle. The poet does not seem to know the name of the Viking leaders (the principal one was no less than Olav Tryggvason himself), and there is no trace of the defeatism and despair of the author of the *Chronicle*. The most important fact the poem reveals about the battle itself is that Byrhtnoth got his army to Maldon before the Vikings had the chance to come off the tidal island on which they were encamped. Byrhtnoth agreed to let them do so, so that they could fight a pitched battle, and this cost him his life and the English a major defeat.

Byrhtnoth has been called foolhardy by armchair military critics; others have thought it so improbable a gesture that it never happened and must be written off as a convention of heroic poetry. But Byrhtnoth was not being foolhardy. He had really little choice. The critics do not ask themselves where the Viking ships were. The poem never suggests that the English had got between the Vikings and their ships. The ships were almost certainly beached by the Blackwater. The Vikings were offering Byrhtnoth a chance to fight at a place where he was obviously prepared to fight; otherwise they would sail away and leave him to chase their trail of looting and destruction.

The battle was lost, and it is difficult not to feel that the defeat was the turning point of the reign. That it was felt as a national, not a local, affair, is shown by the sequel. The *Chronicle* not quite accurately claims that now for the first time the English paid tribute to the Vikings. The English negotiators who advised this course were not local Essex thegns, but the archbishop of Canterbury and the ealdorman of the south-western provinces. Further tribute, in every increasing sums, was also paid in 994, 1002, 1007 and 1012. Then a colossal tribute was raised by Cnut in 1018, presumably to pay off his army and fleet; the last such tribute was raised by Cnut's son, Harthacnut, in 1040 for the same purpose. In some 50 years the English paid £250,000 to the Vikings, suffering in addition local levies and much looting. It also seems that the amount of tribute they could extract impressed the Danes with the advantages of taking over rather than simply plundering England. By 994 the leader of the Vikings was King Sweyn of Denmark himself, and he was to conceive the ambition of making himself king of England.

It took more than 20 years of campaigning by the Vikings before they could credibly aim at full conquest. As the campaign came to its climax there is evidence of division and disloyalty amongst the English nobility. The magnate of worst repute, according to the *Chronicle*, was Eadric Streona of Mercia. Significant for his unreliability

174 The Heggen vane, height 19 cm (Oslo, University Museum of National Antiquities). Of heavily gilt copper or bronze, it was probably originally mounted to a ship's prow by the slanting vertical edge so that streamers attached to the curved edge would indicate wind speed and direction (cf. fig. 183).

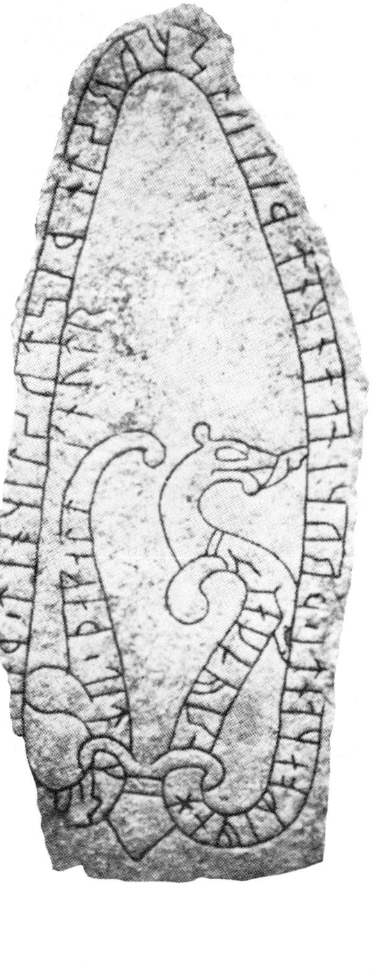

175 Runic stone from Yttergärde, Uppland, Sweden. Raised in memory of Ulf, it records how he took three payments of geld in England – the first that Tosti paid, then Thorkell (the Tall), then Cnut. That a Swede should have fought for Thorkell and Cnut is valuable evidence that famous warlords attracted followers from far afield.

is the fact that one of Cnut's first acts as king of England was to have him killed. It has already been suggested that his attitude might be partly explained by the politics of the period (see above, p. 192). It is also the case that until the campaign by which Cnut gained the English crown the Mercians were largely spared the ravages of the Vikings. Treachery was also endemic in what had once been loyal Wessex. The ealdorman of Hampshire betrayed English plans to the Vikings in 992, and in revenge Aethelred had his son blinded the next year. A powerful South Saxon thegn, Wulfnoth, went into the Viking business on his own account in 1009, and judging by the extraordinary position his family attained under Cnut (he was probably the father of Earl Godwine and grandfather of King Harold and Earl Tostig), perhaps he soon teamed up with the Danish Vikings. In the last years of Aethelred and the brief reign of Edmund Ironside (April–November 1016) there was a good deal of changing of sides, for which some English magnates paid with their lives in the first months of Cnut's reign.

There was treachery on the Viking side too. Sweyn first came with Olaf Tryggvason, but Olaf made a treaty with Aethelred by which he accepted Christianity and never fought for the Danes again, though he fought against them. By about 1010 the principal Viking leader after Sweyn was Thorkell the Tall. In 1011 some Vikings seized the archbishop of Canterbury and held him to ransom. The archbishop, Saint Aelfheah, refused to allow the men of Kent to ransom him because they had been soaked enough to pay the tribute. He was foully murdered (April 1012). The Vikings were Christian by this time; Sweyn had been brought up a Christian since his birth and was even pious in his own way. Allegedly disgusted by this murder, Thorkell and some 40 shipfuls of warriors changed sides and took service, very well-paid service, under Aethelred. To judge by the *Chronicle*, Thorkell was not a popular ally. But he stayed faithful to Aethelred till about 1015 when he went over to Cnut. He played a major role in the military operations that gained Cnut the crown. Not surprisingly, he was never much trusted by Cnut; such warlords were useful allies but over-mighty subjects.

In 1013 Sweyn opened the last phase of the Viking assault; by the summer it was obviously his intention to replace Aethelred as king of the English. He needed, too, revenge for Thorkell's defection. Politics in Denmark are obscure at this time, but Thorkell's later career suggests that he had a power base of his own, and Sweyn probably had no choice. By the end of the summer Aethelred had sent Queen Emma and their two sons to her family in Normandy, and then followed himself. London submitted to Sweyn, and the *Chronicle* says that all the English received him as full king. Sweyn himself died on 2 February 1014. He left two sons: Cnut, almost certainly the elder, who was meant to succeed him as king of the English, and Harold, who succeeded him as king of Denmark. There was, however, an upsurge of anti-Danish feeling, and Thorkell's brother was probably murdered in the resulting pogrom. Cnut, not feeling strong enough on his own, went to his brother in Denmark, where he was joined by Thorkell, who not surprisingly realized he had no future as a 'new Englishman'.

In the meantime the English magnates had sent for Aethelred to return as their king, 'if he would govern them better than he did before'. He did return, but from now on the principal English leader was his eldest son by his first marriage, Edmund Ironside. In 1015 Cnut returned with Thorkell and an army. He was joined by Eadric Streona and 40 ships, probably manned by Danish mercenaries. Aethelred lay at London nearing the end of his tragic life. Edmund went north and made an alliance with the Northumbrian earl, Uhtred. Eadric Streona had also intervened in Northumbrian politics and murdered two important landholders from the north Mercian borderlands. He may have had Aethelred's support here, because when Edmund married the widow of one of them and seized all the property of the murdered men, it was against his father's wishes. Earl Uhtred had some connection with the two murdered thegns and joined Edmund in a punitive raid on Mercia, which experienced war on a large scale for the first time since the mid-tenth century. Cnut attacked York, and Earl Uhtred was forced to turn back to defend his main stronghold. He was driven to change sides and join Cnut, which was foolish since it forced Cnut to choose between him and Eadric Streona. At Eadric's instigation, Cnut had Uhtred murdered.

The Northumbrians, none the less, stayed with Cnut and accepted his nominee, Eric, as their earl. Eric was very close to Cnut; he was Norwegian and had served Sweyn as a sort of viceroy of Norway and the leader of the opposition to the anti-Danish Olaf Tryggvason. Eric lasted as earl of Northumbria until 1023, though he never wholly overcame the challenge to his rule of Earl Uhtred's brother. After 1023 he disappeared from history without trace, but alongside Thorkell he seems to have masterminded Cnut's bid for the crown; he and Thorkell seem to have won the battles.

On Saint George's Day 1016 Aethelred died. His son Edmund was hailed as king by the people of London and such great men as were there; later by Eadric Streona and the West Saxon thegns. Edmund and his allies lost a decisive battle against Cnut in Essex at what is usually identified as Ashingdon. Eadric again turned his coat and the Danes won, but the casualties on both sides were heavy; the Danish losses being so great as to persuade Cnut to be moderate in his victory. He made a treaty with Edmund, recognizing him as king of Wessex but making himself king of Mercia, which was to include London. In the autumn Edmund died. His own young children were taken off, ultimately, to Hungary, out of Cnut's reach; his young stepbrothers were left at the Norman court to be brought up. All the English now accepted Cnut, who promptly took a leaf out of Aethelred's book and married his widow Emma, the Norman princess, who had been queen of England for more than a dozen years by now.

Aethelred's Legislation

There is no question that Cnut was a more successful ruler than Aethelred, and he did give the English 20

176 Aethelred II's charter granting lands to Muchelney Abbey, Somerset, in 995 (Taunton, Somerset Record Office, DD/SAS PR 502, 489 × 381 mm). There is dispute as to who wrote most charters (see p. 176). This one was certainly the work of a Christ Church, Canterbury, scribe. Its abnormality in lacking a description of the estate boundaries in Old English hinders generalization from it.

years or so of the peace they so needed. His policies were much the same as Aethelred's, except that for him they worked. But the reign of Aethelred did leave an important legacy in some respects. In particular, the powerful governmental machine built up by his predecessors was left virtually intact to the new Anglo-Danish dynasty.

The long reign produced much legislation, some of it pious exhortation to make the English behave better. Traditional scholarship recognized 10 legal codes as Aethelred's, but in fact he seems to have legislated on only six occasions. It is obvious that the main influence on Aethelred's legislation was that of his father's four codes. Law was still primarily oral, and it was pious and learned churchmen of the second generation of monastic reform who made written versions of Aethelred's codes, probably for polemical reasons. The only such churchman we can certainly identify is Archbishop Wulfstan of York (1003–23), to whom we are indebted for the survival of most of Aethelred's later legislation. Earlier, Aethelred provides the most detailed account of Anglo-Saxon monetary law to date. We have already seen how important that law and system were under Edgar (see above, p. 173). The text of the laws and the coins themselves show that Aethelred fully maintained his father's policy of strict control until nearly the last years of his reign. In taxation policy there were important innovations.

The English bought the Danes off from time to time. In 1012 they hired some 40 shipfuls of Vikings. The *Chronicle* is adamant that this was the origin of the permanent land tax known as the geld. It is often called the Danegeld, though not in any pre-Conquest source, and while it was sometimes used to raise tribute for the Danes, its main purpose, as its original name, *heregeld*, army money, implies, was to provide Thorkell's troops with the regular payments they required. It was levied at so much per hide. The hide, as we have already seen (see above,

p. 58), was the basic unit by which land was rated for public burdens and military service. In some cases the geld was collected through the hundred by the senior official of the shire, now beginning to be called the sheriff. It is evident from the huge sums it raised that it was efficiently levied and that the collectors or exactors had lists of local landholders and the rating, or hidage, of their estates.

There was also a central treasury that seems to have been permanently sited at Winchester until some time after the Conquest. Not improbably there was an efficient, and foolproof, method of recording receipts on wooden tallies, that partially overcame the difficulty of making calculations with the roman numerals that were the only number system known in the West. The geld, for which the tallies were perhaps invented as part of the mechanism of collection, was a remarkable achievement in itself. But before 1012 the government from time to time raised large capital sums for payments of tribute that after 1012 could have been met out of the geld. How was this done? There may have been levies on a hidage basis before *heregeld* was permanently established *c.* 1012. It has also been plausibly conjectured that another source of funds was the manipulation of the coinage, which the royal control of minting made possible (see above, p. 176; below, pp. 204–5). There was, too, deepening royal control of the *burh* as it progressed from garrison town to urban centre. The control was exercised by reiterating the king's right to any fines incurred by their inhabitants, to the tolls they had to pay, and so on. What was being given legal shape was the primacy of royal lordship in towns. A special connection between town and crown was of crucial importance in England throughout the Middle Ages; its origins were pre-Conquest. The profits of justice were something King Aethelred was quite as familiar with as his great-great-great-great-great-great grandson, Henry II; and they may have been very considerable.

The most famous of Aethelred's laws relates to the jury of 12 senior thegns of the neighbourhood whose job it was to accuse evil-doers of their crimes, arrest them and bring them to trial. This provision is from a code directed to the Danelaw, and it anticipates pretty exactly the famous legislation of Henry II in the twelfth century, establishing (or perhaps simply re-emphasizing) the 'jury of presentment' whose function was that which Aethelred's law lays down. The more one looks at Henry II's assizes the more they seem to owe to earlier example. King Aethelred's 'jury' may be a Scandinavian import confined to the north and east of England at first, but it also seems of a piece with the Carolingian-style intention to strive for the maintenance of law in the localities that is apparent in earlier tenth-century codes (see above, p. 180). Aethelred certainly had compelled local juries to supply him with information about his rights. His so-called fourth law code seems in fact to embody the answers of just such a jury in London. This may well be nothing new. What is clear is that whatever the catastrophes of the reign, Aethelred brooked no diminution of his concern for government at a distance and was just as interested in what went on in the neighbourhoods as any of his predecessors.

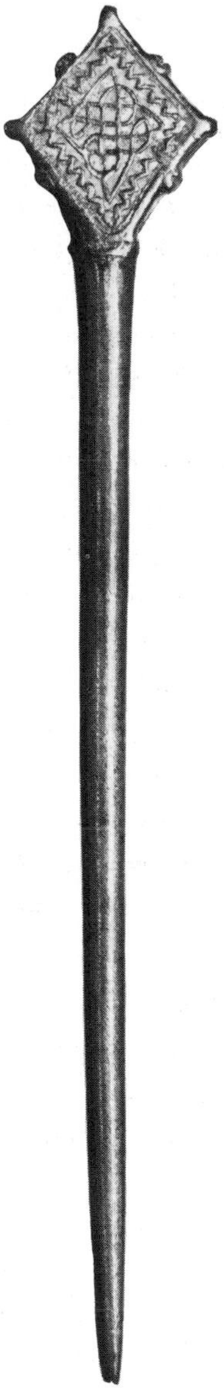

177 Bronze pin found in the tomb of Archbishop Wulfstan (died 1023), length 13.2 cm (London, Society of Antiquaries).

178 (*right*) Christ in Majesty in the church of Saint John the Baptist, Barnack, Northamptonshire, height about 102 cm. Late Saxon (possibly just post-Conquest), it closely resembles a statue in St Radegund's, Poitiers.

Church Learning: Wulfstan and Aelfric

Even more unexpected are the very considerable cultural achievements of the reign, though Aethelred can claim no personal credit for them. Archbishop Wulfstan has already been mentioned as the recorder of Aethelred's later legislation. He and his fellow-monk, Abbot Aelfric of Eynsham, were the principal English intellectuals of the age. Wulfstan and Aelfric were monks of the second generation of the monastic reformation, and their literary output (prodigious for those days) bears testimony to the efficiency of a monasticism based on 'chastity, abstinence from meat, and the holding of property in common' as a means of renewal for the Church.

Wulfstan was clearly of distinguished family, probably of East Anglian origin. He was certainly a monk, and perhaps an abbot, though of which abbey we are ignorant, before he became a bishop. However, he plainly had an affection for Ely and had himself buried there, which is probably significant. He first comes to notice as bishop of London in 996. Coming from the same part of the world as Saint Oswald, Wulfstan too became bishop of Worcester and archbishop of York in 1002. One of his nephews was also elected to Worcester in Cnut's reign. He, in turn, received another Wulfstan into the Worcester community, starting a career that led to Wulfstan II's election as bishop of Worcester in Edward the Confessor's day, a post he held until the time of William Rufus, when he was the only English-born bishop in the kingdom. There is a tradition extending from Oswald's day to the eve of the twelfth century.

Wulfstan was a noted sermon writer, and his sermons have been preserved in some quantity. They have a style of a kind. It has been fairly described as 'long-winded and repetitive', and might also be called soporific and parsonical. The sermons were admired in their day and long afterwards. The most famous of them is the 'Sermon of the Wolf to the English' preached late in Aethelred's reign and clearly directed to a lay audience. In it he attributes the sufferings of the English, about which he goes into interesting detail, to their neglect of religion, the ruin of some of the monasteries and the unpunished murder of Edward the Martyr. For Wulfstan, it is not their king but the English themselves whose inadequacies have brought miseries upon them. More immediately important to the historian are Wulfstan's legal writings, which also express his desire for the moral regeneration of his fellow countrymen.

There can be no doubt that Wulfstan was a legist, and even more a canonist, of the first importance. There is much in his canonical writings that seems—at least to us—inappropriate to a time when a nation was fighting for its life. It is notable that the payment of tithes was a matter of importance to both Aethelred and Wulfstan, as they were to Edgar before them. Tithes were meant for the support of parishes and parish priests. By 1066 we know from Domesday Book and related documents that England was covered in parishes, but it is not clear that they were very old. It looks very likely that the tenth century, and especially the later part of it, was the key period in parish history. Wulfstan's writings were partly written to meet the new needs created by a network of parishes. Early in his pontifical career he wrote the so-called *Canons of Edgar*. This was a book of canon law aimed at parish priests. He seems to have assumed that parish priests will meet annually in synods of three days' duration. The *Canons of Edgar* were designed as a work of reference for such synods. If these synods actually took place, then it was long after 1066 before the English Church recovered this degree of discipline.

Wulfstan's sources are also interesting. Like his Continental counterparts, he shows an extensive knowledge of, and borrowing from, Carolingian legislation. All canonists of the reformed party had trouble with their sources. Custom and usage, often attached to the names of saints and popes, were on the side of the traditional clergy whom they opposed. The tendency was to make the texts read what the reformers thought they ought to have meant, not what they actually said. Bishop Burchard of Worms, the most notable contemporary canonist, was an unscrupulous 'improver' of texts to the extent of outright forgery. Because the reforming monks had a virtual monopoly of literacy their 'improvements' went undetected. On the whole Wulfstan, to his credit, if not free from all such taint, was not such an improver. Because his canons were backed by a powerful king and a united episcopate he does not have to justify the procedures he enjoins. Wulfstan very seldom cites his sources by name, but simply states the rule.

Wulfstan was probably influenced by the reforming abbot of Fleury, Abbo, who spent a period in exile at Ramsey in the mid-980s. Abbo was an exceptionally able canonist and ideologue, and on the whole an honest one. He singled out the ecclesiastical legislation of Charlemagne and Louis the Pious, which was very much of a reforming cast, and instead of forging acceptable texts with names of special sanctity attached, justified his preference for these texts by stating baldly that the 'utility' of the Church had never been so well served by law-makers. Some of the Carolingian legislation actually goes back to legislation of Visigothic synods of the sixth and seventh centuries, helping to form a curious link between kingdoms so remote in time and place as the Spain of Isidore of Seville and the England of Archbishop Wulfstan. Wulfstan seems to have followed Abbo, taking Carolingian texts as his main models and making the utility of the Church his justification.

Abbot Aelfric had a different, more private, career. For the most part he wrote for monks, and his view looks inward to the monastery not outwards to the larger kingdom. He had been a pupil of Saint Aethelwold, and was always proud of it. He wrote rather a dull and disappointing *Life* of Aethelwold and compiled a Latin grammar and a Latin primer, the first examples of such aids to study to be produced in England, so far as we know. His main fame and his main talent, however, lay in his vernacular works. Apart from a number of occasional sermons, he wrote a set of what he called 'catholic' homilies, supplemented by a series of saints' lives; the whole thing was conceived of as a unity. He was probably bringing the *Rule* of Saint Benedict up to date here. Saint Benedict had prescribed a very restricted intellectual diet for monks, consisting mainly of the Bible (and even then the exciting parts like the Book of Kings were not to be read just before going to bed), the lives of the Desert Fathers and improving monastic homilies, like those of John Cassian. Aelfric was offering something more modern in the same mode. He also included one of the lives of the Desert 'fathers', that of a lady, if such she could be called, Saint Mary of Egypt. This life illustrates an important limitation imposed by lifelong existence, from babyhood to the grave, in a single-sex community entirely run by celibates. Saint Mary was a whore who after many years of prodigious fornication underwent a conversion and ended her life in a burst of even more prodigious chastity. It does not seem to have occurred to Aelfric that after a life such as the one she is described as leading, conversion or no conversion, she was unlikely to have much attraction as what would now be described as a sex object.

Aelfric was, within his limitations, a formidable and important writer. He is the father, the inventor, of the rich tradition of plainly stated, undecorated, but vigorous and powerful English prose. In a sense King Alfred is the father of English prose, but where he has to be deciphered, Aelfric can be read. His style is much more impressive than Wulfstan's, and if he had a delivery to match, some of his sermons, such as the powerful one on Saint Oswald (of Northumbria), culled from a few passages in Bede, must have been very effective in the pulpit.

Aelfric wrote very much in the Benedictine tradition. His hearers, or readers, would have learned, fairly painlessly, a lot of not too fanciful Christian history, monastic-centred of course, and within the monastic world, Fleury-centred. There is a life of Saint Maur that turns out to be simply the Fleury version of the abbey's origins and of how it obtained the bones of Saint Benedict. These monks found no barrier between the spiritual and the business side of the new monasticism, and Aelfric was no exception. Saint Aethelwold probably drew up the splendid foundation charter for his re-foundation of the great abbey of Ely (Birch, *Cart.*, no. 1266); a few years later Aelfric supplemented it by a vernacular version. This was all part of the same enterprise: the presentation of the new spirituality, of a new form of monasticism, as part of the essential tradition of the Church. Aelfric's works present essentially a picture of the Church of the martyrs, associating the new ideas with the great figures of the Christian past. Running all the way through is the idea—and the idea can be defended historically—that the monastic movement from the days of Saint Benedict embodied the best in Catholic tradition. It is not surprising that some monks of the day celebrated New Year on 21 March, the 'anniversary of creation' thinly disguised as Saint Benedict's day.

Not much can be said here about Aelfric's theology in detail though something must. It is thoughtful and some of its ideas were new, though not probably original to Aelfric, who derived his ideas from those current in more advanced circles on the Continent, notably Fleury. The ultimate source for the new theology is almost certainly late Carolingian religious thought, with a special importance for Archbishop Hincmar of Rheims, whose changing thought reached Abbo of Fleury through Hincmar's intellectual descendant Flodoard, and was much altered and developed *en route*. Aelfric made this new theology readily available in digestible form and in the vernacular to a generation of churchmen who had almost lost their Latin.

At the centre of what such men wrote was a theology of kingship. The reformers, particularly of the English, West Frankish and Lotharingian movements, all relied in various degrees on royal power to protect their liberties

179 Page from a Herbal produced in Christ Church, Canterbury, early in the 11th century (British Library, MS Cotton Vitellius C.iii, fol. 56v, 290 × 190 mm).

and keep the local magnate and the local bishop from interfering within the monasteries if they were ill-disposed (not all local magnates and bishops, of course, were ill-disposed). At the same time, as the most casual reading of Aelfric will demonstrate, men such as he were well aware that the kind of kings monks could approve of and rely on were exceptions rather than rules. It has been pointed out in connection with Edgar's rather theatrical coronation how this problem was tackled by equating the role of a Christian king with that of Christ himself, thus at once hedging the decrees of a 'good' king with a kind of vicarious divinity and providing a platform for charges of blasphemous tyranny against kings who manifestly were not imitations of Christ (see above, p. 189).

In arguing this case the reformers had to spell out in some detail what they thought about Christ. They anticipated some of the insights more usually associated with part of England most accessible to Normans. The desire to placate Emma's Norman relatives may have played some part in his decision. The duke of Normandy, Robert the Magnificent (or the Devil, it is a matter of taste), had already quarrelled with Cnut and broken the Anglo-Norman alliance. Norman charters show that, towards the end of Cnut's reign, Robert had recognized Edward, the elder son of Emma and Aethelred, the Confessor, as king. One of the major Norman sources, William of Jumièges (see below, p. 221) says Robert led an expedition to England intended to replace Cnut by Edward. The expedition remains a probability rather than a certainty, though a difficult charter seems to confirm its reality. What is certain, however, is that Duke Robert died about the same time as Cnut leaving his duchy to his infant son William, whose combination of disadvantages—bastardy, infancy, and maternal relatives of very low degree—made it inevitable that some years must pass before the young duke or any other Norman, could have an English policy. Thus Earl Godwine had breathing space and some freedom of action in 1035.

It must be borne in mind, though, that cross-Channel politics, like English politics, had their symmetries. Although after 1066 the royal family of France, the Capetians, and the Norman ducal-royal family were usually at odds, before 1066 they were normally friends and allies. The Normans were the enemies of the counts of Anjou with whom they contested the rule of Maine, and were also enemies of the counts of Flanders. The Capetians' ambitions lay more towards the counties of Blois-Chartres, and Champagne and the duchy of Burgundy. The French king could be relied on to support the young Norman duke, and this support was important and would be taken as important at the time. The early Capetians, while limited in resources and possibilities, were within these limits effective enough. They had power as well as status, and it must always have seemed likely that with royal backing Duke William would secure Normandy in the end, provided he shaped up well as we know that he did.

Turning to the 'northern' party, one can guess why Leofric and Siward decided to support Harold I, even though their doing so could only intensify the threat from Scandinavia while offering no hope of a Norman alliance. Harold, was, however, on the spot, and no one knew when Harthacnut would come or even if he would ever come. Harold and his mother Aelfgifu, seem to have been related to those members of the Mercian and Northumbrian aristocracies who had been persecuted by Aethelred II and who, either as a cause or a consequence, were strongly pro-Danish. Thus Leofric and Siward the latter of whom was now very much a part of the old 'English' Establishment in Northumbria (see above, p. 209–12), may have had local and family reasons for supporting Harold. Fear of Earl Godwine's growing wealth and power probably played some part also. A man like Harold (who may well have been related to Siward), with a northern base, was an admirable counterpoise to Godwine's domination of the kernel of the English kingdom, Wessex. It needs to be remembered that in the late Anglo-Saxon period most of the royal estates lay in Wessex. Harold I, with the backing of the earls of Mercia and Northumbria, could not be denied the possession of the numerous widely distributed royal estates south of the Thames, and so would have represented a powerful brake on the ambition of Godwine and his family.

Something of the strength of Godwine's position can be seen from the record of William I's great survey of 1086, Domesday Book, because it records the state of landholding 'on the day King Edward was living and dead' that is 6 January 1066 (see below, pp. 226–7). In that year the royal estates brought in about £5,000 per annum. The holdings of the Godwine family, not counting those of Tostig, Godwine's son and formerly earl of Northumbria (see below, pp. 231–2) brought in £4,000; Earl Tostig, before his fall in October 1065, had an annual income of £1,300, the same as that of the earl of Mercia. By 1066 the Godwine family held land in all parts of England, with the exception of certain Mercian shires (fig. 190), and in part of the heart of Mercia they had a great estate. Again, by 1066 many of the estates of the Godwine family had been beneficially hidated, that is the number of hides on which they were assessed for public obligations and taxes had been reduced. In 1035 this vast accumulation had just begun, but rather more than the foundations had been laid. A very great deal more was at stake in the succession crisis of 1035 than personal bickering (see fig. 190).

Within months of Cnut's death, Harthacnut's failure to appear totally disqualified him as a candidate. The sources are clear that this was what made the English turn against him. Very soon Godwine and Emma gave him up too. What follows is obscure, which is a pity since it sets another pattern that was to be worked out in 1066. Our main source here is the *Encomium of Queen Emma* (see above, p. 208). Its third book presents Emma's version of her part in the events of 1035 and 1036. It is evident that it was meant to silence criticisms of her conduct from unnamed contemporaries, one of whom seems to have been her eldest son, Edward the Confessor. What is being whitewashed, and it clearly is whitewash, is Emma's behaviour after she realized that Harthacnut was a non-starter.

She seems to have summoned one or both of her sons by Aethelred II, Edward and Alfred, to England. Her encomiast says the letter of summons was forged by Harold I or his partisans, but these princes were the last persons Harold would want to see in England. There seems little room for doubt that the letter was genuine; presumably the encomiast sought to explain it away because of its disastrous result. The elder prince Edward stayed in Normandy; the younger, Alfred, turned up and was met by Earl Godwine, who was supposed to take him to his mother. Presumably Godwine and Emma were still in alliance against Harold when the invitation was sent; if so, by the time the prince arrived Godwine had decided he had no option but to accept Harold I. Godwine diverted the young prince to Guildford, became his vassal, laid on plenty of food and drink for his men, then billeted

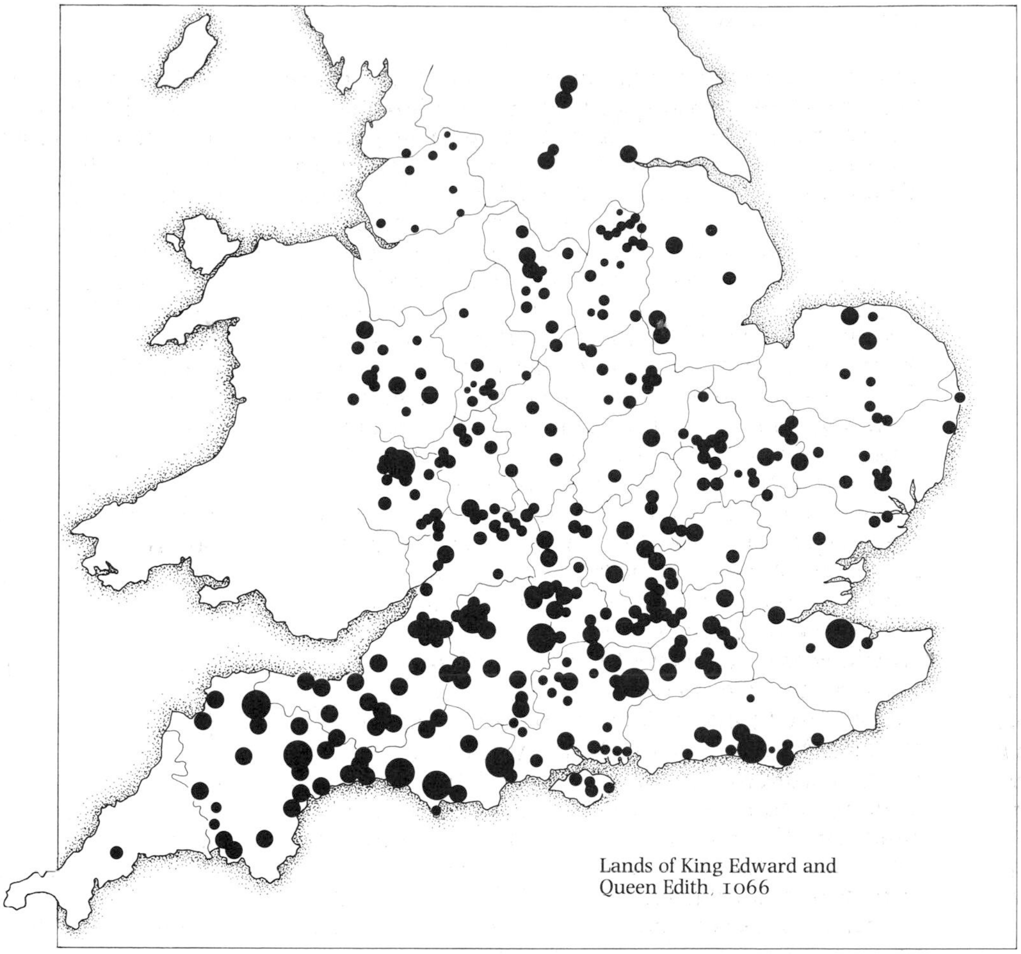

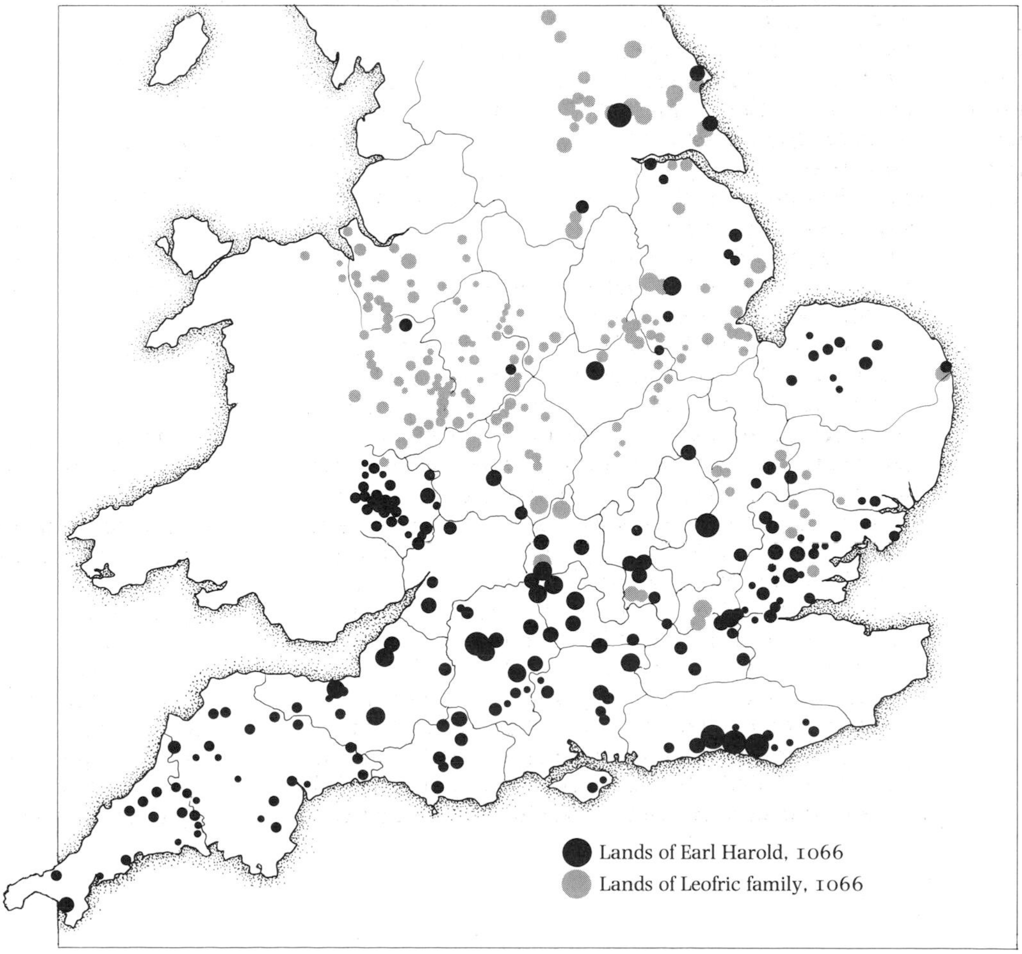

190 Maps showing the distribution of lands held by King Edward and Queen Edith (above), and by Harold and Leofric (below) (from D. Hill, *An Atlas of Anglo-Saxon England* (Blackwell, 1981)). The size of estates (indicated approximately by the size of the dots) ranges from 1 to 100 hides.

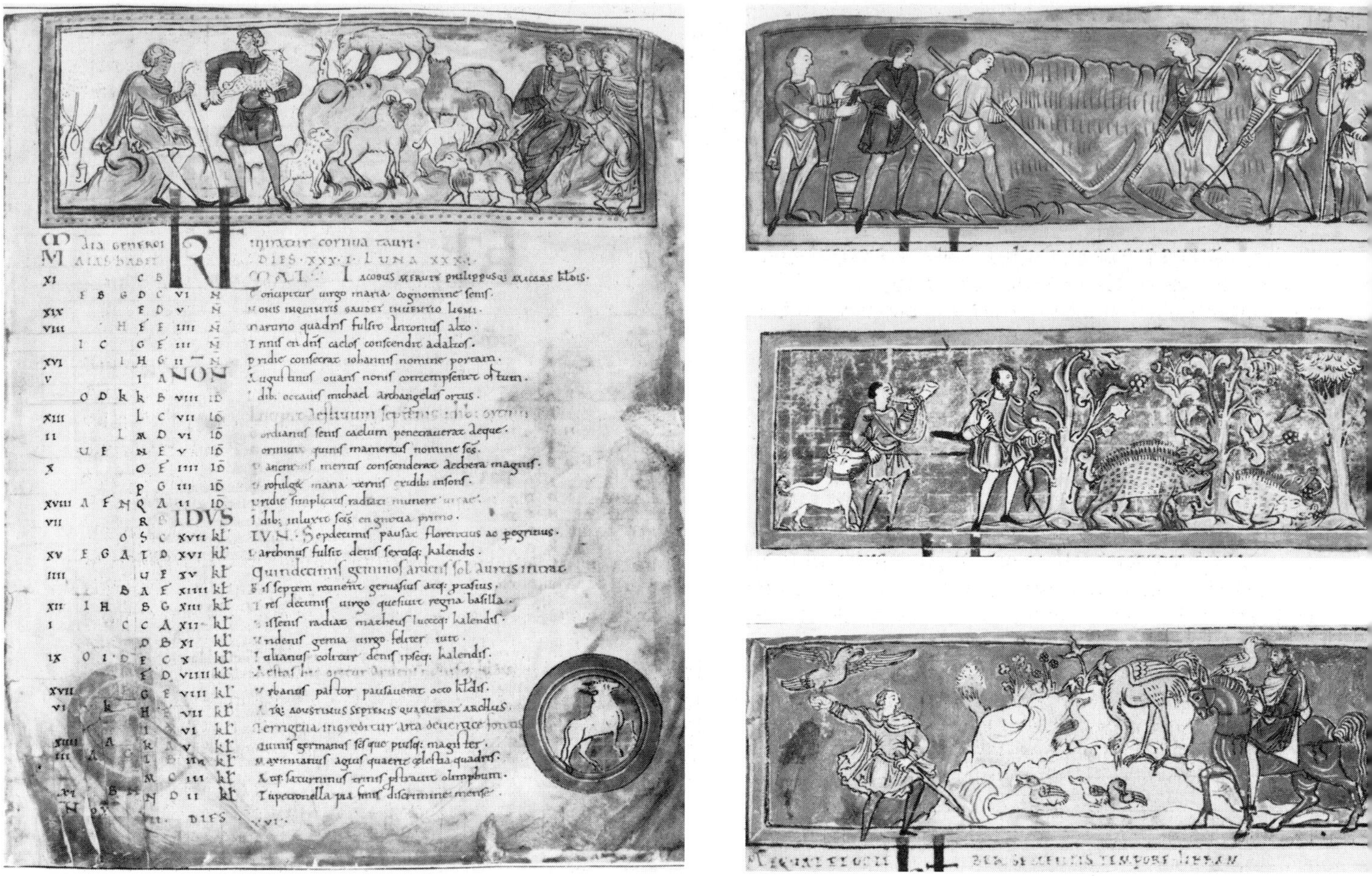

193 Scenes from a calendar illustrating the Labours of the Months (British Library, MS Cotton Tiberius B.v). The full page (left, fol. 5r) shows shepherds with their flock; in the circular panel below is the sign of the zodiac. The three other scenes represent reaping (top; August, fol. 6v), pigs feeding (centre; September, fol. 7r), and hawking (bottom; October, fol.7v). Of particular interest are the iron tools and the whetstone being used by the reapers cf. pp. 170–1).

them in scattered groups. During the night Harold's men fell on the camp, killed many and maimed and blinded Alfred, who died soon afterwards at the abbey of Ely.

Earl Godwine was later tried by Alfred's half-brother, Harthacnut, for his part in the affair and excused himself by saying he was only obeying his lord, King Harold's, orders. The encomiast, who never goes into trivial details unless he has a point to make, reveals in a very circumspect way (when he wrote Godwine was still very much a power in the land) that Godwine had first become Alfred's vassal so that the excuse was false. Godwine, however, got away with it because the other great earls stood as sureties for him; they too had supported Harold and could not let Godwine fall on such an issue. Godwine had to give the head of Alfred's family, now King Harthacnut, a great present that looks very much like a wergeld, composition for a blood-feud. What Harthacnut thought of all this we shall never know, but it follows from his subsequent actions that Alfred's full brother, Edward the Confessor, never forgave Earl Godwine.

It is not easy to shed many tears over Alfred's fate, appalling as it was. He was playing for very high stakes and he must have known they included his life. Godwine, Leofric and Siward could remember very well the havoc a Viking invasion could wreak on England and on such as them. The invasions of a previous generation had put them where they were; if there were to be a renewed invasion they could well suffer the fate of much of Aethelred II's aristocracy. In 1035 they were the men in possession, they were the men with all to lose. By 1040 the English had paid over £250,000 to buy Vikings off or to pay Cnut's armies. They remained burdened by the *heregeld*, the only general land tax in western Europe (see above, pp. 200–1). This tax bore on all classes of society, though perhaps those with a little, rather than those with nothing, suffered the most. (The late Professor Galbraith once remarked that the function of the poor in the Middle Ages was to provide for the rich.) Thus though the politics of the period were conducted in dynastic and personal terms, there was something of a recognizable national interest, and in their selfish ways the great earls were trying to serve it.

By the murder of Alfred the crisis was temporarily resolved, and Harold I was accepted by all the English as king. Of his reign, what he did and what he was like, we know nothing. The main threat to his security must have been Harthacnut, who by 1038 had come to terms with his immediate rival, Magnus of Norway, in a treaty that contained the curious provision that each could be the other's heir should either leave no issue. One of the Norman chronicles says that Harthacnut was a sickly young man, and this may have been in King Magnus's mind. Harthacnut was now free to raise a fleet, and sailed for Bruges to meet his mother, Queen Emma, who never recognized Harold I and had gone into exile in Flanders. He dallied there for six months, perhaps waiting for Harold to die, which he did in March 1040.

Harthacnut was now accepted by all the English, though they never liked him very much. He sent for his half-brother, Edward, and, according to the *Encomium*, associated Edward with him in the kingship, which seems to be confirmed by the *Chronicle*. Harthacnut was a young man—in his early twenties—and might be expected to marry and have children, whose interests this arrangement might seem to hurt. But Edward was probably already known to be a dedicated celibate. If not, why had he not married? His very high birth and his interesting, if uncertain, prospects would have made him a good match. In 1042 Harthacnut fell down dead. One Swedish scholar has suggested Edward poisoned him, which is to go far beyond the evidence. The English were left with no alternative to Edward but Magnus of Norway, who had little attraction for them. The crisis had deepened. Now the English had a bachelor king just entering middle age, penniless and without any military reputation. All he had to offer was the hope of friendship with the still distracted Norman duchy. This is the measure of the crisis in the English political structure.

The Sources for Edward the Confessor's Reign and the Norman Conquest

Before going on to look at Edward's reign and the catastrophe which followed it, it is important to emphasize that there is no agreed interpretation of its politics. The dominant Victorian view, that of Freeman, was that Edward was a French quisling who helped to displace the pure Germanic Godwine family and to put a foreigner, and a French foreigner at that, on the throne: William, who then proceeded to overturn the democratic constitution of Old England. For the great Cambridge historian, Maitland, Edward was a 'holy simpleton' and his reign a concatenation of follies. Since the publication of Sir Frank Stenton's volume in the Oxford History of England historians have come to take a more sympathetic view of Edward and to regard his policies more seriously. Even so, the most recent biography, that by Professor Frank Barlow, still inclines to an interpretation of the reign which takes the English sources more seriously than the Norman. The nub of debate about the politics of the reign is whether or not the Norman sources are to be taken, as Freeman took them, essentially as retrospective propaganda, or whether they are to be regarded, as here they are, as containing a large part of the truth.

We have three narrative sources for the reign, besides the annals of the *Chronicle*. Two of these are Norman, the earlier being an account of Norman history up until shortly after the Conquest by William of Jumièges. It was written no later (and not much earlier) than 1075. It is generally thought, though no one has conclusively proved it, to have been used by William, archdeacon of Poitiers, in his *Gesta Guillelmi*, or *Deeds of Duke William*. This is a much more important and critical work than that of William of Jumièges. Written not much more than two years later than his, it corrects and supplements him, and is composed in much more elegant and incisive Latin.

The third source is ine a sense English. It is the *Vita Ædwardi* or *Life of King Edward*, and is probably the work of a Flemish cleric resident at the royal court. It is in fact an encomium of Edward's queen, Edith, and her family (she was the daughter of Earl Godwine), and has some resemblance to the earlier *Encomium of Queen Emma* (see above, p. 208), though it is not by the same author. It seems clear that it was begun before 1066, largely completed in the short reign of Harold, then modified in the light of the events of 1066. Edith was not in Harold's favour in 1066, and was indeed in some personal danger (see below, p. 232). The anonymous author consoled her for the loss of her earthly hopes and the ruin of her family by presenting her late husband as a saint in heaven. (The cult of Edward began immediately after his death but was at first confined to a very small circle. It did not, curiously, spread to Westminster Abbey, which he refounded, until a generation after his death.) The *Life* is the most nearly contemporary of all the sources and among the most biased. It is very pro-Godwine, but when Harold quarrelled with Godwine's brother Tostig, it takes Tostig's side, which was also the queen's. Moreover, it is positively venomous to Archbishop Stigand of Canterbury, who was probably an ally of Godwine's (see below, p. 230).

The most famous source is the *Anglo-Saxon Chronicle*. It is really three sets of annals, all partly independent and all partly interdependent, known for convenience as C, D, and E. They are presented in the form of year-by-year records with entries for most, but not all, of the years of Edward's reign. (There are other smaller and not very important off-shoots of the *Chronicle* which I shall ignore here.) Each version of the *Chronicle* survives in only one manuscript. That of E was copied at Peterborough half a century after the Conquest, with later additions, mostly of local interest. During Edward's reign, E was probably being kept at St. Augustine's, Canterbury, and like C shows few if any signs of hindsight; if its annals reflect prejudice it is that of contemporaries, not that of a later generation. It is very Godwinist in tone; Kent seems to have been pro-Godwinist in sentiment. The community at Christ Church, Canterbury, certainly was, and so presumably was St. Augustine's.

C is, for this reign, an Abingdon chronicle, and is very hostile to the Godwine family. This cannot be explained by local patriotism. Abingdon, as a community, got on with Earl Godwine well enough. It has been fairly argued that its author was a man of independent judgement, and by and large it is the most honest English source. Unfortunately C ceases to record events after 1056 and does not begin again until 1065; that is, the gap extended from the time Godwine's oldest surviving son, Earl Harold, made himself virtually supreme in England until the beginning of the train of events that led to the ruin of the whole Godwine family (see below, pp. 231–3). The gap may well reflect this annalist's disinclination to record events of which he did not approve.

The D text presents a much more difficult problem. It emanates from the entourage of Ealdred, who was for much of the reign both bishop of Worcester and archbishop of York. Not surprisingly, it contains information from the north, including Scotland, and the west country. Much ink has been spilt over whether D comes from York or Worcester. Since Worcester was a much more literate community than York at this date, and since Ealdred was bishop of Worcester for some years before he got York as well, it is more probable that D's author was a Worcester monk or clerk. In any case what matters is that it is connected with Archbishop Ealdred, who played a very great part in the events of the reign.

D survives in a manuscript of the late eleventh century. It is the shiftiest and most misleading of the three versions, probably because Ealdred continued active in politics for the first years of William I's reign. Usually mildly critical of the Godwines, it occasionally takes their part in a tepid way. But no one would suppose that Archbishop Ealdred played any great part in the reign of the Confessor if he had to rely on D. In fact, Ealdred was instrumental in allowing Harold to escape to Ireland during the temporary eclipse of the family in 1051, and he also played a major part in recruiting the Hungarian-raised son of Edmund Ironside as potential heir to Edward, a policy favoured at the time by the Godwine family: none of this is mentioned by D. It is difficult to escape the conclusion that the necessities of political life under the Conqueror have had some effect on what D says, and even more on what it leaves out.

The problems of D are complicated by the existence of a Latin chronicle attributed to a Worcester monk, Florence, and written little, if at all, before 1100. This is based on a number of sources, one of them a version of the *Anglo-Saxon Chronicle* much like D, but it is often much fuller than any extant version of the *Chronicle*, and this may mean that 'Florence' used a fuller *Chronicle* text (an unexpurgated D?), though he certainly had other sources. In any case, 'Florence's' account of the Confessor's reign draws directly or indirectly on a source connected with Ealdred. He is the only author who tells us why the Godwines were so hated in the north of England—Ealdred was archbishop of York while Tostig was earl of Northumbria (see below, p. 228)—and the only author who reveals that Queen Edith acted as hit-woman for her brother Tostig and had a Northumbrian thegn murdered on his behalf.

The nature of the sources is of the utmost relevance for the interpretation of Edward's reign. The traditional view, the 'Whig' view if one likes, was pro-Godwinist (see above, p. 221). It only gains credibility if the E text of the *Chronicle* is regarded as the National Record, to which the other recensions are merely supplementary. Freeman called the author of E the democrat of Peterborough, wholly misrepresenting his intentions (as well as putting him in the wrong abbey). This traditional school ignores or rejects the Norman sources out of hand. In very few cases do the English sources directly contradict the Norman, but the traditional view has repeatedly assumed that when the *Chronicle* is silent the Norman sources are lying. This is manifestly wrong.

No version of the *Chronicle* provides a dispassionate interpretation of events. Consider, for example, the account which the different versions give of the brief exile of Aelfgar (earl of East Anglia and son of Leofric, earl of Mercia) in 1055. C says he was 'outlawed without any guilt'; D that he was 'outlawed, having committed hardly any crime'; and E that he was 'charged with being a traitor to the king and all the people of this country. And he admitted this before all the people who were assembled there, though the words escaped him against his will.' That is all we know of the circumstances of Aelfgar's first exile: varied opinions about an unknown charge. In 1058 Aelfgar, by then earl of Mercia, was again banished for a time. Only the D version of the *Chronicle* has anything to say about this. 'Earl Aelfgar was banished, but he came back forthwith through Griffith's help. And a naval force came from Norway. It is tedious to relate fully how things went.' Irish and Welsh sources show that the reality so negligently sketched was a major Norwegian attempt on England in which Magnus, son of Harald Hardrada king of Norway, was allied with Aelfgar and Gruffydd, prince of Powys and Gwynedd. The E version of the *Chronicle* has nothing at all to say of this episode. This is a demonstration that its silence is no basis for an argument against an event having taken place; just as its tale of the supposititious parentage of Harold (see above, p. 214) shows how tendentious it could be. The demonstrable inadequacies and uncertainties of the English annals, not least the E version of the *Chronicle*, are such as to ensure that serious consideration should be given to the Norman version of the bases of William the Conqueror's claim to England.

What is at issue in particular is that the Norman authorities, mainly William of Poitiers backed up by the Bayeux Tapestry (which while not a source in the ordinary sense does provide an illuminating pictorial commentary on the principal events, composed not very long afterwards), suggest (a) that Edward offered the English succession to Duke William, and (b) that at some point Harold swore allegiance to William (see below, p. 232). The E text is silent on both those points. Some therefore have argued that they did not happen, others that perhaps they did but they did not matter. If they happened, they mattered, and some explanation of what Edward thought he was doing, and why, is required. That they did happen is strongly suggested by the picturesque, impossible and conflicting accounts that circulated after Harold's death, seeking to explain away his oaths to William. There must be fire behind all the smoke. In addition, one English source, the D text,

VBI HAROLD: SACRAMENTVM: FECIT:
VVILLELMO DVCI:
HIC HA

194 Harold takes the oath by which, according to Norman sources, he confirmed Edward's promise of the kingdom to William and himself swore fealty (Bayeux Tapestry, Bayeux Museum, height 50 cm).

without providing any context, does reveal that during the months Godwine spent in exile, Duke William appeared and did homage to Edward. This can only be explained as the aftermath to an offer of the succession made by the king and accepted by the duke (see below, p. 225).

It is sometimes argued that the Norman sources are suspect as propaganda. There is also no doubt that the E text was engaged in propaganda for the Godwine cause, but there is a difference. There is so little trace of hindsight in the E text as to make it virtually certain it is a contemporary source. The E text is propaganda before the event, the Norman sources propaganda after the event. If there is one thing that strikes the reader about William of Poitiers's *Deeds*, it is the arrogance of success and the brutality of triumph. By the time he wrote (and the Bayeux Tapestry was stitched), William was a king, secure on his throne, with the reputation of being the greatest soldier in Christendom, and probably having the largest income. Successful parties, especially utterly triumphant ones like William's, generate their own propaganda of course. There seem to be traces of this in William of Poitiers, especially his account of the battle of Hastings, where he presents the Duke as running the battle like a Russian grandmaster winning a chess tournament. But William's other observations on English affairs, which amount to no more than two sustained passages, are not like this. They have an unmistakably legal flavour. William is telling us that the crown was offered to the Conqueror; that the offer was confirmed by all the great men in England, including Earl Harold and his father; that Harold came and did homage to William personally, confirming the homage by going on a short campaign with his new lord to Brittany; and finally that in the weeks after Edward's death the two claimants to the crown exchanged legal arguments.

These precise statements and arguments cannot be brushed aside as mere propaganda. In a practical sense William's claim did not require legalistic argument by the time William wrote in about 1075. In 1066 it had done, when his case was argued at Rome and the Pope had recognized him as the legitimate claimant, giving him a holy banner, which made his cause something like a proto-crusade. Ten years later William held England by the strongest of *de facto* titles, overwhelming power. This is not to say that his biographer might not, in seeking to establish the righteousness of his hero's cause, have fabricated a case. But one should not leap to the conclusion that he did. On the balance of evidence it is more probable that he did not have to: that the Conqueror's claim was as William of Poitiers stated it, and based on fact. (It is noteworthy that his account of Harold's claim gives him a strong case that tallies with what other sources tell us.)

What is striking about these sources—and why they require a rather different treatment from those of earlier chapters—is that they ensure that for the Confessor's reign we can seek to follow a political narrative, or rather alternative narratives, according to our judgement of their value. For this reign, unlike its predecessors, we can learn something of the detail rather than simply construct the drift of political events.

195 The late Anglo-Saxon tower of All Saints, Earls Barton, Northamptonshire. Decorative strip work is a characteristic of Saxon architecture. The battlements are later medieval.

The Years 1042–1052

Edward became king in 1042 because there was no real alternative. By 1066, a man born in the reign of Edgar, that is before 975, would have lived under eight different kings drawn from three different families. We have only to compare the steady progress of the French monarchy under the Capetians from 987 until the high Middle Ages, when they produced generation after generation of healthy, able, comparatively long-lived kings (three sufficed for most of the twelfth century), with the initially much stronger German monarchy, whose resources were wasted in a constant succession of dynastic crises, to see how important dynastic stability was. The Confessor represented the oldest royal family in Europe, but he was head only of a junior line. The senior line was represented by Edward the aetheling, son of Edmund Ironside, now to all intents and purposes a Hungarian prince with a very small part to play in English history. His descendants, curiously, did have a part to play. His grand-daughter, Saint Margaret, was queen of Scotland, her daughter married Henry I of England and was in turn grandmother of Henry II and a direct ancestress of all the Plantagenets. In 1042 the English had to make do with a prince of copious pedigree but limited and threatened power

There was still danger from Scandinavia. The Norwegian king Magnus, son of Saint Olaf, had a claim not only to Denmark, but also, probably, to England by his treaty with Harthacnut (see above, p. 221). Until his death in 1047 Englishmen had cause to fear a Norwegian invasion. Indeed such fears did not die with Magnus (see below, p. 233). From the beginning of his reign Edward could count on Norman goodwill, and that had been important to every English government since the 990s. He was half-Norman and had been brought up in Normandy. But in 1042 the young Duke William's supporters were masters of a part only of his duchy, and that not the vital Channel coast. In 1047, however, William gained control of all Normandy at the battle of Val ès Duncs.

It is interesting that the Godwinist E text of the *Chronicle* (see above, p. 221) is the only English source to record William's victory. Godwine would have had cause to take note of it. In the earliest years of the reign he had Edward under his thumb. In 1045 the king married his daughter, Edith. Probably he did not do so willingly, for, in 1051, when he had Godwine at his mercy (see below, p. 225), the first thing Edward did was to pack Edith off to a convent. After Val ès Dunes Edward could look to Duke William as an effective ally; for he had something to offer him, the succession to the English crown.

Old tensions and the new possibility of a Norman alliance made the crisis of 1051–2. It seems to have begun with the appointment of a new archbishop of Canterbury in early 1051. Edward prevented the election of a Canterbury monk who was a kinsman of Godwine and appointed a Norman, Robert, bishop of London, formerly abbot of the Norman abbey of Jumièges. Robert at once set off for Rome to collect his *pallium*.

On the way, so William of Poitiers says, and he is probably right, he conveyed to William of Normandy an offer of the succession to England.

This offer made sense. Edward had no obvious successor; it must have been clear by now that he was unlikely to have children. The elder line of the house of Cerdic was represented only by a Hungarian prince, who presumably could speak no English. Nobody wanted the Norwegian king; for over two centuries the prime function of an English king had been to keep the Vikings out. The rivalry between the 'northern' earls and Godwine, already apparent in the struggles which followed the death of Cnut (see above, p. 215), was such as to make it unlikely that an English earl could succeed. Godwine was powerful enough, now the balance of power in England had once more swung to the south, to prevent either Leofric or Siward from even thinking of the succession; but they in turn were sufficiently powerful to defeat any hopes he might have. A Norman succession fitted into the political pattern of the last half century, and would ensure that the Channel was kept closed to the Vikings.

The crisis, and not improbably the offer, had been in the air for some time. Godwine's establishment of closer ties with Flanders at about this time may have been an attempt to prepare for a struggle. In 1050 or 1051 (but in any case before September 1051) his son Tostig married the count of Flanders's half-sister, Judith. One cannot be sure that the count's policy was unambiguous; for at about this time he married his daughter to William of Normandy. (It would be easier to know what to deduce from this if one knew whether the marriage took place in 1050, 1051 or 1052.) In any case it is certain that access to Flanders mattered to Godwine, for he took refuge after his temporary fall in 1051 at Bruges. The election of the Norman Robert to the see of Canterbury, dominating east Kent, would have impeded this access, just as it would have ensured communication between Normandy to London and Mercia. Edward took another step to secure control of cross-Channel communication at about this time, if, as is possible, he sought to give Dover to his brother-in-law, Eustace, count of Boulougne. Certainly it was Eustace's activities in Dover which touched off a crisis.

In the late summer of 1051 Eustace was returning to his county after a visit to Edward. His men became embroiled with the men of Dover, with deaths on both sides. Then (according to the E text of the *Chronicle*) Edward ordered Godwine, within whose earldom Dover lay, to harry it. Godwine refused. Civil war nearly broke out; but Edward mastered Godwine without bloodshed, so far as we can tell for two main reasons: first, he was supported by Leofric of Mercia and Siward of Northumbria; second, many of the men of military significance in the earldoms of Godwine and his sons would not stand against the king. Godwine and three of his sons fled to Bruges; Harold (Godwine's second son, but to become the oldest surviving one in 1053) fled to Ireland. While they were in exile William of Normandy came to England. 'It is in every way probable that the duke came in order to receive recognition of his standing as successor designate to the crown' (F. M. Stenton). The *quid pro quo* was that he did homage to Edward and became his man.

So far, so good for Edward. But the next year Godwine forced his way back from his Flemish base with the aid of the ships and seamen of the ports of his former earldom of Wessex. Archbishop Robert was sent packing, as were other Normans. He was replaced by Stigand, who seems to have passed from Emma's connection into Godwine's when she fell from power in 1035 (see below, p. 230); at any rate he got the great West Saxon see of Winchester, representing the main religious power in the area where Godwine was the main secular authority. Now he got Canterbury but was not required to surrender Winchester.

It is likely that Godwine's family accepted conditions. At any rate William of Poitiers says that both Stigand and Earl Godwine were among the great men who publicly assented to the Norman succession. If this was so it was mere lip-service. The realities of power were shown by Godwine's ability to force the restoration of his second, and ablest, son Harold, to the old superior earldom of East Anglia; during the period of Godwine's fall it had been held by Leofric's son and heir, Aelfgar.

In the crises of 1051–2 it is plain that the great men of England were anxious to avoid civil war if they could. Godwine and his family might be at daggers drawn with Edward. But there were other great men in England, if none so great as Godwine. Theirs was an organized state and a society which had survived great traumas. The richest landowners, important king's thegns (see above, p. 212), had estates which could lie in more earldoms than one. Conflict between earls was not to their advantage. Lesser men with property had a status and a say in county and hundred courts which brought them into a relationship with the central authority, and they recognized or suffered fiscal and military obligations which were national, not local. Towns prospered, and the extent to which some of them sprawled outside their fortifications in Edward's reign suggests an expectation of peace. Perhaps only just, but still truly, so far as we can guess and glimpse, England was what historians are pleased to call a nation-state. Some historians have regarded nation-states as creations of the Renaissance. England is not so late a creation. If you ask what held it together, a large part of the answer is, unsurprisingly, fear.

There is no doubt that when Englishmen made political calculations in the reign of Edward the Confessor fear of a renewed Viking assault weighed heavily. The great earls might be at odds; but they did not want to return to the days of Aethelred II. When the D chronicler explained how it was that Leofric and Siward on the one hand, and Godwine on the other, did not fight in 1051, he says it was because '. . . they would be opening a way for our enemies to enter the country and cause ruin among ourselves'. This opinion was shared by West Saxon thegns, since they deserted Godwine in 1051 in numbers large enough to force him into exile. The same chronicler, the next year, describing the circumstances

Edward the Confessor's England

In 1086 King William, wishing to know the value of what he had conquered, ordered the making of Domesday Book. This detailed record describes the state of the country both at the time of the inquest and at that of the Confessor's death in January 1066. The surveyors did their work well, much to the resentment of a contemporary, who considered it shameful that not so much as one ox, cow or pig escaped their attention. The modern historian, however, owes them an immense debt. Domesday Book enables a reconstruction of their society to be made on a scale not possible for any other medieval state. Few of the many statistics it provides are without interest. The pattern of landholding, for example, appears in great detail. The possessions of King Edward and his great earls can be mapped (see fig. 190). Their values are given, and reveal the significant fact that the Godwine family's landed wealth, at over £4,500, was little less than that of the king, but twice that of Leofric of Mercia's family. The remarkable effect that the tenth-century monastic reformation had on land ownership is also clear. A sixth of Domesday landed value was in monastic hands. The richest house was Glastonbury, with estates worth over £820, followed by Ely, Christ Church, Canterbury (whose pre-Conquest monks are said to have lived like earls), Bury St Edmunds, St Augustine's, Canterbury, Old Minster, Winchester, and Westminster. Of the bishoprics, Canterbury was the wealthiest, with almost five times York's landed value of about £370.

Towns were important (see p. 176), but most people lived on the land. 13,418 settlements contained 268,984 recorded individuals, which suggests a total population of about 2 million. The annual agricultural cycle which dictated their lives is illustrated in calendars and described in an eleventh-century manual for estate managers. These sources tie in well with each other, and with Domesday. All refer, for example, to the cultivation of vineyards (see no. 2). The manual also mentions mills, of which the country had a recorded total of 6,082. Together with the iron tools which appear in the calendars, they remind us that agricultural communities often have needs which agriculture alone cannot meet. Hence, Anglo-Saxon England knew both trade and industry. Some millstones were brought from the Rhineland. The exploitation of iron, however, was native, widespread and ancient. Domesday mentions renders of iron and iron workers, while an iron mine was granted by Oswine of Kent to St Augustine's, Canterbury, as early as 689. If lead, in contrast, appears to have been mined only in Derbyshire in 1086, this at least says a great deal about the

2 Further miniatures from the calendar in the British Library, MS Cotton Tiberius, B.v, showing the use of iron tools (see also fig. 189). (a) February (fol. 3v): work in the vineyard; (b) November (fol. 8r): smithying (?).

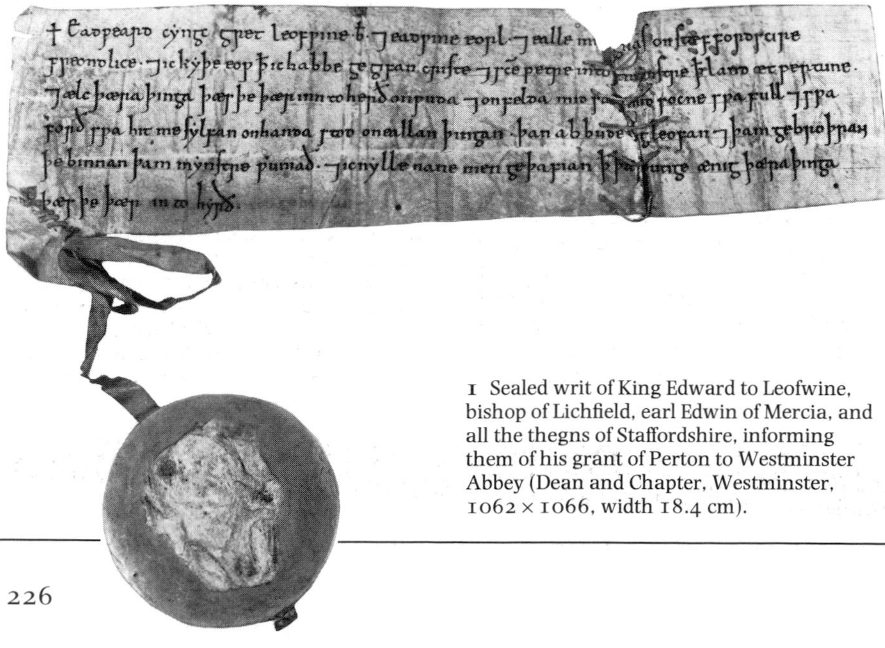

1 Sealed writ of King Edward to Leofwine, bishop of Lichfield, earl Edwin of Mercia, and all the thegns of Staffordshire, informing them of his grant of Perton to Westminster Abbey (Dean and Chapter, Westminster, 1062 × 1066, width 18.4 cm).

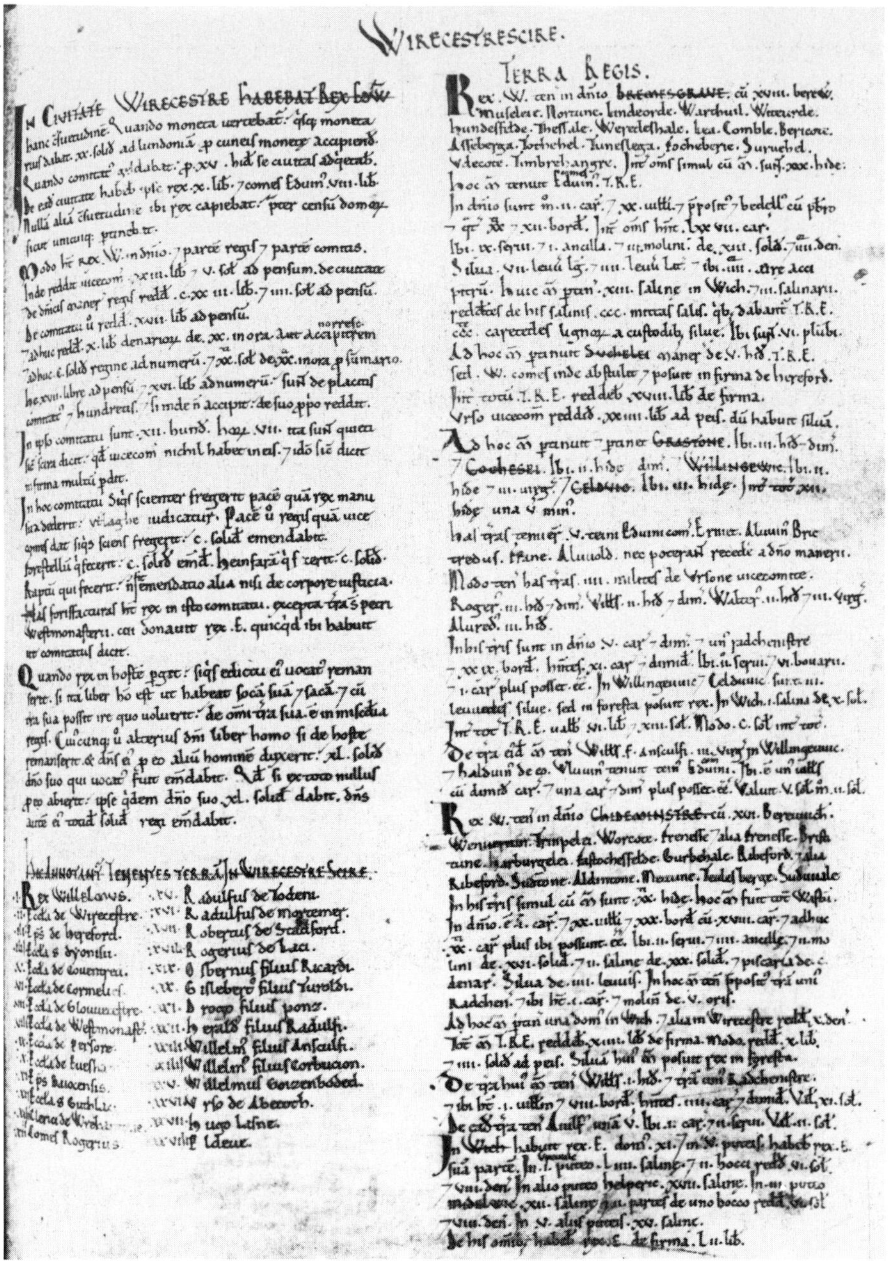

3 The first page of Worcestershire Domesday (Public Record Office, Domesday Book, vol. I, fol. 172). A brief description of the city of Worcester is followed by a list of the landholders under whose names the estates of the shire are arranged and described. The account then begins with the lands of their head – the king.

existence of long-distance transport. Wirksworth, Derbyshire, was already supplying lead to Christ Church, Canterbury, in the ninth century. Similarly, the Worcestershire salt industry, centred on Droitwich, supplied this vital commodity to most of the south-west midlands, and as far afield as Buckinghamshire.

The shires through which the traders passed were very diverse. Berkshire, for example, with an average value of 70 shillings per square mile, was second in wealth only to Oxfordshire, and slightly ahead of Wiltshire, Dorset and Essex. The King had large estates there, as in many of the southern shires (see fig. 190), and so too did Abingdon Abbey, which with a landed value of about £460 was the eighth richest house in England (see above). Staffordshire on the other hand, in area more than half as large again as Berkshire, had nearly double the number of settlements (342 against 189) but only half the recorded rural population (3,028 against 6,139). It had an average annual value of 8 shillings per square mile; only Cheshire and Yorkshire were poorer. This poverty the government had taken into account in its assessment at just over 500 hides, compared with Berkshire's almost 2,500. As in other northern and midland shires, royal estates were somewhat thinly scattered. Lincolnshire and Cheshire had none at all (though neither did Essex). Also like some of its fellows, Staffordshire was less familiar with monks than with secular canons. It had one abbey—Burton—which held 40th place in the table of monastic landed value, with estates worth £37 8*s*. 6*d*. However, it was once wealthier, having been endowed in the early eleventh century by its founder Wulfric Spot with 46 estates. The 34 which can be traced in Domesday were assessed at over 80 hides. Only 13, however, were still in the abbey's hands. Wulfric's descendants may have fallen on bad times, or regarded Burton with disinterest. If so, its history indicates, as from the opposite point of view does that of Godwine landed wealth, the rapidity with which lands could be lost by the friendless and acquired by the influential.

Despite their diversity the shires were a chief instrument of the royal government that bound the country together. Their courts, presided over by earl and bishop, heard land disputes and dispensed secular and ecclesiastical law. Together with their hundredal subdivisions, the shires could mobilize either fleet or army through the system of national assessment based on the hide. They could also collect a national tax, the *geld*, whose payment was facilitated by ready availability of the silver coinage produced by the numerous mints (see map, p. 180). Whatever the King's desire, a communication to the shires (see the Staffordshire writ illustrated) was enough to set the machine in motion.

M. K. Lawson

4 An Exchequer tally inscribed 'stock from Richard Hunilane: for the fine of Jordan, nephew of Gervase'; late 12th-century, of London origin; 13 shillings on lower edge, 4 pence on the upper (Public Record Office). It seems likely that such tallies (or very similar) were already in use in Anglo-Saxon times.

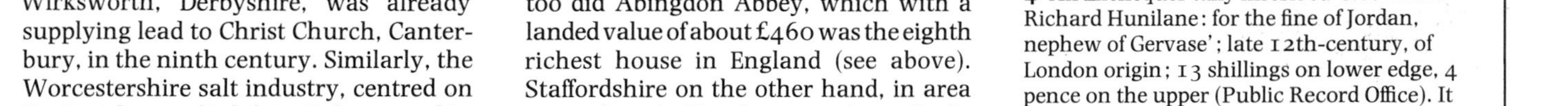

in which the boot was on the other foot, and Godwine got back, says it came about through concern 'lest the country be laid the more open to foreigners through their [the English magnates] destroying one another.' A few years later, when the unknown author of the *Life* of Edward the Confessor sought to explain why Harold would not back his brother Tostig against the grandsons of Earl Leofric (1065), he said, 'in that race horror was felt at what seemed to be civil war'. Nobody dared upset the applecart except those who faced ruin, as Godwin did in 1051 and Leofric's grandsons did in 1065. The enemies feared were, of course, the Vikings, and by now the traditional policy of containing them implied a Norman alliance.

Godwine died soon after his restoration, and his son Harold succeeded him as earl of Wessex. Harold was still not the master of England, and he had to permit Aelfgar to return to East Anglia, although Aelfgar had, in turn, to accept the appointment of Gyrth, a younger brother of Harold, as a subordinate earl in the province. In 1055 Earl Siward died, his eldest son having been killed in the war against Macbeth and his younger son being still a child. Aelfgar seems to have wanted to succeed him, but another of Godwine's sons, Tostig, was preferred and Aelfgar exiled. He was, however, restored and succeeded his father, the longest lived of the great earls of Cnut's reign, as earl of Mercia in 1057 (see above, p. 209). Earl Gyrth got the whole of East Anglia, and Mercia was now completely encircled. At some point after 1058, almost certainly 1062, Earl Aelfgar died or was killed, and his young son Edwin became earl of Mercia. In 1061 Bishop Ealdred of Worcester—as the man who allowed Harold to escape to Ireland in 1051 he was presumably part of the Godwine connection—became archbishop of York

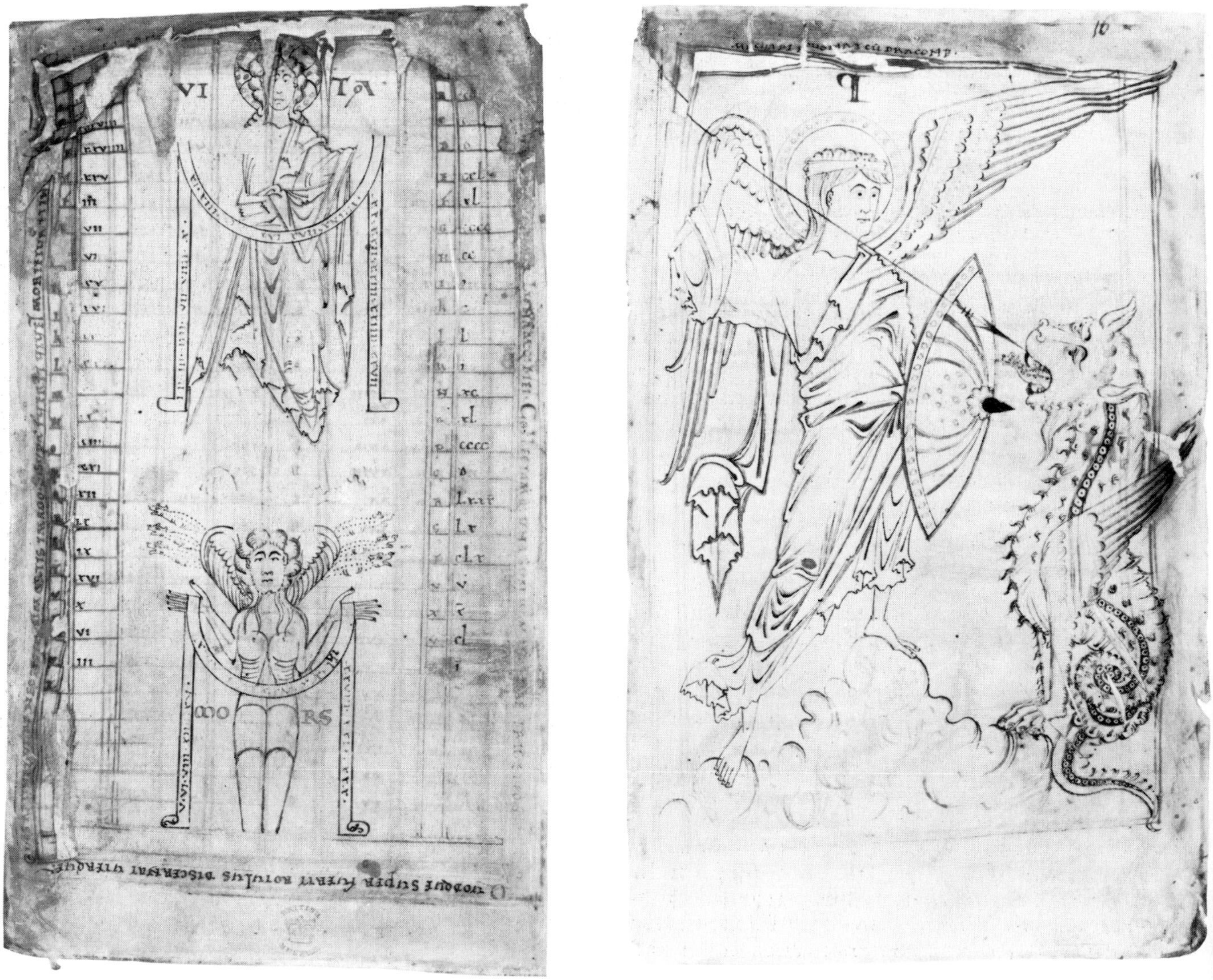

196 Life and Death, and St Michael, from a Psalter produced in Winchester, *c.* 1050 (British Library, MS Cotton Tiberius C.vi, fols. 6v, 16r). Life and Death illustrate the *Sphere of Apuleius*, a formula to foretell the outcome of illness. The numerical value of the letters of the patient's name were added to the day of the moon on which he fell sick. The total was divided by 30, and if the remainder was found among the numbers held by Life, the sick man would recover. If it was among the numbers held by Death, he would not.

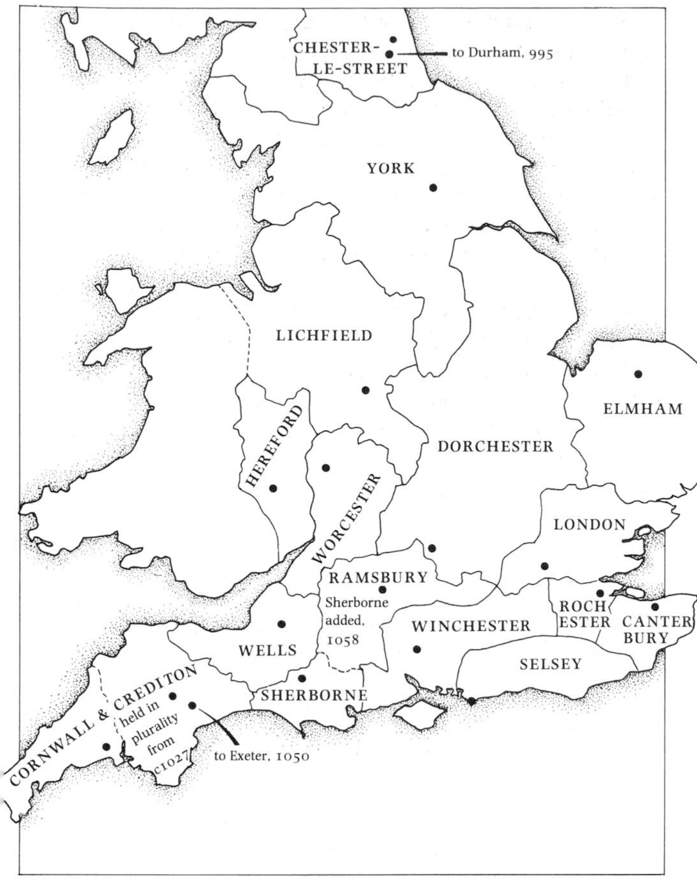

197 Map showing the dioceses of England in the late Anglo-Saxon period (from D. Hill, *An Atlas of Anglo-Saxon England* (Blackwell, 1981)).

as well. Although he was forced by Rome to allow the election of the most distinguished of the English-born prelates of the reign, Wulfstan (see above, p. 229), to Worcester in 1062, he seems to have treated him as a suffragan. Ealdred, then, was in the same position *vis à vis* Earl Tostig as Stigand was *vis à vis* Earl Harold, as well as being lord of Oswaldslow and the most important landholder in south-west Mercia.

The Church under Edward the Confessor

This is perhaps the point at which to say something about the Church. No one would argue that the last generations of Anglo-Saxon churchmen were among the most distinguished in the Old English Church. Aelfric and Wulfstan had no successors of like distinction, but then, of course, neither did Bede. Periods of intense literary and scholarly activity are the exception in England until the early twelfth century, when there begins a tradition of varied literary composition that has not so far dried up. There was some interesting writing: for example, a vernacular version of the classical romance, *The History of Apollonius of Tyre*, written, perhaps, in the reign of Cnut. Unlike anything written previously, this is pure entertainment literature and very felicitous. The Winchester tradition of manuscript illumination and calligraphy, going back ultimately to Carolingian models, as so much in the cultural history of England under West Saxon hegemony does, continued with some notable examples, of which the New Minster Psalter is particularly fine. Fine manuscripts were written elsewhere, and in general late Old English visual art was in a better state than Old English literature. Intellectually the most important compositions were the various histories already discussed as sources. Whatever the shortcomings of the *Chronicle*, for the first time we find history written by men with an interest in political explanation and some notion of causality.

The bishops were a mixed bunch. All the bishops appointed by previous kings had gone by 1051. They were replaced by monks and priests, in about equal proportions, mostly connected with the royal household. Normandy was something of a cultural backwater until

198 Cosmological Diagram, *c.* 1110 (Oxford, St John's College, MS 17, fol. 7v). A summary of Time and Nature, it represents the Zodiac, Months, Seasons, Elements, Four Ages of Man, Cardinal Points and Winds. Part of the Manual by Byrhtferth, an early 11th-century Ramsey monk, it demonstrates late Saxon scientific interests.

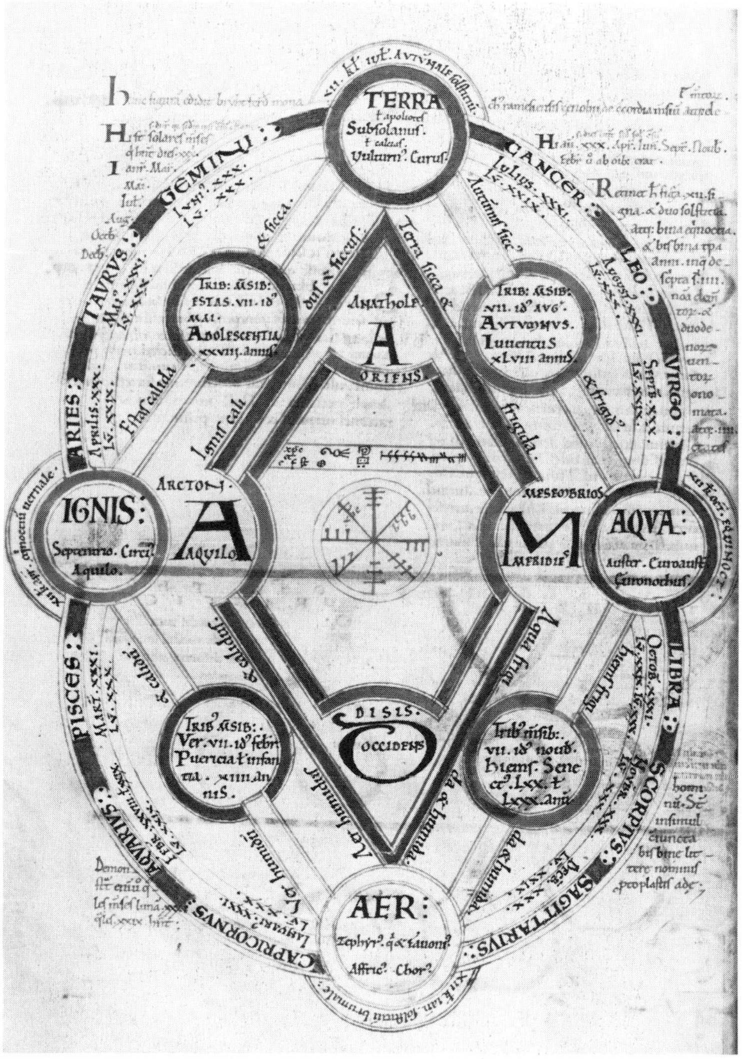

199 Frontispiece to a text of Gregory the Great's *Dialogues*, produced in the mid 11th century perhaps in Worcester (Oxford, Bodleian Library, MS Tanner 3, fol. 1v, 271 × 170 mm). Gregory, here accompanied by Petrus, the interlocutor of the *Dialogues*, was always venerated by the English (cf. p. 45).

the monastic revival reached the duchy, as it did in Edward's boyhood. Not surprisingly we find Norman bishops in England. There was one Norman monk, Robert Champart, whose brief but dramatic career as archbishop of Canterbury has already been noticed (see above, p. 224). Two Norman clerks, Ulf and William, were appointed to Dorchester and London respectively. Ulf (who succeeded three monks of Ramsey in the see) was said to be incompetent. Bishop William left little mark on London though he ruled the see for almost a quarter of a century.

The four other foreign bishops were all either Lotharingian-born or Lotharingian-trained or both. Lower Lotharingia (what are now the Benelux countries plus a small part of north-west Germany) was one of the most important centres of church reform, and Lotharingian clerks and monks are found in sees from Rome itself to Wells in this period. Of the 'English' Lotharingians the most distinguished was Leofric, who was made bishop of Devon and Cornwall in 1046, who compiled one of the most important service books of the English Church, the Leofric Pontifical, moved his see to Exeter, and effected permanent reform of his cathedral community. Leofric seems to have been a Godwine supporter. Although some of these Lotharingian bishops had been royal clerks, it needs to be remembered that it was Earl Godwine, not the King, who was the ally of the count of Flanders, the focus of Lotharingian reform.

The English-born bishops were not very distinguished. In 1070, when a papal legate held a synod at Winchester, five bishops were deposed, resigned, or fled in anticipation, and in only one case is there any likelihood that injustice was perpetrated. Only one English bishop, Wulfstan of Worcester, was really distinguished, above all as a pastor, Ealdred of York and Stigand of Winchester/Canterbury were spectacular prince-prelates.

Naturally the political tensions of the reign affected the bishops. Stigand and Ealdred both showed by their actions that they counted themselves as part of the Godwine connection: they must have owed something for their promotions to Earl Godwine, if only gaining his passive assent. Stigand was an Anglo-Dane from East Anglia. His first benefice was the minster erected by Cnut to commemorate the battle of Ashingdon (see above, p. 199). He seems to have been a royal clerk connected with the queen mother, Emma, and to have owed his first see, Elmham, to her. His promotion to the chief see of Wessex, Winchester, in 1043 almost certainly indicates that he was then in Godwine's favour. His intrusion into Canterbury on the restoration of the Godwine family in 1052 could not have taken place without Godwine's consent. He was succeeded at Elmham by his brother, and it does rather look as though the waxing of the Stigand family had something to do with Godwine ambitions in East Anglia.

Ealdred was originally a West Saxon abbot, of Tavistock. He never put a foot wrong. He was made bishop of Worcester in 1046, allowed Harold to escape to Ireland in 1051, and was promoted to York in 1061. He crowned King Harold II and King William I, and continued important until his death in 1069.

If all this smacks of the turning of coats, we should at least realize that contemporaries did not hold it against these men. None of Aethelred II's bishops jibbed at serving Cnut, and if challenged, would probably have replied that their responsibility to their dioceses and their flocks came first. Kings recognized this. They could distinguish between committed opposition, not common but found, and a prudent regard for the *status quo*, and needed to so distinguish. A king like William the Conqueror demanded loyalty up to a point, or rather would not brook disloyalty; but a certain, indeed a considerable, amount of self-interest was tolerated, in layman and churchman alike. Above all William I demanded competence. The career of an important cleric of the second rank will illustrate this. His name was Regenbald, suggesting he was not of English birth. Post-conquest sources say he was the Confessor's chancellor, and if this was so he was the first head of the royal writing office to bear this title. He was obviously important and had the rank of a bishop without a see. He presumably served King Harold II and certainly served William I, one of whose earliest writs is in his favour. He accumulated land in five counties and no fewer than 20 churches; most of it seems to have gone to Circencester Abbey in the end. If we had to judge the Norman Conquest in the light of Regenbald's career we should not think it very catastrophic. It was catastrophic, but for many a tempered catastrophe, and the career of Regenbald is a useful illustration.

The Years 1053–1066

To return to the narrative of events. Soon after Harold succeeded his father as earl of Wessex, new moves about the succession to the throne were afoot. In 1054 steps were taken to have Edmund Ironside's son Edward brought back from Hungary (see above, p. 199). The instigators of this policy seem to have been Earl Harold and Ealdred of Worcester, since they did the negotiating. The King never saw his nephew, who died soon after his arrival in 1056. By the end of the 1050s, Harold and his brothers held all the earldoms of England except Mercia, Harold's brother Tostig having been made earl of Northumbria on the death of Siward in 1055. After the death of Aelfgar in (probably) 1062, his son Edwin became earl of Mercia, but was too young to be effective. If Ealdred (see above, p. 230) was Harold's ally, then he would have provided powerful support in Mercia, for he held the see of Worcester till 1062; this made him lord of Oswaldslow (see above, p. 172) and the principal landowner in south-west Mercia. From 1056 and 1060 he also had charge of the see of Hereford, where he had been preceded for a few months by a former clerk of Harold's. Harold could now think of his own succession as king. Nothing is heard of any support for the candidature of Edgar the Aetheling, son of the deceased Edward (see above, p. 224), until after Harold's death.

The French king and other French magnates were clearly worried by the prospects of the Norman duke's succession to the English throne. The pattern of French politics changes, and most unusually we find the French king in alliance with the count of Anjou. We know that Harold made diplomatic moves outside England. William of Poitiers says he negotiated with kings. Henry I of France must certainly be meant, perhaps also the Hiberno-Norse king of Dublin. The C text of the *Chronicle* retreats into silence, and D and E become records of the triumphs of Earl Harold; the king is hardly mentioned. Had the Confessor died in 1060 instead of Henry I of France, nothing could have kept Harold from succeeding.

Harold had atrocious luck. After 1060 the French king was a minor under the tutelage of Baldwin of Flanders, who, if he had long-standing and friendly connections

200 Chirographic Latin lease, with estate boundaries in English, Bishop Ealdred of Worcester to his *minister* Dodda, 1058 (British Library, Add. Ch. 19801, approx 33 × 18 cm). Two copies were made, separated by the word CYROGRAUUM, and the parchment cut at this point. The authenticity of either could thus be checked.

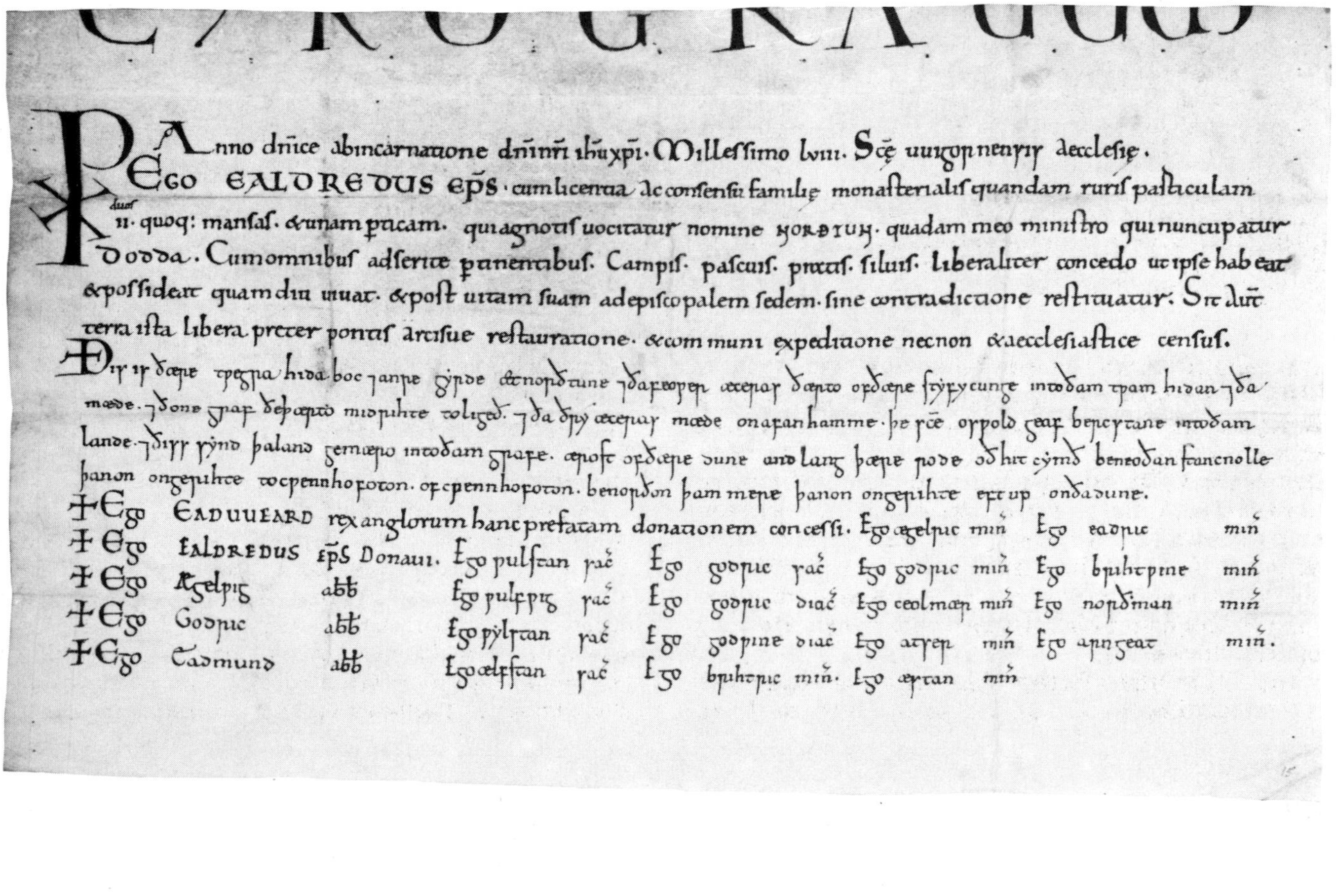

201 Chancel arch, Holy Trinity, Bosham, West Sussex. Late Saxon and possibly depicted on the Bayeux Tapestry (fig. 202).

with the Godwine family, was also William's father-in-law (see above, p. 225). Thus the possibility of an effective French alliance, which could have been the lynch-pin of Harold's policy, was removed. In England, when the King died in January 1066, it was about three months too late for Harold. Towards the end of 1065 the Northumbrians revolted against Earl Tostig. Siward's son, Waltheof, was still too young to act as the head of the party of the traditional nobility, who did not like Tostig's centralizing and 'southernizing' policy. They asked Edwin of Mercia's younger brother, Morcar, or Morkere, to be their earl. Edwin's future cannot have looked very bright at the beginning of the year and this was an opportunity he could not miss. The Mercian and Northumbrian thegns joined forces and made it clear they would fight to the end. By autumn of 1065 it was clear that the West Saxon thegns would not fight Edwin and Morcar, and that the King could not live much longer. Harold acquiesced, thus making a mortal enemy of his brother Tostig, who fled to his brother-in-law, the count of Flanders, and from there joined the Norwegian invasion army in 1066.

The Norman sources make it clear that at some point Harold formally recognized William as Edward's heir and his own lord. If we may believe William of Poitiers, as I have suggested we may (see above, p. 220), Harold went to William expressly for this purpose. William gives no dates precisely but he clearly shows the visit could not have been earlier than 1064 and gives indications suggesting that it was in fact late 1065. What seems to have happened is that the fall of Tostig and the wavering loyalties of the West Saxon thegns gave the old king his chance. He sent Harold to Duke William in Normandy to be humiliated, seeking to do the maximum damage he could, and it was quite a lot, to his chances of the succession. It seems likely that Harold went to Normandy about 1 November and was back in time for the consecration of Westminster Abbey on 28 December. Edward died on 6 January. (It is not impossible that, as Sir Frank Stenton thought, Harold went to Normandy in 1064. The weight of the argument against this earlier date is that Harold is much more likely to have made the major concession he did in 1065 when his power was weakened, than in 1064 when it was at its height.)

Edward died muttering prophecies, unintelligible to us, but terrifying to those who heard them. Harold justified his repudiation of his oath of only a few weeks before by claiming, with the testimony of Archbishop

202 Part of the Bayeux Tapestry (Bayeux Museum) in which Harold arrives at Bosham and feasts there on his way to France in 1064 or 1065 (see p. 232). The picture appears to show the chancel arch of the church (see fig. 201), although somewhat schematized. The hall, which was probably at Bosham, is also schematized, but the arcade is suggestive of the scale of some secular buildings in stone.

Stigand, who was also present at the king's deathbed, that the king had given succession to him in his last hours. The author of the *Life* of Edward, whose probable informant was the queen herself, goes out of his way to discredit this testimony; the queen was involved in her brother Tostig's infamy in Northumbrian eyes, and after the Confessor's death her position under a king Harold who needed to placate northern opinion was not likely to be a happy one.

On Edward's death on 6 January 1066 Harold became king. Whether he would remain king could be decided only by battle. He was threatened not only by William but also by Harold Hardrada, king of Norway. Once again William had all the luck. The wind that would not let him embark his troops in Normandy for the voyage to England blew Harold Hardrada and his Norwegians to the north of England and a catastrophic defeat at Stamford Bridge. The wind now changed and allowed William to cross the Channel and land in the heart of Harold's earldom and the centre of his property and his connections. Harold moved south with great speed. Neither Edwin nor Morcar came with him, and Harold faced William at Hastings with only a small portion of the forces he had at Stamford Bridge. Even so, it was a close-run thing. On 14 October Harold and William met in battle at Hastings. They fought all day. At the end William was victorious and Harold dead.

The Aftermath of the Conquest

With Harold's death at Hastings and Tostig's at Stamford Bridge, the Godwine family was leaderless. Queen Edith, as William of Poitiers' says she did, may have preferred King William to King Harold. She was certainly safer with him and, ended her days in honourable retirement. Edwin and Morcar for a time played with the idea of promoting the succession of Edgar the Aetheling (see above, p. 231), but submitted to William quickly enough. They got nothing out of him. Edwin was eventually killed by his own men; Morcar fled to the Fens to join the outlaw Hereward the Wake and was never heard of again. Siward's youngest son, Waltheof, on the contrary, was treated very well by William and was soon made earl of Northumbria. For reasons still not understood he rebelled, and in 1076 was executed. He was the only prominent Englishman William killed other than in battle: a very striking contrast with the first months of Cnut's reign. Of course, two such great battles as Stamford Bridge and Hastings in one year killed off an important section of the English nobility anyhow. They were largely replaced by Normans of William's trusted circle.

Though the ruling nobility of England became, soon after 1066, almost entirely Norman, Englishmen still mattered. A proportion of the knightly class were English, and it cannot be without significance that the English word 'cniht', or knight, ultimately displaced the French *chevalier*. The extent to which the English mattered is made plain in the account which the *Anglo-Saxon Chronicle* gives of the decisive nature of English support for the Conqueror's son William Rufus in his struggle against his elder brother Robert in 1088. It is likely that when Rufus's successor, Henry I, married a princess of the Old English royal house in 1100 (see above, p. 224), a wish to conciliate the English was among his motives. If the English lost much by the Norman Conquest (and most of the greatest of them lost everything), still there were gains. For example, the alliance between William

The Battle of Hastings

1 The battlefield today, looking from the Norman to the English lines. Battle Abbey, founded by William to commemorate his victory, is in the background. The high altar, to the right of the picture, occupied the spot at which King Harold set up his standards, and was killed.

2 A Norman ship landing at Pevensey, 28 September 1066. The mast is lowered, the horses led ashore.

3 King Harold is struck down. In the border below a corpse is stripped of its armour.

4 Duke William's cavalry charge the English position, 14 October 1066.

The battle of Hastings was the climax and finale of the last disastrous months of Harold Godwineson's life and career: it was the essential prelude to the glorious royal career of William of Normandy that made him the most famous soldier of his day. Most information about the battle comes from Norman sources, the main ones being the account of the deeds of William by the archdeacon of Liseux, William of Poitiers (see p. 221) and most famous of all, the Bayeux Tapestry, from which the illustrations are taken. Neither source tells precisely the same story and neither is likely to be wholly true. The Tapestry (technically an embroidery not a tapestry) was made for Odo, Bishop of Bayeux, whether to adorn his castle or his cathedral is disputed. It was of English provenance and is connected with Canterbury and St Augustine's abbey.

The English sources are few and brief: the D text of the *Chronicle* has, a short and powerful passage. 'William earl of Normandy came into Pevensey on the eve of Michaelmas (28 September 1066), and as soon as his men were ready to move, they constructed a castle at the town of Hastings. This was told to King Harold, and he then collected a large army, and met William at the grey apple tree, and William came upon him unexpectedly before his army was arrayed. Even so, the King fought with William very bravely with the men who would stand by him, and there was much slaughter on both sides. King Harold was slain there, and Earl Leofwine his brother, and Earl Gyrth his brother, and many good men, and the Frenchmen had possession of the place of slaughter.'

It is evident that William was a much better tactician than Harold. It must be remembered that Sussex was the heart of Harold's patrimony, the place where he was most at home, although of course Harold had just fought another bloody engagement at Stamford Bridge little less than three weeks before (see p. 233). It is usually thought that about 7,000 men were involved on each side; this is conjecture, if plausible conjecture. The English took position on a ridge and formed a wall of shields. If they had cavalry they did not use them, nor, surprisingly, archers in any force. The Normans had a 'mix of horse soldiers, infantry and archers'. According to the traditional

2

3

view, based it must be admitted on several sources (not all of them contemporary), the Normans broke the shield wall by tempting Harold and the English with a feigned retreat. The Tapestry gives no support to this theory, and it is difficult to see how, with 14,000 men, many clad in metal and all wielding metal weapons, the orders could have been conveyed by William to his troops above the noise. In the last resort we cannot tell just what happened.

The Tapestry's graphic account of Harold's end has occasioned much dispute. The difficulty is that it is here our sole authority, presenting the problems a purely pictorial record must inevitably create. Two English warriors are represented in the act of falling and over them is written *Hic Haroldus rex interfectus est* ('Here King Harold was slain'). The figure under the word 'Haroldus' is pulling an arrow from his eye and until recently was taken to be the dying Harold. The 'was slain' is placed over a second Englishman being cut down by a Norman knight: some scholars still maintain that this second figure is Harold. It could be maintained however, that both figures are Harold at different stages of his fall, an opinion that has support from the twelfth-century historian, William of Malmesbury, although he was writing long after the battle and may in fact be basing his story on the Tapestry. With the death of Harold and virtually all the adult male members of his family the Norman victory was complete and decisive, although the ease with which William established himself—he met only scattered and local resistance—suggests that the strong and peaceful rule he could obviously provide mattered more to the English than the loss of King Harold.

E. John

a shire—and half of them are addressed to the sheriff or equivalent official (burhreeve or staller).

More evidence of the importance of shire and sheriff in the last years of the Anglo-Saxon state is provided by William the Conqueror's great survey of 1086 that produced Domesday Book. Although Domesday Book is rightly regarded as an Anglo-Norman achievement—it was largely complete by the Conqueror's death in 1087—the more one looks at it the more Anglo-Saxon it seems. It was written up in two volumes and covered all of England except the extreme north. It was compiled shire by shire, and the statistics it contains, given by local juries of local, quite small men, were compared with returns about their own honors submitted by the barons themselves. The enormous job of comparison, compilation and compression was done by obviously highly efficient royal clerks at Winchester. The even more onerous job of empanelling the juries, producing them at the right time and place, was done by the sheriffs. Finally, the crucial importance of sheriff and shire for Anglo-Norman government is that in Domesday Book the information is not presented in terms of Anglo-Norman honors but of Anglo-Saxon shires.

It is certain, then, that crucial elements in English local and central government not only began, but were well-developed before 1066. There are other elements in English government as we see it in the light of abundant twelfth-century documents which may go back so far, and which it is important to consider, not least because they are a reminder of how much of what went on in the Confessor's England may be hidden because the sources are sparse. This is particularly true of the administration of justice.

For example, during the reign of Henry II (1154–89) the Crown developed a system whereby groups of judges were sent round the shires at regular intervals to judge crimes and to hear pleas. There is no doubt that the origins of this go back at least as far as the reign of Henry I. He sent groups of royal agents into the shires to do justice and to perform any other task the king imposed (though on how regular a basis they were sent we cannot tell). It is possible that such activities were older still. The Domesday Survey of 1086 had features in common with such visitations. The main function of its itinerant commissioners was fiscal inquiry; but they performed judicial functions as well. Furthermore, their inquiries were pursued largely by inquest, that is to say by getting groups of informed local men to give evidence on oath. Procedure by inquest was of basic importance to twelfth-century justice. We cannot be sure how far the techniques of the Domesday Survey were of Anglo-Saxon origin; though we can be reasonably sure that the pre-Conquest kings used the sworn inquest, and certain that they sometimes did justice via delegates. It is at least possible that the origins of the itinerant justice of the twelth century go back before the Conquest.

Another example of such early origins may be the writ of right. By the twelfth century the principle was established that no man need answer for his free tenement without the king's writ. That is to say that if a man wished to bring a suit against another in relation to freehold land, even though the case were to be held in a lord's rather than the king's court, he could not do so without a royal writ, the relevant writ being called the writ of right. This was a very important principle indeed. We can infer from records of lawsuits (and confirm our inference from the laws of Edward the Elder) that as late as the tenth century litigation about 'bookland' (see above, p. 97) was heard by the king in person. Later in the Anglo-Saxon period we find records of suits, probably or certainly involving bookland, which were held in the shire court (not before the king) and involved the production of a royal seal (which almost certainly means a royal writ). One may guess that what had happened was that as the kingdom grew too large for the king to judge every case involving bookland, so such cases were relegated to the shire courts, but with insistance that all should be royally authorized. A land charter was known as a *freolsboc*, a freedom charter. It is not difficult therefore to imagine a link between bookland in the late Anglo-Saxon period and the free tenement of the twelfth century. So it could be that a major principle of English land law, and some of the processes involved with it, were established before the Conquest.

In any case what cannot be doubted is that, long before 1066, the problems of government at a distance were well on the road to solution, through the network of shires and the body of local officials responsible to the crown, which was developing the means both of communicating with them and of bringing them to account. Very important in the governmental system were the towns (see above, p. 176). The commercial and urban element in English society seems to have developed rapidly in the generations before the conquest. Already by 1066 something like a tenth of the population may have lived in towns (see the Picture Essay, pp. 174–5). Towns were the local capitals for shire government, which is why most of the castles which William the Conqueror built were urban. Their wealth, and the special relationship which nearly all had with the crown, made them a major source of income. By early in Henry II's reign, when first we have a series of royal accounts, the king could often get more by taxing his towns than by taxing his nobility.

It was government in the Old English style, not *à la Française*, which was the basis of the power of kings of England after the Conquest. That is why kings could prevent Anglo-Norman magnates reaching positions of quasi-independent power such as many of their relatives and counterparts enjoyed in France. If anyone doubts the efficacy of Old English government, let him compare those parts of the Anglo-Norman state which had been brought under the rule of the Old English kings, to those, in particular the Welsh marches, which were added after 1066. The contrast is between regularity and order on the one hand, *ad hoc* arrangements and disorder on the other. It is likely, as has been argued in regard to aspects of the legal system, that the origin of various instruments of government, though doubtful, may lie in the Anglo-Saxon past. The silence of early sources does not necessarily imply a later rather than an earlier origin. There are far more documents surviving from the twelfth century than from the eleventh; not least because the number of religious houses increased so much in the twelfth century. In any case enough is known for certain to put this conclusion beyond argument. The tenth-century kings of the house of Wessex laid the foundations of the English state, not only by unifying England, but also by devising the enduring institutions which made England governable.

204 The density of population in 11th-century England as recorded in Domesday Book (from H. C. Darby (ed.), *A New Historical Geography of England before 1600* (Cambridge University Press, 1976). Note that to estimate the true population the recorded figure must be multiplied to allow for women and children and, probably, for a considerable number of unrecorded men.

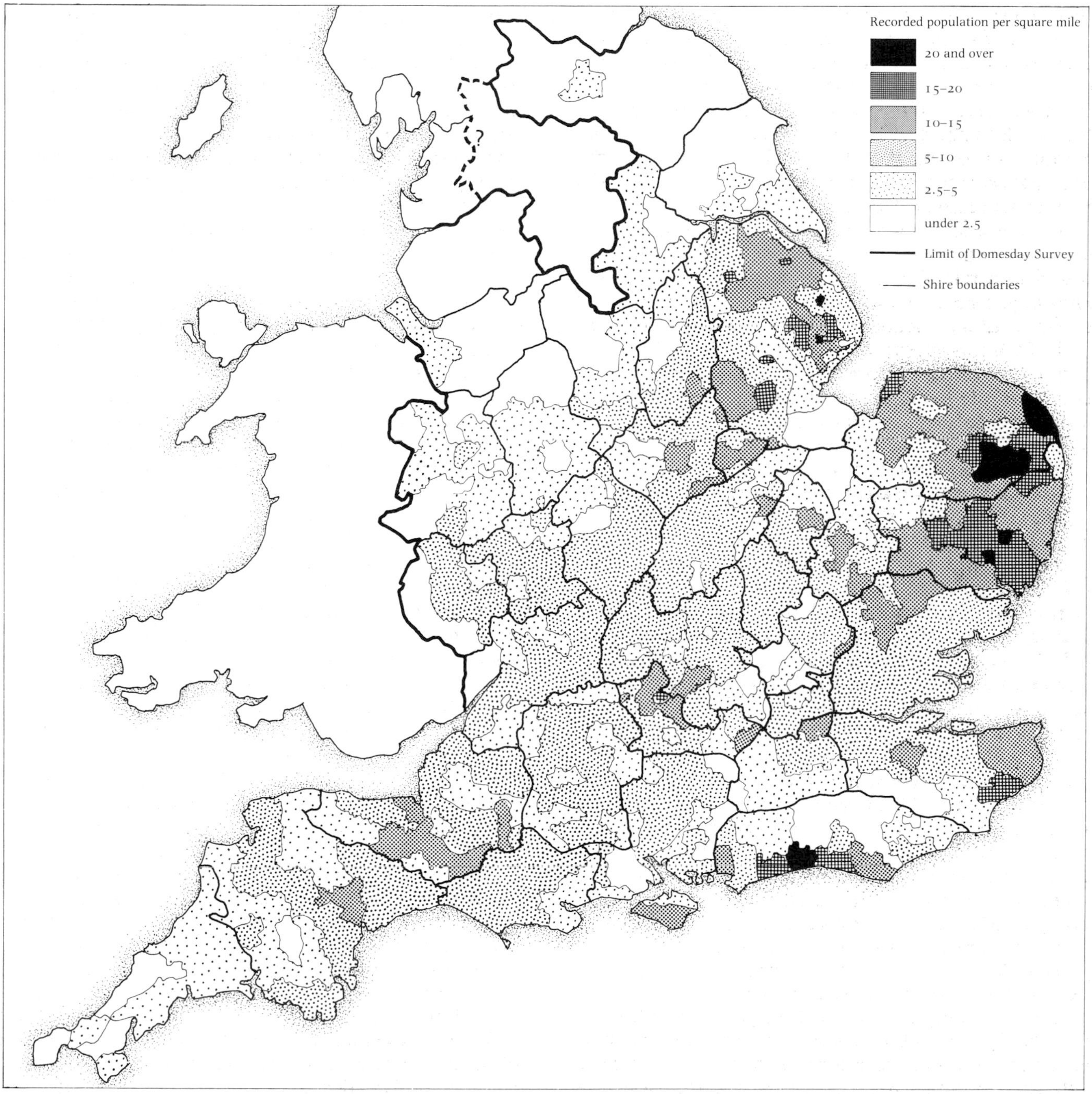

Epilogue

The 14th of October 1066 was a fatal day for many Englishmen and for much in England. It may not have been William's original intention to displace the whole of the English aristocracy. Nevertheless, by the end of his reign he had done so. Only two Englishmen appear as major landowners in Domesday Book. In 1087 of the bishops only one was English, and of the abbots of major abbeys only two. What had happened to the great men of Anglo-Saxon England? Many must have been killed in the three great battles of 1066. Others perished in later rebellions. Some fled to Scotland, whose king, Malcolm, in 1070 married an English princess; others went to Denmark, including, as seems likely, Harold's daughter Gyda, who went on to marry Vladimir Monomach, prince of Kiev (1113–25). Yet others fled further afield, to Byzantium, there to take service in the Scandinavian guard (the Varangians) of the emperors. These wild geese fought the Normans again, at Durazzo in 1081, when the emperor Alexius Comnenus sought to check an invasion by Robert Guiscard, the Norman conqueror of southern Italy. Again they lost. Most of the Anglo-Saxon aristocrats who remained in England seem simply, and no doubt painfully, to have sunk in society. The Norman Conquest was indeed a conquest. Few countries have so sharp a break in their history as that which broke Harold in 1066.

205 Part of a wood and copper gilt cross once in Lundø church, Denmark (Copenhagen, National Museum). An inscription names the maker as Ailmar, whose name suggests that he was English. It may well have been made by an Englishman in Denmark somewhat after 1066. The depiction of the Archangel Michael fighting the dragon is incised on the back of the cross, whose dimensions are 65 × 40 cm.

Yet in no country has the extent and nature of the continuity between the Dark Ages and modern times been more seriously considered than in England; and in none does it deserve more serious concern. It is possible to take an interest in the Anglo-Saxons and their land as one might in other ancient peoples and places, the Incas or the Aztecs, Angkhor Wat or Mohenjo Daro: with fascinated detachment. For the inhabitants of those large parts of the world to which the late General de Gaulle used frequently to allude, not always with affection, as *les pays Anglo-Saxonnes* the interest should be sharper.

An indication as to why this might be so was afforded by de Gaulle himself, when on 8 April 1960 he addressed both Houses of Parliament in Westminster Hall. He made an observation which, if it was not of the kind which falls pleasingly on English ears, was doubtless meant to please; and which was true. 'At the worst moments', he said, 'who ever contested the legitimacy or the authority of the state?' The origins of the security of the English state lie in the length of its history. This is the determinative contrast between England and the other great states of Europe. In no other has there been such continuity in the exercise of effective authority over so wide an area for so long. Cnut's writ ran from Yorkshire to Sussex and from Norfolk to Cheshire. So has that of all his successors, brief intervals of civil war apart. Continuity in the exercise of power brought with it, and was sustained by, continuity in the institutions of government.

Among those institutions the counties mattered very much. They were reordered in 1974. Until those sad changes (and to a considerable extent still) large elements in the administrative geography of England had remained unchanged from the eleventh century or earlier (see above, pp. 172–3). To compare England and France in the eighteenth century is to be struck by the contrast between the variation and complication of French provincial government and the regularity and uniformity of English shire government. Those qualities were a result, not of the modernity of the English shires, but of their antiquity.

Two things deserve emphasis about Anglo-Saxon governmental systems. First, not only were they long-enduring, but elements in them may have been very old indeed. Second, much of what survived in England was of a kind which had once existed in wide areas of the Continent, but had largely disappeared there.

So far back as our knowledge of Anglo-Saxon kingdoms goes, the power of their rulers seems to have extended to large enterprises and their organization to have included elements of order and of complexity. Offa's Dyke demonstrates the orderly exercise of extensive power; its predecessors tell a similar story on their lesser scale (see above, pp. 120–1, figs. 61, 67). There is reason to suppose that the lands of all or most of the early kingdoms were elaborately assessed for services and renders on systems which were the direct ancestors of those which Domesday proves to have been fundamental to English government in the eleventh century (see above, pp. 226–7). One can too easily assume that the development of the Anglo-Saxons and of other peoples in northern Europe was from the chaotic to the orderly, from the *ad hoc* to the schematized, and from weaker rule to stronger. To consider the organization of such peoples as they emerge into the light of documents, beginning with the Irish laws, is to discover extensive traces of integrated systems in which the distribution, assessment and measurement of land, the gradations of society, and the institutions of government were elaborately related together. Much of the nature and power of Dark Age states may have derived from institutions and habits of mind whose origins were prehistoric; and in particular from systems for the provision of services and renders which were nearly as integral to society as those for the conduct of feud. That is to say that the systematization which was so marked a feature of the late Anglo-Saxon state may have had very ancient origins.

Many of the institutions of government in tenth- and eleventh-century England seem to resemble those of the Carolingian Empire in the eighth and ninth centuries. English counties and hundreds with their courts recall their Carolingian counterparts. The general oath for the maintenance of peace which the Carolingians imposed on all free men appears in England also. The assessment systems used for taxation and military service south of the Channel in the ninth century bear general resemblances to those used north of the Channel by the eleventh. Such resemblances raise hard questions and wide possibilities. It is not easy to tell what represents derivation, what parallel development. But the comparison does suggest a generalization: that late Anglo-Saxon England was a state of what might be called a Carolingian type, some of whose characteristics persisted after the Conquest and formed part of the framework of the modern state. By contrast, in the Carolingian lands themselves Carolingian order crumbled, and the principles and development of government came to differ from those of England.

In weighing their debt to and links with the Anglo-Saxon past Englishmen were for many centuries chiefly concerned not so much with the power of the state as with the liberty of the subject. The notion that the roots of a free constitution were Anglo-Saxon appears as early as the early thirteenth century, and strikingly in the fourteenth, when Andrew Horn (died 1328) produced his *Mirror of Justices*, in which King Alfred is held up as a model. Alfred summoned his parliament every two years; he took the advice of his *comites*; he hanged many judges: he was a good king.

The search for Anglo-Saxon precedents and proto-

206 The Horn dance at Abbots Bromley, Staffs. Although there is no reference to the performance of this dance before the 17th century, the horns themselves suggest it has a remote origin, for they are reindeer antlers, and carbon analysis of one set gives dates centring on the 11th century. It is likely that many folk customs which are recorded only in recent centuries had an Anglo-Saxon origin.

207 This sculpture of the Virgin and Child at York Minster is of uncertain date. While some believe it to be of the 12th century others think it more likely that it is of the 11th. One of the arguments put forward for the earlier date is the similarity between it and the carving on the handle of the Godwine seal (p. 197, no. 5).

types did not, however, get strongly under way until the sixteenth century. It began with the wish to find in the Anglo-Saxon or Celtic past evidence for the existence in this island of churches which were independent of Rome, or even Reformed. It was partly because he was interested in such possibilities that archbishop Mathew Parker (1559–75) made the great collection of Anglo-Saxon manuscripts which is now in Corpus Christi College, Cambridge (see, for example, fig. 45). The idea that the battles of the Reformation had their precursors in Anglo-Saxon times still flourished in the nineteenth century. Witness, for example, the Reverend W. Foxley Norris's view of Wilfrid's role at Whitby (see p. 83 above) as expressed in his *Lays of the Early English Church* (1887):

> For the Conference of Whitby
> Held to the Roman school
> And Wilfrith, zealous champion,
> Was the willing papal tool.

It was in the seventeenth century that the secular polity of the Anglo-Saxons became much involved in political controversy. Particularly important was the doctrine of the Norman Yoke: that is to say that a free constitution had been subverted by the Normans at the Conquest and should be restored. Alternatively, it could be held that English constitutional liberties had a continuous history from Anglo-Saxon times. Such views were argued with vehemence and were a stimulus to learning.

When, in the nineteenth century, related questions were again raised it was against a background of much more secure learning. Of particular importance was the work of German scholars who had put the study of Germanic institutions, languages and antiquities on a firm basis. It was largely thanks to them that J. M. Kemble was able to write the first modern book on the Anglo-Saxons, *The Saxons in England* (1849). Its main contents remain fresh; much of its preface sounds very oddly in modern ears. For example: 'On every side of us thrones totter and the deep foundations of society are convulsed. Shot and shell sweep the streets of capitals which have long been pointed out as the chosen abodes of order . . . Yet the exalted Lady who wields the sceptre of these realms sits safe upon her throne, and fearless in the holy circle of her domestic happiness, secure in the affections of a people whose institutions have given to them all the blessings of an equal law. Those institutions they have inherited from a period so distant as to excite our admiration . . .'

Kemble saw the Anglo-Saxon past as having determined much of the course of English history, and continuity with that past as the basic cause of England's freedom from revolution. A greater historian, William Stubbs, held views which were essentially the same. In his *Constitutional History* (1873–8) Stubbs was less strident than Kemble had been, concerned with a wider span of history, more subtly cautious; but he too was not concerned simply to describe, but to explain the past, and in explaining to sustain a claim about the present: that determinants of the English constitution and of English liberty were Anglo-Saxon. His argument, to which no thumb-nail sketch can do justice (compare p. 236 above) was that the institutions of Anglo-Saxon England, as revealed from the time of the earliest laws, were genuinely derived from and reflected the values of, the German world described by Tacitus in the first century.

This was a world in which power did not reside chiefly in kings, but came from below, from warriors who were free and in important senses equal, with their say and their share in decisions. Stubbs saw the early Anglo-Saxon polity as one in which at all levels, and particularly in courts, decisions were taken by assemblies of the free. Kings had important functions, but the root of power lay in the folk. Though well aware that the six Anglo-Saxon centuries saw many changes and believing that they saw the powers both of kings and of lords grow greater, he held that, nevertheless, the participatory element remained very important.

He laid special emphasis on the significance of that element in the courts of shire and hundred (see above, pp. 172–3), and on its surviving the Conquest with them. When the House of Commons came into being in the late thirteenth century the shire members were chosen by the county courts. Thus he saw the development of the representative assembly which had so splendid a future before it as linked to that of local assemblies which had a history extending back beyond the Conquest and which were directly connected to the institutions and the attitudes of the early Germans.

Stubbs is not a fashionable author. His interest in the Germanic past and some of his attitudes towards it have dated to the extent that their context is that of the Victorian love affair with the early Germans; it had Romantic origins, and some aspects which are ridiculous, and others which are ominous to us, who know what was to happen in our own century. (The popularity in Victorian England of the Anglo-Saxon past can be seen, for example, in the reintroduction of Anglo-Saxon Christian names; even Karl Marx called one of his children Edgar.) At a more precise level Stubbs's interpretation (and, still more, later simplifications of it) are questioned by those who, rightly, wish to emphasize the importance of lordship and of great lords in the Anglo-Saxon polity and

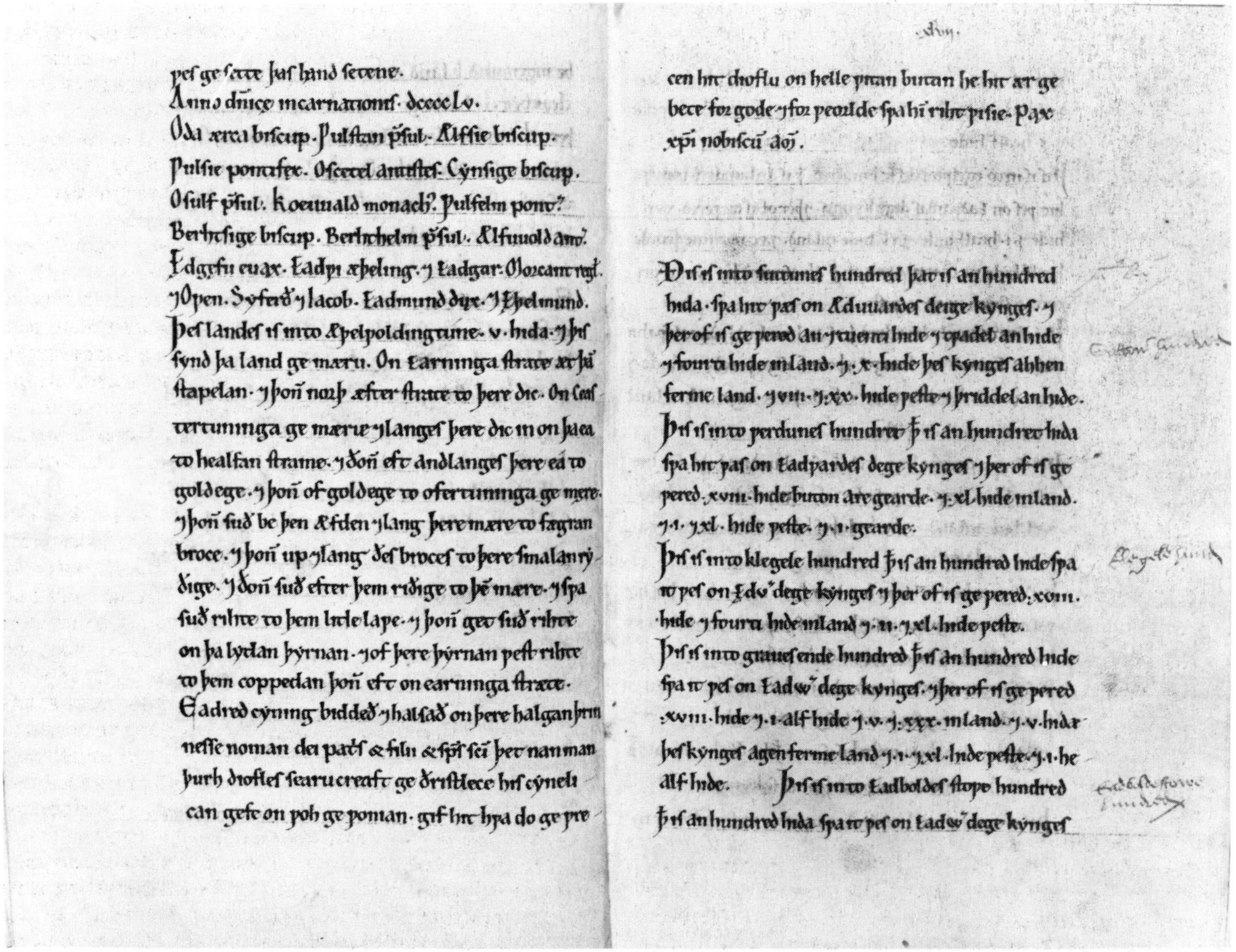

208 The beginning of the Northamptonshire Geld Roll transcribed into the 'Black Book of Peterborough' (London, Society of Antiquaries, MS 60, fol. 52, below right). This document, post-Conquest, but earlier than 1084, gives the hidage assessment of the Northamptonshire hundreds, stating for each how many hides had paid, how many were in demesne, how many were the king's food-rent land, and how many were waste. Plainly the record of an administrative inquiry, it is a very rare survivor from what may have been very numerous administrative documents in Anglo-Saxon.

who distrust views which could suggest that at certain stages and in certain ways it was something like a peasant commonwealth (see above, p. 168).

More generally, such large questions as Stubbs asked about the institutions and attitudes of a society over many centuries can themselves seem anachronistic. For example, in his brilliant account of Stubbs, J. W. Burrows (*A Liberal Descent*, Cambridge, 1981) concludes that while Stubbs may enjoy 'respectful remembrance in the small circle of medievalists', his works, like those of his contemporaries, are 'the triumphal arches of a past empire', interesting, moving, but not providing answers to questions about the past such as we might wish to ask.

Stubbs's questions and his answers matter more than that. Consider another recent book: A. Macfarlane, *The Origins of English Individualism* (Oxford, 1978). Dr Macfarlane emphasizes the extent to which the English seem to have been unusual in their relationship to property, to the family and to the law. He sees more social mobility, greater involvement in the market, in sum more 'individualism' in England than elsewhere; and believes that by the seventeenth century, and indeed before, Englishmen were right in believing that their 'economy, social structure and political system were radically different from those of neighbouring nations' (p. 175). He believes that many of the differentiating characteristics were already there by the thirteenth century and suggests, very tentatively, that their origins were much older: 'I have my own suspicions as to where the "origins" were . . .; and they are similar to those of Montesquieu', from whom he quotes this statement: 'In perusing the admirable treatise of Tacitus *On the Manners of the Germans* we find it is from that nation that the English have borrowed their idea of political government. This beautiful system was invented first in the woods.' So, perhaps Stubbs's ideas belong not so much to the well-appointed zoo which students of intellectual history keep, but rather to the jungle of real debate, in which they are active, and can bite.

In such debate the nature of the continuity between pre- and post-Conquest England raises crucial questions. Though William replaced the Old English aristocracy he maintained most of the governmental system. The shires and hundreds remained with their courts. William raised gelds and so did his sons. He used the Anglo-Saxon system of military service, the *fyrd*, to supplement his mercenaries and his feudal host. The coinage system was maintained, though somewhat simplified.

Why should he not preserve Anglo-Saxon institutions, since they were the essence of the powerful state which he had seized? Certainly; but it is important that he could hardly have preserved them had not numerous Anglo-Saxons survived with *some* wealth, *some* status, and *some* power. For example, most of the moneyers remained Saxons. That the one post-Conquest and pre-Domesday document relating to the collection of the geld is in English is proof that the maintenance of the taxation system must have depended on having Englishmen to run it. It is not easy to see how the king, or his magnates, could have exploited their English gains without English agents. The use of the *fyrd* implied the survival of considerable numbers of Anglo-Saxon landowners of at least modest substance. Above all, the survival of the courts of shire and hundred and the continued use of Anglo-Saxon law in those courts implies the presence of many free Englishmen to work them.

In considering this continuity, questions about the nature of late Anglo-Saxon society arise which cannot be answered, because they have hardly been asked. Something is known of the aristocracy; and much more will soon be known. Considerable thought has been given to the peasantry, but largely with a view to answering questions about the origins of the manor and of villeinage. But the number and nature of the men who were free, had more land than was required for subsistence, and yet were of nothing like the substance of the *antecessores* of Domesday tenants-in-chief, is hardly investigated. In this period, and later, the darkest area of English society is that which included the lower gentry and the upper peasantry, and it is the least studied. (The terms 'gentry' and 'peasantry' both dodge issues and blur distinctions; they have to serve for what they are worth.) It is plain that medieval English government depended on the existence and participation of a substantial class or classes of free men who attended courts and sat on juries. These were men such as attended county courts, gatherings 'of at least 150 men and occasionally very many more at most sessions of most county courts from the thirteenth century to the fifteenth'; or the 'free tenants and many yeomen sufficient in patrimony to make a jury' whose importance Sir John Fortescue emphasized when he commented, in the fifteenth century, on the relationship between English law and English society.

The survival of the institutions of the English state after the Conquest would not have been possible had not such men had numerous Anglo-Saxon predecessors. To emphasize the importance of such men is not to subscribe to the notion that Anglo-Saxon England was a 'peasant commonwealth'. It is to protest against any inclination to believe that Anglo-Saxon society was essentially a two-tier one of 'lords' and 'peasants'. It was much more complex and there were men in the middle who counted. Great lords and lordship mattered very much in late Anglo-Saxon England; they mattered very much in fourteenth-century England also. Their importance in the earlier period need not imply the governmental, or even to an extent political, insignificance of other classes, any more than it does in the later. (Whom was the Confessor seeking to please when he abandoned the *heregeld* in 1051?) Modern scholarship increasingly emphasizes the extent to which late Anglo-Saxon England resembled its Continental neighbours. It is important, however, to remember how far eleventh-century England was *not* like eleventh-century France. One crucial difference could be this: that the English kings, like the Carolingians but unlike most of the Carolingians' successors, maintained a system of rule in which their contact, via public courts, with a fairly large number of free classes mattered for them, and for those classes. That those courts and classes survived the Conquest may well have done much to determine the later history of England.

English survival was also important in the towns and in the Church. Some towns were hard hit by the Conquest, not least by the Conqueror's programme of urban castle-building. Nevertheless, the urban wealth which had been so important in late Anglo-Saxon England seems to a large extent to have remained in English hands. For example, in the twelfth-century English names, and so, presumably, English families, were strongly represented among the aldermen of London. In the Church, if the highest offices were soon nearly monopolized by foreigners, Englishmen remained important, and by no means only at the lowest levels. They mattered as monks in the great abbeys. (It was no small thing to be such a monk; at the Conquest, if the wealth of the abbeys was to be measured in tens of thousand acres, there were probably no more than a thousand monks all told.) A version of the *Chronicle* was kept up in Anglo-Saxon in the abbey of Peterborough until 1154.

Some abbeys remained the homes of English traditions. What happened at St Augustine's, Canterbury, is instructive. The English had considerable reverence for old buildings. At St Augustine's they still preserved until the eleventh century at least three of the small churches built there in the seventh. The last Anglo-Saxon abbot but one started to put into effect a scheme for joining two of these together by a rotunda. But his death in 1059 was attributed to the Virgin Mary's displeasure at his having interfered with the west end of her church, and the scheme was left unfinished. The Conquest brought a new Norman abbot, Scotland. What Norman ecclesiastics liked was large new buildings, impressive in the most up-to-date ways, and costing the earth. Scotland demolished the old buildings and began a brand new church. Yet that church was made into a great shrine for the archbishops and saints of early Kent. Westminster, as the burial place of the Confessor (whose cult, from Henry I's time, was very important to the kings of England), naturally became a home of English memories. In the late thirteenth century its monks drank two-handed because, they said, that was how the English had drunk. Perhaps the most striking feature of the English church in 1066 was the great number of parishes and parish churches recently established, especially in the south and east. Of the 9,000 or so parishes in England in 1700 a very large majority had been established before 1150, and a very high proportion of those before 1066. If Normans often took the better livings, most ordinary parish priests remained English. In the Church as in the state, continuity depended above all on the status and functions of many thousands of Englishmen.

No banality could be more secure than that every country and people are the product of their past. The English connection with the Dark Age past is, however, of a different order because of the continuity of the state and its institutions. Some of these institutions have travelled far, not only in time but in space. Consider the singular history of the sheriff. The origins of his office are obscure, but by the early eleventh century he was there as the king's officer in the shire; important among the local agents by whose employment the late Anglo-Saxon kings, though having in their *ealdormen* the equivalent of the *duces* of sub-Carolingian Europe (see above, p. 172), did without the equivalent of *comites*, aristocrats whose authority over a county often became hereditary. The Normans kept the sheriffs, though they called them something else: in French *viscounts*, in Latin *vicecomites*. By the thirteenth century the sheriff is sometimes again called by his English name: as Maitland pointed out, the continuity of the word, which is not found written down in English for several generations, is revealing.

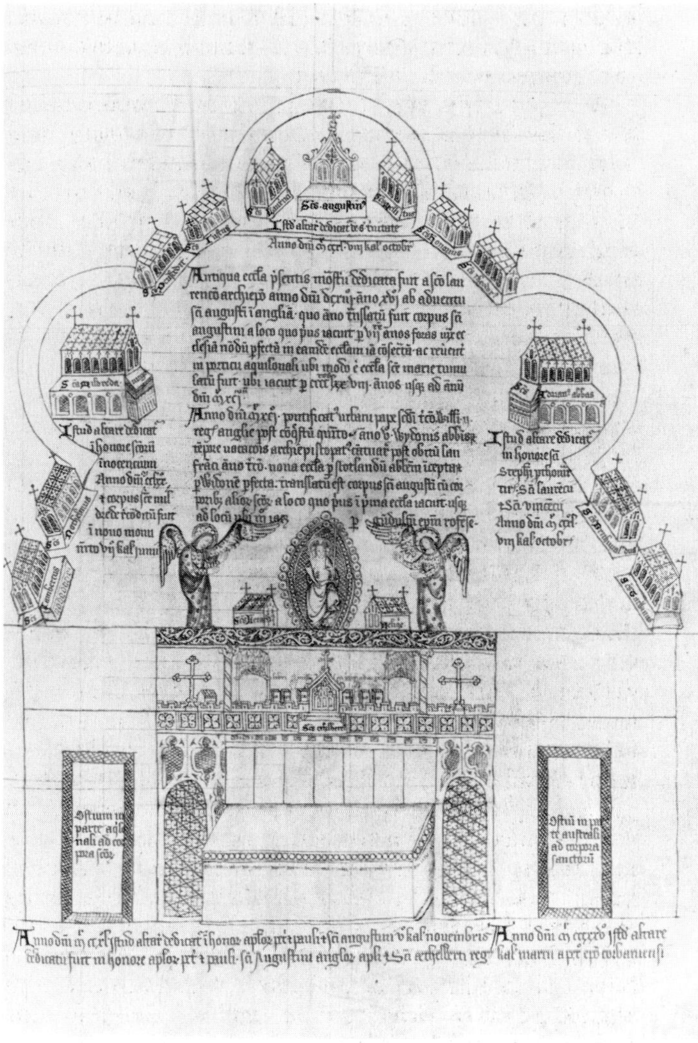

209 A 14th-century plan of the high altar and east end of the abbey church of St Augustine, Canterbury (Cambridge, Trinity Hall, MS 1, fol. 77a). At the far east end stood the altar-tomb of Augustine, flanked by those of his immediate successors as archbishop, Laurentius, Mellitus, Justus, Honorius, Deusdedit and Theodore. Other Anglo-Saxon archbishops were buried further west. On the high altar lay 'the books sent by Gregory to Augustine'. The bodies of the early archbishops were moved to these positions in the new Norman church on its completion in the early 12th century.

For many centuries the sheriff's office was a key one. By the nineteenth century it had become less important. Less important in England, but look some thousands of miles to the west. Whom do we find, famed in song, story and film, sustaining the rule of law and the power of the state, and chasing cattle-thieves, but the sheriff? His functions in the American west more closely resembled those of his Anglo-Saxon predecessors in his office than they did those of his English contemporaries. Indeed it may be that one reason why English institutions proved so resilient in the United States is that they often had their origin in conditions not too dissimilar from those of the New World. Such continuities and coincidences have the power to move. They relate to the institutions of free societies; and raise again the Stubbsian question about the origins of English liberties: 'Why is it that, when half the world awaits the pleasure of generals, no country for the study of the ultimate origins of whose institutions Stubbs's *Constitutional History* is required reading, has ever fallen under despotism?'

Stubbs's great book was not illustrated. He was little concerned with art or archaeology. Yet they bear on his contentions. Perhaps most important are the forts built by Alfred and Edward (see above, pp. 152–3); for, taken in conjunction with the arrangements for their maintenance outlined in the Burghal Hidage, they prove that Dark Age government could work effectively and on a very large scale. Hardly less important is the reformed coinage in use from the reign of Edgar onwards (see above, pp. 204–5); the complexity of its management again demonstrates both power and intelligence. It is only within the last 25 years that archaeologists and numismatists have made the discoveries which have transformed our knowledge of Anglo-Saxon government. They add to the force of Stubb's contentions. Arguments from the continuity of the English state and its institutions have the greater weight in that it is possible to demonstrate that the kings were so powerful, so early.

Behind their power lay wealth; behind that wealth a developing economy. The Anglo-Saxon economy must always have been of some considerable sophistication. Even in the pagan period the survival of thousands of brooches cast from moulds, very few of them cast from the same mould as another, indicates an abundant supply of goods which cannot have been home-made and suggests fairly complicated mechanisms of exchange (though see p. 44 above). In the later period major developments took place, perhaps more important than those in several succeeding centuries. So humble an object as a Thetford-ware cooking pot may have considerable, if indirect, relevance to constitutional history. The abundant production of such wares reflects economic developments which involved both the growth of towns and the widespread use of coin in the countryside. A complex economy means a complex society; that in turn may be one in which what may be termed, not so much anachronistically as too vaguely, the middle classes mattered; and this in some degree may explain why the state was organized as it was.

Here, as very often, to consider the Anglo-Saxons is to end in speculation. Nothing is more sobering than to consider how much of our knowledge of them depends on survivals which are unique, or nearly so: for example, the Sutton Hoo treasure, *Beowulf*, the Alfred Jewel, the Northamptonshire Geld Roll. Above all, there is a very great deal of the highest importance of which we would know nothing at all were it not for the fortunate chances which led to the making and the preservation of the Domesday Book. Our knowledge of so much hangs by so narrow a thread that it is certain as certain can be that there was a great deal about Anglo-Saxon England about which we do not know, and never will know, anything. This we can know. Those six centuries were not simply a barbarous prelude to better things. They are an integral part of the history of one of the most successful human organizations there has ever been.

Notes

ABBREVIATIONS

ASC	C. Plummer and J. Earle (ed.), *Anglo-Saxon Chronicle*, 2 vols., 1892, 1899 (reprinted with additions by D. Whitelock, 1952).
Birch, Cart.	W. de G. Birch (ed.), *Cartularium Saxonicum*, 3 vols., 1885–93; index 1899.
EHD	D. Whitelock (ed.), *English Historical Documents*, vol. 1, 2nd edn., 1979.
EHD 2	D. C. Douglas and G. W. Greenaway (ed.), *English Historical Documents*, vol. 2, 2nd edn., 1981.
HE	Bede, *Historia Ecclesiastica . . . Gentis Anglorum.* All references are to C. Plummer's edition of 1896.
Settimane	*Settimane di Studio del Centro italiano per Studi sull' alto Medioevo* (Spoleto).

For further abbreviations used in the notes to chs. 4–6, see the introductory note to ch. 4.

GENERAL

The single most important guide to Anglo-Saxon England is Stenton 1971. Other useful works dealing with the whole period are Whitelock 1952, Hunter Blair 1978, Loyn 1962. Kirby 1967, Fisher 1973, Sawyer 1978a. The collections of translated sources and the bibliographies in *EHD* and *EHD* 2 are invaluable. Bonser 1957 is the most extensive bibliography. *Anglo-Saxon England* and *Anglo-Saxon Studies in Archaeology and History* are periodicals devoted to Anglo-Saxon studies. The former provides an annual bibliography. So too does *The Old English Newsletter. Medieval Archaeology* is specially useful for its annual survey of archaeological discoveries.

CHAPTER ONE

The End of Roman Britain

The best general books on Roman Britain are Frere 1978, Todd 1981, Wacher 1978 (thematically arranged) and Salway 1981 (which was published too late for proper consideration in preparing the present work). Johnson 1980a is a stimulating account of its period. *Dossiers de l'Archéologie*, 1979, is a well-illustrated collection of popularizing essays by experts. Mann and Penman 1977 translate the narrative sources; Collingwood and Wright 1965 collect the inscriptions. The key periodical is *Britannia*.

p. 8 The quotation is from G. M. Young, *Last Essays* (1961), p. 9.

p. 9 The most recent survey of Romano-British demography is that of M. E. Jones in Casey (ed.) 1979, pp. 231–45. Jones puts the population at between 3 and 4 million 'at its peak', and would put the peak late rather than early, attaching importance to the absence in the late period of 'severe and frequent epidemics' (p. 238). The Nene valley: Taylor 1975, pp. 113–14; Wharram Percy: M. W. Beresford and J. G. Hurst in Sawyer (ed.) 1976, pp. 139–44, Hurst 1981. Rivet (ed.) 1969 and Todd (ed.) 1978 provide excellent surveys of villas; the contributions to these volumes by their respective editors are important for social implications of villas. Mosaics: D. J. Smith in Rivet (ed.) 1969, esp. pp. 79–82, 114–16.

For many aspects of the pottery industry: Dore and Green (ed.) 1977. Import of pottery in the early period and the transformation of the balance of trade by the fourth century: Frere 1978, pp. 328–30 and Rivet in Rivet (ed.) 1969, p. 202.

pp. 10–11 Towns: esp. Wacher 1975, and 1978, pp. 62–105, Rodwell and Rowley (ed.) 1975, and Frere 1978, pp. 273–300, from whom I have taken the statements of area and estimates of population.

Baths, shopping centres, etc.: Wacher 1978, esp. pp. 48–9, 59–60. *Durobrivae*: Wacher 1978, pp. 408–9, and J. P. Wild in Todd (ed.) 1978, p. 66, especially for prosperity in the 4th century.

Summaries of 4th-century urban developments: Todd 1981, pp. 221–3, Wacher 1978, pp. 102–5. Wacher detects considerable indications of decline after the middle of the century. It has been held that such decline was great and general: for comment, Salway 1981, pp. 411–12.

p. 11 For the distribution of villas in general, Rivet (ed.) 1969, Todd (ed.) 1978, and also Wacher 1978, ch. 4, K. Branigan in Branigan and Fowler (ed.) 1976, pp. 120–41, and Ordnance Survey, *Map of Roman Britain.*

The inscriptions mentioned: Birley 1979, p. 127. The development of villas: e.g. D. S. Neal in Todd (ed.) 1979, pp. 33–58.

The basic account of the use of Latin in Roman Britain is that of Jackson 1953, chapter 3; for recent work which has tended to modify his conclusions in particular on the distinction between the Vulgar Latin of Britain and that of Gaul see, e.g., Rivet and Smith 1979, pp. 13–18. Todd in Todd (ed.) 1978, p. 207 and Todd 1981, pp. 203–4 has indicated the likelihood of many army officers, especially in the auxiliary troops, being, by the 4th century, British.

pp. 11–13 The latest and best account of Christianity in Roman Britain is Thomas 1981a. He argues powerfully for a chronology for Patrick's life which puts his death in about 491. Sidonius on the Saxons: Anderson (ed.) 1936, 1965, 8, 6. The quotation from Tacitus has been taken from Rivet and Smith 1979, p. 94.

pp. 13–14 The estimate of the strength of the army is that of Frere 1978, pp. 181–6. The quotation is from Frere 1978, p. 269. The observation about the size of the relieving force of 369, as indicated by Ammianus, is that of Kent, in Casey (ed.) 1979, p. 16. The Saxon Shore forts: Johnson 1976.

The river wall at London: Marsden 1980, pp. 170–80. Mr Marsden thinks it possible that the latest section of the wall so far discovered, by the Tower, could be as late as the first decade of the fifth century. Casey in Casey (ed.) 1979, pp. 66–79, puts the case for Magnus Maximus having returned after 383.

p. 16 The relevant passages of Zosimus are translated by Mann and Penman 1977, pp. 52–3. They have been much discussed; see Demougeot 1979, pp. 436–9 and Johnson 1980, pp. 105–7 for summary accounts with references. Honorius's letter of 410 does not imply a formal 'abandonment' of Britain (Salway 1981, pp. 442–3) and may in any case have been directed to *Brettia* in Italy (loc. cit.). Salway, pp. 426–46 provides an important account of these years.

Coinage: Kent, in Casey (ed.) 1979, pp. 15–27. Chrysanthus and Victorinus: Birley 1979, pp. 55–6 and Birley 1981, pp. 326–8.

p. 17 The only possible reference to a council of the *civitates* of 5th-century Britain is in Gildas, ed. Winterbottom 1978, pp. 97, 26, quoted on p. 23. Gildas on Ambrosius: ed. and trans. Winterbottom 1978, p. 28.

p. 18 Breeze and Dobson 1978 provide the best account of the Wall in the last years of Roman rule. The Sixth Legion: A. R. Birley in Butler (ed.) 1971, pp. 81–96; *Ad Legionem Sextam*: Rivet and Smith 1979, pp. 219–20. Vegetius on the navy: Lang (ed.) 1885, 4, 37; he describes these light vessels as having 20 oars on each side, i.e. they were as big as Viking ships of the 9th century.

p. 19 The fate of villas in the last generations of Roman Britain: esp. Webster in Rivet (ed.) 1969, pp. 222–36, from whom the observations about the apparent effects of the crisis of 367 are taken. Wacher 1978, p. 133, observes that new construction after 367 was 'more modest than earlier in the century'. For Fig. 3: Rivet (ed.) 1969 and Todd (ed.) 1978; p. 79. The problem of what happened to villas in the last Roman decades naturally merges into that of 'continuity'. See, for example, Hadmain's summary account of Godmanchester in Todd (ed.) 1978, pp. 193–4, the interesting account of the villa at Shakenoak, Brodribb and others 1968–78 (esp. V, pp. 205–10), and the thought-provoking observation by Webster (op. cit., p. 235): 'It would not . . . be at all unreasonable to suppose that rural life continued, for example, in the Cotswolds, based on the villas, for at least two centuries after 400.'

ILLUSTRATIONS

Fig. 3: Rivet (ed.) 1969 and Todd (ed.) 1978; bibliography Rivet (ed.) 1969, p. 120.

5: Collingwood and Wright (ed.) 1965, no. 6. 6: Painter 1977. 7: Painter 1976. 8: Bruce Mitford 1974, pp. 175–87. 9: Alexander 1976. 10: Johnson 1976. 11: Royal Commission on Historical Monuments, *York*, 1962, pp. 13–14. 12: Wacher 1975, pp. 255–77. 13: Rivet (ed.) 1969, Todd (ed.) 1978 and Branigan 1977, esp. pp. 100–1. 14: Dove 1971 argues the vessel is a light type (?like a curragh) used for scouting.

CHAPTER TWO

The Lost Centuries: 400–600

Among the more important general works on Britain in this period are Myres, in Collingwood and Myres 1937 (now out of date, but providing a clear starting-point), Stenton 1971, Alcock 1971 (particularly useful for archaeology and for the Celtic peoples), Morris 1973 (full of ideas and learning, but too imaginative and wayward to be a safe guide for beginners), Johnson 1980 and Salway 1981. Ahrens (ed.) 1978, Hills 1979 (a most useful survey), Wilson (ed.) 1976 (which has a comprehensive bibliography), and Wilson 1981 are the most useful guides to the archaeological evidence and the first of them provides a comprehensive account of the Angles and Saxons in the migration period. For the Continental background Musset 1975, Demougeot 1979 and *À l'Aube de la France* 1981 are especially useful. Chadwick 1907 is still important as an interpretation of the period derived from a wide knowledge of the written sources for the Germanic world as a whole. The principal written sources from Britain are Gildas, 'Nennius', Bede and the *Anglo-Saxon Chronicle*, for which see below, notes to ch. 6. Dumville 1977a provides a useful survey of many of their problems.

p. 20 Gildas's hint on the descendants of Ambrosius Aurelianus (he does not actually say they were kings): Winterbottom (ed.) 1978, p. 98.
p. 22 Alcock 1972 describes his excavation at South Cadbury. Gildas on Vortipor: Winterbottom (ed.), p. 101. The inscriptions from Wales: Nash Williams (ed.) 1950 (the Vortipor inscription is his no. 138). See also Jackson 1953, ch. 5. The term *protector*: cf. fig. 18 and Bartrum 1966, p. 4. The Book of Llandaff: Davies 1978, 1979. For all aspects of the British church: Thomas 1981.
The most recent account of the origins of Brittany is Fleuriot 1980. Britons in Galicia: Thompson 1968. Pottery imported from the Mediterranean: Thomas 1981b. Inscriptions showing influence from southern France: Nash Williams 1950, pp. 8, 10 and no. 104. Procopius's remarks on *Brettania* and *Brittia*: Rivet and Smith 1979 and Burn 1955. Thompson 1980 argues for *Brettania*'s being Brittany.
p. 25 The most recent discussions of Gildas on Britain are Miller 1975 (very important though not always convincing) and Thompson 1979.
p. 26 The text of 'Nennius' provided by Morris (ed. and trans.) 1980 is inadequate; a better is expected from Dr Dumville whose work on this source is most important; see Dumville 1975–6, 1977a, 1977c.
The best text of the *Chronicle* is Plummer (ed.) 1952; the best trans. Whitelock, Douglas and Tucker 1961. Dr Whitelock's supplementary ch. to the former and introduction to the latter are very valuable. See also notes to ch. 6. The earliest surviving *dindshencus* are 10th-century but thought to have earlier origins. Jordanes's three ships, Mommsen (ed.) 1882, p. 82, cf. Kemble 1849, I, p. 16. Possible early annals preserved in late sources: see esp. Davies 1977.
Morris 1973 provides the most imaginative, sometimes indeed wild, account of Arthurian possibilities. The most astringent views are those of D. M. Dumville, see e.g. Dumville 1977a, pp. 187–8.
p. 29 The rough figures given for burials derive from Alcock 1971, pp. 310–11, and Hills (1979), pp. 318–19, who emphasizes the large size of some recently discovered cemeteries. For remarks on Bede's source for his statement on the Angles, Saxons and Jutes: Campbell 1979a, p. 9 n.
p. 30 Pagan pottery: see above all Myres 1969, 1977. For analyses of some of the major cremation cemeteries see e.g. Myres and Green 1973 and Hills and Penn 1977, 1981. S. Chadwick Hawkes 'Anglo-Saxon Kent *c.* 425–725' forthcoming in a Council for British Archaeology Research Report on Kentish archaeology, ed. P. Leach, will provide a valuable survey of the archaeology of pagan Kent. I am much obliged to Mrs Hawkes for allowing me to see this paper in advance of publication. Villages deserted in north Germany at this time: Parker 1965 and Ahrens (ed.) 1978, pp. 345–86.
p. 31 Procopius on the inhabitants of *Brittia*: Dewing (ed. and trans.) 1914–40, V, pp. 254–5. The peoples mentioned in *HE*, V.9: Demougeot 1979 provides the best recent survey. Franks in England: esp. Evison 1965; see fig. 37. Immigration from Norway and Denmark: Hawkes and Pollard 1981. (I am obliged to Mrs Hawkes for the opportunity to read this paper in advance of publication.) Bede's dates for the coming of the Saxons: Miller 1975. The earliest cremation urns: Myres 1969, pp. 71–83.
pp. 34–6 Evison 1981 provides the most recent discussion of many of the objects bearing on early 5th-century German settlement. For the significance of 'chip-carved' belt-furniture, see fig. 19 and note. In talking of the number of early graves, it is important to bear in mind that a high proportion of cremation urns cannot be dated with any precision; Hills 1979, pp. 324–7, Eagles 1980.
Early finds near Cirencester: Brown 1976.
p. 37 Constantius: Krusch and Levison (ed.) 1919. Riothamus: Demougeot 1979, pp. 506–7, 596–7, 634, 635, 685 and Fleuriot 1980, esp. pp. 170–6. See also Ashe 1981. Morris 1973, pp. 88–93 provides an imaginative interpretation of events of the 460s in Gaul; the suggestion about Cerdic is his. Gregory of Tours: Krusch and Levison (ed.) 1951, p. 161. The translation is Dalton's 1927, vol. 2, p. 57. Gregory is writing a century after what he purports to describe. Franks in England: see e.g. fig. 37.
p. 38 Procopius's story: Dewing (ed.) 1914–40, V, pp. 252–67; cf. Bruce-Mitford 1975, pp. 694–5. Migration to the Continent: ibid., p. 255. Thompson 1980 is sceptical. For the Varni see Demougeot 1979, pp. 262–4. Procopius on diplomatic relations: Dewing (ed.) 1914–40, V, p. 255, VI, p. 233. The story about Childebert is from the *Life* of St Leonorus, Morice 1742–6, I, col. 194. Fleuriot 1980, pp. 189, 280–1, drew attention to this passage. For Leonorus see Chadwick 1969, pp. 210–12. For English relations with the Merovingians in general: Lohaus 1974.
Place-names: Gelling 1978 is the best general guide.
p. 39 York: Hope-Taylor 1971; Phillips 1975. For Wroxeter see fig. 40.
p. 40 *Verulamium* water-pipe: Frere 1966, pp. 97–8. St Alban's: esp. Levison 1941.
pp. 40–1 Bath: Morris (ed. and trans.) 1980, pp. 81, 40; *HE*, I.1, p. 10; cf. Cunliffe 1980.
p. 41 Early Kent: Jolliffe 1933 is basic, though his arguments on origins are questionable. The survival of Celtic institutions: Rees 1963, Barrow 1975, pp. 7–68, G. R. J. Jones 1976b. For a different approach to rural 'continuity': Bonney 1972, 1976.
British cemeteries: Thomas 1981a, ch. 9; Faull 1977; cf. Hope Taylor 1977 and Alcock 1981. Lindsey: Stenton 1970, p. 129.
p. 42 Droitwich: Hook 1981. Lead: *HE*, III.25, p. 181.
p. 43 Kingston brooch: fig. 48.
p. 44 Kentish brooches: I owe the observation to Mrs Hawkes's forthcoming paper on early Kent. See note to p. 30. Slave-trade: Pelteret 1981.

ILLUSTRATIONS
Fig. 15: Alcock 1972. 16: See above, p. 22. 17: Thomas 1981a, pp. 283–4. 18: *À l'Aube de la France* 1981, no. 317. 19: Mucking: Jones 1979. Chip-carved belt-furniture: Hills 1979, pp. 298–308. Continental Saxons who had returned home after Roman service: *À l'Aube de la France* 1981, nos. 327–30. 20: Myres and Green 1973, pp. 114–17 (by R. I. Page); Wrenn 1965, pp. 42–6. 21, 22: Ahrens (ed.) 1978, p. 590; Myres and Green 1973, p. 90, where it is suggested that this brooch may have been brought by a settler from the Continent. 23: For Sarre: Hawkes 1969, p. 191. 24: Ahrens (ed.) 1978, p. 582. 25: Ahrens (ed.) 1978, p. 642, Vierck 1978. 26: Hills 1979, pp. 306–8. 27, 28: Myres and Green 1973, pp. 237–8. 29: See note to p. 30 above. 31: See pp. 48–9 above. 32: Hills 1980. 33: Harden 1956, pp. 143, 146; in general see Thieme 1978. 35: Green, Milligan and West 1981. 36: Briscoe 1981. 37: Evison 1965, pp. 23, 32; *À l'Aube de la France*, nos. 182–5, cf. 189–91. 38: See notes to p. 39. 39: Speake 1981, pp. 47, 52 ff. 40: Barker 1975, 1979. 41: See pp. 48–9 above. 42: Grierson 1952–4. 43: Bruce-Mitford 1974 (with M. Luscombe), pp. 236–42. 44: Hills 1979, p. 324.

PICTURE ESSAY 1 (pp. 24–5): **Finglesham** Chadwick 1958, pp. 1–71; Hawkes 1977, pp. 33–51; Hawkes and Pollard 1981, pp. 1 ff.: Rahtz, Dickinson and Watts (ed.) 1980.

PICTURE ESSAY 2 (pp. 32–3): **Sutton Hoo** Bruce-Mitford 1974, 1976, 1978, 1979; Green 1968; Werner 1982, Evison 1980; Brown 1981.

CHAPTER THREE

The First Christian Kings

The principal narrative sources for the first three quarters of the seventh century are Bede and the *Anglo-Saxon Chronicle*: see below, notes to ch. 6, and above, p. 54. Some of the hagiographies and charters from the last generation of the century and the beginning of the next cast light on earlier decades; most important among these are Eddius, the *Lives* of Cuthbert and of Guthlac (see below, notes to ch. 4). The early laws are best ed. and trans. (German) Liebermann 1903–16 and Attenborough 1922 (cited here). Archaeological evidence remains important. The principal guides to it are listed in the notes to ch. 2. Mayr-Harting 1972 provides the best account of the conversion. Hunter Blair 1970 and Deanesly 1964 are valuable guides to ecclesiastical history.

p. **45** Gregory's letter: *EHD*, no. 163. Italian clerics in England: Levison 1946, pp. 15–16.
p. **47** Cuthbert's dying words: Colgrave (ed.) 1940, p. 284. Wilfrid and Benedict Biscop: see notes to ch. 4.
p. **50** Augustine's Gospels: fig. 45. Bede's knowledge of the date of the Augustinian mission: Hunter Blair 1970, pp. 68–9. Canterbury: Brooks 1977, arguing that St Martin's and Christ Church had, as Bede suggests, been Roman churches, and for the possibility of some continuity of cult in Canterbury and elsewhere in Kent. Bubonic plague: MacArthur 1959.
p. **51** The identification of *Cnobheresburg* with Burgh Castle rests only on a plausible guess of Camden's and some ambiguous archaeology. Cuthbert's tours: Colgrave (ed.) 1940, c. 9; cf. Levison (ed.) 1905, p. 5. Progress of conversion: Campbell 1973, pp. 20–4. Wessex and Glastonbury: Finberg 1964b, pp. 83–115, Slover 1935. Britons on Wilfrid's estates: Jones 1976, pp. 68–74. St Alban's: above, p. 40; later St Alban's traditions are adamant that Offa founded the abbey at a time when the site of the martyr's grave was forgotten, Wats (ed.) 1639, pp. 26–7. Christian survival in the Rhineland: e.g. Kempf and Reusch (ed.) 1965.
p. **52** Place-names in Elmet: Smith 1979, pp. 4–5.
p. **53** Sources: see the introduction to the notes for this chapter and ch. 4. Kings and kingdoms: Campbell 1979a. Bede's list of kings with extensive power: *HE*, II.5, p. 89. It is probable that although Bede's statement on the extent of Edwin's power is ambiguous he means not that it covered the whole island but rather all the British and English peoples; cf. the rephrased version II.9, p. 97. He repeats elsewhere, III.24, p. 180, that Oswy subjugated most of the Picts. It is important that Edwin's empire extended over the Britons as well as the Anglo-Saxons; cf. II.20, p. 124. When his power broke it was by the rebellion of a British king allied to a Mercian prince, loc. cit. It is similarly important that the authority of the Northumbrian kings extended far into modern Scotland. It is likely that by 638 Edinburgh was under attack. Before the end of the century Northumbrian power was established on the Firth of Forth. In Bede's day there was an English bishopric at Whithorn in Galloway. In 752 Kyle was added to Northumbria. Although Egfrith's defeat at the hands of the Picts seems to have put an end to Northumbrian power in the far North, Bede's evidence is that for about a generation it had been real there. Anglo-Saxon kings could be more deeply involved with Celts, indeed more Celtic, than mental pictures derived from later political geography or dominated by the idea of almost perpetual hostility between Britons and Saxons sometimes seem to allow. Edwin's court must have been frequented by British princes. Oswald and Oswy became Christians while in exile among the Picts and Scots. Their nephew Talorcan became a king of the Picts. One of Oswy's wives was a British princess. Duncan 1978, pp. 53–4, 60–5, provides a good account of Northumbrian power in the North. The term *bretwalda* has passed into currency for Bede's seven rulers. It is not unlikely that the *brytenwalda* form, with less 'imperial' connotations, is the right one: Yorke 1981, pp. 171–4.
p. **54** The most convenient ed. of *Beowulf* is Klaeber (ed.) 1950; the translation quoted is Crossley-Holland 1968. For the date see Chase (ed.) 1981 and below, p. 128. Hrothgar's followers: lines 64–7; his generosity: lines 1684–6, 1749–51; the gift of a sword: lines 1900–3 (much of what is written here is from Campbell 1979). The Sutton Hoo helmet: Cramp 1957, pp. 61–2, Brady 1979, pp. 85–90.
p. **56** The East Anglian kings: these events are known only from Bede *HE*, II.5, p. 89; II.12, pp. 107–10; II.15, pp. 115–16; III.18; III.19, pp. 163, 164; III.24, p. 178. (In all editions of *HE* Bede is made to say that Anna's brother Aethelhere was the instigator of the war which culminated in 655. Prestwich 1968 proves that it was Penda whom Bede called *Auctor . . . belli*.) Killing captured kings and nobles: *HE*, IV.22, pp. 249–51, a captured noble seeks to save his life by pretending to be a peasant; Krusch (ed.) 1902, p. 449, having captured a monastic community Penda intends to kill the abbot but sell the monks.
Successions: see below, pp. 114 ff. Exiles: *HE*, III.15, p. 116 (Sigbert); II.12, p. 107 (Edwin); III.1, p. 127 (Oswald and Oswy); Plummer's note, *HE*, II, p. 263 (Aldfrith); *HE*, III.7, p. 140 (Cenwalh); IV.15 (Caedwalla). Oundle: Colgrave (ed.) 1927, c. 67. Beowulf's arrival in Denmark: lines 338–9. Guthlac: Colgrave (ed.) 1956, p. 80. Edwin's kingdoms: *HE*, III.6, pp. 137–8. Sigbert of East Anglia: *HE*, III.18. Sigbert of Essex: III.22, p. 173.
pp. **56–7** Yeavering: Hope-Taylor 1977, who has been followed above; Miket 1980, pp. 301–3 argues that Hope-Taylor's evidence is insufficient to prove that the earliest timber buildings on the site were British rather than Anglian. 'Heorot' ('Hart'): line 78. Edwin's council: *HE*, II.13 (though Bede's reference to the priest Coifi's riding from the council to Goodmanham, over 20 miles from York, suggests that the venue may have been elsewhere; a point I owe to Dr Lawson).
p. **58** Edwin's peace: *HE*, *II.18*. Oswald and the silver dish, *III.6*, p. 138; Campbell 1971, p. 18. Charter for 38 hides: Birch, *Cart.*, no. 78.
Royal vills, or halls, as centres: laws of Hlothere and Eadric c. 7 and c. 16; and note the reference to the reeve on p. 22; if each royal vill had a reeve in charge the possible number and status of such men raises important questions throughout Anglo-Saxon history. Specified food-rents: laws of Ine c. 70/1.
Ealdormen and *scirs*: laws of Ine c. 8, c. 36/1, c. 50; the most important discussion of the possibilities is Chadwick 1905, esp. pp. 282–90. The essential problem is that although the laws seem to treat the ealdorman as a functionary, there is other reason to suppose that he was also a member of the royal clan, of the kind Latin sources sometimes call *rex* or *subregulus*; for more recent comments see Sawyer 1978, esp. pp. 45–7 and Campbell 1979a, pp. 5, 8.
p. **59** Wergelds: most recently Sawyer 1978, pp. 172–3. Free peasants: Stenton 1971, pp. 275–7; he nowhere says that he regards the 200 wergeld payers as a majority of the population. If such men really did have holdings of 40 acres or more then they were by later standards very rich peasants and there is room for many poorer men beneath them.
Selling oneself into slavery: 'If he is compelled by necessity, a father has the power to sell his son of seven years of age into slavery . . . A person of fourteen years can make himself a slave' (*Penitential* of Theodore II.13, 1 and 2: McNeill and Gamer 1929, p. 211). Summoning an army: *HE*, II.12, p. 110. This relates to Aethelfrith of Northumbria; so great a king might be thought of as summoning subordinated rulers with their retinues; Penda's thirty *legiones* with *duces regii* at the Winwaed were probably such contingents (*HE*, III.24, p. 178); the same is less likely true of the army *congregatus* by Oswine of Deira in 655 (*HE*, III.14, p. 155). Possibility that ordinary freemen performed ancillary services: John 1966, pp. 136–7. East Wansdyke: Myres 1964 and fig. 61. Penda's raids: Sawyer 1978, p. 31. Horses: Campbell 1979a, pp. 11–12.
Tribal Hidage: Davies and Vierck 1974 provide the most recent extended discussion. Russell 1947 is important in showing that it may include part of Wales.
p. **61** Bede's hidages: Hart 1971, pp. 146–7. Ine's law on baptism: c. 2. Paulinus at Yeavering: *HE*, II.15, p. 115. Earconberht: *HE*, III.8, p. 142. Rights of Kentish kings: laws of Aethelbert, c. 6. Association of churches with royal vill: Deanesly 1941. *Tributum*: Campbell 1971, p. 13. East

Anglian royal house pp. 32–3. Cissa: Colgrave (ed.) 1956, pp. 148–9. Styles of ornament: Speake 1980. Frankish pottery: above, p. 22. Conversions at Nantes: Levison 1946, p. 4. Saxons at Iona: Anderson and Anderson (ed.) 1961, pp. 486, 512. Edwin's family: *HE*, II.20, p. 125. Ceolfrith's voyage: *Historia Abbatum* (see notes to ch. 4), c. 17, p. 382.
The princess from Kent: *HE*, III.15. Bronze vessels: fig. 44. Ivory: Myres and Green 1973, pp. 100–3. Missionaries taking ship: Levison (ed.) 1905, p. 16. The slave trade: Pelteret 1981. Bede's story: *HE*, IV.22, pp. 249–50. English slaves in Gaul: Levison 1946, pp. 9–10. England and Gaul: Levison 1946, pp. 4–11, Campbell 1971, pp. 16–29.
p. **66** Gregory of Tours: Krusch and Levison (ed.) 1951, p. 254. Aethelbert's laws: *HE*, II.5, p. 90. Sutton Hoo: Picture Essay 2; 'Roman depiction', fig. 66; helmet of a cavalry officer, fig. 65.
p. **67** Childeric's tomb: *A l'Aube de la France*, 1981, pp. 241–5. The East Anglian genealogy and Romulus and Remus: *HE*, II.15, p. 116; Dumville 1976, p. 31; fig. 68. Pseudo-Roman claims: Wallace-Hadrill (ed.) 1960, pp. xi–xii. For the influence of Roman art in the north cf. Vierck 1981.

ILLUSTRATIONS
Fig. 45: Wormald 1954. 46: See pp. 48–9 above. 47: Fletcher 1981, pp. 79–80. 48: Avent 1975, no. 179, see I, p. 53. 49: Taylor and Taylor 1965–78, pp. 91–3 and 1075. 51, 52, 53: Speake 1970. 54: Sawyer 1957, 1962. 55: Gilmour 1979. 56: Maryon 1960, Anstee and Bick 1961, Wilson (ed.) 1976, pp. 265–6. There were variations from the technique described in the caption. The essential element in the 'pattern welding' was the employment of sandwiches of iron and steel strips twisted together and hammered flat to produce the characteristic pattern here seen on the surface of the blade. 57: Bruce Mitford 1974 (here with M. Luscombe), pp. 223–52; Swanton 1980; Bruce-Mitford 1978, plate 23, shows a reconstruction. 58: Hope Taylor 1977. 59: Jones 1979; P. Rahtz in Wilson (ed.) 1976, pp. 49–98 provides the best survey of early Anglo-Saxon timber buildings. 60: Werner 1954 for the significance of such balances. 61: Myres 1964; Green 1971. 62: Vierck 1970, who argues that the model (which he dates *c.* 700) shows a keel more developed than that of the Sutton Hoo ship. See also D. Elmers in Ahrens (ed.) 1978, pp. 495–510. 64: Longley 1975. 65: *À l'Aube de la France* 1981, no. 216; Johnson 1980. 66: Wright and Collingwood (ed.) 1965, no. 1172. 67: Fox 1923, pp. 89–90, 124–5. It is disputed whether this dyke is Dark Age, or earlier. 68: Green 1971. 69: Bruce-Mitford 1978, pp. 311–93; Simpson 1979; Reynolds 1980. 70: Bruce-Mitford 1978, pp. 138–231.

PICTURE ESSAY 3 (pp. 48–9): **Cemeteries**
Baker 1969; Boddington and Cadman 1981, pp. 103–22; Bruce-Mitford and Luscombe in Bruce-Mitford 1974, pp. 223–52; S. Chadwick Hawkes in Philp 1973, pp. 186–201; Hawkes and Grove 1963, pp. 22–38; Hawkes *et al.* 1965, pp. 17–32; Hyslop 1963, pp. 161–2; Meaney and Hawkes 1970; Rigold 1960, 1966; Vierck in Ahrens (ed.) 1978, pp. 225–62; Wade-Martins 1980. The Crundale buckle (no. 3) is hollow, like the great buckle from Sutton Hoo (p. 33, no. 2).

PICTURE ESSAY 4 (pp. 62–3): **Anglo-Saxon Coins 1**
Rigold in Bruce-Mitford 1975, pp. 653–77; Stuart in Carson and Kraay 1978, pp. 143–72; Rigold 1960, pp. 6–53; Rigold and Metcalf 1977, pp. 31–52; Pagan 1969, pp. 1–15; Blunt, Lyon and Stewart 1963, pp. 1–74.

CHAPTER FOUR
The Age of Bede and Aethelbald

The main source for the period 670–750 remains Bede, *HE*. Together with the *Continuation of Bede*, *HA* (*Historia Abbatum*), *VC* (*Vita Ceolfridi*), and *Ep. ad Egb.* (*Epistola ad Egbertum episcopum*), it is edited, with priceless commentary, by Plummer 1896. *HE* is translated by Colgrave and Mynors 1969, *HA* by Campbell 1968, and *Continuation of Bede*, *VC* and *Ep. ad Egb.* by *EHD*, nos. 5, 55, 170. The main Saints' Lives are *Life of Wilfrid* (Eddius), ed. and tr. Colgrave 1927; *Two Lives of Cuthbert* (Anon., Bede), ed. and tr. Colgrave 1940; *Life of Guthlac* (Felix), ed. and tr. Colgrave 1956; *Life of Boniface* (Willibald), ed. Levison 1905, tr. Talbot 1954. The correspondence of Boniface is ed. Tangl 1916, tr. Emerton 1940; the works of Aldhelm, ed. Ehwald 1919, tr. (prose only) Lapidge and Herren 1979. The *Penitential of Theodore*, the *Dialogue of Egbert*, and the decrees of the councils at Rome (679) and Clovesho (746/7) are ed. Haddan and Stubbs 1871, the first two tr. McNeill and Gamer 1929. The laws are best ed. and tr. (German) Liebermann 1903–16; English editions and translations used here are Attenborough 1922 and Robertson 1925. Charters are ed. Birch, *Cart.*, and invaluably listed with bibliography and concordance to Birch by Sawyer 1968; the charters of Rochester are now ed. Campbell 1973, and those of Burton ed. Sawyer 1979, the first in a new series of definitive editions, cartulary by cartulary; for translations of selected charters see *EHD*. The *ASC* is splendidly translated by Whitelock in *EHD* (see notes on ch. 6), from which citations in this chapter are taken. The best general account of most issues of the period is Stenton 1971, chs. 2–3, 5–7. For the Church, see Deanesly 1962, and especially Mayr-Harting 1972. Useful introductions to learning and the arts are Hunter Blair 1970, and 1976a. The secular context of early Christian growth is discussed by Wormald 1978a; Green 1965 is an important linguistic study of the Church as it affected lordship. For politics, Stenton 1918 is fundamental.

pp. 72–8 *HE*, V.23, pp. 349–51 is Bede's summary of his own times, and V.24, pp. 356–60 is his 'autobiography'. Campbell 1966 is basic for Bede as historian, and for Saints' Lives see Jones 1947. Bibliography for the other themes summarized here is given below.
p. **78** Benedict Biscop, *HA*, cc. 1–7, pp. 365–70, c. 9, p. 373, c. 11, pp. 374–6; see also bibl. on Picture Essay 5. Hilda, Whitby and double monasteries, *HE*, IV.23–4, pp. 252–62; Bateson 1899; Campbell 1971, pp. 18–26; Cramp 1976b, pp. 223–9, 453–62. The Whitby *Life of Gregory*, Colgrave 1967; Caedmon, Plummer 1896, II, pp. 251–2, and Wrenn 1946.
p. **79** *Life of Cuthbert* (Bede), cc. 9–11, pp. 184–95, cc. 17–20, pp. 214–25, c. 37, pp. 270–81. See also bibl. on Picture Essay 6.
p. **82** *Life of Guthlac*, cc. 1–2, pp. 72–5, cc. 16–18, pp. 80–3, c. 31, pp. 100–7, c. 34, pp. 108–11, cc. 36–8, pp. 114–17; Whitelock 1951, pp. 80–1; Mayr-Harting 1972, pp. 229–39.
Life of Boniface, cc. 1–2, pp. 4–11, c. 4, pp. 13–18, c. 8, pp. 45–56. See also Levison 1946 (basic), Mayr-Harting 1972, pp. 226–8, and Reuter 1980; for the vernacular at Fulda, Wormald 1978a, pp. 47, 50, 53.
Life of Wilfrid, cc. 2–6, pp. 4–15, cc. 10–17, pp. 20–7, c. 22, pp. 44–7, c. 26, pp. 52–3, cc. 29–32, pp. 57–67, c. 41, pp. 80–5, cc. 45–7, pp. 92–9, cc. 50–5, pp. 102–21, c. 62, pp. 134–5; *HE*, III.25, pp. 181–9, III.28, pp. 194–5, IV.13, pp. 230–2, IV.15, p. 236, IV.19, p. 243, V.19–20, pp. 321–32. The best account of Wilfrid is Mayr-Harting 1972, ch. 9 and pp. 156–9, 166–7, 174–81; Isenberg 1978 is very important; see also Kirby 1974, and Wormald 1978a, pp. 54–5.
pp. **84–6** Gregory's scheme, *HE*, I.29, pp. 63–4; Theodore's council and resistance to it, IV.5, pp. 214–17, IV.6, p. 218, IV.12, p. 229, and *EHD*, p. 793, *Life of Wilfrid*, cc 29–32, pp. 57–67, cc. 50–5, pp. 102–21. For episcopal *mores* see the decrees of Rome (679), p. 133; *Penitential of Theodore* I.vii.2, p. 182, II.xiv.4, 7, 10, pp. 202–3; and *Ep. ad Egb.*, cc. 7–8, pp. 410–12. Discussion: Campbell 1971, pp. 13–14, Mayr-Harting 1972, pp. 130–9, Biddle 1976, pp. 103–12, and Wormald 1978a, pp. 52–5.
pp. **86–8** Proliferation of monasteries, Campbell 1971, pp. 14–16. Resting-places, Rollason 1978, and Sawyer 1978a, ch. 7. The traditional view of early monasticism, Thompson 1935, pp. 60–101. The cathedral monastery, *HE*, I.27, pp. 48–9, IV.27, pp. 270–1, with Deanesly 1964, pp. 1–22. Wilfrid's monastic empire, John 1971, pp. 53–62. Charters of exemption, Wormald 1976, pp. 146–9; for other Gallic symptoms, Sims-Williams 1975.
The spread of the *Rule of St Benedict*, Wormald 1976, and Mayr-Harting 1976; for the earliest MS, Farmer 1968, and Engelbert 1969. Birch, *Cart.*, no 156 (*EHD*, no. 68) is the resolution of the Withington dispute, and *Dialogue of Egbert*, c. 11, p. 408 shows partition of a monastery between heirs. For the *Eigenkirche*, Wormald 1978a, pp. 52–4, Böhmer 1921.
pp. **88–9** Missions: Levison 1946, Reuter 1980, Charles-Edwards 1976a (on the Irish), Mayr-Harting 1981 (on Wilfrid). *Andreas*, ed. Brooks 1961.

Bede's library, Laistner 1935, Hunter Blair 1976b, pp. 242–50. Bede as scholar, Laistner 1933, Mayr-Harting 1972, pp. 204–19, Jones 1976, Meyvaert 1976. The Inkberrow Jerome, Lowe 1961, Pls. I, V, and Sims-Williams 1976. Aldhelm, Mayr-Harting 1972, pp. 192–204, 214–19. Winterbottom 1977, and Lapidge and Herren 1979. Brooks 1983 discusses the Canterbury school, and for abbot Hadrian see also Brown 1975, pp. 298–9.

pp. 90–3 Greenfield 1966 is the best introduction to Anglo-Saxon literature; Stanley 1966 has more specialized discussions; see also Shippey 1972. The *Dream of the Rood* is ed. Swanton 1970; the translation in the text is from Alexander 1966, pp. 106–9; the poem's Christian background, Woolf 1958 and O'Carrigain 1978, pp. 140–1.

The arts at Monkwearmouth–Jarrow, Picture Essay 5. Wilfrid's churches, Taylor and Taylor 1965, pp. 297–312, 516–18, Gilbert 1974; Hexham sculpture, Cramp 1974. Brixworth, Taylor and Taylor 1965, pp. 108–14, Parsons 1977, with Stenton 1933, p. 185, for the documentary references. Lindisfarne Gospels, Kendrick *et al.* 1960, Alexander 1978, no. 9, and Backhouse 1981. The arts in general, Bruce Mitford 1967.

pp. 93–5 Egfrith: *HE*, III.14, p. 154, III.24, p. 178, IV.5, p. 214, IV.12, p. 229, IV.21, p. 249, IV.26, pp. 266–8; *HA*, c. 4, pp. 367–8, c. 7, p. 370; *Life of Cuthbert* (Bede), c. 24, pp. 235–9, c. 27, pp. 242–9; *Life of Wilfrid*, cc. 17–21, pp. 40–5, c. 24, pp. 48–9, cc. 34–9, pp. 70–9, c. 44, pp. 90–1.

Caedwalla: *HE*, IV.15–16, pp. 236–8, V.7, pp. 292–4; *Life of Wilfrid*, c. 42, pp. 84–5; *Anglo-Saxon Chronicle*, years 661, 685–8, pp. 165–8 (and on Ine, years 688, 694, 710, 715, 721, 722, 725, 726, pp. 168–72); Birch, *Cart.*, nos. 72 (*EHD*, no. 58), 82 (Hart 1966, pp. 135–41), 89 (Stenton 1933, pp. 189–90).

Aethelbald: *HE* V.23, p. 350; *Life of Guthlac*, c. 40, pp. 124–7, c. 49, pp. 148–51, cc. 51–2, pp. 162–7. (For Bishop Haedde in this *Life* see cc. 46–7, pp. 142–7; Tatwine, c. 25, pp. 88–9; Wilfrid, Pr., pp. 64–5, c. 28, pp. 92–5, c. 37, pp. 116–19, cc. 39–40, pp. 120–7—Wilfrid is described as an abbot, which would rule out his identity with the bishop of Worcester who acceded *c.* 718, if, as is commonly supposed, the *Life of Guthlac* was not written until the 730s; but all that suggests this is the extravagant language used of Aethelbald's prophesied power, and this may owe more to Biblical parallels than political realities.)

Aethelbald (cont.): *ASC*, years 716, 733, 737, 743, 752, 757, pp. 171–6; *Continuation of Bede*, years 740, 750, 757, pp. 362–3; Birch, *Cart.*, nos. 149, 150, 152 (Campbell 1973, no. 2, *EHD*, no. 66), 154 (*EHD*, no. 67), 157, 162 (a forgery; see note to ch. 5, pp. 125–8), 163, 164, 171, 177, 181. On the extent of Aethelbald's power, compare Stenton 1918, pp. 53–8, with Vollrath-Reichelt 1971, pp. 122–51. On Haedde see further Dornier (ed.) 1977, p. 155; Aethelbald's mausoleum, compare Taylor 1971, p. 388, with Gilbert 1974, pp. 100–1; his posthumous fate, Tangl 1916, no. 115, p. 249. Kings and churchmen in general, Wallace-Hadrill 1971, pp. 59–66.

pp. 95–8 Charter study, Stenton 1955, Brooks 1974, *EHD*, pp. 369–82. Fundamental work, generally followed here, is Chaplais 1965–9, but see Keynes 1980 for the central production of diplomas at a later period. Affinities of Anglo-Saxon charters, Levison 1946, pp. 226–33, with Sims-Williams 1975. On the chancery issue, Brooks 1969 shows that 9th-century charters were produced in cathedral *scriptoria*, but note that Birch, *Cart.*, no. 149 (Aethelbald for Minster-in-Thanet in Canterbury's diocese) is almost identical with Birch, *Cart.*, no. 152 (Aethelbald for Rochester). Script of the Ismere charter, Engelbert 1969, pp. 406, 410. For the legal rights conveyed by charter see the revolutionary conclusions of John 1960, defended in John 1966, ch. 2; also, Charles-Edwards 1976b. The view taken here is the author's sole responsibility, and will be defended in a future publication.

pp. 98–9 Laws in General, *EHD*, pp. 357–69, Wallace-Hadrill 1971, pp. 32–4, and Wormald 1977a; on the blood-feud Wormald 1980 includes a survey of most historical and anthropological literature. Sources for wergelds: e.g. Laws of Aethelbert, cc. 21, 25, 26, pp. 6–7, laws of Hlothere, cc. 1, 3, pp. 18–19, laws of Ine, cc. 19, 23/3, pp. 42–3, cc. 32–3, 34/1, pp. 46–7, c. 70, pp. 58–61. Injury tariffs: laws of Aethelbert, cc. 34–72, pp. 8–15, laws of Alfred, cc. 44–77, pp. 86–93. The kinless man, laws of Ine, cc. 23–23/2, pp. 42–3. The captured thief, laws of Wihtred, c. 25, pp. 28–9, laws of Ine, c. 12, pp. 40–1, cc. 24/1, 28, pp. 44–5. Trade, laws of Hlothere, cc. 15–16, pp. 20–3, laws of Wihtred, c. 28, pp. 30–1, laws of Ine, c. 25, pp. 44–5. The Church, laws of Aethelbert, c. 1, pp. 4–5, laws of Wihtred, cc. 1–1/1, 4–7, pp. 24–7, laws of Ine, cc. 2–4, pp. 36–7.

pp. 99–100 *Bretwaldas*: Stenton 1918, John 1966, ch. 1, Vollrath-Reichelt 1971, Yorke 1981; the view taken here will also be defended in a forthcoming publication. Relevant passages of *HE* are II.5, pp. 89–90, II.12, p. 110, III.24, pp. 177–80, IV.21, p. 249. Other sources: *Life of Wilfrid*, c. 20, pp. 42–3; Birch, *Cart.*, nos. 89 (title claimed for Aethelred of Mercia), 154 (*EHD*, no. 67), 157, 163, 164, 181 (Aethelbald charters, the last not necessarily from Worcester, though the bishop of Worcester witnessed it); *EHD*, no. 164 (Bishop Waldhere's letter); Aldhelm, *Carmen Ecclesiasticum*, iii, lines 2–3, 15, 36, pp. 14–16 (poetic licence on Kings Centwine, Caedwalla and Ine of Wessex?); laws of Wihtred, Pr., pp. 24–5 (Archbishop Berhtwald's title); Dümmler 1895, p. 191 (Alcuin's letter, though Mr. Campbell points out to me that the phrase may mean only that the English conquest began in Kent). Tara, Byrne 1973, chs. 4, 12.

Council of Clovesho, Tangl 1916, no. 10, p. 14; nos. 73–5, pp. 146–8; no. 78, pp. 161–70. Relevant canons of the council: 5, p. 364, 8, p. 365, 11, p. 366, 16, p. 368, 19–21, p. 369, 28, p. 374, 30, pp. 375–6. Gumley privilege, Birch, *Cart.*, no. 178; for its interpretation compare John 1960, pp. 67–74 with Brooks 1971, pp. 76–7.

ILLUSTRATIONS (other than those discussed in text, for which see above)

Fig. 71: Arngart 1952, Lowe 1958 (with critique by Wright and Meyvaert 1961), Meyvaert 1964, pp. 3–4, Alexander 1978, no. 19, Parkes 1982. 72: cf. Ryan 1939, which I was unable to use. 73: Taylor and Taylor 1965, pp. 86–9, Taylor 1973; cf. Hamilton (ed.) 1870, p. 346. 74: Alexander 1978, no. 6. 75: Cramp 1970, 1976b, pp. 239–41. 78: Peers and Ralegh Radford 1943, Cramp 1976b, pp. 453–7. 79: *Codices Latini Antiquiores*, V.606A, Levison 1946, p. 65. 81: Wilson 1961, p. 214. 82: Bailey 1974, pp. 155–8. 86: Taylor and Taylor 1965–78, pp. 234–8. 87: Cramp 1965, pp. 8–9. 88: Alexander 1978, no. 65, Levison 1946, p. 133. 89: Cramp 1965, pp. 9–12, O'Carragain 1978. 91: see Picture Essay 5. 93: Beckwith 1972, pp. 14–18. 96: Chaplais 1965–9, pp. 317–27.

PICTURE ESSAY 5 (pp. 74–5)
Monkwearmouth and Jarrow
Sources: *HA*, *VC* (see note at beginning of chapter); Tangl 1916, nos. 76, pp. 158–9, 116, pp. 250–2, 127, pp. 264–5; Dümmler 1895, nos. 19, pp. 53–6, 67, pp. 110–11, 282, pp. 440–1; Northern Annals, year 794, *EHD*, p. 273. Secondary: Buildings and excavations, Taylor and Taylor 1965–78, pp. 378–49, 432–46, Cramp 1969, 1976a, 1976b, pp. 229–41. The *Codex Amiatinus* and its authorship, Lowe 1961, pp. 8–13, and Pls. VIII–X, Bruce Mitford 1969, but also Nordhagen 1977. On other manuscripts, Lowe 1958, criticized in one respect by Wright and Meyvaert 1961, and Parkes 1982. Sculpture, Cramp 1965, pp. 9–12. General, Wormald 1976, Meyvaert 1979.

PICTURE ESSAY 6 (pp. 80–1) **The Tomb of Saint Cuthbert**
The essential guide is Battiscombe (ed.) 1956, in which the contributions by Kitzinger, Bruce-Mitford, Lasko, Flanagan and Radford are especially important. For the Gospel book see Brown 1969.

CHAPTER FIVE
The Age of Offa and Alcuin

The major sources for this ill-served period are: (1) the northern annals incorporated in the *Historia Regum* attributed to the 12th-century Symeon of Durham, and now known to be contemporary annals, written up *c.* 1000 by the great late Saxon scholar Byrhtferth: ed. Arnold 1882–5, vol. 2, trans. *EHD*, no. 3, discussed by Hunter Blair 1964, and in Lapidge 1982; (2) the correspondence of Alcuin, ed. Dümmler 1895, and selectively translated in *EHD*; (3) charters: see above on ch. 4, plus Harmer 1914 and Robertson 1939 for the increasingly common vernacular texts. Also valuable because, like Symeon, he incorporated otherwise lost early material is Roger of Wendover, ed. Luard 1890. The Welsh Annals are ed. and trans. Morris 1980, and discussed by Hughes 1973.

See notes on ch. 4 for Bede, laws and Church councils (though Dümmler 1895, no. 3 is the best edition of the 786 council); see notes on ch. 6 for the *ASC*, and for Asser's *Life of Alfred*; citations of the *ASC* in this chapter are from *EHD*, no. 1.
Secondary discussion of the period 750–830 is also scanty. Exceptions are: Stenton 1971, ch. 7 (to be read with Stenton 1918, and 1955), Levison 1946, chs. 5–6, Wallace-Hadrill 1965, 1971, ch. 5, and Sawyer 1978a, ch. 2. On Alcuin, Gaskoin 1904 is still the best book, but Donald Bullough's forthcoming study, kindly lent me before publication, will supersede it in most respects. On Charlemagne, Bullough 1965, Ganshof 1968, and Ganshof 1971. Of the works listed below on specific topics, Brooks 1983 is of considerable general importance.

pp. **101–14** Many of the themes discussed in this section are treated in detail with references below. Note that there is one other (short) letter by Charlemagne to Offa: Dümmler 1895, no. 87. On the Carolingian creation of archbishoprics see Levison 1946, p. 96. For another example of English exiles at Charlemagne's court see Dümmler 1895, no. 85, *EHD*, no. 196. Alcuin's York poem is ed. Dümmler 1881, pp. 169–206; an improved edition with translation is forthcoming from Peter Godman. For the abiding English commitment to the Continent see Levison 1946; on the Gandersheim casket, Beckwith 1972, pp. 18–19, and no. 2; on the Rupert Cross and Tassilo Chalice, Wilson 1978, pp. 14–16; on Cathwulf, Dümmler 1895, pp. 501–5, and Wallace-Hadrill 1971, pp. 100–2. For the burial place of Offa see Roger of Wendover, pp. 402–3. For Offa's possible interest in learning see Dümmler 1895, no. 64, *EHD*, no. 195, and for the copy of Bede to which he had access, Levison 1946, p. 245. On the question of Mercian *scriptoria* see Sisam 1956–7 and Dumville 1972, who give reasons for connecting most allegedly Mercian manuscripts with Canterbury, if anywhere. For Alcuin's learning and its York background see the York poem, lines 1540–56, pp. 203–4, with Hunter Blair 1976b and Bullough forthcoming; for Aethelwulf see Campbell 1967; for Breedon, Dornier 1977, pp. 155–68 and Cramp 1977.
pp. **114–17** The early Anglo-Saxon genealogical collection is ed., with important discussion, Dumville 1976; the original breakthrough was Sisam 1953a. See also Dumville 1977b for the principles of genealogical study, and Dumville 1979 for the royal succession.
pp. **117–18** Unction and its early history in the British Isles, Levison 1946, pp. 117–19, John 1966, pp. 27–35, Nelson 1980. The Irish background, Byrne 1973, pp. 159–60.
pp. **118–19** Coins and trade, Picture Essays 4, 7. Of special importance to my text are: the seminal study of Offa's coinage by Blunt in Dolley (ed.) 1961; the 'compromise' to the dispute on the extent of money and trade between himself and Grierson in Metcalf 1974; the survey of Charlemagne's coinage in Grierson 1965; the argument for a royal coinage before Offa in Rigold 1960 and Metcalf 1977; Lyon 1967 on the question whether Offa was really responsible for the first signed coinage; and Dolley and Morrison 1963 on the exclusion of foreign coin from the later 8th century. Trade and towns: *EHD*, nos. 20, 192 give evidence of Charlemagne's trade embargo; the toll charters are Birch, *Cart.*, nos. 138, 149, 150, 152 (Campbell 1973, no. 2, *EHD*, no. 66), 171 (Robertson 1939, no. 1), 173, 188, 189, plus Sawyer 1968, no. 1788. For other sources on wics and towns, plus an illuminating general discussion, see Biddle 1976b, pp. 112–20; and in general Sawyer 1978a, ch. 6.
pp. **119–22** The dyke: see bibliography on Picture Essay 8. Anglo-Welsh relations, Lloyd 1939, pp. 194–202. The *Danevirke*, Graham-Campbell 1980a, pp. 208–9; the *Karlsgrab*, Hofman 1965. *Widsith* (lines 35–44), Chambers 1912, pp. 202–4. Fortification in general, Brooks 1971; for Tamworth and Hereford, Rahtz 1977.
pp. **122–3** The charters of Beornwulf's 825 council are Birch, *Cart.*, nos. 384 (an 'original' in a Canterbury hand), 386 (Robertson 1939, no. 5), 387.
Worcester estates in general, Dyer 1981, ch. 1. English immunities, Brooks 1971; their judicial dimension (unmodified, in my view, by subsequent criticism), Maitland 1897, pp. 269–79. Aethelmund's Westbury charter is Birch, *Cart.*, no. 274; his death in battle is recorded in *Anglo-Saxon Chronicle*, year 802, p. 183. Deerhurst, Taylor and Taylor 1965, pp. 193–209.
pp. **124–5** The account given here of Canterbury and Wulfred is heavily based on Brooks 1983, especially his brilliant account of the great dispute over the Kentish minsters; I am most grateful to the author for pre-publication sight of it. On almost all matters connected with Canterbury, Brooks supersedes earlier work, which is not therefore referred to here. The professions of faith to Canterbury archbishops are ed. and discussed Richter 1972–3.
Dümmler's 1895 edition of the 786 council is cited here (see above); *EHD*, no. 191 provides a partial translation. The secular decrees of the council are nos. XI–XVI, pp. 23–5; the reference to their being read out *'tam latine quam theotisce'* is on p. 28 (*EHD*, p. 839, and cf. Levison 1946, pp. 126–30). Alfred refers to Offa's laws in his preface, and his laws on nuns and inheritance (c. 8/1, 2, pp. 68–9) may be compared to canon XVI of 786; similarly, Alcuin's remarks (Dümmler 1895, p. 180) about the proper activity of bishops and the just judgements, chastity and fidelity to their lord of great laymen, may be compared to 786, canons III–IV, XIII, XV, XII.
pp. **125–8** Offa's relations with Kentish kings and treatment of Kentish property, Stenton 1918, pp. 58–64, and 1971, pp. 36, 206–10, plus John 1966, pp. 25–6, and Vollrath-Reichelt 1971, pp. 152–79; a comparable Selsey case, Birch, *Cart.*, no. 387. I will return to this subject in a forthcoming paper. *Acta* of the Clovesho council of 803 are recorded in Birch, *Cart.*, nos. 308, 309, 310, 312; Cenwulf is not recorded as present in the last three (all dated 12 October), but he does attest the first (6 October). The relevant canons of Chelsea are nos. IV, V, VII, VIII, pp. 580–3. Brooks 1983 shows that Wulfred or his assistants forged Birch, *Cart.*, nos. 91, 162 (the privileges for the Kentish churches of Wihtred and Aethelbald respectively); cf. fig. 119. As Brooks 1983 shows, the *Anglo-Saxon Chronicle* telescopes the chronology of the dramatic events of 825–9 (*EHD*, pp. 185–6); a more convincing chronology (which there was no reason to invent) is preserved by Roger of Wendover, pp. 413–14.
On the date of *Beowulf* and the possible relevance of the Offa digression see Whitelock 1951, pp. 57–64; Wormald 1978a, pp. 94–5 discusses this and other points, but the papers in Chase 1981 generally favour a later date. On this suggestion my only comment at this stage is that it is somewhat surprising to find a 10th-century work in praise of Danes which is entirely devoid of Danish linguistic influence. For the view that the poem looks back nostalgically on the noble hopelessness of heathen times see Tolkien's fine essay of 1936.

ILLUSTRATIONS (other than those discussed in text, for which see above)
Fig. 97: Wright 1967, Alexander 1978, no. 29. 98: Alexander 1978, no. 52. 99, 100: Taylor and Taylor 1965–78, pp. 503–9, Peers 1927. 103: Kendrick 1938, p. 169; Cramp 1977, pp. 210–11. 104: Williams 1977, pp. 104–7. 105: Wilson 1964, pp. 20–2, and no. 41. 106: Alexander 1978, no. 17, Bailey 1978, plus Bullough's forthcoming study of Alcuin. 107: Kendrick 1938, pp. 140–2. 108–9: Cramp 1977. 110: Okasha 1971, no. 93. 111: Kendrick 1938, pp. 150–2. 112: Hinton 1974, no. 8. 113, 114: Beckwith 1972, pp. 20–2, and no. 3, p. 25, and no. 9. 115: Alexander 1978, no. 21. 117: Sisam 1956–7, Campbell in Wright 1967, pp. 81–90. 120: Wilson 1964, pp. 11–14, and no. 19.

PICTURE ESSAY 7 (pp. 102–3): **Hamwih**
Addyman and Hill 1968, 1969 review all work before 1970. Holdsworth (ed.) 1980 has important contributions by various hands. Cherry and Hodges 1978 review the chronology. See also Hill 1967 and Hinton 1978.

PICTURE ESSAY 8 (pp. 120–1): **Offa's Dyke**
Sources: Asser, c. 14, p. 12.
Secondary: The standard work is Fox 1955; see also Stenton 1971, pp. 212–15. I am most grateful to David Hill for giving me the up-to-date findings of himself and his unit in modification of Fox; because these are by no means complete as yet, their publication cannot be expected for some time, but see meanwhile Hill 1974 and Hill 1977.

PICTURE ESSAY 9 (pp. 130–1): **Anglo-Saxon Coins 2**
Dolley and Blunt in Dolley (ed.) 1961, pp. 77–95. Pagan 1965, pp. 11–27; Blunt 1970, pp. 234–55, 1974, pp. 35–160; Lyon 1968, pp. 216–38, 1970, pp. 193–204.

CHAPTER SIX
The Ninth Century

See bibliography of chapter 4 for Bede, laws and charters, and that of chapter 5 for northern annals, the correspondence of Alcuin, vernacular charters, Welsh annals, and Roger of Wendover. Viking activities in Europe can be followed in *Royal Frankish Annals*, ed. Kurze 1895, in the *Annals of St Bertin*, ed. Grat 1964, and in *Annals of Ulster*, ed. and tr. Hennessy 1887. As stated in the text, no 'saga' can be considered a contemporary witness, but something may be gained atmospherically from *Egils Saga*, tr. Fell and Lucas 1975, and from Snorri Sturlasson's *Heimskringla* (a history of the Norwegian kings), tr. Hollander 1967. The *Historia de Sancto Cuthberto*, a neglected because partly late and legendary account of Northumbria before and during the Viking invasions, is ed. Arnold 1882–5, vol. 1, and partly translated in *EHD*, no. 6; discussion: Craster 1954, Morris 1977. Other than the *Anglo-Saxon Chronicle* (see below), the most important Alfredian source is Asser's *Life of King Alfred*, ed. Stevenson 1959; for discussion see the bibliography in *EHD*, p. 141, plus Brooke 1970, pp. 231–5, and Bullough 1972, pp. 454–5. Alfred's will is Harmer 1914, no. 11 (*EHD*, no. 96). Alfred's *Pastoral Rule* is ed. and tr. Sweet 1871–2; for editions and translations of the other 'Alfredian' translations see Whitelock 1966, pp. 101–2.

Much the most important source for the period is the *Anglo-Saxon Chronicle*, and now that it is for the first time a contemporary source as it stands something must be said of its many problems (by no means all yet resolved). As Plummer 1952 was the first to stress in his standard edition, it should more properly be called the *Anglo-Saxon Chronicles*, since it survives in a series of related but independent texts (see above, pp. 221 ff. for the situation under Edward the Confessor). All texts draw on a common original down to the early 890s, a version of which, the 'A' text, is extant in near contemporary script and language (cf. Picture Essay 11, pp. 158–9). But nearly all texts interpolate information from other sources into this common original; thus the 'northern recension', represented by the 'D' and 'E' texts, has northern material, including its account of the 793 raid, which is not in any other. The great merit of Dorothy Whitelock's translation in *EHD*, no. 1, used throughout this chapter, is that she prints the parallel texts where relevant, so that one may see what was probably in the 890s original, and what was added later. Whitelock also gives a lucid account of these problems, and a full bibliography: *EHD*, pp. 109–25, 139–41. The most difficult and perhaps the most important question is, who was responsible for the original compilation? Most scholars have been unable to resist the temptation to connect it with Alfred: e.g. Plummer 1952, pp. civ–cv, Wallace-Hadrill 1950, pp. 209–11, 214–15, Davis 1971, and Parkes 1976. But Whitelock herself strongly disputes this (*EHD*, pp. 123–4, 140), following Stenton 1925, who preferred to ascribe the enterprise to a West Country nobleman. The arguments are too complex for further discussion here, but two things can be said. First, the *Chronicle* is not in Alfred's own prose style (Bately 1979), but this does not rule out some connection; it is now known that Alfred did not write some other 'Alfredian' translations, with which he nevertheless probably had some connection. Second, even opponents of sponsorship admit the probability of his role in circulating the *Chronicle*, and there is not a lot of difference between commissioning and circulating a text. To this it may be added that, while the *Chronicle* differs in significant ways from the *Royal Frankish Annals*, which were in a sense official, there is no known early medieval parallel to a mere nobleman's commissioning this sort of chronicle on this sort of scale. Among secondary discussions of the period, the best guide remains Stenton 1971, ch. 8, especially for the military side. For the Vikings in general see Gwyn Jones 1968, Loyn 1977, and, among the splendidly illustrated works inspired by the British Museum exhibition of 1980, Graham-Campbell and Kidd 1980 (the exhibition catalogue) and Graham-Campbell 1980a; Bailey 1980 is an excellent discussion of Viking Age sculpture which is also of considerable general importance. The most important modern discussion of the Vikings is Sawyer 1971; see also Sawyer 1969 for a sample of the controversy he aroused, plus Sawyer 1978b and 1982 for his new approach, which should culminate in another full-length book. Wormald 1982 takes issue with many aspects of the original Sawyer thesis, and what is written here is essentially a digest of my conclusions. Plummer 1902, and Lees 1915 are still good biographies of Alfred; Whitelock's forthcoming study in the Eyre Methuen series on English monarchs should provide a definitive statement of the traditional view of the king. See also Wallace-Hadrill 1950, and 1971, ch. 6, on Alfred's kingship and its background.

pp. 132–5 See below for bibliography on the themes adumbrated here and more fully developed later. The translation of St Cuthbert's relics to Norham, *Historia de Sancto Cuthberto*, p. 201, Rollason 1978, p. 68. Kentish charters relating to early Viking incursions in Kent, Brooks 1971, pp. 79–80.

p. 135 East Anglian coinage, Blunt *et al.* 1963, pp. 25–30; pottery, Hurst 1976, pp. 299–307. The radical and interesting revision of 9th-century Northumbrian chronology proposed on numismatic grounds by Pagan 1969 has not been accepted by numismatists or historians and is not followed here. Northumbrian coinage in general, Lyon 1956; the robbery of St Cuthbert's lands, *Historia de Sancto Cuthberto*, pp. 201–2.

pp. 138–40 The Welsh campaign of 853, Lloyd 1939, p. 325. Ceolwulf's charter, Birch, *Cart.*, no. 540. On the relevance of royal cults see forthcoming articles by David Rollason (in *Anglo-Saxon England*, 11, 1982), and Alan Thacker. For the Mercian coinage see Blunt *et al.* 1963, Pagan 1965.

Egbert's seizure of Mercia, Blunt *et al.* 1963, p. 34, Dumville 1977, p. 100. There is a seminal discussion of the Council of Kingston in Brooks 1983. Aethelwulf's arrangements for the succession, John 1966, pp. 37–44, Dumville 1979, pp. 21–4. Aethelbald's rebellion, Asser, c. 12, pp. 9–10, Stafford 1979, p. 89.

9th-century Kent, Brooks 1983; Badanoth's will is ed. and tr. Campbell 1938; see also Harmer 1914, nos. 2, 4, 5, 6, 7, 8, 10 for other transactions by the Kentish aristocracy. The decimation of Aethelwulf, Stevenson 1959, pp. 186–91, Finberg 1964a, pp. 187–213. Abingdon charters, Stenton 1913, pp. 25–7.

pp. 141–2 Alfred's munificence, *EHD*, p. 536, Asser, c. 91, p. 77, cc. 99–100, pp. 85–7. Coinage of Aethelwulf and Alfred, Dolley and Skaare, and Dolley and Blunt respectively, in Dolley 1961, pp. 63–95, and on Alfred's heavy penny, Lyon 1976, pp. 183–90. Egbert's Welsh victories, Roger of Wendover, p. 409. Pope John VIII's letter to Archbishop Aethelred, *EHD*, no. 222. Aethelwulf's marriage, *Annals of St Bertin*, p. 73, Asser, c. 13, p. 11, c. 17, p. 16 and Stafford 1979, pp. 85–6.

Status of the Worcester peasants, Dyer 1981, p. 34; Alfredian use of *ceorl*, Finberg 1964b, pp. 144–7; Alfred on lordship, laws of Alfred c. 37, pp. 80–1, with which cf. laws of Ine, c. 39, pp. 48–9: the penalty for desertion of a lord is increased and enforced by royal officers.

pp. 143–4 Canterbury charters before 850, Brooks 1983; probably Canterbury illuminated manuscripts of the same period, see figs. 122, 124 (I am also grateful to Dr M. Budney for advice on the Royal Bible, of which she is preparing a study). The Wirksworth slab, Cramp 1977, pp. 218–25; its possible connections with Cynewulf, Clemoes 1971, pp. 293–304; Cynewulf's other work, Sisam 1932.

pp. 144–5 Apart from the evidence in Frankish, Irish and English annals (see above) for early Viking attacks, see also Dümmler 1895, p. 309 for Alcuin's anxiety in 799, and Dümmler 1895, nos. 16–17 (*EHD*, nos. 193–4) for famous examples of his reaction to the sack of Lindisfarne. The saga of St Philibert's relics, Bloch 1961, p. 20; Irish coin-hoards, Dolley 1966, p. 20; Shetland and Orkney, Wainwright 1964, pp. 126–40, Graham-Campbell 1980a, pp. 68–9. The concentration of Viking attacks on England in the 860s, Hill 1981, pp. 33–4; the Croydon hoard, Thompson 1956, no. 111, and a forthcoming paper by Nicholas Brooks and James Graham-Campbell. Ivarr, Healfdene and the former's descendants, Smyth 1975, 1977, 1979; this thesis has attracted severe criticism (e.g. O'Corrain 1979), but Wormald 1982 attempts to justify its basic elements. It should be noted that the *Anglo-Saxon Chronicle* at this period seems to have begun its year in September; thus, the martyrdom of King Edmund, which it dates to 870, actually happened in late 869, and is

accordingly dated in my text: see Whitelock's note in Plummer 1952, pp. cxl–cxli, and Smyth 1977, pp. 170–1.
p. **147** This view of the Vikings is put by Sawyer 1971, *passim*, and is general in modern literature on the subject. For trade see also Blindheim 1978. On numbers, Brooks 1979 is a powerful counter-blast to Sawyer's views. The reality of Viking destruction in Francia (and elsewhere), Wallace-Hadrill 1974. The evidence of English episcopal lists is in O'Donovan 1972–3, and for Normandy see Musset 1965, pp. 218–22. The fullest (somewhat legendary) account of the flight of St Cuthbert's community is in Symeon's *Historia Dunelmensis Ecclesiae*, ed. Arnold 1882–5, vol. 1, pp. 56–69, but *Historia de Sancto Cuthberto*, pp. 207–8, has its essential elements.
Cultural collapse in Kent, Brooks 1979, pp. 14–16; for a less pessimistic view, not available to me when this chapter was written, see a forthcoming paper by Jennifer Morrish.
Gneuss 1980 list *c.* 950 manuscripts written or owned in England before 1100. A *very rough* calculation indicates that *c.* 130 may be prior to the Alfredian revival, but *c.* 60 of these survive on the Continent and raise the possibility that they were taken there in the 8th century; of the 774 in English libraries only *c.* 70 may have been written and/or preserved in England before 850. Half of these are Northumbrian and probably bound up with the precarious survival of Lindisfarne and perhaps York; of the other half, *c.* 10 seem to have survived at Canterbury, and *c.* 5 at Winchester and Worcester respectively, leaving *c.* 15 (2%) to be possibly assigned to other S. English *scriptoria*, none of them known to have been in the Danelaw.
pp. **148–9** Viking paganism, Fell's contribution to Graham-Campbell 1980a, pp. 172–93. Sculpture, Bailey 1980. The 'blood-eagle', Smyth 1977, pp. 189–94, 209–23. Abbo's *Passio* of St Edmund is ed. Winterbottom 1972. The positive side of the Vikings is well put by Graham-Campbell 1980a. Replacement charters, Sawyer 1979, pp. 4–5.
pp. **149–50** On the contrasting campaigns of the 870s and 890s see Hill 1981, pp. 40–1. Later Anglo-Saxon military and naval organization, Hollister 1962, pp. 38–58, 103–15; the Carolingian army, Ganshof 1968, pp. 59–68; Charlemagne's fleet, Holder-Egger (ed.) 1911, p. 21.
pp. **154–5** *Burhs*, see bibliography to Picture Essay 10; for the administrative implications, Brooks 1979, pp. 17–20, and for Continental parallels, Vercauteren 1936, and Jäschke 1975. Pippin of Acquitaine, *Annals of St Bertin*, pp. 74, 105, 113, and for the Irish evidence, Hughes 1966, pp. 203–5, and Smyth 1977, pp. 129–53.
Aethelwold's rebellion, *EHD*, pp. 207–9. Charlemagne and the oath, Ganshof 1971, pp. 111–24; later English legal evidence, laws of Edward, II, c. 5, pp. 120–1, and laws of Edmund, III, c. 1, pp. 12–13. Aethelred's grants to Wulfhere, Birch, *Cart.*, nos. 508, 886.
Charters giving Alfred's titles, Birch, *Cart.*, nos. 561, 564, 565, 567, 568, 581; Alfred's charters in general, Whitelock 1978. Coinage, Dolley 1961, p. 81. Alfred's treaty with Guthrum, *EHD*, no. 34, and on its interpretation, Stenton 1971, pp. 260–2. Alfred's posthumous reputation in the north, *Historia de Sancto Cuthberto*, pp. 204–7, 210–11.
pp. **156–7** Alfred's choice of Worcester scholars, Stenton 1971, pp. 270–1. Welsh manuscripts that may or may not be part of Asser's background, Lindsay 1912, nos. 2, 4, 6, 7; Asser's Latin, Stevenson 1959, pp. xci–xcv. John the Old Saxon, Raw 1976 (though without specific reference to John), and Lapidge 1980, pp. 72–83; Grimbald, *EHD*, no. 223, Grierson 1940, and Parkes 1976. The view of Alfred's educational ideals taken here was originally expounded in Wormald 1977b. For the manuscripts see Picture Essay 11, and on Alfred's prefatory letter see Shippey 1979, and Morrish forthcoming. For a sound survey of Alfredian literature see Whitelock 1966, and for the identification of Alfred's 'own work', Bately 1970. The best discussion of an Alfredian translation is Otten 1964 (on the Boethius); see also the contributions by M. Godden and M. B. Parkes in M. T. Gibson (ed.) 1981; in general see Wallace-Hadrill 1971, pp. 141–8. Alfred's reference to Nebuchadnezzar is Sweet 1871, pp. 38–9; cf. Gregory's original in *Patrologia Latina*, vol. 77, col. 18.
The Alfred Jewel, Hinton 1974, no. 23, and Howlett 1975. Alfred and the judges, cf. Asser c. 106, pp. 92–5, with c. 24, p. 21, c. 76, pp. 60–2. Only Liebermann 1903–16 prints Alfred's law-book in the form transmitted by all the manuscripts; for a fuller discussion see my forthcoming *Kingship and the Making of Law in Anglo-Saxon England.*

ILLUSTRATIONS
Fig. 122: Alexander 1978, no. 32. 123: Wilson 1964, pp. 80–1, and no. 18; Okasha 1971, no. 38. 124: Alexander 1978, no. 30. 125: For the Minster Lovell jewel, Hinton 1974, no. 22; for the Alfred Jewel see above. 126: Wilson 1964, pp. 30 1, 91 8, and no. 153. 127: Bailey 1974, pp. 141–50. 128, 129: Wilson 1964, pp. 22–3, 82, and nos. 1, 31; Okasha 1971, nos. 70, 107. 130: Alexander 1978, no. 66; Dumville 1972. 131, 132: Wilson 1964, pp. 24–7, and nos. 90, 94, 95. 133: Wilson 1964, p. 35, n. 1. 134: Alexander 1978, no. 41, and cf. Mayr-Harting 1972, pp. 187–9. 135: Alexander 1978, no. 33. 137: Gotland picture stone: Graham-Campbell 1980b, no. 479. 138: Graham-Campbell 1980b, no. 301; Lyon and Stewart in Dolley (ed.) 1961. 139: Wilson 1964, p. 13; Graham-Campbell 1980b, no. 309. 140: McGrail in Graham-Campbell 1980a, pp. 38–63. 141: Graham-Campbell 1980a, pp. 120–1. 143: Wilson 1964, no. 66. 144: Hinton 1974, no. 1.

PICTURE ESSAY 10 (pp. 152–3): **The Burhs**
Asser, c. 91, p. 77; *Anglo-Saxon Chronicle*, year 892, in *EHD*, p. 201; *William of Malmesbury, Gesta Pontificum*, ed. Hamilton (1870), p. 186. Later *burh* building, *Anglo-Saxon Chronicle* from year 911 (*EHD*, pp. 211 ff.). Legislation, laws of Edward, I, c. 1-1, pp. 114–15, laws of Aethelstan, II, c. 12, pp. 134–5, IV, c. 2, pp. 146–7. The transcript text of the Burghal Hidage is ed. and tr. Robertson 1939, pp. 246–9, but it is best to refer to the textual discussion in Hill 1969. For the Continental parallel see Widukind, I. xxxv, pp. 48–9.
Secondary: Stenton 1971, pp. 264–5 is good on the *burhs*, but modern work really began with Brooks 1964, and Hill 1969. The seminal article is Biddle and Hill 1971, further developed in Biddle 1976b, pp. 124–34. See also Ralegh Radford 1970, and on the growth of towns in general, Sawyer 1978a, ch. 6.

PICTURE ESSAY 11 (pp. 158–9): **Alfredian Manuscripts**
The manuscripts discussed here are Ker 1959, nos. 39, 133, 195, 324. Full facsimiles: of the 'Parker Chronicle', Flower and Smith 1941; of the Helmingham Orosius, Campbell 1953; of the Oxford *Pastoral Rule*, Ker 1956. The Rochester charter is no. 24 in Campbell 1973, and discussed by him (somewhat inconsistently) on pp. xiv, xxiv; but see also Brooks 1969, pp. 147–50. On the general Kentish situation see Brooks 1979, pp. 14–16. On the publication of Alfred's translations, with particular reference to the *Pastoral Rule*, see Sisam 1953b, pp. 140–7; on Winchester connections, Wormald 1945, pp. 118–19, and Parkes 1976, *passim.*

CHAPTER SEVEN
The Age of Edgar

The best general work on the late Old English period is Stenton 1971. The *Chronicle*, trans. *EHD* 1 and *EHD* 2 remains a major source; see notes to ch. 6. The laws are translated Robertson 1925, the wills Whitelock 1930 and some of the charters *EHD* 1, *EHD* 2 and Robertson 1939.

pp. **160–1** *ASC* D, E for 975; *EHD* 1, p. 228; on the marriages of Aethelstan's half-sisters, Stenton 1971, pp. 339–40, 344–7. *ASC* for 886: *EHD* 1, p. 199.
Welsh submission to Edward; *ASC* A for 921, *EHD* 1, p. 216. Post-Conquest sources on the Danelaw: Chadwick 1905, pp. 198–201. East Anglia possibly not being part of the Danelaw: Davis 1955, see also Picture Essay 12.
pp. **164–8** The standard account of Aethelstan's reign, followed here, is Stenton 1971, pp. 339–56. Brunanburh: Campbell 1938. West Saxon rule in the North: Whitelock 1959. The use of 'earl'; Chadwick 1905, pp. 161 ff.
Florence on Edgar's navy, Thorpe (ed.) 1848, pp. 143–4. Henry the Fowler and the ending of the partible inheritance of the German crown: Fleckenstein 1978, p. 114. Henry's fortifications: Fleckenstein, pp. 132–5, is conservative; Baaken 1961 is important, but cannot be followed all the way. Mid-10th-century Carolingians and Capetians: Lot 1970, pp. 435 ff. St Ursula and Cologne: Levison 1928. Duckett 1955, p. 36 provides

an English summary of the argument.
pp. 168–72 The traditional view of Anglo-Saxon England as a *ceorl*-centred society is most fully worked out in Stenton 1971; see above, p. 59. For the wealth of some Anglo-Saxon magnates see the wills ed. Whitelock 1930. One such, that of Wulfric Spot, is discussed in Sawyer 1979. The ceorl as slave owner: Stenton 1971, p. 314. The bonds of lordship: John 1966, pp. 128–153. Edmund's fealty oath, III Edmund 1. King Sigeberht: *ASC* s.a. 755; the misfortunes of the Godwines: below, chapter 9. The meeting of the *witan*, see map in Stenton 1971, p. 350. For what follows, Campbell 1975a. 12th-century peripatetic government, Jolliffe 1966, pp. 139 ff.
pp. 172–3 The main source for the history of Aethelstan Half-King and his family is the *Vita Oswaldi*, Raine 1879; valuable comments, Hart 1973. The political nomenclature of East Anglia: the first life of Oswald, Raine 1879, *passim*. The author of this life is thought to be the Ramsey monk Byrhtferth. The disappearance of Aethelstan Half-King's family, Hart 1973. The military function of the hundred: John 1960, p. 115. Aethelweard's Chronicle, Campbell 1962, p. 28, reads: '. . . and there Ealdorman Weohstan met him with hundreds of the people of Wiltshire.' The shipfyrd is discussed: John 1960, p. 115.
Florence on Edgar's navy, ed. Thorpe 1848, pp. 143 4. 'Laws of Henry I', Downer 1972, pp. 96–7. The bishop of Sherborne's letter: Harmer 1952, no. 63. In her commentary, p. 483, Dr Harmer first elucidated the significance of *scypscot*. *Archiductor*: Birch, *Cart.*, no. 1136: *semper illius archiductoris dominatui et voluntati qui episcopatui presidet*, 'always at the will and command of that *archiductor* who rules the diocese'. *Archidux*: Ruotger's Life of Bruno, c. 20, ed. Ott 1951, p. 19. Maitland 1897, '. . . they (the Oswaldslow thegns) will follow the banner of St. Mary of Worcester'. On Edgar's naval activities see the early 12th-century letter from a Worcester monk (Stubbs (ed.) 1874, p. 422) claiming that Edgar regularly circumnavigated Britain and that his power extended to Dublin. This information is presumably connected with but not entirely dependent on the Oswaldslow charter.
Law as status-symbol: Wormald 1977, pp. 105–38. Outlawing of feud: II Edmund 7 and also V Aethelred 9/1 on rewards for celibate priests. The 5 hide unit and thegnly status: *Of People's Ranks and Laws*, in Stubbs (ed.) 1913, p. 88. Anglo-Saxon coins: see Picture Essay 17.
pp. 176–7 Keynes 1980 is for the existence of a chancery, Chaplais in Ranger (ed.) 1973 is not. John 1966, pp. 181–209, defends the authenticity of some eccentric documents, which Keynes, pp. 98 ff., prefers to reject. I am unconvinced but agree that the problem needs more airing. *Burh* and *port*, see Loyn in Clemoes and Hughes (ed.) 1971.
Laws of Aethelstan, Attenborough (ed.) 1922.
pp. 180–1 The *Chronicle*'s comment on London for 1097: *EHD* 2, p. 182. Henry the Fowler's *Burgen*: Erdmann 1941–3, who cites the sources *in extenso*; Baaken 1961, and Leyser 1968. The *Ordinance of the Hundred* is ed. Robertson 1925. Scalping slaves: III Edmund 4. Archbishop Wulfstan's *Sermo Lupi* complains of thralls joining the Vikings; trans. *EHD* 1, pp. 929–34.
pp. 181–5 For the 10th-century Reformation the best summary of work on the liturgical and spiritual side is Duckett 1955. John 1966 is a collection of studies on political and economic aspects; see also John 1964–5 and 1965. Parsons 1975 is interesting. On reformed monasticism generally, see especially Hallinger 1950–1; also Tellenbach 1959.
Columba and Iona: Anderson and Anderson 1961, pp. 90 ff. Alcuin: the opening of his life of St Willibrord, ed. Krusch and Levison 1919, p. 116, tr. Talbot 1954, p. 3. Oswald's early career: the first life, ed. Raine 1879, p. 411.
St Benedict's intentions: Vogüé 1961. The reform of Christ Church Canterbury: Birch, *Cart.*, nos. 342 and 402. Alcuin's letter: ed. Dümmler 1895, no. 19. Odo's intentions: John of Salerno's *Life*, iii.9, conveniently in Sitwell 1968, p. 81. Debauchery amongst the clergy: Weigle (ed.) 1949, *passim*, and Petrus Damiani, *Liber Gomorrhianus*, Migne (ed.) 1853, vol. ii, cols. 159–90. This must be the most detailed account of perverse sexual practices before Kraft-Ebbing. It is impossible to suppose that Peter Damian had personal experience of his subject-matter; it looks as though he was drawing on his experience of the confessional.
pp. 185–9 For most of these details: Armitage Robinson 1923 and Duckett 1955. Aethelwold and Abingdon: especially Stenton 1913. No one disputes that Aethelwold 'converted' Winchester to monasticism, but there is controversy about what Oswald did, if anything, at Worcester; cf. John 1966, pp. 234–48 and Sawyer, in Parsons (ed.) 1975, pp. 84–93.
The new episcopate: Barlow 1963. On Edgar's coronation cf. John 1966, pp. 276–89 and Nelson 1977b. The Dunstan *Ordo*: Schramm (ed.) 1937, and Bouman 1957. I have not seen Kleinschmidt 1979, which has a substantial amount on Edgar's coronation. Edgar's 'durbar' at Chester: Florence of Worcester, ed. Thorpe 1848, p. 142 and Aelfric, *Lives of the Saints*, ed. Skeat 1881, p. 469.
Edgar as Good Shepherd: *Regularis Concordia*, ed. Symons 1953, p. 2. The Anglo-Saxon empire: Drögereit 1952, pp. 58–71, summarized by Loyn 1955, and criticized by John 1960, pp. 95–8, and cf. the remarkable discussion in Erdmann 1951.

ILLUSTRATIONS
Fig. 145: Taylor and Taylor 1965–78, pp. 52–7. 146: Bailey 1980, pp. 85–100. 147: Wilson 1964, no. 64. 149, 154: Temple 1976, no. 5. 150: Royal Commission on Historical Monuments 1972, p. 16. 151, 152: Taylor and Taylor 1965–78, pp. 94–6. 153: Battiscombe 1956, pp. 379–432. 156: Temple 1976, no. 13. 157, 159: Wilson 1964, nos. 56, 10. 158: Temple 1976, no. 23. 160: Beckwith 1972, no. 20. 162: Rahtz 1979. 163, 164, 165, 166: Temple, nos. 11, 16 (also Birch, *Cart.*, no. 1190), 100, 23. 167: Okasha 1971. 168, 169: Temple, nos. 68, 66.

PICTURE ESSAY 12 (pp. 162–3): **Scandinavian Settlements**
Sources: *ASC*, years 876, 877, 880, *EHD*, pp. 195–6; laws of Aethelred III, pp. 64–71 (and for discussion, Wormald 1978b, pp. 61–2). For the archaeology and art see Wilson 1967, 1968, 1976, pp. 393–403; Evison 1969, pp. 336–41; Bailey 1980.
Secondary: The basic statement was Stenton 1927, redeveloped in Stenton 1971, pp. 502–25. The first critique was Davis 1955, developed by Sawyer 1958 and amplified in Sawyer 1971, pp. 149–76. Sawyer's views are themselves criticized in Sawyer 1969, Fellows-Jensen 1975 and Wormald 1982, and are modified in Sawyer 1981.

PICTURE ESSAY 13 (pp. 166–7): **Anglo-Scandinavian York**
Hall 1978, 1980; MacGregor 1982.

PICTURE ESSAY 14 (pp. 170–1): **Late Anglo-Saxon England and the Continent**
Edgar's coronation, Nelson 1977, pp. 67–70; Henry II's prohibition, Thietmar, ed. Holtzmann, pp. 306–8; Aethelred's laws: V Aethelred 2; *Regularis Concordia*, ed. Symons 1953, p. 3; Irish merchants, *Liber Eliensis*, ed. Blake 1962, p. 107; IV Aethelred, Robertson 1925, pp. 72–3. Illustrations; Temple 1976, nos. 32, 42, 64, 105; Lasko 1972, p. 125.

PICTURE ESSAY 15 (pp. 174–5): **Norwich and Winchester**
Campbell 1975, Carter 1978 (from whom the map is taken), Biddle 1975, 1976a. For the spoon see Collis and Kølbye-Biddle 1979.

CHAPTER EIGHT
The Return of the Vikings

In addition to the general works and collections of sources bearing on the late Anglo-Saxon period, and already mentioned, Hill (ed.) 1978 and Keynes 1980 are specially useful for Aethelred II's reign. Larson 1912 is the most recent published monograph in English on Cnut.

pp. 192–3 See generally Fisher 1952. Byrhtferth as author of the *Vita Oswaldi*: Crawford 1929; Lapidge 1975; and on Byrhtferth in general, Hart 1972; Raine 1879, p. 448. The *Vita Oswaldi* is the major source here. The *Liber Eliensis*: ed. Blake 1962, pp. ix–xii; John 1966, pp. 271–5. Oswald's family: Hart 1964, p. 61. Wicklow: John 1966, pp. 210–34. The sources are reticent about the murder of Edward: *ASC* E for 979; Raine (ed.) 1879, vol. i, p. 450, and Wulfstan, *Sermon of the Wolf to the English*, *EHD* 1, p. 931. However, it seems reasonable to interpret Aelfhere's translation of the body in 980 as expiation, *ASC* E for 980; especially in light of the *Vita Oswaldi*, ed. Raine 1879, p. 451, which implies a penitential flavour. This source suggests that the murder may have been done by Aelfhere's minions rather than Aelfhere himself.

p. 193 Authorship of the *Chronicle*: Keynes 1978; for its style, Clark 1971.
p. 194 The Jomsviking Saga, ed. N. F. Blake 1962. In John 1977, p. 176, n. 15, I was ignorant of Dr Blake's excellent edition. For relevant passages with other saga material relating to the Jomsvikings, Ashdown (ed.) 1930; see also Napier and Stevenson 1895, pp. 139–42.
The 'treaty' text is ed. Stubbs 1874, pp. 397–8; and see John 1977, p. 189. On Aethelred's invasion of Normandy, William of Jumièges, ed. Marx 1914, pp. 76–7; on his marriage, *ASC* for 1002.
pp. 197–8 For the battles of Maldon, see John 1977, pp. 173–95. On the MS of the *Vita Oswaldi*, John 1966, p. 290; Lapidge 1979, pp. 331 ff.; Lapidge 1975, p. 91. The poem is ed. Gordon 1937 and trans. Ashdown 1930; *EHD* I. For the MS see Gordon 1937, pp. 30–3. For Byrhtnoth's family and Barking, Whitelock 1930, no. xv. For Olaf Tryggvason at Maldon, John 1977, p. 175, n. 13. Recent work on Maldon includes Petty and Petty 1976, on the site; Gneuss 1976, and Blake 1978. Dr Blake's thesis that the poem has little historical value leaves me unconvinced. I hope to take the matter up elsewhere. For Sweyn's coming, *ASC* for 994.
pp. 199 The treachery of the ealdorman of Hampshire: *ASC* for 992. Wulfnoth: *ASC* for 1009; that he was father of Earl Godwine, *ASC* F for 1009, and Whitelock 1930, p. 171. Olaf and Aethelred: *ASC* for 994. Thorkell: John 1980, pp. 65 ff.; and *ASC* C for 1009, 'there came at once after Lammas the immense raiding army which we called Thorkell's army.' The murder of St Aelfheah: *ASC* for 1012, and Thietmar, ed. Holtzmann 1935, pp. 448–450. Thorkell's unpopularity, Sweyn's victory and Aethelred's plight, *ASC* for 1013.
On Aethelred's return, *ASC* for 1014. Cnut and Thorkell: John 1980, pp. 65 ff. Edmund's marriage: Sawyer 1979, pp. xxii–xxiii. Uhtred: *ASC* for 1016 and Duncan 1976, who argues that Uhtred was killed in 1018. Appointment of Earl Eric: *ASC* for 1016, and the full account of his career, Napier and Stevenson (ed.) 1895, pp. 142–8. The sagas say he died from natural causes after a pilgrimage to Rome. The best source for Cnut's 1016 campaign is the *Encomium* of Queen Emma, ed. Campbell 1949, bk. ii; and cf. Campbell's discussion, pp. liii–lxi, and John 1980, pp. 70–6. For the death of Aethelred and for Ashingdon, *ASC* for 1016. The aftermath of Ashingdon: Campbell (ed.) 1949, bk, ii.
pp. 200–1 For Aethelred's legislation see Robertson 1925, and the important discussion of Wormald 1978, pp. 47–80. On Wulfstan, see especially Jost 1950; Bethurum 1957. Their Wulfstan canon is rejected Hohler 1975. Without accepting all Mr Hohler's arguments, I agree that rather more reserve in attributing anonymous works to Wulfstan would certainly be welcome.
On the geld, Harmer 1952, pp. 439–40. Origins of the office of sheriff: Morris 1927 is essential though in many ways out of date. For what follows on Aethelred's government, see Campbell 1975a; *Burh* and government: Metcalf in Hill (ed.) 1978, pp. 159–212, and Hill in Hill (ed.) 1978, pp. 213–26, and Loyn in Clemoes and Hughes (ed.) 1971, pp. 115–28. Aethelred and the jury: the authoritative account is Hurnard 1941. For IV Aethelred see Wormald, in Hill (ed.) 1978, p. 62.
pp. 201–3 The principal editions of Aelfric's works are those of Thorpe (1844), Skeat (1881), Pope (1967) and Godden (1979). The definition of monasticism is from John of Salerno's *Life* of St Odo of Cluny, ed. Sitwell 1968, p. 81. On Wulfstan's career see the works cited above and Whitelock 1942. Abbo was at Ramsey for almost two years, 986–8, Duckett 1955, pp. 212 ff. Abbo as canonist, Fournier and Le Bras 1931, pp. 320–30. Importance of Visigothic legislation: Ewig, in Kempf *et al.* 1969. St Benedict's notions as to suitable reading matter: *Regula*, cap. xlii, e.g. most conveniently in McCann (ed.) 1952. Aelfric's life of St Mary of Egypt is in Skeat (ed.) 1881, ii, pp. 2–53. Skeat thought it was not by Aelfric. The problems are discussed by Clemoes in Clemoes (ed.), 1959, p. 219, n. 2. Nonetheless the life expresses the Aelfrician ideology. Hincmar of Rheims's ideology, see Nelson 1977a.
pp. 206–7 The 'new' theology of the Atonement, Southern 1963, cap. 3. The life of St Martin: Skeat (ed.), 1881, no. xxxi. The original story is found in Fontaine (ed.), 1967, i, p. 307. The history of the crucifix: Thoby 1959 and Bloch and Schnitzler 1969, ii, pp. 118–21: Thoby seems to be wrong in maintaining that Ottonian, unlike English crucifixes, do not show Jesus as dead; see Bloch and Schnitzler 1969, i, p. 99, the Gero crucifix at Cologne and especially the late 10th-century ivory at Munich. Holzmann 1943, plate 19. Abbo's *Life* of Edmund is now available in a good modern edition, M. Winterbottom 1972, pp. 67–87. Aelfric's version was ed. by G. I. Needham 1966, pp. 43–59, and trans. Skeat (ed.) 1881, no. xxxii. *The Sermon of the Wolf to the English* is trans. in *EHD* I. Aethelweard, see A. Campbell 1962.
pp. 207–13 Cnut and Emma: Campbell (ed.) 1949, pp. 33–5: Cnut's brother: Campbell (ed.), 1949, pp. lv–lvii and John 1980, p. 65, n. 2.
Cnut's writ is easily accessible in Stubbs (ed.), 1913, pp. 90–2. *ASC* for 1017: 'In this year King Cnut succeeded to the whole realm of England, and divided it into four parts. . . .' Leofric, see John 1979, pp. 243–4.

ILLUSTRATIONS
Fig. 170: Wilson 1964, no. 60. 171: Hinton 1974, nos. 25, 26. 172: Okasha 1971, no. 58. 174: Graham-Campbell 1980b, no. 283. 175: Jansson 1966. 176: Sawyer 1968, no. 884. 177: Wilson 1964, p. 6. 178, 181: Talbot Rice 1952, pp. 82–3, 231–3. 179, 180, 182: Temple 1976, nos. 63, 41, 78. 183: Graham-Campbell 1980b, no. 499; Bailey 1980, p. 26. 184, 185, 187: Temple 1976, nos. 47, 24, 58.

PICTURE ESSAY 16 (pp. 196–7): **Anglo-Saxon Ivories**
Beckwith 1972. See also fig. 68 and p. 103, no. 3. See Myres and Green 1973, pp. 84–5 for early bone caskets. For pre-Reformation losses of Anglo-Saxon art see Dodwell 1973.

PICTURE ESSAY 17 (pp. 204–5): **Anglo-Saxon Coins 3**
Dolley 1964; Galster 1964–75; Lyon 1976, pp. 173–224; Metcalf in Hill (ed.) 1978, pp. 159–212; Smart 1968, pp. 191–276.

CHAPTER NINE

The End of Anglo-Saxon England

The period covered in this chapter is dealt with in Stenton 1971. Brown 1969 is interesting, although dismissive of the Old English state. Matthew 1966 is important and independent. Barlow 1965 is a short, compressed account of importance. Barlow 1970 offers an alternative view of the Confessor's reign. Barlow 1963 is a standard account of the Church, and Barlow 1955, although its author later changed his mind on some points, is valuable for setting the reign in context.

pp. 214–16 Stenton 1971, pp. 401–7, for Scandinavian affairs. Emma of Normandy: Campbell (ed.) 1949, pp. xl–l; John 1980. Aelfgifu: Stenton 1971, pp. 397, 405–6, 420–1; Sawyer 1979, p. xliii. Harthacnut's succession: John 1980, p. 64.
Duke Robert's expedition: Marx 1914, pp. 109–11. The charter is in Fauroux 1961, no. 76, and cf. John 1980, p. 83, n. 5 for the evidence that Edward assumed the title of king about this time.
Aelfgifu's connection with Leofric's family: the discussion of Wulfric Spot's will in Sawyer 1979. The statistics about incomes are from Barlow 1970, p. 74. For Cnut's letter of 1027, Robertson 1925, pp. 146–153. For Emma's letter of summons and Alfred's murder, *Encomium*, ed. A. Campbell 1949, pp. 40–7.
pp. 220–1 That Edward never forgave Godwine is suggested by the fact that at the point at which he had the upper hand, in 1051, he raised the old charge and clearly intended to kill Godwine, Barlow 1962, pp. 20–3.
Harthacnut and Edward: *Encomium*, p. 52, *ASC* C for 1041. Edward's celibacy: John 1979, p. 248. Harthacnut's death: Körner 1964, p. 73. The writs are ed. Harmer 1952. Norman charters before 1066: Fauroux 1961. William of Jumièges: Marx 1914; William of Poitiers, Foreville 1952; *Vita Edwardi*, ed. Barlow 1962. Edward's cult: John 1979.
pp. 221–3 Provenance of the E text for the Confessor's reign: Plummer 1899, pp. xlv, xlix ff.; Levison 1946, p. 201, and Clark 1970, pp. xxi, xxiv. Whitelock 1961 summarizes the then state of affairs on *Chronicle* studies. The provenance of the D text: Whitelock 1961, pp. xv–xvi; John 1964, p. 102, n. 1.
Florence of Worcester, ed. Thorpe 1848. The exile and restoration of Aelfgar: *ASC*, especially D, for 1058, and Stenton 1971, pp.

574–6. This business shows how dangerous it is to rely on the silence of any *Chronicle* version. D has: 'In this year Aelfgar was banished but came forthwith by violence through Griffith's help. And a naval force came from Norway. It is tedious to relate fully how things went.' E never mentions the matter. Using the Welsh and Irish annals Sir Frank Stenton was able to show that the campaign was a major assault on the English and caused much damage; Stenton 1971, p. 575. For the *Bayeux Tapestry*, Stenton 1965, supplemented by Brooks and Walker 1979, pp. 1–34.
pp. **224–9** The Canterbury election, Barlow 1962, p. 18.
The quotations: *ASC* D for 1051 and 1052 and the *Vita Edwardi*, Barlow 1962, p. 53. For the crisis: Douglas 1953; Oleson 1957; John 1979.
Eustace of Boulogne: Brown 1969, p. 123. Dover Castle and the Dover *burh*: Brown 1976, p. 46.
Stigand and the Norman succession: Foreville 1952, pp. 174–6; Barlow 1970, p. 107, n. 2 and John 1979, pp. 255–6.
Ealdred and Harold's escape: *ASC* D for 1051. Ealdred's career: Barlow 1963.
pp. **229–31** Wulfstan II: Barlow 1963 and Darlington 1928, introduction. Apollonius of Tyre: Goolden 1958.
The intellectual grasp of the *Chronicle*: Clark 1971, pp. 215–236. The English bishops of the reign: Barlow 1963. I have followed the English tradition of accepting Florence of Worcester's authority for Harold's coronation by Ealdred, Thorpe (ed.) 1848, p. 224. William of Poitiers, Orderic Vitalis and the Bayeux Tapestry say that Stigand officiated. Barlow 1963, p. 60, n. 4, and Brown 1969, p. 134, n. 129, argue powerfully that the Norman sources should be believed. Regenbald: Campbell 1979b, p. 131; and Round 1909, pp. 421–30.
pp. **231–3** The return of Edward the Aetheling: Oleson 1957, p. 225; and John 1979, p. 257. Harold's negotiations: Barlow 1962, p. 33; Freeman 1877, ii, app.EE. Northumbrian revolt: Barlow 1962, pp. 50 ff., discussed in Barlow 1970, pp. 233–239. Harold's visit to William: the view taken here is defended: John 1979. Brooks and Walker 1979, pp. 10–11, suggest, on the basis of the Bayeux Tapestry and Eadmer's *Historia Novorum*, that Harold really went to Normandy to reclaim his brother and nephew, who were being held hostage there. I disagree, and hope to deal with the matter at length elsewhere. Stenton's chronology: Stenton 1971, p. 578. The terms of the 'treaty' Harold made with William: William of Poitiers, ed. Foreville 1952, p. 104. Edward's deathbed: Barlow 1962, pp. 74 ff.; John 1979, pp. 264–7. William of Poitiers' account of Hastings, Foreville (ed.) 1952, pp. 183–205.
pp. **233–7** On the Queen's views, Foreville (ed.) 1952, p. 168. English activities in 1088: *EHD* 2, pp. 173–4. Henry I's marriage: Southern 1963, p. 188.
The literature on the origins of English feudalism is enormous. The traditional view that the Normans introduced feudalism into England is most powerfully expounded in Jolliffe 1937 and Stenton 1932, chapter on Thegns and Knights. More recently it has been defended in Brown 1969, 1973. It is opposed by Barlow 1965, John 1960, 1966. Somewhere in between comes Hollister 1962, 1965. Mathew 1966 is independent and fair-minded. Stubbs's views were expounded in vol. I of his *Constitutional History* and Freeman's in his *Norman Conquest.* On the significance of the heriot in this connection: Brooks 1978.
pp. **237–9** For the sheriff: Morris 1927. The exchequer: Poole 1912; and Liebermann's review in *English Historical Review.* Litigation about bookland: Laws of Edward the Elder (I Edward 2/1) and especially the lawsuit heard by King Alfred; Harmer 1914, no. 18. Urban population: Loyn 1962, p. 384. Stone 1966 supposes the urban population stood at a steady 5 per cent of the population for centuries. It tends to depend on what one means by a town.

ILLUSTRATIONS
Figs. 188, 189, 191, 192, 193: Temple 1976, nos. 86, 87, 93, 94. 194: Stenton 1965. 195: Taylor and Taylor 1965–78, pp. 222–6. 196: Temple 1976, no. 98. 198: Singer and Singer 1917; Hart 1972. 199: Temple 1976, no. 89. 200: Sawyer 1968, no. 1405. 201: Taylor and Taylor 1965–78, pp. 81–4. 202, 203: Stenton 1965.

PICTURE ESSAY 18 (pp. 226–7): **Edward the Confessor's England**
General: Darby 1977. Monastic values, Knowles 1963, pp. 702–3. Bishoprics' values: Corbett 1926, pp. 509–11. Estate manual, Cunningham 1910, pp. 571–6. Millstones, Hill 1981, p. 120. Oswine's grant and Wirksworth, Sawyer 1968, nos. 12, 1624; cf. pp. 143–4 above. Burton, Sawyer 1979, pp. xliv–xlv. Illustrations: Harmer 1952, no. 96, Temple 1976, no. 87.

PICTURE ESSAY 19 (pp. 234–5): **The Battle of Hastings**
Stenton 1965; Brooks and Walker 1979.

CHAPTER TEN
Epilogue
p. **240** Fate of the English after the Conquest: Stenton 1970, pp. 325–34; Varangian Guard, Shepard 1973. 13th- and 14th century views: Jolliffe 1963, p. 323; Whitaker (ed.) 1895, pp. 8, 166–71; Catto 1981, p. 387.
pp. **241–3** The history of Anglo-Saxon scholarship: Douglas 1951, Pocock 1957, McKisack 1971. Parts of this section are quoted directly from Campbell 1975a, 1975b.
p. **244** Attendance at shire courts: Maddicott 1978, p. 30. Fortescue: Chrimes (ed.) 1942, pp. 68–9.
p. **245** St Augustine's Canterbury: Taylor and Taylor 1965–78, I, pp. 134–43. Monks at Westminster: W. A. Pantin in McCann and Cary-Elwes 1952, p. 33.
County and hundred courts: the best, though in some respect an outdated, account is that of Maitland, Pollock and Maitland 1898, I, pp. 532–60.

ILLUSTRATIONS
Fig. 205: Oman 1954. 206: Buckland 1980. 207: Talbot Rice 1952, pp. 114–21. 208: Northants. Geld Roll: Robertson (ed.) 1939, pp. 230–5.

Bibliography *of works mentioned in the notes*

Place of publication of books is London unless otherwise stated.

ADDYMAN, P. V., and HILL, D. H., 1968, 1969. 'Saxon Southampton: a Review of the Evidence', *Proc. of the Hampshire Field Club and Archaeological Soc.*, 25, pp. 61–93 and 26, pp. 61–96.

AHRENS, C. (ed.), 1978. *Sachsen und Angelsachsen* (Hamburg), catalogue of an exhibition in the Helms Museum, Hamburg, Nov. 1978–Feb. 1979.

À l'Aube de la France, Paris, 1981, catalogue of an exhibition held at the Musée de Luxembourg, Paris, 1981.

ALCOCK, L., 1971. *Arthur's Britain. History and Archaeology A.D. 367–634.*

ALCOCK, L., 1972. *'By South Cadbury is that Camelot . . .' The Excavation of Cadbury Castle 1966–70.*

ALCOCK, L., 1981. 'Quantity or Quality: the Anglian Graves of Bernicia', in Evison (ed.) 1981, pp. 168–86.

ALEXANDER, J. J. G., 1976. 'The Illustrated Manuscripts of the Notitia Dignitatum', in Goodburn and Bartholomew (ed.) 1976, pp. 11–50.

ALEXANDER, J. J. G., 1978. *Insular Manuscripts from the Sixth to the Ninth Centuries.*

ALEXANDER, M. (tr.), 1966. *The Earliest English Poems* (Penguin Classics).

ANDERSON, A. O., and ANDERSON, M. O. (ed.) 1961. *Adomnan's Life of Columba.*

ANDERSON, W. B., (ed. and tr.), 1936, 1945. *Sidonius. Poems and Letters* (2 vols.).

ANDERSSON, A. and SANDRED, K. I. (ed.), 1978. *The Vikings* (Uppsala).

ANSTEE, J. W. and BICK, L., 1961. 'A Study in Pattern-welding', *Medieval Archaeology*, 5, pp. 71–93.

ARMITAGE ROBINSON, J., 1923. *The Times of Saint Dunstan* (Oxford).

ARNGART, O. (ed.), 1952. *The Leningrad Bede* (Early English Manuscripts in Facsimile, Vol. 2, Copenhagen).

ARNOLD, T. (ed.), 1882–5. *Symeoni monachi Opera*, 2 vols (Rolls series, Vol. 75).

ASHDOWN, M. (ed.), 1930. *English and Norse Documents, Relating to the Reign of Ethelred the Unready* (Cambridge).

ASHE, G., 1981. '"A Certain Very Ancient Book". Traces of an Arthurian source in Geoffrey of Monmouth's *History*', *Speculum*, 56, pp. 301–323.

ASTON, T. H., 1958. 'The Origins of the Manor in England', *Transactions of the Royal Historical Society* (Fifth Series, 8), pp. 59–83.

ATTENBOROUGH, F. (ed.), 1922. *The Laws of the Earliest English Kings* (Cambridge).

AVENT, R., 1975. *Anglo-Saxon Garnet Inlaid Disc and Composite Brooches* (2 vols., Oxford).

BAAKEN, G., 1961. *Königtum, Burgen und Königsfreie* (Constance).

BACKHOUSE, J., 1981. *The Lindisfarne Gospels* (Oxford).

BAILEY, R. N., 1974. 'The Anglo-Saxon Metalwork from Hexham', in Kirby (ed.) 1974, pp. 141–67.

BAILEY, R. N., 1978. *The Durham Cassiodorus* (Jarrow lecture 1978).

BAILEY, R. N., 1980. *Viking Age Sculpture in Northern England.*

BAKER, D., 1969. 'Excavations at Elstow Abbey, Bedfordshire, 1966–8', *Bedfordshire Archaeological Journal*, 4, pp. 27–41.

BARKER, P. A., 1975. 'Excavations on the site of the Baths Basilica at Wroxeter 1966–74: an Interim Report', *Britannia*, 6, pp. 106–117.

BARKER, P. A., 1979. 'The Latest Occupation of the Baths Basilica at Wroxeter', in Casey (ed.), 1979, pp. 175–81.

BARLEY, M. W. (ed.), 1977. *European Towns, their Archaeology and Early History.*

BARLEY, M. W. and HANSON, R. P. C. (ed.), 1968. *Christianity in Britain, 300–700* (Leicester).

BARLOW, F., 1955. *The Feudal Kingdom of England 1042–1216.*

BARLOW, F. (ed.), 1962. *Vita Aedwardi Regis.*

BARLOW, F., 1963. *The English Church 1000–1066.*

BARLOW, F., 1965. *William I and the Norman Conquest.*

BARLOW, F., 1970. *Edward the Confessor.*

BARLOW, F. and others, 1972. *Leofric of Exeter* (Exeter).

BARROW, G. W. S., 1975. *The Kingdom of the Scots.*

BARTRUM, P. C. (ed.), 1966. *Early Welsh Genealogical Tracts* (Cardiff).

BATELY, J., 1970. 'King Alfred and the Translation of Orosius', *Anglia*, 88, pp. 434–60.

BATELY, J., 1979. 'The Compilation of the Anglo-Saxon Chronicle', *Proceedings of the British Academy* 64, pp. 93–129.

BATESON, M., 1899. 'The Origin and Early History of Double Monasteries', *Transactions of the Royal Historical Society*, N.S., 13, pp. 137–98.

BATTISCOMBE, C. F. (ed.), 1956. *The Relics of Saint Cuthbert* (Oxford).

BECKWITH, J. G., 1972. *Ivory carvings in Early Medieval England.*

BETHURUM, D. (ed.), 1957. *The Homilies of Wulfstan* (Oxford).

BIDDLE, M., 1975a. *'Felix urbs Winthoniae*: Winchester in the Age of Monastic Reform', in Parsons (ed.) 1975, pp. 123–40.

BIDDLE, M. (ed.), 1975b. *Winchester Studies*, I, (Oxford).

BIDDLE, M., 1976. 'Towns', in Wilson (ed.) 1976, pp. 99–150.

BIDDLE, M. and HILL, D., 1971. 'Late Saxon Planned Towns', *Antiquaries Journal*, 51, pp. 70–85.

BIRCH, W. DE G. (ed.), 1885–99. *Cartularium Saxonicum*, 4 vols.

BIRLEY, A. R., 1979. *The People of Roman Britain.*

BIRLEY, A. R., 1981. *The Fasti of Roman Britain* (Oxford).

BLAKE, E. O. (ed.), 1962. *Liber Eliensis* (Camden Society, Third Series, 92).

BLAKE, N. F. (tr.), 1962. *The Saga of the Jomsvikings.*

BLAKE, N. F., 1978. 'The Genesis of *The Battle of Maldon*', *Anglo-Saxon England* 7, pp. 119–129.

BLINDHEIM, C., 1978. 'Trade Problems in the Viking Age', in Andersson and Sandred (ed.) 1978, pp. 166–76.

BLOCH, H. P. and SCHNITZLER, H., 1967. *Die ottonische Kölner Malerschule* (Düsseldorf).

BLOCH, M., 1961. *Feudal Society.*

BLUNT, C. E., 1970. 'The St Edmund Memorial Coinage', *Proc. of the Suffolk Inst. of Archaeology*, 31, pp. 234–55.

BLUNT, C. E., 1974. 'The Coinage of Athelstan 924–939. A Survey', *British Numismatic Journal*, 42, pp. 35–160.

BLUNT, C. E., LYON, C. S. S., and STEWART, B. H. I. H., 1963. 'The Coinage of Southern England 796–840', *British Numismatic Journal*, 32, pp. 1–72.

BODDINGTON, A., and CADMAN, G., 1981. 'Raunds: an Interim Report on Excavations 1977–1980', *Anglo-Saxon Studies in Archaeology and History*, 2, pp. 103–22.

BÖHMER, H., 1921. 'Das Eigenkirchentum in England', in H. Böhmer (ed.), *Festgabe für Felix Liebermann* (Halle), pp. 301–53.

BONNER, G. (ed.), 1976. *Famulus Christi: Studies in Commemoration of the Thirteenth Centenary of the birth of the Venerable Bede.*

BONNEY, D. J., 1972. 'Early Boundaries in Wessex', in Fowler (ed.) 1972, pp. 168–86.

BONNEY, D. J., 1976. 'Early Boundaries and Estates in Southern England', in Sawyer (ed.) 1976, pp. 72–82.

BONSER, W., 1957. *An Anglo-Saxon and Celtic Bibliography 450–1087* (Oxford).

BOUMAN, C. A., 1957. *Sacring and Crowning. The Development of the Latin Ritual for the Anointing of Kings and the Coronation of an Emperor before the 11th century* (Groningen).

BRADY, C., 1979. '"Weapons" in *Beowulf*: an Analysis of the Nominal Compounds and an Evaluation of the Poet's Use of Them', *Anglo-Saxon England*, 8, pp. 79–141.

BRANIGAN, K., 1977. *The Roman Villa in South-West England* (Bradford-on-Avon).

BRANIGAN, K. and FOWLER, P. J. (ed.), 1976. *The Roman West Country* (Newton Abbot).

BRAUNFELS, W. (ed.), 1965. *Karl der Grosse*, vol. I (Dusseldorf).

BREEZE, D. J. and DOBSON, B., 1978. *Hadrian's Wall* (revised edn., Harmondsworth).

BRISCOE, T., 1981. 'Anglo-Saxon Pot Stamps', *Anglo-Saxon Studies in Archaeology and History*, 2, pp. 1–36.
BROADRIBB, A. C. C., HANDS, A. R. and WALKER, D. R., 1968–78. *Excavations at Shakenoak* (5 vols., Oxford).
BROOKE, C. N. L., 1970. 'Historical Writings in England, 850–1150', *Settimane*, 17, pp. 223–47.
BROOKS, K. R., 1961. *Andreas and the Fates of the Apostles* (Oxford).
BROOKS, N. P., 1964. 'The Unidentified Forts of the Burghal Hidage', *Medieval Archaeology*, 8, pp. 74–90.
BROOKS, N. P., 1969. *The Early Charters of Christ Church Canterbury* (Oxford, unpubl. D.Phil. thesis).
BROOKS, N. P., 1971. 'The Development of Military Obligations in Eighth- and Ninth-century England', in Clemoes & Hughes (ed.) 1971, pp. 69–84.
BROOKS, N. P., 1974. 'Anglo-Saxon Charters: the Work of the Last Twenty Years', *Anglo-Saxon England*, 3, pp. 211–31.
BROOKS, N. P., 1977. 'The Ecclesiastical Topography of Early Canterbury', in Barley (ed.) 1977, pp. 487–96.
BROOKS, N. P., 1978. 'Arms, Status and Warfare in Late-Saxon England', in Hill (ed.) 1978.
BROOKS, N. P., 1979. 'Ninth-century England: the Crucible of Defeat', *Transactions of the Royal Historical Society*, 5th series, 29, pp. 1–20.
BROOKS, N. P., 1983. *The Early History of Christ Church Canterbury* (Leicester).
BROOKS, N. P. and WALKER, H. E., 1979. 'The Authority and Interpretation of the Bayeux Tapestry', *Proceedings of the Battle Conference on Anglo-Norman Studies 1, 1978*, ed. R. A. Brown (Ipswich and Totawa).
BROWN, D., 1976. 'Archaeological Evidence for the Anglo-Saxon Period', in A. McWhirr (ed.), *Archaeology and History of Cirencester* (Oxford), pp. 19–45.
BROWN, R. A., 1969. *The Normans and the Norman Conquest.*
BROWN, R. A., 1973. *Origins of English Feudalism.*
BROWN, R. A., 1976. *English Castles* (3rd edn.).
BROWN, T. J., 1969. *The Stonyhurst Gospel of St John* (Oxford).
BROWN, T. J., 1975. 'Historical Introduction to the Use of Classical Latin Authors in the British Isles from the Fifth to the Eleventh Centuries', *Settimane*, 22, pp. 237–99.
BRUCE-MITFORD, R. L. S., 1967. 'The Reception by the Anglo-Saxons of Mediterranean Art', *Settimane*, 14, pp. 797–825.
BRUCE-MITFORD, R. L. S., 1969. 'The Art of the Codex Amiatinus', (Jarrow Lecture, 1967), *Journal British Archaeological Association*, 3rd series, 32, pp. 1–25.
BRUCE-MITFORD, R. L. S., 1974. *Aspects of Anglo-Saxon Archaeology.*
BRUCE-MITFORD, R. L. S. (with contributions by others), 1975, 1978. *The Sutton Hoo Ship burial*, I, *Excavations, Background, the Ship, Dating and Inventory* (1975), II, *Arms, Armour and Regalia* (1978).
BRUCE-MITFORD, R. L. S., 1979. *The Sutton Hoo Ship Burial: a Handbook* (3rd edn.).
BUCKLAND, T., 1980. 'The Reindeer Antlers of the Abbots Bromley Horn Dance: a Re-examination', *Lore and Language*, 3 (2), pt. A, pp. 1–8.
BULLOUGH, D. A., 1965. *The Age of Charlemagne.*
BULLOUGH, D. A., 1972. 'The Educational Tradition in England from Alfred to Aelfric', *Settimane*, 19, pp. 453–94.
BUTLER, R. M. (ed.), 1971. *Soldier and Civilian in Roman Yorkshire* (Leicester).
BURN, A. R., 1955. 'Procopius and the Isle of Ghosts', *English Historical Review*, 70, pp. 258–61.
BYRNE, F. J., 1973. *Irish Kings and High Kings.*

Codices Latini Antiquiores, 1934–72. Ed. E. A. Lowe (Oxford, 12 vols.).
CAMPBELL, A., 1938. 'An Old English Will', *Journal of English and Germanic Philology*, 27, pp. 133–52.
CAMPBELL, A. (ed.), 1938. *The Battle of Brunanburh.*
CAMPBELL, A. (ed.), 1949. *Encomium Emmae Reginae* (Camden Society, Third Series, 72).
CAMPBELL, A., 1953. *The Tollemache Orosius* (Early English Manuscripts in Facsimile, Vol. 3, Copenhagen).
CAMPBELL, A. (ed.), 1962. *Chronicon Aethelweardi.*
CAMPBELL, A. (ed.), 1967. *Aethelwulf, De Abbatibus* (Oxford).
CAMPBELL, A. (ed.), 1973. *The Charters of Rochester.*
CAMPBELL, J., 1966. 'Bede', in T. A. Dorey (ed.), *Latin Historians*, pp. 159–90.
CAMPBELL, J. (tr.), 1968. *Bede* (New York).
CAMPBELL, J., 1971. 'The First Century of English Christianity', *Ampleforth Journal*, 76, pp. 12–29.
CAMPBELL, J., 1973. 'Observations on the Conversion of England', *Ampleforth Journal*, 78, pp. 12–26.
CAMPBELL, J., 1975a. 'Observations on English Government from the Tenth to the Twelfth Century', *Transactions of the Royal Historical Society* (Fifth Series, 25), pp. 39–54.
CAMPBELL, J., 1975b. Review of John Morris, *The Age of Arthur. Studia Hibernica*, 15, pp. 177–85.
CAMPBELL, J., 1975c. 'Norwich', in M. D. Lobel and W. H. Johns (ed.), *The Atlas of Historic Towns*, vol. 2.
CAMPBELL, J., 1978. 'Die Sozialordnung der Angelsachsen nach den Schriftquellen', in Ahrens (ed.) 1978, pp. 455–62.
CAMPBELL, J., 1979a. *Bede's* REGES *and* PRINCIPES (Jarrow Lecture, 1979).
CAMPBELL, J., 1979b. 'The Church in Anglo-Saxon Towns', in D. Baker (ed.), *The Church in Town and Countryside* (Studies in Church History, 16).
CAMPBELL, J., 1979c. 'Bede's Words for Places', in Sawyer (ed.) 1979, pp. 34–53.
CARSON, R. A. G., and KRAAY (ed.), 1978. *Scripta Nummaria Romana: Essays Presented to Humphrey Sutherland.*
CARTER, A., 1978. 'The Anglo-Saxon Origins of Norwich: the Problems and Approaches', *Anglo-Saxon England*, 7, pp. 175–204.
CASEY, P. J. (ed.), 1979. *The End of Roman Britain* (Oxford).
CATTO, R. J. I. A., 1981. 'Andrew Horn: Law and History in Fourteenth-century England', in R. H. C. Davis and J. M. Wallace-Hadrill (ed.), *The Writing of History in the Middle Ages* (Oxford), pp. 367–92.
CHADWICK, H. M., 1905. *Studies on Anglo-Saxon Institutions* (Cambridge).
CHADWICK, H. M., 1907. *The Origin of the English Nation* (Cambridge).
CHADWICK, N. K., 1969. *Early Brittany* (Cardiff).
CHADWICK, S. E., 1958. 'The Anglo-Saxon Cemetery at Finglesham, Kent: a Reconsideration', *Medieval Archaeology*, 2, pp. 1–71.
CHAMBERS, R. W. (ed.), 1912. *Widsith* (Cambridge).
CHAPLAIS, P., 1965–9. 'The Origin and Authenticity of the Royal Anglo-Saxon Diploma'; 'The Anglo-Saxon Chancery: from the Diploma to the Writ'; 'Some early Anglo-Saxon Diplomas on Single Sheets'; 'Who introduced Charters into England?', *Journal of the Society of Archivists*, 3, pp. 48–61, 160–76, 315–36, 526–42; reprinted in Ranger (ed.) 1973, pp. 28–107.
CHARLES-EDWARDS, T. M., 1976a. 'The Social Background to Irish *peregrinatio*', *Celtica*, 11, pp. 43–59.
CHARLES-EDWARDS, T. M., 1976b. 'The Distinction between Land and Movable Wealth in Anglo-Saxon England', in Sawyer (ed.) 1976, pp. 180–7.
CHASE, C. (ed.), 1981. *The Dating of Beowulf* (Toronto).
CHERRY, J. F. and HODGES, R., 1978. 'The Dating of Hamwih, Saxon Southampton Reconsidered', *Antiquaries Journal*, 58, pp. 299–309.
CHRIMES, S. B. (ed.), 1942. *Sir John Fortescue, De Laudibus Legum Anglie* (Cambridge).
CLARK, C., 1970. *The Peterborough Chronicle 1070–1154* (2nd edn., Oxford).
CLARK, C., 1971. 'The Narrative Mode of *The Anglo-Saxon Chronicle* before the Conquest', in Clemoes and Hughes (ed.) 1971.
CLEMOES, P. (ed.), 1959. *The Anglo-Saxons. Studies Presented to Bruce Dickins.*
CLEMOES, P. and HUGHES, K. (ed.), 1971. *England before the Conquest: Studies in Primary Sources Presented to Dorothy Whitelock* (Cambridge).
COLGRAVE, B. (ed.), 1927. *Eddius, Life of Wilfrid* (Cambridge).
COLGRAVE, B. (ed.), 1940. *Two Lives of Cuthbert* (Cambridge).
COLGRAVE, B. (ed.), 1956. *Felix, Life of Guthlac* (Cambridge).
COLGRAVE, B. (ed.), 1967. *The Earliest Life of Gregory the Great* (Kansas).
COLGRAVE, B., and MYNORS, R. A. B. (ed.), 1969. *Bede's Ecclesiastical History of the English People* (Oxford).
COLLINGWOOD, R. G. and MYRES, J. N. L., 1937. *Roman Britain and the English Settlement* (Oxford).
COLLINGWOOD, R. G., and WRIGHT, R. P. (ed.), 1965. *The Roman Inscriptions of*

Britain, I (Oxford).
COLLIS, J., and KJØLBYE-BIDDLE, B., 1979. 'Early Medieval Bone Spoons from Winchester', *Antiquaries Journal*, 59, pp. 375–391.
CORBETT, W. J., 1926. 'The Development of the Duchy of Normandy and the Norman Conquest of England', *Cambridge Medieval History*, vol. 5, pp. 481–520.
CRAMP, R. J., 1957. 'Beowulf and Archaeology', *Medieval Archaeology*, I, pp. 55–77.
CRAMP, R. J., 1965. *Northumbrian Sculpture* (Jarrow Lecture, 1965).
CRAMP, R. J., 1969. 'Excavations at the Saxon Monastic Sites of Wearmouth and Jarrow: an Interim Report', *Medieval Archaeology*, 13, pp. 21–64.
CRAMP, R. J., 1970. 'Decorated Window-glass and Millefiori from Monkwearmouth', *Antiquaries Journal*, 50, pp. 327–35.
CRAMP, R. J., 1974. 'Early Northumbrian Sculpture at Hexham', in Kirby (ed.) 1974, pp. 115–40.
CRAMP, R. J., 1976a. 'Monkwearmouth and Jarrow: the Archaeological Evidence', in Bonner (ed.) 1976, pp. 5–18.
CRAMP, R. J., 1976b. 'Monastic Sites', in Wilson (ed.) 1976, pp. 201–52, 453–62.
CRAMP, R. J., 1977. 'Schools of Mercian Sculpture', in Dornier (ed.) 1977, pp. 191–231.
CRASTER, E., 1954. 'The Patrimony of St Cuthbert', *English Historical Review*, 69, pp. 177–99.
CRAWFORD, S. J. (ed.), 1929. *Byrhtferth's Manual.*
CROSSLEY-HOLLAND, K. (tr.), 1968. *Beowulf* (Cambridge).
CUNLIFFE, B., 1980. 'The Excavation of the Roman Spring at Bath. A Preliminary Description', *Antiquaries Journal*, 60, pp. 187–206.
CUNNINGHAM, W., 1910. *The Growth of English Industry and Commerce*, I (5th edn., Cambridge).

DALTON, O. M. (tr.), 1927. *The History of the Franks by Gregory of Tours* (2 vols., Oxford).
DARBY, H. C., 1977. *Domesday England* (Cambridge).
DARLINGTON, R. R. (ed.), 1928. *The Vita Wulfstani of William of Malmesbury* (Camden Society, 40).
DAVIES, W., 1977. 'Annals and the Origin of Mercia', in Dornier (ed.) 1977, pp. 17–30.
DAVIES, W., 1978. *An Early Welsh Microcosm. Studies in the Llandaff Charters.*
DAVIES, W., 1979. *The Llandaff Charters* (Aberystwyth).
DAVIES, W. and VIERCK, H., 1974. 'The Contexts of the *Tribal Hidage*: Social Aggregates and Settlement Patterns', *Frühmittelalterliche Studien*, 8, pp. 223–93.
DAVIS, R. H. C., 1955. 'East Anglia and the Danelaw', *Transactions of the Royal Historical Society*, 5th series, 5, pp. 23–39.
DAVIS, R. H. C., 1971. 'Alfred the Great: Propaganda and Truth', *History*, 56, pp. 169–82.
DEANESLY, M., 1941. 'Early English and Gallic Minsters', *Trans. Royal Hist. Soc.*, 4th. ser., 23, pp. 25–53.
DEANESLY, M., 1962. *The Pre-Conquest Church in England* (2nd edn.).
DEANESLY, M., 1964. *Saint Augustine of Canterbury.*
DEMOUGEOT, E., 1979. *La Formation de l'Europe et les invasions barbares* (Part 2, 2 vols., Paris).
DEWING, H. B. (ed. and tr.), 1914–40. *Procopius* (7 vols.).
DOBSON, B., and MANN, J. C., 1973. 'The Roman Army in Britain and Britons in the Roman Army', *Britannia*, 4, pp. 191–205.
DODWELL, C. R., 1973. 'Losses of Anglo-Saxon Art in the Middle Ages', *Bulletin of the John Rylands Library*, 56, pp. 74–92.
DOLLEY, R. H. M. (ed.), 1961. *Anglo-Saxon Coins: Studies Presented to Sir Frank Stenton.*
DOLLEY, R. H. M., 1964. *Anglo-Saxon Pennies.*
DOLLEY, R. H. M., 1966. *The Hiberno-Norse Coins in the British Museum.*
DOLLEY, R. H. M. and BLUNT, C. E., 1961. 'The chronology of the Coins of Alfred the Great' in Dolley (ed.) 1961, pp. 77–95.
DOLLEY, R. H. M., and METCALFE, D. M., 1961. 'The Reform of the English Coinage under Eadgar', in Dolley (ed.) 1961, pp. 136–68.
DOLLEY, R. H. M. and MORRISON, K. F., 1963. 'Finds of Carolingian Coins from Great Britain and Ireland', *British Numismatic Journal*, 32, pp. 75–87.
DORE, J. and GREEN, K. (ed.), 1977. *Roman Pottery Studies in Britain and Beyond: Papers Presented to John Gillam, July 1977* (Oxford).
DORNIER, A. (ed.), 1977. *Mercian Studies* (Leicester).
Dossiers de l'Archéologie, no. 37 (1979). 'Les Romains en Grande Bretagne'.
DOUGLAS, D. C., 1939. *English Scholars* (2nd revised edn., 1951).
DOUGLAS, D. C., 1953. 'Edward the Confessor, Duke William of Normandy, and the English Succession', *English Historical Review*, 68, pp. 526–43.
DOUGLAS, D. C., and GREENAWAY, G. W. (ed.), 1981. *English Historical Documents 1042–1189* (2nd edn.).
DOVE, C. E., 1971. 'The First British Navy', *Antiquity*, 45, pp. 15–20.
DOWNER, L. J. (ed.), 1972. *Legeds Henrici Primi* (Oxford).
DRÖGEREIT, R., 1952. 'Kaiseridee und Kaisertitel bei den Angelsachsen' *Zeitschrift der Savigny-Stiftung für Rechtsgeschichte*, 69, Germanistische Abteilung, pp. 24–73.
DUCKETT, E. S., 1955. *Saint Dunstan of Canterbury.*
DÜMMLER, E. (ed.), 1881. *Poetae Latinae . . .*, Vol. I (Mon. Germ. Hist.).
DÜMMLER, E. (ed.), 1895. *Alcuini Epistolae* (Mon. Germ. Hist., Epist. Karolini Aevi, 2).
DUMVILLE, D. N., 1972. 'A Re-examination of the Origins and Contents of the Ninth-century Section of the Book of Cerne', *Journal of Theological Studies*, n.s., 23, pp. 374–406.
DUMVILLE, D. N., 1975–6. 'Nennius and the *Historia Brittonum*', *Studia Celtica*, 10–11, pp. 78–95.
DUMVILLE, D. N., 1976. 'The Anglian Collection of Royal Genealogies and Regnal Lists', *Anglo-Saxon England*, 5, pp. 23–50.
DUMVILLE, D. N., 1977a. 'Sub-Roman Britain – History and Legend', *History*, 62, pp. 173–92.
DUMVILLE, D. N., 1977b. 'Kingship, Genealogies and Regnal lists', in Sawyer and Wood (ed.) 1977, pp. 72–104.
DUMVILLE, D. N., 1977c. 'On the North British Section of the *Historia Brettonum*', *Welsh Hist. Rev.*, 8.
DUMVILLE, D. N., 1979. 'The *Aetheling*', *Anglo-Saxon England*, 8, pp. 1–33.
DUNCAN, A. A. M., 1976. 'The Battle of Carham, 1018', *Scottish Historical Review*, 55, pp. 20–8.
DUNCAN, A. A. M., 1978. *Scotland, the Making of the Kingdom* (rev. edn., Edinburgh).
DYER, C., 1981. *Lords and Peasants in a Changing Society* (Cambridge).

EAGLES, B. N., 1979. *The Anglo-Saxon settlement of Humberside* (Oxford).
EAGLES, B. N., 1980. 'Anglo-Saxons in Lindsey and the East Riding of Yorkshire in the Fifth Century', in Rahtz, Dickinson and Watts (ed.) 1980, pp. 285–7.
English Historical Documents, *see* Douglas and Greenaway 1981, Whitelock 1979.
EHWALD, R. (ed.), 1919. *Aldhelmi Opera* (Mon. Germ. Hist., Auctores Antiquissimi, 15).
ELLMERS, D., 1978. 'Die Schiffe der Angelsachsen', in Ahrens (ed.) 1978, pp. 495–510.
EMERTON, E., 1940. *The Letters of Saint Boniface* (New York).
ENGELBERT, P., 1969. 'Paläographische Bermerkungen zur Facsimileausgabe der ältesten Handschrift der *Regula Sancti Benedicti*', *Revue Benedictine*, 79, pp. 399–413.
ERDMANN, C., 1941–3. 'Beiträge zur Geschichte Heinrichs', *Sachsen und Anhalt*, 18, pp. 14–61.
ERDMANN, C., 1951. *Forschungen zur politischen Ideenwelt des Frühmittelalters* (Berlin).
EVISON, V. I., 1965. *The Fifth-Century Invasions South of the Thames.*
EVISON, V. I., 1969. 'A Viking Grave at Sonning, Berks', *Antiquaries Journal*, 49, pp. 330–45.
EVISON, V. I., 1979. 'The Body in the Ship at Sutton Hoo', *Anglo-Saxon Studies in Archaeology and History*, I, pp. 121–38.
EVISON, V. I. (ed.), 1981. *Angles, Saxons and Jutes. Essays Presented to J. N. L. Myres* (Oxford).
EVISON, V. I., 1981. 'Distribution Maps and England in the First Two Phases', in Evison (ed.) 1981, pp. 126–67.

FARMER, D. H., 1968. *The Rule of St Benedict* (Early English Manuscripts in Facsimile, Vol. 15, Copenhagen).
FARRELL, R. T. (ed.), 1978. *Bede and Anglo-Saxon England* (Oxford).
FARRELL, R. T. (ed.), 1982. *Viking Civilization.*
FAULL, M. L., 1977. 'British Survival in Anglo-Saxon Northumbria', in Laing (ed.) 1977, pp. 1–56.
FAUROUX, M., 1961. *Recueil des actes des ducs*

de Normandie de 911 à 1066 (Caen).
FELL, C. and LUCAS, J. (tr.), 1975. *Egils Saga.*
FELLOWS-JENSEN, G., 1975. 'The Vikings in England: a Review', *Anglo-Saxon England*, 4, pp. 181–206.
FINBERG, H. P. R., 1964a. *The Early Charters of Wessex* (Leicester).
FINBERG, H. P. R., 1964b. *Lucerna* (Leicester).
FISHER, D. J. V., 1952. 'The Anti-Monastic Reaction in the Reign of Edward the Martyr', *Cambridge Historical Journal*, 12, pp. 254–70.
FISHER, D. J. V., 1973. *The Anglo-Saxon Age c. 400–1042.*
FLECKENSTEIN, J., 1978. *Early Medieval Germany* (Oxford).
FLETCHER, E., 1981. 'The Influence of Merovingian Gaul on Northumbria in the Seventh Century', *Medieval Archaeology*, 24, pp. 69–86.
FLEURIOT, F., 1980. *Les Origines de la Bretagne* (Paris).
FLOWER, R. and SMITH, A. H. (ed.), 1941. *The Parker Chronicle and Laws: A Facsimile.*
FONTAINE, J. (ed.), 1967. *Sulpicius Severus, Vie de Saint Martin* (Paris).
FOREVILLE, R. (ed.), 1952. *William of Poitiers, Histoire de Guillaume le Conquerant* (Paris).
FOURNIER, P. E. L., and LE BRAS, G., 1931. *Histoire des collections canoniques en Occident depuis les fausses décrétales jusqu'au décret de Gratien* (Paris).
FOX, C., 1923. *The Archaeology of the Cambridge Region* (Cambridge).
FOX, C., 1955. *Offa's Dyke.*
FOWLER, P. J. (ed.), 1972. *Archaeology and the Landscape.*
FOWLER, P. J. (ed.), 1975. *Recent Work on Rural Archaeology* (Bradford-on-Avon).
FREEMAN, E. A., 1877. *The History of the Norman Conquest of England* (3rd edn., Oxford).
FRERE, S. S., 1966. 'The End of Towns in Roman Britain', in Wacher (ed.), 1966, pp. 87–100.
FRERE, S. S., 1978. *Britannia, a History of Roman Britain* (2nd edn.).
FULFORD, M., 1979. 'Pottery Production and Trade at the End of Roman Britain: the Case against Continuity', in Casey (ed.) 1979, pp. 120–32.

GALSTER, G., 1964–75. *The Royal Danish Coin Collection, Copenhagen*, Parts I–V, 7 vols.
GANSHOF, F. L., 1968. *Frankish Institutions under Charlemagne* (Providence).
GANSHOF, F. L., 1971. *The Carolingians and the Frankish Monarchy.*
GASKOIN, C. J. B., 1904. *Alcuin, His Life and his Work.*
GELLING, M., 1978. *Signposts to the Past. Place-names and the History of England.*
GIBSON, M. T. (ed.), 1981. *Boethius. Studies in his Life, Work and Influence* (Oxford).
GILBERT, E., 1974. 'St Wilfrid's Church at Hexham', in Kirby (ed.) 1974, pp. 81–113.
GILMOUR, B., 1979. 'The Anglo-Saxon Church at St. Paul-in-the-Bail, Lincoln', *Medieval Archaeology*, 23, pp. 214–18.
GNEUSS, H., 1976. 'Die "Battle of Maldon" als historisches und literarisches Zeugnis', *Bayerische Akademie der Wissenschaften, Philosophisch-historische Klasse, Sitzungsberichte* (Munich).
GNEUSS, H., 1980. 'A Preliminary List of Manuscripts Written or Owned in England up to 1100', *Anglo-Saxon England*, 9, pp. 1–60.
GODDEN, M. (ed.), 1979. *Aelfric's Catholic Homilies. The Second Series* (Early English Texts Society, 2nd series, no. 5).
GOLLANCZ, I., 1927. *The Caedmon Manuscript* (Oxford).
GOODBURN, R. and BARTHOLOMEW, P. (ed.), 1976. *Aspects of the Notitia Dignitatum* (Oxford).
GOOLDEN, P. (ed.), 1958. *The Old English 'Apollonius of Tyre'* (Oxford).
GORDON, E. V. (ed.), 1937. *The Battle of Maldon.*
GRAHAM-CAMPBELL, J., 1980a. *The Viking World.*
GRAHAM-CAMPBELL, J., 1980b. *Viking Artefacts: a Select Catalogue.*
GRAHAM-CAMPBELL, J. and KIDD, D., 1980. *The Vikings.*
GRAT, F. *et al.* (ed.), 1964. *Annales de Saint Bertin* (Société de l'histoire de France, Paris).
GREEN, B., 1971. 'An Anglo-Saxon Bone Plaque from Larling, Norfolk', *Antiquaries Journal*, 51, pp. 321–3.
GREEN, B., MILLIGAN, W. F. and WEST, S. E., 1981. 'The Illington/Lackford Workshop', in Evison (ed.), 1981, pp. 187–226.
GREEN, C., 1968. *Sutton Hoo. The Excavation of a Royal Ship-Burial* (2nd. edn.).
GREEN, D. H., 1965. *The Carolingian Lord* (Cambridge).
GREEN, H. S., 1971. 'Wansdyke Excavations, 1966 to 1970', *Wiltshire Archaeological and Natural History Magazine*, 66, pp. 129–46.
GREENFIELD, S. B., 1966. *Critical History of Old English Literature.*
GRIERSON, P., 1940. 'Grimbald of Saint Bertin', *English Historical Review*, 55, pp. 529–61.
GRIERSON, P., 1952–4. 'The Canterbury (St. Martin's) Hoard of Frankish and Anglo-Saxon Coin-Ornaments', *British Numismatic Journal*, 27, pp. 39–51.
GRIERSON, P., 1961. 'La Fonction sociale de la monnaie en Angleterre aux VIIe–VIIIe siècles', *Settimane*, 8, pp. 341–85.
GRIERSON, P., 1965. 'Money and Coinage under Charlemagne', in Braunfels (ed.) 1965, pp. 501–36.

HADDAN, A. W. and STUBBS, W., 1871. *Councils and Ecclesiastical Documents relating to Great Britain and Ireland*, Vol. 3 (Oxford).
HALL, R. A. (ed.), 1978. *Viking Age York and the North.*
HALL, R. A., 1980. *Jorvik: Viking Age York* (York).
HALLINGER, K., 1950–1. *Gorze-Kluny, Studien zu den monastischen Lebensformen und Gegensätzen im Hochmittelalter* (Rome).
HAMILTON, N. E. S. A. (ed.), 1870. *William of Malmesbury, Gesta Pontificum* (Rolls Series, 52).
HARDEN, D. B., 1956. 'Glass Vessels in Britain and Ireland', in Harden (ed.) 1956, pp. 132–67.
HARDEN, D. B. (ed.), 1956. *Dark Age Britain. Studies presented to E. T. Leeds.*
HARMER, F. E. (ed), 1914. *Select English Historical Documents of the Ninth and Tenth Centuries* (Cambridge).
HARMER, F. E. (ed.), 1952. *Anglo-Saxon Writs* (Manchester).
HART, C. R., 1964. 'Eadnoth, First Abbot of Ramsey, and the Foundation of Chatteris and St Ives', *Cambridge Antiquarian Society Proceedings for 1962–1963*, 56–7, pp. 61–7.
HART, C. R., 1966. *The Early Charters of Eastern England* (Leicester).
HART, C. R., 1971. 'The Tribal Hidage', *Trans. Royal Hist. Soc.*, 5th. ser., 21, pp. 133–58.
HART, C. R., 1972. 'Byrhtferth and his Manual', *Medium Aevum*, 41, pp. 95–109.
HART, C. R., 1973. 'Athelstan "Half King" and his Family', *Anglo-Saxon England*, 2, pp. 115–44.
HAWKES, S. CHADWICK, 1969. 'Early Anglo-Saxon Kent', *Archaeological Journal*, 126, pp. 186–92.
HAWKES, S. CHADWICK, 1977. 'Orientation at Finglesham: Sunrise Dating of Death and Burial in an Anglo-Saxon Cemetery in East Kent,' *Archaeologia Cantiana*, 92, pp. 33–51.
HAWKES, S. CHADWICK, 1979. 'Eastry in Anglo-Saxon Kent; its Importance and a Newly-Found Grave' *Anglo-Saxon Studies in Archaeology and History*, 1, pp. 81–113.
HAWKES, S. CHADWICK, *et al.*, 1965. 'The Finglesham Man', *Antiquity*, 39, pp. 17–32.
HAWKES, S. CHADWICK, BROWN, D., and CAMPBELL, J. (ed.), 1979–. *Anglo-Saxon Studies in Archaeology and History.*
HAWKES, S. CHADWICK, and GROVE, L. R. A., 1963. 'Finds from a Seventh-Century Anglo-Saxon Cemetery at Milton Regis', *Archaeologia Cantiana*, 78, pp. 22–38.
HAWKES, S. CHADWICK and POLLARD, M., 1981. 'The Gold Bracteates from Sixth Century Graves in Kent in the Light of a New Find from Finglesham', *Frühmittelalterliche Studien*, 15.
HENNESSY, W. M. (ed.), 1887. *The Annals of Ulster*, Vol. 1 (Dublin).
HILL, D., 1967. 'The Burghal Hidage—Southampton', *Proc. of the Hampshire Field Club and Archaeological Society*, 24, pp. 59–61.
HILL, D., 1969. 'The Burghal Hidage: the Establishment of a Text', *Medieval Archaeology*, 13, pp. 84–92.
HILL, D., 1974. 'The Relationship of Offa's and Wat's Dykes', *Antiquity*, 48, pp. 309–12.
HILL, D., 1977. Offa's and Wat's Dykes: Some Aspects of Recent Work', *Transactions of the Lancashire and Cheshire Antiquarian Society*, 79, pp. 21–33.
HILL, D., 1978. 'Trends in the Development of Towns during the Reign of Ethelred II', in Hill (ed.) 1978, pp. 213–26.
HILL, D. (ed.), 1978. *Ethelred the Unready: Papers from the Millenary Conference* (Oxford).
HILL, D., 1981. *An Atlas of Anglo-Saxon England* (Oxford).
HILLS, C., 1979. 'The Archaeology of

England in the Pagan Period', *Anglo-Saxon England*, 8, pp. 297–330.

HILLS, C., 1980. 'Anglo-Saxon Chairperson', *Antiquity*, 54, pp. 52–4.

HILLS, C. and PENN, K., 1977, 1981, in progress. *The Anglo-Saxon Cemetery at Spong Hill, North Elmham*. East Anglian Archaeology, Report nos. 6 and 11 (2 vols., Gressenhall).

HINTON, D. A., 1974. *A Catalogue of the Anglo-Saxon Ornamental Metalwork, 700–1100, in the . . . Ashmolean Museum* (Oxford).

HINTON, D. A., 1978. 'Late Saxon Treasure and Bullion', in Hill (ed.) 1978, pp. 135–58.

HOFMANN, H., 1965. 'Fossa Carolina', in Braunfels (ed.) 1965, pp. 437–53.

HOHLER, C. E., 1975. 'Some Service Books of the Later Saxon Church', in Parsons (ed.) 1975, pp. 60–83, 217–27.

HOHLER-EGGER, O., 1911. *Einhardi Vita Caroli Magni* (Mon. Germ. Hist., Hannover and Leipzig).

HOLDSWORTH, P. (ed.), 1980. *Excavations at Melbourne Rd., Southampton 1971–6.*

HOLLANDER, L. (tr.), 1967. *Heimskringla* (Austin).

HOLLISTER, C. W., 1962. *Anglo-Saxon Military Institutions* (Oxford).

HOLLISTER, C. W., 1965. *The Military Organization of Norman England* (Oxford).

HOLTZMANN, R. (ed.), 1935. *Thietmari Mersebergensis . . . Chronicon* (Berlin).

HOLTZMANN, R., 1943. *Geschichte der sächsischen Kaiserzeit 900–1024* (Munich).

HOOK, D., 1981. 'The Droitwich Salt Industry', *Anglo-Saxon Studies in Archaeology and History*, 2, pp. 123–70.

HOPE-TAYLOR, B., 1971. *Under York Minster: Archaeological Discoveries 1966–71* (York).

HOPE-TAYLOR, B., 1977. *Yeavering. An Anglo-British Centre of Early Northumbria.*

HOWLETT, D., 1975. 'The Iconography of the Alfred Jewel', *Oxoniensia*, 39, pp. 44–52.

HUGHES, K., 1966. *The Church in Early Irish Society.*

HUGHES, K., 1973. 'The Welsh Latin Chronicles', *Proceedings of the British Academy*, 59, pp. 233–58.

HUNTER BLAIR, P., 1964. 'The *Historia Regum* Attributed to Symeon of Durham', in N. K. Chadwick (ed.), *Celt and Saxon* (Cambridge), pp. 63–118.

HUNTER BLAIR, P., 1970. *The World of Bede.*

HUNTER BLAIR, P., 1976a. *Northumbria in the Age of Bede.*

HUNTER BLAIR, P., 1976b. 'From Bede to Alcuin', in Bonner (ed.) 1976, pp. 239–60.

HUNTER BLAIR, P., 1978. *An Introduction to Anglo-Saxon England* (2nd edn., Cambridge).

HURST, J. G., 1976. 'The Pottery', in Wilson (ed.) 1976, pp. 283–348.

HURST, J. G., 1981. 'Wharram: Roman to Medieval', in Evison (ed.) 1981, pp. 241–55.

HUTCHINSON, J. and PHILLIPS, D., 1972. 'York Minster, the Excavations', in Pevsner 1972.

HYSLOP, M., 1963. 'Two Anglo-Saxon Cemeteries at Chamberlains Barn, Leighton Buzzard, Bedfordshire', *Archaeological Journal*, 120, pp. 161–200.

ISENBERG, G., 1978. *Die Wüordigung Wilfrieds von York in der Historia Ecclesiastica Gentis Anglorum Bedeas und der Vita Wilfridi des Eddius* (Weidenau/Sieg).

JACKSON, K. J., 1953. *Language and History in Early Britain* (Edinburgh).

JANSSON, S. B. F., 1966. *Swedish Vikings in England, the Evidence of the Rune Stones.*

JÄSCHKE, K.-U., 1975. *Burgenbau und Landesverteidigung um 900* (Sigmaringen, Vorträge und Forschungen, SB 16).

JOHN, E., 1960. *Land Tenure in Early England* (Leicester).

JOHN, E., 1964–5. 'The Church of Winchester and the Tenth Century Reformation', *Bulletin of the John Rylands Library*, 47, pp. 404–29.

JOHN, E., 1965. '*Secularium Prioratus* and the Rule of St Benedict', *Revue Benedictine*, 75, pp. 212–39.

JOHN, E., 1966. *Orbis Britanniae and Other Studies* (Leicester).

JOHN, E., 1971. 'Social and Economic Problems of the Early English Church', in J. Thirsk (ed.), *Land, Church and People: Essays presented to H. P. R. Finberg* (*Agricultural History Review*, Supplement to Vol. 18), pp. 39–63.

JOHN, E., 1977. 'War and Society in the Tenth Century: the Maldon Campaign', *Transactions of the Royal Historical Society*, Fifth Series, 27.

JOHN, E., 1979. 'Edward the Confessor and the Norman Succession', *English Historical Review*, 94, pp. 241–67.

JOHN, E., 1980–1. 'The *Encomium Emmae Reginae*: a Riddle and a Solution', *Bulletin of the John Rylands Library*, 63, pp. 58–94.

JOHNSON, S., 1976. *The Roman Forts of the Saxon Shore.*

JOHNSON, S., 1980a. *Later Roman Britain.*

JOHNSON, S., 1980b. 'A Late Roman Helmet from Burgh Castle', *Britannia*, 11, pp. 303–12.

JOLLIFFE, J. E. A., 1933. *Pre-feudal England. The Jutes* (Oxford).

JOLLIFFE, J. E. A., 1937. 'Alod and Fee', *Cambridge Historical Journal*, 5, pp. 225–34.

JOLLIFFE, J. E. A., 1966. *Angevin Kingship.*

JONES, C. W., 1947. *Saints' Lives and Chronicles* (2nd edn., Ithaca).

JONES, C. W., 1976. 'Bede's Place in the Medieval Schools', in Bonner (ed.) 1976, pp. 261–85.

JONES, GWYS, 1968. *A History of the Vikings* (Oxford).

JONES, G. R. J., 1976a. 'Historical Geography and our Landed Heritage', *Univ. of Leeds Rev.*, 19.

JONES, G. R. J., 1976b. 'Multiple Estates and Early Settlement', in Sawyer (ed.) 1976, pp. 15–40.

JONES, M. E., 1979. 'Climate, Nutrition and Disease: an Hypothesis of Romano-British Population', in Casey (ed.) 1979, pp. 231–51.

JONES, M. V., 1979. 'Saxon Mucking—a post-Excavation Note', *Anglo-Saxon Studies in Archaeology and History*, 1, pp. 21–28.

JOST, K., 1950. *Wulfstanstudien* (Bern).

KEMBLE, J. M., 1849. *The Saxons in England* (2 vols.).

KEMPF, F., *et al.*, 1969. *The Church in the Age of Feudalism.*

KEMPF, T. F. and REUSCH, W., 1965. *Frühchristliche Zeugnisse in Einzugsgebiet von Rhein und Mosel* (Trier).

KENDRICK, T. D., 1938. *Anglo-Saxon Art (to 900).*

KENDRICK, T. D., 1949. *Late Saxon and Viking Art.*

KENDRICK, T. D., *et al.*, 1956, 1960. *Evangeliorum Quattuor Codex Lindisfarnensis*, 2 vols. (Olten-Lausanne).

KER, N. R. (ed.), 1956. *The Pastoral Care* (Early English Manuscripts in Facsimile, Vol. 6, Copenhagen).

KER, N. R., 1959. *A Catalogue of Manuscripts containing Anglo-Saxon* (Oxford).

KEYNES, S. D., 1978. 'The Declining Reputation of King Aethelred the Unready', in Hill (ed.) 1978, pp. 227–53.

KEYNES, S. D., 1980. *The Diplomas of King Aethelred the Unready* (Cambridge).

KIRBY, D. P., 1967. *The Making of Early England.*

KIRBY, D. P. (ed.), 1974. *St Wilfrid at Hexham* (Newcastle-upon-Tyne).

KLAEBER, F. (ed.), 1936. *Beowulf and the Fight at Finnsburg* (3rd edn.).

KLEINSCHMIDT, H., 1979. *Untersuchungen über das englische Königtum im 10. Jahrhundert* (Göttingen).

KNOWLES, D., 1963. *The Monastic Order in England* (2nd edn., Cambridge).

KÖRNER, S., 1964. *The Battle of Hastings, England and Europe 1035–1066* (Lund).

KRUSCH, B. (ed.), 1902. *Additamentum Nivialense de Foilano* (Mon. Germ. Hist., Hannover and Leipzig), pp. 449–91).

KRUSCH, B. and LEVISON, W. (ed.), 1919. *Passiones Vitaeque Sanctorum Aevi Merovingici* (Mon. Germ. Hist., Script. Rer. Mer., vol. 7, part 1, Hannover and Leipzig).

KRUSCH, B. and LEVISON, W. (ed.), 1951. *Gregorii Episcopi Turonensis Libri Historiarum X* (Mon. Germ. Hist., Hannover).

KURZE, F. (ed.), 1895. *Annales Regni Francorum* (Mon. Germ. Hist. Hannover).

LAING, L. R. (ed.), 1977. *Studies in Celtic Survival* (Oxford).

LAISTNER, M. L. W., 1933. 'Bede as Classical and Patristic Scholar', *Transactions of the Royal Historical Society*, 4th series, 16, pp. 69–94.

LAISTNER, M. L. W., 1935. 'The Library of the Venerable Bede', in Thompson (ed.) 1935, pp. 237–66.

LANG, C. (ed.), 1885. *Flavi Vegeti Renoti Epitoma rei militari* (Leipzig).

LAPIDGE, M., 1975. 'The Hermeneutic Style in Tenth Century Anglo-Latin Literature', *Anglo-Saxon England*, 4, pp. 67–111.

LAPIDGE, M., 1979. 'Byrhtferth and the *Vita S. Ecgwini*', *Mediaeval Studies*, 41, pp. 331–53.

LAPIDGE, M., 1980. 'Some Latin Poems as Evidence for the Reign of Aethelstan', *Anglo-Saxon England*, 9, pp. 61–98.

LAPIDGE, M., 1981. 'Byrtferth of Ramsey and the Early Sections of the *Historia Regum* Attributed to Symeon of Durham', *Anglo-Saxon England*, 10, pp. 97–122.

LAPIDGE, M. and HERREN, M., 1979.

Aldhelm: The Prose Works.
LARSON, L. M., 1912. *Canute the Great.*
LASKO, P., 1972. *Ars Sacra 800–1200* (Harmondsworth).
LEES, B. A., 1915. *Alfred the Great, the Truth-teller.*
LEVISON, W. (ed.), 1905. *Vita Sancti Bonifatii Archiepiscopi Moguntini* (Mon. Germ. Hist.) Scriptores in usum scholarum Hannover.
LEVISON, W., 1927. 'Das Werden der Ursula Legende, *Bonner Jahrbücher*, 132, pp. 1–164.
LEVISON, W., 1941. 'St Alban and St Alban's', *Antiquity*, 14, pp. 337–59.
LEVISON, W., 1946. *England and the Continent in the Eighth Century* (Oxford).
LEYSER, K., 1968. 'Henry I and the Beginnings of the Saxon Empire', *English Historical Review*, 83, pp. 1–32.
LIEBERMANN, F. (ed.), 1903–16. *Die Gesetze der Angelsachsen*, 3 vols. (Halle).
LINDSAY, W. M., 1912. *Early Welsh Script* (Oxford).
LLOYD, J., 1939. *History of Wales to the Edwardian Conquest*, 2 vols. (3rd. edn.).
LOHAUS, A., 1974. *Die Merowinger und England* (Munich).
LONGLEY, D. M. T., 1975. *Hanging Bowls, Penannular Brooches and the Anglo-Saxon Connexion* (Oxford).
LOT, F., 1970. *La Naissance de la France* (Paris).
LOWE, E. A., 1958. 'A Key to Bede's Scriptorium', *Scriptorium*, 12, pp. 182–90.
LOWE, E. A., 1961. *English Uncial* (Oxford).
LOYN, H. R., 1962. *Anglo-Saxon England and the Norman Conquest.*
LOYN, H. R., 1971. 'Towns in Late Anglo-Saxon England', in Clemoes and Hughes (ed.) 1971, pp. 115–28.
LOYN, H. R., 1977. *The Vikings in Britain.*
LUARD, H. R. (ed.), 1890. *Roger of Wendover, Flores Historiarum* (Rolls Series, 95).
LYON, C. S. S., 1956. 'A Reappraisal of the Sceatta and Styca Coinage of Northumbria', *British Numismatic Journal*, 28, pp. 227–42.
LYON, C. S. S., 1967. 'Historical Problems of the Anglo-Saxon Coinage', I, *British Numismatic Journal*, 36, pp. 215–21.
LYON, C. S. S., 1968. 'Historical Problems of the Anglo-Saxon Coinage: (2) The Ninth Century—Offa to Alfred', *British Numismatic Journal*, 37, pp. 216–38.
LYON, C. S. S., 1970. 'Historical Problems of Anglo-Saxon Coinage: (4) The Viking age', *British Numismatic Journal*, 39, pp. 193–204.
LYON, C. S. S., 1976. 'Some Problems in Interpreting Anglo-Saxon Coinage', *Anglo-Saxon England*, 5, pp. 173–224.

MACARTHUR, W., 1959. 'The Identification of some Pestilences of the Past', *Trans. Royal Soc. of Tropical Medicine*, 53, pp. 423–39.
MCCANN, P. J. (ed.), 1952. *The Rule of Saint Benedict.*
MCCANN, [P.] J. and CARY-ELWES, C. (ed.), 1952. *Ampleforth and its Origins.*
MACGREGOR, A., 1982. 'Anglo-Scandinavian Finds from Lloyds Bank, Pavement and other Sites', in P. V. Addyman (ed.), *The Archaeology of York*, 17/3, pp. 67–174.
MCKISACK, M., 1971. *Medieval History in the Tudor Age* (Oxford).
MCNEILL, J. and GAMER, H. (ed.), 1929. *Medieval Handbooks of Penance* (New York).
MADDICOTT, J. R. L., 1978. 'The County Community and the Making of Public Opinion in Fourteenth Century England', *Trans. Royal Historical Soc.*, 5th series, 28, pp. 27–44.
MAITLAND, F. W., 1897. *Domesday Book and Beyond* (Cambridge).
MANN, J. C. and PENMAN, R. S. (tr.), 1977. *Literary Sources for Roman Britain.*
MARSDEN, P., 1980. *Roman London.*
MARYON, H., 1960. 'Pattern-welding and Damascening of Sword Blades', *Studies in Conservation*, 5, pp. 25–35, 52–60.
MARX, J. (ed.), 1914. *William of Jumièges, Gesta Normannorum Ducum* (Rouen and Paris).
MATTHEW, D. J. A., 1966. *The Norman Conquest.*
MAYR-HARTING, H., 1972. *The Coming of Christianity to Anglo-Saxon England.*
MAYR-HARTING, H., 1976. *Bede, the Rule of St Benedict and Social Class* (Jarrow Lecture, 1976).
MAYR-HARTING, H., 1981. 'Saint Wilfred in Sussex', in M. J. Kitch (ed.), *Studies in Sussex Church History*, pp. 1–17.
MEANEY, A. L., 1964. *A Gazeteer of Early Anglo-Saxon Burial Sites.*
MEANEY, A. L., and HAWKES, S. CHADWICK, 1970. *Two Anglo-Saxon Cemeteries at Winnal, Winchester, Hampshire* (Soc. for Medieval Archaeology, monogr. 4).
METCALF, D. M., 1974. 'Monetary Expansion and Recession', in J. Casey and R. Reece (ed.), *Coins and the Archaeologist* (Oxford), pp. 206–23.
METCALF, D. M., 1977. 'Monetary Affairs in Mercia at the Time of Aethelbald', in Dornier (ed.) 1977, pp. 87–106.
METCALF, D. M., 1978. 'The Ranking of Boroughs: Numismatic Evidence from the Reign of Aethelred II', in Hill (ed.) 1978, pp. 159–212.
MEYVAERT, P., 1964. *Bede and Gregory the Great* (Jarrow Lecture, 1964).
MEYVAERT, P., 1976. 'Bede the Scholar', in Bonner (ed.) 1976, pp. 40–69.
MEYVAERT, P., 1979. 'Bede and the Church Paintings at Wearmouth–Jarrow', *Anglo-Saxon England*, 8, pp. 63–77.
MIGNE, J.-P. (ed.), 1853. *S. petri Damiani . . . Opera Omnia* (Patrologia Latina, vols. 144, 145, Paris).
MIKET, R., 1980. 'A Restatement of Evidence for Bernician Anglo-Saxon Burials', in Rahtz, Dickinson and Watts (ed.) 1980, pp. 289–306.
MILLER, M., 1975. 'Bede's Use of Gildas', *English Hist. Rev.*, 90, pp. 241–61.
MILLER, M., 1977. 'Starting to Write History: Gildas, Bede and Nennius', *Welsh Hist. Rev.*, 8, pp. 456–65.
MOMMSEN, T. (ed.), 1882. *Iordanis Romana et Getica* (Mon. Germ. Hist., Berlin).
MORICE, H., 1742–6. *Memoires pour servir de preuves à l'histoire . . . de Bretagne* (3 vols., Paris).
MORRIS, C., 1977. 'Northumbria and the Viking Settlement', *Archaeologia Aeliana*, 5th series, 5, pp. 81–103.
MORRIS, J., 1973. *The Age of Arthur, a History of the British Isles from 350 to 650.*
MORRIS, J. (ed. and tr.), 1980. *Nennius.*
MORRIS, W. A., 1927. *The Medieval English Sheriff to 1300* (Manchester).
MUSSET, L., 1965. *Les Invasions germaniques, II, le second assaut contre l'Europe chrétien* (Paris).
MUSSET, L., 1975. *The Germanic Invasions: the Making of Europe A.D. 400–600.*
MYRES, J. N. L., 1964. 'Wansdyke and the Origin of Wessex', in H. R. Trevor-Roper (ed.), *Essays in British History presented to Sir Keith Feiling.*
MYRES, J. N. L., 1969. *Anglo-Saxon Pottery and the Settlement of England* (Oxford).
MYRES, J. N. L., 1977. *A Corpus of Anglo-Saxon Pottery of the Pagan Period* (2 vols., Cambridge).
MYRES, J. N. L. and GREEN, B., 1973. *The Anglo-Saxon Cemeteries of Caistor-by-Norwich and Markshall, Norfolk.*

NAPIER, A. S. and STEVENSON, W. H. (ed.), 1895. *The Crawford Collection of Early Charters and Documents now in the Bodleian Library* (Oxford).
NASH-WILLIAMS, V. E., 1950. *The Early Christian Monuments of Wales* (Cardiff).
NEEDHAM, G. I. (ed.), 1966. *Aelfric, Lives of Three English Saints.*
NELSON, J. L., 1977b. 'Kingship, Law and Liturgy in the Political Thought of Hincmar of Rheims', *English Historical Review*, 92, pp. 241–79.
NELSON, J. L., 1977b. 'Inauguration Rituals', in Sawyer and Wood (ed.) 1977, pp. 50–71.
NELSON, J. L., 1980. 'The Earliest English Coronation *Ordo*', in B. Tierney and P. Linehan (ed.), *Authority and Power: Studies Presented to Walter Ullmann* (Cambridge), pp. 29–48.
NORDHAGEN, P., 1977. *The Codex Amiatinus and the Byzantine Element in the Northumbrian Renaissance* (Jarrow Lecture, 1977).

O'CARRIGAIN, E. O., 1978. 'Liturgical Innovations associated with Pope Sergius and the Iconography of the Ruthwell and Bewcastle Crosses', in Farrell (ed.) 1978, pp. 131–47.
O'CORRAIN, D., 1979. 'High Kings, Vikings and other Kings', *Irish Historical Studies*, 21, pp. 283–323.
O'DONOVAN, M. A. O., 1972, 1973. 'An Interim Revision of Episcopal Dates for the Province of Canterbury, 850–950', *Anglo-Saxon England*, 1, pp. 23–44, 2, pp. 91–113.
OKASHA, E., 1971. *Handlist of Anglo-Saxon Non-Runic Inscriptions* (Cambridge).
OLESON, T. J., 1957. 'Edward the Confessor's Promise of the Throne to Duke William of Normandy', *English Historical Review*, 72, pp. 221–8.
OMAN, C., 1954. 'An Eleventh Century English Cross', *Burlington Magazine*, 96, pp. 383–4.
ORDNANCE SURVEY, 1966. *Map of Britain in the Dark Ages* (2nd. edn., Chessington).
ORDNANCE SURVEY, 1974. *Britain before the Norman Conquest* (Southampton).
ORDNANCE SURVEY, 1979. *Map of Roman Britain* (4th. edn., Southampton).

O'SULLIVAN, T. D., 1978. *The De Excidio of Gildas – its Authenticity and Date* (Leiden).
OTT, I. (ed.), 1951. *Ruotgeri Vita Brunonis Archiepiscopi Coloniensis* (Mon. Germ. Hist., Weimar).
OTTEN, K., 1964. *König Alfreds Boethius* (Tübingen).

PAGAN, H. E., 1965. 'Coinage in the Age of Burgred', *British Numismatic Journal*, 34, pp. 11–27.
PAGAN, H. E., 1969. 'Northumbrian Numismatic Chronology in the Ninth Century', *British Numismatic Journal*, 38, pp. 1–15.
PAINTER, K. S., 1976. 'The Design of the Roman Mosaic at Hinton St. Mary', *Antiquaries Journal*, 56, pp. 49–54.
PAINTER, K. S., 1977. *The Water Newton Early Christian Silver.*
PARKER, H., 1965. 'Feddersen Wierde and Vallhager: a Contrast in Settlements', *Medieval Archaeology*, 9, pp. 1–10.
PARKES, M. B., 1976. 'The Palaeography of the Parker Manuscript of the Chronicle . . .', *Anglo-Saxon England*, 5, pp. 149–71.
PARKES, M. B., 1982. *The Scriptorium of Wearmouth–Jarrow* (Jarrow Lecture, 1982).
PARSONS, D. (ed.), 1975. *Tenth Century Studies* (London and Chichester).
PARSONS, D., 1977. 'Brixworth and its Monastery Church', in Dornier (ed.) 1977, pp. 173–90.
PEERS, C., 1927. 'Reculver; its Saxon Church and Cross', *Archaeologia*, 77, pp. 241–56.
PEERS, C. and RALEGH RADFORD, C. A., 1943. 'The Saxon Monastery at Whitby', *Archaeologia*, 89, pp. 27–88.
PELTERET, D., 1981. 'Slave Raiding and Slave Trading in Early England', *Anglo-Saxon England*, 9, pp. 99–114.
PETTY, G. R. and PETTY, S., 1976. 'Geology and *The Battle of Maldon*', *Speculum*, 51, pp. 435–45.
PHILLIPS, D., 1975. 'Excavations at York Minster 1967–73', *Friends of York Minster, 46th Annual Report*, pp. 19–27.
PHILP, B., *et al.*, 1973. *Excavations in West Kent.*
PLATT, C., 1976. *The English Medieval Town.*
PLUMMER, C. (ed.), 1896. *Venerabilis Baedae Opera Historica*, 2 vols. (Oxford).
PLUMMER, C., 1902. *Life and Times of Alfred the Great* (Oxford).
PLUMMER, C. (ed.), 1952. *Two of the Saxon Chronicles Parallel* (vol. 1, 1892; vol. 2, 1899; reprinted with additions by D. Whitelock, 1952, Oxford).
POCOCK, J. G. A., 1957. *The Ancient Constitution and the Feudal Law* (Cambridge).
POLLOCK, F. and MAITLAND, F. W., 1898. *The History of English Law* (2 vols., Cambridge).
POOLE, R. L., 1912. *The Exchequer in the Twelfth Century* (Oxford).
POPE, J. C., 1967, 1968. *Homilies of Aelfric*, Early English Texts Society, nos. 259, 260.
POWICKE, F. M. and FRYDE, E. B. (ed.), 1961. *Handbook of British Chronology* (2nd. edn.).
PRESTWICH, J. O., 1968. 'King Aethelhere and the Battle of the Winwaed', *English Historical Review*, 83, pp. 89–95.

RAHTZ, P., 1976. 'Buildings and rural settlement', in Wilson (ed.) 1976, pp. 23–48, 405–52.
RAHTZ, P., 1977. 'The Archaeology of West Mercian Towns', in Dornier (ed.) 1977, pp. 107–29.
RAHTZ, P., 1979. *The Saxon and Medieval Palaces at Cheddar* (Oxford).
RAHTZ, P., DICKINSON, T. and WATTS, L. (ed.) 1980. *Anglo-Saxon Cemeteries* (Oxford).
RAINE, J. (ed.), 1879–94. *The Historians of the Church of York and its Archbishops* (Rolls Series, no. 71, 3 vols.).
RALEGH RADFORD, C. A., 1970. 'The Later Pre-conquest Boroughs and their Defences', *Medieval Archaeology*, 14, pp. 83–103.
RANGER, F. (ed.), 1973. *Prisca Munimenta.*
RAW, B., 1976. 'The Probable Derivation of Most of the Illustrations in Junius 11 from an Illustrated Old Saxon Genesis', *Anglo-Saxon England*, 5, pp. 133–48.
REES, W., 1963. 'Survivals of Ancient Celtic Custom in Medieval England', in Tolkein and others 1963, pp. 148–68.
REUTER, T. A., 1980. *The Greatest Englishman* (Exeter).
REYNOLDS, N., 1980. 'The King's Whetstone: a Footnote', *Antiquities*, 54, pp. 232–6.
RICHTER, M., 1972–3. *Canterbury Professions* (Canterbury and York Society, Vol. 67).
RIGOLD, S. E., 1960, 1966. 'The Two Primary Series of Sceattas', *British Numismatic Journal*, 30, pp. 6–53, 35, pp. 1–6.
RIGOLD, S. E., 1975. 'The Sutton Hoo Coins in the Light of the Contemporary Background of Coinage in England', in Bruce-Mitford (ed.) 1975, pp. 653–77.
RIGOLD, S. E. and METCALF, D. M., 1977. 'A Checklist of English Finds of sceattas', *British Numismatic Journal*, 48, pp. 31–52.
RIVET, A. L. F. (ed.), 1969. *The Roman Villa in Britain.*
RIVET, A. L. F. and SMITH, C., 1979. *The Place-Names of Roman Britain.*
ROBERTSON, A. J. (ed.), 1925. *The Laws of the Kings of England from Edmund to Henry I* (Cambridge).
ROBERTSON, A. J. (ed.), 1939. *Anglo-Saxon Charters* (Cambridge).
RODWELL, W., 1975. 'Trinovantian Towns and their Setting', in Rodwell and Rowley (ed.) 1975, pp. 85–95.
RODWELL, W. and ROWLEY, T. (ed.), 1975. *Small Towns of Roman Britain* (Oxford).
ROLLASON, D. P., 1978. 'Lists of Saints' Resting-places in Anglo-Saxon England', *Anglo-Saxon England*, 7, pp. 61–93.
ROUND, J. H., 1909. *Feudal England* (1895; reprinted 1909).
Royal Commission on Historical Monuments, 1962. *An Inventory of the Historical Monuments in the City of York*, vol. 1, *Eburacum.*
Royal Commission on Historical Monuments, 1972. *County of Dorset*, vol. 4.
RUSSELL, J. C., 1947. 'The Tribal Hidage', *Traditio*, 5, pp. 193–209.
RYAN, A. M., 1939. *A Map of Old English Monasteries and Related Ecclesiastical Foundations, 400–1066* (Ithaca).

SALWAY, P., 1981. *Roman Britain* (Oxford).
SAWYER, P. H., 1957–8. 'The Density of Danish Settlement in England', *University of Birmingham Historical Journal*, 6, pp. 1–17.
SAWYER, P. H., 1957, 1962. *The Textus Roffensis* (2 vols., Copenhagen and Baltimore).
SAWYER, P. H., 1968. *Anglo-Saxon Charters: an Annotated List and Bibliography.*
SAWYER, P. H., 1969. 'The Two Viking Ages: a Discussion', *Medieval Scandinavia*, 2.
SAWYER, P. H., 1971. *The Age of the Vikings* (2nd. edn.).
SAWYER, P. H., 1975. 'Charters of the Reform Movement: the Worcester Archive', in Parsons (ed.) 1975, pp. 84–93, 228.
SAWYER, P. H. (ed.), 1976. *Medieval Settlement.*
SAWYER, P. H., 1978a. *From Roman Britain to Norman England.*
SAWYER, P. H., 1978b. 'Wics, Kings and Vikings', in Andersson and Sandred (ed.) 1978, pp. 23–31.
SAWYER, P. H. (ed.), 1979a. *The Charters of Burton Abbey.*
SAWYER, P. H. (ed.), 1979b. *Places, Names and Graves* (Leeds).
SAWYER, P. H., 1981. 'Conquest and Colonization: Scandinavians in the Danelaw and in Normandy', in H. Bekker-Nielsen *et al.* (ed.), *Proceedings of the Eighth Viking Congress* (Odense), pp. 123–31.
SAWYER, P. H., 1982. 'The Causes of the Viking Expansion', in Farrell (ed.) 1982.
SAWYER, P. H. and WOOD, I. N. (ed.), 1977. *Early Medieval Kingship* (Leeds).
SCHMID, P., 1978. 'Siedlungs- und Wirtschaftsstruktur auf dem Kontinent', in Ahrens (ed.) 1978, pp. 345–62.
SCHRAMM, P., 1937. *A History of the English Coronation* (Oxford).
SHEPARD, J., 1973. 'The English and Byzantium: a Study in their Role in the Byzantine Army in the Later Eleventh Century', *Traditio*, 29, pp. 53–92.
SHIPPEY, T. A., 1972. *Anglo-Saxon Verse.*
SHIPPEY, T. A., 1979. 'Wealth and Wisdom in King Alfred's Preface to the Old English Pastoral Care', *English Historical Review*, 94, pp. 346–55.
SIMPSON, M., 1979. 'The King's Whetstone', *Antiquity*, 53, pp. 96–100.
SIMS-WILLIAMS, P., 1975. 'Continental Influence at Bath Monastery in the Seventh Century', *Anglo-Saxon England*, 4, pp. 1–10.
SIMS-WILLIAMS, P., 1976. 'Cuthswith, Seventh-century Abbess of Inkberrow . . .', *Anglo-Saxon England*, 5, pp. 1–21.
SINGER, C. and SINGER, D., 1917. 'Byrhtferth's Diagram', *The Bodleian Quarterly Record*, 2, pp. 47–51.
SISAM, K., 1932. 'Cynewulf and his Poetry', *Proceedings of the British Academy*, 18, pp. 303–31; repr. in Sisam 1953b, pp. 1–28.
SISAM, K., 1953a. 'Anglo-Saxon Royal Genealogies', *Proceedings of the British Academy*, 39, pp. 287–346.
SISAM, K., 1953b. *Studies in the History of Old English Literature* (Oxford).
SISAM, K., 1956–7. 'Canterbury, Lichfield and the Vespasian Psalter', *Review of English Studies*, n.s., 7, 1956, pp. 1–10, 113–31; 8, 1957, pp. 37–40.

SISAM, K., 1965. *The Structure of Beowulf* (Oxford).

SITWELL, G. (tr.), 1958. *The Life of Saint Odo by John of Salerno and the Life of Saint Gerald of Aurillac by Saint Odo* (Oxford).

SKEAT, W. W. (ed.), 1881–1900. *Aelfric's Lives of the Saints* (Early English Texts Society, vols. 76, 82, 94, 114).

SLOVER, C. H., 1935. 'Glastonbury Abbey and the Fusing of English Literary Culture', *Speculum*, 10, pp. 147–59.

SMART, V., 1968. 'Moneyers of the Late Anglo-Saxon Coinage', *Commentationes de Nummis Saeculorum IX–XI in Suecia Repertis*, ii, pp. 191–276.

SMITH, C., 1979. 'Romano-British Place-names in Bede', *Anglo-Saxon Studies in Archaeology and History*, 1, pp. 1–20.

SMYTHE, A. P., 1975. 1979, *Scandinavian York and Dublin* (2 vols., Dublin).

SMYTH, A. P., 1977. *Scandinavian Kings in the British Isles, 850–80* (Oxford).

SOUTHERN, R. W., 1963. *Saint Anselm and his Biographer* (Cambridge).

SPEAKE, G., 1970. 'A Seventh-Century Coin-Pendant from Bacton, Norfolk and its Ornament', *Medieval Archaeology*, 14, pp. 1–16.

SPEAKE, G., 1980. *Anglo-Saxon Animal Art and its Germanic Background* (Oxford).

STAFFORD, P., 1979. 'Family Politics in the Early Middle Ages', in D. Baker (ed.), *Medieval Women* (Oxford, Ecclesiastical History Society), pp. 79–100.

STANLEY, E. G. (ed.), 1966. *Continuations and Beginnings.*

STENTON, D. M. (ed.), 1970. *Preparatory to Anglo-Saxon England: The Collected Papers of Frank Merry Stenton* (Oxford).

STENTON, F. M., 1913. *The Early History of the abbey at Abingdon* (Reading).

STENTON, F. M., 1918. 'The Supremacy of the Mercian Kings', *English Historical Review*, 33, pp. 433–52; repr. in D. M. Stenton (ed.) 1970, pp. 48–66.

STENTON, F. M., 1925. 'The South-western Element in the Anglo-Saxon Chronicle', in A. G. Little and F. M. Powicke (eds.), *Essays in Medieval History Presented to T. F. Tout* (Manchester), pp. 15–24; repr. in D. M. Stenton (ed.) 1970, pp. 106–15.

STENTON, F. M., 1927. 'The Danes in England', *Proceedings of the British Academy*, 13, pp. 203–46; repr. in D. M. Stenton (ed.) 1970, pp. 136–65.

STENTON, F. M., 1932. *The First Century of English Feudalism 1066–1166* (Oxford).

STENTON, F. M., 1933. 'Medeshamstede and its Colonies', in J. G. Edwards *et al.* (ed.), *Essays in honour of James Tait* (Manchester), pp. 313–26; repr. in D. M. Stenton (ed.) 1970, pp. 179–92.

STENTON, F. M., 1955. *Latin Charters of the Anglo-Saxon Period* (Oxford).

STENTON, F. M. (ed.), 1965. *The Bayeux Tapestry* (2nd edn.).

STENTON, F. M., 1971. *Anglo-Saxon England* (Oxford, 3rd edn.).

STEVENSON, W. H. (ed.), 1959. *Asser's Life of King Alfred* (Oxford, reprint with supplement by D. Whitelock).

STEWART, I., 1978. 'Anglo-Saxon Gold Coins', in Carson and Kraay (ed.) 1978, pp. 143–72.

STONE, L., 1966. *The Crisis of the Aristocracy* (Oxford).

STUBBS, W., 1873–8. *The Constitutional History of England* (3 vols., Oxford).

STUBBS, W. (ed.), 1874. *Memorials of Saint Dunstan* (Rolls Series, 63).

STUBBS, W. (ed.), 1913. *Select Charters* (Oxford, 9th. edn., rev. by H. W. C. Davis).

SWANTON, M. J., 1970. *The Dream of the Rood* (Manchester).

SWANTON, M. J., 1980. 'The Manuscript Illumination of a Helmet of Benty Grange Type', *Journ. of the Arms and Armour Society*, 10, pp. 1–5.

SWEET, H. (ed.), 1871–2. *King Alfred's West Saxon Version of Gregory's Pastoral Care* (Oxford).

SYMONS, T. (ed.), 1953. *Regularis Concordia.*

TALBOT, C. H. (tr.), 1954. *The Anglo-Saxon Missionaries in Germany.*

TALBOT RICE, D., 1952. *English Art 871–1100* (Oxford).

TANGL, M. (ed.), 1916. *Die Briefe der heiligen Bonifatius und Lullus* (Mon. Germ. Hist., Berlin).

TAYLOR, C., 1975. 'Roman Settlements in the Nene Valley: the Impact of Recent Archaeology', in Fowler (ed.) 1975.

TAYLOR, H. M., 1971. 'Repton Reconsidered', in Clemoes and Hughes (ed.) 1971, pp. 351–89.

TAYLOR, H. M., 1973. 'The Anglo-Saxon Chapel at Bradford-on-Avon', *Archaeological Journal*, 129, pp. 89–118.

TAYLOR, H. M. and TAYLOR, J., 1965–78. *Anglo-Saxon Architecture* (Cambridge, 2 vols., with vol. 3, 1978).

TELLENBACH, G., 1959. *Church, State, and Christian Society* (Oxford).

TEMPLE, E., 1976. *Anglo-Saxon Manuscripts 900–1066.*

THIEME, B., 1978. 'Importierte Gläser', in Ahrens (ed.) 1978, pp. 179–84.

THOBY, P., 1959. *Le Crucifix des origines au Concile de Trente* (Nantes).

THOMAS, C., 1981a. *Christianity in Roman Britain to AD 500.*

THOMAS, C., 1981b. *A Provisional List of Imported Pottery in Post-Roman Western Britain and Ireland* (Institute of Cornish Studies Special Report 7, Redruth).

THOMPSON, A. H. (ed.), 1935. *Bede, His Life, Times and Writings* (Oxford).

THOMPSON, E. A., 1968. 'Britonia', in Barley and Hanson (ed.) 1968, pp. 201–6.

THOMPSON, E. A., 1979. 'Gildas and the History of Britain', *Britannia*, 10, pp. 203–26.

THOMPSON, E. A., 1980. 'Procopius on Brittia and Britannia', *Classical Quarterly*, 30, pp. 498–507.

THOMPSON, J. D. A., 1956. *An Inventory of British Coin-hoards* (Oxford).

THORPE, B. (ed.), 1844. *The Homilies of the Anglo-Saxon Church: the First Part, Containing the Sermones Catholici, or Homilies of Aelfric, in the Original Anglo-Saxon, with an English Version.*

THORPE, B. (ed.), 1848–9. *Florentii Wigorniensis Monachi Chronicon ex Chronicis.*

TODD, M. (ed.), 1978. *Studies in the Romano-British Villa.*

TODD, M., 1981. *Roman Britain 55 BC–AD 400.*

TOLKIEN, J. R. R., 1936. 'Beowulf: the Monsters and the Critics', *Proceedings of the British Academy*, 21, pp. 245–95.

TOLKIEN, J. R. R., and others, 1963. *Angles and Britons* (O'Donnell Lectures; Cardiff).

VERCAUTEREN, F., 1936. 'Comment s'est-on défendu au IXe siècle dans l'empire franc contre les invasions normandes?', *Annales du XXXe congrés de la Féderation archéologique de Belgique*, pp. 117–32.

VIERCK, H., 1970. 'The Origin and Date of the Ship's Figurehead from Moerzeke-Mariekerke, Antwerp', *Helinium*, 10, pp. 139–49.

VIERCK, H., 1978. 'Zur angelsächsischen Frauentracht', in Ahrens (ed.) 1978, pp. 245–54.

VIERCK, H., 1981. '*Imitatio imperii* und *interpretatio Germanica* von der Wikingerzeit', in R. Zeitler (ed.), *Les Pays du Nord et Byzance* (Uppsala), pp. 64–113.

VOGÜÉ, A. DE, 1961. *La Communauté et l'abbé dans la Règle de Saint Benoît* (Bruges).

VOLLRATH-REICHELT, H., 1971. *Königtum und Königsgedanke bei den Anglesachsen* (Köln).

WACHER, J. S. (ed.), 1966. *The Civitas Capitals of Roman Britain* (Leicester).

WACHER, J. S., 1975. *The Towns of Roman Britain.*

WACHER, J. S., 1978. *Roman Britain.*

WADE-MARTINS, P., 1980. *North Elmham* (East Anglian Archaeology, report no. 9).

WAINWRIGHT, F. T., 1964. *The Northern Isles* (Oxford).

WALLACE-HADRILL, J. M., 1950. 'The Franks and the English in the Ninth Century', *History*, 35, pp. 202–18; repr. in Wallace-Hadrill 1975, pp. 201–16.

WALLACE-HADRILL, J. M. (ed.), 1960. *The Fourth Book of the Chronicle of Fredegar.*

WALLACE-HADRILL, J. M., 1965. 'Charlemagne and England', in Braunfels (ed.) 1965, pp. 683–98; repr. in Wallace-Hadrill 1975, pp. 155–80.

WALLACE-HADRILL, J. M., 1971. *Early Germanic Kingship in England and on the Continent* (Oxford).

WALLACE-HADRILL, J. M., 1974. 'The Vikings in Francia' (Stenton Lecture, Reading, 1974); repr. in Wallace-Hadrill 1975, pp. 217–36.

WALLACE-HADRILL, J. M., 1975. *Early Medieval History* (Oxford).

WATS, W. (ed.), 1639. *Vitae duorum Offarum . . . et abbatum Sancti Albani.*

WEIGLE, F. (ed.), 1949. *Die Briefe des Bischofs Rather von Verona* (Mon. Germ. Hist., Weimar).

WERNER, J., 1954. 'Waage und Geld in der Merovingzeit', *Sitzungsberichte der Bayerischen Akademie der Wissenschaften, Philosophisch-historische Klasse*, 1.

WERNER, J., 1982. 'Schiffsgrab von Sutton Hoo. Forschunsgeschichte und Informationsstand zwischen 1939 und 1980', *Germania*, 60, pp. 1–17.

WHITAKER, W. J. (ed.), 1895. *The Mirror of Justices* (Selden Soc.).

WHITELOCK, D. (ed.), 1930. *Anglo-Saxon Wills* (Cambridge).
WHITELOCK, D., 1942. 'Archbishop Wulfstan, Homilist and Statesman', *Transactions of the Royal Historical Society* (Fourth Series, 24), pp. 25–45.
WHITELOCK, D., 1951. *The Audience of Beowulf* (Oxford).
WHITELOCK, D., 1952. *The Beginnings of English Society* (Harmondsworth).
WHITELOCK, D., 1959. 'The Dealings of the Kings of England with Northumbria in the Tenth and Eleventh Centuries', in Clemoes (ed.) 1959.
WHITELOCK, D. (with D. C. Douglas and S. I. Tucker), 1961. *The Anglo-Saxon Chronicle: A Revised Translation.*
WHITELOCK, D., 1966. 'The Prose of King Alfred's Reign', in Stanley (ed.) 1966, pp. 67–103.
WHITELOCK, D., 1978. 'Some Charters in the Name of King Alfred', in M. H. King and W. M. Stevens (ed.), *Saints, Scholars and Heroes: Studies in Medieval Culture in Honour of Charles W. Jones* (Collegeville, Minnesota), vol. 1, pp. 77–98.
WHITELOCK, D. (ed.), 1979. *English Historical Documents*, vol. 1 (2nd. edn.).
WILLIAMS, J., 1977. 'The Early Development of the Town of Northampton', in Dornier (ed.) 1977, pp. 131–52.
WILSON, D. M., 1961. 'An Anglo-Saxon Book-binding at Fulda', *Antiquaries Journal*, 41, pp. 199–217.
WILSON, D. M., 1964. *Anglo-Saxon Ornamental Metalwork, 700–1100, in the British Museum.*
WILSON, D. M., 1967. 'The Vikings' Relationship with Christianity in Northern England', *Journal of British Archaeological Association*, 3rd. series, 30, pp. 437–47.
WILSON, D. M., 1968. 'Archaeological Evidence for the Viking Settlements and Raids in England', *Frühmittelalterliche Studien*, 2, pp. 291–304.
WILSON, D. M. (ed.), 1976. *The Archaeology of Anglo-Saxon England.*
WILSON, D. M., 1976. 'Craft and Industry', in Wilson (ed.) 1976, pp. 253–82.
WILSON, D. M., 1978. 'The Art and Archaeology of Bedan Northumbria', in Farrell (ed.) 1978, pp. 1–22.
WILSON, D. M., 1981. *The Anglo-Saxons* (2nd. edn., Harmondsworth).
WINTERBOTTOM, M. (ed.), 1972. *Three Anglo-Saxon Saints.*
WINTERBOTTOM, M., 1977. 'Aldhelm's Prose-style and its Origins', *Anglo-Saxon England*, 6, pp. 39–76.
WINTERBOTTOM, M. (ed. and tr.), 1978. *Gildas, The Ruin of Britain and Other Works.*
WOOLF, R., 1958. 'Doctrinal Influences on the Dream of the Rood', *Medium Aevum*, 27, pp. 137–53.
WORMALD, C. P., 1976. 'Bede and Benedict Biscop', in Bonner (ed.) 1976, pp. 141–69.
WORMALD, C. P., 1977a. '*Lex Scripta* and *Verbum Regis*: Legislation and Germanic Kingship from Euric to Cnut', in Sawyer and Wood (ed.) 1977, pp. 105–38.
WORMALD, C. P., 1977b. 'The Uses of Literacy in Anglo-Saxon England and its Neighbours', *Transactions of the Royal Historical Society*, 5th. series, 27, pp. 95–114.
WORMALD, C. P., 1978a. 'Bede, Beowulf and the Conversion of the Anglo-Saxon Aristocracy', in Farrell (ed.) 1978, pp. 32–95.
WORMALD, C. P., 1978b. 'Aethelred the Lawmaker', in Hill (ed.) 1978, pp. 47–80.
WORMALD, C. P., 1982. 'Viking Studies: Whence and Whither?', in Farrell (ed.) 1982, pp. 128–53.
WORMALD, F., 1945. 'Decorated Initials in English Manuscripts, 900–1100', *Archaeologia*, 91, pp. 107–35.
WORMALD, F., 1954. *The Miniatures in the Gospels of St. Augustine* (Cambridge).
WORMALD, J., 1980. 'Bloodfeud, Kindred and Government in Early Modern Scotland', *Past and Present*, 87, pp. 54–97.
WRENN, C. L., 1946. 'The Poetry of Caedmon', *Proceedings of the British Academy*, 32, pp. 277–95.
WRENN, C. L., 1965. 'Some earliest Anglo-Saxon Cult Symbols', in J. B. Bessinger and R. P. Creed (ed.), *Medieval and Linguistic Studies in Honor of Francis Peabody Magoun*, pp. 40–55.
WRIGHT, D. H., 1967. *The Vespasian Psalter* (Early English Manuscripts in Facsimile, vol. 14, Copenhagen).
WRIGHT, D. H. and MEYVAERT, P., 1961. Reviews of Lowe on Bede's *scriptorium*, *Revue Benedictine*, 71, pp. 265–86.

YORKE, B., 1981. 'The Vocabulary of Anglo-Saxon Overlordship', *Anglo-Saxon Studies in Archaeology and History*, 2, pp. 171–200.

Index

Numbers in italic refer to illustrations and their captions